NEW YORK STATE GOVERNMENT

Second Edition

Robert B. Ward

The
Rockefeller
Institute
Press

Albany, New York

Cover photo by Michael F. Joyce, NYS Office of General Services Photographer

Dustjacket Author Photo by Tim Raab/Northern Photo

Rockefeller Institute Press, Albany, New York 12203-1003
© 2006 by the Rockefeller Institute Press
All rights reserved.
Printed in the United States of America

The Rockefeller Institute Press
The Nelson A. Rockefeller Institute of Government
411 State Street
Albany, New York 12203-1003

Library of Congress Cataloging-in-Publication Data

Ward, Robert B.
    New York State government / Robert B. Ward. -- 2nd ed.
        p. cm.
    ISBN 1-930912-15-3 -- ISBN 1-930912-16-1 (pbk.)
    1. New York (State)--Politics and government. I. Title

JK3416.W37 2006
320.4747--dc22

                                                              2006050402

ISBN: 1-930912-16-1 (softcover)
           1-930912-15-3 (hardcover)

To Deborah Hormell Ward

With gratitude
from her fortunate husband.

TABLE OF CONTENTS

FOREWORD

This second edition of Robert B. Ward's book on *New York State Government* comes at a propitious time. Eliot Spitzer's election as New York's 54th governor has produced high expectations about major policy and governmental reforms. A new *Chapter Two* of this book describes the cacophony of voices calling for governmental reform and plans and proposals that have been advanced. The book contains four other new chapters — one on strengthening the state's economy, with a special focus on the upstate region; one on debt and public authorities; and two chapters on local governments. Updates are provided throughout the book, and a new feature has been added this year listing key points at the head of each chapter.

Ward's book covers the waterfront of New York State and local government activities and issues. It explains the history and highlights of major issues and at the same time serves as a source book on the way governments carry out their functions and provide services that are vital to the everyday life of New Yorkers. A detailed *Table of Contents* allows for ready reference.

Like it or not, we could not live five minutes without the things state and local governments do. This is not to say that all is well. Good citizens can help to produce good government by keeping a close eye on the activities of state and local governments. As a way to assist citizens (especially students) and governmental leaders to do this, the Rockefeller Institute is proud to publish this new edition. We thank Bob Ward for undertaking this project and carrying it out so effectively. He is wise and knowledgeable and a pleasure to work with. We are in his debt.

Richard P. Nathan

ACKNOWLEDGMENTS

I am grateful to numerous individuals in and outside New York State government who contributed to this book by providing ideas, granting interviews, reviewing drafts, and helping in other ways.

Rockefeller Institute Director Richard Nathan initiated both the first edition of this book, published in 2002, and this updated and expanded edition. He provided consistently wise and patient counsel during the development of each. He envisioned the two most important new chapters in this book, those on reforming Albany and on the challenges facing the Upstate economy. In addition to meeting the demands of running a highly regarded think tank, Dick is one of the nation's ranking experts in areas including social welfare and federalism; he provided valuable guidance in the treatment of those two subjects.

I've long respected the Rockefeller Institute as a source of wide-ranging knowledge on public policy, and writing this book provided the opportunity to find out first-hand the breadth and depth of that expertise. Brian Stenson took on the task of researching and writing this edition's new chapter on the state's debt and its public authorities, and provided expert advice on other portions of the book. Michael Cooper shepherded production through a tight timetable and delays from the author; I am deeply indebted to Mike and to his highly capable assistant, Michele Charbonneau. Donald Boyd, David Wright and Thomas Gais were generous sources of guidance. Irene Pavone edited and proofread much of the new edition, improving it throughout; Barbara Stubblebine assisted with proofreading. Talin Saroukhanian provided capable research assistance, and Sandra Hackman served as editor of the text, for the first edition. Much of their valuable work carries over to the present book.

Along with the Rockefeller Institute, I am grateful to the Governor's Office of Employee Relations for its role in making both editions of this book possible. Besides helping get the first edition off the ground,

Linda Angello, the former director of GOER, and Administrative Officer Paul Shatsoff provided important insights into the complicated world of New York State's civil-service system and employee relations.

Several experts were generous sources of advice for updates of the first edition. I'm grateful to Richard Briffault, Sharon Carpinello, Frank Maresca, Bob McEvoy, Richard Mills, Ken Pokalsky, Patricia Salkin, Sandra Shapard and Carole Stone.

Within state government, the following commissioners and other key officials in state government gave generously of their time for interviews and/or reviewed sections of the book (some have now moved on from the positions they held when I interviewed them): John Bacheller, Joseph Boardman, Patricia Bucklin, Albert Caccese, Bernadette Castro, John Clarkson, Jill Daniels, Charles Dawson, James T. Dillon, Gavin Donohue, Peter Finn, Amelia Foell-Stern, Maureen Helmer, William Howard, Richard Jackson, Abraham Lackman, Richard Mills, Nancy Palumbo, David Pietrusza, Arthur Roth, Maurice Satin, Gregory Serio, Sandra Shapard, George Sinott, James L. Stone, Alexander Treadwell, Nicholas Vagianelis, Dennis Whalen, and Brian Wing.

Several individuals who know more about New York State government than I do — Gerald Benjamin, Dall Forsythe, Frank Mauro, and John Carter Rice — read draft sections of the first edition and provided insightful advice. Others who were kind enough to read parts of the book and improved it with helpful comments included Robert Freeman, Blair Horner, Lawrence Justice, E.J. McMahon, Ken Pokalsky, and Rus Sykes.

James D. Folts of the New York State Archives provided answers to several nagging research questions, and his online history of state government's educational activities was particularly helpful. Any serious student of New York State government should become familiar with the wide variety of useful information available through the State Archives.

Peter J. Galie provided helpful guidance on New York State's constitutional history, on which his works are authoritative source materials.

Each of the above individuals helped make this book better than it otherwise would have been; any errors that may appear are solely mine.

I'm especially grateful to David Shaffer, the corporate secretary of The Business Council of New York State and president of its Public Policy Institute, who encouraged me to undertake this project and made it possible to do so. For 17 years I've been privileged to have David and Ed Reinfurt, the vice president of The Business Council, as mentors who together have provided the equivalent of a Ph.D. program in the study of government and politics. Elliott Shaw, who knows as much as anyone about the ways of New York State's Legislature and health-care policies, read the original chapters on those topics and provided helpful comments. My appreciation also goes to Dan Walsh, the former president of The Business Council, who approved my taking extensive time away from regular duties to research and write this book.

Finally, my deepest gratitude to my beloved wife and best editor, Deborah Hormell Ward. She not only read and substantially improved much of both editions, but generously encouraged and supported me through long months of work.

R.B.W.
Albany, NY
October 2006

Chapter One

A BROAD IMPACT

The sun rises on the Empire State each day at Montauk Point.

Here, at the eastern end of Long Island, New York State government gets an early start. Montauk Point State Park — 1,276 acres of woods, beaches, nature trails, and picnic areas — attracts 1 million visitors a year. They explore the historic Montauk Lighthouse, enjoy surf-fishing on the beach, and ski cross-country trails in the winter.

From sunrise to sunset, 365 days a year, employees of the state Office of Parks, Recreation and Historic Preservation are at work welcoming, guiding, educating, and cleaning up after the visitors.

Elsewhere across New York, state government is busy through the night. State police officers are on the road. In institutions, small group homes, and other residential settings, state workers and employees of private agencies funded by the state care for some 40,000 individuals with developmental disabilities and mental illness. The lights are also on 24 hours a day at 69 state prisons.

As the sun rises in the sky across Suffolk and Nassau counties, hundreds of thousands of cars, trucks, and school buses crowd the Long Island Expressway, Southern State Parkway, and other state highways on their way to work and the classroom. These roads, like many in other regions of the state, were built and are maintained by the New York State Department of Transportation.

Tens of thousands of Long Island commuters, joined by additional thousands from New Jersey to the west, cross into Manhattan via bridges, tunnels, and rail lines operated by the Port Authority of New York and New Jersey, and the Metropolitan Transportation Authority and its subsidiaries. Each of these agencies is controlled entirely or largely by New York State. Throughout the city's five boroughs, state government plays the major role in bringing hundreds of thousands of commuters to work and to school.

The skyscrapers of New York City are known around the world. From 1973 until September 11, 2001, the tallest in the city — and, for a time, the highest-reaching structures on earth — were the twin towers of the World Trade Center. The center was owned by, and redevelopment will be significantly controlled by, the Port Authority. Another state-controlled public corporation, the Hugh L. Carey Battery Park City Authority, developed the neighborhood immediately west of the World Trade Center that is home to scores of businesses and some 9,000 residents.

A few blocks away in downtown Manhattan are the main offices of the state Banking Department and Insurance Department — regulatory agencies whose influence is felt nationwide and around the world.

Into New York Bay flows the Hudson River, perhaps the single most important element in the economic and social history of the city and state of New York. At the mouth of the river, and along its 240 miles of shoreline to the north, state workers monitor the condition of the water and regulate the municipalities, businesses, and individuals who use the Hudson for drinking, waste disposal, transportation, recreation, and industrial purposes.

A northbound traveler, driving the New York State Thruway or riding the state-subsidized Amtrak train, soon comes to Albany, the state capital. Here, government is the key player in the local economy. Some 50,000 state employees work in and around the capital city at sites including the Governor W. Averell Harriman State Office Campus and the Nelson A. Rockefeller Empire State Plaza.

North of Albany lies Saratoga Springs. It is home to the world- renowned Saratoga Race Track, a magnet for 1 million visitors during a typical recent season. Gambling at the track is conducted under license of — and is heavily regulated by — state government. Just a few miles still farther north is the southern boundary of the Adirondack Park, which totals 5.8 million acres. The state owns huge swaths of land here, some 2.5 million acres in all; it tightly regulates use of the rest. Some 4,800 residents here work for the state — as prison guards, forest rangers, helping to run the taxpayer-owned ski centers at Whiteface and Gore mountains, or in other jobs. State government represents roughly 12 percent of total employment, compared to 3 percent statewide. State government also supports tourism, the largest private-sector industry, through taxpayer-funded marketing and strict regulation of forestlands and waterways.

On a line west of Albany lies the string of cities and towns once thought of as the Erie Canal Corridor, and now as the Thruway Corridor. Utica, Rome, Syracuse, Rochester, and Buffalo all were built, in part, to handle merchandise and passenger traffic on the Erie Canal. The artificial waterway — which led to development of not only Upstate New York but much of the American interior — was built by New York State government.

Near Syracuse, the New York State Fair attracts 1 million or so visitors over 12 days in late summer. The Fair is an activity of the Department of Agriculture and Markets.

Some 35 miles to the southwest is the city of Auburn, home to the 190-year-old Auburn Correctional Facility. It's the longest-operating of 69 Department of Correctional Services facilities scattered throughout the state that, together, house some 63,000 state prisoners.

The beautiful Finger Lakes region boasts, among other attractions, a wine industry that is increasingly respected nationally. State government assists the industry — with promotion and research into areas such as vineyard productivity — through the New York Wine and Grape Foundation.

A few miles from where the original Erie Canal ended is the campus of the University at Buffalo, the largest of the State University of New York's 64 colleges and university centers. In a typical year, SUNY and the state-supported City University of New York together enroll more than half of the state's post-secondary students. Those who attend private campuses also benefit from scholarships and other assistance funded by state taxpayers; many live in buildings financed by the state Dormitory Authority. Buffalo is home, too, to Roswell Park Cancer Institute. The world's first cancer research facility and a pre-eminent treatment center, Roswell Park was for decades part of the state Health Department and is now operated by an independent state authority.

At the northwestern boundary of the Empire State is the world-renowned Niagara Falls. The American Falls is part of Niagara Reservation State Park, the oldest state park in the country. In addition to attracting visitors from around the world, the Falls produces 2,400 megawatts of electricity, which the New York Power Authority sells at low cost to businesses and residents.

An Increasingly Important Role

From one end of New York to the other, state government directly affects the lives of virtually every resident. Its broadest functions are at work in every part of the Empire State:

- Guiding and helping pay for the education of some 3 million children in public schools (and, to a lesser extent, overseeing private schools that educate another 500,000 or so young New Yorkers).

- Providing the courts that serve as arbiters, and finders of guilt or lack thereof, in more than 3.5 million civil and criminal cases each year.

- Paying for health insurance for the poor, and nursing homes and other long-term care for the elderly, at a cost of some $45 billion a year.

- Regulating the products and services provided by banking, insurance, telecommunications, and electric companies, and regulating every company's relationships with its employees.

- Telling local government officials much of what they must do, and how they must do it.

- Raising the money to pay for all these services — and allocating those dollars by program and by region.

In sum, there is barely an area of life that New York State government does not touch. To be sure, state governments throughout the country play an increasingly important role as governments at all levels assume more responsibilities, and as the federalist balance of power between Washington and the states continues to shift.

At the founding of America, states retained most governmental power; the 10th Amendment to the national Constitution provided strong protection for states' rights. The 14th Amendment, enacted in the wake of the Civil War, helped propel a significant shift of authority to the federal government. Creation of the federal income tax and new regulatory agencies, and Washington's enactment of wide-ranging social legislation in the first two-thirds of the 20th century, further shifted the balance of power.

At the start of the 21st century, the federalist system that divides power between the national government and the states is shifting more power to the latter in major areas such as welfare and transportation. In at least one key area, education, Washington is flexing its muscles as never before. In the newly conceived area of homeland security, both federal and state governments — and some large municipal governments — are assuming new challenges as well.

The role of state government is especially important in New York. The tax dollars citizens pay to the state and its localities (which are largely creatures of state government) constitute a bigger share of the economy in New York than in any other state. To put it another way, New Yorkers have historically assigned more responsibilities to their state government than residents of many other states. For instance, the state takes a significantly greater role in paying for health care and providing transportation. On the other hand, other state governments provide some services, such as running liquor stores, that New York leaves to the private sector.

Why This Book?

The premise of a democratic government is that elected leaders and the officials they appoint carry out the will of the people, at least in broad terms. To hold government accountable, citizens must, at a minimum, know enough so they can develop informed opinions about its performance. Beyond that minimum level of knowledge, those who best understand government are best equipped to influence it if they so desire. The unusually large role that state government plays in the economic and social life of the Empire State makes such an understanding especially important for New Yorkers.

Current and future public managers may profit from learning broadly about the state's governance, including areas beyond their immediate responsibilities. The same is true of rank-and-file employees who deliver services and represent the state in most face-to-face dealings with citizens.

Understanding what happens in Albany and in the other reaches of state government can be useful for non-New Yorkers as well. Historically, the Empire State has often been a national leader in developing public policy. Examples abound: universal, free public schools; civil service based on merit; government-owned electrical service; a strong chief executive office, including dominance over the budget process; and a broad-based tax structure. Even where they have made mistakes or gone too far — many would argue that examples include high taxes and an overly complex civil service system — leaders in Albany have achieved national recognition for taking steps toward reform.

Finally, as leaders in Washington, D.C., continue to debate the idea of returning power to the states in areas from social services to environmental regulation, an understanding of government in a major state such as New York becomes more important to understanding national issues as well.

A Key Question:
What Does State Government Do?

A central purpose of this book is, simply, to describe *what state government does* in New York. A complete description of every activity could fill an encyclopedia, of course; fully explaining New York State's role in any one of numerous areas would require a book larger than this. Still, it is possible to capture, in relatively brief form, the state's most important and far-reaching activities. While doing so, the book offers ways to think about the activities of New York State government — context of why things are as they are, how they came to be this way, and how they might change.

This book is written on the assumption that citizens *should* know what their government does. Yet most New Yorkers will learn little about that subject from news reports, which tend to focus on politics and process to the exclusion of policy. Because understanding how the institutions of government became what they are today is essential to seeing where they might go in the future, each chapter includes some historical perspective on the topic at hand.

One way to summarize what New York State government does is to say that it:

- *Makes the rules.* Most of the laws governing relationships among individuals and organizations — marriages, business incorporations, contracts — are state enactments, rather than federal statutes or local ordinances. The same is true of most criminal laws.

- *Provides certain basic services, and supervises others.* States are the primary governmental actors in key areas of social policy such as education and health care. Although candidates for national office routinely talk, for example, about education, most broad policies regarding curriculum, graduation requirements, and schools' business arrangements are still made in Albany and other state capitals — and the overwhelming majority of dollars spent on public schools come from taxes collected within the state, not by Washington. (Even after major increases in recent years, federal funding accounted for less than 8 percent of revenues for K-12 public schools in New York in 2004.) State government takes care of many who cannot take care of themselves, such as developmentally disabled individuals. In other cases, it makes sure that someone else provides key services — such as requiring counties to inspect restaurants and other public food sources for cleanliness. Other vital services that state government generally does not handle directly, such as fire protection and water and sewer service, are provided by local governments with some oversight and assistance from the state.

- *Raises money and decides how to allocate it.* Many would argue that this function — the collecting and spending of taxpayer dollars — is the most important role state government plays, especially in New York. "The intentions of governments are written in their budgets," former Assemblyman Arthur O. Eve has written. Budget negotiations produce decisions on major programmatic as well as fiscal issues. This book will examine where our tax dollars come from and where they go. It will also look at how the budget process works, so that those seeking to understand or influence its contents will know how to make a difference.

How does government in New York go about *accomplishing* its tasks? The book will address that question as well. State government is not only big but highly complex — more so than all but the largest private corporations. Its complexity means, among other things, that many different individuals play important roles. The governor, legislative leaders, and the chief judge oversee the three major branches of state government, making decisions that affect all the wide-ranging services described above. Still, the imprint of these individuals on the overall organization has its limits; activities of mid-level managers and "line" workers have enormous impact as well. Closest to home for most New Yorkers, state government is the tens of thousands of individuals who plow the roads, care for the disabled, run the prisons, and process the paperwork that makes the bureaucracy operate. Because the subject is complex, the text touches on some key topics more than once. For instance, the state Constitution's protection of forestlands as "forever wild" is discussed in both the chapter on the Constitution and that on the environment.

Government Responds

Government changes dramatically over time, both reflecting and shaping the society it serves. As Thomas Jefferson wrote in the Declaration of Independence, people create governments for certain purposes. New York State government continually evolves in response to the will of the people and the goals of its elected leaders. In recent years, Albany has expanded its role in some areas (Medicaid and other health coverage, for instance) while reducing its role in some other areas (such as regulation of the electric industry).

Why does government do certain things in particular ways? *What* makes it change? The answers to the two questions are identical: individuals and institutions. From the 20th century alone, it's easy to identify major reforms that occurred because of the first governor, Theodore Roosevelt, or the century's last, George E. Pataki (*see Chapter Three*). Individuals outside of government, sometimes working through organizations and sometimes almost alone, have also made a difference. In every case, these men and women set their minds to changing something about New York State government and used its institutions to do so.

The relative influence of the governor and the Legislature over state spending varies over the course of decades, and sometimes from year to year. As the 20th century ended, the office of attorney general assumed a major new source of power through lawsuits filed with other state attorneys general against tobacco companies and other businesses. On an operational level, state agencies now commonly use computer technology to make information and some services — such as renewal of motor vehicle registrations, and reservation of state campground space — available online 24 hours a day, seven days a week.

Citizens should know how government *decides* things — which jobs to take on and which to leave to the private sector; how to accomplish the tasks it sets for itself; how to raise and spend taxpayer dollars; and so on. The book examines the structure of governance in the Empire State — similar in some ways to our national government and those of other states, yet different in key ways as well. An understanding of the structure and process of government is based on the written law — which, in turn, starts with our state Constitution. (For instance, the Constitution makes the office of governor in New York far more powerful than those in most states.) Also influential are the folkways and traditions of how institutions and individuals in government work.

In New York as elsewhere, average people often feel disconnected from government. That need not, and should not, be the case. Individuals change the course of government every day. Citizens who know more about what their government does, and how it works, will be more capable of making it better.

Chapter Two

REFORM: IS THIS THE TIME?

Key points:

- A popular new governor promises to bring dramatic change to Albany; the state Constitution grants the chief executive extensive powers to initiate and carry out reforms.

- This chapter examines four major categories of process-related reforms: the budget process, the legislative process, the influence of money in campaigns and lobbying, and legislative redistricting.

- Those issues will have to compete for priority attention with substantive policy reforms in, for example, Medicaid, education, economic development, and tax law.

- In pushing for structural and legal changes, reformers often ignore the role leaders play in making government work better.

While campaigning for governor, Eliot Spitzer proclaimed that "everything" would change starting on the first day of his administration. Given the power that New York's Constitution grants to the governor, a new chief executive starts with significant political capital — particularly if elected with a large margin, as Spitzer was on November 7, 2006. Unofficial results showed Democrat Spitzer defeating Republican John Faso with some 69 percent of the vote, a modern record. Spitzer carried nearly every county, including many that generally vote Republican. Although Republicans retained control in the Senate, and Democrats in the Assembly, several incumbents lost — an unusual development in Albany.

With the advent of a new governor for the first time in 12 years, there was a widespread sense in Albany that dramatic changes may well be coming. Interest groups with varied perspectives were energized and in many cases a bit nervous over the prospect.

This chapter reviews major proposals for process reforms that have arisen in Albany over the last decade, starting with key areas identified by the new governor. It also examines the question of whether fundamental reform — major change to the state Constitution — is needed or likely in the near future. Some topics that frequently enter the discussion of reform in New York State are discussed in more detail in other chapters, such as those on Medicaid, the Upstate economy, the judiciary, the state budget, and debt and public authorities.

Talk of systemic reform in Albany has been building for years — at least since 1997, when voters last considered calling a constitutional convention. Given the dominant role of the governor's office, though, major change is most likely to emerge when an incoming chief executive has campaigned on reform themes. A year before Election Day 2006, at the Rockefeller Institute of Government in Albany, candidate Spitzer gave a detailed presentation on his vision for government reform.[1] Having built a national reputation by driving structural changes in major financial-services industries, Spitzer declared: "In Albany — as it was on Wall Street — the status quo is a system that lacks accountability. It is a system that is controlled by special interests. It is a system that is not efficient, is not open and transparent." Promising dramatic change, he added: "What happened on Wall Street … can also happen on State Street here in Albany."

---

1   "Government Reform," remarks at the Nelson A. Rockefeller Institute of Government, Albany, NY, November 21, 2005.

The address touched on many of the major issues facing the state. For instance, Spitzer called for:

- "Accountability" reforms such as banning campaign contributions to state candidates from those who "do business with" the state. Other proposals included "a dramatic reduction" in maximum campaign contributions; public financing for some campaigns; and a nonpartisan commission to redistrict the Legislature.

- "Efficiency" concerns such as limiting overall state debt, enacting a "false claims act" for Medicaid, and appointing "the best people" to run the state's public authorities.

- Changes to the court system, promoting the "rule of law" with reforms such as merit appointment rather than election of judges; consolidation of the "Balkanized" system of trial courts; and creation of more integrated courts to reduce costs and improve the quality of judicial decisions.

Even given the extensive powers of New York's gubernatorial office, there are limits on how much a new governor can achieve. Which reforms are more important — those that change the process in Albany, or those that change major state policies in education, taxation, regulation, economic development, health care, and other areas? Candidate Spitzer argued that the two go together:

(I)n order to improve opportunity for all New Yorkers, we need reform in many substantive areas — from job creation to education to health care.... But the key for success in all these areas is having a government that is seen as a catalyst, not an impediment to change.[2]

Rising Calls for Reform

New Yorkers are known for political disputes based on Upstate-Downstate rivalries and other competing interests. Traditional disagreements on issues such as education funding, the level and distribution of taxes, and treatment of criminals show no sign of fading away. But many New

---

2   Eliot Spitzer remarks, November 21, 2005.

Cornerstones of Governmental Reform

It is helpful to think of four key aspects of governmental reform — process, people, policy, and results.

Process reforms address such issues as campaign finance, internal operational rules for the Legislature, reporting requirements for public authorities, and administrative-procedure requirements for state agency regulations. Such steps do not directly influence public services or policies, but supporters say they make government more accountable, responsive, and inclusive. Thus, such changes may make public policies more reflective of popular will and increase confidence in government. Process reforms are most valuable when they reduce the power of narrow, entrenched interests. Examples are civil-service laws that reduced cronyism in state appointments and the Executive Budget system that initiated more responsible use of taxpayer dollars.

People — individual leaders in elected and appointed positions in the public sector — make a huge difference in what government does and how it works. Elections matter. So do appointments to key posts. Individuals who serve in public office respond to different constituencies, have different priorities, and pursue them with varying levels of dedication to the broader welfare. "Good-government" groups, which set much of the agenda for what constitutes reform, seek to maintain a nonpartisan image. As a result, they too often ignore the obvious role of specific individuals, and focus instead on improving processes. When former Senator Alfonse D'Amato earned a $500,000 lobbying fee for influencing a decision by the Metropolitan Transportation Authority, for instance, critics said it showed the need for more legal restrictions on public authorities. Such changes may be justified, but the "pay for play" aspect of the incident primarily reflected the express or implied approval of Governor Pataki, whose direct or indirect appointees responded favorably to D'Amato's phone call.

Policy decisions by those individuals determine whether taxes go up or down; whether the government executes criminals or restricts abortion; the nature of our children's education; our markets for electricity; and the size and quality of our health-care system. Discussions of reform too often ignore policy implications. That's partly because "good-government" groups and the news media are reluctant to be perceived as taking sides on many policy questions.

> ***Results*** count. Do programs work? Are their outcomes good or
> bad? Recent discussion of New York's vast Medicaid system, for in-
> stance, has focused on the program's cost and problems with fraud.
> Those issues deserve close attention. But equally important are ques-
> tions about the value that New Yorkers receive for their $45 billion
> Medicaid program — improvement in health outcomes for poor fami-
> lies, the impact on privately insured individuals, and the quality of life
> for older residents of the state, to name just a few. Such questions about
> the performance of the program receive very little attention outside
> government, and too little attention at the Capitol. (*For more on perfor-
> mance measurement, see Chapter Twenty.*)

Yorkers of differing perspectives agree on one thing: They don't like
the way state government works.

In a January 2006 poll for the Empire Center for New York State
Policy, the Siena College Research Institute found that 58 percent of
surveyed voters were dissatisfied with Albany's performance. A similar
percentage said interest groups "such as labor unions, trial lawyers and
business organizations" have too much influence on elected officials in
state government.[3] A Marist Institute for Public Opinion poll sponsored
by the Center for Governmental Research found residents giving Albany mostly negative ratings for 18 of 20 high-priority issues related to
the economy, taxes, health care, and other areas.[4]

Some criticisms of Albany are longstanding. Each year from 1985
through 2004, the Legislature failed to act on the budget until days,
weeks, or even months after the start of a new fiscal year. Other criticisms are newer, or have grown in intensity — for instance, the complaint that state leaders have done too little to strengthen the struggling
Upstate economy (*see Chapter Three*).

By 2004, relatively poor economic conditions combined with frustration at years of late budgets and increasing criticism of Albany from opinion leaders to heighten public attention to problems in state government.

Advocates at various points on the ideological spectrum saw reason
to hold Albany in contempt. For those who support more spending on
programs such as education, it was the failure of Governor Pataki and

---

3   *Ready For Change: A Statewide New York Voter Survey*, available at *www.empirecenter.
    org.*

4   Press release, May 25, 2006, available at *www.newyorkmatters.org.*

the Legislature to act on a court order that they provide billions of dollars in new funding to New York City's schools (*see Chapter Thirteen*). Taxpayers who chafe under New York's tax burden, the highest in the nation by many measures, decried above-inflation spending increases, continuing growth in state debt, and the Legislature's decision in 2003 to impose $2 billion in new taxes (see *Chapter Ten*).

The 2004 elections provided some additional evidence of voter unrest, as several incumbent legislators lost primary- or general-election challenges. To be sure, such losses were not entirely driven by discontentment with Albany. For instance, state Senator Nancy Larraine Hoffmann, a member of the Republican majority, lost her seat to Democrat David J. Valesky, who had campaigned on a reform theme. But Hoffmann had emphasized reform issues as well, and more traditional party politics may have been the chief factor in Valesky's narrow, 742-vote victory. A third candidate, Thomas V. Dadey, Jr., took 13,234 votes, more than 11 percent of the total, on the Independent and Conservative lines. The new Working Families Party played a role, too, delivering 2,771 votes for Valesky.

Whatever the cause, incumbent losses in Albany are unexpected. Many news accounts portrayed the handful of incumbent losses as portents of broader change. The state's risk-averse political establishment took the 2004 developments as a warning from voters. The bottom line was additional impetus for reform in 2005. In September 2006, five incumbent legislators lost primary elections. There was little evidence, though, that any of those losses indicated general unhappiness with state government.

Four Categories of Process Reform

From late budgets to legislative "dysfunction," many of the most common criticisms of Albany in recent years have focused on the processes of state government. In these areas, reform may require elected leaders to change the structure of the process, change the way that they use the process, or both.

The Budget Process

For typical voters, Albany's most noticeable failure was its inability for 20 years in a row to enact an on-time budget. Voters tend to see this issue as a simple matter: Elected officials are failing to do their job on time.

In 1984, Governor Cuomo and the Legislature completed action on the 1984-85 budget on March 31. The next year, final action did not occur until April 4. In 1986, final legislative action was five days late; in the next two years, delays stretched to 10 days, and then 20. By 2004, the Legislature completed its budget work on August 11, after more than one-quarter of the fiscal year had passed.

Voters who read newspapers regularly can hardly fail to notice when the state budget is late. Most newspapers outside New York City report on budget developments once or twice a week while negotiations continue; editorials criticize the legislature year after year for failing to adopt the budget on time. In recent years, some newspapers have editorialized on the issue half a dozen times or more each year, as the statutory budget-making period of three months or so stretched into six months or more. (Such criticisms had limited impact. As with most editorials that take "the Legislature" to task, those criticizing late budgets seldom mentioned the names of Senate and Assembly members in the newspapers' own locales.) Over time, because it was consistently seen as a governmental failure and because of its status as a process issue on which critics from various perspectives could agree, late budgets became well known as the preeminent example of Albany's dysfunction.

One other development, near the end of 2004, added even more momentum for change: The Court of Appeals' split decision in a case involving the division of budget powers between the governor and the Legislature.

In *Pataki* v. *Assembly*,[5] the court held that Governor Pataki did not overstep his Constitutional budget powers in writing statutory language into an appropriation bill; and that the Legislature did go beyond Constitutional limits on its powers in amending such proposals in the Executive Budget bills. The Senate and Assembly had argued that the state Constitution does not explicitly give governors the power to include extensive lawmaking in appropriation bills, and that allowing such action by the chief executive weakens the Legislature's position as the originator of changes to the laws of the state.

---

5   The Court of Appeals decision actually covered two related cases. *Pataki* v. *Assembly* grew out of disputes involving the 2001 budget; *Silver* v. *Pataki* emerged from the 1998 budget negotiations.

Voter Opinions and the Economy

Public opinion on whether the governor and legislators are doing a good job (and thus whether major reform is needed) is strongly influenced by the economy — a factor that, in the short run at least, is largely driven by forces outside Albany's control. Public opinion polls by Zogby International and the Marist College Institute for Public Opinion found more than half of New Yorkers saying the state was heading "in the right direction" in every poll taken from 1997 into mid-2002. Only a third, at most, said the state was headed in the wrong direction.

The state's economy, like the nation's, was performing well for most of the period. Most regions of the state were adding jobs — a condition that, fairly or not, tends to reflect well on incumbent officials. With Wall Street enjoying extraordinary growth, Albany's revenues were rising sharply. Governor Pataki and legislators were able to enact popular measures such as a state funded reduction in school property taxes, major expansion of taxpayer-funded health programs and billions of dollars in funding for local projects.

The issue that helped crystallize voter and editorial-page anger — late budgets — seemed to matter little to voters during the 1997-2002 period. Not a single budget was completed on time, and several stretched more than two months into the new fiscal year. Yet New Yorkers seemed to accept the status quo when they entered the voting booth. Governor Pataki won re-election easily in 1998 and 2002, and the few losses for legislators were widely perceived as reflecting local factors rather than budget issues.

Voters' perception of "right track" or "wrong track" also appears to track differences in regional economies. In Marist's September 2005 poll, more than half of New York City and downstate suburban residents said the state was on the "right track." Fewer than one-third of Upstate residents said so, with 62 percent seeing New York on the "wrong track." Downstate, job growth was strong, while most of Upstate continued to struggle economically.

Economic conditions may have played a role in regional votes on Proposal One, the 2005 Constitutional amendment that would have changed the budget process. Critics of the proposal argued it would result in higher taxes and hurt the state's economy. Erie County, suffering long-term economic stagnation, rejected the proposal by nearly 4-to-1, a far greater margin than in prosperous Nassau, Suffolk and Westchester counties.

Senators and Assembly members reacted with outrage to the court decision. Speaker Sheldon Silver said the decision "reduced New York's budget process to a one-sided charade" and "has sounded the death knell for public education."[6]

The years of criticism over late budgets and the *Pataki v. Assembly* decision helped lead to two new developments in 2005: a mostly on-time budget for the first time in two decades and the Legislature's proposal to change the budget process under the state Constitution.

Just three weeks after finalizing the 2005-06 budget, the Senate gave final legislative approval to a proposed constitutional amendment that was to spark a bitter debate between the governor and legislative leaders, and among supporters of each side. Both houses had already given first passage to the budget-powers amendment in 2004. Proposal One, as the amendment was known, represented the most dramatic change to the budget process since voters approved the Executive Budget system in 1927. But when the Legislature's amendment went on the ballot in 2005, voters rejected it overwhelmingly. (*See Chapter Ten.*)

The Legislature has advanced a related amendment that could go to voters in 2007. That proposed amendment — much less complex and likely to be less controversial than the 2005 Proposal One — amends the existing Article VII to specify that the governor may not include legislative language in appropriation bills. Both houses gave first passage to the amendment in 2005, and could give the required second passage as early as 2007. Governor-elect Spitzer is believed to oppose that amendment and to prefer making any changes to the budget process in statute and practice rather than constitutional amendments. Meanwhile, Comptroller Hevesi and others are arguing for another constitutional amendment to restrict state borrowing (*see Chapter Eleven*).

Aside from constitutional rules relating to state finances, critics point to the increasing use of grants that are allocated by the governor and legislative leaders outside the normal budget process. Such targeted funding gives elected officials maximum political benefit with minimal accountability. In September 2006, for instance, the Albany *Times Union* reported that Senate Republicans and Assembly Democrats were secretly distributing some $85 million a year to favored school districts

---

6   Assembly press release, December 16, 2004, available at *http://www.assembly.state.ny.us/Press/20041216/*.

under a funding program called General Legislative Operations Programs, or GLOP.[7]

As both a Constitutional issue and a question of legislative practice, budget reform appears likely to remain on Albany's agenda for some time.

Legislative Process

After years of late budgets had left many voters cynical about New York's state government, several major new voices emerged in 2004 to demand broad change in Albany.

In July 2004, scholars at New York University extended popular criticism of Albany from the budget to the internal workings of the Senate and Assembly, attacking the Legislature as "the most dysfunctional in the nation." A detailed report issued by the Brennan Center for Justice at NYU Law School did not quantify such a finding, but did report measurements such as these, for the Legislature's activity from 1997 to 2001:

- Fewer than 5 percent of the "major" bills passed by the Assembly or Senate were debated on the floor of the respective chambers.

- During the same period, only 0.5 percent of the major bills passed by the Assembly, and only 0.7 percent of the major bills passed by the Senate, received a committee hearing.

- The Senate voted on 7,109 bills, and the Assembly took action on 4,365 from 1997 to 1999. Not a single bill was voted down in either house, the report found.[8]

The report's specific findings were new, but its conclusions echoed what most observers of Albany had recognized for years: The Legislature's operational practices keep individual members from playing meaningful roles by concentrating authority in the legislative leaders, and thus limit real representation in Albany. Newspapers around the state, long critical of the Legislature's leadership-driven processes, rallied even more strongly to the cause.

---

7   James M. Odato, "GLOP fills up pork barrel," *Times Union*, Albany, NY, September 17, 2006.

8   See *www.brennancenter.org*.

In early 2004, Nassau County Executive Tom Suozzi announced a political committee called Fix Albany that would pressure state legislators to reform New York's Medicaid program, which contributes to high property taxes on Long Island and elsewhere in the state. Suozzi later claimed credit for helping a legislative challenger defeat an incumbent member of the Assembly from Nassau County in November 2004. News media paid special attention to the county executive's proposals for change because he was a likely candidate for governor.

Another new voice for reform was a Central New York businessman, Mark Bitz, who attacked both Albany's governmental processes and its policies that affect businesses. Bitz, who created his own pro-reform website, endorsed the Brennan Center proposals for internal legislative changes. He also criticized the state's heavy tax burden, and higher-than-average costs for energy and workers' compensation. Bitz warned that he and other business owners were considering leaving the state to find more hospitable locations elsewhere. In numerous op-eds and on his political website, Bitz estimated that his company, Plainville Farms, spent $600,000 more annually on such costs than it would if it were located in a competing state.[9] Such criticism hit home in much of Upstate New York, where employment and population trends remain among the most discouraging in the nation.

The Brennan Center report, and the concurrent efforts by others such as Suozzi and Bitz, galvanized critics from varied perspectives. Supporters of the Brennan Center proposals demanded procedural changes that would force more meaningful policy debates in the Legislature, disperse authority from leaders to rank-and-file members, and make enactment of new policies more likely. In its report, the Brennan Center said legislative dysfunction had blocked action on issues such as a minimum-wage increase, gay and lesbian rights, reform of costly rules governing public construction, and mandated inclusion of mental-illness treatment in health-insurance policies. Chambers of commerce, nonprofit groups representing social-service agencies, and other interest groups endorsed the Brennan Center proposals. The report's criticisms became campaign issues in some 2004 legislative campaigns.

After those campaigns resulted in several losses by incumbents, Senate and Assembly members returned to Albany in January 2005 to announce that the time for reform had come. Both houses adopted new internal rules that responded to some of the criticisms in the Brennan

---

9   The site is *www.freenys.org.*

Center report. The Assembly began requiring that members be physically present to have votes counted; creating open meetings of the powerful Rules Committee; and requiring that committees engage in oversight of executive-branch agencies. The Senate banned "empty-seat" voting for nonroutine bills, among other changes. Both houses agreed to more regular use of open conference committees, instead of closed leaders' meetings, to negotiate two-house differences on legislation.

The Brennan Center and its supporters welcomed the changes to internal legislative rules, but said they did not go far enough. For instance, the center said, majority- and minority-party legislators should receive equal funding for staff and office space, and conference committees should be called at the request of bill sponsors, rather than by the leaders. Such steps would reduce the majority-party members' ability to deliver politically attractive funding to their home districts, and bring significant shifts of power from the legislative leaders to individual members. Neither house acted on those proposals, and as of 2006 there was no apparent public pressure for them to do so.

The internal legislative rules changes appeared to make little, if any, difference from a policy perspective. None of the issues that the Brennan Center suggested were being ignored because of an unaccountable Legislature were acted upon as a result of the rules changes. The Legislature enacted a minimum-wage increase after release of the report, but that action was driven more by traditional concern about the pending legislative elections than by changes in the houses' internal rules. In October 2006, the Brennan Center issued a follow-up report declaring that "some has changed, but not enough" in Albany. The new report added:

> On the other hand, New York is on the edge of major change. Nearly all candidates for statewide offices speak of reform. A new governor will enter office. Voters have made clear they want action. Rarely will the political planets align for reform as they will over the next year.

The Role of Money in Lobbying

As long as there has been a New York State government, individuals in positions of power have been known to use public office and taxpayer dollars to help friends and political supporters. DeWitt Clinton, the most important governor in the state's early decades, used political patronage to build and maintain influence. Martin Van Buren did the same from positions as governor (briefly, in 1829) and U.S. Senator before being elected president. Other examples are too numerous to list.

Government in Albany has grown larger and more powerful in recent decades. So, too, has the lobbying industry. Organizations and individuals whose mission is to influence the executive and legislative branches of state government play a larger role than ever in shaping budget actions, legislation, and regulations.

At the start of the 21st century, such efforts have become highly specialized. In addition to long-established organizations that represent broad-based interests — education, health care, business, labor, environmental groups, and so on — Albany is home base for an increasing number of lawyers and former high-ranking government officials who represent various individual clients. (*See Chapter Twenty for further discussion.*)

Lobbyists who have close personal relationships with state leaders have drawn particular attention. The son of Senate Majority Leader Joseph L. Bruno and the top staff assistant to Assembly Speaker Sheldon Silver both became highly paid lobbyists. One example of their high-profile clients was Cablevision, a corporation that owns Madison Square Garden in New York City. The company strongly opposed a 2004 proposal by New York Mayor Michael Bloomberg to build a stadium on Manhattan's West Side that would be used for the Jets football team and, the mayor hoped, for the 2012 Olympics. Cablevision saw the new stadium as a threat to its own interests and spent more than $13 million lobbying against the proposal, according to the state Lobbying Commission. Firms established by Kenneth Bruno, son of the majority leader, and Patricia Lynch, former top aide to the speaker, received consulting contracts with Cablevision for $10,000 a month in 2005.[10] Close associates of Governor Pataki, such as political adviser Kieran Mahoney and former Public Service Commission Chairman John O'Mara, also became successful lobbyists.

In May 2002, *The New York Times* reported on problems in the development of a new headquarters for the Metropolitan Transportation Authority. The article mentioned that former U.S. Senator Alfonse D'Amato had earned $500,000 for lobbying the chairman of the author-

---

10 Details on lobbying contracts are available from the Temporary State Commission on Lobbying's website, *www.nylobby.state.ny.us*.

ity in relation to a contract for financing of the project.[11] The former senator, who had lost a reelection bid in 1998, was a close political ally of the MTA chairman, E. Virgil Conway; and of Governor Pataki, who appointed the MTA chairman and several other board members. Some months later, other news media revealed that the $500,000 fee was for a single telephone call. Editorialists and "good-government" groups used the story as the basis for new criticisms of political favoritism in Albany.

The D'Amato-MTA story embodies, and helped stimulate debate over, three strands of the modern "reform Albany" movement:

- Political favoritism in lucrative lobbying deals.

- Public authorities, the "fourth branch of state government," which are less accountable to the Legislature than traditional state agencies.

- And the increasing use of high-paid lobbyists not only to persuade the Legislature with regard to legislation, but to persuade executive agencies regarding the awarding of valuable procurement contracts.

Widespread criticism of the D'Amato deal helped prompt state leaders to broaden the state Lobby Law in 2005 to include procurement contracts within the scope of the law. Both houses voted unanimously to approve the changes, and Governor Pataki signaled its high priority by signing the bill as Chapter 1 of the Laws of 2005.

"Bidders and potential bidders often attempt to influence procurement contract decisions by hiring lobbyists to advocate on their behalf before procurement officials," the legislative memo in support of the bill stated. "Contacts in the context of the procurement process should be regulated by the Lobby Commission to ensure that there is public disclosure of such arrangements and that they are subject to the same restrictions placed on lobbyists who appear before government on other policy matters."

Much of the criticism that led up to passage of procurement reform focused on the merits of the Lobby Law and of public authorities. But such critiques may be misdirected if they ignore the governmental

---

11 Charles V. Bagli, "Sweet Deal for M.T.A. Home Turns Sour, Beset by Cost Overruns and Indictments," *The New York Times*, May 29, 2002.

leaders whose decision-making processes are already covered by the Lobby Law, and who create and oversee the authorities Major decisions at the MTA, for instance, are seldom made without approval of the governor. If the MTA and other public authorities have worked well in the last decade, much of the credit goes directly to Governor Pataki — not simply to the earlier generation of leaders who created the authority's structure. If the authorities do not function properly at any given time, much of the blame lies with the governor as well.

The Role of Money in Campaigns

In Albany, as in many other centers of government, individuals and organizations typically contribute to political campaigns for one primary reason: to help elect candidates whose policies already are, or might become, favorable to the donors. As a corollary, donors tend to give most to incumbents and likely winners who will be able to repay the favor in some way. In 2002, for example, Governor Pataki spent more than $45 million, nearly triple the amount raised by his challenger, H. Carl McCall. In 2006, political observers were virtually unanimous in expecting a big win by Attorney General Spitzer. He ultimately raised more than $40 million, some ten times the amount donors gave to Republican candidate John Faso.

Such trends in contributions tend to reinforce already strong candidates, creating even bigger disparities with those who have few resources. Numerous critics of the current campaign system have proposed addressing such disparities by reducing the maximum donation levels for candidates seeking state office. Governor-elect Spitzer called for "a dramatic reduction" in contribution limits, to help create "a level playing field."[12] To be sure, limits on cash contributions would leave untouched some other ways that Albany insiders use big money to influence policy — for instance, the multimillion-dollar ad campaigns by health-care and teacher unions. Many observers agree, though, that reducing contribution limits is at least worth consideration; such proposals will likely be on the table in 2007.

Spitzer and others have also called for public financing of state-level campaigns, in the form of matching grants for candidates who attract a certain level of private contributions. New York City has such a system in place, tied to candidates' acceptance of limits on overall spending.

---

12 Remarks at the Rockefeller Institute.

Under rulings from the U.S. Supreme Court, such spending limits must be voluntary. Michael Bloomberg, for instance, chose to forego spending limits and public funding in his successful 2001 and 2005 campaigns for mayor. Critics of public campaign financing argue such systems tend to result in wealthy candidates running for office. Supporters say public financing enhances democracy by reducing candidates' reliance on special-interest donors.

Redistricting

As critics from varying perspectives note, members of the Senate and Assembly in New York have built one of the most effective incumbent-protection systems in the nation. Since the early 1980s, a key element has been the once-every-decade redrawing of legislative districts to favor majority-party incumbents, Republicans in the Senate and Democrats in the Assembly.

Under the current system, in New York as in many other states, legislators essentially choose their voters rather than vice versa. Reformers such as Citizens Union, the New York Public Interest Research Group (NYPIRG), and Mark Bitz have called for anindependent redistricting commission to make legislative elections more competitive — and make legislators more accountable to voters.

Legislators have introduced some such proposals. In 2005, for example, Assemblyman Michael Gianaris and 22 colleagues introduced legislation (A.6287) based on redistricting procedures in Iowa. The bill would create a reapportionment commission whose members would be chosen by legislative leaders from candidates named by an appointment committee whose members would first be appointed by statewide elected leaders, legislative leaders, and the state's chief judge. The commission would recommend a redistricting plan that the Legislature could accept or reject without amendments. If legislators rejected two such proposals, the commission would then submit a third plan that the Legislature could amend before adoption.

While removing political considerations entirely from the redistricting process is impossible, NYPIRG and other groups favor the Iowa approach. The Brookings Institution's Thomas Mann finds that the Hawkeye State enjoys "timely completion of redistricting, no court challenges, mostly competitive seats, and no blatant incumbent or partisan gerrymandering." Mann suggests, though, that Iowa's political culture plays a key role:

> The legislature has never chosen to exercise its authority to draw its own maps, even when a majority believed that the neutral process had produced a partisan outcome. It appears that the "good government" norms in the state, and the popularity of the nonpartisan redistricting process, has constrained the self-interested behavior of incumbents and parties.[13]

Examination of cultural norms is a helpful reminder that constitutional and statutory rules are not the only things that affect the quality of government. Decisions by elected officials matter as well. Spitzer said during the 2006 gubernatorial campaign that if elected he would refuse to sign any redistricting bill that went too far in protecting incumbents. That would represent a major change from the recent practice of governors signing whatever reapportionment plan the Legislature adopted.

Policy Reforms

Beyond process reforms, major changes in the policies of New York State government will be debated intently in 2007 and beyond. Such changes may affect vitally important concerns such as the strength of the state's economy and availability of good jobs; the quality of education for poor children in the state; and the size of the tax burden on individuals and businesses. While Albany has addressed each of these areas in recent years, the reform agenda will include discussion of proposals to:

- Balance spending and revenues consistently. The state has a structural budget gap in the billions of dollars, debt has soared in the last decade, and state leaders are expanding use of undesirable revenue sources such as state-sponsored gambling.

- Control the cost of, and effectively manage, the $46 billion Medicaid program. Governor Pataki and the Legislature took steps to ease the burden on local governments, but costs

---

13 "Redistricting Reform: What is Desirable? Possible?" paper prepared for Conference on "Competition, Partisanship, and Congressional Redistricting," April 16, 2004, available via *www.brookings.edu*.

continue to rise — and little is done to ensure maximum benefit from the nation's most generous public health-care programs.

- Ensure new resources for New York City schools, as ordered by state courts. (The Court of Appeals has ruled the state doesn't have to pay the whole cost itself; state leaders can require the city to spend more on schools if they so choose.) Albany's traditional method of increasing education aid in one region is to do the same in all regions — but using that approach to resolve the Campaign for Fiscal Equity case would cost billions of dollars. The Court of Appeals also suggested greater accountability for education spending, with little response from state leaders.

- Make New York more competitive for new businesses and jobs. Spitzer has said he will implement "an aggressive strategy to reduce the cost of doing business in New York." He called for reducing costs of workers' compensation, energy, and health insurance while streamlining the state's regulatory system.

Like beauty, reform is in the eye of the beholder. "Good-government" groups that strongly support proposals for limits on campaign spending, for instance, might not endorse his policies on reforming workers' compensation. Business and other groups that argue for shrinking New York's hospital system — a policy Spitzer has also endorsed — may have less interest in taxpayer financing of political campaigns. That change is coming to Albany is virtually certain. But what changes? The answer to that question will have to wait for a third edition of this book.

The State Constitution

In 1997, voters had an opportunity to demand major reform of state government by calling a constitutional convention. Advertising campaigns by public-employee unions and others helped persuade voters to reject the proposal. To be sure, dismissal of the call for a convention (which was placed on the ballot automatically, as happens every 20 years) was not unexpected. Aside from the well-financed campaign urging rejection, times seemed relatively good. New York was participating in the national economic boom and even starting to catch up to its competitor states, if still lagging behind the nationwide job-growth rates in most years. Crime rates were falling, and new leadership in Albany was enacting popular tax cuts and new programs.

The automatic opportunity for voters to call a constitutional convention will appear on the ballot in 2017. The Legislature could place such a proposal on the ballot any year. However, that possibility seems remote; most legislators strongly opposed the 1997 question on calling a convention. A popular governor might be able to force legislative consideration of the issue. While Spitzer has called for some constitutional changes, he has said such reforms might occur more easily through legislative action on individual amendments rather than at a convention.

Since the 1938 Constitutional Convention, the last to propose changes that were ratified by the people, the Legislature and voters have approved more than 130 individual amendments. Some emerged as single-issue proposals; others came from the 1967 proposed Constitution that voters rejected; and still others were from a commission appointed by Governor W. Averell Harriman and chaired by future Governor Nelson A. Rockefeller. Today, some supporters of constitutional change urge creation of a new "blue-ribbon" commission to propose reforms in numerous sections of the state's fundamental law.

With that backdrop, an issue that was last on the agenda almost a decade ago — the question of constitutional change — returned to the debate. New York State's fundamental law has a number of major flaws. For example:

- Key provisions of Article III, the section of the Constitution that defines the powers of the Legislature, have been dead letters for 40 years. In the 1960s, the U.S. Supreme Court ruled that state legislative districts must be drawn to give approximately equal weight to each citizen's vote. As has been true since New York's first Constitution, the text of the present charter directs the drawing of state Senate districts in ways that limit representation in the most populous counties. It also guarantees almost every county at least one Assembly district, creating overrepresentation for residents of lightly populated regions. As a result of the federal and state court decisions, those provisions of the state Constitution are no longer in force. Making the Constitution relevant and understandable to today's citizens would mean stripping the dead letters from the state's fundamental law and, at a minimum, replacing the outmoded provisions with language reflecting the legal reality today. As mentioned above, many observers argue for a further, more far-reaching, change to Article III: taking the redistricting power from sitting legislators and giving it to an independent commission such as Ohio and some other states do.

- The Judiciary article creates a court system that a succession of judicial leaders, including Chief Judge Judith Kaye, have described as so complex and inefficient that it harms the cause of justice. Major elements of the system are three centuries old. Judge Kaye has asked the Legislature to make major changes, some of which would require constitutional change. The Legislature has refused most such proposals.

- State debt, among the highest in the country, continues to rise sharply. In the mid-1800s, concern over increasing state debt prompted constitutional restrictions on Albany's ability to borrow. Those restrictions, including a requirement that most borrowing be approved by voters, worked as intended for a century or so. The debt restrictions effectively acted to restrict state spending, given elected leaders' desire to avoid voter wrath by raising taxes too much. In the middle of the 20th century, Nelson A. Rockefeller and succeeding governors found the debt restrictions unacceptable. Rockefeller raised taxes sharply to pay for new programs such as expansion of the State University system and Medicaid, but the new tax revenue was not enough. Thus the state turned increasingly to borrowing carried out through its public authorities. Unless New Yorkers hold governors and legislators accountable for high and rising debt — or elected leaders decide of their own volition to change recent practices — the only way to limit future borrowing may be to update and strengthen the constitutional restrictions created in the Civil War era.

Numerous other proposals for constitutional change have emerged. Frustrated by the lack of legislative action on favored issues, advocates from various ideological perspectives have called for use of initiative and referendum, which allow voters to place policy proposals directly on the ballot. Organizations concerned about the state's tax burden suggest a constitutional limit on taxes, state spending, or both. Supporters of greater flexibility for local governments urge prohibition against new state mandates on municipalities and school districts. While there are arguments for each of these proposals, there are also arguments against. None appear likely to attract strong support soon from the Legislature. Without legislative approval, any amendments would have to await a constitutional convention before going to voters.

The Political and Governmental Culture of Albany

Beyond particular issues such as those involving budgets and legislative operations, there is the broader question of whether the political and governmental culture of New York State serves the people well. Political scientists in New York and elsewhere have given little attention to such issues, but the topic may be gaining attention. A good way to view the governmental culture of the American states is

> ...the degree to which state governments have a serious and substantive commitment to the functions and activities of government on a basis that emphasizes community values and the public service, and on issues of consequence is capable of transcending narrow partisan and personal interests.[14]

Using the following definition, research by the Rockefeller Institute of Government surveyed experts on the governmental culture of 17 states.

> States rank high ... for a good-government culture if they have leaders and leadership practices and traditions that are seen as transcending partisanship and calculations of personal political advantage, not on all matters, but in important situations such that substantive considerations are highlighted in the governmental process in a way that is widely recognized and accepted in the behavior of leading members of the legislature and leaders in the executive branch, and furthermore that this good-gov-

---

14 Richard P. Nathan, "Striking While the Iron is Hot: State and Local Transitions and the First 100 Days," in Udai Tambar and Andrew Rachlin, eds, *From Campaigning to Governing: Leadership in Transition*, Princeton, NJ: Princeton University, 2006, pp. 9-12.

ernment culture is reflected in the way state government is viewed by the public and in the way it is viewed and treated by the media.

The experts the Rockefeller Institute surveyed classified state governments in Maine, Michigan, South Dakota, Virginia, and Washington as having a tradition that emphasizes deliberative political processes focused in a serious way on the substance of government. All are also "relatively scandal free," according to the survey.

While the concept of "scandal free" leaves plenty of room for interpretation, New York State's government could hardly be considered in such a category. As noted in Chapter Four, Governor Cuomo initiated enactment of a state Ethics Law in 1987 after numerous scandals in both state and New York City government. A 2002 review of the law's implementation, by the executive director of the state Ethics Commission, concluded that "for those citizens and government officials who thirst for integrity in government, they may reasonably view the glass of reform as half full."[15]

As of 2006, nine members of the Legislature had been charged with bribery or other crimes within the past five years. All represented districts in New York City, where voters are particularly unlikely to be aware of their representatives in the Senate and Assembly — let alone the activities of those individuals. For these voters, state government is hardly "viewed by the public" at all. If democracy is designed to bring public pressure to bear on elected officials, it's not surprising that lack of public scrutiny — or even awareness — may be associated with a lack of good-government culture.

Criticisms of the political-governmental culture in Albany go beyond prominent cases. As discussed above, high-paid, special-interest lobbying by political allies and former top staff to the governor and legislative leaders convinces many observers that "narrow partisan and personal interests" are too much at play in Albany. Observers in the public and the media believe that state government often acts (or decides not to act) based on other than substance factors.

---

15 Karl J. Sleight, "With the Benefit of Experience: An Examination of the Ethics in Government Act of 1987 and the New York State Ethics Commission," in Patricia E. Salkin and Barbara F. Smith, eds., *Ethics in Government, The Public Trust: A Two-Way Street*, Albany, NY: New York State Bar Association, 2002.

The Road Ahead

Governments change over time because of the influence of two factors — institutions and individuals. Institutions include both organizational structures — political parties, legislative caucuses, interest groups — and legal structures, such as laws and regulations. The crucial human factor, individual leadership, is often overlooked in discussions of governmental reform. Ignoring it leaves a gap in our understanding of how government can and does change — for better or worse.

In the Legislature, calls for reform often focus on changing the operating rules of the Senate and Assembly. Yet legislators have proven that when they choose to do so, they can act the way voters want — for instance, by approving a budget on time — despite the presence of the same procedural framework that prevailed during 20 years of late budgets. The 2005 and 2006 budgets were adopted in a timely manner not because the Legislature changed its procedures, but because individual legislators and their leaders decided that timeliness was crucial.

In specific issue areas, elected leaders have been known to declare victory for "reform" by adopting new procedural rules, rather than new policies. Rising concern about Albany's growing debt prompted Governor Pataki and the Legislature to enact the Debt Reform Act of 2000, which created statutory limits on most future borrowing. Rather than enact new rules, state leaders could have simply decided to reduce the level of new debt.

To be sure, legal and organizational institutions are important. Governor Smith initiated the Executive Budget system in the 1920s because he believed it would help him and other governors achieve important policy goals, including more responsible budgets. The legislative budgeting system he inherited made such results impossible, no matter how much political will and legislative wisdom Smith brought to bear. Yet even the Executive Budget system — widely regarded as one of the most important reforms in the state's history — does not guarantee sound budgets. Individual governors and individual legislators still decide on the policies that the budget reflects.

A longtime observer of Albany, journalist Jay Gallagher, published a book-length explication of criticisms, linking governmental failure to weakness in New York's economy, in late 2005.

...the Empire State has been slowly declining for the past half-century, losing much of its political and economic clout. Much of the blame ... can be laid at the feet of the men and women we send to the Capitol to serve us.

All too often they have acted in their own self-interest and that of the thousands of lobbyists who spent $144 million last year trying to influence them and less for the general good.

New York's government, Gallagher wrote, "seems to be lacking the principle that should be its focus: a dedication to the prosperity and well being of its citizens."[16] Many voters agree strongly with that sentiment.

All the criticisms of Albany, of course, do not change the fact that state government manages to accomplish enormous good every day. Children are educated; the elderly, poor, and incapacitated are cared for; the roads are paved and plowed. Citizens expect such services as the basics of government — and they pay for them. They reasonably expect that government will pursue its mission with appropriate standards of integrity, efficiency, and accountability. Rising demands for reform in recent years are based on widespread belief that Albany has not been meeting these standards.

16 Jay Gallagher, *The Politics of Decline: A Chronicle of New York's Descent and What You Can Do to Save Your State*, Albany, NY: Whitston Publishing Co. Inc., 2005.

Chapter Three

THE UPSTATE CHALLENGE

Key points:

- Longstanding economic, social and political differences between Upstate and Downstate New York are among the most important elements of the state's political and governmental culture.

- Most of the Upstate region has suffered from chronic economic problems for more than a decade, and debates over how to address such problems are now a top public-policy concern.

- Reducing the overall cost of doing business, developing high-tech industries, and restoring vitality to downtowns are among the most commonly cited solutions to Upstate's economic woes.

When the young United States of America considered building a union that would be stronger than the one created by the Articles of Confederation, the outcome was highly uncertain. The flaws of the nation's first charter were clear — starting with the lack of authority to raise revenue or do much else without consent of the states. Yet distrust of centralized governmental power remained strong when Congress sent the proposed Constitution to the states for ratification in 1787.

No state was more split over the federalist issue than was New York. After months of debate and elections for a state convention in Poughkeepsie, delegates voted 30-27 in favor of ratification on July 26, 1788. The Federalists, led by Alexander Hamilton and others, supported a stronger central government. They included most wealthy landowners, leading merchants and professionals such as lawyers who served them. George Clinton's Antifederalists, many of them farmers and other small-business owners, were motivated largely by fear that a far-off, national government would restrict their liberty to live as they chose, and would impose taxes they could not afford.

When the votes were counted, all the delegates from what we now call Upstate opposed the more powerful central government. All those from south of Orange and Dutchess counties were in favor.[1]

More than two centuries later, the political and economic divide between Upstate and Downstate retains some of that historical flavor. Downstate is far wealthier, on average; it's home to higher proportions of rich as well as poor. Upstaters tend to be more socially and fiscally conservative, and Downstaters more liberal. The pace of life is faster in New York City and its environs. West of Albany, Upstate becomes progressively more Midwestern and middle American. The Big Apple is one of the world's great centers of immigration; nearly half of its residents are foreign-born, while in most Upstate cities the proportion is less than 5 percent. International migration into the big city makes its population younger than it would otherwise be; outmigration of the young from much of Upstate means that its residents tend to be relatively older.

The differences are not only social and economic, but political — especially those between Upstate and New York City. In 1994, voters in the Big Apple favored Democratic Governor Mario Cuomo more than 2-to-1 over Republican challenger George Pataki; north and west of Westchester County, the numbers were nearly reversed. When the Legislature puts a borrowing proposal on the ballot, supporters plan big get-out-the-vote efforts in New York City to overcome the sizable "no" vote they expect from Upstate.

---

1   David M. Ellis et al., *A History of New York State*, Ithaca, NY: Cornell University Press, 1967, p. 127.

Key Indicators, Upstate and Downstate New York			
	Upstate	*Downstate*	*U.S.*
Population growth, 1940-90	44%	28%	89%
Population growth, 1990-2000	1.1%	8.2%	13%
Population change, ages 20-34, 1990-2000	-22.4%	-5.9%	-5.4%
Change in private-sector employment, 1990-2005	3.5%	5.0%	22.6%
Personal income, 2004 (millions)	$206,385	$531,371	$9,731,400
Poverty rate, 2000	11%	16%	11.3%
Percentage of total votes cast for George W. Bush, 2004	48.8%	33.7%	50.7%

Sources: U.S. Census Bureau; U.S. Bureau of Labor Statistics; Public Policy Institute of New York State; Brookings Institution; Federal Elections Commission

Through the decades, public discussion of Upstate-Downstate relations has frequently been characterized by acrimony and derision. New York Mayor Ed Koch famously called rural Upstate "a joke," insulting the men's department-store suits and the women's "gingham dresses." Upstate legislators periodically proposed establishing the region as a separate state, to break away from the perceived negative effects of association with the big city. After more than a decade of economic troubles facing Upstate, though, the discussion has taken on new seriousness and urgency. Two lengthy articles in *The New York Times* in June 2006 signaled the end of any debate over whether the Upstate economy was in trouble, and whether the issue required special attention in Albany.[2]

This chapter outlines the now-chronic economic difficulties facing Upstate New York — an ongoing loss of jobs and people rivaling any in the country. It also examines the attendant loss of political influence for

---

2   Sam Roberts, "The Upstate Economy, the Problem That Still Plagues Politicians and Their Promises," June 11, 2006; and "Flight of Young Adults Is Causing Alarm Upstate," *The New York Times*, June 13, 2006.

Upstate — which some observers say has led to public policies in Albany that make it even more difficult for Upstate to make a comeback.

A Dramatic Reversal of Economic Fortunes

After completion of the Erie Canal in 1825 laid the foundation for New York to become the Empire State, the following century brought a flood of growth that created good jobs by the thousands. The canal made partners of Upstate and the counties that would later become New York City, each enjoying enormous profits and growth from the grain and manufactured goods that were shipped from heartland America to the world.[3] From a combined 223,000 residents in 1830, New York and Kings counties grew to over 1 million 30 years later. By then, Erie (Buffalo) and Oneida (Utica) counties were each home to more than 100,000. With continued growth, New York City's population reached 3.4 million by the turn of the 20th century. It was by far the nation's biggest city, and Buffalo was the 8th-largest, with well over 300,000 people.

The entire state, and particularly its cities, continued to boom in the first decades of the new century. Buffalo, Rochester, Syracuse, and other major cities reached their all-time high populations in 1950. The state's economy was more than up to the task of providing jobs for millions of new residents. New Yorkers enjoyed rising incomes and improving quality of life. Wealthy, home-grown philanthropists sponsored major cultural institutions such as Buffalo's Albright Art Gallery (now the Albright-Knox); even smaller cities such as Schenectady were able to create sizable urban parks and other amenities with their growing tax revenue.

By World War II, New York State's economic and population growth had begun to slow relative to the rest of the nation's. And conditions within the state changed as Upstate began to outpace the New York City metropolitan area. From 1940 to 1990, the number of Upstate residents rose by 44 percent — significantly more than Downstate's 28 percent. During the devastating 1970s, Downstate shrank by 6.5 percent, with New York City in particular watching jobs and people seek better opportunities in lower-cost, lower-tax locations. Upstate's population rose slightly over the decade.

---

3   Peter L. Bernstein argues that the great canal not only produced a booming American economy, but led to repeal of tariffs, reduced costs of production and industrial development in Great Britain and Europe. See *Wedding of the Waters: The Erie Canal and the Making of a Great Nation*, New York, NY: W.W. Norton & Co., 2005.

Changes In Population, Regions of New York State
(population in thousands)

Year	Downstate		Upstate	
	Population	Change from 10 years earlier	Population	Change from 10 years earlier
1910	5,292	39%	3,822	10%
1920	6,256	18%	4,129	8.0%
1930	7,989	27%	4,599	11.4%
1940	8,724	9.2%	4,755	3.4%
1950	9,576	9.8%	5,254	10.5%
1960	10,729	12%	6,053	15.2%
1970	11,632	8.4%	6,609	9.2%
1980	10,880	-6.5%	6,678	1.0%
1990	11,156	2.5%	6,834	2.3%
2000	12,068	8.2%	6,908	1.1%

Source: U.S. Census Bureau

Although the faltering of the Empire State had begun mid-century, the first major academic review of New York State's failure to keep pace with the nation was a 1981 book that grew out of the State Museum's bicentennial planning. Its authors wrote:

> In the postwar era, three developments are particularly striking. From the very first, the growth of the New York economy lagged behind that of the nation: in population, in employment, and in per capita income. Second, this retardation accelerated sharply in the 1970s as total employment actually declined and population growth turned negative. Third, all of these developments were particularly marked in New York City.[4]

The Big Apple suffered further in the recession of the early 1990s — a mild recession in most of the country that hit much harder in New York State, particularly New York City. Yet the city boomed again starting in mid-decade. With record gains on Wall Street, favorable federal tax policies, sharp reductions in crime, major increases in immigration, and tourism, the city's population reached all-time highs at more than 8 million.

Upstate, though, the trends were heading in the opposite direction. Over the 15 years ending in 2005, Upstate's economic performance was among the worst in the country:

- If considered as a separate state, Upstate's population growth during the 1990s would have ranked 49th in the nation, ahead of only North Dakota and West Virginia. And one study found that nearly 30 percent of Upstate's growth reflected increases in state prison populations.[5]

- Upstate's personal income rose at half the national pace during the 1990s — and most of its new income came from gains in Social Security, public and private pensions and other transfer payments, rather than new economic activity.[6]

---

4   Peter D. McClelland and Alan L. Magdovitz, *Crisis in the Making: The Political Economy of New York State Since 1945*, New York, NY: Cambridge University Press, 1981.

5   Rolf Pendall, *Upstate New York's Population Plateau: The Third-Slowest Growing 'State,'* Brookings Institution Center on Urban and Metropolitan Policy, Washington, DC, August 2003.

6   Rolf Pendall and Susan Christopherson, *Losing Ground: Income and Poverty in Upstate New York, 1980-2000*, Brookings Institution Center on Urban and Metropolitan Policy, Washington, DC, September 2004.

- While manufacturing has been the region's economic bedrock for over a century, industrial employment throughout Upstate fell by nearly a third from 1990 through 2005 — a greater loss proportionally than almost any state, and significantly worse than trends in comparable areas such as Michigan and Ohio. Meanwhile, almost all net new jobs in Upstate were either on public payrolls, or in sectors such as health care and social services that largely depend on taxpayer funding.[7]

Upstate's economic woes are especially visible west of Albany. From 1996 to 2005, according to Empire State Development, private-sector employment in the "Upstate West" region rose by less than 2 percent. The comparable growth nationwide was more than 16 percent, and in New York City-Long Island, around 10 percent.[8] From 2001 to 2006, while U.S. employment rose by 2 percent, metropolitan areas such as Binghamton, Buffalo-Niagara Falls, Elmira, Rochester, and Utica lost jobs, as shown in data compiled by the Fiscal Policy Institute. If the Binghamton area had kept pace with nationwide growth over the five years, it would have gained 2,400 jobs by 2006, instead of losing 8,100. In the Buffalo-Niagara region, matching the nation's pace would have meant an additional 18,000 jobs in 2006.[9]

A Rising Tide, Then an Ebb, of Manufacturing Jobs

For Upstate in particular, the rise and fall of fortune over more than a century largely reflected the flow of manufacturing activity. Much of the United States boomed with the industrial revolution in the late 1800s and early 1900s. That growth in factory-based employment continued through World War II and well into the post-war era, reaching a high of 19.4 million in 1979. Nowhere was the term "industrial powerhouse" more appropriate than in New York. Home to one in 10 Americans in 1940, the state accounted for one in seven U.S. industrial jobs.

7   David F. Shaffer, *Could New York Let Upstate Be Upstate?*, Albany, NY: The Public Policy Institute, May 2004.

8   John Bacheller, *Structural Change in the Upstate Economy*, presentation at the Rockefeller Institute of Government, Albany, NY, September 15, 2006.

9   Author's calculations from Fiscal Policy Institute data in *The State of Working New York 2006: An Uneven Recovery*, Latham, NY, September 2006.

Manufacturing employment in New York reached a high of more than 2 million in the mid-1950s, but the state's share of the national total started declining. By 1980, population had dropped noticeably relative to other states.

Manufacturing declined even more precipitously. From 1959 through 1979, New York lost 400,000 manufacturing jobs — while the United States as a whole gained 4 million. Through the start of the 21st century, factory-related employment declined nationwide, due to sharp increases in both labor productivity and global competition. New York continued to suffer disproportionately. For much of the period, the state lost an average of 100 manufacturing jobs a day.[10]

Besides losing more industrial jobs, New York did far worse than most states in keeping and attracting the highest-paying jobs. Nationwide, reductions in manufacturing employment were concentrated in lower- and mid-skill positions, according to the Buffalo Branch of the Federal Reserve Bank of New York. The number of high-skilled manufacturing jobs across the country rose dramatically, by 37 percent, from 1983 to 2002, as factory workers increasingly came to use sophisticated machinery that added value to their work while eliminating the need for many lower-paid jobs. In New York, though, even high-skilled jobs declined by 14.3 percent over the period. While other northern, historically industrialized states also suffered large losses in overall employment, most gained skilled jobs while New York was losing them. Employment in such positions rose by more than 20 percent each in Massachusetts, Pennsylvania, Ohio, and Michigan, although it declined 10 percent in Connecticut.[11]

Overall manufacturing losses were heavy throughout New York State, but the economic and social damage was greatest west and north of Albany where, unlike Downstate, employment in other sectors was also relatively flat. As of 2005, the statewide total of 580,000 manufacturing jobs represented just over 4 percent of the national total — roughly a third of the comparable share half a century earlier.

The loss of industry devastated many small Upstate communities where one or more local factories had provided the best paychecks and benefits, with each job supporting one to three others in supply,

---

10 Robert B. Ward, "100 Lost Jobs a Day," *New York Post*, November 7, 2003.

11 Richard Deitz, "Restructuring in the Manufacturing Workforce: New York State and the Nation," *The Regional Economy of Upstate New York*, Winter 2004, Buffalo Branch, Federal Reserve Bank of New York, Buffalo, NY.

services, retail, government, and other sectors. While some residents moved away to seek opportunity, others remained, struggling to survive on reduced incomes that often required public and/or private support (see sidebar on next page).

Sharp Decline in Upstate Cities

While many of Upstate's small towns and rural areas were in decline in the second half of the 20th century, most of the region's cities lost population as well. Among the 61 cities statewide, 25 experienced five consecutive decades of population losses from 1950 through the end of the century, according to the Office of the State Comptroller. The average population drop in those localities was 26 percent. Major cities that had anchored Upstate's boom suffered even greater losses.

> In terms of population loss, the large upstate cities have been particularly hard hit. For example, the City of Buffalo lost approximately half of its population from 1950 to 2000. This population loss is the fourth highest among large cities nationwide. Rochester (34 percent decline) and Syracuse (33 percent decline) experienced significant population reductions for the same period. Like Buffalo, these cities have had five consecutive decades of declining population levels. [12]

The comptroller's report put the cities' decline in the context of industrial shifts Upstate and nationwide. "Manufacturing-focused cities," it said, "have steadily lost ground to lower-cost competitors in other states and foreign countries."

> The steel industry provides a good illustration of the forces behind these trends. While the demand for steel has remained strong, production technology and corporate practices have shifted. The proliferation of "mini-mills" in lower cost, non-unionized regions of the U.S. has enabled smaller start-up companies to produce steel at a more competitive rate. As a result, steel-centered metropolitan areas such as Buffalo, Youngstown and Pittsburgh — areas which were home to the less competitive, larger, integrated and heavily unionized steel production firms — have all experienced a virtual disappearance of their steel production facilities. [13]

---

12 Office of the State Comptroller, *Population Trends in New York State's Cities*, Albany, NY, December 2004.

13 Ibid.

"We Are in Desperate Times"

Experts in the private sector, government and academia have written detailed analyses of the weak Upstate New York economy in recent years. None of those reports, though, captures the human impact of economic stagnation better than did the Salvation Army in a fall 2005 newsletter. An excerpt follows.

"We are in desperate times here in Canton — really all around Upstate New York," says Shari Wilcox, Chairman of The Salvation Army Service Unit in Canton, NY, and Executive Director of the Church and Community Program.

"Meghan is just one example of how the children have been affected by the stress their parents are going through. She was a troubled high school student from a single-parent home. She was put in my care while doing her community service for her crime," explains Shari. "She got caught stealing toilet paper. Why did she do it? She overheard her mom say times were so bad they couldn't even afford toilet paper," says Shari....

Shari described how the Canton community was once a thriving area with a major food manufacturer providing plenty of good-paying jobs. That company left years ago along with all of the major grocery stores and department stores that catered to the working class....

(W)here do the people live?

"Predominantly in trailers and substandard housing," says Shari. "And one of the biggest problems we have is keeping these people warm, especially the ones in trailers," she says. "There's no insulation."

And going hungry is always an issue. "The nearest grocery store is over five miles away!" Shari raises her voice. "People can't afford cars, and there are no buses — no taxis. So they go to the convenience store at the gas station where everything costs a small fortune and it's basically junk food," she says, shaking her head.

From "Young Meghan Gets Caught Stealing for Her Family: What Made Her Do It?", *On The March*, The Salvation Army Empire State Division, Syracuse, NY, Fall 2005.

As jobs and residents moved away, most cities saw their tax bases stagnate or decline. With revenues flat or barely increasing, continual increases in public-employee compensation and other expenses, and lack of productivity improvement, mayors were forced into service reductions that prompted more residents — disproportionately those who were more affluent — to depart. Cities such as Buffalo, Syracuse, and Niagara Falls now have "severely constrained revenue streams, high levels of debt and high fixed costs — suggesting that they are so negatively affected by fiscal stress that they have very little local capacity to attain long-term fiscal stability and growth," the comptroller's office said.[14] With their population down by a third or even half in recent decades, most Upstate cities saw housing quality decline and numerous local service businesses close their doors. Once-lively neighborhoods deteriorated into communities of concentrated poverty, often afflicted with high levels of crime and family dysfunction.

The Upstate Economy Becomes a Political Issue

One of the first observers to point out the decline in Upstate's economic fortunes was then-Assemblyman Charles Schumer, who made the Upstate economy an issue in his 1998 campaign for the U.S. Senate.[15] Two years later, then-First Lady Hillary Clinton echoed the call for special attention to Upstate in her campaign for Senate. Her opponent, U.S. Rep. Rick Lazio, spoke more positively about trends in the region, drawing harsh criticism from some editorial pages and perhaps damaging his electoral chances. In an endorsement editorial, for instance, *The Buffalo News* wrote: "The decisive factor for Western New Yorkers in this tightly contested and closely watched race should be Clinton's early and strong grasp of the economic challenges faced by this region."[16]

Since then, candidates for statewide office or legislative seats from most of Upstate have considered it essential to talk about proposed solutions to the region's economic stagnation. In 2006, both gubernatorial candidates spoke repeatedly on the issue, offering detailed plans to reduce taxes and take other steps that would reinvigorate the region.

---

14 Office of the State Comptroller, *Analysis of Fiscal Stress in New York State's Cities*, Albany, NY, February 2006.

15 See, for example, Adam Nagourney, "Schumer Tours Upstate to Counter Attacks by D'Amato," *The New York Times*, September 28, 1998. In 1994, state Senator George E. Pataki made rebuilding the state's economy a central plank of his ultimately successful run for governor. With New York City still early in its rejuvenation, however, he made little distinction between the state's overall economic trends and those in Upstate.

16 "Clinton for Senate," editorial, *The Buffalo News*, October 30, 2000.

What Explains Upstate's Long Decline?

Upstate's longstanding reliance on manufacturing has been a major factor in the region's failure to keep pace with Downstate and the nation. Manufacturing employment across the country is down some 20 percent since 1998. Although the Midwest and other regions that historically depend heavily on industry have also suffered, national manufacturing trends cannot fully explain Upstate's troubles. During the mid-1990s, Upstate lost tens of thousands of factory jobs while the nation gained several hundred thousand. Over a longer period, from 1990 through 2005, manufacturing employment declined 20 percent nationwide — and by 35 percent in Upstate New York. States such as Illinois, Ohio, and Michigan have enjoyed double-digit percentage gains in overall private-sector employment since 1990, while Upstate's increase was less than 4 percent.[17]

Using a statistical technique called shift-share analysis, federal labor economists concluded that New York lost the equivalent of 1.8 million jobs due to its failure to match nationwide growth levels in each of its employment sectors from 1983 to 1995. The analysis is designed to eliminate statistical effects from such factors as nationwide economic trends and differences in industry mix among states.[18]

> New York … had the worst overall share index. With the exception of mining (a very minor industry in New York), employment in all major industry groups grew at rates substantially less than the national average over all periods examined.[19]

In other words, employment in the Empire State suffered dramatically for reasons that had nothing to do with the national economy or the state's unique combination of industries. Among other relevant factors, the economists concluded, in a time of increasing global competition, "firms and industries are less constrained by geographic factors than was previously the case." New York also had a relatively low level

---

17 Bureau of Labor Statistics data.

18 William G. Deming, "A decade of economic change and population shifts in U.S. regions," *Monthly Labor Review*, U.S. Department of Labor, Washington, DC, November 1996.

19 Ibid.

Is Upstate Becoming Appalachia?

"If you drive from Schenectady to Niagara Falls," Eliot Spitzer said during the 2006 gubernatorial campaign, "you'll see an economy that is devastated. It looks like Appalachia. This is not the New York we dream of."

While political opponents criticized the comparison to the region that had come to symbolize American poverty, employment and population data support the observation — which did not originate with Spitzer. Assemblyman Joseph Morelle, a Monroe County Democrat, had made a similar comment not long before. A 2004 report by the Public Policy Institute of New York State reviewed employment and population trends in the region and asked, "Is Upstate New York going the way of Appalachia?"*

Indeed, some key indicators show Appalachia far outpacing Upstate in recent years. The Appalachian region — all of West Virginia and parts of 12 other states, including 14 counties along New York's Southern Tier — saw its population rise by 9.1 percent in the 1990s, according to the Appalachian Regional Commission. Even central Appalachia, the poorest section, enjoyed a 6 percent increase in population. By contrast, the number of Upstate New York residents rose 1.1 percent; excluding the Hudson Valley, the region lost population during the decade.

Appalachia gained a net 700,000 new residents from elsewhere in the United States during the 1990s. Upstate New York lost some 400,000 more than it gained in domestic migration.

Overall employment in Upstate rose 0.2 percent in 2005. Eleven of the other 12 states included in the Congressionally designated Appalachian region did better. West Virginia, the heart of Appalachia, produced new jobs at a rate of 1.4 percent; if Upstate had matched that pace, it would have gained an additional 36,000 jobs.

Still, Upstate New York retains some of its historic economic strength. Average annual wages in the New York counties considered part of Appalachia were far higher, just over $40,000, than the Appalachian median of $29,000, in 2000. More people live in poverty throughout Appalachia (13.6 percent, as of 2000) than in Upstate New York (11 percent).

---

*   Shaffer, *Could New York Let Upstate Be Upstate?*, ibid.

> Broome, Chemung, Chautauqua, and other counties that represent Appalachian New York boast higher educational levels, with 83 percent of residents holding high-school diplomas and 21 percent college degrees as of 2000. Throughout Appalachia, those figures were 77 and 18 percent, respectively. Still, the educational gap between Appalachian New York and the overall Appalachian region was smaller than it had been in 1980.

of federal defense spending, as a share of gross state product, and its share fell by more than half during the period studied.

Analysis of the Upstate economy by the Buffalo Branch of the Federal Reserve Bank of New York points to a cycle in which "people follow jobs and jobs follow people."

> Manufacturing employment has been moving from the Northeast to other parts of the country to pursue lower cost resources, such as labor and land, and has tended to avoid unionized labor in the Northeast. Service sector employment in support of manufacturing, such as transportation and warehousing jobs, has followed.[20]

Lifestyle factors such as warmer weather to the south have contributed to the problem, according to the Buffalo Fed. Yet those factors also affect states where, as noted earlier in this chapter, employment trends have been more favorable.

Business leaders and many economists point to high business costs in New York, including Upstate, as the key disadvantage in global and national competition for jobs. One of the most prominent critics of the state's business environment has been the chairman of Buffalo-based M&T Bank, Robert G. Wilmers. Among other comments, Wilmers has compared his company's marketplace in Upstate New York with areas such as neighboring Pennsylvania, where M&T acquired Allfirst Financial Inc. in 2003.

> (L)ocal government taxes as a percentage of personal income in Upstate New York are fully 35% above the national average, a level higher

---

20 Richard Deitz, "Population Out-Migration From Upstate New York," *The Regional Economy of Upstate New York*, Winter 2005, Buffalo Branch, Federal Reserve Bank of New York.

than any state except New York as a whole (including downstate). In contrast, central Pennsylvania — a market in which the Allfirst acquisition has increased M&T's presence — stands 31% below the national average in the bite taken by local taxes. This is just one of the many reasons we are more hopeful about that region's economic prospects.[21]

New York's high business costs go beyond a combined state and local tax burden that studies consistently rank as the highest or second-highest in the nation. Electric prices for commercial and industrial users are often 20 to 30 percent lower elsewhere in the United States. Workers' compensation premiums are significantly higher in New York; in 2006, the chief executive officer of Delphi Corp. cited the issue in discussion of whether the company would retain a major auto-parts factory in the Buffalo area. Upstate property taxes, particularly on commercial and industrial property, are also higher than those in many competing locations.

Extensive anecdotal and research evidence indicates that business executives and investors react to high costs. Mark Bitz, a Central New York business owner, estimated that energy, property taxes, employee health insurance, and workers' compensation cost his company a total of $600,000 more in New York than would have been the case in a typical competing state.[22] With gross sales of $20 million, that figure would represent a substantial difference in annual profits. Separately, a corporate site-selection consultant concluded that opening a bank data center with 75 employees in the Buffalo-Niagara region would require an investment of $11.6 million, nearly $2 million more than the cost in Sioux Falls, South Dakota.[23]

While business costs are especially high in the New York City metropolitan region, companies there typically can overcome high costs by virtue of the city's global status in financial and business services, corporate headquarters and other high-value activities. Most of Upstate has relatively high costs, but lacks those advantages.

Gubernatorial candidates Eliot Spitzer and John Faso both cited Upstate's high business costs frequently during their 2006 campaign. More detailed comments by Spitzer appear later in this chapter.

---

21 Robert G. Wilmers, "Message To Stockholders," *2004 Annual Report*, M&T Bank Corp.

22 Mark W. Bitz, *Creating A Prosperous New York State*, 2006.

23 David Robinson, "Cheap power, incentives clinched deal for data center," *The Buffalo News*, Buffalo, NY, October 15, 2006.

Still, Some Key Advantages

While its recent history is discouraging, Upstate New York retains much of the long-term economic and human capital built up over more than a century — significant advantages in a national and global marketplace that increasingly values education, innovation and quality of life.

The region remains an economic force on a par with states such as Virginia and North Carolina, with a gross product — the total value of goods and services produced — of $262 billion in 2000.

With institutions such as Cornell, the University of Rochester, SUNY campuses at Buffalo and Albany, Syracuse University, and others, Upstate is home to a disproportionate share of respected colleges and universities. The initiative by Governor Pataki and the Legislature to develop Centers of Excellence in nanotechnology, biotechnology, and other advanced fields is expected to attract billions in private investment and significant numbers of new jobs — and, in limited fashion, has already begun to do so. Long-established research locations include Saranac Lake's Trudeau Institute, in the heart of the Adirondacks, as well as major corporate research/development centers such as General Electric's outside Schenectady and IBM's in the Hudson Valley.

New York's rich cultural and economic heritage leaves Upstate home to nationally and internationally respected centers of culture such as the Chautauqua Institution, where more than 140,000 visitors attend summertime programs and classes on public issues, the arts, science, foreign affairs, and other topics. Museums such as the Women's Hall of Fame in Seneca Falls, birthplace of the women's movement, recall Upstate's historical leadership in advancing human rights. The Corning Glass Museum, International Museum of Photography and Film, and Albany Institute of History and Art educate 21st-century students and tourists on industrial advances that built Upstate's economy decades ago and remain important today. For the increasing number of history buffs across the country, the Saratoga battlefield and Fort Ticonderoga are among dozens of important landmarks.

Home prices in most of Upstate are relatively affordable, compared to those in many other metro areas (although, as mentioned, high property taxes reduce buyers' purchasing power). Visitors from regions such as Atlanta and Los Angeles envy Upstate's easier commutes and shorter distances to lakes and wilderness. Outsiders often find Upstaters generally nicer than people in many other areas; Buffalo, for example, was named the nation's "friendliest city" in a 2001 poll by *USA Today*. Other quality-of-life advantages include breathtaking natural environments, from the 6-million-acre Adirondack Park to Genesee County's Letchworth Gorge and Niagara Falls.

There are some signs that these and other advantages are producing more positive results for the region. The number of Upstate residents moving out declined, and those moving in rose, after the mid-1990s, according to the Brookings Institution.[24] In the year ending in August 2006, the Elmira region added jobs at a faster pace than the nation, while the Syracuse region showed some strength as well. Binghamton added manufacturing jobs during the same period. In Buffalo, development of the Lake Erie waterfront and other projects held promise of better times ahead.

Looking Ahead

If the level of attention given to the Upstate economy is any indication, there may be reason to hope for broader recovery. After years of increasing agitation by business executives, editorial writers and citizen activists, no issue commands a higher ranking on the must-do list for Albany.

What to do, precisely?

Business advocates are more united than ever in urging state leaders to "let Upstate be Upstate," or to "unshackle Upstate," by changing policies to reduce business costs in the region.

> Left to its own devices, for example, Upstate would never have a Medicaid program that is by far the most expensive in the country — helping to push property taxes to the highest levels in the nation. Upstate wouldn't have kept tolls on the Thruway after the early 1990s, when the last bonds were being paid off and the late Sen. Daniel Patrick Moynihan was extracting $5 billion in federal funds to help remove the tolls. Upstate probably wouldn't have laws (e.g., the Triborough provision) giving public-employee unions such decisive leverage to drive up local government costs, and to block consolidation or privatization of services.

---

24 Pendall, *Upstate New York's Population Plateau*, ibid.

Upstate wouldn't choose energy policies that push basic industrial electric rates about 17 percent above the national average — while a competitor like Ohio has rates below the national average.[25]

Business groups and taxpayer advocates argue that Albany's political and ideological culture has become more reflective of Downstate's traditional approach to public policy, one dominated by public-sector unions and other voices that favor higher spending and taxes, and more government regulation of private businesses. Clearly, with the state's population shifting Downstate in recent years, the metropolitan region has gained seats in the Legislature at the expense of Upstate; that trend is likely to continue after the 2010 Census. Assembly Democrats, with the city as their primary stronghold, were in their fourth decade of control. Republicans, with an Upstate and suburban base, retained the majority in the Senate, but many political observers expected that to change in coming years due to ongoing population and demographic shifts.

Some community activists blame New York's high taxes on its complex, costly array of local governments and lack of regional cooperation on planning and economic development. They urge giving county governments more authority to limit local tax abatements that reduce government revenue, and to develop comprehensive land-use and transportation plans to push investment to core urbanized areas.[26]

The state's economic-development efforts rely heavily on tax exemptions and other financial incentives provided by programs such as Empire Zones. Using tax revenues that flow disproportionately from the New York metropolitan area, state officials spend a majority of economic-development dollars in Upstate, according to statistics from the state business-promotion agency, Empire State Development. From 1995 through 2005, some 992 companies in New York City and Long Island received funding from the state's major economic-development programs, compared to more than 2,200 companies in, or north and west of, the Capital Region. Funding for major projects totaled $431 million in the "Upstate-West" region, $275 million in the Hudson Valley and $225 million in New York City and Long Island.[27]

---

25 Shaffer, *Could New York Let Upstate Be Upstate?*, ibid.

26 David Rusk, *Upstate New York: A House Divided*, May 20, 2005.

27 Bacheller, "Structural Change in the Upstate Economy," ibid.

The New Governor's Plan For Upstate

In numerous formal addresses and other settings, gubernatorial candidate Eliot Spitzer outlined his ideas for improving the Upstate economy. This statement, published in the Utica Observer-Dispatch on October 1, 2006, is one typical example of his comments.

The decline of manufacturing over the last few decades has left upstate hemorrhaging jobs, people and its tax base. From 1990 to 2004, upstate lost 33 percent of its manufacturing base, more than any other state. Since 1990, upstate lost 25 percent of its young people ages 20 to 34. This cannot continue. Revitalizing the upstate economy requires a co-ordinated and sustained effort. Our government should have no higher priority than standing up for New York State's economic future and making New York the best place to do business in America.

First, we must make business more competitive by improving New York State's business climate. Second, we must foster innovation and cultivate the growth of strategic industries and expand the research capacity at our colleges and universities in areas with direct commercial applications.

Third, we must revitalize our cities and downtowns to make them economically vibrant places to live and work. Fourth, we must implement a focused program to support small businesses. Fifth and finally, we must develop a transportation, energy and broadband Internet infra-structure that will create and support economic expansion. With dedicated leadership, New York will emerge as a state where ideas are born, companies are raised and jobs and careers thrive.

Upstate's "good living" could be an important attraction as many Americans' rising incomes and increased mobility create competition for residents. Some observers suggest a broad initiative to develop communities with a "New Urbanism" approach of mixed residential and small-business properties, pedestrian-friendly streets, and high levels of amenities.

(T)here's good living in upstate New York, you can get a nice house for modest prices, good schools, you can commute easily. There are nodes in Saratoga, Albany, the Finger Lakes, where you can build on the am-biance. New strategies might be ripe for these times: not smokestack-chasing, not big factories, but communities that can attract people.[28]

Some new Americans are discovering the good living of Upstate as a result of invitations from longtime residents. Over the last 20 years, two Upstate cities — Utica and Schenectady — have bolstered population counts and urban vitality by attracting thousands of international immigrants. Refugee groups in Utica encouraged more than 10,000 individuals from Bosnia, other areas of Eastern Europe, Southeast Asia, and elsewhere to move to Oneida County. Schenectady officials traveled to neighborhoods in Queens where many immigrants from Guyana had made homes, inviting families and individuals to move to the Electric City. More than 1,000 Guyanese did so in the past decade. Such immigrants have strengthened housing prices, created small businesses, and provided qualified workers for established manufacturing companies in the two areas. While refugees may drive up local social-services and educational costs in the short run, the Utica and Schenectady experiences are among the most positive steps local officials in Upstate have taken on their own to reverse discouraging population trends.

Each effort to build a better future carries its own challenges. None alone will return Upstate to its historic position as a driver of economic growth for the Empire State and the nation — and perhaps no combination of steps will do so. Clearly, though, frustrated Upstate residents who consider current economic and political conditions intolerable are being heard in Albany. State leaders pledge a combination of a more competitive business environment, and focused efforts to stimulate economic development, that together will lead to new jobs and good reasons for young New Yorkers to stay New Yorkers. If those promises come true, and if a new Upstate generation can rediscover the entrepreneurial genius of the past, the region's best days lie ahead.

---

28 Richard P. Nathan, quoted in "The Upstate Economy, the Problem That Still Plagues Politicians and Their Promises," ibid.

Chapter Four

THE GOVERNOR AND OTHER STATEWIDE ELECTED LEADERS

Key points:

- The governor of New York is one of the most powerful elected executives in the nation, with particularly extensive authority over the state budget.

- In addition to formal powers, governors can focus public and political attention on key issues — but they tend not to use the "bully pulpit" to its potential.

- Pension and regulatory powers make the comptroller and attorney general increasingly important.

The colonial leaders who created the American presidency — and, in New York and other states, the office of governor — distrusted executive power after living under kings whom they considered tyrants. The chief executive offices they created reflected that distrust, with most power given to the other branches of government. Yet, for a variety of reasons — some written in law, others that are matters of political practice — the office of governor in most states acquired significant new influence during the 20th century.

That was true in the Empire State, which even from the earliest days of the nation vested more power in its chief executive than most other states. Of the original 13, "Only in New York, Massachusetts and Connecticut did governors have much power or serve for any length of time" during the early years of the Republic, James Q. Wilson has written.[1]

Today, New York's governor is among the most powerful state leaders, and one of the most influential governmental leaders in the nation at any level. The state Constitution and statutes give the chief executive enormous control over the budget and administration of state agencies and criminal justice, as well as more limited influence over legislation. Beyond the written law, political folkways strengthen the governor's hand in dealing with the Legislature over the passage of laws.

This chapter will review the powers of the governor and explore how he or she can use those powers. The chapter will also look at two of the three executive departments not directly controlled by the governor: the Department of Audit and Control (the Office of the State Comptroller), and the Department of Law (the Office of the Attorney General). The third such agency, the Department of Education, overseen by the Board of Regents and Education Commissioner, will be examined in Chapter 12.

A Powerful Executive

In terms of its formal power within a state government, New York's chief executive office today is consistently ranked among the most powerful in the country. For example, a 2005 analysis by political scientist Thad L. Beyle concluded that no governor in the nation has greater "institutional" powers than New York's governor.[2] Chief-executive offices in Alaska, New Jersey, and West Virginia were tied with New York's at the top of the power list. The Beyle study includes six institutional indicators of gubernatorial power:

---

1   James Q. Wilson, *American Government: Institutions and Policies*, Lexington, MA: D.C. Heath and Co., 1980; p. 308

2   Available online at *http://www.unc.edu/~beyle/*.

- Number of separately elected officials with executive-branch responsibilities.

- Length of, and limits on the number of, terms in office.

- Appointment powers in major areas such as education, health, and corrections.

- Veto power and the possibility of legislative overrides.

- Budgeting power.

- Congruence of political party control of the executive and legislative branches.

Beyle's analysis gives the Empire State's chief-executive office its highest possible score for tenure and veto power, and a high score for influence over the budget. On a scale of 1 to 5, the overall New York rating was 4.1 — significantly higher than the 50-state average of 3.5. As Frank J. Thompson wrote of the ratings, originally published in 1995 and since updated, "If Gov. Pete Wilson of California is to provide leadership comparable to that of Gov. George Pataki in New York, he will need to be much more adroit at manipulating the informal levers of power."[3]

A second rating, published in conjunction with an earlier version of the Beyle study, examined "enabling" resources available to governors in each state. Such resources include gubernatorial staff and office budget in relation to overall state government employment and spending, power to appoint cabinet members, and time available to prepare a state budget. New York's executive office ranked among the most powerful in the nation by these measures as well.[4]

In addition to the legal powers and institutional resources granted it, the governor's office in New York is unusually influential in several other ways:

---

3   Frank J. Thompson, "Executive Leadership as an Enduring Issue," *State and Local Government Review* 27, 1 (Winter 1995): 15.

4   "A Comparative Analysis of Gubernatorial Enabling Resources," *State and Local Government Review*, ibid., pp. 118-126. Other studies that have reached similar conclusions include Joseph A. Schlesinger, "The Politics of the Executive," in Herbert Jacob and Kenneth N. Vines, *Politics in the American States*, 2nd ed., Boston: Little, Brown, 1971, p. 232.

Institutional Powers of the Governorship, 2005			
State	*Total Score*	*State*	*Total Score*
Alabama	2.8	Nebraska	3.8
Alaska	4.1	Nevada	3.0
Arizona	3.4	New Hampshire	2.8
Arkansas	3.1	New Jersey	4.1
California	3.2	New Mexico	3.7
Colorado	3.6	New York	4.1
Connecticut	3.6	North Carolina	2.9
Delaware	3.5	North Dakota	3.9
Florida	3.6	Ohio	3.9
Georgia	3.2	Oklahoma	2.8
Hawaii	3.4	Oregon	3.3
Idaho	3.5	Pennsylvania	3.7
Illinois	3.8	Rhode Island	2.6
Indiana	3.1	South Carolina	3.0
Iowa	3.7	South Dakota	3.8
Kansas	3.3	Tennessee	3.8
Kentucky	3.5	Texas	3.2
Louisiana	3.4	Utah	4.0
Maine	3.6	Vermont	2.5
Maryland	3.8	Virginia	3.2
Massachusetts	3.6	Washington	3.6
Michigan	3.6	West Virginia	4.1
Minnesota	3.8	Wisconsin	3.3
Mississippi	2.9	Wyoming	3.1
Missouri	3.6		
Montana	3.6	Average, all states	3.5

Source: *http://www.unc.edu/~beyle/*

- The population and economy of the Empire State are larger than almost any other state's. Only California is larger in both these respects; while Texas passed New York in number of residents during the 1990s, its gross state product and total personal income — two key measures of economic strength — are still below New York's.

- New York State government exerts influence over more of its citizens' social and economic activity than do most state governments. In New York, the governor's legislative, appointment, and budgetary powers extend into major arenas — including marketing of electricity, pricing of rental apartments, and provision of medical care — far more than in most other states.

- New York State government exerts extraordinary control over local governments. Several studies have shown that Albany imposes more mandates on localities than do most other state capitals. And local taxes per capita in New York are by far the highest in the country — a reflection, in large part, of governors' and legislators' decisions to force localities to provide certain services or manage their operations in certain ways.

Taken together, these factors mean that the governor of New York may be the second most powerful chief elected executive in the nation, behind only the president.

True, decisions by the state government in Sacramento influence an economy and population far larger than those in any other state. The Golden State has also led the nation on cutting-edge issues such as reducing property taxes and scaling back affirmative-action programs in recent decades. On the other hand, such actions in California often arise from popular initiative rather than elected leaders. Political scientists tend to rank the executive office in California far behind New York, and even below the national average in terms of institutional power. The California governor's office is weakened by separately elected statewide officials who compete with the chief executive for governmental power and political leadership. Voters in the Golden State separately elect, for example, the lieutenant governor, the superintendent of public instruction, the insurance commissioner, and the secretary of state, whose duties include overseeing elections and corporate registration.

Governors and the Presidency

In recent decades, American voters have been comfortable with electing governors to the highest office in the land. From 1976 through 2004, former governors (Jimmy Carter, Ronald Reagan, Bill Clinton, and George W. Bush) won seven of eight presidential elections. Before Carter's campaign in 1976, no governor had been a major-party candidate for president since New York's Thomas E. Dewey in 1952.

New York governors were not among the candidates during that period, even though the other state leaders who were nominated and elected all had held less powerful offices than that of the chief executive of the Empire State. The governor's office in Arkansas, for example, is regarded as one of the least powerful in the nation. The office that was Clinton's springboard to the presidency has relatively weak powers of appointment and shares a relatively high level of power with other elected officials. In Texas, where Bush served as governor before assuming the presidency, the chief executive's office cedes extensive powers to other, separately elected officials. It also has relatively weak budgetary authority.

Massachusetts' executive office is considered weak in relation to appointments, but possessed of a strong veto power. Governor Michael Dukakis was the Democratic candidate for president in 1988. In Georgia, Carter's home state, Beyle rates the executive's overall powers below average. California, which sent Reagan to the White House, gives the governor extensive veto authority but shares executive power with numerous other statewide elected officials.

As the 2008 presidential elections approached, current or former governors who were mentioned as potential candidates included Republicans George Allen of Virginia, Mitt Romney of Massachusetts and George Pataki of New York; and Democrats Bill Richardson of New Mexico and Mark Warner of Virginia.

The nation's other most populous states, Texas and Florida, also rank far behind New York on most political scientists' scales of gubernatorial power. In Texas — the only state besides California with a population larger than New York's — the lieutenant governor is widely considered more powerful than the governor, having extensive power over legislation by virtue of presiding over the state Senate.[5] The Texas comptroller, an independently elected official, oversees tax collections and estimates revenues for the coming year — functions that in New York are under the authority of the governor; the comptroller also must certify that appropriations are within estimated revenue collections, an influential function that does not exist in New York. Texas has a separately elected commissioner of agriculture, while New York's is appointed by the governor. Florida's chief executive office also ranks behind the Empire State's in each of the six types of powers ranked by Beyle. And neither Texas nor Florida has a state government with overall powers as large and pervasive as those of New York State.

Gerald Benjamin explains the tradition of a powerful executive in New York this way: "Perhaps there is an underlying consensus among those attentive to politics and government in New York that a strong governor is needed to deal with a socially diverse, economically complex state's broad array of powerful interest groups and institutions."[6] On the other hand, California is just as diverse socially, and at least as economically complex.

The strength of the governor's office is one reason that New York governors have almost always been considered for national leadership. More presidents have served as governor of New York — Martin Van Buren, Grover Cleveland, Theodore Roosevelt, and Franklin Delano Roosevelt — than of any other state. During the 20th century, two leaders from the Empire State served as president, and virtually every other elected governor in New York either was nominated, or received serious consideration, as a candidate on the national ticket.[7] Besides the Roosevelts, Democrats nationwide nominated or looked closely at Governors Smith, Carey, and Cuomo; Republicans did the same with Governors Hughes, Dewey, Rockefeller, and Pataki.

---

5 For a summary of the powers of the Texas lieutenant governor, see
    http://www.ltgov.state.tx.us/Duties/.

6 Gerald Benjamin, "Structures of New York State Government," in Gerald Benjamin
    and Henrik N. Dullea, eds., *Decision 1997: Constitutional Change in New York*, p. 74.

7 Other states have dominated top leadership positions in Congress. Four representatives from Massachusetts served as speaker of the House for a total of 28 years during the 20th century, while three Texans led the House for a total of 22 years. The only New Yorker ever to serve as speaker, John W. Taylor, left the office in 1827.

Who Becomes Governor of New York?

The state's chief executive serves a four-year term, elected in even-numbered, nonpresidential years. There is no legal limit on the number of terms. As of 2006, the salary for the office was $177,984.[8]

The state's chief executive has typically had extensive government experience, either in the state or at the federal level. That was true of both major-party candidates for governor in 2006 – Attorney General Eliot Spitzer and former Assembly Minority Leader John Faso. Governor Pataki served in the Legislature for eight years and was mayor of the city of Peekskill. Mario M. Cuomo was secretary of state and then lieutenant governor to Governor Carey, who had moved to the Executive Mansion after representing part of Brooklyn in Congress for 14 years. Significant government service also appears in the backgrounds of Malcolm Wilson, Nelson Rockefeller, W. Averell Harriman, and most of their predecessors. That work is not always elective office; Harriman and Rockefeller had high-level appointive experience in the federal government but had never run for office before their gubernatorial campaigns.

In the latter part of the 20th century, several individuals with extensive experience in the private sector but little government service ran for governor unsuccessfully. Republican candidate Lewis Lehrman came the closest to victory, losing to then-Lieutenant Governor Cuomo in 1982 by 52 to 48 percent.

Partisan control of the governor's office was exactly evenly split during the 1900s — 50 years of governors who were Republicans, and 50 years of Democrats.[9]

---

8   Salaries for the governor, other statewide elected officials and the Legislature were last changed in 1999. The salary of the governor is set by legislative resolution, while salaries for members of the Senate and Assembly (along with stipends or "lulus") are in statute, part of the Legislative Law.

9   From the start of New York State government through 2002, Democratic governors held an edge of 138 years to 69 for Republicans. (The Democratic party was originally known as Republican and then Democratic-Republican.) Members of the Whig party, considered a forerunner to the Republican party, served for a total of 12 years, and Federalist governors for six.

What Does the Governor Do?

The common perception is that a governor "runs" state government. In reality, of course, the powers and responsibilities of the state's chief executive are more nuanced. The governor exerts little direct control over elementary and secondary school curricula, for instance, even though education is one of the state's chief concerns. What, then, does the governor *do*?

The most important function of the office, as with any chief executive position, is to take the lead in *setting the agenda*. The governor of New York does so primarily in the roles of:

- The top official who is best-known and considered most responsible for whatever state government does, and therefore is assumed to speak for state government. In fact, as noted in Chapter One, the Constitution requires the governor to inform the Legislature annually on the "condition of the state," and to recommend "expedient" actions.

- Originator and primary driver of each year's budget, with particularly substantial power to limit spending. *(See a more detailed discussion in Chapter Eight.)*

- Chief administrator of the state's huge bureaucracy — in effect, ultimate boss of some 260,000 employees in agencies and public authorities.

Much of the power vested in New York's governor today stems not from the Constitution but from … the Legislature. After all, it's up to the chief executive to administer the governmental programs and policies established by the Legislature (with the approval, in most cases, of the governor as well). Over the last century, New York's leaders have continually expanded the role of state government (sometimes at the initiative of the governor, sometimes under proposals from the Legislature). When a new law decrees, for instance, that the state will expand its regulation of environmental matters, that power is generally vested in the Department of Environmental Conservation. The governor appoints the commissioner of the department and serves as the ultimate authority who can approve or disapprove its regulations and other activities.

Enacting Laws:
Constitutional Powers, Political Influence

The governor can veto legislation (subject to override by both houses) and can require the Legislature to consider specific legislation by calling lawmakers into special session. The Constitution also gives the chief executive powers that can be used to help create a favorable climate for enacting desired legislation. But only the Legislature can actually pass legislation.

Still, governors sometimes can exercise their influence such that they virtually force favored legislation through the Senate and Assembly. One such instance, if critics of Governor Rockefeller are to be believed, occurred in 1969, when he proposed a budget that would have increased spending by more than 16 percent — and called for a tax increase to balance the financial plan.

"During the past 10 years, New York State has led the Nation in the development of sound innovative and effective programs to meet the social, economic, and physical needs of its people," Governor Rockefeller said in his budget message of January 21, 1969. "In the past, we have squarely faced the demands for expanded State services by providing the necessary additional revenues. Now that expectations and demands are outpacing our ability to meet them on a sound economic basis, we must face with equal courage the need to reorder and reschedule our priorities so that pressing needs are met while a healthy climate for economic growth is preserved.... We will continue to allocate resources so that justice and progress are assured."

The proposed budget included a sizable jump in expenditures. Education spending, by far the largest element of the budget, would have increased nearly 20 percent, to $3.6 billion. State aid to school districts, financial aid for college students, and continued expansion of the State University and City University of New York systems accounted for much of the increase. The category that Rockefeller's Budget Division called "social development" — welfare, Medicaid, and other elements of what today would be called the social services budget — received an even bigger increase, 29 percent, rising to a total of $2.3 billion. Medicaid, created just three years earlier, was budgeted at $907 million even though, as the governor's summary of the enacted budget pointed out: "The rapidly rising cost of Medicaid ... compelled the State this year to impose certain limitations."

To help pay for the new spending, Governor Rockefeller proposed an increase in the state sales tax from 2 to 3 percent. The sales tax proposal was unpopular, partly because it came on top of numerous tax increases adopted over the previous decade. The 2 percent state sales tax itself had been enacted, at Rockefeller's urging, just four years earlier in 1965. It was the first state sales tax in New York's history except for a one-year, 1 percent levy during the depth of the Depression, in 1933. Personal income taxes, business taxes, and New York's estate tax had also grown at Rockefeller's initiative.

The proposed extra penny of sales tax would provide an estimated $350 million in new revenue for the 1969-70 fiscal plan. With normal revenue growth and additional borrowing, that would be enough to cover the recommended increase in spending. But some of Rockefeller's fellow Republicans, who held majorities in both the Senate and Assembly, opposed the measure, and the minority Democrats were nearly unanimous in opposition.

When the budget vote was held on March 28, 1969, two Democrats joined most of the Republican majority in the Assembly in support of the governor's proposal, and the tax hike passed by three votes.

"Charges had circulated among the Democrats for several hours before the balloting that the two (Democrats) had exchanged their votes for consideration in patronage appointments," *The New York Times* reported later. The state Democratic chair, John J. Burns, and Assembly minority leader, Stanley Steingut, accused the two legislators of seeking "political plums," as Burns put it. Sure enough, on July 3, the governor's office announced that one of the Democrats, Charles F. Stockmeister of Rochester, had been named a member of the state Civil Service Commission.

The salary of $27,500 was substantial (equivalent to roughly $150,000 in 2006 dollars), especially for a part-time job. Contributing to skepticism surrounding the appointment, "The announcement of Mr. Stockmeister's appointment came at the beginning of a holiday weekend, when many vacationers are out of touch with the news," according to the *Times*.[10] The other legislator, Albert J. Hausbeck, also was rewarded by the Rockefeller administration.

---

10   "Rebel Democrat Gets State Post," *The New York Times*, July 4, 1969, p. 1.

Whether or not there was a deal, Governor Rockefeller had won the much-criticized increase in the sales tax.

The Agreement to Create Charter Schools

Another instance of a governor pushing through legislation in the face of strong opposition occurred nearly 30 years later. As part of his January 1998 budget proposal, Governor Pataki recommended legislation to create charter schools — public schools that would be free from many state-mandated regulations in exchange for greater accountability. Supporters said the charter schools, directly accountable to a unit of the State University or to the Board of Regents rather than to local school boards and administrators, would offer innovation and more choice for parents, leading to better student achievement. Opponents argued that the new institutions would divert resources from struggling urban schools and weaken existing state efforts to raise standards for all students.

Opponents included many members of both houses in the Legislature. New York State United Teachers, the principal statewide teachers' union, which had a long record of contributing financial and other support to members of both parties in both the Senate and the Assembly, strongly opposed the governor's bill. Still, Senate Majority Leader Joseph L. Bruno, a fellow Republican who at the time was generally a loyal ally of Governor Pataki, indicated his conference's willingness to enact a modified version of the legislation. The ultimate dispute, then, arose primarily between the governor and the Democratic Assembly, led by Speaker Sheldon Silver.

At the same time, many legislators were quietly urging their leaders to bring to the floor a measure raising lawmakers' salaries. As rumors of a pay increase floated during the course of several weeks, Governor Pataki said he did not see the need for a raise and might veto such a bill if it reached his desk. Given voters' opposition to raising legislators' pay, it was clear that neither house would pass such a bill unless the leaders knew it would be worth the political pain — in other words, that the governor would sign it into law.

In late December, after extensive negotiations, Governor Pataki, Senator Bruno, and Speaker Silver announced agreement on a charter-schools bill that supporters said was one of the strongest in the nation — exactly the type that many legislators had said they would oppose. The legislative leaders also announced they would bring to their respective houses a measure raising lawmakers' pay by 38 percent. The governor said he would not oppose the bill, and quickly signed it into law.

Persuading Legislators on an Ethics Law

Besides agreeing to what legislators want in one area in exchange for their support on another issue, governors can use the "bully pulpit," as Theodore Roosevelt called the presidency, to force action by lawmakers. A good example was Governor Cuomo's insistence, in the mid-1980s, on a new state ethics law.

The battle over ethics arose after several years of scandals, both at the state level and in major municipalities. Cuomo himself, as lieutenant governor, had seen his chief of staff plead guilty in November 1981 to putting fictitious employees on the state payroll and converting the fraudulent paychecks to his personal use. Major scandals also erupted in New York City government in 1985 and 1986. Then in 1987 a Republican state senator was convicted of tax evasion, and a Democratic Assemblyperson's staff member was convicted in connection with charges of no-show jobs and payroll padding.

Newspapers across the state carried numerous reports critical of the Legislature's internal finances and outside activities that allowed some members to profit from political and legislative connections. Gannett News Service, which served daily newspapers in Westchester County, Rochester and several other markets, ran a series of articles on the "Solid Gold Legislature." *The New York Times* followed in 1987 with a series called "Public Business, Private Interests." The *New York Post* carried numerous reports, including one in which a staff member of Senate Minority Leader Manfred Ohrenstein said he collected pay from the Legislature for doing no work.

Governor Cuomo announced in early 1986 he would seek legislation to create new limits on the intersection between the public offices and private finances of elected and political party officials. He proposed a bill in April, and the state Senate announced its own proposed measure shortly after. The Legislature ultimately did not agree on any legislation that year.

Throughout the first few months of 1987, the governor stepped up his attacks on the Legislature for failing to enact a new law, while several criminal investigations — including one by the Manhattan district attorney, Robert Morgenthau, and several by the United States attorney, Rudolph Giuliani — continued to attract media attention. In March, Senate and Assembly leaders announced agreement on new ethics legislation, which passed both houses. Governor Cuomo vetoed the bill, saying it was too weak.

The next several weeks brought mutual criticism by the governor and legislative leaders, along with intense negotiations. Senate Majority Leader Warren Anderson, Assembly Speaker Mel Miller and their close aides gradually agreed to virtually all of the governor's demands. At one point, legislative negotiators reportedly made a proposal they believed would force the governor to back off — a permanent prohibition on former executive branch officials dealing with their former agencies on issues they had addressed while in state employment. Much to their surprise (and chagrin), Governor Cuomo accepted the proposal.

On July 2, 1987, the legislation passed unanimously in both the Senate and Assembly. Legislators, many of whom criticized the new restrictions bitterly, clearly believed they could not afford to oppose ethics legislation that 18 months earlier had not been on the radar screen. The difference was determined action by a governor who used the bully pulpit to the fullest, and whose actions were shaped by outside circumstances such as the scandals in New York City government and the Legislature itself.

The Power of the Spotlight

Governor Cuomo's success in pushing for ethics legislation is among the best recent examples of a governor's use of the ability to command attention. Other governors have wielded the same power to win unlikely battles at least as far back as Theodore Roosevelt's successful fight for civil-service laws.

More recent governors have used the State of the State address in early January to promote their program. While the timing and the trappings of the address are similar from governor to governor, the form varies widely (as do, of course, the proposals). Governor Cuomo was known for lengthy addresses that included dozens of separate policy recommendations. Governor Pataki preferred much shorter, more thematic speeches that concentrate on a few key policy initiatives.

As is true of the president's annual State of the Union address, the State of the State presentation captures the attention of all state leaders. It marks one of the few days each year when virtually all of the state's daily newspapers, and even many television news reports, include significant coverage of state government (the days when the budget is first proposed, and then passed, are the only others that capture such attention). Thousands of New Yorkers with a direct stake in state policies look for the news reports.

For the governor's actual speech, members of both houses gather in the Assembly chamber on the third floor of the Capitol. The lieutenant governor, comptroller, attorney general, and members of the Court of Appeals attend as well. Even political opponents of the governor are required by custom to listen respectfully — although the event also gives them an occasion to criticize the governor's policies if they so wish, when reporters seek comments in response to the address.

Governors and their staffs hope that the State of the State speech will dominate news coverage across the state. Success depends on a combination of relevance to pressing news of the day and sharp imagery. Governor Carey clearly succeeded in capturing statewide attention with his first address as the New York City and state fiscal crises were emerging in early 1975. Citing the need to control spending to avoid financial disaster, the governor warned that "the days of wine and roses are over."[11]

While there are numerous examples of governors using their "bully pulpit" to push the Legislature to action, it remains a relatively little-used power of the office. While succeeding in enacting a strict ethics law, Governor Cuomo failed to mount effective campaigns for other issues he declared to be priorities — for instance, reallocating significant amounts of school aid from richer to poorer districts. Governor Pataki proposed cost-saving reforms to Medicaid every year, but never took the issue to the public. Governors, like other chief executives, only have so much political capital to call upon. To the extent they fail to use the resources they do have, however, they fail to provide the leadership citizens have a right to expect.

Besides the State of the State and other means of shining a bright spotlight on key issues, the governor has the power to appoint special

---

11 The pungent phrase became so clearly associated with Governor Carey that it is the title of a biography by Daniel C. Kramer, published by University Press of America in 1997.

investigatory bodies known as Moreland Act commissions.[12] Such commissions can subpoena witnesses to testify, and organizations or individuals to produce documents for review. The very act of naming such a commission draws attention to a perceived problem, and its findings can be shaped to produce further publicity. Governor Carey used the power to investigate the nursing home industry in the mid-1970s, while Governor Cuomo did so to examine ethics and accountability in state and local government in 1987 and school districts' management and spending in 1993. More recently, Governor Pataki appointed a Moreland Act commission in 1998 to investigate how efficiently New York City schools use taxpayer dollars.

The ability of governors to control the public agenda rests, in part, on the tendency of the news media to focus on individual leaders at the top of the government. Newspapers around the state typically report on bills and budget items of local interest but focus their coverage of broad statewide issues mainly on the governor and, to a lesser extent, legislative leaders *(see Chapter Fifteen for more on this subject)*. In New York City, most state legislators complete their entire careers without a mention in the daily newspapers. Both in the city and elsewhere, television reports that are the only source of news for many voters pay little attention to state government; whatever coverage they do provide often focuses on the governor.

The Administrator-in-Chief

As the administrative head of state government, the governor has enormous power to direct the workings of agencies and public authorities across the broad spectrum of state government activities described in Chapter One. The governor can:

- Revise the structure of the executive branch through executive action alone or, when needed, in laws enacted through the Legislature.

- Influence the quality of public services through the quality of individuals appointed to run agencies.

---

12 The name refers to Assemblyman Sherman Moreland of Chemung County, who served only four years in the Legislature. The law, part of Section 6 of the state's Executive Law, was enacted in 1907 as one of the first steps toward giving the governor control of the state bureaucracy.

- Set a tone or theme for state agency leaders and employees. Governors Carey and Pataki, for instance, repeatedly urged agencies to work more cost-effectively as part of broader efforts to restrain spending. Several agencies in Governor Cuomo's administration adopted an initiative to improve management and operations that, much like efforts undertaken by many private companies, relied in part on empowering employees to participate in decision making.

The governor appoints the heads of almost all state agencies. (The most important exception is the Education Department. Even there, however, some governors have exerted influence, as discussed in Chapter Ten.) In all but the smallest agencies, a given administration also can appoint second-ranking and other high-level officials.

Knowing that constituency groups and the press will pay the most attention to those who are appointed as agency heads, governors usually consider political ramifications and public opinion in naming agency leaders. Besides ability to do the job, governors often consider whether a candidate for commissioner is favored by an important constituency, provides political balance (geographic, racial, or gender), or otherwise helps shape a favorable opinion of the administration. Governor Cuomo reflected on his aspirations for administration officials in his diary on November 5, 1982, three days after winning election to his first term: "Some things are clear. I want to reflect our entire coalition: Women — Blacks — Hispanics — Italians — Disabled — Business People — Unions. It's important to distinguish my administration from Carey's, so I can't have too many holdovers. It's also important that the transition effort not function as a patronage machine. Above all, I must have the very best available."[13]

Because governors sometimes choose commissioners based partly on political considerations, the No. 2 official at a given agency often has more day-to-day power than the commissioner. That is particularly true because an executive deputy commissioner at a large agency such as Labor or Environmental Conservation is likely to be a trusted extension of the governor's closest staff. Sometimes the result is friction between commissioners and the governor's immediate staff. In 1987, for instance, then-Labor Commissioner Lillian Roberts resigned after complaining that she seldom met with Governor Cuomo and was not

---

13 Mario M. Cuomo, *Diaries of Mario M. Cuomo: The Campaign for Governor*, Random House, New York, NY, 1984, p. 356.

allowed to choose her top staff. Governor Pataki's labor commissioner, James J. McGowan, left in 2000 with similar complaints.

The governor's appointees to head most agencies are subject to approval by the Senate. The approval process is one of the key areas where governors benefit when their party controls the upper house. Governor Cuomo found, after Health Commissioner David Axelrod suffered a stroke and died in 1989, that it was difficult to attract a highly qualified successor because of the salary. His administration and a desirable candidate for the position agreed that the next commissioner would receive a second salary as the head of the state's nonprofit health research agency. Republicans in the state Senate sharply questioned the move before ultimately confirming the new commissioner. When Governor Pataki took office in 1995, he was confronted with the same salary problem and similarly arranged for two salaries. This time, some Democrats in the Senate complained. (Governor Pataki, at least, did not have to worry about his candidate being rejected — the Senate was controlled by members of his party, who were unlikely to block the governor's nominees.)

Under the state Constitution, the governor is commander-in-chief of the state's military. In recent decades, that primarily meant having ultimate authority for the work that the state's National Guard members performed during and after civil emergencies such as flooding, hurricanes and blizzards. The nation's response to terrorist attacks on and after September 11, 2001, brought a new level of urgency to the work of the National Guard. Several hundred members were called to duty, for instance, to support recovery efforts in lower Manhattan after 9/11. Some New York National Guard volunteers were among those called to overseas duty when the United States went to war in Afghanistan and Iraq. When mobilized for such federal duty status, members of the Guard are under the jurisdiction of U.S. military leadership and, ultimately, the president.

Under Section 29-a of the Executive Law, the governor also has the power to "temporarily suspend specific provisions of any statute, local law, ordinance, or orders, rules or regulations, or parts thereof, of any agency during a state disaster emergency, if compliance with such provisions would prevent, hinder, or delay action necessary to cope with the disaster." Governor Pataki invoked the power with regard to a number of laws, to speed assistance to injured individuals and families of victims, after the September 2001 attacks on the World Trade Center.

Limits to Executive Authority

For all of the office's legal and political powers, the influence of the governor has limits. Perhaps the most important is the practical reality that there are only so many battles any chief executive can wage. Priorities must be set, and even issues that are highly important may remain unaddressed if others are even more crucial. For instance, numerous commissions and other independent observers have concluded that complex, outmoded civil service rules create enormous difficulty for public managers at both the state and local levels throughout New York. However, reform can prove difficult. For example, Stephen Berger was Governor Carey's appointee as executive director of the Emergency Financial Control Board during the New York City fiscal crisis, when Carey and his associates were working day and night to convince leaders of the city's banks, unions, and other institutions to take steps to resolve the crisis. Berger reportedly said that "he wanted to institute significant reforms in the City's civil service system to make service delivery more effective." The governor rejected the idea "on the grounds that it would unnecessarily irritate labor."[14]

The governor's final power over legislation — the veto — is limited by the Legislature's ability to override vetoes with a two-thirds vote in each house. Historically, overrides have been extremely rare, (as, presumably, the founders of the state government intended). In 1976, Governor Carey vetoed a measure protecting the education component of the New York City budget from spending cuts. The Legislature's successful override was the first in 104 years. In 1982, when Carey vetoed hundreds of millions of dollars in spending added by the Legislature, lawmakers restored significant sums via override. That effort, however, left some of the vetoes untouched.

In Governor Pataki's last term, the Legislature overrode numerous vetoes. A 2004 veto override by both houses raised the minimum wage from $5.15 to $7.15 an hour. Most other overrides involved the budget — either appropriations or, as in 2005, legislation that changed the budget process to shift more power to the Legislature. (That legislation was contingent on voter approval for a Constitutional amendment, which failed on Election Day. For more on that subject, see Chapter Nine.)

---

14 Berger interview related in Kramer, *The Days of Wine and Roses Are Over*, p. 111.

Ultimately, of course, the governor's power is limited by the will of the voters. Three of the last six governors to serve in the 20th century — Harriman, Wilson, and Cuomo — left office after losing on Election Day. Knowing their every action may be subject to voters' scrutiny, governors impose their own limits on the use of their power by ensuring that their decisions are at least defensible — and, preferably, looked upon favorably by a majority of New Yorkers.

The Governor's Staff: The "Second Floor"

Traditionally, the closest and most important assistants to the governor are not the heads of major agencies but people who hold the top positions in the Executive Chamber on the second floor of the Capitol. (The "Second Floor" is commonly used as shorthand for the governor's top staff members and their assistants.) The secretary to the governor is considered the chief of staff. Perhaps the single most powerful gubernatorial aide in recent decades was Robert Morgado, who served as secretary to Governor Carey and was widely considered the day-to-day overseer of much of state government.

The position of counsel to the governor has been important at least since the days of Franklin Roosevelt, who appointed Samuel Rosenman to that position after the lawyer played an important role as researcher and speechwriter during Roosevelt's first campaign. The counsel continues to be one of the most influential aides in part because he or she oversees the flow of legislation and recommends approval or disapproval. The counsel may play an especially vital role when a governor is contemplating an unprecedented or unusual action that might arouse legal opposition, or require interpretation of the Constitution or statutes.

Politics nationwide has become more media-focused in recent years, and political communication more sophisticated. Shaping and communicating the governor's "message" has thus grown in importance and the role of the communications director has taken on additional influence. Governor Pataki's first communications director and senior policy advisor, Zenia Mucha, functioned as a top adviser on virtually all matters, including policy and appointments.

In recent decades, governors have named a director of state operations whose duties include overseeing day-to-day operational decisions by state agencies. Like the secretary, the director of state operations has several top assistants who specialize in various program areas. These aides help draft and negotiate passage of the governor's program bills in addition to coordinating policy in the respective agencies.

One other position in the Capitol — that of budget director — plays a key advisory role. The director is always at least the administration's primary negotiator in budget discussions with the Senate and Assembly. Depending on the individual and his or her relationship with the governor, the director may also provide an important voice on other issues with a fiscal impact — encompassing a broad agenda in state government. Patricia A. Woodworth and Robert L. King, who both served as budget director under Governor Pataki, played another key role that was unusual for the position — that of chief public speaker on the governor's budget priorities. Despite such close ties at the top, many of the Budget Division's 400 or so staff are career employees, and its offices are on the first floor of the Capitol. Thus the division is institutionally not as close to the governor and other Executive Chamber officials as the program associates and other staff on the second floor.

Another important assistant to the governor is the appointments secretary. Governors must appoint hundreds of individuals to positions in state service — perhaps several thousand, in the case of a multi-term governor. These appointees work not only as top-level advisers and lower-level support staff but also as the members of dozens of unpaid advisory boards, committees, and councils. The appointments office screens each of these for qualifications both professional and political, and acts as a main point of contact for political party leaders around the state. The office must also review potential appointees' personal lives to avoid associating the administration with criminal or simply embarrassing incidents; the State Police Bureau of Criminal Investigation also investigates candidates for higher-level jobs.

Staff who work in the Executive Chamber typically include individuals who have worked on the gubernatorial campaign and thus can be known as competent and loyal. Others may come from the legislative branch; for instance, Governor Pataki's first director of state operations, James Natoli, previously served as staff director for the Republican minority in the Assembly. Each administration typically includes some individuals brought in from outside government because they contribute particularly useful knowledge of a key issue.

New governors often restructure the Executive Chamber to reflect their own priorities or organizational approaches. Governor Pataki created a position of deputy secretary to oversee a new Office of Public

Authorities. Governor Cuomo created an Office of Management and Productivity to help agencies cut costs while improving services.

Alton G. Marshall, who served as secretary to Governor Rockefeller, said the internal structure of an administration can significantly affect the policies that emerge.

"The very fact that we set up this system of program associates in the governor's office caused ... this constant drive by the associates for new programs in their particular social field," Marshall said. "The concept was that established operating agencies were more apt to want to keep things status quo in government than to change them. Therefore, the program associates needed to reach in and excite that group to come up with some new ideas and also to encourage them to know that they had a friend in court for any new program they might wish. That structure alone led to the goddamnedest number of programs!"[15]

Governor's Legislation

In addition to initiating the Legislature's action on the annual budget, governors develop an annual legislative program — a set of policy-related bills on which they seek action. The most important such proposals are called "program bills." The administration's legislative initiatives also include proposals of lesser or narrower importance championed by an individual executive agency. Such "departmental bills" reflect agency managers' needs to update programs, transfer state property or take other action requiring statutory authorization. As these bills are less likely to merit personal lobbying by the governor or top staff, their passage may depend on good relations between agency officials and the relevant committee chairs, legislative leaders, or top legislative staff.

The Budget Division reviews, and may comment on, all bills submitted to the governor, regardless of fiscal impact. The division screens for consistency, program implications, and administrative problems as well as financial impact. The governor's Counsel's Office also examines all bills and helps determine which will be incorporated into the governor's legislative program.

---

15 Comments from Alton G. Marshall in "Experimentation in Social Policy: Medicaid, Community Mental Health, Drug Abuse" in Gerald Benjamin and T. Norman Hurd, eds., *Rockefeller In Retrospect: The Governor's New York Legacy*, Rockefeller Institute of Government, Albany, NY, 1984, p. 31.

Except budget bills, every bill must have a legislative sponsor or group of sponsors — the governor cannot introduce legislation directly. Important bills are often sponsored by a committee chair or a member recommended by the Senate or Assembly leadership.

Assessing Governors

New York State has clearly been home to a number of governors who have been dynamic, occasionally visionary, even giants among their national peers. Ironically, the two 20th-century governors who rose to the greatest height on the national stage — the presidency — were not among the best New York leaders. Theodore Roosevelt served as governor only two years; while he pushed through important laws in areas such as labor and civil service, perhaps his most important contribution was reminding New Yorkers that a determined leader in the executive branch could overcome the Legislature on an issue the public cares about. Franklin Roosevelt served twice as long as his distant cousin and initiated important changes including several that presaged federal New Deal government protections for the needy. Historians and political scientists generally agree, though, that other governors surpass the two Roosevelts in importance.

Alfred E. Smith, a Democrat, is clearly in this category. He introduced the modern governorship — a significantly stronger office that offers voters clear accountability for what is right or wrong about state government. Smith fought and won a long battle to create the Executive Budget system, under which the governor presents a unified plan of expenses and revenues to the Legislature. Previously, the Legislature enacted appropriations with relatively little regard to the state's overall fiscal position. Smith also reorganized the executive branch, putting most agencies directly under the control of the governor. (Former Governor Charles Evans Hughes, who left his own longstanding mark on the state, assisted Smith in the latter effort by chairing a citizens' commission on government reform.)

Thomas E. Dewey, a Republican, is often included among the great governors. At a time when education and transportation were becoming more important than ever to social progress and economic growth, he brought together disparate colleges under the umbrella of the State University and led the push to build the State Thruway.

Notable New York Governors of the 20th Century		
Governor	*Leg. Control*	*Selected Accomplishments*
Theodore Roosevelt (R) 1899-1900	Senate – R Assembly – R	Enacted laws reforming civil service, promoting labor safety and instituting a corporate franchise tax.
Charles Evans Hughes (R) 1907-10	Senate – R Assembly – R	Created Public Service Commission; enacted workers' compensation law.
Alfred E. Smith (D) 1919-20; 1923-28	Senate – R, D Assembly – R	Restructured state government to make it more accountable to the governor; created parks system; increased welfare and education spending; enacted income tax and reduced state property tax.
Franklin D. Roosevelt (D) 1929-32	Senate – R Assembly – R	Won Court of Appeals decision implementing Executive Budget; created old-age pensions; created Home Relief and work relief for the needy.
Herbert H. Lehman (D) 1933-42	Senate – D, R Assembly – R, D	Expanded and consolidated welfare programs in Department of Social Services; enacted numerous labor measures; expanded civil-service protections.
Thomas E. Dewey (R) 1943-54	Senate – R Assembly – R	Created SUNY; initiated Thruway; enacted first state law banning job discrimination; doubled aid to education.
Nelson A. Rockefeller (R) 1959-73	Senate – R, D Assembly – R, D	Expanded state services, including creating Medicaid and expanding SUNY and environmental programs; built Empire State Plaza; enacted sales tax; increased personal and corporate taxes.
Hugh L. Carey (D) 1975-1982	Senate – R Assembly – D	Resolved New York City and state fiscal crises; cut taxes; reformed programs for mentally disabled; enacted major environmental laws.
Mario M. Cuomo (D) 1983-1994	Senate – R Assembly – D	Expanded prison system; expanded Medicaid; initiated state ethics law; cut taxes and later raised them.
George E. Pataki (R) 1995-2006	Senate – R Assembly – D	Cut taxes; reduced regulatory burdens; reformed welfare; added to Forest Preserve; expanded Medicaid and other health programs; increased state debt.

Nelson A. Rockefeller left a huge impact on the Empire State, which he led longer than any governor in history except George Clinton, New York's first chief executive. Rockefeller expanded the size and influence of state government dramatically in areas from education to health care to regulation of businesses. Under his leadership, for instance, enrollment at the State University exploded, from 73,000 in 1960 to 385,000 in 1973. He created the state's Medicaid system, now the single largest expenditure in the budget. To pay for expanded state government, he raised taxes sharply, including personal income taxes, corporate taxes, and a new sales tax.

Observers of the presidency commonly say that great national leaders arise from crisis and can be measured by their response to it. Using that measure, Hugh L. Carey clearly ranks among the great governors of New York, dealing effectively with the fiscal crises that hit both the state and New York City governments during the economic woes of the mid-1970s. As *The New York Times* editorialized upon his leaving office: "It is hard to imagine how anyone else could have done so well in leading the state through its hardest winter."[16]

What is the proper measure of a chief executive? There are many, but perhaps the one that is most important — and often ignored — is results. Consider two governors, Nelson A. Rockefeller and Hugh L. Carey, in this light.

Rockefeller spoke often about the need to address critical problems facing the state, from providing high-quality education to ensuring human rights. His accomplishments as a builder and a visionary of new programs to address social ills were enormous. For instance, he began to clean up state waterways that were badly polluted with household and industrial wastes. Yet many observers agree, in hindsight, that the costs associated with Rockefeller's projects created new problems. Certainly the state's economic performance relative to the rest of the nation worsened during the 1960s and early 1970s; some blame for that lies in the heavy tax increases Rockefeller introduced. Gerald Benjamin wrote that Rockefeller's "emphasis on large solutions sometimes led to large mistakes.... [For example] Rockefeller's spending in a variety of program areas left New York with a tax structure and debt burden that ultimately came to threaten the very viability of its private sector

---

16   "A Governor for hard winters," *The New York Times*, December 30, 1982, p. A-14.

economy."[17] Considering that a healthy private sector is the fundamental strength of any state — and given New York's dominant historical role in the nation's commerce — such criticism is damning.

When Carey took office, he inherited Rockefeller's bold commitments to expanded government as well as three major crises. (Wilson's short tenure as governor between Rockefeller and Carey, lasting barely more than a year, was characterized by initial steps to reduce taxes and otherwise get the state back on a stronger footing.) Most importantly, the state's economic troubles were hurting tens of thousands of state residents and threatening others with loss of job opportunities. Second, the weakening of the state's economy was diminishing tax revenues, which combined with growing spending produced the fiscal crisis that is still the best known feature of the mid-1970s. Third, the Rockefeller era left the tragic conditions for mentally disabled individuals that became most notorious at the state hospital known as Willowbrook.

Carey addressed each of these crises. After implementing a tax increase his first year to balance the budget, he persuaded the Legislature to reduce taxes and hold down spending during the remainder of his administration.[18] He refinanced state and city debt and imposed fiscal oversight on New York City and the state's public authorities. As a result of all those efforts, the state and New York City emerged financially secure. The state's economy began growing again. Carey also signed a consent order reforming operations not only at Willowbrook, but throughout the state's facilities for the developmentally disabled.

To be sure, such a brief discussion cannot convey the legacy that a governor leaves the state. The important point is that every governor, like every other public official, should be assessed mainly in terms of results.

---

17 Gerald Benjamin, "Nelson Rockefeller and the New York Governorship," in *Rockefeller in Retrospect*, 1984, p. 298.

18 Fiscal analyst E.J. McMahon of the Manhattan Institute concludes that Carey held state-funded spending (not including federal funds) essentially flat, after adjusting for inflation, over his eight years in office. See "Deja Vu All Over Again: The Right Way to Cure New York's Looming Budget Gap," October 2002, accessed online at *www.manhattan-institute.org/html/cr_29.htm*.

The Lieutenant Governor

Among political observers, the office of lieutenant governor traditionally receives respect equal to that given the U.S. vice presidency — in other words, not much. One who held the latter office, John Nance Garner, is famously reputed to have said that it was "not worth a pitcher of warm spit," although some reports indicate that his actual quote was slightly more vulgar.

As a matter of law, the No. 2 executive office in New York is even weaker than its federal counterpart. Both officials preside over the Senate. The vice president, though, has the power to vote on any bill in the Senate, when necessary to break a tie. The state Constitution gives the lieutenant governor a "casting vote" — historically interpreted to mean a vote that can be used only on procedural matters. As noted in the previous chapter, the Constitution assigns the office no other direct powers. Statutes give the lieutenant governor several duties, including membership on the Committee on Open Government and service as a trustee of Cornell University.

Still, the office of lieutenant governor can be important. First, of course, like the vice president, the lieutenant governor assumes the chief executive office upon the death or resignation of the incumbent. The state Constitution also provides that the lieutenant governor becomes acting governor when the governor is temporarily incapacitated or away from the state. (The latter provision is often criticized as outmoded given modern communications and transportation; no such provision applies to international travel by the president.)

Six lieutenant governors have ascended to the top office when governors did not complete the terms to which they had been elected. Most recently, Malcolm Wilson followed Nelson Rockefeller as governor when the latter resigned in 1973.[19] Other lieutenant governors (Mario Cuomo being the most recent) have ascended to the top job through election.

Aside from succession, the lieutenant governor's office has performed another main function that is, again, analogous to the vice

---

19 Others in the past century: Horace White succeeded to the office when Charles Evans Hughes moved to the U.S. Supreme Court in October 1910; Martin H. Glynn replaced William Sulzer, who was removed via impeachment in October 1913; Charles Poletti served briefly as governor after Herbert Lehman joined the Roosevelt Administration in December 1942.

presidency: it acts as a surrogate for the chief executive. When the governor and the lieutenant governor have a strong relationship, the latter will represent the governor at numerous public functions and will receive important policy assignments. During Rockefeller's 15 years in office, Lieutenant Governor Wilson was a trusted political and policy advisor. He helped strengthen relations between Rockefeller and members of the Legislature, where Wilson had served for 20 years before moving to the executive branch; and with local political leaders around the state.

Governor Cuomo's tenure included both strong and weak relationships between the state's top two officials. When he took office for his first term, the lieutenant governor was Alfred DelBello. Cuomo had not sought DelBello for his ticket; he had supported H. Carl McCall (who would later become state comptroller). DelBello won the Democratic nod, though, and he and Cuomo were elected together in November 1982. DelBello served less than two years, resigning in apparent frustration at the lack of interesting work given to him. In January 1986, when preparing for his re-election campaign, Cuomo told reporters he wanted his next lieutenant governor to serve in a Cabinet capacity as well as elective office. "Why can't the lieutenant governor be health commissioner? Why can't he or she be secretary of state? Or criminal justice coordinator?"[20] In the event, Cuomo chose then-Congressman Stan Lundine as his running mate; the two were elected that year and again in 1990. Governor Cuomo did not pursue having the lieutenant governor serve as a department head. By all accounts, though, the professional relationship was fairly strong; Cuomo assigned Lundine a number of important responsibilities, including overseeing the state Job Training Partnership Council and several high-tech initiatives.

Governors sometimes find that a higher political profile for a lieutenant governor comes back to haunt them. Governor Carey's choice for the job during his first term, former state Senator Mary Anne Krupsak, became disillusioned with the governor and his staff and challenged him in the Democratic party primary in 1978 (losing by a large margin). According to Carey's biographer Daniel C. Kramer, the governor treated Lieutenant Governor Krupsak well in terms of her office budget and in introducing legislation she recommended. The lieutenant governor was prepared to stay on the ticket less than a week before the Democratic party's nominating convention in June 1978. Several

---

20 Maurice Carroll, "Cuomo Would Broaden Lieutenant Governor Job," *The New York Times*, January 28, 1986, p. B-4.

factors, including events that highlighted policy differences within the administration as well as perceived personal slights by the governor and his top staff, prompted Krupsak to change her mind.

Governor Pataki, too, had both good and bad relations with lieutenant governors. Betsy McCaughey was a valued part of his first administration early on; he called on her reputation as an expert on health care in support of his proposals to restructure the Medicaid system in 1995. Within months thereafter, though, Lieutenant Governor McCaughey had a complete falling-out with Governor Pataki and his aides. She not only was not renominated by the Republican party but challenged the governor's re-election effort in 1998 by running on the minor Liberal party line. Lieutenant Governor Mary O. Donohue, Governor Pataki's running mate that year, established a good working relationship with the governor and was nominated for a federal judgeship with his support.

Beyond the Governor

The executive branch includes not only the governor and the lieutenant governor but the other two statewide officials, the comptroller and the attorney general. Each is the head of a key department — the Department of Audit and Control, and the Department of Law, respectively. (Over the past two decades, these elected officials have adopted the practice of referring to their departments as the Office of the State Comptroller and the Office of the Attorney General, but the official department names remain.)

In addition, one major state agency — the Education Department — is ultimately responsible not to the governor, but to the Legislature. The Constitution makes the Board of Regents, who are appointed by a vote of the Legislature, the head of the department. The Regents in turn appoint a commissioner of education, who is responsible for providing the department's vision and administrative leadership. On the other hand, the governor does appoint the trustees of the State University, subject to Senate confirmation.

For the first decades of American independence, the offices of comptroller and attorney general served largely as support agencies for the Legislature and the governor — just as a corporate chief financial officer and general counsel do for the board of directors and chief executive officer of a modern corporation. Each officer was expected to provide some independent review of the actions of elected policy makers. That responsibility was strengthened in 1846 when a new Constitution made both offices elective rather than subject to appointment by the Legislature. In 1938, the terms of both were lengthened from two to four years, along with those of the governor and lieutenant governor.

In the 20th century, the dramatic growth of state government vested extensive new powers in both offices. The comptroller was given sole responsibility for investing the pension funds of most state and local government employees; that task has since grown enormously with sharp increases in the number and compensation of public employees. The Executive Law, the General Business Law, and other statutes assigned the attorney general a variety of powers in consumer protection and other areas.

As statewide elected officials, both the comptroller and the attorney general have the power to capture press and public attention. A biography of Franklin Delano Roosevelt indicates that this element of the job was important at least as far back as 1928, when FDR won his first term as governor. During the campaign, professional gamblers laid 2-1 odds for Republican Richard Ottinger against Roosevelt. Among other reasons,

> Ottinger as attorney general had gained much favorable publicity for himself by warring effectively against loan sharks, adulterated-food dealers, dealers in phony stocks, and petty grafters of all kinds. This enabled him to campaign as champion of "little people" against those who would defraud them; it lent weight to his promise of stern action against graft and crime once he was in the governor's chair.[21]

Such responsibilities can provide a springboard to higher office. Martin Van Buren served as New York's attorney general for four years before serving briefly as governor and later moving to the White House.[22] More recently, Jacob K. Javits served as attorney general for two years before his election to the U.S. Senate in 1956. Having gained national attention while serving as attorney general started in 1999, Eliot Spitzer became the frontrunner for the governor's office in 2006.

---

21 Kenneth S. Davis, *FDR: The New York Years 1928-1933*, Random House, New York, NY, 1985, p. 31.

22 Van Buren ran for governor as part of a successful plan to help Andrew Jackson carry New York and the nation in his 1828 campaign for president against John Quincy Adams. The understanding was that Van Buren would resign shortly after taking office to become Jackson's secretary of state – which he did, leaving the governor's office to Enos Throop.

The Comptroller

The auditing powers assigned to New York's comptroller and the office's sole control of pension funds for state and local government employees make the position among the strongest of its kind in the 50 states.

The auditing responsibilities of the Office of the State Comptroller (OSC) fall into two major categories generally described as "pre-audit" and "post-audit." Both powers create a strong (and, because the comptroller is elected separately, an independent) check on executive agencies.

Before making any payment, the department reviews payment vouchers to ascertain whether they appear to be supported by valid documentation. In addition, no state department, board, or institution can enter into a contract for more than $10,000 without the department's prior approval.

From October 1997 through September 2002, the department conducted more than 700 audits of state agencies and public authorities. Collectively, these are the state's most comprehensive effort to identify financial and operational weaknesses and to promote continuous improvement. *(See Chapter Fifteen for further discussion of accountability efforts in state government.)*

OSC's Management Audit Group estimated that its recommendations to state agencies in 1999 could save New York State taxpayers about $69 million by reducing costs and increasing revenues, and cut costs to the federal government by an additional $47 million. The audit group also maintains that its reports produce benefits that cannot be quantified, such as substantial new internal controls and management procedures. OSC's auditors point out that they also identify areas in which state agencies are doing a good job. The agency's 1999 report on audits of state agencies and public authorities stated:

> During the past year we noted that the Banking Department was generally effective in regulating the mortgage banking industry; the Office of Mental Retardation and Developmental Disabilities was effective in redeploying institutional staff into community-based programs; the New York State Thruway Authority initiated changes in toll collection practices that virtually eliminated traffic congestion in one of the most heavily traveled sections of the Thruway; and by conducting on-site reviews of the actions taken by utility companies in addressing potential

data processing difficulties related to the year 2000, the Public Service Commission appeared to have exceeded the extent of monitoring provided by other state regulators.[23]

The department audits municipalities from New York City to small villages and fire districts. From 1995 through 1999, the department audited 40 of the state's 57 counties and 679 of 932 towns. Every unit of local government is subject to periodic audit to identify fiscal problems and to test for compliance with finance-related laws, regulations, and guidance from OSC itself. The department also conducts performance and program audits.

OSC gives officials of audited agencies an opportunity to review a draft report. The final report typically states that officials agree with certain findings and recommendations, and often that they have begun to implement some recommendations; the reports often note disagreement on other findings as well.

The audits are conducted according to long-established accounting and management principles. Still, any given report — particularly those in the management arena — may include subjective judgments. Even the initial decision to audit a given program reflects the judgment of individuals in the department. The department's auditors have long been viewed as nonpartisan, but the same direct accountability to voters that gives the comptroller's office its independence also allows other elected officials to claim that audits are influenced by political considerations. In 1998, New York City Mayor Rudolph Giuliani criticized OSC's audits of city government as politically motivated (Giuliani was Republican, and then-Comptroller H. Carl McCall a Democrat). When the mayor refused to give OSC staff access to certain records, the comptroller filed suit, asking the courts to require that the city comply with auditors' requests for information. In April 1999, the Court of Appeals affirmed the comptroller's authority to audit the city.

Audit reports are typically read only by the state or local-government agencies being reviewed and, perhaps, a few members of the governor's and legislative staff responsible for the relevant program area. Only on rare occasions — most often when reporters believe a critical audit may have potential political impact — do the news media pay attention. Still, the possibility of such attention often makes the auditing

---

23 See *http://www.osc.state.ny.us/audits.*

Auditing: A Powerful Role

The comptroller's auditing power is comprehensive, as shown by a partial listing of audits conducted in recent years. Such examinations are not exhaustive in scope, however. The comptroller's staff conducted 100 audits of Health Department programs from October 1997 to September 2002, with more than half of those involving the Medicaid program. Yet the office did not uncover the extensive fraud and abuse revealed in press reports in 2004.

Other agencies subjected to numerous audits from October 1997 to September 2002 included:

- *Civil Service Department (42)*. Most addressed the state health-insurance program for state employees.

- *Department of Correctional Services (37)*. Most examined payroll or other practices at individual prisons.

- *Department of Environmental Conservation (15)*. Subjects included costs and revenues from air-permit and waste-site remediation programs.

- *Labor Department (22)*. Unemployment insurance and welfare reform were among the programs several times.

- *Department of Taxation and Finance*. Employer satisfaction with the withholding-tax process, and privatization of certain services, received repreated attention.

- *Higher Education Services Corp. (42)*. Tuition-assistance programs at individual colleges made up most such audits.

process uncomfortable for agency managers and serves as an incentive to avoid problems.

The $128 Billion Job

The comptroller's audit responsibilities address the details of government in every municipality, right down to the smallest special districts with annual budgets of a few hundred dollars. The office's other major responsibility is international in scope, requiring oversight of one of the biggest financial assets in the world.

Under New York's Finance Law, the comptroller is the sole trustee of the Common Retirement Fund, which provides pension benefits for state employees and many local government workers, including those of police and fire departments around the state. The fund is the second largest public pension plan in the country, behind only the California Public Employees Retirement System. As of March 31, 2005, its net assets totaled more than $128 billion — or roughly one-quarter larger than the state's 2004-05 budget. The fund paid current benefits for some 334,000 retirees and held assets for future benefits payable to 648,000 working men and women. Almost 3,000 public employers – the state itself, local governments and school districts – participate in the fund.

Total payouts in 2004-05 were around $5.6 billion, for an average annual pension of $16,766. The Common Retirement Fund includes two large systems – the Police and Fire System, and the Employees Retirement System. New retirees in ERS received average annual pensions of $19,231 in 2005. In the Police and Fire System, the average annual pension was $33,375 in 2005, with new retirees averaging $53,604 per year.

The number and cost of retired public employees is rising sharply. In the report on the 2004-05 fiscal year, pension administrators wrote: "Benefit payments continue to rise, reflecting improvements in final average salaries over the past decades, cost-of-living adjustment (COLA) payments and benefit improvements enacted over the years. For example, in 1996, benefit payments were approaching $2.9 billion, while this year's payments totaled more than $5.6 billion."

Forbes magazine has said the New York State comptroller "controls more money than anyone else on the planet."[24] (Boards of trustees oversee the California fund and most other large state pension funds.) As of March 2005, some 64 percent of the New York fund was invested in stocks and other equity investments. As trustee, Comptroller Hevesi held more than $1 billion in Citigroup, Exxon/Mobil, General Electric and Microsoft Corp., and hundreds of millions of dollars in companies such as Intel, WalMart, Pfizer, and AT&T. Some 19 percent of the fund was invested in government and corporate bonds and other debt, with smaller amounts in real estate and other investments.

---

24 Tyler Maroney, "McCall to Duty," *Forbes*, May 1, 2000, p. 302.

Investing the huge assets of the Common Retirement Fund is a major responsibility with direct ramifications for taxpayers and government workers. Like other investors, the fund is affected by both up and down markets. In 2004-05, annualized return on all investments was 8.5 percent, with international stocks, private equity and real-estate investments providing especially strong returns.

Greater investment returns can reduce contributions from taxpayers and public employees; allow higher benefits for retirees; or both. In 1980, the state and local governments had to set aside the equivalent of more than 30 percent of workers' salaries for pension benefits, according to OSC. That figure fell to around 2 percent as of 2001. By 2005, the contribution was back up to 12.9 percent. The difference meant sharp variations in taxpayer costs, totaling billions of dollars annually. During some periods, retirees from state and local governments elsewhere have gone more than a decade with no increase in pension benefits because their public pension funds were poorly invested. That has not been the case in New York.[25] Retirement funds in numerous other states are seriously underfunded, due to elected leaders' failure to ensure that taxpayer contributions and investment returns are sufficient to pay promised benefits. New York's public pension funds hold adequate reserves, according to their audited financial reports. Those reports assume continuation of strong investment gains, typically 8 percent or so a year. Absent such returns, taxpayer costs could rise sharply.

As costs and volatility rose in recent years, some observers suggested public employers in New York should follow private-sector trends and move gradually to defined-contribution, rather than defined-benefit, retirement plans. Such a move would replace traditional pension funds with individually managed 401(k)-style investment plans. Given strong opposition from the state's powerful public-employee unions, such a change is not likely in the near future. It may, however, become difficult to avoid as pension obligations for the state and local governments continue to rise in coming years.

The fund's huge assets make the comptroller a potentially powerful player in the affairs of hundreds of corporations in which the fund is one of the largest single investors. Recognizing the fund's huge investment power, the New York Stock Exchange named then-Comptroller McCall as the only public official to sit on its board of directors in June 1999.

---

25 See, for example, Jeff D. Opdyke, "West Virginia Pensioners Are Coming Up Short," *The Wall Street Journal*, June 5, 2000.

Comptrollers traditionally have been careful to use the investment power for the sole purpose of achieving the highest return for retirees and taxpayers. Interest groups occasionally urge the comptroller to use stockholder pressure against corporate managers for various purposes, but generally meet firm resistance.

In most states, boards of trustees with representation from unions, local governments, taxpayers, and other interest groups make investment decisions for public pension funds. Various legislators in Albany have introduced proposals over the years to create such a board in New York, but those proposals have not come close to passage. Comptrollers and others have argued that the current system creates clear accountability for managing and investing the pension funds — accountability that might be diffused with a multi-member board of trustees. There is little question that the California retirement fund, for instance, has taken the lead on politically charged issues more than New York's.

The Attorney General

As the state's chief legal officer, the attorney general represents the governor, all executive branch officials, the Legislature, state employees and other state entities in thousands of lawsuits each year. Some two-thirds of the attorneys working in the state's Department of Law are assigned to the Division of State Counsel, which handles litigation by or against the state, suits to recover delinquent accounts such as unpaid student loans, and monetary claims including tort and contract disputes. A Division of Appeals and Opinions prepares and argues appeals of court decisions involving the state, and provides legal opinions to state agencies and others. Agencies occasionally request that private firms be assigned to handle specialized topics.

During recent electoral campaigns, the attorney general's role has been presented to voters as something akin to chief crime-fighter. If there is such an official in New York, it is the governor, who oversees the State Police, police and peace officers in a number of other agencies, and the state prison system. As mentioned above, the attorney general has some responsibility for criminal investigations and prosecutions, but those areas are limited.

Better known to many New Yorkers because of the press attention it often attracts is the attorney general's role as "the people's lawyer."

"The Attorney General serves as the chief guardian of the legal rights of the citizens of New York, its businesses and its natural resources," according to the department's own description. "The Attorney General's Office is charged with the statutory *and common law* [emphasis added] powers to protect consumers and investors against fraud, the public health and environment against polluters, human and civil rights, and the rights of wage-earners and businesses across the State."[26]

For instance, the department's Bureau of Investor Protection and Securities is charged with enforcing the New York State Securities Law. Known as the Martin Act, this law protects the public from fraud by regulating sales of investment securities in New York, and by requiring brokers, dealers, and investment advisors to register with the Attorney General's Office. The bureau's attorneys can undertake investigations, criminal prosecutions, and civil litigation on behalf of investors.

Attorney General Eliot Spitzer, who took office in 1999, used the Martin Act and related powers more than any predecessor to undertake large-scale investigations and prosecutions of individuals and companies in the financial sector. Results included heightened sensitivity on Wall Street to problems of conflict of interest between corporate managers and small investors; significant operational changes in the mutual-funds industry; billions of dollars in corporate fines and settlements; and dismissal of chief executives at major companies. The investigations also left some companies badly weakened. Marsh & McLennan, for instance, laid off some 3,000 workers, many of them in New York, in the wake of the attorney general's probe into its insurance brokerage business.

The new approach to consumer protection purposefully relied not only on legal action against companies that were suspected of cheating their customers, but on negative publicity and the possibility of resulting damage to corporations' stock values and strength in the marketplace. A 2006 biography of Spitzer recounted the attorney general's investigation into the brokerage firm UBS Paine Webber, contrasting his approach with those of the federal Securities and Exchange Commission (SEC) and the industry's self-regulatory agency, the National Association of Stock Dealers (NASD).

The SEC and NASD had historically prided themselves on carrying out investigations discreetly, lest they harm public companies or frighten investors before all the facts were known. Spitzer tended to go public

---

26 *The New York Red Book 1999-2000*, p. 792.

much faster. When criticized, he would cite Louis Brandeis' adage that "Sunlight is said to be the best of disinfectants." His staffers also argued that they weren't the only ones talking to the media.

A lawyer for UBS Paine Webber, Theodore Levine, complained about leaks to the news media, apparently coming from New York State investigators or those from other states, during a meeting with securities regulators from several states.

Though Levine had carefully not singled out Spitzer or anyone else, the New York attorney general took it personally. He lashed out, blaming the banks themselves for the leaks. "This investigation is costing you billions of dollars in market cap," Spitzer said, referring to the banks' dropping stock prices. "If you want to continue to lose it, well, this can continue."[27]

Many observers of politics and of New York's financial sector expect future attorneys general to emulate the Spitzer approach to corporate oversight. Some critics have argued that such an approach by government investigators is inappropriate, and that any corporate malfeasance should be handled through official channels, including legal action when necessary.

Such investigations into the financial sector are one illustration of how New York State's attorney general and those in other states have taken on a major national role in recent years — with New York often leading the way. State attorneys general filed the lawsuits that led to the nationwide settlement with tobacco companies in 1998 and payments of billions of dollars to states. Mississippi Attorney General Mike Moore filed the first suit in 1994, alleging that Mississippi, like other states, "spends millions of dollars each year to provide or pay for health care and other necessary facilities and services on behalf of indigents and other eligible citizens whose said health care costs are directly caused by tobacco." Attorneys general in other states, including New York, echoed the suit's request that tobacco companies be ordered to repay the taxpayers. The overall settlement reached in November 1998, along with details ironed out in succeeding weeks, required the approval of Dennis Vacco, who served as New York attorney general through 1998, and his successor Eliot Spitzer. The tobacco settlement

---

27 Brooke A. Masters, *Spoiling For A Fight: The Rise of Eliot Spitzer*, Henry Holt & Co. LLC, New York, NY, 2006, p. 115.

brought a major new source of revenue to the states — with New York's share estimated at roughly $1 billion a year for the foreseeable future.

Along with the U.S. Department of Justice, 19 state attorneys general also filed an antitrust suit against Microsoft in 1998, arguing that the software giant waged an unlawful campaign to preserve a monopoly position in the market for operating systems on personal computers using Intel chips. The states (South Carolina later dropped its suit) sought a court ruling against Microsoft on their antitrust laws. In April 2000, U.S. District Judge Thomas Penfield Jackson found the company liable under state laws, including Section 340 of New York State's General Business Law, as well as federal antitrust law. Part of that decision was overturned on appeal, and the U.S. Justice Department and Microsoft reached a settlement in October 2001. State attorneys general, however, demonstrated their ability to continue the suit independent of the federal government.

Such multistate actions by attorneys general "fit into a long list of similar efforts" over decades, the National Association of Attorneys General said at the time of the Microsoft case. "Joint actions are now an integral part of the way that State Attorneys General fulfill their role as the ultimate state-level guardian of the law and the consuming public." Other targets of coordinated action by attorneys general have included automakers, airlines, food manufacturers, footwear companies, the insurance and oil industries, fast-food chains, and America Online.

Some of the growing activity by attorneys general puts those officials — including New York's — in a policy oversight position that has historically been reserved to the governor and the Legislature. Such policymaking extends to the details of implementation, and can create controversy. In the case of the national tobacco settlement, *State Policy Reports* newsletter observed: "For state policymakers, one of the biggest problems in understanding the impact of the [settlement] is the lack of information available to the public. Most information travels between the independent auditor, the participating manufacturers and state attorneys general. It does not always find its way into budget offices and other agencies that must estimate payments pursuant to the [settlement] and develop policy recommendations for the use of those funds."[28]

---

28 "Tobacco Settlement Update," Marcia Howard, ed., *State Policy Reports* 18, 7 (April 2000): p. 22.

The responsibilities and public profile that accompany such suits can boost the careers of attorneys general. One commentary observed that "The 1980s were a political boom decade for the ambitious politicians who held the reins of law enforcement in state capitols of America." It noted that, in 1985, 10 of 50 governors had moved directly into the chief executive's office from the attorney general's desk. One of those was Arkansas Governor and future President Bill Clinton.[29]

---

29 "Blocked Path to the Big Job," Governing, March 1996 (reprinted in *State Government: CQ's Guide to Current Issues and Activities 1996-97*).

Chapter Five

THE LEGISLATURE

Key points:

- When its members are united, the Legislature has nearly complete power over state government — but for various reasons, it seldom uses its full authority.

- Members of the Senate and Assembly choose to cede most decisions to a single leader of each house.

- Legislators have adopted numerous practices to maximize their chances of re-election, and relatively few legislative elections in New York are competitive.

"New York State legislative procedures remain an arcane mystery to many of even the most sophisticated counsel."[1]

---

1 Richard A. Givens, "Practice Commentaries: A Primer on the New York State Legislative Process: And How It Differs from Federal Procedure," *McKinney's Consolidated Laws of New York Annotated, Legislative Law*, West Publishing Co., St. Paul, MN, 1991, p. 67.

$\mathbf{M}$any citizens will not be surprised that even the "most sophisticated" lawyers cannot understand how New York's Legislature works. As is true in Washington and in other state capitals, the news media report relatively little on what occurs on the third floor of the Capitol in Albany, where the Senate and Assembly meet. Those New Yorkers who know only what they read in the newspapers might be considered fortunate simply to know *what* happens on major issues. Those who rely on television news generally will know even less. As to *why* and *how* any given law is passed or not passed, interested citizens may be told nothing beyond the fact that one or more legislators had a political need for a particular outcome. Clearly, such information is important — but it is by no means the entire story.

Understanding state legislatures is essential to understanding American government, given the broad range of ways in which they affect society. "Their involvement in our lives runs the gamut from womb to tomb," Alan Rosenthal, a leading observer of legislatures across the country, has written.[2] Certainly that's true in New York State, with its long tradition of activist government.

Any exploration of the Legislature must start, of course, with the state Constitution. As outlined in Chapter Two, New York's charter creates the legislative branch in Article III, and lays out or limits its powers and responsibilities in numerous other provisions.

Beyond the Constitution, the Legislature is governed by the provisions of the state's Legislative Law, internal rules adopted by resolution in each house, and folkways that have developed over the course of more than two centuries. Perhaps most importantly, the Senate and Assembly, like any democratically elected body, act according to political imperatives.

This chapter examines the legal and political context in which the Legislature operates. Key concepts include:

- *How legislation is shaped and passed.* The traditional charts that show "how a bill becomes law" are useful guides to the formal process. Relying on them, however, means missing key elements. The single most important of these is...

---

2   Alan Rosenthal, *Legislative Life: People, Process, and Performance in the States*,
    Harper & Row, New York, NY, 1981, p. xi.

- *The powerful role of the Senate and Assembly leaders.* These two individuals are, after the governor, far and away the most influential in state government. The power of the leaders flows from — and is directly accountable to — the members of the Legislature, as recent history in each house makes clear. If the leader wants a bill to pass, it almost always will. Although strong legislative leadership is often criticized, it may be necessary to avoid another failing of which legislatures are sometimes accused — the inability to get things done.

- *The evolving nature of the Legislature.* New York's people and its economy are constantly changing, altering the political and social environment in which the Legislature operates. Given this changing context, leaders and members of the two houses continually seek ways to maximize their institutional influence over state policy, the power of their party conference within the house, and individual members' opportunities to remain in power. One important evolution in recent decades has been...

- *The "professionalization" of the Legislature.* Growing numbers of long-term legislators, increased "incumbent protection" efforts, dramatic growth of legislative staff, more time on the job, and other factors have returned to the Legislature some of the influence that had shifted to the executive branch during much of the 20th century.

- *The nearly constant political pressure of being a legislator.* Elected every two years, members of the Senate and Assembly often feel they must work day in and day out to build voter support — even though the re-election rate for incumbents in New York is among the highest in the country.

The Basics

When New Yorkers created their first state government, they made certain that the overwhelming balance of power resided in the Legislature. Today, as the previous chapters outline, that is not always the case. Largely as a result of changes in the 20th century, the governor has assumed the dominant power over the direction of state agencies and the budget.

The Legislature still exerts its own significant influence on the budget and, to a lesser extent, the operation of state agencies. Most importantly, it initiates most of the hundreds of statutes enacted each year to govern the lives of New Yorkers.

As is true in every state except Nebraska, the legislature in Albany is composed of two houses. Bills may originate in either house (including tax bills, which at the federal level can only start in the House of Representatives). The Senate has some institutional powers the Assembly does not — primarily, consenting to cabinet and other major appointments made by the governor. The Senate has fewer members — as of 2006, 62 compared with 150 in the Assembly. Thus, other things being equal, each senator has a greater chance than individual Assembly members to influence the budget and legislation.

The number of Assembly seats is fixed by the Constitution, which provides for a 50-member Senate but allows a greater number based on population. The Constitution does not specify a maximum number of seats, and various court decisions affecting its districting provisions leave the question open to debate. The current number of seats in the Senate dates to 2002, when Republicans, who controlled the Senate, saw an opportunity to add a seat that could increase their majority while meeting federally mandated guidelines on districting. During reapportionment in 2002 Senate Republicans initiated creation of a 62nd seat again, with the expectation they could win the seat in November. Given New York's population of just under 19 million, each Assembly member represent some 128,000 constituents, on average, compared with 311,000 in the average Senate district.

The Constitution reserves to the Assembly the power of impeachment. The Legislature as a whole appoints members of the Board of Regents, the state's education policy-setting body; as a practical matter, the Assembly's Democratic majority has been large enough in recent decades to control such appointments.

As of 2006, Republicans had controlled the Senate continuously since 1966, and Democrats the Assembly since 1975. That represented the longest divided partisan control of any legislature in the country.

From Royal Control to the Will of the People

The early history of the New York State Legislature is a microcosm of the American Revolution itself — a story of the people (only some of them, at first) taking power from colonial rulers. It's one of the earliest such narratives in the Western Hemisphere; the first Assembly gathered in 1683, nearly a century before the creation of the U.S. Congress.

It was a far different world for representative democracy then, just as the community itself differed from today's. The early European settlers in the area of the Hudson River were here only because they had the blessing, and in some cases the financial backing, of monarchs and wealthy investors across the Atlantic.

The Dutch settlers came first, in 1609, when the Dutch West India Co. sent Henry Hudson on his unsuccessful mission to find a faster trade route to Asia than around the southern tip of Africa. Preoccupied with other colonial efforts from Brazil to Java, however, the company did not establish the first permanent European settlement in the area until 1624, at Fort Orange in what is now Albany. The company's investors reaped the benefits of trading beaver furs and other goods from the rich lands bordering the Hudson.

The company, ruled by a board of directors, was empowered by the Dutch crown to make its own laws in the territory it called New Netherland. The board in turn appointed a governor, or director-general, to administer its colony. During the 40 years of Dutch rule, governors appointed councils to give advice and lend political support for potentially controversial policies such as new taxes or relations with Native Americans. Often, the members of these councils would attempt to establish some power independent of the appointed governor. Invariably, they failed.

In 1664, the Dutch surrendered New Netherland to the British.[3] King Charles II gave virtually total control of the colony to his brother James, the Duke of York (later King James II). Like his Dutch predecessors, James had concerns beyond what was now called New York, and

---

3   David M. Ellis writes that the Dutch were supplanted partly for lack of colonists, which reflected well on conditions back home: "Why should men and women leave Holland with its stable republican government, its religious toleration, its thriving economy, for a life of danger in the rude settlements along the Hudson?" See Ellis et al., *A History of New York State,* 1967, p. 18.

appointed governors to run the territory. By this time, the residents of
the colony — particularly many on Long Island, where settlement patterns resulted in a feeling of separation from New Netherland — were
pushing hard for a representative assembly.

Eventually they convinced Governor Edmund Andros to propose
such an assembly to the duke, but James refused. In retaliation, merchants refused to pay import duties. The duke capitulated and sent a
new governor, Thomas Dongan. He was told to call a general assembly
to pass laws subject to the approval of the governor and the duke. The

Governors vs. the Legislature

Modern observers of New York State government are used to seeing the
governor and the Legislature argue over policy decisions, as well as
broader questions of where to draw the line between the powers of each
branch. Such battles go back nearly to the earliest days of European settlement more than a third of a millennium ago.

In 1641, colonial settlers made what historians often term the first
attempt at representative government in the future Empire State. One of
the early governors appointed by the Dutch West India Co., Willem
Kieft, faced a series of crises, including bad relations with Native
Americans, who were still a powerful force. Kieft wanted to tax Algon-
kian natives for repairs to Fort Amsterdam and called a council of 12
men for support. The council members approved the action against the
Indians but demanded additional powers over taxes and other policies.
The governor, displeased, dismissed the group.

One of the best-remembered governors, Pieter Stuyvesant, appointed a nine-member council of advisers who agreed to his request
for new taxes. Later, however, they drew up a list of criticisms that
asked for more settlers, more free trade, and more protection from the
Native Americans.

Under the British, as early as 1755, New York's Assembly had established "committees of correspondence" to maintain contacts with
other English colonies concerning the Stamp Act, the Sugar Act, and
other "intolerable acts" pressed upon them by the London government.
In 1766, Governor Moore suspended the Assembly and would not allow it to do business until New York furnished barracks and supplies
for British troops.

Assembly met for the first time for three weeks starting October 17, 1683, at Fort James, near the present Battery in Manhattan. It adopted a Charter of Liberties and Privileges, which included freedom of worship, trial by jury, and a court system. After the Duke of York became King James II two years later, he rejected this charter as too strong a challenge to his powers. He also abolished the Assembly *(see sidebar)*.

The Assembly functioned periodically and in various forms under the English until New York and the other 12 colonies declared their independence in 1776. The first New York State Constitution created the following year established the two-house Legislature we know today, continuing the Assembly and giving birth to the state Senate.

The Legislature first met in the Bogardus Tavern in Kingston on September 1 of that year. During and after the Revolution, the Legislature convened up and down the Hudson Valley, in Kingston, Poughkeepsie, Fishkill, Albany, and New York City, finally settling in Albany in 1797.

The representative bodies of the founders' era differed from those of today in important respects. Eligibility to vote and run for election was restricted to roughly half of the white men and a tiny minority of black men — those who owned property and met residency requirements. Women and most non-whites were prohibited from voting.

Among the institutional differences from the current Legislature, members of the Senate originally were elected for four years, and Assembly members, one year. The difference was somewhat analogous to the structure of the U.S. Congress, where six-year terms give senators a longer-term perspective than members of the House of Representatives. (Some commentators believe the state Senate was intended to protect the interests of wealthy landowners against the potentially more populist Assembly.) The Constitution of 1846 changed the term of senators to two years, while Assembly terms remained a single year until an amendment that took effect in 1938 established two-year terms. For more than a century and a half, in other words, senators were far more privileged politically than members of the Assembly.

The Senate, under the state's first Constitution, consisted of 24 members elected by and from landowners whose net worth was at least 100 pounds. Additional senators were to be added to each district as population grew.

Like members of the U.S. Senate whose "districts" are their constituent states, New York's state senators originally were elected from large regions — four "great districts" — rather than individual communities. Like the U.S. Constitutional guarantee that each state will have at least one seat in the House of Representatives, New York's original Constitution also guaranteed that every county (except Fulton and Hamilton) would be represented by at least one member of the Assembly.

That provision and several others gave voters in less populated areas of the state (especially the most rural counties) proportionally greater electoral power than those in the most densely populated areas — in particular, New York City. U.S. Supreme Court decisions in the mid-1960s rendered such rules obsolete, but some of those provisions remain in the state Constitution today.

"One Man, One Vote"

For nearly two centuries, legislatures in New York and other states distributed political power unevenly. Urban residents saw this as inherently wrong and discriminatory. Rural representatives, on the other hand, perceived it as necessary protection against tyranny by the more densely populated areas, comparable to the U.S. Constitution's provision for a Senate with equal representation from every state regardless of population.

Across the nation, "Rural areas, if we consider population as the basis of representation, have been disproportionately strong in legislative bodies; the urban voice, far weaker than its numbers of people allow it to be," Charles R. Adrian wrote shortly after the major Supreme Court cases on such apportionment.[4]

In 1958, *Magraw* v. *Donovan*, a federal district court decision, established the principle of judicial involvement in questions of state legislative apportionment. For several decades previously, the courts had considered apportionment decisions to be solely legislative in nature, or a "political question" that the judiciary could not properly address under the separation of powers.

In 1962, the U.S. Supreme Court accepted jurisdiction in an apportionment case for the first time. In *Baker* v. *Carr,* the high court ruled

---

4   Charles R. Adrian, *State and Local Governments,* McGraw-Hill Inc., New York, NY, 1967, p. 358.

"New York City Is Pie For The Hayseeds"

The view of New York City politicians regarding legislative apportionment was captured in the classic *Plunkitt of Tammany Hall: A Series of
Very Plain Talks on Very Practical Politics**, a 1905 book based on interviews with George Washington Plunkitt. Ward leader in Manhattan's
Fifteenth Assembly District, and one of the powers of Tammany Hall
when Tammany was supreme in the city, Plunkitt granted the interviews to William Riordon of the *New York Evening Post.*

Plunkitt's comments on how upstate legislators took advantage of
the city, under the heading "New York City Is Pie For The Hayseeds,"
included:

> This city is ruled entirely by the hayseed legislators at Albany. ... You
> hear a lot about the downtrodden people of Ireland and the Russian
> peasants and the sufferin' Boers. Now, let me tell you that they have
> more real freedom and home rule than the people of this grand and im-
> perial city. In England, for example, they make a pretense of givin' the
> Irish some self-government. In this State the Republican government
> makes no pretense at all. It says right out in the open: "New York City
> is a nice big fat Goose. Come along with your carvin' knives and have a
> slice." They don't pretend to ask the Goose's consent.

> Did you ever go up to Albany from this city with a delegation that
> wanted anything from the Legislature? No? Well, don't. The hayseeds
> who run all the committees will look at you as if you were a child that
> didn't know what it wanted, and will tell you in so many words to go
> home and be good and the Legislature will give you whatever it thinks
> is good for you.... Then the Legislature goes and passes a law increasin'
> the liquor tax or some other tax in New York City, takes a half of the
> proceeds for the State Treasury and cuts down the farmers' taxes to
> suit. It's as easy as rollin' off a log – if you've got a good workin' ma-
> jority and no conscience to speak of.

At the time of Plunkitt's interviews, New York City held roughly 47
percent of the state's population. That meant that, even if legislative
seats had been apportioned equitably, the city's representatives would
not have made a majority. By the time of the 1940 Census, though, the
city's population accounted for more than 55 percent of the statewide
total. Yet its seats in the 1945 Senate (25 of 56) and Assembly (67 of
150) were each less than 45 percent of the total.

---

*   William L. Riordan, *Plunkitt of Tammany Hall*, E. P. Dutton & Co., New York, NY,
        1905.

that lower courts should consider whether the Tennessee Legislature's apportionment violated the equal-protection clause of the Fourteenth Amendment.[5] In a 1964 case involving state legislatures' drawing of lines for Congressional seats, the court invoked the relevant language that was to become well-known in discussion of apportionment, saying legislatures must make sure that, as much as possible, "one man's vote in a Congressional election must be worth as much as another's."[6] Finally, in *Reynolds* v. *Sims,* the Supreme Court ruled that both houses of a state legislature must be apportioned as strictly as possible according to population.[7]

The case of *WMCA* v. *Lorenzo* applied the rule particularly to New York.[8] Later that year, New York's Court of Appeals decided that, based on the Supreme Court rulings, a full Assembly seat could no longer be guaranteed to each county, and that because some districts would cross county lines, local legislatures would no longer have the power to draw Assembly districts.[9] A new constitution proposed by the Constitutional Convention of 1967 would have eliminated its unenforceable districting provisions, but voters rejected the proposal because of controversy over other provisions. Thus Article III of New York's fundamental law retains the old language, now dead letters.

In New York State as in many others, the impact of the apportionment cases was huge; it still reverberates in the early 21st century. In the Empire State, the imperative to take political power from Upstate and shift it to New York City played a key role (along with Lyndon Johnson's landslide victory over Barry Goldwater in the presidential election) in allowing the Democrats to take control of the Legislature in 1965 for the first time in state history. By the 1960s, however, the state's largest city had dropped below a majority of the population — to 46.4 percent — for the first time in the 20th Century. The Republicans quickly regained the Senate in 1966 and have held it ever since. In the Assembly, the GOP recaptured the majority in 1969 but lost it again in the post-Watergate elections of 1974. Democrats have held control of the lower house ever since.

---

5   *Baker* v. *Carr*, 369 U.S. 186 (1962)

6   *Westberry* v. *Sanders,* 376 U.S. 1 (1964)

7   *Reynolds* v. *Sims,* 377 U.S. 533 (1964)

8   *WMCA* v. *Lorenzo*, 377 U.S. 633 (1964)

9   *Matter of Orans*, 15 NY 2nd 339 (1965)

The courts' rulings requiring equitable representation in both houses of the Legislature played a key role in other major changes:

- *More minority-group members* were elected to both houses, partly because many of the districts newly apportioned to New York City had large proportions of minority residents.

- *For the same reason*, some more politically conservative lawmakers were replaced by others who were more politically liberal. This shift has resulted in state leaders expanding the role of government in welfare, health care, the environment and other areas. The leadership of Governor Rockefeller and his successors was important in bringing those changes, but the new makeup of the Legislature played a role as well.

- *The Senate and Assembly* became more "professionalized." Both houses added more and better-trained staff, while members' service grew longer and their compensation increased. These developments helped boost the power of the Legislature relative to that of the governor.

Today, Republicans who control the state Senate have drawn districts that discriminate slightly against New York City by including more residents in each district there than in upstate districts. In the Assembly, the opposite is true; majority Democrats strengthen their hold on power by drawing district lines to favor New York City. In 2002, as in the past two decades, the two houses approved redistricting plans written by the majority in each chamber. Courts in New York and other states have generally allowed small differences in population among legislative districts — as much as 10 percent difference from the least to most populated districts — in accord with U.S. Supreme Court rulings.[10]

One of the oldest democratically elected legislative bodies in the world, the New York Legislature continues to evolve, often in ways that affect the balance of power between lawmakers and the governor. As the 21st century began, for instance, the leaders and some individual

10 David I. Wells, "Legislative Districting and the New York State Constitution," in Benjamin and Dullea, eds., *Decision 1997: Constitutional Change in New York*, 1997, p. 113.

members of the Senate and Assembly had assumed more direct control than ever before over hundreds of millions of dollars in capital and other spending each year. As part of budget agreements with the governor, these dollars were allocated for projects identified by members of the Legislature with little input from the executive branch, contrary to the normal give-and-take. In return, the governor was allocated a certain amount of funding, for projects he deemed important, without the need for legislative approval. For legislators and communities favored by the process, this development represented a high point of legislative power to rival any of those during the Legislature's 300-plus years.

The Powers of the Legislature

The Legislature has enormous *potential* power, although it seldom exercises that power fully. The state Constitution gave it more power than the governor because lawmakers are elected "closer to home" and are subject to more frequent review by the voters. That remains the case today despite creation of the executive budget process and other 20th-century steps toward a stronger executive.

While budget and policy proposals made by the governor often capture attention, most of the hundreds of laws enacted in any given year originate with individual legislators. Most of these receive little or no attention from the press, but each new law represents some shift in the way public policy affects New Yorkers' lives. *(For one example, see Appendix.)*

The state's major statutes, many of which go through some significant changes in a typical year, include:

- *The Penal Code and Criminal Procedure Law.* Through these and other laws, the Legislature decides what is and is not a crime in the state, the police and judicial procedures that establish guilt or innocence, and the punishment imposed for all crimes.

- *The Business Corporations Law, Not For Profit Corporations Law, Civil Practice Law and Rules, and other statutes.* These laws outline how New Yorkers can form various types of business firms and other organizations, and how individuals and organizations deal with each other in ways that will be enforced by the broader society.

- *The Vehicle and Traffic Law*, which sets rules to promote safe and efficient transportation on New York's public roads.

- *The Environmental Conservation Law, and the Parks and Recreation Law.* Under these statutes, the Legislature makes a wide variety of decisions on how individuals, businesses, units of government, and others use and protect the natural environment of the state.

Other key statutes make rules regarding public health, the powers and responsibilities of local governments and school districts, care for those who are disabled or financially needy, the employment of workers in both the private and public sectors, and a myriad other matters.

Besides setting public policy in all of these important areas, the Legislature, of course, shares the budgeting role with the governor. What's more, while the Constitution gives the governor the initiative in the budget process, the Legislature can spend the state's dollars in almost any way it wants — *if* its members are united enough to agree on a two-thirds override vote in each house. After dealing with the governor's budget proposals, members of the Senate and Assembly can also originate their own individual appropriation bills. On the revenue side of the budget, they have the power to rewrite the tax law entirely, and change or enact new fees and other charges, if they so wish. (*See more detailed discussion, Chapter Ten.*)

The Legislature has the power to revise the Constitution, subject to approval of the voters (two separately elected legislatures must give approval first). The governor has no official role in that process, although his "bully pulpit" can be influential in shaping public opinion.

Sitting jointly, members of the Senate and Assembly elect the members of the Board of Regents, one of the most important agencies in state government. The Regents in turn appoint the commissioner of education, oversee the Education Department, and set education policy for the state. Again, the governor has no formal role.

In a power-sharing arrangement similar to that in our national government, the state Senate confirms or rejects nominations made by the governor for certain state and judicial offices. The Senate majority leader, or temporary president, follows the lieutenant governor in succession to the governorship if necessary. If the Senate leader is incapable of serving, the Assembly speaker is next in line. (That order of succession is the reverse of the federal government's, where the speaker of the House follows the vice president in the line of succession, and then the leader of the U.S. Senate.)

The Senate and Assembly also oversee the performance of the executive branch. This is a natural outgrowth of the Legislature's role in appropriating taxpayer dollars, and its role (the Senate's role, at least) in reviewing and approving appointments to the top positions in executive agencies.

As part of this responsibility, in the case of "enemy attack or ... disasters (natural or otherwise)," the Legislature has the power "and the immediate duty" under the Constitution to "provide for prompt and temporary succession to the powers and duties of public offices, of whatever nature and whether filled by election or appointment." The Assembly has the power to impeach state officials. The Senate, along with members of the Court of Appeals, sits as a court of impeachment in such cases.

The Legislature's sphere of influence extends even into the federal government, as it enacts legislation drawing districts for the state's delegation to the House of Representatives (subject to gubernatorial veto and potential override). Particularly in the year or two leading up to each decade's redistricting, members of Congress tend to be attentive and even solicitous to members of the Legislature who may have a voice in drawing the new lines. The Legislature's writing of state Election Law also governs when political parties hold primaries for offices that include the presidency; an earlier or later date may give one or another national candidate an advantage.

Finally, legislators perform constituent service. Especially if they chair a committee, otherwise occupy a leadership position, or are of the same political party as the governor, members may be able to help constituents resolve difficulties with state agencies. Legislators also disseminate a great variety of information about state programs. Most legislators' offices are well stocked with brochures from state agencies and other sources such as tourist attractions in the state.

Limits on Power

For all of that, the full *potential* powers of the Legislature are seldom used. For instance, overrides of gubernatorial vetoes are relatively rare, despite the fact that almost all vetoed bills originally passed both houses with more than the two-thirds votes needed for override. In Governor Pataki's first two terms in office, the Legislature did not override a single veto — even though his vetoes targeted, for instance, more than $1 billion in spending the Legislature included in the 1998-99 budget. Sometimes, legislators work around vetoes by negotiating changes with the executive branch — but, just as often, a veto is the end of action on a given issue for that year.

As the previous chapter pointed out, after all, the power of the governor is not based only on written law. An effective governor enhances executive power by appealing to popular opinion. Members of the Legislature, who must run for reelection every two years while the governor has the comparative luxury of a four-year term, must be particularly sensitive to such opinion.

Further, the Legislature, while acting as a unit when it passes bills, is not by nature a unified entity but rather a gathering of various individual players and groups of interests. Passage of legislation requires, at the broadest level, action by two separately elected houses. Within each house are two party conferences, majority and minority. Within each of the four party conferences are smaller groupings based on shared regional, ideological, or other interests. Like other men and women, legislators think about issues based on their own and their constituents' political needs, life experiences, biases, and visions of the future. In addition, interests that oppose a bill have numerous opportunities to block its passage; proponents must win at each step of the process.

To promote full consideration of legislation before passage, the Constitution requires that bills be on lawmakers' desks for three days before voting. Exception can be made on certification from the governor that an immediate vote is necessary. During the last day or two of each legislative session, this provision effectively gives the governor the power to decide whether last-minute bills can be acted upon. Each house can bypass the restriction simply by extending its session by a day or two, but legislative leaders often will not do so unless a high-priority bill hangs in the balance.

As noted in Chapter Two, the state Constitution limits the lawmaking power of the Legislature and the governor through the Bill of Rights and other provisions. In the budgetary area, for instance, the Constitution restricts the Legislature's authority to appropriate taxpayer dollars.

Legislators are sometimes criticized for perceived failure to act — or to act quickly enough — on issues important to some New Yorkers. To cite one obvious example, the Legislature as an institution receives widespread criticism (along with the governor) when the state budget is not enacted on time. Such lack of action reflects the competing interests that individual legislators face before they make a decision, and that the two houses as institutions face before they can reconcile the positions of their members. Those individuals and groups who criticize lawmakers for failure to act should keep in mind that the Legislature is not designed to act quickly. Perhaps critics can be comforted by reflecting on other issues the Legislature has not addressed and *should* not. Different observers, of course, will have different opinions regarding what those issues may be.

The other common criticism of the Legislature is that its leaders have too much power. It's certainly true that the leaders of New York's Senate and Assembly dominate their institutions far more than leaders in most other states, or in Congress. On the other hand, the leaders are elected by the members of the Legislature — who have an opportunity to replace them at least every two years. Senators and Assembly members themselves often explain any faults in their institutions with reference to centralized leadership, the suggestion being that individual legislators cannot improve things. Their proven ability to replace leaders, and to shape legislative action, proves such claims wrong.

As an independent branch of government, the Legislature has wide latitude to manage its own affairs. The Constitution provides that "each house shall determine the rules of its own proceedings, and be the judge of the elections, returns and qualifications of its own members; (and) shall choose its own officers." It also protects members' speech on the floor, saying "For any speech or debate in either house of the legislature, the members shall not be questioned in any other place." In other words, statements made in the course of debate may not form the basis of a libel suit or prosecution in any other tribunal. No legislator may be arrested during session. The Legislative Law allows either house to "punish by imprisonment not extending beyond the same session of the legislature, as for a contempt" anyone who bribes a member, refuses to give evidence in response to a legislative subpoena, or commits certain other offenses. The Penal Law provides other sanctions against corruption by legislators and other officials.

Still, the Legislature does not have total control of its own affairs. Items in its own budget are subject to gubernatorial veto (with the same possibility for legislative override as other measures), although such vetoes are virtually unknown in recent history. Legislators are also subject, of course, to enforcement of the laws they enact; members have been found guilty of criminal offenses for such actions as filing false claims for travel reimbursement and putting no-show employees on the payroll.

How Do the Houses Work?

The Senate and Assembly generally meet, in their respective chambers on the third floor of the Capitol, on two to four days a week from January through June, with sessions more frequent during the last month or two. The two houses were scheduled to be in session on 65 days in 2006, ending on June 22, according to the joint session calendar both houses adopted at the start of the year. The two houses adjourned June 23 and planned to return to the Capitol later in the year to act on some additional issues.

Since the late 1970s, the Legislature has adopted the practice of never formally adjourning, a change that affects the balance of legislative power relative to that of the governor. The state Constitution provides that any bill not acted upon by the governor within 10 days of its being sent to him (not counting Sundays) automatically becomes law — unless the Legislature has adjourned. If it has adjourned, the governor has a "pocket veto," meaning he can effectively veto the bill simply by taking no action.

By remaining officially in session, even during periods when members do not actually meet, the Legislature prevents a governor from exercising a pocket veto. One of the Assembly members from the Albany area — in recent years, Assemblyman John J. McEneny — bangs the gavel at the speaker's desk in the Assembly chamber once a week to indicate continuation of session. Similar formalities are followed in the Senate.

To permit the public to follow its deliberations, the Constitution requires that sessions of the Legislature be open. Section 18 of the legislative article, enacted in 1975, gives the Legislature the power to call itself into extraordinary session upon petition to the leaders of the houses, signed by two-thirds of the members of each house. Previously only the governor had the power to call an extraordinary session. (With the later practice of never adjourning, Section 18 has little practical import.)

On days they are not in session, members are most likely to be in their districts. There, on any given day, a member might attend one or more functions addressing or meeting with constituents. Nonsession days may also bring activities such as hearings on legislative issues and political party functions. With elections every two years, even many long-tenured legislators feel the need to "campaign" more or less continually. However, while many legislators classify their job as full-time, others devote most off-session days to work in law, business or other fields.

The Legislature operates on several cycles. One cycle is based on the two-year terms between elections, another on the six months of each year's regular legislative session. Each year's session starts with the State of the State address by the governor (held, by custom, on the first Wednesday of the year). When a new Legislature forms every two years, the legislative slate is clean. Bills introduced during the first year of a term carry over into the second year, but all bills die at the end of each Legislature on December 31st in even-numbered years. Each house has internal rules governing the introduction of legislation, including limits on bill introductions during the final weeks of the session. For instance, after April 25, 2006, members of the Senate were limited to introducing 10 bills for the remainder of the session. Members of the Assembly faced such a limit on and after May 2.

The Rules Committee in each house serves as an arm of the leadership, controlling the flow of legislation, especially toward the end of session.

The operations of the Senate and Assembly are governed by the Legislative Law and by internal rules adopted by resolution in each house. In addition to specifying the leadership positions in each house and their compensation, the Legislative Law lays out procedural requirements for introducing and passing bills. It provides for internal financial controls over the legislative budget, and establishes the Administrative Regulations Review Commission to monitor executive agency regulations. The Legislative Law also creates the Legislative Commission on Expenditure Review, although the commission has not functioned since 1993 because the two houses stopped funding it that

	Bills Introduced and Enacted in New York			
Year	Senate Bills Introduced	Assembly Bills Introduced	Bills Sent to Governor	Number (%) Signed into Law
1929-30	3,501	4,043	2,127	1,592 (75%)
1939-40	4,428	4,782	2,492	1,843 (74%)
1949-50	5,512	6,405	2,370	1,683 (71%)
1959-60	7,715	9,171	2,592	1,969 (76%)
1969-70	9,497	14,050	2,863	2,203 (77%)
1979-80	9,782	12,289	1,914	1,690 (88%)
1989-90	9,184	12,219	1,782	1,731 (97%)
1999-2000	8,230	10,875	1,441	1,268 (88%)

Source: Mary Ann Ryan-Germani, ed., *The New York Red Book 2001-02*, New York Legal Publishing Corp., Albany, NY, 2001.

year. The commission published widely respected analyses of state programs. Its elimination represented one of the few times in recent decades a legislative commission has gone out of business.

The Senate and Assembly's internal rules are subject to change by vote of the respective house — unlike the Legislative Law, which can be amended only as any other statute, by action of both houses and approval of the governor. The internal rules lay out further procedural guidelines for action on legislation, set policies on subjects such as affirmative action and sexual harassment, and otherwise direct the operations of the two houses. As with most other elements of the Legislature's work, the rules of each house are determined mainly by the leaders.

How a Bill Becomes Law: The Basics

Any member of the Senate or Assembly can introduce a bill on any subject. After introduction, the bill must pass at least three major hurdles to become law: it must pass in the house of origin, pass in the other house, and gain approval by the governor or successful override of a gubernatorial veto. The overwhelming majority of bills must win a vote in at least one committee before going "to the floor" for a vote by the entire house. Some go to more than one committee — in the Assembly, for instance, any bill with fiscal impact will go to the Ways and Means Committee, and those carrying criminal sanctions will go to the Codes Committee.

Given those hurdles, the odds that any individual bill will become law are low. Legislators introduce some 10,000 bills in a typical two-year session.[11] With some bills, sponsors have little intention of pushing for passage, advancing them simply to satisfy a constituent or interest group. Other bills are understood to be "one-house" bills — proposals that, for ideological or political reasons, can easily pass one house but would never be considered by the other. Sometimes the chair will refuse to bring a bill to a vote in committee, effectively halting its advance, and the sponsor may be unable or unwilling to persuade house leaders to overrule the chair's decision. Generally, the leaders do not schedule a vote unless they support the bill's passage.

The Role of the Leadership

A simple rule of thumb in Albany is this: *If the leadership in a given house wants a bill to pass, it will.* The question for supporters of any bill is how to get the Senate majority leader and the Assembly speaker to want a bill to pass. One way outside supporters attempt to do so is to get a significant bloc of legislators to ask the leadership and top staff members to bring it to the floor for a vote.

The power of the leaders over each house is often described as near-total. Each leader — along with a few top staff members he appoints — plays the dominant role *outside* the house, communicating and negotiating positions on the budget and other legislative matters. The majority leader and the speaker also maintain virtually complete control over *internal* matters — they name legislators to other leadership positions and committee chairs, which often makes a difference of

---

11 "Session" has several meanings. Each two-year term is, technically, one session, given that the houses do not adjourn. Observers commonly refer to each year's work as, for instance, "the 2006 session." And on a given day when lawmakers are meeting, they are said to be "in session."

$10,000 or more in salary. Leaders approve the appointment and compensation of all legislative staff, and designate which office space will be given to which members.

"Strong legislative leadership has traditionally been considered a necessity in New York state both because of its large legislative body and because of its extremely powerful governorship," according to one analysis.[12]

As is true in Congress and other American legislatures, Democrats and Republicans in each house choose their leaders before electing the leadership of the entire house. Whichever party has a majority in effect elects the house leader, who in turn appoints deputies, committee chairs, other leaders and key staff.

The leader makes decisions on legislation and other matters in consultation with the party conference. Each of the four conferences (members of the two parties in each of the two houses) typically gather one or more times each week the house is in session so conference leaders can update members on plans for the coming week. At the same time, leaders and rank-and-file members discuss the conference's position on potentially controversial issues.

Meetings of the two majority conferences are often the most important events in determining what will happen on a given issue, particularly one that is controversial. Members usually have some idea of which direction the leadership is leaning on a particular issue. If several legislators want a different decision, the conference meeting is their chance to air the issue. Such discussions affect the outcome of legislative and budgetary decisions far more often than debates in committee or on the floor of the house.

Many Albany observers tend to forget that the members elect the leaders because of the common wisdom that legislative leaders have total control of their houses. From time to time, one or more members take action that reminds everyone that the leaders are not elected for life. In mid-2000, Assembly Majority Leader Michael Bragman attempted to oust Speaker Sheldon Silver. The effort would have required a majority of the house's Democratic majority. While a number of other Democrats said they were unhappy with certain conditions in the

---

12 Abdo I. Baaklini and Charles S. Dawson, *The Politics of Legislation in New York State: How A Bill Becomes A Law*, Comparative Development Studies Center, Graduate School of Public Affairs, SUNY Albany, Albany, NY, 1979, p. 19.

Assembly, such as the influence of central staff, the Bragman effort failed. Still, Speaker Silver appointed a committee of members to propose procedural changes in the house, and some changes were put in place as a result. At the end of 1994, Republican members of the Senate decided to oust Majority Leader Ralph J. Marino, who was considered antagonistic to the governor-elect, George E. Pataki.

More often than not, when the leadership position in either house opens as a result of retirement or death, two or more members vie for it. Once in place, however, legislative leaders are virtually never dethroned. Some pundits call the legislative leadership position "the hardest job in Albany to get, and the easiest to keep."

Another key role for the Senate and Assembly leadership is that of political leader. Like the leaders of Congress, leaders in the New York Senate and Assembly shape their conference's policy agenda, in part to help lay the groundwork for appealing to voters. They often participate in selecting candidates for seats held by the opposition or where an incumbent is leaving; in many cases they provide the bulk of the financial and other support candidates need in an election. When Democrats Hugh Carey and Mario Cuomo were governor, the Republicans who served as majority leader of the Senate (Warren Anderson from 1973-1988, and Marino from 1989-94) were often described as the most powerful members of their party in the state. After Pataki became governor, Silver was recognized as the leading Democrat in New York. For instance, he formally announced the New York delegation's vote to nominate Al Gore for president during the 2000 National Democratic Convention.

Legislative leaders' political involvement is sometimes seen as a natural function of working to achieve legislative goals. After all, if the party in control of one house were to lose control, its legislative agenda would have little to no chance of passage. Defenders of the status quo in Albany sometimes use this argument to justify the Legislature's extensive use of tax dollars to promote members' popularity and prospects for re-election.

In addition to the Senate majority leader and the speaker of the Assembly, a small number of other legislators hold positions that are especially important. These individuals are typically viewed as potential successors to the leader.

In the Assembly, the majority leader is the second-ranking member of the majority party and oversees floor action, as well as participating in leadership deliberations and negotiations. The chair of the Ways and

Means Committee is a key voice in the majority's decisions and negotiations on tax and spending issues. Another committee with broad responsibility is the Codes Committee, which reviews all legislation with any impact on criminal laws. A senior member of the majority party usually presides over the Assembly's proceedings from the speaker's chair on the podium.

The lieutenant governor is charged by the Constitution with presiding over the Senate; in a typical year, she or he might actually do so on a dozen or fewer occasions because of other responsibilities. The deputy majority leader for legislative operations manages floor action. The chair of the Finance Committee is another key leadership position in the Senate, like that of the Ways and Means chair in the Assembly.

One way the leaders exercise control is through legislative staff. All employees serve at the pleasure of the majority leader in the Senate and the speaker in the Assembly. Members generally receive a fairly limited budget for their personal staff — for newer legislators who are not committee chairs, typically two to three assistants in Albany and a similar number in the district office. Chairmanships and other leadership positions usually come with additional staff. These assistants are often hired and assigned by the leaders or their top staff members.

The highest-ranking legislative staff members have more influence than most lawmakers, a source of periodic rancor among members. The leader in each house typically has two to four aides with whom he works especially closely. These generally include the leader's counsel and/or chief of staff, the top fiscal advisor (secretary to the Senate Finance or Assembly Ways and Means Committee), and the communications director. In conjunction with the house leadership, the counsel or chief of staff oversees preparation of legislation, negotiation with the other house and the governor's staff on nonfiscal issues, and scheduling of bills for floor action. Given the nature of the Legislature, each of these individuals' duties may involve political counsel. The leader generally will also have one or more political aides whose chief responsibility is to help members win re-election by assuring passage of popular legislation, assisting with constituent services, encouraging legislative staff to spend personal time on campaigns and otherwise promoting preservation of the majority.

Normally, as mentioned earlier, the leaders decide what happens in each house on any given day, and use the formal process to implement their decisions. The process sometimes trumps other considerations, however. Near the end of the 2000 Senate session, a bill to ease the tax burden on railroads did not pass because the printed bill was not at the desk of the Senate clerk when the time came to vote on it. The bill had already passed the Assembly, was agreed upon for Senate passage, and was supported by Governor Pataki. Senate Majority Leader Joseph L. Bruno had made a commitment to members that he would not keep the session going beyond a certain time. When the time came and the bill had not been printed and copied, the Senate adjourned. The bill remained in limbo until 2002.

Leaders also control when bills that have passed both houses go to the governor, with the house that passes a bill first controlling such timing. Assembly rules provide that bills passed by both houses, and returned from the Senate to the Assembly before May 1, be sent to the governor within 10 legislative days. Bills returned from the Senate in May must be sent to the second floor within 30 days, and those received in June or later transmitted within 45 days. The Senate has no such requirements for bills under its control.

In committee, chairs and their staffs typically will not bring a bill to a vote unless it has sufficient votes to pass. On occasion, more often in the Assembly than in the Senate, bills will come up in committee when one or more supporters are absent, and united opposition will defeat the bill. Leaders have the power to change or add committee memberships at will. In 2006, Speaker Silver added three members to the Assembly Judiciary Committee just before the panel was to vote on a bill to limit "double dipping" by local-government employees who collect both jury awards and disability benefits for on-the-job injuries. The bill was opposed by trial lawyers, a favored constituency in the Assembly, but the Judiciary Committee appeared ready to approve the bill. The three new members — Ronald Canestrari, Deborah Glick, and Catherine Nolan — voted in the negative, and the committee defeated the bill. The move sparked criticism as a stifling of democracy, but the leadership — with the support of individual members — carried the day.

The Committee System

As it does in Congress and most other state legislatures, the committee system serves several important functions in Albany.

It organizes consideration of, and preliminary action on, most bills. A proposal dealing with curricula in public schools, for instance, is automatically referred to the Education Committee in each house. Members of committees, and the staff that leadership assigns to them, develop expertise in both the substance and political aspects of particular subject areas.

The committees also screen bills so that every member does not have to deal with each of the 10,000 or so bills introduced in a typical two-year session.

Allocation of chairmanships at the start of each two-year legislative term is a key part of the leaders' responsibility to distribute policy influence and leadership stipends. Loyalty to the leader, seniority, geographic distribution, and other factors come into play in such allocations.

As of 2006 session, the Senate had 31 committees. The Assembly's website listed 42 committees (although that number included groups such as Majority Program and Steering which were not legislative committees in the traditional sense). Most of the committees are similar in both houses, reflecting the policy areas historically addressed by the Legislature and the structure of executive agencies — from Agriculture to Labor, Banks to Social Services, Judiciary to Local Government. Other committees reflect issues of particular interest to one house. The Assembly has a Committee on Libraries and Education Technology; the Senate has no analogous panel. Some committees that are essentially the same in both houses have different names to reflect different emphases — for example, the Committee on Corrections in the Assembly, but the Committee on Crime Victims, Crime and Correction in the Senate.

A dozen or so joint legislative commissions focus on special issue areas. One granted particular powers by statute is the Administrative Regulations Review Commission *(for additional information, see Chapter Six)*. Other commissions examine areas such as health-care financing, science and technology, solid waste management, and development of rural resources. For instance, the Legislative Commission on Government Administration conducted detailed research on conference committees before the Senate and Assembly used that approach to work on the budget in 1998. While the commissions are created by law with joint membership from the two houses, in practice the staff is in effect an extension of the central staff for one house. The Government Administration, Solid Waste Management and Tax Study commissions, for instance, are in effect controlled by the Assembly; those dealing with Critical Transportation Choices and Rural Resources are run by the Senate. Exceptions to one-house control are the regulations review

Why Hearings Are Valuable

Michael J. BeVier, a former staff member in the California Legislature, wrote a book about his experiences in the mid-1970s trying to pass legislation creating a new housing program (an idea modeled on New York State's Housing Finance Agency). One of the steps to building support for the plan was holding a public hearing. BeVier explained the need for the hearing this way:

I suppose an ostensible purpose of such hearings is to serve as a forum in which citizens can directly express their opinions to the Legislature, but there is not enough time in a day or two or even three to provide any kind of reliable survey of the state's eight million voters.... In short, hearings serve as a cumbersome and awkward forum for exchange of information between legislators and constituents. They do have some value as a symbolic gesture indicating the desire of the Legislature to elicit opinions from the citizenry and emphasizing the importance of communication between representatives and the people they are elected to represent. More important for our purposes, though, was the public exposure which hearings would provide the committee members. We wanted the members to be publicly associated with the issue of housing, believing this would increase the amount of real support we could get from them when housing finance agency legislation was introduced.

Michael J. BeVier, *Politics Backstage: Inside the California Legislature*, Temple University Press, Philadelphia, PA, 1979; p. 40.

commission and the Legislative Task Force on Demographic Research and Reapportionment. Both have co-chairs from the two houses, and both are involved in work that the leadership and members of each house consider important.

Beyond committees and commissions, each house organizes less formal groups known as task forces, caucuses, subcommittees or the like. The Assembly, with its larger membership and broader range of interests, has more of these groups, including the Black, Puerto Rican and Hispanic Legislative Caucus; the Democratic Study Group, which examines legislation from a liberal/progressive perspective; the Legislative Women's Caucus; and task forces on the homeless, New Americans, the Mohawk Valley, people with disabilities and university-industry cooperation. Senate groups include the Special

Committee on Arts and Cultural Affairs, and the Subcommittee on the Long Island Marine District.

Committees and task forces often use public hearings to gather information on, and attract attention to, issues they consider important. "At the institutional level, hearings may allow the legislature to protect its prerogatives, often by asserting itself in its relationship with the executive. From a partisan perspective, hearings are opportunities for the parties to develop and advance alternative policy agendas. And finally, hearings provide a platform upon which individual politicians may build their careers."

Conference Committees:
What Was Old Is New Again

In 1995, with new leadership in both houses (Sheldon Silver took office as Assembly speaker in early 1994, and Joseph L. Bruno became Senate majority leader in January 1995), the Senate and Assembly used a conference committee to resolve differences over legislation for the first time in several decades. The state's first Constitution called for conference committees "whenever the assembly and senate disagree," with members to be chosen by ballot. Albany used the process during the early 1900s and as late as 1938, according to research by the Legislative Commission on Government Administration· Senate-Assembly rules included provisions governing use of conference committees until 1980. In 1995, renewing the process to negotiate a bill raising the speed limit on portions of the Thruway, the two houses reinserted a rule governing appointment and operation of conference committees. One difference from the previous procedures: a lesser role for minority members. The 1995 rule requires that "at least one member shall represent the minority in each House"; the previous rules specified at least two minority representatives from each house.

The Legislature again used conference committees in 1996 to reach compromise on legislation establishing mandatory minimum maternity care coverage, giving residents of small city school districts the right to vote directly on school budgets, and creating a state registry of pesticides. In 1997, a conference committee negotiated agreement on the Power for Jobs program delivering low-cost electrical power for economic development.

Conference committees have also used in the budget process in recent years. Some longtime critics of Albany's legislative processes hailed the budget conference committees as an important step toward greater democracy at the Capitol. Public discussions among members of the committees, though, were limited to arguments in favor of previously stated positions or scripted announcements of agreements that had been made privately by the leaders.

The Minority: An Important Voice

As the common wisdom has it, few things in Albany are more discouraging than being a minority-party legislator. The majority party in each house controls most of the things that are important to lawmakers: funding for local projects, action on bills, office space, the budget for staff and equipment, even the communities that will be included in a given legislative district.

One thing the majorities do not control, however, is *ideas*. At their best, minority parties in New York's Legislature or any other serve as sources of new policy proposals that may not emerge from the majority because of ideological differences, adherence to tradition, or inertia. During the 2000 budget negotiations, for instance, the Senate Democratic Conference advocated elimination of the state's "marriage tax penalty," under which married couples pay more than the same individuals would if they were not married. Senate Republicans, who were in the majority and thus in a position to negotiate the budget with Governor Pataki and the Assembly Democratic majority, had previously advanced a broad package of other tax cuts, including a deduction for college tuition and elimination of a tax on electricity. After Senate Democrats proposed repeal of the marriage penalty, the Assembly majority included a similar proposal in its budget program — and the proposal was enacted into law.

Similarly, the Assembly Republican conference tends to advocate stricter criminal penalties than the Democratic majority. From April through mid-June 2000, Assembly Republicans attempted to apply political pressure on the majority party with a stream of press releases and other efforts. At the end of session, the governor and the two majority conferences agreed to several major new crime bills.

It's often impossible to say precisely why a given issue gathers enough political momentum to propel a legislative proposal into law. It's clear, though, that advocacy by the minority party can play a role.

Members of the majority party know that their term is for only two years. In particular, those who come from "marginal" districts — those where either party might win — are sensitive to potential criticism that they are not reflecting the will of their constituents. They also know that action during the legislative session — or lack of action — is fair game during electoral campaigns.

Minority parties in the Legislature develop more than ideas; they develop *people*. Governor Pataki's service in state government began in such a role: He was a member of the Assembly minority for eight years before moving to the Senate and then the Executive Mansion. Comptroller McCall was elected to two terms in the Senate minority before serving as commissioner of the state Division of Human Rights. When control of the governorship moves from one party to the other, the new administration commonly looks to legislative staff for expertise — for instance, Governor Pataki appointed former legislative staff members to key positions in the Labor, Environmental Conservation, and Insurance departments.

A "Professional" Legislature

Political scientists often characterize state legislatures by their degree of "professionalism," which typically is meant to include elements such as length of session, size of legislative staffs, and lawmakers' salaries. One study of conditions in legislatures in the late 1980s found that, combining the three factors, New York's was the most professionalized legislature in the country; those in Michigan, California, and Massachusetts were not far behind.[13] As of 2003, National Conference of State Legislatures data showed New York's Senate and Assembly had by far the largest combined payroll, with 3,428 staffers. California, with fewer legislators and a population 84 percent larger than New York's, managed with 2,359 legislative staff.

Up to a point, larger staffs, longer sessions and higher salaries strengthen the Legislature's ability to function as an effective and independent component of the policy making arena. Political scientists agree that state legislatures in virtually all the 50 states are more professional today than a generation ago.

---

13 Peverill Squire, cited in Christopher Z. Mooney, "Measuring U.S. State Legislative Professionalism: An Evaluation of Five Indices," *State and Local Government Review* 26, 2 (Spring 1994): 70-78.

Among other effects, those changes have helped produce more leg-islation — at least, more *proposed* legislation. As Table 1 earlier in this chapter shows, the number of bills introduced in the two houses has roughly doubled since the mid-20th century, although the number en-acted into law is approximately the same. More time that legislators spend on the job, and more staff to provide assistance, mean greater op-portunity to turn ideas into draft legislation. Critics say the result is sim-ply wasted taxpayers' dollars. As mentioned earlier, it's clear that many bills are introduced with no expectation of further action. It can also be said, though, that the Legislature is *supposed* to consider a wide variety of ideas for changing state government and public policy. Perhaps the additional cost of printing thousands of extra bills (a small part of the Legislature's budget) is worthwhile, if the process surfaces good ideas that might otherwise be lost.

The growing professionalization of legislatures in New York and other states has a political impact as well. "By providing more institu-tional resources to members, professional legislatures serve to reduce the impact of other variables (for example, presidential coattails or a poor economy) on election outcomes."[14] That's one key reason both the Senate and Assembly have maintained one-party control for three de-cades. The relatively high pay and strong-incumbency aspects of New York's Legislature give it one of the lowest rates of turnover — through both retirement and losses on Election Day — in the country.

In New York, professionalization of the Legislature began exerting a dramatic impact in the 1960s. Both houses began to hire more staff, starting with the fiscal committees. Over two decades or so, the combi-nation of more expert staff, longer-tenured members, and other changes gave the Legislature more of an equal footing with governors. By the 1970s, roughly one in four lawmakers officially listed their occupation as legislator; by 1988, more than half did so. (In some cases, the change of publicly identified career may reflect what members perceive as a good image to project to voters.)

Several observers have suggested that professional state legislatures may have different effects on the recruitment patterns of Democrats compared with Republicans. The argument is that Republicans find full-time legislative service less enticing because they are more likely to have more lucrative positions in the private sector. For Democrats in

---

14 Virginia Gray et al., eds., *Politics in the American States: A Comparative Analysis*, 1999, pp. 144-146.

more professional legislatures, "legislative service now becomes an attractive career, probably better compensated and more highly regarded than their present careers."[15]

Who Are They?
Members of the Legislature Today

The state Constitution requires that each member of the Legislature be a U.S. citizen and have lived in the state for at least five years before taking office. Senators and Assembly members must have lived in the district they represent for at least a year. Exception is made in the first election after a redrawing of district lines; in that case, members must have lived for a year in the county that contains the district.

Some members have made a career out of the Legislature. Assemblyman Richard N. Gottfried of Manhattan was first elected in 1970, at the age of 23, while a student at Columbia Law School. Others come to the Senate or Assembly well into middle age, or even after retiring from an earlier career. Many — though by no means all — members have been elected to local office at the municipal or county level. In the past decade or so, a number of legislative staff members have sought and won election when the incumbent for whom they worked has left office.

As of 2006, women accounted for 22.6 percent of the members of the Legislature, the same as the average for all states. Some 21 percent of New York lawmakers were black or Hispanic, nearly double the average nationwide. At this writing, neither house has ever elected a woman or racial-minority member to its top leadership position. David Paterson became the first member of a racial minority to become minority-party leader in either house, elected Senate Democratic leader in November 2002.

While serving in the Legislature, members may not hold any other elective office except as delegate to a constitutional convention. They may not be appointed to any office that was created, or had its salary increased, during their legislative term.

Starting in 1999, members received a base salary of $79,500 a year (payable, under the Legislative Law, every other week). Under a

---

15 Alan Ehrenhalt, *The United States of Ambition: Politicians, Power and the Pursuit of Office*, Random House, New York, NY, 1991.

Elements of Legislative Life			
	Salary, 2004	Average Session Days, 1996-97	Total staff, 2003
Alabama	$1,050	103	496
Alaska	24,012	128	449
Arizona	24,000	96	682
Arkansas	13,751	55	493
California	99,000	264	2,359
Colorado	30,000	119	385
Connecticut	28,000	119	539
Delaware	34,800	177	131
Florida	29,916	66	1,803
Georgia	16,200	72	823
Hawaii	32,000	105	652
Idaho	15,646	68	183
Illinois	55,788	133	906
Indiana	11,600	133	307
Iowa	21,380	110	370
Kansas	9,214	135	340
Kentucky	16,468	52	628
Louisiana	16,800	119	739
Maine	9,555	152	190
Maryland	31,509	90	965
Massachusetts	53,380	363	935
Michigan	79,650	351	1,153
Minnesota	31,140	105	684
Mississippi	10,000	109	195
Missouri	31,351	128	349
Montana	6,758	54	247
Nebraska	12,000	131	239

Elements of Legislative Life (Continued)			
	Salary, 2004	Average Session Days, 1996-97	Total staff, 2003
Nevada	$7,800	84	498
New Hampshire	100	165	165
New Jersey	49,000	364	1,265
New Mexico	0	45	648
NEW YORK	**79,500**	**193**	**3,428**
North Carolina	13,951	125	629
North Dakota	12,625	48	124
Ohio	54,942	360	506
Oklahoma	38,400	129	433
Oregon	15,396	87	465
Pennsylvania	66,204	347	2,947
Rhode Island	12,286	256	454
South Carolina	10,400	162	421
South Dakota	6,000	67	75
Tennessee	16,500	123	284
Texas	7,200	70	2,268
Utah	5,400	44	181
Vermont	10,349	139	82
Virginia	18,000	53	682
Washington	34,227	82	826
West Virginia	15,000	60	410
Wisconsin	45,569	365	756
Wyoming	3,250	36	114

Sources: Salaries, *CQ's State Fact Finder 2005*; session days and staff, *Politics in The American States: A Comparative Analysis*; legislative staff, National Conference of State Legislatures.

measure enacted in 1998, along with the most recent pay raise, legislators are not paid after the first day of the state fiscal year until both houses have acted on that year's Executive Budget.

Most legislators also receive what the Legislative Law calls an "allowance" for serving as "an officer" or in "special capacity." Such allowances are more familiarly known as "lulus," because they were originally considered payments in lieu of expenses. The largest stipends go to the majority leader in the Senate and the speaker of the Assembly; each receives $41,500 on top of the base salary. The smallest extra allowance is $9,000, payable to ranking minority members of several committees in each house.

Under the salary schedule included in the 1998 legislation, and still effective in 2006, the Senate has 87 stipends. That's more than enough for each of the 61 senators to receive a special allowance; the Legislative Law prohibits any member from collecting more than one. The Assembly has 108 stipends available. All told, 169, or 80 percent, of legislators are eligible for one of the additional payments.

Members receive an allowance, determined by the leadership, for staff and other expenses. Leadership also assigns office space in the Capitol or the Legislative Office Building in Albany; members are free to choose where to locate their district offices but receive a fixed amount to spend on rent. Some high-ranking members are assigned a state automobile, and may have a staff member who serves as driver (but has a different title, such as community-affairs assistant).

In recent years, many legislators have effectively augmented their compensation by using campaign donations to pay for personal expenses. Cars, meals, and cell phones are typical examples. The reform organization Common Cause reported that one senator, Martin Connor, spent $11,966 of campaign funds on a parking space "located over two miles from his district office in Manhattan but just one block from his Brooklyn residence."[16]

Members of the Legislature often move to higher political office, including that of the governor. The Assembly, for instance, has seen 18 of its members become governors of New York (Governor Pataki being the most recent), eight become U.S. senators, four become

---

16 Common Cause/NY, *The $2,100 Club: What New York State Political Campaigns Cost, How Much Those Costs are Rising and Who's Footing the Bill*, New York, NY, March 2006.

vice-presidents, and two (Millard Fillmore and Theodore Roosevelt) become president.

Representative Democracy = Politics

If understanding the Constitution and key statutes is essential to understanding the Legislature, so, too, is an awareness of the political imperatives that are always a reality in a representative democracy.

Members of the Senate and Assembly go before the voters every two years. Their re-election rate is extraordinarily high — in many election cycles, not a single incumbent is defeated at the polls, and critics have said that turnover of seats in Albany was less than that in the Politburo of the former Soviet Union. Still, rejection of incumbents does happen. Sometimes, a legislative seat held by a member of one party is taken by a challenger from the other party; in other cases, a member of the same party defeats an incumbent in an intra-party primary.

Average Length of Service in the Legislature (Years)		
	Senate	*Assembly*
1960	7.9	8.2
1970	8.0	6.7
1980	8.6	6.8
1990	13.0	10.5
2000	15.8	11.4

Source: *The Modern New York State Legislature*, Benjamin and Nakamura, 1991; 2000 data from *The New York Red Book, 1999-2000*.

In fact, a sitting speaker of the Assembly, Stanley Steingut, lost his seat as a result of a Democratic party primary defeat in his Brooklyn district in 1978. Speaker Steingut ran in the general election on the Liberal line, but lost to the Democratic candidate, Moses Weinstein. In an interview years later, Steingut explained his defeat this way: "I didn't do anything (to campaign). If I had done in the primary what I did in the election I would have won that very easily.... I was there too long. My voting record and the things I stood for, my positions — the death

penalty, abortion, the other legislative initiatives I was involved with —
were no longer very popular in my district."[17]

If the most powerful member of the Assembly can lose an election,
is it any wonder that legislators run scared?

Members of the Legislature respond to the electoral imperative in
every way they can. They work to bring home the largest possible share
of the state budget through school aid and "member items" for local
capital projects and community groups. They make sure to communicate a positive message to voters through legislative newsletters and by
seeking favorable coverage in the hometown news media. They arrange
to have buildings named after them, such as the Joseph L. Bruno Stadium in Troy, and the Senator Mike Nozzolio Soccer Complex in Web-
ster. They reach out to important constituent groups, whether those are
issue-oriented, ethnic, religious, or other organizations. Often they play
a major role in their local political party, which can help solidify
partisan support and reduce the possibility of intra-party challenges.

Most importantly, as far as the state as a whole is concerned, members of the Senate and Assembly respond to political influences through
legislation. They are there, after all, to represent voters' wishes. In recent years, leaders and rank-and-file members in both houses have
modified   policy   positions   in   response   to   changing   political
circumstances.

In 1995, for instance, Governor Pataki took office promising to reduce state spending and cut personal income taxes dramatically. One of
his major spending targets was Medicaid. The Democratic majority in
the Assembly opposed the Medicaid reductions and sharply criticized
the Pataki tax plan as benefitting wealthy New Yorkers at the expense
of the needy. Ultimately, though, most of the governor's proposed tax
cuts were enacted, as was a smaller program of reductions in Medicaid
funding for hospitals and other institutions. (The Assembly proposed,
and the governor and the Senate embraced, a major expansion of
Medicaid four years later.)

During the 2000 session, the Republican majority in the Senate approved several major bills that many of its members had opposed and
Democratic sponsors had pushed — measures promoting gun control,

---

17 Comments by Stanley Steingut in Benjamin and Nakamura, eds., *The Modern New
York State Legislature,* 1991, p. 103.

tougher criminal penalties for "hate crimes," and creation of a public database on disciplinary actions against physicians.

In a representative democracy, legislators are assumed to represent their constituents, but this can get complicated. Richard Fenno has theorized that various constituencies can be pictured as a set of concentric circles, some closer to the lawmaker than others. The largest is the geographic constituency — all the residents of the member's district. Even the most popular legislators know that they will not win every resident's vote, for a number of reasons (for instance, some voters will vote only for one party). Thus elected officials often think, Fenno says, in terms of the *reelection* constituency, made up of known or potential supporters. This list starts with registered voters in the same political party and may include residents of the legislators' hometown and members of particular community or interest groups with which the member has been active or friendly. A subset of the re-election constituency is the *primary* constituency, the legislator's strongest supporters or loyalists. Finally, there is the *personal* constituency, the political confidants and advisors and close personal friends.[18]

Getting Elected

Compared with other states, New York ranks high in the proportion of races where both parties nominate a candidate, but low in the proportion of those where both candidates have a realistic chance of winning. From 1968 through 1995, some 90 percent of legislative races in the Empire State offered voters a candidate from at least two parties; only four states ranked higher. On the other hand, only 22 percent of races in New York were considered "competitive," with the loser receiving at least 40 percent of the vote; New York ranked 33rd in this measurement.[19] In the November 2000 legislative elections, only one incumbent lost, while 195 were re-elected (several others did not seek re-election). Why do so many candidates run in elections they know they are likely to lose? One answer: New York's large public sector gives political party leaders more power to reward losing candidates with jobs or other favors.

---

18 Richard F. Fenno Jr., *Homestyle: House Members in Their Districts,* Addison-Wesley Educational Publishers Inc., 1997.

19 Keith E. Hamm and Gary F. Moncrief, "Legislative Politics in the States," in Gray et al., *Politics in the American States*, 1999.

As part of its growing professionalization, the New York Legislature has added some elements that often help incumbents win reelection. For instance, communication with constituents is itself highly professionalized, with trained staff available to work on newsletters, brochures on special topics, and even television shows broadcast on local cable stations. Incumbents hold fund-raising receptions near the Capitol — some within the state's own Empire State Plaza — hours after legislative session. Challengers to incumbent lawmakers often criticize these and other institutional provisions that enhance incumbents' chances of re-election.

Fundraising for campaigns — perhaps more important now than ever — includes extensive centralized efforts by the party conferences. The Senate Republican Campaign Committee and the Democratic Assembly Campaign Committee, as the political arms of the majority conferences, can make available hundreds of thousands of dollars to a candidate in an important race. The campaign committees for the Senate Democrats and Assembly Republicans — the two minority parties — do not raise as much money, but can still provide significant funding and technical assistance.

Ultimately, of course, the voters decide who will represent them in Albany's halls of power. That means it is they who are responsible for the men and women serving in the Senate and Assembly, and the laws they produce.

Chapter Six

THE JUDICIARY

Key points:

- While federal courts receive more attention, state courts adjudicate most cases — more than 4 million a year in New York.

- In recent decades, authority over the court system has moved incrementally from the local level to Albany.

- Still, the system's basic structure is largely the same as a century ago, and judicial leaders have asked the Legislature repeatedly to streamline the trial courts.

A judicial system that is independent of the executive and legislative branches — and yet accountable to those elected officials and, through them, to the people — is a basic part of democratic government in America. Article VI of the state Constitution guarantees New Yorkers such an independent, accountable judiciary.

It is no idle boast to say that the Empire State has been a leader in establishing judicial policy and process throughout the history of the United States. George Washington appointed John Jay, a New Yorker and one of the leading figures in establishing the state's first Constitution, as the nation's first chief justice in 1789. Two others from the Empire State — Charles Evans Hughes and Harlan F. Stone — served consecutively as chief justice from 1930 to 1946, a period of key decisions in the development of modern American government. Eleven other New Yorkers have been associate justices, including historic names such as Benjamin Cardozo and Thurgood Marshall and current Justice Ruth Bader Ginsburg. The total of 14 New Yorkers who have served on the high court is greater than that for any other state.

Rulings in the state's own courts have long influenced decisions in federal and other state courts. Throughout much of the 20th century, in particular, New York State's pre-eminence in business and industry helped set the stage for its Court of Appeals to become a national leader in developing commercial and business law. One study ranked New York's high court along with those in California and New Jersey as state courts that "stand out from the rest" in judicial activism — a combination of policymaking and overturning statutory provisions enacted by legislatures and governors.[1]

Today, New York's courts deal with well over 4 million cases each year, including those in town and village courts — an average of more than one case for every five New Yorkers.

"The subject matter of this caseload is as broad as human experience itself: from suits over sophisticated financial transactions to disputes over simple leases; from homicides to charitable trusts; from litigation involving the breakup of families to cases creating new caring homes for children," Chief Judge Judith Kaye wrote.[2] Effects of the courts' decisions range from relatively small fines for traffic violations to life-changing outcomes in criminal, family, and other cases. Many individuals involved in these cases find that the actions of the court system have a much greater impact on their lives than any decisions by the governor or the Legislature. And some decisions by the Court of Appeals can have an impact equal to major legislation.

---

1   Henry R. Glick, "Courts: Politics and the Judicial Process," in *Politics in the American States: A Comparative Analysis*, Washington, DC: CQ Press, 1999.

2   State of the Judiciary Address, New York State Unified Court System, February 8, 1999.

Given the continually changing nature of government, it's no surprise that New York's courts have evolved over two centuries. Long-standing debates over whether judges should be elected or appointed, and what the most efficient structure of the various courts might be, have made "court reform" one of the most familiar phrases to anyone who pays attention to policy debate in Albany. (The phrase, of course, means different things to different people.)

Still, the basic structure of the judiciary has remained largely the same for well over a century. Cases are heard by judges and juries in communities across the state. Appeals can be taken to multi-judge courts sitting in regional centers, with the possibility of ultimate appeal to the state's highest court, the Court of Appeals, across the street from the state Capitol in Albany.

In the latter half of the 20th century, authority over the court system moved incrementally from the local level to Albany. Administrative control of the courts is under the ultimate authority of the chief judge, through a chief administrator of the courts (known as the chief administrative judge, if the appointee is a jurist). Yet the court system is not analogous to an executive-branch agency where the chain of command and responsibility is strictly hierarchical, up through the agency commissioner to the governor. Responsibility for on-site management of the trial courts is vested in local administrative judges. Individual judges on the Court of Appeals also have important responsibility beyond writing and voting on opinions. For instance, each judge reviews requests from convicted criminals for permission to appeal to the court.

This chapter reviews the types of cases heard in state courts as opposed to the federal courts; summarizes the structure of New York's court system, including its "absurdly complex" mix of trial courts; describes the many responsibilities of the Court of Appeals; examines the powers of the courts and checks on those powers; and describes the roles played by judges and jurors.

State Courts:
The Mainstream of the U.S. Judiciary

The U.S. Supreme Court, with its majestic building in the nation's capital and legal pronouncements that are sometimes treated as if handed down from Olympus, often comes to mind when the subject is the American judicial system.

Yet all of the federal courts — which also include the trial courts, known as district courts, and mid-level federal appeals courts — are the venue for only a small minority of cases nationwide. In terms of numbers, at least, state courts are where the action is. The 4 million-plus cases heard each year in New York courts alone are more than 10 times the entire caseload in federal courts nationwide.

Have a problem with your landlord or tenant? If you want to sue, you'll probably apply to state court. If you are charged with a crime, the case will likely be heard in a state court. The same is true if you leave an estate large enough to be reviewed by a judge, if you and your spouse decide to divorce, or if your company sues or is sued by another business.

Federal courts have a limited area of "original" jurisdiction — areas where they are the first to hear a case (outlined later in this chapter). They do not exist as higher authorities to which someone dissatisfied with the decision of a state court can automatically appeal. In rare circumstances, a case will start in a state trial court, wind its way to the highest state court, and then make its way through the federal courts. In these instances it's very likely that the federal case will be based on different issues than the state case — turning on a federal statute that does not exist at the state level, for example. Where the determining factor is state law or a state constitution, the federal courts generally will decline to hear the case, leaving the state courts' decision as the final word.

Some cases can be heard in either state or federal courts. Bank robbery, for instance, violates both state and federal laws and can be prosecuted at either level. As Congress enacts more federal crimes from year to year, the number of areas with dual potential for prosecution grows.

Structure of the Courts

The courts in New York and other states, like those at the federal level, fall into two broad categories: trial courts, and appellate courts.

Trial courts provide legal forums for both criminal cases, which establish whether a person accused of an offense is legally guilty; and civil cases, which resolve disputes between private or public parties — individuals, businesses, government agencies, and other organizations

— over noncriminal matters. In 2004, New York trial courts, excluding town and village courts, disposed of about 1.6 million criminal cases and 1.4 million civil cases *(see table on page 138)*. The facts of such cases are usually determined by a jury, although judges make the determination in some trials. (Family and surrogate's courts brought the state-system total to 3.7 million dispositions.)

Appellate courts hear appeals from decisions of trial courts. The "loser" in a lower court does not automatically go on to appellate court, as evidenced by the fact that the state's appeals courts disposed of some 19,600 cases in 2004 — a fraction of 1 percent of the trial court caseload. The jurisdiction of the Court of Appeals is limited and, on appeal, the scope of review is generally limited to questions of law. Judges generally give preference to cases that have the broadest impact or are most likely to establish important precedents for other cases.

The Constitution on the Courts

Much of the current Judiciary article of New York's Constitution was adopted by statewide referendum in November 1961, replacing sections adopted in 1925 and amended numerous times. In both years, proposed changes emerged from the Legislature, not through a constitutional convention. The 1961 changes included creation of a "unified court system," in name at least, and elimination of eight types of trial courts.

Reflecting the complicated nature and convoluted historical development of the state's court system, the Judiciary article is the longest in the Constitution, making up more than 11 pages of the 47-page document printed by the state Department of State. (The Legislature article is 3½ pages and the Executive, barely more than one.) While the judicial system is designed to be nonpolitical, judges and attorneys historically have been well represented in the making of New York's Constitutions and statutes. Much of the detail of the Judiciary article reflects efforts over the decades "protecting some judges and courts from encroachments by other judges and courts, and keeping them in their places."[3]

---

3   Frederick Miller, "New York State's Judicial Article: A Work in Progress," in Gerald Benjamin and Henrik N. Dullea, eds., *Decision 1997: Constitutional Change in New York*, Albany, NY: The Rockefeller Institute Press, pp. 127-146.

Filings and Dispositions in the Trial Courts, 2004		
Criminal Courts	Filings	Dispositions
Supreme and County Courts	63,217	60,445
NYC Criminal Court	786,540	686,550
City/District Courts Outside NYC	702,079	669,921
Parking Tickets	153,533	139,276
Criminal Subtotal	1,705,369	1,556,192
Civil Courts		
Supreme Courts	415,132	434,675
NYC Civil Court	756,852	561,715
City/District Courts Outside NYC	292,925	279,485
County Courts	30,333	30,416
Court of Claims	1,694	1,729
Arbitration Program	21,387	17,499
Small Claims Assessment Review	85,324	42,933
Civil Subtotal	1,582,260	1,368,452
Family Courts	695,842	704,348
Surrogate's Courts	145,749	119,702
Total	4,129,220	3,748,694

Source: New York State Unified Court System, *Twenty-Seventh Annual Report of the Chief Administrator of the Courts,* Albany, NY, 2004.

The article does not directly establish the state's highest court, the Court of Appeals, which was founded in 1846, but says "The court of appeals is continued." The court is to consist of the chief judge and six associate judges. Each serves a term of 14 years, and may be reappointed. Five members constitute a quorum, and a majority of four can issue decisions.

The governor appoints members of the Court of Appeals with the advice and consent of the Senate from among candidates recommended by a bipartisan Commission on Judicial Nomination, which must consider such candidates "well qualified."

In case of temporary disability of any judge on the Court of Appeals, the court itself may designate any justice of the state Supreme Court to serve as associate judge. The court may also ask the governor to name up to four Supreme Court justices to serve as associate judges on the Court of Appeals if a case backlog makes it impossible for the court to hear and dispose of cases "with reasonable speed." When such additional judges sit on the hight court — which has not occurred in recent years — no more than seven may participate in any case.

The Commission on Judicial Nomination is to have twelve members — four appointed by the governor, four by the chief judge, and one each by the four leaders of the Legislature. The governor appoints the chair, who traditionally plays a strong leading role in selecting candidates. The commission is intended to be insulated from partisan politics; no member can hold office in any political party, and among the four appointments of the governor and the chief judge, no more than two in each group can be from the same political party. The commission must also include at least four representatives who are lawyers, and four who are not.

Judges must retire by the last day of December the year they turn 70. If they are able, retired judges of the Court of Appeals and of the Supreme Court may be certified for service as Supreme Court justices for two-year periods until the last day of December in the year they reach 76.

The Judiciary article limits the jurisdiction of the Court of Appeals to questions of law except in extraordinary circumstances: "where the judgement is of death," and where the Appellate Division changes a lower-court ruling based on finding of new facts.

Jury trials are guaranteed by the Constitution's Bill of Rights. That article also allows defendants to waive the right except in cases where the penalty may be death. The Constitution generally requires that felonies be tried before 12-person juries. In nonfelony cases, the Judiciary article authorizes the Legislature to provide that juries in any court of original jurisdiction may be six or 12 persons.

A 10-year requirement for membership in the bar applies to justices of the Supreme Court and the Court of Claims as well as the Court of Appeals. Judges in the other courts must have been admitted to the state bar for at least five years, or a greater number that the Legislature may determine. The Legislature has imposed a 10-year requirement on Family Court judges, surrogates, and judges of the New York City civil and criminal courts. Judges are barred from holding any other public office except delegate to a constitutional convention, and from holding office in any political organization.

The Judiciary article creates a Commission on Judicial Conduct to investigate complaints about the "conduct, qualifications, fitness to perform or performance of official duties" of any judge in the unified court system. The commission may admonish, censure, or remove from office any judge for causes including misconduct, persistent failure to perform duties, "habitual intemperance," and "conduct, on or off the bench, prejudicial to the administration of justice." Judges may appeal the commission's rulings to the Court of Appeals, which may make the sanction more or less severe or impose none. The Court of Appeals can also suspend a jurist who is charged with a felony or who is under investigation by the Commission on Judicial Conduct. The Legislature may remove judges of the Court of Appeals and justices of the Supreme Court through concurrent resolution approved by two-thirds majorities in each house. The Senate may remove judges of the lower courts on recommendation of the governor. Neither legislative process has been used since creation of the Commission on Judicial Conduct.

An "Absurdly Complex" System

Reflecting its origins in local courts established in different communities for a variety of purposes, the system of trial courts in New York State is a patchwork quilt that Chief Judge Judith Kaye calls "absurdly complex ... difficult to understand, hard to navigate and a burden to administer."[4] Most observers agree.

By way of comparison, the system of federal trial courts around the United States is easy to describe and understand. At the federal level, almost all trials are held in district courts. These courts are the judicial venue for individuals charged with federal crimes, civil suits under federal law, civil suits between residents of different states, bankruptcy cases (bankruptcy courts are units of the district courts), maritime cases, certain appeals from decisions of federal regulatory agencies, and other matters assigned by Congress. Every state has at least one district court. New York includes four districts — based in Brooklyn, Manhattan, Syracuse, and Buffalo — with a total of 51 judgeships.

---

4   State of the Judiciary Address, *ibid.*

Above the federal district courts are 12 regional circuits, each of which has a U.S. Court of Appeals. These courts hear appeals from the district courts within their circuits, as well as appeals from federal regulatory decisions. At the apex of the federal court system is the U.S. Supreme Court, whose caseload consists mainly of appeals. (For more information, see *www.uscourts.gov.*)

The overall structure of New York's judicial system is basically similar to the federal system, with the three levels of trial courts, appellate courts, and finally an ultimate appeals court.[5]

Somewhat confusingly to those learning it for the first time, the highest court in the state is the Court of Appeals. The Supreme Court in New York is the primary lower state court, the tribunal of original jurisdiction. The mid-level appellate courts are the Appellate Division (and appellate terms) of the Supreme Court.

Why is New York's Supreme Court a lower court, while the Court of Appeals is the name of the top court? When the state's first Constitution was written in 1777, the Supreme Court *was* supreme among the various trial courts that existed at the time. The highest tribunal, the Court for the Trial of Impeachments and the Correction of Errors, was a quasi-judicial body that included the temporary president of the Senate, Supreme Court judges and others. The 1846 Constitutional Convention abolished that court while creating the Court of Appeals. The convention also initiated election of judges, and abolished independent chancery and circuit courts by merging them into the Supreme Court. "General terms" of the Supreme Court, created as mid-level appeals courts, eventually developed into the current Appellate Divisions.

The trial courts of the time were financed, and in some cases established, by local governments. As such, they were subject to relatively little oversight from Albany, and a variety of trial courts evolved around the state.

While the 1961 constitutional changes streamlined the court system somewhat, a complicated array of trial courts remained. In the mid-1970s, Governor Carey and leaders of the court system pushed through the Legislature, and voters approved, major additional changes to the structure of the judiciary. Henceforth, Court of Appeals judges

---

5   While the structure is also similar to those in most other states, some states differ. For instance, Texas and Oklahoma each have two supreme courts, one for criminal and one for civil cases.

would be chosen through merit selection (appointment by the governor, based on recommendations from a screening panel, and subject to Senate confirmation). At the same time, the office of chief administrator of the courts was written into the Constitution. The Commission on Judicial Conduct was created, with its disciplinary rulings subject to final review by the Court of Appeals. A new law unified the court system's budget, an important step toward state-level funding.

Today, as a result of legislation adopted in 1977, state taxpayers fund all operational costs for the court system (not including town and village courts). Local governments are responsible for constructing court facilities, although the state provides some financial aid and pays for ongoing maintenance.

Under the Constitution, the Court of Appeals must approve a proposed budget for the judicial branch, and the governor must include the proposal without change in the Executive Budget (he may recommend changes). The Legislature can change appropriations for the judiciary, and the governor can veto elements of the judicial budget. Leaders of the court system typically conduct informal discussions with the governor's office — often rising to the level of negotiations — before submitting proposals to be included in the Executive Budget.

The Trial Courts

Court cases generally start at the trial level. One individual or organization sues another, police officers charge someone with a crime, a married couple files for divorce — each of these events occurs hundreds of thousands of times each year in New York State.

In many of the areas that require New Yorkers to interact with their state government, the particular agency involved is the same regardless of the specific nature of the activity or the region where it occurs. Obtaining a driver's license means dealing with the Department of Motor Vehicles whether the individual drives a tractor-trailer, a school bus, or a two-door compact. If taxes must be paid, the state's Department of Taxation and Finance is the place to go whether the bill is for personal income taxes, corporate taxes, sales tax, or any of a dozen others; property owners generally send local property tax payments to one office even though the tax bill may include charges from a half-dozen local government entities.

When New Yorkers go to court, though, things get complicated. Depending on the nature of the case and the location within the state, one (or perhaps more) of nine separate courts may be involved. Four types of trial courts operate everywhere in New York State. They differ primarily in the nature of cases they hear:

- The Supreme Court has unlimited original jurisdiction — under the law, its justices can hear virtually any type of case. Generally, though, these courts hear civil cases that the more specialized courts do not. In New York City and some other parts of the state, the Supreme Court also hears more serious criminal cases, those involving felony charges.

- The Court of Claims hears all claims for monetary damages against the state government. For instance, someone who is injured in a highway accident and claims that highway conditions were to blame would sue the state Department of Transportation in the Court of Claims.

- Family courts in each county and in New York City hear matters involving children and families. The caseload for these courts largely concerns foster care placements, support of dependent relatives, custody and visitation, juvenile delinquency, child protection, persons in need of supervision, paternity determinations, and family offenses.

- The surrogate's court in each county handles cases involving the affairs of deceased individuals, including probate of wills and administration of estates. It shares, with family courts, jurisdiction in adoption proceedings.

In addition to the four trial courts that operate throughout the state, other courts hear trials in particular locales.

In New York City, the Civil Court has jurisdiction over civil cases involving amounts up to $25,000 and other civil matters referred to it by the Supreme Court. The Civil Court includes a "part," or division, for small-claims matters not exceeding $5,000, and another for housing cases. The city Criminal Court has jurisdiction over misdemeanors and violations; its judges also conduct arraignments and preliminary hearings in felony cases, although trials for the latter are moved to Supreme Court.

Each county outside New York City has a county court. These courts handle prosecution of felonies and some misdemeanors. They also have limited jurisdiction in civil cases, generally involving amounts up to $25,000.

Trials for misdemeanors and minor offenses, along with arraignments and other preliminary proceedings for felonies, are generally handled by the courts with more limited jurisdiction. The latter include city courts, in 61 cities across the state; town and village courts; and district courts in Nassau County and the western part of Suffolk County. These courts also have civil jurisdiction over relatively small claims.

The Supreme Courts also include a number of specialized divisions, sometimes known as "parts." In 1995, a Commercial Division of state Supreme Court began operating on an experimental basis in Manhattan and Rochester. The new courts were intended to reduce the backlog of commercial disputes and increase the expertise among judges hearing them. The division has since expanded to Erie, Nassau, Westchester, Albany, Kings, and Suffolk counties. Cases assigned to the Commercial Division have court-imposed time frames for completion of pre-trial activities and the trial itself. Court officials say technology and "advanced case management techniques" have reduced the time needed to resolve such cases by more than a third.[6]

In addition to a network of "problem-solving" courts *(see more detailed discussion on next page)*, the court system also funds a network of nonprofit Community Dispute Resolution Centers which provide mediation, conciliation, arbitration, and related services. In 2004, such centers served 108,553 individuals in minor criminal, small-claims, housing, and family cases.

Structural Reform?

As mentioned above, the current structure of the court system has been in place for more than four decades. That complexity has prompted at least six comprehensive reform proposals since 1953, according to Gerald Benjamin.[7] Like many of her predecessors, Chief Judge Kaye has proposed sweeping reorganization of the trial court system to make it

6   Judith S. Kaye, State of the Judiciary Address, New York State Unified Court System, Albany, NY, March 23, 1998.

7   Benjamin, "Structures of New York State Government," p. 76.

"Problem-Solving" Courts

Over the past decade, a major source of change in New York's court system, as in some other states, has been development of "problem-solving" courts. The purpose of such special courts, Chief Judge Kaye says, is similar in all cases: to "reduce recidivism and help non-violent offenders reclaim their lives."*

The trend began in 1989 with the Midtown Community Court in Manhattan. Individuals charged with low-level crimes such as vandalism, prostitution, and minor drug possession are sentenced to community service such as cleaning streets and parks. Often, the courts order self-improvement efforts such as drug treatment and job training.

As of early 2006, more than 160 drug courts operated in Family Courts, municipal courts, and other local venues. Nine mental-health courts were in place, and 128 integrated domestic-violence courts. New York is the first state to create special courts for sex-offense cases, now operating in Oswego, Nassau, and Westchester counties.

> In this small but rapidly growing world ... you can find Judge Jaya K. Madhavan in the Bronx, trying to help a pregnant woman facing eviction clear up her housing crisis. You can find Justice Matthew J. D'Emic in mental health court, dealing with murder, kidnapping — and whether or not an arsonist needs to change his psychiatric medicines.
>
>   And you can find Judge Miriam Cyrulnik giving a young man in her Brooklyn domestic violence court the choice between jail and anger-management classes.**

The court system's Center for Court Innovation, responsible for much of the thinking behind creation of such courts, has won awards from the Kennedy School of Government at Harvard University and the Citizens Budget Commission in New York City. But some criticisms have been raised, as well.

Most of the specialized courts are creatures of the judiciary itself, rather than changes in the statutory — let alone Constitutional — rules for structure of the court system. Some observers say the lack of legislative

---

*   State of the Judiciary Address, February 6, 2006.

**   Leslie Eaton and Leslie Kaufman, "In Problem-Solving Courts, Judges Turn Therapist," *The New York Times*, New York, NY, April 26, 2005.

approval for such courts, and the nature of their work, may raise legal questions about the disposition of matters there. Traditionally, for instance, criminal charges are resolved in an adversarial setting. In drug and other courts, judges may encourage defendants to give up the right to a plea of not guilty as part of a settlement, creating potential grounds for later appeals.

And some legal scholars have raised concerns about judges — who are mostly middle class and often politically connected — imposing some of their personal values on people from very different backgrounds.

Lawyers who represent poor clients say that these courts, whatever their good intentions, have left judges intimately — and uncomfortably — involved in the everyday lives of an increasing number of people....

"We are sliding backward, without even realizing it, toward an inquisitorial system of justice," James A. Yates, a state Supreme Court judge in Manhattan, told an audience of criminal defense lawyers...***

***   Ibid.

easier for citizens to understand and more flexible for court administrators to manage. One such proposal, for instance, would consolidate the nine trial courts into two: a Supreme Court with unlimited jurisdiction, and a District Court with limited jurisdiction over civil and criminal matters.

After years of unsuccessful efforts, and approaching retirement, the chief judge created a Special Commission on the Future of the New York State Courts in mid-2006. The commission was charged with examining "the effects of the current constitutional structure as it relates to a wide range of important objectives such as productivity, efficiency and access to justice." Judge Kaye cast the effort in the context of a similar commission whose work in the 1950s helped produce major revisions of the Judiciary Article in 1961. The new commission is to report in early 2007.

Appellate Courts

When decisions of New York's lower courts are appealed, the landscape is considerably less confusing than at the trial level.

Judicial Departments and Judicial Districts

When courts were created — most of them between one and two centuries ago — in what is now New York State, the top levels of state government provided much less centralized direction. Judges were more likely to look to their peers in nearby communities to establish cooperative efforts and common methods of operation.

Starting in the mid-1800s, constitutional reforms and changes in judicial practice gradually expanded oversight from Albany. Still, though, it made sense to retain regional appeals courts. The regional structure also was useful in administrative terms — judges might serve temporarily in nearby communities as needed or establish procedural guidelines that made sense in one area of the state more than in another.

Hence the courts are divided into four judicial departments and 12 judicial districts. Each department represents an Appellate Division, which hears appeals from both civil and criminal cases in the Supreme Court and other trial courts. Seats of the four divisions are in Manhattan, Brooklyn, Albany, and Rochester.

Because of the heavy caseload in the metropolitan New York area, some Supreme Court justices there sit as appellate judges, hearing appeals from civil and criminal cases in New York City, and from local trial courts on Long Island and the northern reaches of the metropolitan region.

The Appellate Division of the Supreme Court serves as an intermediate appellate court with the power to review both the law and facts in civil and criminal cases. It also serves as a court of original jurisdiction for limited areas, including discipline, admission, and disbarment of attorneys; and Article 78 proceedings (cases seeking to require the government to take a particular action) brought against a Supreme Court justice. The Appellate Division's justices are designated by the governor from among elected Supreme Court justices. They serve five-year terms.

In addition to hearing cases involving individual lawyers' professional activities, the presiding justices of the Appellate Division oversee rules regulating the bar. In June 2006, for instance, the four presiding justices issued new restrictions on lawyer advertising, "to safeguard consumers from potentially misleading advertising and overly aggressive or inappropriate solicitation for legal services."[8] Amendments to the Lawyer's Code of Professional Conduct included:

- A required 30-day waiting period after accidents before soliciting wrongful-death or personal-injury clients.

- A ban on paid endorsements and testimonials by current clients.

- A ban on using nicknames, mottos or trade names that "suggest an ability to obtain results."

The Court of Appeals

The seven members of the Court of Appeals, including the chief judge, are appointed by the governor to 14-year terms. The 1867 Constitutional Convention chose the 14-year term based on the average service of federal judges, who at the time were appointed for indefinite terms defined as "during good behavior." Five members of the court constitute a quorum, and agreement of at least four members is required for a decision.

Judges of the Court of Appeals act together to decide all appeals and motions. They also vote as a body on "certified questions" — requests from federal courts for interpretation of New York's Constitution or statutes that must be taken into account in a federal case. Individual judges rule on applications for permission to appeal in criminal cases and on emergency requests for certain court orders.

In addition to serving as the state-level court of last resort, the Court of Appeals has significant administrative powers over the legal profession. These include regulating admission of attorneys to the bar and appointing members of the State Board of Law Examiners. The full court approves statewide administrative standards and policies established by the chief judge after consultation with the Administrative Board of the Courts, a body chaired by the chief judge that also includes the presiding justices of the four Appellate Divisions.

---

8   New York State Unified Court System, press release, June 15, 2006.

The court sits in Albany, in the Court of Appeals building across the street from the state Capitol, typically for two-week sessions throughout the year. During Albany sessions, members of the court meet each morning in conference to discuss the appeals argued the afternoon before, to consider and vote on writings circulated on pending appeals, and to decide motions and administrative matters. In the afternoon, the full court hears oral arguments.

When not in session in Albany, the judges work in "home chambers" in their city or town of residence on opinions and other matters to be decided by the full court upon return to Albany. They also hear requests for permission to appeal criminal-case decisions from lower courts and review their share of the motions the full court must decide. Criminal-leave applications are the single most common type of actions the court decides upon.

In recent years, the court has written opinions in some 175 to 200 cases annually, in addition to deciding approximately 1,200 motions for permission to appeal civil cases and more than 2,000 applications to appeal criminal convictions. The high court grants permission to appeal only in a relative handful of cases each year. In 2005, of 2,383 applications in criminal cases, the court agreed to hear 42 cases, only 1.8 percent of the total. In the early 1990s, the court agreed to hear more than 2 percent of requests each year. The acceptance rate has been below 2 percent every year since 1998.

Once the court agrees to hear an appeal, the odds favor affirmation of a lower-court decision, particularly in criminal cases. From 2001 to 2005, the Court of Appeals affirmed convictions in 67 to 76 percent of criminal cases, with reversals in 14 to 29 percent (several cases are modified or dismissed each year). The disparity between affirmations and reversals in civil cases is usually narrower. In 2005, for instance, the high court affirmed 49 percent of lower-court decisions and reversed 31 percent. Overall, civil cases typically make up more than two-thirds appeals heard by the court.

The number of appeals heard by the court declined after 1985, when the court sought — and Governor Cuomo and the Legislature granted — greater power over its caseload. Leaders of the court system argued that the change would allow the state's highest court to concentrate more on cases with critical statewide significance.

Court of Appeals Judges, 2006 (in order of seniority)			
	Home Chambers	*Law School*	*Prior Experience*
Judith S. Kaye (1983)*	Manhattan	New York University	Private practice, executive committee, Association of the Bar of the City of New York
Carmen Beauchamp Ciparick (1993)*	Manhattan	St. John's University	New York City Criminal Court, Supreme Court
Albert M. Rosenblatt (1998)**	Poughkeepsie	Harvard	District attorney, County Court, Supreme Court, Chief Administrative Judge, Appellate Division
Victoria A. Graffeo (2000)**	Albany	Albany	State Solicitor General, Supreme Court, Appellate Division
Susan Phillips Read (2003)**	Albany	University of Chicago	SUNY, private and corporate practice, deputy counsel to governor, Court of Claims
Robert S. Smith (2004)**	Manhattan	Columbia	Private practice, Columbia Law School
Eugene F. Pigott, Jr.** (2006)	Buffalo	SUNY Buffalo	Private practice, Erie County attorney, Supreme Court, Appellate Division (presiding justice).

*   Appointed by Governor Cuomo
** Appointed by Governor Pataki

While the number of appeals heard by the court is relatively small —
196 in 2005, or slightly less than one for every working day — each appeal requires a significant amount of work. Lawyers for each side file briefs, along with the full record of lower-court action. Oral arguments presented to the full court in most appeals allow the seven judges to

question attorneys. At the end of each afternoon of oral arguments, random assignment distributes cases to individual judges to report on at the next morning's conference of all the judges. During the conference, if a majority of the court agrees with the reporting judge's proposed ruling, that judge is responsible for preparing the court's opinion. If the majority disagrees, one of the judges holding the majority opinion is assigned to draft the opinion. Draft opinions are circulated to all seven judges during their home chambers sessions, and the court's ruling is typically handed down during the next Albany session after further discussion among the judges. An average appeal takes six months from filing to appearance on the court's calendar, and six weeks or less from argument or submission to disposition by the court.

Powers of the Courts

Anyone who has been involved in a court case knows the dramatic impact a court decision can have on an individual, a family, a business, government, or other organization. Even a finding of guilt in connection with a simple speeding ticket can cost a driver well over $100, given a typical fine and the higher insurance premiums that sometimes result. Tens of thousands of New Yorkers are serving long terms in state prison after conviction in court.

In civil courts, parents experience agonizing decisions over child custody and divorcing couples are told how to divide financial resources that may already be painfully limited. Businesses engage in multimillion-dollar disputes that may leave one company dramatically stronger and another much weaker, with implications for owners and workers on both sides. Individuals seek to force public schools and government agencies to provide educational or other services in a particular way.

By definition, every decision of a court relates to a single "case." A fundamental principle of the American judicial system is that cases can arise only from actual "controversies" between adversaries. If an individual is accused of a crime, his adversary is the people, represented by a prosecutor. In civil cases, two parties (or, in unusual instances, more than two) want a court to settle a dispute.

And yet, courts also shape the law by interpreting — and sometimes striking down — the statutes enacted by the Legislature as well as the regulations written by appointees of the governor. Sometimes decisions that interpret the law extend the effect of a statute to situations not previously considered. On occasion, courts essentially create law by applying their understanding of the Constitution to an issue not addressed by Congress or a state legislature, or by decreeing that the legislative action is unconstitutional. In most cases, such policymaking is performed, ultimately, by appellate courts.

Instances of judicial policymaking by the federal courts are well known. Famous U.S. Supreme Court decisions include *Roe* v. *Wade*, the case that sharply limited the states' powers to restrict abortion; and *Brown* v. *Board of Education*, the 1954 ruling that made it illegal for states to prevent black children from attending the same schools as white children.

Such major decisions by New York State courts are relatively rare. The 2004 decision *People* v. *Stephen LaValle*, invalidating the state's death-penalty statute, reversed one of Governor Pataki's signature accomplishments (see "The Ultimate Penalty," page 153). The Campaign for Fiscal Equity case, described elsewhere in this book, is another example of significant judicial intervention into policy-making. Yet it's uncertain that Court of Appeals and lower-court decisions in that case will lead to dramatic change in the state's education system. State funding for New York City schools, and perhaps those in some other cities, will likely be somewhat higher as a result of the case. Whether day-to-day practices in struggling urban schools will change — or, more importantly, whether indicators of student achievement will improve — remains to be seen.

If revolutionary court decisions are rare at the state level, much more common is the case that builds on existing statutes or case law to establish public policy in light of new social or technological developments.

One example is a 1999 case, *Lunney* v. *Prodigy Servs. Co.*, in which the Court of Appeals had to decide whether an Internet service provider (ISP) could be held liable for defamation as a result of messages transmitted through its system. Using the name of Alexander Lunney, an unknown imposter opened a number of accounts in 1994 with Prodigy Services, then one of the largest ISPs in the country. The real Alexander Lunney was a 15-year-old Boy Scout, according to court papers. The fraudulent Lunney sent obscenities and criminal threats of murder and sodomy to various people, including the boy's scoutmaster, via Prodigy's e-mail and bulletin-board services. Police were unable to find the person or people who committed the crime. In suing Prodigy, the real

The Ultimate Penalty

In criminal cases, the job of the courts is to establish guilt or lack thereof—to punish the guilty while protecting the rights of the accused, and to guard against false conviction of innocent individuals. These conflicting demands appear in particularly sharp focus in cases where there is the possibility of the ultimate punishment — execution of an individual by the state.

Like all the laws that underlie the work of the courts, the provisions of New York State's Penal Code that establish capital punishment are products of the Legislature. After the U.S. Supreme Court declared a long-existing death penalty statute unconstitutional (with those in other states) in 1972, the Legislature voted repeatedly through the late 1970s, 1980s and early 1990s to enact a new law. Governors Carey and Cuomo vetoed those bills, as morally unacceptable, more than a dozen times.

In 1995, Governor Pataki promised to sign the death penalty into law. Opponents did not have enough votes to block the measure in the Legislature, but they did force into the statute numerous provisions intended to guard against false conviction and to require serious consideration of a lifetime prison sentence rather than execution. The law required that a trial judge instruct jurors, before their sentencing deliberations, that they must choose unanimously between the death penalty and life imprisonment without parole. If the jurors failed to reach a unanimous decision, the court would sentence the defendant to life imprisonment with parole eligibility after a minimum of 20 to 25 years.

In February 2004, the Court of Appeals overturned the law in the case of Stephen LaValle. He had been convicted of raping and murdering a woman named Cynthia Quinn, who had gone jogging near her home in Yaphank, Suffolk County, in 1997. In a 4-3 decision, the court said the required instructions to jurors violated the Due Process Clause of the state Constitution by creating an unacceptable risk that jurors favoring life without parole would be coerced into voting for execution to avoid the possibility of the killer eventually leaving prison.*

With new questions raised about capital-punishment laws around the country, the Legislature did not act on a new death-penalty statute. In the 2006 gubernatorial election, both the leading candidates — Eliot Spitzer and John Faso — favored restoration of the death penalty. Whether the Legislature would present the next governor with a bill to approve or veto was uncertain.

---

*   *People* v. *LaValle* (3 NY3d 88)

Alexander claimed defamation and infliction of emotional distress. Applying established tort principles, the court held that, like a telephone company, an ISP cannot be held liable in defamation as a publisher of e-mail messages transmitted through its system by a third party. For that and other reasons, the court determined that Prodigy was not the "publisher" of the bulletin board messages and therefore was not liable for defamation.

In the absence of statutory action by the Legislature to determine whether ISPs can be liable for such defamation, the Court of Appeals' decision sets the legal standard for future cases.

Checks on the Courts' Powers

The system of checks and balances at work throughout American government applies to New York's courts. The top judges are appointed by the governor with the assent of the Senate. As mentioned earlier, the governor assigns judges to the Appellate Division, with no input from the legislative branch. Among other things, this gives the governor potentially significant power to shape the operations of the judicial system, given the membership of the Appellate Division's presiding judges in the Administrative Board of the Courts. The Legislature has the power to rewrite the laws on which judicial action is based.

An example of legislation overturning a decision of the courts came in 1996, when Governor Pataki and the Legislature made substantial changes to New York's Workers Compensation Law. Since its inception in 1914, the workers compensation system has prevented employees from suing employers for injuries suffered on the job in return for guaranteed financial benefits, even if a worker's own actions might have contributed to an injury. In a 1973 case, *Dole* v. *Dow*, the Court of Appeals ruled that an injured worker could sue a third party — for instance, a company that manufactured equipment involved in an injury — and that the third party could then sue the employer. Businesses complained that the ruling violated the "no-fault" nature of the workers compensation system and drove up insurance costs. As part of broad reform legislation enacted in 1996 (nearly a quarter-century after the original case), the governor and the Legislature outlawed most *Dole* v. *Dow*-type cases.

The Judges

Courts in New York State are in the hands of approximately 3,500 judges, from the seven who sit on the court of last resort — the Court of Appeals — to those who serve part-time in 1,250 village and town courts.

In that latter group, some 2,000 justices who serve four-year terms make up the majority of judges in the state. Unlike judges in the state-wide court system, these officials are paid by the local government in which they serve. Close to 75 percent of these individuals are nonlawyers, according to the Office of Court Administration. New justices who are not attorneys are required to complete a six-day basic certification course covering the fundamentals of law and their responsibilities as justices. Approximately 150 did so in 1999. Town and village justices are also required to attend continuing education programs each year. The court system's City, Town and Village Courts Resource Center offers guidance to judges and clerks of such courts; it handles 200 or more inquiries in a typical week.

Some 1,100 judges were assigned to the state trial courts, and another 73 jurists served on the Appellate Division or in Appellate Terms, as of 2004.

The governor appoints the chief judge, other members of the Court of Appeals, and members of the Court of Claims, subject to the consent of the Senate. The governor also chooses Supreme Court justices for elevation to the Appellate Division, with no Senate confirmation needed.

Voters choose the majority of judges in New York — town and village justices, Supreme Court justices, and those in county courts, surrogate's courts, most family courts, the New York City Civil Court, and the district courts — after nomination by political parties. Family and Criminal Court judges in New York City are appointed by the mayor, as are some city court judges in other cities.

Involvement of political parties has often been criticized as injecting an unseemly taint of political favoritism into the judiciary. For example, *Newsday* ran a series of articles in 1999 analyzing the involvement of many judges in Nassau and Suffolk counties in local Republican politics. Other newspapers around the state have reported periodically on surrogate's courts appointing politically involved lawyers to lucrative positions as guardians or receivers. In March 2000, Chief

Administrative Judge Jonathan Lippman directed state judges to supervise more closely the court-appointed receivers who oversee bankrupt or mismanaged businesses and property.

A different type of concern over judicial elections helped lead to the mid-1970s constitutional amendment providing for gubernatorial appointment of Court of Appeals judges. For more than half a century, the two major political parties had generally cross-endorsed candidates in campaigns for the high court, including the office of chief judge. In 1973, a Manhattan trial attorney, Jacob Fuchsberg, ignored the tradition by which sitting Associate Judge Charles Breitel would have been elected chief judge unopposed. Although Breitel won the contested election, and Fuchsberg won election as an associate judge, the campaign left ill feelings among members of the bar. The following year, the only African-American member of the Court of Appeals, Harold Stevens, was defeated in a primary. The two events helped create the necessary momentum to take Court of Appeals appointments out of the electoral process.

More recently, the process for political-party nominations of judicial candidates has come under attack. In early 2006, a federal judge in Brooklyn ruled that party leaders had too much power to dictate nominations. Citing the First and 14th Amendments to the U.S. Constitution, Margarita Lopez Torres and other plaintiffs had argued that the long-standing nominating system of nominating conventions deprived voters of the right to choose their parties' candidates, and imposed insurmountable burdens on candidates who ran without local leaders' support. The ruling ordered use of direct primaries for such nominations pending statutory change by the Legislature.

Along with 38 other states, New York retains the practice of electing all general-jurisdiction trial judges (in New York, the Supreme Court). However, only nine of the states conduct partisan elections, while others conduct elections with no party labels, use a merit-selection system or have a hybrid approach. Among states that use partisan elections, all the others allow insurgents to run in primary elections "by filing a notice, gathering a reasonable number of signatures, paying a filing fee, or fulfilling some combination of these requirements."[9] New York allows such primaries for county courts and most other trial courts, but not Supreme Court.

---

9   *Lopez Torres* v. *New York State Board of Elections*, issued January 27, 2006.

In February 2006, Chief Judge Kaye announced new rules establishing screening panels for all elective judgeships. In each judicial district, a 15-member commission will publish a list of candidates found qualified and of those who declined to participate in such screening. Meanwhile, an advisory commission to the court system recommended retaining judicial nominating conventions, while making them smaller and more independent from political-party leaders. As of mid-2006, the Legislature had not acted on any changes to the nominating system.

Two centuries ago, reform-minded New Yorkers sought election of judges to make them accountable to the people rather than to powerful government leaders. Relying on elections to promote an honest and capable judiciary requires that voters have some knowledge of their judges and court system. It seems fair to say that relatively few New Yorkers have such knowledge today. Instead, whichever candidates can win the support of the locally dominant political party are virtually guaranteed election to the bench.

Under the state Constitution, jurists of the Court of Appeals and state Supreme Court can be removed by a two-thirds vote in each house of the Legislature. Judges of most lower courts may be removed by a two-thirds vote of the Senate, on recommendation of the governor.

The People's Courts: The Juror's Role

The second paragraph of New York State's Constitution (following only the securing of rights and privileges to all citizens) guarantees the right to a trial by jury. Aside from voting, jury service is the most common way individuals actively participate in their government. Today it's often perceived, at best, as a necessary chore — or, worse, as a harmful intrusion in the busy life of modern Americans.

Only a small proportion of cases filed in the courts end up before a jury. In 2004, of 197,926 civil cases disposed of in Supreme Court, fewer than 3 percent ended in jury verdicts and decisions. In felony criminal cases decided in Supreme and county courts, jury convictions and acquittals accounted for fewer than 4 percent of dispositions (roughly another 1 percent ended in nonjury verdicts). Fully 87 percent of criminal cases ended when defendants pled guilty, often in exchange for consideration in sentencing. The parties in most civil suits settled before a jury verdict.

Juries are charged with considering the facts and circumstances presented in a case and applying the law to reach a decision. In a criminal trial involving a felony charge, twelve jurors and up to six alternates may be chosen; misdemeanor cases require a jury of six. Juries in civil trials usually have six members and one or two alternates. Judges usually designate the first juror chosen in a criminal trial as the foreperson; in civil trials, the judge will often allow the jury members to make the choice. The foreperson typically speaks for the jury in the courtroom and often (but not always) leads discussion in deliberations on a verdict.

Judges may allow jurors to take notes during the trial, but are not required to do so; many judges believe note-taking diminishes jurors' ability to pay full attention to witnesses while they are on the stand. In 2005, an advisory group recommended that judges routinely allow note-taking and provide materials. The group examined other issues such as allowing jurors to submit written questions for witnesses, and providing judges' final instructions in writing.[10]

For decades before 1994, lawyers and numerous other professionals were automatically exempt from jury duty. The list of exemptions, which included pharmacists, embalmers, podiatrists, and prosthetists, diminished the pool of potential jurors by 1 million or so, according to the Office of Court Administration. At the initiative of Chief Judge Kaye, the Legislature eliminated automatic exemptions effective January 1, 1996. Thousands of lawyers, and even a few judges, have served since, as have other high-profile individuals such as New York City Mayor Rudolph Giuliani. Lawyers are slightly less likely than other individuals to be selected to sit as jurors once they report for duty, according to the advisory committee.

The addition of so many New Yorkers to the overall jury pool and other administrative improvements have paid off in sharply reduced terms of service for jurors. The statewide average term in 1997 was 2.5 days, less than half of what it had been three years earlier.

Juries in criminal trials must agree unanimously on a finding of guilty or not guilty; failure to agree results in a mistrial, which can be followed by a new trial or dismissal of charges. In civil cases, agreement by five of six jury members is sufficient.

---

10 Elissa Krauss, "Jury Trial Innovations in New York State," *New York State Bar Association Journal*, May 2005 (available online via *www.nyjuryinnovations.org*).

Despite the low proportion of cases that go before a jury, such trials are common enough to require continual replenishment of the jury pool in each trial court. More than 600,000 New Yorkers are called as potential jurors, and another 25,000 as members of grand juries, each year. Jurors must meet certain basic qualifications — U.S. citizenship, residence in the relevant county, age of at least 18, no felony convictions, and the ability to communicate in English. The court system obtains each year the names of state residents who are registered voters, state taxpayers, licensed drivers, or recipients of public assistance benefits or unemployment compensation. Prospective jurors who have not served for a given number of years — four in most of the state, two years in Manhattan and the Bronx — are selected randomly from the lists.

Jury trials last an average of three to five days in civil cases and five to 10 days in criminal cases, according to the Office of Court Administration. As of 2006, the state paid jurors $40 a day, minus any salary or wages the individual received from a regular job. State law prohibits employers from penalizing or terminating an employee because of jury service, if given notice when the employee receives a jury summons.

Chapter Seven

THE CONSTITUTION

Key points:

- New York's Constitution is much longer, and more detailed, than the U.S. Constitution.

- The fundamental law changes in response to the times, and to efforts of individual leaders.

- Although voters decided in 1997 not to call a constitutional convention, New Yorkers need not wait until 2017 to pursue major changes in the state's basic charter.

New York State government is, before all else, words on paper. The fundamental authority by which the governor and the Legislature act — and by which they, in turn, create authority for every unit of state and local government in New York — is the state Constitution. Its preamble, reflecting the people's purposeful decision to invest certain powers in government, states:

We the People of the State of New York, grateful to Almighty God for our Freedom, in order to secure its blessings, DO ESTABLISH THIS CONSTITUTION.[1]

The wording, added in 1821, echoes that of the more familiar U.S. Constitution. But New York, like most of the other original colonies, developed its own Constitution in the months immediately following the Declaration of Independence in 1776. The writing and ratification of the national charter followed more than a decade later. After all, the nation began as a confederation of states; its founders thought of themselves as citizens of states before conceiving of what was to become a strong national government. Even the Articles of Confederation, creating a weak national government, were not written until five years after independence.

New York's Constitution starts by reserving rights to the people and then outlines how the people express their will through voting, before detailing the structure of government in Article III and following sections. This is quite different from the national charter, which after a brief preamble gets right to the business of setting up the government and attaches a Bill of Rights only as the first group of amendments.

This chapter outlines the most important elements of the state Constitution. To lay a foundation for understanding today's basic contract between the people and their elected leaders, it first provides national and historical context for the document. It then discusses how the Constitution can be changed, what drives such change, and whether significant constitutional revision is likely in the near future.

Changes Over Time

New York's Constitution has been substantially rewritten four times since the original 1777 document, most recently in 1938.[2] The present document — with core sections dating to the 19th century, and other important provisions coming as late as the 1970s — has been amended more than 200 times. All of those changes represent shifting voter attitudes about powers the people give to the government and the division of authority among the various branches of the government.

---

1   Printed copies of the state Constitution are available from the New York State Department of State, Office of Information Services, Albany NY 12231-0001. The text is also available through the state's website, *www.state.ny.us*.

2   Other major revisions took place in 1821, 1846, and 1894.

The first state Constitution, like later revisions, reflected its times. Written just months after the American colonies had voted to be free of the British crown, its provisions for a relatively weak government — including a governor whose powers were few and limited — reflected a suspicion of centralized power. At the same time, New York's first Constitution continued governmental dominance by the economic and political elite. It limited suffrage to a minority of the population, excluding all women and men who did not own property or pay taxes. (One effect of the latter requirement was that relatively few black New Yorkers were allowed to vote.) The limits of the franchise were reflected in the number of votes cast. In George Clinton's campaign for governor in 1792, he defeated his eventual successor, John Jay, by 8,440 votes to 8,332.[3]

Today's Constitution retains, from the original document, the three major branches of government and many of the rights reserved to the people. At the start of the 21st century, though, New York's basic charter is dramatically different from the 1776 version. It includes provisions for a strong executive and gives the state power to act in areas far beyond those originally envisioned — for example, developing homes, promoting health, and using public money to help businesses grow. The current document includes significant sections approved by voters after action by six constitutional conventions. For example:

- In 1821, much of the Bill of Rights was added.

- In 1846, restrictions were placed on state government's powers to incur debt and impose taxes.

- In 1867, a convention created the current structure of the Court of Appeals.

- In 1894, much of the rest of today's judicial structure, provisions on education and conservation, the merit system of civil appointments, and election rules were approved.

- In 1915, a convention produced proposals to reorganize the executive branch and create an Executive Budget. Although rejected by the voters that year, many of those ideas were en-

---

3   Reported in Mason C. Hutchins, *The New York Red Book 1938*, Albany, NY: J.B. Lyon Company, 1938, p. 484.

acted through legislative action and voter approval over the following decade or so.

- In 1938, voters approved convention proposals regarding the rights of labor and provision for housing, social welfare, and health programs. Specifics are detailed later in this chapter.

Other sections of today's Constitution were enacted piecemeal through individual amendments passed by the Legislature and approved by voters.

The National Context

Compared to the broad language of the U.S. Constitution, the Empire State's charter — like those of most states — is lengthy and detailed. One observer, Henrik N. Dullea, says New York has "not only one of the longest but one of the most complex and intimidating constitutions among the fifty states."[4]

The national document written by James Madison and his counterparts, and amended over two centuries, is some 7,300 words. Today's New York charter is more than six times that long. The two are similar in many ways, particularly the broad structure of the three branches of government and the guarantees of rights.

Like all state constitutions, New York's is subject to preemption by the U.S. Constitution when the two conflict.[5] Among other things, the supremacy of the national Constitution and statutes has produced court decisions outlawing present-day provisions of New York's Constitution for apportioning the Legislature, on the basis that they do not allow the proportional representation required by the U.S. Constitution.

At the same time, state constitutions are autonomous of federal enactments. States generally have a free hand to act where the U.S. Constitution and laws are silent, and to establish rights that go beyond those that are federally guaranteed. "Aid, care and support of the needy," for

---

4   Henrik N. Dullea, *Charter Revision in the Empire State: The Politics of New York's 1967 Constitutional Convention*, Albany, NY: The Rockefeller Institute Press, 1997.

5   Article VI of the U.S. Constitution states: "This Constitution, and the Laws of the United States which shall be made in Pursuance thereof … shall be the supreme Law of the Land; and the Judges in every State shall be bound thereby, any Thing in the Constitution or Laws of any State to the Contrary notwithstanding."

instance, are "public concerns" under the Constitution of the Empire State, and must be addressed by the Legislature as such.

State constitutions differ markedly in the governmental processes and structures they create. Unlike some states, New York has no state-level provision for citizen initiative in the legislative process, or limits on the terms that elected officials can serve. A hallmark of the state's strong governorship is the low number of statewide elected officials, compared to many other states.

The U.S. Constitution created a government where none had existed previously; before American independence, the 13 colonies were separate entities with no domestic political superstructure uniting them. New York in the early 1770s, on the other hand, had a colonial governor and other offices making decisions for what was to become the state of New York. In some measure, the first state Constitution represented simply a metamorphosis of that existing government — albeit in the context of a revolutionary switch of ultimate authority from the British crown to the people of New York.

New York's First Constitution

After representatives of the 13 colonies agreed in Philadelphia on July 4, 1776, to declare independence, each colony faced the need to establish new governmental authority. In New York, the Fourth Provincial Congress declared New York independent five days later. The representatives, who had planned to assembly in Kingston to discuss relations with Britain even before the Philadelphia declaration, changed the name of their gathering to the Convention of the Representatives of the State of New York. It was the first formal use of the "state" designation.

John Jay, who was to become the first chief justice of the United States, is credited with a primary role in writing a draft constitution. After months of drafting and debate, the first Constitution of New York State was adopted on April 20, 1777. With a Revolutionary War going on — and many battles in New York territory — the historic charter was not subjected to voter approval. Its text, however, spoke of the people's support: "This convention, therefore, in the name and by the authority of the good people of this State, doth ordain, determine, and declare that no authority shall, on any presence whatever, be exercised over the people or members of this State but such as shall be derived from and granted by them."

The Constitution provided for the strongest executive among the new American states. New York's governor was to be elected directly, rather than by the legislature as in some states, and therefore was directly accountable not to other officials but to the people. He could be elected to more than one term; and shared veto power with members of the judiciary through a Council of Revision. The New York judiciary, too, was given more power than many of its counterparts in other states. Another important body, the Council of Appointment, gave the governor and the Senate shared authority over nomination of lower state officials. The Council of Appointment represented an unusual balance of powers: the Assembly elected the senators who would sit on the council along with the governor.

A new convention in 1801 enacted changes in the makeup of the Legislature and clarified the governor's role in the appointments process. "By placing effective power in the hands of the legislature the way was opened for the creation of a powerful party machine for the control of political patronage.... It is fair to say that these decisions enabled the 'spoils system' to reach its state of development in New York. The 'clean sweep' of office-holders, a practice which did not precede the 1801 convention, became routine."[6] Like the state's first Constitution, the new charter took effect without voter approval. It was the product of the only Constitutional Convention in New York's history to be called by the Legislature for limited purposes.

The 1821 Constitutional Convention: Historic Changes

Nearly two decades later, the Legislature responded to calls for greater suffrage and other reforms by placing on the ballot a question as to whether there should be a constitutional convention. That action "established the tradition in New York of making constitutional conventions the creature of the people, not of the legislature," according to Peter J. Galie.[7]

---

6   Peter J. Galie, *Ordered Liberty: A Constitutional History of New York*, New York: Fordham University Press, 1996, p. 68.

7   Peter J. Galie, *The New York State Constitution: A Reference Guide*, Westport, CT: Greenwood Press, 1991, p. 7.

The resulting 1821 convention began a century-long process of concentrating, in the chief executive's office, significant powers that the state's founders had purposefully distributed among the Legislature and the multibranch councils. The Council of Revision and the Council of Appointment were eliminated; with them went a degree of power-sharing among the three branches of state government that seems strange today. Instead of the Council of Revision, the governor alone was to have the veto power; the Legislature retained a lesser role with the ability to override such vetoes, while the involvement of the judicial branch in legislation was eliminated. (By this time, though, the U.S. Supreme Court had articulated the doctrine of judicial review — the power of the judiciary to determine the constitutionality of statutes — in *Marbury* v. *Madison*.) At the same time, the governor's term was shortened from three to two years. Voters approved the convention's proposals in 1822.

Other changes made as a result of the 1821 convention included broader suffrage, extending to virtually all white men, along with new property requirements for African-American men who wished to vote. The changes had the effect of taking away the voting power from most black men who previously had the franchise.

In response to several scandals, the new Constitution included a number of limits and prohibitions on the power of the Legislature. One example is the requirement for a two-thirds vote of the Legislature for any bill appropriating money or property for local or private purposes. The document was also the first to include a number of specific policy provisions — one of the most notable features of today's Constitution.

The 1821 convention created the state's constitutional Bill of Rights. It drew on similar provisions in England, safeguards recognized under 17th-century law in colonial New York, a statutory bill of rights enacted by the New York Legislature in 1787, and the Bill of Rights in the federal Constitution.

More Power to the People:
The 1846 Convention

Despite eight amendments enacted individually between 1822 and 1845, the middle of the 19th century brought a growing realization that the 1821 charter required fundamental change. Among other things, development of the canal system and other public works had put the state deeply in debt, and state charters for private corporations were granted as political favors.

"By 1842, the financial affairs of the state were rapidly approaching a crisis," Galie writes.[8] The anti-rent wars were also a factor in demand for constitutional change,[9] as were the desire for more direct popular control of the government and backlogs in the courts.

Delegates to the 1846 convention and the voters who approved its work imposed significant new restrictions on the Legislature's ability to spend, borrow, and directly control the creation of corporations. To address anti-rent sentiment, future leases of agricultural lands were limited to 12 years. The new Constitution, sometimes called the "People's Constitution," gave extensive new power to the voters. It made numerous offices elective (including those of state engineer and state prison inspectors) and moved some governmental authority to the local level. The convention proposed suffrage rights for African-American males equal to those for white men. However, that proposal was rejected by the voters, virtually all of whom were white, by a margin of more than 2-1.

The 1846 document also instituted a provision that remains important today: The requirement that voters be asked every 20 years whether a new Constitutional Convention should be called (see page 187).

Overall, the new Constitution represented a significant reduction in the power of the Legislature. More broadly, it brought about a dramatic change in the relationship between state government and the private-sector economy. Until that point, according to Galie, a "tradition of active regulation and encouragement of the economy" characterized New York.

> The significance of the 1846 convention was its retreat from this tradition and its redefining the role of the government in society, ensuring that the transformation of the socio-economic order of New York would take place under the umbrella, but not the active direction, of the government.[10]

---

8   *Ordered Liberty*, p. 96.

9   Tenant farmers engaged in agitation and armed rebellion against wealthy landowners at various times from the 1750s to the mid-1800s, often having an important influence on the political climate in the state and nation.

10 *Ordered Liberty*, p. 113.

Just after the Civil War, concerns about the effectiveness of the state's court system — concerns that had existed for decades — helped lead to a new convention. Voters approved the 1866 question on the calling of a convention under the 20-year rule adopted two decades earlier. The Court of Appeals was re-created in its current form of seven members, including the chief judge (members were elected until the mid-1970s).

In 1872, Governor John T. Hoffman and the Legislature created a constitutional commission to propose amendments that could be acted upon by the Legislature, without the need for a convention. The commission produced a number of recommendations that were later enacted. For example, the governor's office was strengthened with a line-item veto, return to a three-year term, and additional power to appoint department heads. Legislative action after the commission's work also eliminated the discriminatory voting requirements for black citizens that had been in effect for more than half a century.

Development of the Modern Constitution: 1894-1938

The opportunity for voters to call a constitutional convention arose again in 1886, and the call was approved overwhelmingly. Republican legislators and Governor David B. Hill, a Democrat, could not agree on a delegate-selection process. That stalemate ended when Democrats won control of the governor's office, the Senate, and the Assembly in 1892. Delegates were elected the following year, and the convention held one year later.

That convention produced a number of provisions that remain in force today. These include the Conservation article and political reforms such as a requirement for bipartisan boards of elections.

Of broader importance, the convention and voters approved the Education article, which requires the state to provide schools for "all the children of this state." Also enacted was a requirement that civil-service appointments and promotions be made "according to merit and fitness," to be judged as much as possible by competitive examination. In the judiciary, the 1894 changes created the Appellate Division of the Supreme Court to ease the burden on the Court of Appeals, and consolidated some courts, creating a system that largely remains (*see Chapter Six*).

The 1894 convention also produced provisions for apportioning Senate and Assembly seats that remain in today's Constitution, although some are dead letters. Still in effect is the size of the Assembly, at 150 seats. Other provisions that had the effect of giving more representation to rural areas and less to New York City were ruled contrary to the U.S. Constitution in the 1960s (*see Chapter Five*).

Within two decades of the 1894 convention, two major labor-related provisions were added: Giving the Legislature power to regulate wages and hours of employment, and creating a system of workers' compensation under which injured employees would automatically receive benefits in exchange for giving up the right to sue their employers. These and other changes were part of the nationwide "progressive" movement that sought to take power from the government and big corporations, and return it to the people.

A 1915 convention proposed major changes to strengthen the role of the governor by creating an executive budget and consolidating executive agencies under the authority of the chief executive. Those proposals were rejected initially (along with several others), but were enacted incrementally by the late 1920s. Along with a 1937 amendment giving the governor and other statewide officials four-year terms, these changes established the New York governor's office as among the strongest in the nation.

After two centuries of change, what is in the New York State Constitution today? Following is a selection of major elements. Readers are encouraged to consult *The New York State Constitution: A Reference Guide*, from which some of the following discussion is adapted, for a comprehensive analysis.

The Constitution at the Turn of the 21st Century: A Bill of Rights — Right at the Start

Today's state Constitution puts more power in the hands of the government than John Jay and other founders might have imagined. Still, the first Article emphasizes the rights that remain with the people. Indeed, unlike our national charter, the New York State Constitution places the

Bill of Rights at the very beginning, rather than as a series of amendments at the end.

"No member of this state shall be disfranchised, or deprived of any of the rights or privileges secured to any citizen hereof, unless by the law of the land, or the judgment of his peers," Section 1 of Article 1 states, providing a guarantee similar to one enjoyed by the English since the Magna Carta.[11]

In the first of many such instances, Section 1 of the Bill of Rights follows that broad, high-minded statement of principle with a narrow rule added in 1959 to save money on uncontested primaries:

> ... except that the legislature may provide that there shall be no primary election held to nominate candidates for public office or to elect persons to party positions for any political party or parties in any unit of representation of the state from which such candidates or persons are nominated or elected whenever there is no contest or contests for such nominations or election as may be prescribed by general law.

The Bill of Rights goes on to guarantee many of the same rights that appear in the United States Constitution — often in identical or similar language — while continuing to descend occasionally into more mundane provisions.

The right to trial by jury is the second right granted by Article I. Criminal defendants may waive the right, except in cases of charges that may be punishable by death.

Article I also guarantees "free exercise and enjoyment of religious profession and worship, without discrimination or preference." In addition, "no person shall be rendered incompetent to be a witness on account of his opinions on matters of religious belief." These rights are not absolute, however: "the liberty of conscience hereby secured shall not be so construed as to excuse acts of licentiousness, or justify practices inconsistent with the peace or safety of this state."

The following three sections of the Bill of Rights provide various protections against unfair prosecution — protections that go further than those guaranteed by U.S. Supreme Court interpretations of the national charter. Section 6, for example, guarantees criminal defendants a

---

11 Space does not permit including the entire state Constitution in this book. While texts on U.S. government often include the federal Constitution as an appendix, New York's charter would represent the equivalent of several additional chapters.

right to counsel and several other rights. This one section of New York's Constitution has generated so many lawsuits and resulting case law that the summary reports of such decisions fill almost all of an 848-page volume of *McKinney's Consolidated Laws of New York's* annotation of the Constitution.

Section 7 contains a more detailed discussion of concerns relating to private property and eminent domain: "Private property shall not be taken for public use without just compensation." Further provisions relate to public takings of private roads and the use of private property for drainage of swamp or farmlands.

Section 8 guarantees freedom of speech; citizens are made "responsible for the abuse of that right."

Section 9 prohibits laws that would limit the right to peaceful assembly or to petition the government. The same sentence contains two other, unrelated provisions. First, no divorce shall be granted other than through judicial proceedings. Second, lotteries "or any other kind of gambling" are outlawed, except state lotteries to raise money for education and pari-mutuel betting on horse races "from which the state shall derive a reasonable revenue for the support of government."

Notwithstanding the ban on gambling, Section 9 allows localities to permit bingo or similar games of chance operated by religious, charitable, veterans, and similar nonprofit organizations. In a classic illustration of the detail to which state constitutions often extend, New York's fundamental law then stipulates that bingo prizes shall not exceed $250 for single games, and $1,000 for series of prizes on one occasion.

The former Sections 10, 13, and 15 of the Bill of Rights are no longer in effect, having been repealed by popular vote in 1962. Those provisions, considered out of date and unnecessary, dealt with things such as the purchase of lands of Indians, and certain grants of lands and charters made by the king of Great Britain. The remaining sections have not been renumbered, leaving sequential gaps in the Bill of Rights today.

Section 11 guarantees equal protection under the laws of the state and its subdivisions — including protection against private discrimination: "No person shall, because of race, color, creed or religion, be subjected to any discrimination in his civil rights by any other person or by any firm, corporation or institution, or by the state or any agency or subdivision of the state."

"Legislation Frozen Into the Constitutional Mold"

Warren M. Anderson, who served as majority leader of the state Senate from 1973 to 1988, described the Constitution this way:

"We have in New York a Constitution that should more properly be described as legislation that has been frozen into the constitutional mold, covering subjects so diverse that its index alone takes up no less than 68 fine-print pages ranging from absentee voting to workers' compensation." Senator Anderson made his comments in October 1994, as part of a University at Binghamton symposium on the prospect of a 1998 constitutional convention.

The level of detail in the Constitution is one reason so many interest groups oppose the idea of changing it, according to Henrik N. Dullea. Most New Yorkers, he writes, "would never imagine that the state Constitution contains, sometimes in excruciating detail, everything from the width of ski trails in the Adirondacks to procedures for the issuance of local debt for water and sewer systems."

"Changing a Constitution thus creates uncertainty and risk," Dullea, a former top aide to Governor Cuomo, adds. "For every group passionately committed to the reform of a particular constitutional provision, there is an equal and opposite group fiercely determined to preserve that same provision, which has provided it with either an important benefit or protection over the years."[*]

---

[*]   Henrik N. Dullea, "Constitutional Revision in 1967: Learning the Right Lessons from the Magnificent Failure," in Gerald Benjamin and Henrik N. Dullea, eds. *Decision 1997: Constitutional Change in New York*, Albany, NY: Rockefeller Institute Press, 1997, p. 368.

Section 12 protects "the right of the people to be secure in their persons, houses, papers and effects, against unreasonable searches and seizures." Search warrants are to be granted only upon "probable cause" and must be particular in describing the place to be searched, and persons or things to be seized. This section, adopted in 1938, also prohibits "unreasonable interception of telephone and telegraph communications." Like some other parts of the state Bill of Rights, Section 12 has played an important role in state court decisions providing broader

A Direct Impact on Policy

New York State's Constitution has a direct impact on major policy questions in the 21st century. At the start of 2007, recent or pending constitutional decisions by the Court of Appeals promise to influence matters such as:

- **Funding for New York City schools.** The state's highest court must decide whether the Constitution requires a specific additional level of state aid, as lower courts have said, or whether that choice is up to the elected representatives of the people.

- **Marriage between same-sex couples.** The court ruled in 2006 that the Constitution neither prohibits nor requires state approval of gay marriage. During the 2006 gubernatorial campaign, Eliot Spitzer pledged to propose legislation creating authorization for such marriages.

- **The death penalty.** The Court of Appeals ruled unconstitutional a 1995 statute enacted by Governor Pataki and the Legislature, but left the door open to a different law. Whether capital punishment returns to New York after absence of more than 40 years may depend on whether the new governor attempts to persuade an increasingly skeptical Assembly.

protections for criminal suspects than those required by the U.S. Supreme Court's interpretations of identical language in the U.S. Constitution.[12]

Section 14, some of which dates to the 1777 Constitution, reaffirms the effective status of much of the common law and colonial statutes enacted before independence.

Section 16 safeguards the right of individuals to file civil lawsuits "to recover damages for injuries resulting in death"; further, "the amount recoverable shall not be subject to any statutory limitation."

The "labor clause" and related provisions appear in Section 17: "Labor of human beings is not a commodity nor an article of commerce and shall never be so considered or construed." The clause, added in 1938 but with statutory roots dating back to 1897, makes clear that union activity is not to be considered a violation of antitrust laws. This section

12 See Burton C. Agata, "Criminal Justice," in *Decision 1997*, pp. 258-9

guarantees employees "the right to organize and to bargain collectively through representatives of their own choosing." It also limits workers on public works projects to eight hours a day and five days a week, "except in cases of extraordinary emergency," and requires that they be paid the wage "prevailing in the same trade or occupation in the locality within the state where such public work is to be situated, erected or used." According to Galie, "The occupancy of the field by federal law has had the effect of preempting this section, as well as much other state labor law, giving it primarily a standby character. The value of these provisions, aside from their symbolic importance, lies in their potential use should federal policy change radically."[13]

Section 18, the final provision of the Bill of Rights, also focuses on an important labor issue, giving the Legislature authority to create a workers' compensation system. The key tradeoff between workers and employers, reflected in this section, stipulates that payments can be made regardless of whether the employee is at fault for an injury, and that employers can be protected against any other legal liability for employees' injuries or deaths on the job.

After the Bill of Rights, Article II provides rules relating to suffrage. Since a 1995 amendment, the vote is available to citizens 18 or over who have lived in the state at least 30 days before an election.

Structure of State Government: The Legislature

After stating the rights of the people, and laying out the general rules for voting in New York, the Constitution creates the structure of state government in Articles III through VI. As does the U.S. Constitution, it starts with the branch of government that was intended to be most powerful because it is closest to the people — the legislative branch.

The number of senators can vary from a minimum of 50. The text of the state Constitution allows for additional seats to provide the necessary complement of senators to more populous counties. Court decisions that invalidated provisions for apportioning the Senate in the 1960s have left unclear whether there is a maximum number of seats allowable under the Constitution. As of 2006, there are 62 senators. The

---

13 *The New York State Constitution*, p. 66.

number was expanded from 61 after the 2000 census, when majority Republicans saw an opportunity to draw a new district that could help preserve their leadership in the chamber. The Assembly is set at a fixed 150 seats.

Article III lays out a number of procedural rules for the Legislature, including:

- Unlike in Congress, where tax legislation must originate in the House of Representatives because its members are subject to more frequent election than are senators, in New York any bill may originate in either house.

- For any bill to pass either house, a majority of members (not simply a majority of those present) must vote in favor.

- Neither house may pass any bill "unless it shall have been printed and upon the desks of the members, in its final form, at least three calendar legislative days prior to its final passage." The requirement is interpreted such that a bill can be voted upon in its third day of existence, potentially little more than 48 hours after introduction. An exception to the "aging" requirement — one breaching the separation of powers between the legislative and executive branches — allows the governor to certify the need for immediate action. Governors typically agree to such certification only when they support the legislation. On June 23, 2006, for instance, the Senate introduced S.8470, a "budget cleanup" bill. Governor Pataki sent a "message of necessity," both houses passed the bill, and the governor signed Chapter 108 of the Laws of 2006 the same day.

- In a provision that both reflected the founders' distrust of government and foreshadowed the 1970s-era concern for open government, "The doors of each house shall be kept open, except when the public welfare shall require secrecy." Each house today maintains a visitors' gallery above its chamber on the third floor of the state Capitol.

- "Private or local bills" are strictly regulated. The Legislature is to enact no such bill embracing more than one subject. In addition, the Constitution lists 14 cases in which the Legislature may not pass a private or local bill. Such bills include those that change the names of persons; locate or change county seats; or exempt any private corporation, association or individual from taxation of real or personal property.

- Two-thirds of the members of each house must vote for any bill "appropriating the public moneys or property for local or private purposes." If strictly interpreted, this 1821 provision of Article III would appear to cover the "member items" that the Legislature appropriates for specific local organizations and projects.

- A quorum of either house is usually a simple majority. For passage of any tax legislation, appropriation of public money or creation of debt, a quorum is three-fifths of the membership.

Structure of State Government:
The Governor

The Constitution places executive power in the governor, who must be at least 30 years old and a citizen of the United States, and have lived in the state at least five years. Befitting the Constitution's origin at a time when the colonies were at war with England, the first stated power of the governor is serving as commander-in-chief "of the military and naval forces of the state."

As detailed in Chapter Four, the governor has enormous power over legislation and the budget, including veto power. The line-item veto is one of several major constitutional and statutory provisions that, taken together, give the governor by far the most powerful role in the state budget process.

Other powers the Constitution vests in the chief executive include:

- The authority to convene the Legislature, or the Senate only, in extraordinary session. In such sessions the Legislature may act on no measure except those recommended by the governor.

The Commander-in-Chief Today

As commander-in-chief of the state's military forces, the governor has authority over the Army National Guard, Air National Guard, Naval Militia, and New York Guard. The four branches are under the supervision of the Division of Military and Naval Affairs, which provides civilian command of the military in a manner analogous to that of the U.S. Defense Department.

Members of the state's forces traditionally provide a variety of services in times of natural disaster or emergency. Responding to a severe ice storm in the state's northern counties in January 1998, for example, National Guard forces helped locate stranded residents, transport generators and food, and clear roads. In the weeks after the September 11, 2001, terrorist attacks on America, more than 2,000 National Guard members were assigned to provide security in the World Trade Center area, around nuclear power plants, and at other sites.

The state's military forces can be, and occasionally are, involved in the nation's military actions overseas. A New York Army National Guard unit participated in the NATO peacekeeping mission in Bosnia in 1997. The Division of Military and Naval Affairs' website is *http://www.dmna.state.ny.us/*.

- The responsibility to "communicate by message to the legislature at every session the condition of the state, and recommend such matters to it as he shall judge expedient." This is the genesis of the "State of the State" message — an opportunity for the governor to focus the public spotlight on the issues he seeks to address in the upcoming legislative session.

- The power to grant reprieves, commutations, and pardons after criminal convictions, "for all offenses except treason and cases of impeachment," subject to procedural regulations that may be imposed by law.

The Constitution also creates the foundation for what have become significant procedural limitations on the power of the governor and executive agencies to write rules and regulations. The document states that no such rule, except those relating to the organization or internal management of agencies, shall take effect until it is filed with the Department of State. Governors and legislatures have, over the years, written into statute further protections for the people against overweening regulation by state agencies. (*See Chapter Eight for further discussion of administrative law.*)

Article IV also provides for the position of lieutenant governor. As with the U.S. vice president, the most important function of the lieutenant governor is one of potential — of succeeding the governor in case of death, resignation, or removal from office. The last such succession came in December 1973, when Malcolm Wilson became governor upon the resignation of Nelson A. Rockefeller. The lieutenant governor is also to act as governor when the chief executive is "absent from the state." This provision, dating to colonial times, has been widely criticized as outmoded and is often ignored in an age of worldwide telecommunication and rapid transportation. If both the governor and lieutenant governor leave office or are absent from the state, the temporary president of the the Senate becomes acting governor. If that office is vacant, the Assembly speaker follows in the line of succession.

The office of lieutenant governor has no power of its own, other than to cast a vote in the Senate when needed to break a tie on procedural matters. When the lieutenant governor has a good relationship with the governor, typically he or she will be assigned projects of some importance. That was true, for instance, with Governor Mario M. Cuomo and Lieutenant Governor Stan Lundine. In the last two decades, though, strained relations have been more the norm — between Governor Hugh L. Carey and then-Lieutenant Governor Cuomo; between Governor Cuomo and Lieutenant Governor Alfred DelBello; and between Governor Pataki and Lieutenant Governor Betsy McCaughey Ross.

The Comptroller and Attorney General

The Constitution creates two additional statewide elected officers: the comptroller and the attorney general. (Most states have more separately elected statewide officials, diffusing the executive power more than New York does.) They are elected at the same time as the governor and have the same terms of office. Like the governor and lieutenant governor, they must be 30 or older, U.S. citizens, and residents of the state for at least five years.

Unlike the offices of governor and lieutenant governor, those of comptroller and attorney general are filled by the Legislature in case of vacancies. During the early 1990s, Comptroller Edward V. Regan and Attorney General Robert Abrams each resigned. They were succeeded, respectively, by H. Carl McCall, whom the Legislature elected with Governor Cuomo's support; and G. Oliver Koppell, a longtime member of the Assembly. Vacancies are filled through a joint vote of both houses. After the Regan and Abrams vacancies, the Democratic majority in the Assembly effectively held the power to choose successors.

The Constitution gives the comptroller significant procedural controls over the spending of state money. He or she is required to:

- Audit all vouchers before payment, and all official accounts.

- Audit the accrual and collection of all revenues and receipts.

- Prescribe the accounting methods state agencies must follow to make such auditing possible.

The Constitution also allows the Legislature to assign to the comptroller supervision of the accounts of any political subdivision of the state. However, as Gerald Benjamin has pointed out, "The Constitution is silent on the comptroller's very considerable powers in the management of the state retirement system, and his or her role in the incurring of state debt. These are entirely based in statute."[14]

The Constitution is also virtually silent on the powers and duties of the attorney general, other than to make him the head of the Department of Law with responsibility for representing the state in litigation.

The Executive article makes the Regents of the University of the State of New York, collectively, the head of the Department of Education. They are charged with appointing and, at their pleasure, removing the commissioner of education, the chief administrative officer of the agency. The heads of departments other than Audit and Control, Law,

---

14 Benjamin, "Structures of New York State Government," in Benjamin and Dullea, eds., *Decision 1997,* pp. 57-80.

and Education are to be appointed by the governor with the advice and consent of the Senate, as are members of "all boards and commissions, excepting temporary commissions for special purposes."

The Constitution limits the Executive branch to 20 departments, a 1925 change that was intended to limit the sprawl of government. It did not work. Governor Nelson A. Rockefeller told the Legislature in 1960 that the number of agencies reporting to the governor had grown from 65 to 136 since the amendment was enacted, and state government employment from 29,000 to "about 100,000."[15] In practice, governors have created "divisions" and "offices" within the Executive Department to get around the constitutional limit. As of 2006, some 30 agencies included "division" or "office" in their titles — from small agencies such as the Office of the Advocate for Persons with Disabilities and the Division for Women, to large ones such as the Division of State Police. Each is part of the Executive Department, more than doubling the number of state "departments." Agencies with other titles, such as the Council on the Arts and the Consumer Protection Board, add further to the state bureaucracy.

The Constitution's Executive article also creates important provisions regarding employees of the state and local government. Section 6 requires that appointments and promotions "in the civil service of the state" and its localities "shall be made according to merit and fitness to be ascertained, as far as practicable, by examination which, as far as practicable, shall be competitive." Legislation has established the dividing line between those positions that must be filled through competitive examination, and managerial and other exempt employees. Section 6 grants veterans additional points on their civil service exam scores (*see Chapter Eight on the workforce*).

Section 7 provides that membership in any state or local government pension system "shall be a contractual relationship, the benefits of which shall not be diminished or impaired." As a result, any reduction in pension benefits can only apply to employees hired after the change. That provision attained added relevance in 2006, as local-government leaders and fiscal critics of the state argued that public pensions were helping to drive property taxes and state spending to unaffordable levels.

---

15 "Pre-Session Memorandum on Reorganization of the Executive Branch of State Government," in *Public Papers of Governor Nelson A. Rockefeller*, State of New York, 1960.

Impeachment in New York

The Judicial article of the Constitution contains the rules for impeaching high state officials, which requires a simple majority vote by the Assembly. The court of impeachment is to consist of members of the Senate and the judges of the Court of Appeals, with a majority of both bodies required to participate. Conviction after inpeachment requires a two-thirds vote.

In addition to several judges, one governor has been removed by impeachment. William Sulzer was convicted in 1913 for filing false statements regarding the use of campaign funds and for using such funds to speculate in the stock market. The impeachment of Sulzer, a Democrat, was voted by a Democratic-controlled Assembly. "His trial before the Court of Impeachment, which is made up of the judges of the Court of Appeals and the members of the state Senate, clearly established the accusations as true," then-Assembly member and later Governor Al Smith wrote later.* On the other hand, David M. Ellis and other historians called Sulzer "a victim of political vengeance" who "was removed because he refused to obey ... orders" from Tammany Hall leader Charles E. Murphy.**

Section 32 of the Public Officers Law creates a second route to removal of state officials, including the comptroller and attorney general. Under the statute, the governor can recommend removal by the Senate, where two-thirds of all members must vote in the affirmative.

---

* Alfred E. Smith, *Up To Now: An Autobiography,* New York, NY: The Viking Press, 1929, p. 132.

** David M. Ellis et al., *A History of New York State*, Ithaca, NY: Cornell University Press, 1967, p. 388.

Structure of State Government: The Judiciary

The longest article in the Constitution — nearly 10 times as long as the Executive article — lays out the organization of, and procedures for, the state court system.

The Constitution creates a system of self-rule for the courts, with extensive administrative power vested in the chief judge of the Court of Appeals. (Contrary to the practice in federal courts, the highest-ranking jurists in New York are called judges, and many in the lower courts are called justices.) It establishes a unified court system throughout the state, with the chief judge serving as the chief judicial officer. The chief judge chairs the Administrative Board of the Courts; presiding justices of each of the Appellate Divisions of state Supreme Court also serve on the board. The chief judge appoints, with the advice and consent of the Administrative Board, a chief administrator of the courts. The chief judge is also responsible for establishing "standards and administrative policies for general application throughout the state," although the Court of Appeals must approve such rules.

What Government Must, May, and Cannot Do

After the four articles describing the functions and responsibilities of the state's officers and its courts, the Constitution outlines the general powers of the state and local governments, and sets limits on those powers.

State finances. Article VII lays out the Executive Budget process. To promote accountability for the state's taxing, borrowing, and spending policies, the article places clear, primary responsibility for the budget in the office of the governor. Provisions related to the state's finances appear throughout the Constitution, in 12 of the 20 articles. (*For details, see Chapter Ten.*)

Local finances and a Bill of Rights for local governments. Article VIII imposes detailed limits on the authority that counties, cities, towns, villages, and school districts have to borrow and impose real estate taxes. Included are specific, separate rules for New York City, Nassau County, Buffalo, Rochester, and Syracuse. Article IX's Bill of Rights for local governments grants them the power to elect local legislative bodies, adopt local laws, and make agreements with the federal government or other state or local governments. Article IX creates the general scheme of state oversight of local governments, but also attempts to limit the power of the state government over those of local governments. Those constitutional rules have had mixed success at best, and local governmental bodies remain "political subdivisions" subordinate to the state.

Corporations. Article X gives the Legislature the power to pass general laws allowing the formation of corporations, but prohibits the use of special acts to form corporations other than public agencies. In other words, businesses and individuals generally have the right to form corporations without seeking special favor from the Legislature. Charters of savings banks and other savings organizations receive similar treatment. Section 5 of the article regulates "public corporations," more commonly known now as public authorities. "Strictly interpreted, the provisions of this article, along with Article XVI, section 1 and Article VII, sections 8 and 12, would have severely limited the usefulness of public authorities," according to Galie. However, the courts have interpreted the provisions more permissively, resulting in broad devolution of power to public authorities.[16]

Education. For a document that is long and often highly detailed, the Constitution is succinct and general when it comes to establishing governmental authority for education. New York's entire system of support for public schools relies on Article XI, Section 1, which states: "The legislature shall provide for the maintenance and support of a system of free common schools, wherein all the children of this state may be educated." Given the social, economic, and political importance of the issue, governors and legislatures have used that authority broadly. The Education article continues the Board of Regents, originally created in 1784. It also prohibits the use of public property or money to support "any school or institution of learning wholly or in part under the control or direction of any religious denomination," although transportation of children to or from any such school is permitted (*see Chapter Eleven*).

Defense. Article XII holds: "The defense and protection of the state and of the United States is an obligation of all persons within the state. The legislature shall provide for the discharge of this obligation and for the maintenance and regulation of an organized militia." The article was approved by popular vote, after legislative action, in 1962.

Public officers. Article XIII provides the oath or affirmation that legislators, executive branch officers and judges must take, before entering office, to support the constitutions of the United States and of New York State. It stipulates that "no other oath, declaration or test shall

---

16 *The New York State Constitution: A Reference Guide*, p. 228.

be required as a qualification for any office of public trust." In 1938, the latter clause was amended to state that any political party committee may "provide for equal representation of the sexes on any such committee." Article XIII also establishes January 1 as the start of the legislative term and political year; sets the start of each legislative session as the first Wednesday after the first Monday in January; requires the Legislature to provide for removal of public officials "for misconduct or malversation in office"; provides that each state officer named in the Constitution shall be paid compensation, fixed by law, that cannot be changed during the term for which the officer is elected or appointed; and sets various other terms of office. The article also gives the Legislature the power to regulate the wages and hours, and provide for the protection, welfare and safety, of persons employed by public agencies or by contractors performing work for public entities.

Conservation. "The lands of the state, now owned or hereafter acquired, constituting the forest preserve as now fixed by law, shall be forever kept as wild forest lands." So begins Article XIV. After that grand, succinct declaration, it goes on in great detail to do such things as allow specific conveyances of state-owned land to five entities in exchange for lands those parties would convey to the state.

Article XIV grants the Legislature authority to provide for reservoirs and canals built in the forest preserve lands. It returns to broad policy with the provision, "Forest and wild life conservation are hereby declared to be policies of the state," and gives the Legislature the power to buy state land outside the Adirondack and Catskill parks for such purposes, where the "forever wild" provisions shall not apply.

The article provides that any violation of its provisions "may be restrained at the suit of the people or, with the consent of the supreme court in appellate division, on notice to the attorney-general at the suit of any citizen." Environmental groups have lobbied in recent years for legislation allowing such "citizen suits" on a broader range of issues, although the existing constitutional provision is used only rarely.

Canals. Article XV ensures the continuation of a waterway transportation system by prohibiting the sale or disposition of the barge canal system developed in the 1800s — the Erie, Oswego, Champlain, Cayuga, and Seneca canals — except where sections are or may become unneeded. The Legislature is given authority to grant revocable permits or leases for use of any of the canal lands and related structures, and to transfer or lease the canal system to the federal government "for purposes of operation, improvement and inclusion in the national system of inland waterways."

Taxation. Additional rules governing the finances of both the state and local governments, dating mostly from 1938, appear in Article XVI. This article provides that the taxing power of government "shall never be surrendered, suspended or contracted away, except as to securities issued for public purposes pursuant to law." The article also prohibits discriminatory taxation of corporations and declares that pensions of public employees are not subject to taxation. Unlike constitutions in some states, New York's charter does not prohibit income or sales taxes.

Social welfare. Like the Education article, this section is a small part of the Constitution, given its importance in state government today. Most of the article was enacted as part of the 1938 changes, after Franklin D. Roosevelt had championed a more activist role for government, first as governor of New York and then as president. Article XVII gives the state broad powers in caring for the public welfare, public health, and persons with mental disabilities. Seemingly misplaced in the Social Welfare article, but reflecting the historical development of the welfare and prison systems, is a section creating broad authority for a state criminal justice system.

Section 1, probably the best-known section of the article, states: "The aid, care and support of the needy are public concerns and shall be provided by the state and by such of its subdivisions, and in such manner and by such means, as the legislature may from time to time determine." Section 3 provides: "The protection and promotion of the health of the inhabitants of the state are matters of public concern and provision therefor shall be made by the state and by such of its subdivisions and in such manner, and by such means as the legislature shall from time to time determine."

The sections of the article referring to care for the mentally disabled and a criminal justice system are less directive. Neither subject is said to be a "matter of public concern," and each is something that the state "may," rather than "shall," provide for.

Article XVII also continues the state Board of Social Welfare, which inspects institutions ranging from orphanages to adult homes. And, in an amendment enacted in 1969, the article creates authority for the state or municipalities to loan money for hospital construction.

Housing. Also originally adopted by the 1938 convention, Article XVIII creates authority for the state and its localities to "provide ... for low-rent housing and nursing home accommodations for persons of low income," and "for the clearance, replanning, reconstruction and rehabilitation of substandard and insanitary areas." The current text of the article reflects amendments to expand the powers of state and local governments in 1949, 1955, 1957, and 1965. For example, Article XVIII allows the Legislature to grant the power of eminent domain to any city, town, or village, to any public corporation, and even to certain types of private housing corporations regulated by law. It also excludes, from the general limits on debt, borrowings to carry out these powers.

Constitutional amendments. Article XIX provides two methods for amending the Constitution. First, in a three-step process, amendments can be approved by the Legislature, approved a second time by the Legislature after a legislative election, and then submitted to the voters for approval. (The governor's involvement is not required.) Alternatively, changes can be proposed by a constitutional convention, and then submitted to the voters. Approval in the Legislature and by voters require simple majority votes — a significantly lighter burden than that for amending the U.S. Constitution.

New York is one of 14 states with a mechanism for the people to call a constitutional convention, the second method of amendment.[17] The 1846 Constitutional Convention proposed, and voters approved, a section providing that, every 20 years, the statewide ballot would automatically include a question: "Shall there be a convention to revise the constitution and amend the same?" If a majority of voters are in favor, three delegates are to be elected from each Senate district and 15 delegates elected statewide. Delegates convene at the Capitol in April following their election, "and shall continue their session until the business of such convention shall have been completed."

The Amendments article gives preference to the convention method over the legislative amendment process in one respect: If both a constitutional convention and the Legislature submit amendments on the same subject to the voters at the same time, and both are approved, the proposal from the convention supersedes that from the Legislature.

---

17 Robert F. Williams, "New York State's Constitution in Comparative Context," in Benjamin and Dullea, eds., *Decision 1997*, pp. 29-43.

Driving Constitutional Change:
Politics, Society, and Ideas

What forces brought dramatic constitutional revisions over more than two centuries? As with any major change in government, the answer is a combination of individual leaders and the times.

One factor leading up to the important 1846 Constitutional Convention, for instance, was the populist fervor that had spread in New York and throughout the country as farmers, tradesmen, and others sought to broaden political power originally held by a relative few. Andrew Jackson's election as president in 1828 (with key support from New York's Martin Van Buren) marked one major step in the rise of populism. At the state level, popular election of presidential electors (previously chosen by the Legislature) and elimination of property requirements for voting were among other developments.

Tenant farmers' efforts to end the colonial-era leasehold system of land tenure also played a role in building support for the 1846 convention. So did concern over the state's rising debt and a perception that the Legislature was too deeply involved in directing economic activity within the state.

Numerous individuals played important roles, over two decades or more, in building support for the changes that eventually were enacted in 1846. While Van Buren was one, others are largely forgotten today. Historian Milton M. Klein notes, for instance, the role of "Radical Democrat" leaders Michael Hoffman and Arphaxed Loomis in the successful drive for constitutional limits on borrowing.

Much of the agenda of the 1846 convention echoes in calls for reform of Albany today, 160 years later. Klein summarizes its work this way:

> The constitution of 1846 curtailed the legislature's power to distribute public largess to special interests, imposed tighter standards of legislative procedure, and strengthened the mechanisms of popular control.... (I)t prohibited the legislature from lending the state's credit to individuals or corporations and limited total state indebtedness to $1 million. Any new obligation in excess of that amount would require popular approval and new taxes dedicated to its repayment....

The new constitution also expanded opportunities for voter control of the government by reducing senatorial terms from four to two years and creating single-member districts, Klein notes. It provided for election of most judges, and of the state attorney general and comptroller, making those office-holders accountable to the people rather than the Legislature. All in all, according to Klein, delegates "wrought a constitutional revolution."[18]

Another period of major structural change was the Progressive era, personified best by Al Smith, from 1915 through most of the 1920s. Idealistic citizen groups advanced key ideas for change. Individuals with social and/or political standing contributed important support through organizations such as the New York State Association. Reformist leaders from both parties played important roles: Republicans such as Charles Evans Hughes joined with Smith to provide the political power needed to convince a reluctant Legislature.

The last time New Yorkers enacted the proposals of a constitutional convention was 1938 — the first such gathering to include women, who had won the vote nationwide in 1920. Reflecting many of the concerns of Americans during the Depression, the new amendments included articles in support of social-welfare and housing programs and guaranteeing workers the right to organize.

The last convention, in 1967, produced numerous sweeping proposals and presented them to voters as a single ballot question. Voters rejected the convention's work; many analysts believe a major reason was the proposal to allow public support for sectarian schools.

The 1997 Vote Against a Convention

New Yorkers last had the opportunity to call a constitutional convention in November 1997. As the vote on whether to hold a new convention approached, a good case could be made for reform. Even the fundamental direction that New York State's governing charter gave its elected leaders was inconsistent. On the one hand, as Joseph F. Zimmerman wrote, "The Constitution basically is a document reflecting distrust of government and public officials."[19] That analysis could be justified based on the Constitution's extensive provisions limiting the Legisla-

---

18 Milton M. Klein, ed., *The Empire State: A History of New York,* Ithaca, NY: Cornell University Press, 2001, p. 392-3.

19 Joseph F. Zimmerman, *The Government and Politics of New York State*, New York, NY: New York University Press, 1981, p. 58.

ture's ability to incur debt and spend taxpayer dollars. On the other hand, the document required or allowed state government to act in a full spectrum of social areas, from housing to education to conservation.

Since 1960, at least 10 states have adopted new constitutions and several others have undertaken major constitutional review. These changes "have usually resulted in more streamlined constitutions and more effective state governments."[20]

Tough economic times often produce popular demands for change in government. The early 1990s brought significant economic difficulty to New York, including the loss of more than 500,000 jobs from 1990 to 1992. The job losses were far higher, proportionally, than those in the national economy, which suffered only a brief recession before resuming growth. Many business leaders and a number of newspaper editorials complained that the state's tax and other policies were driving jobs and residents elsewhere. *Forbes* printed a cover article with the headline: "One in three Americans who lost their jobs in the recession was a New Yorker. Other states gained jobs. Why?"[21]

Anticipating the 1997 ballot question on a constitutional convention, in 1993 Governor Cuomo appointed a Temporary Commission on Constitutional Revision to study the processes for holding a convention and to recommend issues it might address. "The people of New York State believe that they face a series of deepening problems that government is failing to address," the commission reported in February 1995. "Most New Yorkers are not united or even certain about what the solutions to those problems are.... Many have no confidence that current institutions are capable of finding solutions to those problems."[22] The commission pointed to the need for reform in fiscal integrity, state/local relations, education, and public safety.

Whether voters agreed with those sentiments, they overwhelmingly rejected the question on a convention in November 1997. One major factor was strong opposition by public-employee unions, organizations supporting abortion rights, environmental activists, and others who feared major changes in the Constitution. Still, within five years after

---

20 Galie, *The New York State Constitution*, p. xxii.

21 *Forbes*, January 31, 1994.

22 Temporary New York State Commission on Constitutional Revision, *Effective Government Now for the New Century*, February 1995, p. 1. The commission was chaired by former state budget director Peter C. Goldmark, Jr., and its staff provided by the Nelson A. Rockefeller Institute of Government.

the Commission's report, the state's elected leaders had enacted major changes to state policies in at least three of its areas of concern.

In a step that supporters said would end (or at least minimize) delays in adopting the annual state budget, the Legislature approved a statute withholding members' paychecks from the start of the fiscal year until budget adoption. Additionally, the Senate and Assembly adopted the practice of using joint conference committees to settle differences over the fiscal plan. In 2000, the budget was passed "only" a month past the April 1 start of the fiscal year — less than half the annual delay during most of the 1990s. (In 2001, however, final budget action did not come until October.) The commission identified "keeping the burden of taxation within reason" as a concern; Governor Pataki and the Legislature enacted reductions in most of the state's major taxes.

In education, the commission identified "failing" public schools as a critical concern, pointing to the need for greater focus on performance and results, and mechanisms for allowing parents to move children from schools that fail to others that succeed. The Board of Regents and Education Commissioner Richard Mills created "school report cards" and other significant accountability measures. And in December 1997, Governor Pataki and the Legislature enacted legislation authorizing 100 charter schools statewide, to give families choices outside the regular public school system. Meanwhile, a court challenge to the constitutionality of New York's school financing held the possibility of court-ordered change in that key area (*see Chapter Thirteen*).

Public safety improved substantially between the early 1990s and the turn of the century — crime rates fell sharply, most noticeably in New York City but throughout the state as well. One specific area cited by the commission was the problem of young, violent criminals; Governor Pataki and the Legislature enacted new laws there also.

In the area of state/local relations, the commission's concerns included numerous and overlapping local governments as well as costly and inefficient state mandates imposed on localities and school districts. Little has changed in those areas; the problem of state mandates driving property taxes higher has grown worse with the imposition of new health-care and pension costs.

Constitutional Reform Without a Convention

While much of the history of revision to New York's fundamental law revolves around constitutional conventions, many major changes emerged from the Legislature. Some of those changes — such as creation of the Executive Budget — were not, at first glance, likely to win approval from legislators who are notoriously jealous of their institutional power. But their passage shows that it is possible to shake things up in Albany even in the absence of a convention.

In 2006, for instance, most observers agreed that sharp increases in state borrowing under Governors Cuomo and Pataki showed the need for tighter constitutional restrictions on state debt. Governor Pataki, Comptroller Hevesi, and Senate Republicans proposed amendments that would, in varying ways, limit Albany's total outstanding debt to a fraction of total personal income in the state. None of the proposed amendments appeared likely to go before voters immediately. But they are examples of what might be done, without a convention, if political and other leaders created pressure on the Legislature to act.

Some observers have suggested creation of a constitutional commission, a group of distinguished New Yorkers that would be appointed by the governor and legislative leaders with the understanding that its proposals would receive serious consideration. Such an approach, combined with a campaign-style sales effort by a reform-minded governor, might be necessary to push through proposals such as independent redistricting of the Legislature — a favorite reform idea among many in Albany.

The theory of democratic government would hold that the actions of elected officials — including those that addressed issues raised by the Goldmark commission — generally reflect the demands of the voters. In some measure, then, it can be argued that the "loss" of the convention vote in 1997 did not necessarily mean that voters forfeited the chance to enact significant changes. In government, as in other spheres, tomorrow is always another day.

Chapter Eight

APPOINTED OFFICIALS, ADMINISTRATIVE LAW, AND THE BUREAUCRACY

Key points:

- Appointed officials in state agencies influence both the procedures and policies of government, bringing their own abilities, initiative and beliefs to the task.

- When adopting regulations, agencies must follow administrative procedures designed to give the public adequate opportunity to review and comment.

- Major industries such as banking and insurance are still regulated mostly by states, but Washington's involvement is increasing.

T he ultimate authority for state government is the state Constitution, approved directly by the people of New York. Elected officials hold the power to make wide-ranging decisions about public policy and allocation of state resources through statutes and budgets.

When New Yorkers actually experience state government at work, though, it is usually not through written laws or the political leaders who receive most of the media attention. Rather, it is through state-funded institutions and individuals who operate the various state agencies.

The men and women who are appointed to administer executive-branch agencies in any level of American government — certainly including the state of New York — wield enormous influence over both the procedures and policies of government. Richard P. Nathan calls such individuals "the governing class" and says of them:

> These officials do the heavy lifting of policymaking and management in America's governments.... As government has grown and become more involved in regulating and influencing more and more areas of our national life, so has the role of appointed officials....[1]

Later chapters of this book will look at the major operating agencies of state government. This chapter examines two broader elements common to most executive-branch agencies. It starts with a brief look at the role of top appointed officials in setting the policy priorities and operational style for a department. Then it examines the regulatory process through which agencies exert the power of state government over a wide variety of social and economic activities. The chapter also summarizes much of the economic regulation conducted by state government; some particular areas of such regulation, such as health and environmental protection, are discussed in later chapters. Finally, the chapter covers the extensive regulations that govern how the regulators themselves do their work.

Policy, Powers, and People

What agencies do, how they do it, and how well they achieve their goals reflect a combination of three broad factors.

First, agencies receive policy direction from elected leaders — including the governor as the head of the executive branch, and the Legislature and the governor through statute — as well as rulings handed down by courts. The head of almost every agency is appointed, and

---

1   Richard P. Nathan, *So You Want To Be In Government,* Albany, NY: Rockefeller Institute Press, 2000, p. 3.

most can be dismissed at any time, by the chief executive. The governor has complete authority over departmental budget requests to the Legislature, and controls the number of employees in each agency. Perhaps most importantly, the governor has the very real power to lay out a vision for state government and its agencies — whether it be achieving greater cost-efficiency, extending services to more New Yorkers, or promoting other policy goals.

Agencies are also responsible to the Legislature, and can be held accountable to the courts. Most of their activities are driven by statutes, and the Senate and Assembly have subpoena and other powers to investigate whether departments are fulfilling the will of the Legislature. As described in previous chapters, the Legislature shares with the governor control over every agency's budget; the Senate must approve most agency commissioners, along with members of important boards such as the Public Service Commission, before they take office; and the Legislature appoints the Board of Regents. Anyone can file suit against a state department, and court decisions occasionally require major changes in state policy. One example was the 1970s lawsuit challenging the Department of Mental Hygiene's care of mentally retarded clients, which ended in a settlement producing dramatic reforms.

Secondly, beyond broad policy direction, the state's elected officials give each agency a specific set of powers and responsibilities. Some departments, such as Health, have a long and multifaceted list. Others — Correctional Services, for instance — have a more focused mission.

The third factor that affects what agencies do, how they do it, and how well they achieve their goals is often overlooked. It is the set of human qualities that the people managing and operating the agencies bring to their jobs: their level of ability and personal initiative, commitment to the philosophy of the elected leadership, individual ideologies, and other intangible elements.

The Power of Appointed Officials

An agency executive with a vision, personal drive, and the support of elected leadership can make an enormous impact on state government and the society it serves. Perhaps the best example in New York's history is Robert Moses, who was responsible for developing the state park system as well as building roads and electric power projects in Long Island, New York City, along the Niagara Frontier, and on the St. Lawrence River at the Canadian border. Moses's involvement in these projects extended from creating the original vision to overseeing small details. He also developed and implemented the political strategy needed to secure approval for these projects — or, at least, to neutralize any opposition — from the Legislature, local elected officials, and powerful private individuals. His achievements were possible, though, because he had the support of elected leaders, starting with Governor Alfred E. Smith.

While no one surpasses Moses as an executive agency manager who got things done, countless others have brought about major changes in the state. Examples might include John O'Mara, who initiated the Public Service Commission's recent deregulation of the electric industry under Governor Pataki; Patricia Adduci, who led the customer-friendly transformation of the Department of Motor Vehicles under Governor Cuomo; David Axelrod, who won praise for his activist approach to public health as health commissioner under Governors Carey and Cuomo; and Raymond T. Schuler, who helped create the modern Transportation Department and served as its commissioner under Governors Rockefeller, Wilson, and Carey.

Advisers who do not hold a traditional appointive position sometimes play a major role as well. Belle Moskowitz was considered the most influential counselor to Governor Smith despite having no official position; Governor Carey made a personal friend, Dr. Kevin Cahill, his chief adviser on health issues for many years.

Just below the top rank of appointed officials are the managers who are largely responsible for implementing policy directives. Depending on the size of the agency and other factors, these positions may be part of the civil service or subject to the pleasure of the governor. (*Chapter Nine examines the state workforce at the civil-service level.*) Often, a primary challenge for individuals in such positions is marrying the policy and political dictates from above with the realities of bureaucratic operations below — a challenge faced by mid- to upper-level managers in large private-sector organizations as well. Institutional knowledge is a key resource managers use to succeed, as are the ability to bring disparate individuals and views together to advance a policy or program and good, long-term relationships with peers in other agencies. Managers at this level often have titles such as deputy commissioner or administrative officer.

How many appointed officials work in state government? The broadest definition might include all members of the managerial/confidential (M/C) classification as defined by the state's Civil Service Law. These employees — 12,000 in the regular executive branch agencies — encompass a broad range of occupations, including policymaking managers, middle managers, and specialists in fields as diverse as education, law, computer science, medicine, administrative support, and law enforcement. Civil Service Law treats M/C employees differently from others, in that they are not allowed to organize or bargain collectively on terms and conditions of employment owing to the nature of the work their positions require. Employees may be designated "managerial" if they formulate policy, assist the employer directly in preparing for or conducting negotiations, or play a major role (involving independent judgment) in administering labor agreements. Employees may be designated "confidential" if they assist and act in a confidential capacity to employees designated managerial.

Patronage, or Performance?

A more common measure of appointed positions is those filled at the pleasure of the governor, often through "patronage." The traditional view of patronage holds that top elected officials give jobs to political supporters with little concern for ability or experience. Clearly, governors (and legislative leaders, as well as elected officials at other levels of government) provide jobs directly to individual supporters and to others who have the backing of political patrons. While some such appointees may be unprepared for the job, as a general rule any administration can abide only a minimal level of incompetence before the potential political loss outweighs any gain.

Years before winning elective office himself, Daniel Patrick Moynihan coauthored a study of patronage in New York State during the administration of Democratic Governor W. Averell Harriman.[2] Nearly half a century after Harriman took office, the themes explored in that study remain relevant today.

---

2 The study, "Patronage in New York State, 1955-1959," appeared in *American Political Science Review* 58, 2 (June 1964): 286-301. The article does not define what constitutes a "patronage" appointment.

Harriman had appointed Carmine G. DeSapio, the leader of the Tammany Hall Democratic organization in Manhattan and an important player in the governor's election, as secretary of state. Moynihan, the state's future senator, served as an assistant to the governor, with duties that included involvement in the appointment process. Some five years after the end of the Harriman administration, with full access to its appointment records, the researchers counted 1,765 patronage jobs filled over the four-year term. As might be expected, most — nearly 62 percent — of those individuals were nominated by Democratic party officials, who also "cleared" another 12.1 percent. Roughly 16 percent of patronage appointments were based on personal, nonparty relationships. Another 4.6 percent — 81 new hires — came from Republicans, a greater number than the 3.1 percent from labor unions or 1.6 percent from the Liberal Party, both supporters of Governor Harriman.

Harriman "had only barely won the election, and such unity as the party had achieved during the campaign was evanescent at best," Moynihan and coauthor James Q. Wilson commented in the study. They added:

> ...at least two goals were to be served by the allocation of jobs — staffing the government with competent and attractive administrators, and acquiring and consolidating power over the party apparatus. These goals were obviously not always compatible, particularly when there was a chronic shortage of men whose qualifications would make their appointment contribute to the attainment of the first of these ends.[3]

Party patronage was "greatest in the least visible jobs," according to the study. The Albany Democratic organization, headed by legendary Chairman Dan O'Connell, was well-known for seeking low-paid positions for local party members, on the principle that the party could then demand a greater number of appointments (and win the gratitude of more voters). Among cabinet and "honorific" appointments, Republican party favorites received more than might have been expected given their status as the opposition party.

Often, approval of an appointment by a local county leader "was purely *pro forma*," according to the study: "The prospective appointee would, in the typical case, have to be an outspoken critic of the local leader in order to fail of clearance except in those cases where the leader

---

3   Ibid, p. 286.

Long-Term Appointments

Over many decades, New York's legislators and governors have created important policymaking boards whose members' terms extend beyond those of the elected officials who appoint them. Examples include the State University Board of Trustees, Public Service Commission (PSC), Workers' Compensation Board, Unemployment Insurance Appeals Board, and others.

Such boards are ostensibly intended to make agencies more independent from electoral concerns, and less susceptible to short-term policy changes, than those whose administrators can be removed at the pleasure of the chief executive. Most governors find ways to bend such agencies to their will, however. Immediately after taking office in 1995, for instance, Governor Pataki's appointment power at the SUNY board and the Public Service Commission (PSC) represented a minority of seats in each case. Yet both institutions adopted major changes in policy in fairly short order. Some holdover appointees were willing to go along with the new administration's preferences, while others were persuaded to step down.

In 2006, Governor Pataki made some long-term appointments that critics said violated longstanding tradition of leaving key policymaking positions for a succeeding governor. Examples included Peter Kalikow, reappointed to a six-year term as chairman of the important Metropolitan Transit Authority, and Charles Gargano, to a six-year term on the board of the Port Authority of New York and New Jersey. The criticism reflected broad understanding in Albany that the "independent" agencies aren't expected to be so independent from newly elected officials, after all.

had his own favorite whose candidacy he was actively pressing." If nothing else, the need for even *pro forma* clearance reduces the number of individuals who might become "outspoken critics" of a party leader.

Whatever other role the patronage process served, Moynihan and Wilson wrote, "Governor Harriman surely desired to have enough power over the state government to have a reasonable chance of putting into effect the policies he favored and of making certain that the routine business of government was carried on with reasonable efficiency and honesty."[4] Clearly, the same is true of virtually any elected executive. Most voters, too, are more interested in the policies and efficiency of a given administration than in the backgrounds of those who win patronage appointments.

While patronage has a bad name, many experienced and accomplished leaders in government believe that appointment of political loyalists is essential to achieving elected officials' goals. Certainly an unresponsive civil service has been known to stand in the way of efficient government (*see Chapter Nine*). Some government observers believe *more* appointments made at the pleasure of the elected leader would improve the effectiveness of public services. At the least, it can be said that "good citizenship and political power go together. Although many appointed leaders serve because of their commitment to their country and their community, those who succeed do so because they also have political skills or because they learn on the job how to be effective politically."[5]

State Agency Powers: Regulation

Different areas of state government have widely disparate responsibilities, as outlined in succeeding chapters. Agencies' powers and responsibilities can be classified most broadly as *operational* or *regulatory*. For example, when the Department of Transportation builds or maintains a highway, it's engaging in operational activity. When the department issues a license to a motor carrier or approves rates for a household moving company, that work is regulatory.

Regulatory aspects of government, in turn, include three broad categories:

- *Rulemaking*: Executive-branch agencies perform functions similar to that of the legislative branch — writing rules and regulations that have the force of law and general application. Agency rules must be based on statutory authority granted by the Legislature. Agencies generally must go through a highly detailed process of seeking public input before regulations can take effect.

---

4   Ibid, p. 300.

5   Nathan, *So You Want To Be In Government?*, p. 24.

- *Adjudication*: Agencies also act like courts sometimes — considering evidence and making rulings in specific cases. Examples in New York include adjudication of more than 300,000 disability claims annually by the Office of Temporary and Disability Assistance.

- *Licensing*: The Department of Motor Vehicles licenses some 2.7 million drivers statewide. In 2004, the Education Department licensed 193,079 registered nurses; 15,692 professional engineers; and 178 interior designers.[6] Other licensing agencies include the departments of State, Environmental Conservation, and Insurance.

Precisely because these and other state agencies hold such extensive power over individuals and businesses, they have been made subject to detailed rules and limitations on how they use that power. (Those regulations on the regulators will be described later in this chapter.)

Regulating Business Relationships

Regulating private economic activity has always been a central activity of state government. The first charters granted by Dutch authorities in the early 1600s gave particular companies exclusive rights to do business in the area we now call New York State. These first "constitutions" for the state gave local company directors, as described in earlier chapters, not only economic power but full governmental authority, "subject only to appellate review by the authorities in Holland."[7]

Most of what we think of as regulation today, however, is of much more modern vintage — dating from within the last century. Detailed governmental oversight of business activity emerged as a result of several factors. The Industrial Revolution created huge new sources of wealth, concentration of economic power, and social problems that previously were unknown, or at least of relatively lower priority. Perceptions of the essential role of government evolved to include greater measures of protection for society and individuals. Rising levels of

---

6   *2005 New York State Statistical Yearbook*, Albany, NY: Nelson A. Rockefeller Institute of Government, p. 164.

7   Galie, *Ordered Liberty*, p. 12.

education and income gave more Americans the freedom to focus on broader social issues.

Today state government regulates virtually every organized business activity. Some industries receive particularly close attention from Albany; our review of state regulation starts with them.

Public Service Commission

For most of the 20th century, no industry was more heavily regulated by state government than the energy industry — particularly electricity and natural gas. The first well that was intentionally drilled to obtain natural gas is believed to have been in Fredonia, in the western part of the state. By the late 1800s, most city street lights were fueled by gas. Complaints of high prices prompted the Legislature to appoint an investigative committee in 1905, and Charles Evans Hughes was named committee counsel. The Legislature enacted laws regulating the prices of both gas and electricity as a result of the investigation (federal regulation of the gas industry did not come until 1938). Two years after that inquiry, as governor, Hughes generated strong public support for his proposal to establish an ongoing Public Service Commission, and won approval from the Legislature.

Today, the Department of Public Service has a broad mandate to ensure that all New Yorkers have access to reliable and low-cost utility services. The department is the staff arm of the Public Service Commission, which regulates electric, gas, steam, telecommunications, and water utilities and oversees the cable television industry.

The commission has the legal responsibility to set certain rates as well as ensure that utility companies provide adequate service — a complex mixture of roles that requires a careful balancing of priorities. On the one hand, every state resident — and therefore every elected official — wants utility rates set as low as possible. On the other hand, companies that sell or deliver electricity, for instance, must have adequate revenues to pay for construction and maintenance of generating plants, transmission lines, and other essential parts of the system — as well as profits to attract the investment capital that pays for all that infrastructure.

The commission also exercises jurisdiction over the siting of major gas and electric transmission facilities, and ensures the safety of natural gas and liquid petroleum pipelines.

Bipartisan by law since 1970, the commission consists of up to five members, each appointed by the governor and confirmed by the Senate for a term of six years, or to complete an unexpired term of a former commissioner. The chairman, designated by the governor, is the chief executive officer of the department. Department staff represent all rate-payers and "the public interest" in commission proceedings, set service and operating standards for utilities, and administer regulations issued by the commission. The department helps consumers with complaints against utilities, receiving well over 100,000 calls in a typical year.

In recent years, the PSC's most visible undertakings have included overseeing creation of competitive marketplaces in the electric and natural gas industries, and encouraging development of "renewable" sources of electricity. After taking office in 1995, Governor Pataki charged the commission with giving consumers more choices and the marketplace a greater role in determining prices. The expectation was that, once the marketplace became competitive, the commission would reduce its regulatory oversight further. The dramatic change in state government's approach to this major regulatory issue was accomplished through action by the executive branch. Members of the Assembly majority complained that the issue required legislative action, and passed bills that took a different approach to deregulation, but the Senate did not take up the bills. A decade later, market competition was still developing.

In late 1997 and early 1998, the commission approved rate reductions and industry restructuring plans with each of the state's electrical utilities, covering the entire state outside Long Island. (Governor Pataki and the Legislature had previously enacted legislation creating the Long Island Power Authority, which assumed control of most of the assets of the former utility, the Long Island Lighting Co.) Each agreement set terms for introducing retail competition, under which customers could purchase electricity from any supplier. Each utility divested its generating plants. As of June 2006, about 10 percent of customers in the state had taken advantage of the freedom to have their electricity delivered by a supplier other than the regional utility, according to the PSC. Those customers — mainly large users of electricity — represented 43 percent of all power used in the state. Yet while new companies were making inroads in delivery of electricity, progress on competition in electric generation was slow. After expiration of the state's Article X plant-siting legislation, investors were reluctant to devote the millions of dollars needed to seek regulatory approvals for generating plants.

In his 2003 State of the State address, Governor Pataki directed the PSC to implement a "renewable portfolio standard" to guarantee that, within 10 years, at least 25 percent of electricity bought in the state would come from "renewable energy resources like solar power, wind power, or fuel cells." The commission adopted the mandate in 2005, including hydropower, which already represented more than 15 percent of generation in the state.

By mid-2006, investors were proposing windmill farms for several locations in the Adirondacks and elsewhere. Some such proposals aroused stiff opposition from neighboring residents concerned about noise, impact on scenic views, and other potential impacts on quality of life. It appeared likely that wind power would become more common, yet remain a relatively small contributor to the state's overall energy demand. Given that, it was uncertain how the state would meet the PSC's 25 percent goal for renewable sources of electric power.

Banking and Insurance Regulation

New York State — in particular, New York City — has been one of the world's leading centers of financial services for well over a century. The state agencies that regulate insurance and banking are among the most important overseers of financial firms in the world.

Both banking and insurance, of course, play fundamental roles in the modern economy. Banks facilitate the use of money by providing credit, by transacting payments that in turn make possible the exchange of goods and services, and by giving companies and individuals a secure place for holding financial assets. Insurance gives property owners the ability to minimize the financial risk inherent in purchasing, say, a home that might someday burn down, or a multimillion-dollar ship that might sink in a storm. Economists say those functions encourage investment and wealth creation, which in turn produce job growth and improved standards of living. The fundamental mission of both the Banking Department and the Insurance Department is to ensure that banks and insurers will have the assets to pay creditors and insured losses — providing a second measure of financial stability behind that provided by the regulated companies themselves.

Losing Influence to Washington

In the competition for regulatory authority, state bank regulators — including New York's Banking Department — are losing ground to the federal government. In her 2004 Annual Report, Banking Superintendent Diana L. Taylor wrote:

> ... this was a year of fundamental and tumultuous change in the regulation of the financial industry. The year began with the (Office of the Comptroller of the Currency) making permanent its preemption of lending and deposit laws for national banks; exempting them from the enforcement of any consumer protection laws by any entity other than itself; and granting operating subsidiaries the same preemption rights and visitorial immunity as the parent banks.

For the Department this was troubling: for consumers, the news could not have been worse. The effect of this ruling is that national banks and their operating subsidiaries no longer have to obey state consumer protection laws and no entity other than the Office of the Comptroller of the Currency (OCC) has the right to go into a nationally chartered bank or its operating subsidiaries to enforce any of those laws. The result is that a consumer is protected to a different standard depending on which institution they go to for a financial product, such as a mortgage loan. In New York, that standard is significantly lower for nationally chartered banks than for those chartered by the state.

The increasing federal preemption, Superintendent Taylor wrote, "has highlighted the fact that we state regulators operate in a competitive environment, and we need to add value in our examinations."

In January 2004, the state attorney general's office sued a subsidiary of First Tennessee Bank, a nationally chartered bank, alleging that it improperly sought to foreclose on the home of a Rensselaer County couple, Robert and Marsha Hall. Attorney General Spitzer said the case represented inadequate consumer protection by the Comptroller of the Currency.

Federal regulators agree that they compete with state agencies, but have a different view of their efforts to preempt state regulations. Some such changes in recent years simply codify longstand-

addition, the feds argue, all banks remain subject to state laws regarding contracts, torts, financial crimes, discrimination, and other issues.*

In recent years, two major banks in New York — HSBC and JPMorgan Chase — changed to federal charters. Among other implications, the moves meant a loss to the Banking Department of 30 percent of the fees that provide its operating budget. With approval from the Legislature and Governor Pataki, the department began to assess fees on nonbank institutions. The department's staffing has remained relatively unchanged.

Total assets of institutions regulated by the department have fallen by a third in just a few years, from nearly $2 trillion in 2001 to $1.3 trillion in 2004. That reflects not only a trend toward federal chartering, but movement in the banking industry out of the Empire State. New York's share of the nation's commercial bank assets has fallen from 22 percent of the U.S. total in 2000 to 12 percent in 2006, as assets held in New York have declined and the nationwide total has risen sharply.

---

*   Testimony to Senate Committee on Banking, Housing and Urban Affairs by Comptroller of the Currency John D. Hawke, Jr., April 7, 2004.

The two agencies share another important feature: In addition to regulating key industries, each is charged with promoting New York State as a home for the businesses it regulates. Both departments are aware that other states compete to attract headquarters and regional offices of insurance and banking companies as well as other industries. The Banking Department has another source of "competition" — federal agencies that charter and supervise banks, including the Office of the Comptroller of the Currency (part of the Treasury Department) and the Federal Reserve System. Over the past two decades or so, many banks that had been state-chartered have changed to federal charters to make it easier to do business in several states, or for other reasons. State officials prefer that banks remain New York-chartered, partly to maintain regulatory influence and the fees that pay for department operations, and partly out of a belief that a state charter increases the company's long-term commitment to New York. For both the Banking and Insurance departments, the twin missions of regulating companies, on the one hand, and encouraging their presence and growth in New York on the other hand sometimes are in tension.

The Banking Department

In the first few decades of American independence, when the Empire State grew into the leadership role reflected in its nickname, "banks played a critical role in the state's extraordinary economic growth.... They were the principal mechanisms for pooling capital for investment in transportation, commerce, and manufacturing."[8] Alexander Hamilton, the nation's first treasury secretary, founded the Bank of New York in 1784. It, the Bank of Albany, Manhattan Bank, and others issued bank notes that served as currency and extended credit.

Early state regulation of banks, in New York and elsewhere, was limited largely to chartering of banks through special laws. "Such acts opened chartering to political favoritism, however, and public opinion eventually led to passage of 'free banking' acts. The first free banking acts were passed in Connecticut, Michigan, and New York in 1837 and 1838, and other states later passed similar acts. Essentially incorporation laws, they allowed anyone meeting certain standards and requirements to secure a bank charter."[9]

An 1829 law created the Bank Fund, later renamed the Safety Fund, to guarantee the payment of debts of insolvent banks. All state-chartered banks were required to make an annual contribution to the fund, which was managed by the state treasurer. The same law provided for the appointment of three bank commissioners to examine the financial status of banks and to report annually to the legislature. The 1838 "free banking" law increased regulatory requirements, including an annual report to the comptroller.

The Banking Department was established in 1851 and is the oldest bank regulatory agency in the nation. It is the primary regulator of some 300 depository institutions such as banks and credit unions, and another 3,000 finance companies, money transmitters, licensed lenders, check cashers, mortgage brokers, and other financial institutions operating in the state.

---

8   Milton M. Klein, ed., *The Empire State: A History of New York,* Ithaca, NY: Cornell University Press, 2001, p. 320.

9   Kenneth Spong, *Banking Regulation: Its Purposes, Implementation, and Effects,* Kansas City, MO: Federal Reserve Bank of Kansas City, 2000, p. 17.

A generation ago, New York was home to many of the largest banking companies in the nation and worldwide. That is less true today. Consolidation in banking and the broader financial services industry has reduced the number of banks nationwide from roughly 14,000 to 9,000 or so over the last several decades, and some New York banks have been absorbed into companies headquartered in other states or other countries. But New York City remains one of three worldwide banking centers, along with London and Tokyo. The state remains the national leader in commercial bank assets, with $1.1 trillion — 12 percent of the U.S. total — in 2004.[10] The state is far and away the most important U.S. home for international banking; as of the end of 2000, according to the Banking Department, it supervised more than 80 percent of the assets held by foreign bank entities in the United States.[11] New York's department is unique among American bank regulators in numerous respects. For example, it is the only agency to maintain an overseas office (in London; a Tokyo office closed in 2004), and the only one with a special bureau for criminal investigations. The department also remains a leader in addressing new regulatory areas — for instance, in 2000 it adopted regulations on low-cost home loans that have been adopted in part by other states and by the Federal Reserve system.

The Banking Department's regulatory oversight also includes measuring banks' compliance with the state Community Reinvestment Act. That law encourages banks to invest in local communities by funding community housing and other public projects, and offering mortgage and small-business loans in low- and moderate-income areas. The department's regulations are approved by the quasi-legislative Banking Board, a 17-member group chaired by the superintendent of banks and including eight members from the banking industry and eight from the public.

The Insurance Department

As with banks, insurance companies doing business in New York were chartered by special acts of the Legislature for several decades after the state's founding. Laws enacted in 1849 and 1853 did away with the need for special legislation and required prospective insurance com-

---

10   Federal Deposit Insurance Corp. data; see *www.fdic.gov.*

11   See the department's website, *www.banking.state.ny.us.*

panies to file incorporation papers with the secretary of state. The 1849 statute also vested some regulatory power over insurance companies with the state comptroller, who was authorized to require the companies to submit annual financial statements and to deny a company the right to operate if capital securities and investments did not remain secure.

The Insurance Department was established in 1860 as the first independent regulatory agency in the country. Its most basic mission is to ensure that insurance companies will have the assets to pay any claims for losses — to "ensure the continued sound and prudent conduct of insurers' financial operations," in the department's words. Toward this end, it examines insurance companies' financial condition; regulates rates for most types of insurance; protects policyholders from financially impaired or insolvent insurers; works to eliminate fraud, which drives up costs to honest policy holders; and promotes growth of the insurance industry in the state. The department licenses agents, brokers, consultants, adjusters, and others involved in insurance, and uses that power to fulfill its mission of protecting consumers. In rare instances, the department will assume control of an insurance company that is facing insolvency, attempting to return it to financial stability, and in some cases finding another company to take over the business.

Unlike the banking and securities industries — both of which have significant oversight by federal agencies along with state regulation — insurance is regulated mainly by the states. Given New York's status as a world capital to the industry, the state Insurance Department is among the most important insurance regulators in the world. Insurance companies are chartered under the laws of a single state. Officials in other states where they conduct business typically rely on the home state to be the primary regulator, particularly in New York's case, given the sophistication of the state's Insurance Department. Federal legislation enacted in 1999 allows banking, securities, and insurance activities to be merged within the same company. That law creates new challenges for regulators — for instance, greater concentration of assets — which the Banking and Insurance departments are now addressing.

Both the Banking and Insurance departments are headed by superintendents appointed by the governor with the consent of the Senate. Each is funded by fees on the businesses it regulates. Those assessments, passed on to consumers, represent a modest increase in costs to consumers in exchange for reduced risk of financial losses. In fiscal 2001,

State, or Federal, Regulation of Insurers?

In 1999, Congress passed and President Clinton signed the Gramm-Leach-Bliley Financial Services Modernization Act. Among other things, the law paved the way for continued consolidation of financial-services firms.

The law reaffirmed state leadership in regulation of most insurance products. As banks and mutual-fund companies began competing more directly with insurers, the insurance industry increasingly saw state-level regulation as overly complex and harmful to its competitive position. For instance, securities firms can obtain regulatory approval for new investment products within a month or two, but insurance companies may need two years for 50 state agencies to approve a competing product, insurers say.

"Reform proposals at the national level are moving in two directions," an industry group, the Insurance Information Institute, wrote in 2006. "One is a dual (federal/state) chartering system similar to the banking industry's dual regulatory system that would allow companies to choose between the state system and a national regulatory structure that would eliminate the need to comply with 51 sets of different regulations. The other is modernization of the state system. One proposal would create a framework for a national system of state-based regulation, which would create uniform standards in such areas as market conduct, licensing, the filing of new products and reinsurance. Among those supporting an optional charter are large insurers that sell coverage to major corporations, reinsurers, brokerage firms, life insurers and banks that are moving into the insurance business."[*]

Some state officials and consumer groups argued that complexity and variation in insurance products require preservation of the traditional state-level approach.

"Banking/financial service products tend to have few variations within a product line," state Senator William J. Larkin wrote in 2003. "In contrast, insurance products tend to be complex contracts that provide a wide variety of coverages depending on the fortuitous event that triggers coverage. In addition, each state's tort and common law heritage can help to interpret the same insurance policy

---

[*]   Insurance Information Institute, "Modernizing Insurance Regulation," August 2006, www.iii.org.

contract in different ways depending on the state where the insurable event occurred; for insurance products, it is fitting for the states to be the primary regulator."**

One example of how complex insurance policies, and consumer ignorance of their provisions, came after parts of the Mohawk Valley and Southern Tier suffered extensive flooding in mid-2006. Some homeowners and businesses found their insurance policies providing no compensation — an unexpected and deeply distressing development. Those policies, though, were written under the longstanding system of state regulation.

Future changes in insurance regulation will play out in the context of potential change in partisan control of Congress, voter skepticism about big business, competition among major financial industries and other factors.

**   William J. Larkin and J. Stephen Casscles, "Defending the State Regulation of the Business of Insurance," *Empire State Report*, Mount Vernon, NY, May 2003, p. 27.

the Banking Department had an estimated 619 employees, with a total budget of $67 billion. The Insurance Department employed 944 individuals, with a budget of $118 million, including nearly $20 million paid to the Department of State for costs associated with fire-prevention and building code enforcement efforts.

Securities firms operating in New York are regulated by the attorney general *(see Chapter Four)* as well as by the federal government.

The Department of State

Agencies such as the Public Service Commission, Department of Environmental Conservation, and the Banking and Insurance departments are often in the news because they regulate big businesses that provide services to millions of New Yorkers. But perhaps no state office has a broader impact on business activity than a lesser-known agency, the Department of State.

More than 650,000 individuals are licensed through the department — men and women who make a living as real-estate agents, barbers, cosmetologists, security guards, and bail enforcement agents, to name just a few. Operators of pet cemeteries are regulated by the department, as are telemarketers and manufacturers of bedding.

The department is something of a catch-all for regulatory activity the Legislature considers outside the realm of other agencies. In mid-2006, for instance, the department was preparing to adopt regulations requiring home inspectors to maintain liability insurance coverage of at least $150,000 per occurrence and $500,000 in the aggregate. Other pending regulations would establish energy-efficiency standards for appliances sold in the state — items such as ice-cube machines, ceiling fan light kits, and illuminated exit signs.

The Department of State also oversees the state's fire prevention and building codes. Those rules directly influence the nature and cost of construction for all new buildings in the state.

Corporations that organize in New York — both business and nonprofit — must register with the Department of State. A corporation is a legal entity that is separate, for liability and other purposes, from the individual or persons who form it. Corporations must designate the Secretary of State as an agent for service of legal papers, so anyone seeking legal redress against the corporation will have the opportunity to pursue a claim. The agency also maintains records such as the names of corporate officers and directors, date of organization, and other information. The department's Uniform Commercial Code Bureau maintains records on financial obligations such as Internal Revenue Service liens that are incurred by individuals doing business as sole proprietors, corporations, and other business entities.

Through its Division of Coastal Resources, the agency also has regulatory powers over development and use of property along state coastlines — including estuaries such as much of the Hudson River.

Administrative Law:
Authority Under the Statutes

As Chapter One makes clear, state government touches the lives of millions of New Yorkers every day — through everything from the roads we ride on, to our public schools, to state parks, to regulations for driving motor vehicles and running factories.

Ultimately, every one of those activities must be based on authority that the people have given to government through the state

Constitution.[12] After the Constitution, the functions of state government are driven by New York State's body of written law. For instance, Montauk Point State Park, where the rising sun strikes the eastern tip of Long Island each day, exists by virtue of the state's Parks, Recreation and Historic Preservation Law. The law declares, as a matter of state policy:

> The state of New York is abundant in natural, scenic and other recreational resources, which for over a century have educated, edified, uplifted and delighted our citizens. The establishment and maintenance of a statewide system of parks, recreation and historic preservation are hereby declared to be policies of the state....

The law further provides that the Office of Parks, Recreation and Historic Preservation "shall ... acquire and establish historic sites and objects and ... state parks, parkways and state recreational facilities." The agency shall, the law says, "operate and maintain, either directly, or by contract, lease or license, such historic sites and objects, parks, parkways and recreational facilities." The statute grants the agency further authority in a number of areas, including such detailed powers as leasing bathhouses at the Saratoga Spa State Park "for reasonable consideration and for a term not to exceed forty years."

Whether a state agency makes a decision at the broad policy level or addresses an individual case, *every action that any state government agency or worker takes must ultimately be based in law.* One authority puts it this way: "Governmental actions are defined and controlled by special provisions of the Constitution and laws. As such, government actions must be accomplished in particular ways. The need for responsiveness and responsibility in government agencies requires that legal guidelines be carefully drawn in cases where government acts."[13]

Over time, the courts and elected representatives have prescribed certain procedures that administrators must follow. The earliest of these came from court cases dealing with the tension between the citizen's right to due process and the administrator's legislatively delegated

---

12 Some Constitutional scholars posit that state governments, having descended from royal grants of authority, historically had broad powers that were limited by their constitutions. Such plenary powers would stand in contrast to those of the federal government, where the Tenth Amendment to the Constitution specifically reserves to the states and the people any powers not delegated to the national government.

13 Philip J. Cooper, *Public Law and Public Administration*, Englewood Cliffs, NJ: Prentice Hall, 1988, p. 3

powers. While administrators are granted authority to act in particular areas, the citizen is guaranteed by the 14th Amendment to the U.S. Constitution that:

> No state shall make or enforce any law which shall abridge the privileges or immunities of citizens of the United States; nor shall any state deprive any person of life, liberty or property without due process of law; nor deny to any person within its jurisdiction the equal protection of the laws.[14]

Agencies are required to ensure not only that their actions are affirmatively based in law, but that those actions are not contrary to the various constitutional and other protections citizens have against a government that might take too much power unto itself.

Questions about the very legitimacy of government agencies — to say nothing of their actions — date from the early days of the United States. In 1819, for instance, the Supreme Court was asked to decide whether Congress had the power to create the Bank of the United States as a central financial institution. Such power was not specifically in the Constitution. Chief Justice Marshall, writing for the court, cited powers that the Constitution does grant to Congress as the basis for deciding that creation of the bank was also permissible.[15]

For more than a century, departments of both federal and state governments were primarily operational in nature — dedicated to tasks such as fighting wars, issuing currency, and raising revenue. By the early part of the 20th century, that had begun to change. Responding to public concerns over issues ranging from labor to health, both the national government and states began taking on regulatory powers regarding private economic activity. In 1905, for instance, voters in New York approved a Constitutional amendment that permitted the Legislature to regulate wages, hours, and working conditions for laborers employed by the state or on public contracts; such authority was vested in the Department of Labor.

Before too long, the regulatory agencies themselves had become a source of some concern. The 1938 Constitutional Convention proposed, and voters approved, a new section to the executive article of the

---

14 One good source for the text of, and other formation about, the U.S. Constitution is the National Archives website, *www.archives.gov.*

15 *McCulloch* v. *Maryland*, 17 U.S. (4 Wheat.) 316 (1819)

Constitution ensuring a chance for public review of any agency rule. The provision stipulated that no state agency rule or regulation — aside from internal matters — can take effect before being filed with the Department of State. The section (Article IV, Section 8) instructs the Legislature to "provide for the speedy publication of such rules and regulations."

"Prior to this provision, with few exceptions, there were no public rules or regulations of which the public had any notice," Galie writes. "Its adoption was a reflection of the growing size and importance of the bureaucracy and administrative law in the daily lives of citizens."[16]

Over succeeding decades, reflecting and sometimes leading a national trend, New York's governors and the Legislature assigned more regulatory powers to state agencies.

In 1956, for instance, the Department of Motor Vehicles was given the power to oversee required annual inspection of vehicles more than four years old, and the superintendent of insurance was authorized to oversee union welfare funds, an increasingly important source of insurance and other benefits for workers.[17] In the 1960s and 1970s, Governors Rockefeller and Carey worked with the Legislature to enact major new laws aimed at protecting the state's water, air, and lands; the Department of Environmental Conservation became more powerful in implementing those laws as well as others enacted by Congress.

Regulating the Regulators: SAPA

By the early 1970s, elected leaders were showing more concern about the regulatory authority and practices of state agencies. In 1975, Governor Carey and the Legislature enacted the State Administrative Procedure Act (SAPA), setting clear and consistent rules for agencies to follow in regulatory activities. The statute includes many of the provisions of the federal Administrative Procedure Act, which was enacted in several phases starting in the 1940s.

Although the concept of public access to agency decision-making processes had been established before the passage of SAPA,

---

16 Galie, p. 107.

17 *The New York Red Book 1956*, Albany, NY: Williams Press Inc., 1956 edition, pp. 71-2.

administrators generally had to rely on case law for guidance on how to provide citizens with adequate due process. Given varying interpretations of court decisions, these principles were applied inconsistently.

SAPA might be considered as something of a bill of rights for individuals, local governments, businesses, and other organizations affected by state regulatory agencies. New York's original administrative procedures act included a requirement that agencies print each proposed rule in the *State Register* — a compendium of state government announcements published by the Department of State — at least 30 days before the rule was to become effective. (This was a statutory extension of the constitutional mandate that proposed rules be filed with the Department of State and published for public information.)

Since SAPA's enactment, state leaders have expanded the statute and adopted other requirements for agencies. Today, the law requires that "each agency shall strive to ensure that, to the maximum extent practical, its rules, regulations and related documents are written in a clear and coherent manner, using words with common and everyday meanings." It also creates rules that agencies must follow in each of the three major regulatory areas — rulemaking, adjudicatory proceedings, and licensing.

Rulemaking

Unlike SAPA's provisions regarding adjudication and licensing, those covering rulemaking have been changed numerous times since the statute's original enactment in 1975 — usually, though not always, imposing more rules on those who issue agency rules.

SAPA does not dictate what types of rules agencies may impose. Rather, it creates a process they must follow in adopting new regulations. The process is intended, generally, to ensure that agencies give full consideration to any potential harm that might result from a proposed action, in hopes of minimizing its unintended consequences.

Publication of a proposed rule now generally must take place at least 45 days before a regulation is adopted (the effective date is usually two weeks after the adoption is filed) or before a public hearing is to be held. Agencies may, but are not required to, publish the notice in general-circulation newspapers or specialized publications as well as the *State Register.*

The Eternal Search for Better Regulations

Governors control the state's regulatory departments by appointing their top officials, approving every dollar in their budgets, and overseeing their regulatory activities. Still, virtually every chief executive complains about the work of those agencies. Some of their comments:

> "The time has come for New York to acknowledge and accept the principle that the agencies of government must respond to the needs of the governed, not only substantively, but also procedurally." — Governor Hugh L. Carey, on signing legislation enacting the State Administrative Procedure Act, June 3, 1975.

> "There has been a growing concern over the regulatory burdens and concomitant costs placed upon businesses, professionals and the general public by the State and its regulatory agencies." — Governor Mario M. Cuomo, announcing his approval of legislation to create the Office of Business Permits and Regulatory Assistance, Chapter 698, Laws of 1984, August 3, 1984.

> "We will reinvent regulation by demanding that our agencies care about people and jobs, not just paperwork and rules." — Governor George E. Pataki, announcing a temporary moratorium on regulations that affect the economy, January 5, 1995.

Agencies must also:

- Consider ways to "avoid undue deleterious economic effects or overly burdensome impacts" on affected parties, or upon "the economy or administration of state or local government agencies."

- Prepare a "regulatory impact statement" that indicates the need for the rule, along with the expected benefits and costs to the state, local governments, and regulated parties. Such statement must describe the need for paperwork that the new rule would create; compare the proposed requirements with existing state and federal rules; discuss whether any "significant" alternatives were considered, along with why they

were not used; outline any new mandate on local governments and school districts; and estimate the "time necessary
to enable regulated persons to achieve compliance with the
rule."

• Give particular consideration to a proposed rule's impact on
small businesses (defined as independently owned and operated in New York and employing 100 or fewer individuals),
local governments, and rural areas. Agencies must consider
using compliance or reporting requirements that "take into
account the resources available" to small businesses and local governments. They are also required to consider using
"performance rather than design standards," and exempting
small businesses from new rules "so long as the public
health, safety or general welfare is not endangered."

• Issue a "regulatory flexibility analysis" estimating how many
and what types of small businesses and local governments
would be affected; and describing the compliance requirements and the professional services small businesses and local
governments would need to comply. The analysis is also supposed to estimate the initial capital cost and annual costs of
complying with the regulation, and indicate how the rule is
designed to minimize any financial harm to small businesses
and local governments. The agency must "assure that small
businesses and local governments have been given an opportunity to participate in the rule making" through steps such as
publishing notices in specialized publications.[18]

SAPA gives agencies the power to issue a "declaratory ruling" on request of a regulated person or organization. Such a ruling may be helpful to a business, nonprofit organization, or individual because it can
indicate whether the requesting party is subject to a rule or law
enforceable by the agency.

In 1996, after more than a decade of efforts to use SAPA to convince
regulatory agencies to consider the regulated community, the Legislature placed particular importance on requiring agencies to consider the
impact of proposed rules on job growth. When "it is apparent" that the
rule may have a "substantial adverse impact" (leading to the loss of 100

---

18 Citations are from State Administrative Procedure Act, Sections 202-a and 202-b.

or more jobs over two years), the agency must issue a Job Impact Statement with information including the nature and approximate number of the jobs affected, and any measures taken to minimize job losses. In an Assembly memorandum of support, legislative sponsors wrote: "Unless an agency operates with an awareness of the impact its actions may have on jobs and employment opportunities, its ability to effectively minimize any adverse employment impacts of its rules and regulations will be compromised."[19] As implementation of the requirement depends on agencies acknowledging that a proposal will cause significant economic harm, its usefulness remains uncertain.

Another 1996 addition to SAPA could have greater impact. Section 207 of the statute requires that all rules adopted after January 1, 1997, must be reviewed and justified in their fifth year of existence, and at five-year intervals thereafter. As of 2006, however, few rules had changed as a result of such reviews.

Executive Chamber Oversight of Regulations

Before going through the requirements of SAPA, agencies generally must receive Executive Chamber approval. Under Governor Pataki, the office performing such review was called the Governor's Office of Regulatory Reform. The office was created in 1979 as the Office of Business Permits, a one-stop shopping office for companies seeking a variety of state permits. In 1985 its mission was expanded legislatively and it became the Office of Business Permits and Regulatory Assistance, conducting studies on regulatory problems and offering assistance in some cases.

In addition, agencies may publish a "regulatory agenda" of rules the agencies are considering proposing. A number of major regulatory agencies (Health, Education, Environmental Conservation, Social Services, Insurance, Labor, Banking, Agriculture and Markets, Housing and Community Renewal, and the Workers Compensation Board) are required to publish a regulatory agenda once or twice a year.

Agencies' rulemaking is also subject to oversight by a legislative panel, the Administrative Regulations Review Commission (ARRC). Its staff analyzes proposed rules with respect to statutory authority,

---

19 *McKinney's 1996 Session Laws of New York,* Vol. 2, St. Paul, MN: West Group, 1997, p. 2162.

compliance with legislative intent, impact on the economy and the operations of state and local governments, and impact on affected parties. The commission, created by a 1978 law, has no power to block or amend regulations but can help legislators raise questions about proposed regulations — or, in extreme cases, consider legislation to overturn agency rules.

State rule makers have sometimes been advised to be aware of three questions a court would ask if regulations faced a legal challenge:

- What is the statutory basis for agency authority in this area? This may involve an examination of the agency's interpretation of the statute and an inquiry as to whether the act is within the bounds set by the Legislature.

- Did the agency follow the proper procedures, as established by the State Administrative Procedure Act and elsewhere?

- Was the decision within the realm of reasonableness? Agencies are considered the experts in the field, and judges generally defer to their expertise. To convince a judge to strike down a decision on the issue of unreasonableness, a plaintiff generally must show that the decision was irrational or fundamentally flawed, or went against the weight of evidence.

These questions apply to any official action, whether it stems from the agency's rulemaking, licensing, investigatory, or enforcement powers.[20]

Regulatory agencies sometimes act in ways that are informal but can have essentially the same effect as adoption of official regulations. Agencies have been known to make wide-ranging policy through advisory opinions, memoranda, letters, and even telephone calls. Businesses and other organizations that deal continuously with the Department of Environmental Conservation and other agencies sometimes complain that these forms of informal rulemaking are subject to little legislative and public scrutiny, yet impose requirements on regulated parties nonetheless.

---

20 From *Governing the Empire State: An Insider's Guide*, Albany, NY: State of New York Management Resources Project, 1988.

Adjudication

SAPA imposes a number of requirements on agencies when they perform adjudicatory proceedings. Those requirements are designed to balance the rights of the regulated individual or organization with the agency's responsibilities. They include:

- "All parties shall be afforded an opportunity for hearing within reasonable time," and given reasonable notice of hearings. The state's courts have allowed agencies significant leeway in meeting the demand of timeliness, especially where affected parties could not show that they had suffered as a result of delay. There are limits, however. In 1992, for instance, an Appellate Division panel held that the Education Department's delay of four years in starting disciplinary proceedings against a physician caused "actual prejudice" because of a witness's difficulty in recalling events.[21]

- Agencies must adopt rules governing proceedings and appeals, and make plain-language summaries of those rules available to participants.

- All parties are allowed to present written arguments on issues of law, and evidence on issues of fact; agencies may limit oral arguments to "a reasonable time." In setting the time and place for hearings, agencies must have "due regard … for the convenience of the parties."

- The agency must make a complete record of all adjudicatory proceedings. The record is to include all notices, pleadings, motions, intermediate rulings, evidence presented, and a statement of matters officially noticed.

- "Hearings shall be conducted in an impartial manner." If a party complains "in good faith" of bias on the part of a hearing officer, the agency must determine that question as part of the record in the case.

---

21 *Sharma* v. *Sobol* (3 Dept. 1992), 188 A.D. 2d 833, 591 NYS 2d 572.

Generally, the burden of proof in adjudicatory matters is "on the party who initiated the proceeding." Agencies need not follow rules of evidence used in the courts, and hearing officers may exclude irrelevant or repetitious evidence. Parties have the right to cross-examine witnesses.

Final decisions adverse to a party in an adjudicatory proceeding must be in writing or stated in the record, and include findings of fact, conclusions of law, or reasons for the decision. Parties to a hearing are entitled to have a copy of the decision mailed them "forthwith." To make research on previous decisions possible, agencies must maintain an index by name and subject of all written final decisions; information that is personal or a trade secret may be omitted.

Licensing

SAPA gives license holders — such as motorists, psychologists, and other professionals — some protection from needless delay by state agencies. The law provides that when a licensee has made "timely and sufficient" application for license renewal, the existing license does not expire until the application has been finally determined by the agency. On the other hand, agencies can order summary suspension of a license if "public health, safety or welfare imperatively requires emergency action."[22]

Beyond SAPA

Outside the realm of SAPA, state leaders have gone so far as to restructure some agencies' internal operations to avoid unfair treatment of regulated parties. Until the mid-1980s, for instance, a taxpayer appealing a decision by the Department of Taxation and Finance would take the appeal to the state Tax Commission, which would review the dispute on legal and factual grounds. The tax commissioner served as both head of the department and chair of the commission. In 1986, the Legislature created the Tax Appeals Tribunal, a separate agency within the department. Tax attorneys widely praise the tribunal for its independence and for bringing more consistency and predictability to interpretation of the state's sometimes complicated tax laws.

---

22 State Administrative Procedure Act, Section 401.

Even after extensive reforms, many New Yorkers perceived that regulators continued to go too far. In 1989, for instance, a business advocacy group's magazine complained: "State agencies seem to be stretching the bounds of the laws and constitutional protections which are supposed to ensure that regulations are adopted in a fair and open manner — and that their rules are consistent with the intent of the Legislature." For instance, the group pointed to a Health Department rule requiring motels and campgrounds to have lifeguards on duty whenever swimming pools were open; the rule was thrown out in court for reflecting too little attention to its impact on employers.[23]

To be sure, such observations are by no means limited to New York. Many other states have enacted administrative procedures acts and/or other laws that regulate the bureaucracy. Despite all those legislative actions, one academic observer had this to say in a mid-1990s review of state bureaucracies nationwide:

> Many parts of the state bureaucracy ... appear to be remarkably immune to the vagaries of legislative and gubernatorial politics. The key to successful bureaucratic politics is to keep a low profile. Governors come and go, legislators come and go, but some agencies keep on doing what they have always done with minimum intrusion from outside. State government encompasses so many agencies and activities that it is virtually impossible for the governor and the legislature to keep track of them all.[24]

From SAPA to GORR

The challenge of controlling the regulatory bureaucracy has prompted state leaders to continue to address the issue more than half a century after the state Constitution was amended because of concerns about state agency powers.

Governor Pataki identified regulatory reform as a top issue of his administration as soon as he took office in 1995, issuing an Executive Order that created a months-long moratorium on most new regulations. The governor's Executive Order No. 2 also directed each agency to evaluate all existing rules and regulations for economic impact.

---

23 Robert Ward, "Regulatory Overreach: A Growing Problem for Business," *Business/New York,* May 1989, p. 18.

24 Thad L. Beyle, "State Bureaucracies and Administration," in *State Government: CQ's Guide to Current Issues and Activities, 1996-97.*

In November 1995, the governor announced Executive Order 20, formally creating the Governor's Office of Regulatory Reform and establishing new rules for agency rulemaking. The order gave the director of regulatory reform — along with the secretary and the counsel to the governor, the director of state operations, and the budget director — the power to send proposed rules back to agencies for changes they deem necessary. Several organizations unhappy with some of GORR's involvement in the regulatory process challenged its authority in court, but the agency's power was upheld.[25]

Beyond the powers formally given the office, perhaps even more important were the high level of personal attention the governor gave the issue and the high-profile role played by the first director of regulatory reform, Robert L. King. Formerly a county executive and member of the Assembly, King used the office as a bully pulpit to address the business community, local government leaders, and others concerned about state regulations. He gave the agency an image of vigorous reform, including the motto "Home of New York's Bureaucracy Busters" and a bulldog logo; both appeared on the reception room wall in GORR's office in the Alfred E. Smith State Office Building in Albany.

The agency created a comprehensive plan for agencies' use in performing cost-benefit analyses of major regulatory proposals. King said such analysis helped motivate, among other cases, a decision to void revisions to the state building code proposed by an advisory group to the Department of State. The code changes, intended to strengthen buildings against potential earthquakes, could have increased construction costs in the state by close to 4 percent on an average project, or hundreds of millions of dollars a year, according to GORR. "The risk of serious earthquakes in New York remains unproven," Director King wrote. "In fact, New York has never had a major earthquake," defined as 6.0 or higher on the Richter scale.[26]

GORR pointed out that cost-benefit analysis had already been required in many cases but had been little used. The very nature of the agency indicated the difference that changes in elected government can make. For all the laws limiting regulatory power enacted over two decades, the new administration's fundamental approach to regulation was substantially different. It attempted to meet public policy goals in

---

25 *Rudder et al.* v. *Pataki et al.,* 93 NY 2d 273 (1999).

26 Governor's Office of Regulatory Reform, *Cost-Benefit Handbook: A Guide for New York State's Regulatory Agencies*, January 1996.

ways that did not impose burdensome costs on the private sector, local governments, and the state itself. Within a few years, however, agencies were routinely adopting major regulations with no detailed cost-benefit analysis. The initiative within the Pataki administration for limiting new regulatory activity had diminished noticeably.

Regulatory Agencies and the Courts

If individuals or organizations are unhappy with actions by regulatory agencies, they can (and regularly do) go to court. Article 78 of the state's Civil Practice Law and Rules gives citizens the power to "challenge action (or inaction) by agencies and officers of state and local government."[27] Enacted in 1962, the statute amended previous laws written decades earlier and continued rights that were based in common law developed in England and the United States over centuries of practice. A number of the statutes governing individual agencies also include specific provisions for judicial review of decisions. For example, state Labor Law allows direct review by the Appellate Division of decisions made by the Unemployment Insurance Appeals Board.[28]

State residents sometimes complain they are over-regulated by government agencies. The people who operate the agencies retort — with some justification — that *their* actions are also regulated heavily through laws, regulations, and judicial decisions meant to limit governmental authority. Still, such limits are mostly procedural in nature, leaving agencies plenty of room to act — as long as they are carrying out the will of the elected governor and/or Legislature.

One expert on administrative law writes that regulation of regulators advances the agencies' own purposes: "Administrative law is not merely a set of constraints but also a collection of tools which can be used to do the people's business more fairly, effectively, and perhaps even more efficiently."[29]

---

27 Vincent C. Alexander, "Practice Commentaries: The Prerogative Writs, in General," *McKinney's Consolidated Laws of New York, Annotated: Civil Practice Law and Rules*, 1994, p. 25.

28 Ibid.

29 Cooper, p. xiii.

Chapter Nine

THE WORKFORCE

Key points:

- After decades of growth, the size of the state workforce declined modestly starting in the late 1990s.

- New York was a national leader in civil-service reform a century ago, but its system has earned sharp criticism more recently.

- The Taylor Law, governing public-employee relations, is likely to remain a topic of fierce debate.

State government is by far the biggest employer in New York. Depending on how its payroll is measured (for instance, whether quasi-independent public authorities are included), the state employs three to four times the number of people who work for the largest individual private companies. Large state agencies such as the Department of Correctional Services and the Office of Mental

Retardation and Developmental Disabilities, individually, provide more jobs than any but a few employers in the private sector.

Over many decades, state government has developed extensive legal and management structures to hire, negotiate with, discipline, and otherwise handle relations with individual employees and the unions that represent them. At the same time — particularly since 1967, when the labor-relations statute known as the Taylor Law was enacted — unions representing public employees have grown in membership and political influence.

This chapter describes the people who work for New York State, the unions that represent them, the state's major laws and agencies that affect employee relations, and the labor-management structures that shape those relationships.

Who Are the State's Workers?

According to the authoritative count by the U.S. Labor Department's Bureau of Labor Statistics, some 261,000 individuals worked for New York State government during an average month in 2005. Some 63,000 of those positions were in education, another 17,500 in hospitals, and the remainder in other branches of state service.

The total includes the men and women who work for the public authorities that are both part of state government and, to an extent, outside of it. For instance, the Metropolitan Transportation Authority employs some 63,000 individuals, while another 7,000 work for the Port Authority of New York and New Jersey. Each agency is governed by a board whose members are appointed by the governor (with additional members named by the governor of New Jersey, in the case of the Port Authority).

The state Department of Civil Service counted 163,460 employees in the state's "classified service" as of January 2005. Its tally represents only the executive branch and omits public authorities as well as faculty of the State University, the State Police, and employees of the legislative and judicial branches of state government. The table on the next page shows the largest state agencies and their employment totals as of 1995 and 2005.

The most common job title on the state payroll is corrections officer, of whom 19,453 were employed in January 2005. Next were

Employment by 10 Largest State Agencies, 1995 and 2005
(Ranked by 2005 Employment)

Agency	1995 Employment	2005 Employment	Change
Correctional Services	31,632	31,769	0.0%
Mental Retardation	27,545	23,793	-13.6%
Mental Health	26,764	17,436	-34.9%
SUNY (classified)	17,258	16,798	-2.7%
Transportation	12,889	9,825	-23.8%
Health	7,443	6,597	-11.4%
Taxation & Finance	6,442	4,986	-22.6%
Labor	5,122	4,153	-18.9%
Children & Family Services*	4,819	4,072	-15.5%*
Environmental Conservation	4,459	3,930	-11.9%

*   Office of Children and Family Services created in 1996. First number shown is for 2000; percent change is for 2000 to 2005.

Source: New York State Department of Civil Service, *Workforce Management Report 2005.*

developmental aide, with 11,162 positions, and keyboard specialist, with 4,875 individual jobs.

By any measure, the size of the state workforce has declined in the past decade, after many years of growth. As of 1967, the earliest reported data from the U.S. Labor Department, New York State employed 173,000. The payroll grew almost continually over the next 23 years, except for two years in the mid-1970s, when the state's economy and tax revenues were in a slowdown. By 1990, the total was 286,000, an increase of nearly two-thirds from a quarter-century earlier (Labor Department data include all three branches of state government and public authorities). When state revenues declined in the early 1990s, Governor Cuomo reversed the trend of his first two terms in office and reduced the workforce. That process continued under Governor Pataki.

The largest geographic center of state employment is, not surprisingly, the Capital Region, with some 53,400 state workers as of 2005, according to the comprehensive BLS data. New York City was second, with more than 49,000 state employees, followed by Long Island with some 25,000.

As with the American workforce in general, the average age of New York State's workers has risen over the last two decades. The average age rose from 41.8 to 46.5 years from 1991 to 2005, according to the Civil Service Department. Just over 51 percent of employees are male.

Nearly 73 percent of the executive-branch workforce is white, while just under 15 percent of employees are black, 4.1 percent Hispanic, and 2.7 percent Asian/Pacific Islanders, the department's data show. Civil Service reports that the ethnicity of another 6.2 percent of employees is "unknown." If we assume that those workers include proportionate numbers of differing ethnic backgrounds, the shares of the state workforce represented by whites and blacks are close to those of New York's population. Hispanic New Yorkers make up a significantly smaller share of the workforce than their 15.6 percent of the overall state population.

The Legal Environment: Yesterday and Today

Almost from the earliest days of state government, the method of hiring individuals for public positions — and the qualification of those individuals — was a matter of some controversy. Unlike the modern system in which executive-branch employees report to the governor, the Council of Appointment chose employees during the first several decades of New York's history. The council's makeup, with representation from the Senate as well as the governor's office, made the hiring of key state officials an exercise in both political horsetrading and obstruction of individuals loyal to the opposition. One of the resulting political battles in 1801 led to a duel between DeWitt Clinton, a Republican leader who would later serve as governor, and John Swartwout, a Federalist supporter of Aaron Burr. Swartwout suffered two leg wounds, while the future governor emerged with merely a bullet hole in his coat.

By the post-Civil War period, according to one leading historian of the state,

(C)ivil servants or bureaucrats correctly assumed that their jobs were nothing more than rewards for the services that they had rendered to the party in power.... Every autumn the Democratic and Republican parties waged bitter and relentless campaigns for control over some part of the state government. Both parties were "plunderbirds" whose principal objective was to get at the booty that was theirs for the taking after a victory at the polls. Victory meant jobs for the faithful who had got out the vote and an opportunity for graft for those who got the jobs. For the electorate it meant little more than a change in names without a change in policies. Upstate Republicans could be as corrupt as Tammany Democrats, and officials from both parties received kickbacks from contractors, falsified their accounts, and exacted political contributions from their subordinates on the public payroll.[1]

The situation was similar, to varying degrees, in other states and the federal government. Across the country, reformers began pressing for change. The pressure became irresistible after President James A. Garfield was assassinated in 1881 by Charles Guiteau, who had unsuccessfully sought a job as a federal attorney (and may have been mentally ill). Within months, the Pendleton Act, requiring merit appointment for certain federal jobs, was signed into law by Garfield's successor, Chester A. Arthur of New York.

Two years later, New York became a national leader in enacting statutory reform of the civil service at the state level, and numerous other states followed with similar laws. (Two state leaders who eventually moved to the White House — Grover Cleveland and Theodore Roosevelt — built national reputations partly on their role in achieving civil service reform in New York.) In 1894, the reformers' ideal was written into the state Constitution with an amendment providing that "Appointments and promotions in the civil service of the state and all of the civil divisions thereof, including cities and villages, shall be made according to merit and fitness to be ascertained, as far as practicable, by examination which, as far as practicable, shall be competitive...."[2]

An 1883 statute created the Civil Service Commission, which remains in existence today. The Department of Civil Service is the central personnel agency for the executive branch of state government. The department also provides technical services regarding administration of the state's more than 100 municipal civil service agencies (excluding

---

1   Ellis et al., *A History of New York State*, 1967, pp. 351, 353-4.
2   New York State Constitution, Article V, section 6.

New York City), which covered approximately 383,000 local government employees as of the start of 2001.

The agency administers health, dental, accident, and life insurance programs covering state employees and retirees, as well as some local government employees. The health insurance program is one of the largest in the world, covering 1.1 million state and local employees, retirees, and their families. Also provided by the department are on-the-job health programs such as nursing services, medical examinations, wellness promotion programs, and occupational health services.

In the decades following its enactment, the Civil Service Law was amended numerous times, with significant recodification in 1909 and 1958. Major sections divide state jobs into "classified" and "unclassified" positions for civil-service purposes, and create the rules for hiring, promoting, transferring, and disciplining employees. Other sections in today's law address issues such as special rights for veterans and volunteer firefighters, and the structure of the state Civil Service Department and local civil service commissions.

The Taylor Law

Perhaps the most significant changes to the statute since its 1883 enactment stemmed largely from conflicts between public employees and the new administration of New York City Mayor John V. Lindsay in 1965. City welfare workers walked off the job for 28 days early in the year, seeking higher wages, lighter caseloads, and better working conditions. On New Year's Day 1966, some 30,000 employees of the city Transit Authority went on strike for 12 days. Tens of thousands of city residents could not get to work in what some observers called the worst economic catastrophe in New York since the Depression.

Existing law provided that each employee would be penalized two days' pay for every day on strike, given no raises for six months, and placed on probationary status for a year. After both strikes, the Legislature approved bills granting amnesty to the striking employees. Three days after the transit strike ended, Governor Rockefeller appointed a committee led by a University of Pennsylvania professor, George W. Taylor, to study the state's relations with its employees. Within three months, the committee proposed amendments to the Civil Service Law that were, in large part, adopted in 1967.

The resulting Public Employees Fair Employment Act, commonly known as the Taylor Law, also covers most local government employees in the state. The law was the first comprehensive labor relations law for public employees in the state, and among the first in the United States. As with the Empire State's establishment of civil-service law in the 1880s, the Taylor Law became a model for many other states.

Major provisions of the law grant public employees the right to be represented by employee organizations of their own choice, require public employers to negotiate agreements with public employee organizations regarding terms and conditions of employment, and prohibit strikes by public employees. The law also establishes procedures for resolving collective bargaining disputes, defines and prohibits improper practices by public employers and public employee organizations, and establishes a state agency, the Public Employment Relations Board (PERB), to administer these provisions.

PERB's three members are appointed by the governor with the consent of the Senate. The board resolves disputes between unions and public employers arising from the Taylor Law. Other responsibilities include mediating impasses in contract negotiations, adjudicating improper practice charges, designating employees as management/confidential, determining whether employee organizations are responsible when members strike, and administering grievance and interest arbitration panels.

The Taylor Law has been controversial from the start — at first, from the perspective of some labor leaders and later from that of public managers. One union critic labeled it the "Rockefeller-Travia Slave Labor Act," after the governor and Assembly Speaker Anthony Travia, because of the prohibition against strikes. Unions that had not already established bargaining rights, however, benefited greatly from the requirement that public employers negotiate terms and conditions of employment. The Civil Service Employees Association, now the largest union representing state and local government employees in New York, says the law "turned CSEA from an informal, socially-oriented organization into a powerful labor union with the goal of negotiating — and strongly enforcing — contracts for its members."[3] In the years after enactment of the Taylor Law, CSEA and other public-employee unions in the state increased in membership and, as a result, financial strength.

3   CSEA website, *http://www.cseainc.org/yesterdy.html*

Their thousands of members made them a potent political force that can raise millions for campaign contributions, operate telephone banks on behalf of political candidates, and provide votes for favored candidates. For instance, CSEA's endorsement of Lieutenant Governor Cuomo in 1982 was considered a key element in Cuomo's victory in the Democratic primary for governor against New York City Mayor Edward Koch and the general-election victory over Republican Lew Lehrman.

The Taylor Law underwent significant change in 1982, when Governor Carey and the Legislature enacted additional provisions known as the Triborough amendment (after a dispute involving the Triborough Bridge and Tunnel Authority). The statute requires public employers to continue all the terms of an expired agreement until a new one is negotiated, unless the expired agreement states otherwise.

"This requirement is unique in public-sector collective bargaining," one observer commented in 1992. "Coupled with the broad interpretation afforded it by PERB and the New York courts, this provision has drastically changed the face of public-sector negotiations in New York."[4] The Triborough amendment represented a significant shift in the balance of negotiating power away from government employers and toward public-employee unions. Perhaps as a result, the number of public-employee strikes has fallen sharply. Such strikes in New York numbered 15 to 25 annually from the late 1960s to 1981, but have since declined to five or fewer a year, according to PERB.

Some representatives of public employers, such as the New York State School Boards Association, argue that the Triborough amendment gives employee unions an incentive to shun contract settlements and continue the status quo of expired contracts. One result, according to the association, is that school boards have greater difficulty negotiating such things as changes in benefits and work rules. To obtain such changes, the association argues, school districts must agree to higher salary increases than they would otherwise, thus requiring higher school property taxes. The New York State Conference of Mayors and some other critics, meanwhile, argue that the Taylor Law's requirement of binding arbitration in contract disputes involving police and

---

4   Mary Helen Moses, "Scope of Bargaining and the Triborough Law: New York's Collective Bargaining Dilemma," *Albany Law Review* 56, 1 (1992): 53-118.

firefighter unions drives up costs unreasonably.[5] Public employee unions respond that the law takes away a right that employees in the private sector retain — the right to strike for better conditions of employment — and that the law's other provisions keep the system fair to workers.

In December 2005, the union representing most Metropolitan Transportation Authority employees went on strike, shutting down the transit system for three days during the Christmas season. At the request of city officials, a judge invoked the Taylor Law's prohibition against strikes to fine the Transit Workers Union and send its president, Roger Toussaint, to jail for several days. The TWU and other unions criticized the action as unfair, saying MTA executives had pushed the union into striking by refusing to bargain in good faith.

Union leaders urged the Legislature to rewrite the Taylor Law, and more than a dozen bills giving public-employee unions new rights under the law passed the Senate and Assembly in 2006. For instance, one bill, S. 3178, would have reduced the penalties for illegal strikes and created automatic pay raises for unionized workers if PERB determined that a public employer was not bargaining in good faith. Governor Pataki vetoed that bill and a number of others the Legislature had passed at the behest of the unions (both major gubernatorial candidates, Eliot Spitzer and John Faso, also criticized the unions' proposed changes to the Taylor Law). It appeared likely, however, that the issue would remain a contentious one in 2007 and beyond.

Resolving Disputes Under the Taylor Law

Generally, under the Taylor Law there are four ways to resolve an impasse between a public employer and an employee union. Each system starts with mediation. Either or both parties may request mediation assistance from PERB, which acts as liaison between the parties and seeks to bring about a settlement through persuasion and compromise.

If mediation fails, a PERB fact-finder may attempt to resolve the dispute through a second mediation effort. If unsuccessful in that effort, the fact-finder then holds a hearing, takes testimony, accepts briefs from the parties, and makes a written, nonbinding recommendation for settlement to both parties.

---

5   See, for example, "Taylor-Made Taxpayer Abuse," in *City Journal*, Manhattan Institute, Autumn 2000, p. 7.

In cases where binding or interest arbitration is not permitted, if one or both parties do not accept the fact-finding report in its entirety, the next step is a hearing before the appropriate legislative body. (That provision does not apply to public employees of educational institutions, police, firefighters, corrections officers, certain transit employees, and other workers.) Legislative bodies usually direct both parties to resume negotiations but, occasionally, impose employment terms. Such imposition may last for no more than a single fiscal year. A legislative determination cannot change the terms of an expired agreement unless the employee organization has waived its right to stand on those terms. PERB also offers conciliation, mediation assistance provided if an impasse continues after a fact-finding report has been issued.

Bargaining Units and Unions

Roughly 94 percent of employees of the state's executive branch are unionized, in 14 bargaining units. Those whom PERB deems to be managerial or confidential include employees who formulate policy, assist directly in the conduct or preparation of negotiations, or assist, in a confidential capacity, employees who have employee relations responsibilities. (Many of the Unified Court System's 15,000 or so nonjudicial employees are also unionized; no legislative employees are.)

Two years after adoption of the Taylor Law, Governor Rockefeller and the Legislature established the Office of Employee Relations to act as the governor's agent in collective bargaining. The office's mission is defined in the Executive Law as "to promote harmonious and cooperative relationships between the state and its employees to protect the public by assuring, at all times, the orderly and uninterrupted operations and functions of state government."[6] Now known as the Governor's Office of Employee Relations, the agency negotiates collective bargaining agreements for 14 negotiating units. It also reviews terms and conditions of union contracts with public authorities such as the Metropolitan Transportation Authority.

Agency staff coordinate and support the administration of employee contracts, including interpreting contract clauses for state agencies, overseeing labor-management programs, and providing advice on employee relations. GOER also helps agencies develop, coordinate, and implement

---

6   NYS Executive Law, Article 24.

comprehensive management improvement initiatives and organizational re-engineering for improved performance and service to the general public.

Repairing a "Calcified" Civil-Service System

The crises in public employee relations that led to strikes and then passage of the Taylor Law in the 1960s masked another emerging problem. The civil service system, after three-quarters of a century, was suffering from the accretion of too many rules and strictures. More than 25 studies issued over a quarter-century starting in 1970 identified problems such as too many job titles and difficulty of transferring employees from one title to another.

By the start of the 1990s, state government encompassed more than 7,000 job titles, and 4,000 of those had only a single employee. More than 3,000 state workers had been serving in "provisional" appointments (while awaiting examination) longer than the statutory limit of nine months; 500 individuals had been provisional for more than five years. The Rockefeller Institute of Government's Richard P. Nathan concluded that "New York represents an extreme" among rigid systems that prevent public administrators from exercising effective leadership.[7] *Governing* magazine, in a report on outmoded civil service systems nationwide, wrote: "For decades, the king of the calcified and recalcitrant beasts has been the New York state civil service system, a monster off whose chest comprehensive reports on reform bounded like Wiffle balls — 27 of them in all since the 1970s. For public managers in the Empire State, it was simply one of the larger complications of government service to be worked around on a regular basis."[8]

When a sagging economy weakened revenues for several years, Governor Cuomo was forced to reduce the state payroll starting in 1990. Civil-service rules made the bad news worse, giving managers little flexibility to move employees from one agency that was downsizing to another that had openings because of attrition or essential growth. As a result, nearly 6,000 employees were laid off between April 1990 and March 1992 as part of an overall workforce reduction of 17,800 positions.

---

7   Richard P. Nathan, "Deregulating State and Local Government: What Can Leaders Do?" paper presented at the Association for Public Policy Analysis and Management's 14th annual research conference, October 1993, Washington D.C.

8   Jonathan Walters, "Untangling Albany," *Governing*, Washington, DC, December 1998.

In 1995 and 1996, the state faced another major fiscal challenge and Governor Pataki planned to restructure several administrative agencies — two factors that would result in significant workforce reductions. To minimize harm to state workers, the governor created a task force to co-ordinate staff-reduction efforts and find ways to avoid layoffs.

The task force developed strategies for liberalizing the cumbersome employee-transfer process to allow rapid redeployment of employees. The new approach was designed to allow workers to move from agencies that were shrinking to those that needed additional staff. Since a change in Civil Service Law was needed, the task force brought together interested parties to obtain their support for a new Section 78 of the statute. The task force members met with leaders of the state's largest public-employee unions and discussed how the changes would benefit employees. With the unions' support, the Governor's Office of Employee Relations and Department of Civil Service went to the Legislature to gain passage of needed changes in the law.

In addition to the Section 78 transfer legislation, the task force proposed early-retirement incentives that would increase protections against layoffs. Both measures sailed through the Legislature. Reflecting the unions' sensitivity to such major changes, however, both laws were made effective for only a year, and were extended in 1997 and 1998. The Section 78 transfer legislation was made permanent by Chapter 70 of the Laws of 1999.

As with all legislation, the 1995 changes to the Civil Service Law were only the start of a process that depended on administrative implementation. Over the following three years, the Governor's Office of Employee Relations took the lead in working with the governor's executive staff, agency managers, and union leaders to transfer more than 2,400 employees to new positions using the new Section 78.

Throughout the first several years of the Pataki administration, agency restructuring and consolidation provided additional challenges for GOER. A major challenge throughout the administration, with workforce implications addressed by GOER and the Department of Civil Service, was the restructuring of social-service agencies. The Department of Social Services was separated into major functional areas, with pieces going to the new Office of Children and Family Services (which also took over the former Division for Youth), Office for Temporary and Disability Assistance, Health (which took over the Medicaid program), and Labor (employment-related services).

Employee Relations in the 21st Century

At the start of a new century, state government's relations with employees and their unions are, in various ways, entering a new era. Greater flexibility for employees to move from one department to another, outlined above, is an example. The Civil Service Department has identified several major trends affecting the state workforce. Those trends include:

- Continued consolidation and merging of programs.

- Integration of new technologies, such as decentralizing information processing from mainframe computers to individual and networked personal computers.

- Expansion of the state Office for Technology and the consolidation of state data centers and applications services.

- Ongoing shifting of the client population of mental health and mental retardation service agencies from institutional settings to community-based programs.

The Civil Service Department and the Governor's Office of Employee Relations use human-resource approaches common in leading private-sector corporations to promote a higher-quality workforce. For instance, GOER oversees the Workforce Champions program, which recognizes outstanding performance by state employees. Fellow workers — supervisors, colleagues, or subordinates — may nominate teams in the same or another agency as "champions." Award ceremonies provide reinforcement for excellent work and a signal to other employees that good performance is recognized. In 2005, the program's honorees included managers and union representatives in the Office of Mental Retardation and Developmental Disabilities who developed an expedited resolution process for disciplinary cases involving workers represented by the Civil Service Employees Association. Previous winners included staff of the Division of Criminal Justice Services who developed the ability to receive digital live-scan fingerprints from law-enforcement agencies.

Another initiative is the Leadership Classroom, which helps participants explore leadership principles and practices. The 12-month program includes two week-long residential seminars, an on-the-job project that puts classroom principles into practice, and individual leadership development plans for participants. Employees have used the projects to improve internal communications, change a department's organizational structure to improve workflow, and bring about other operational improvements in state agencies.

Chapter Ten

STATE GOVERNMENT'S BIGGEST JOB: THE BUDGET

Key points:

- The Constitution gives the governor enormous budgetary power, but the Legislature can have its way, too; court decisions have failed to clarify the precise balance between the branches.

- New York is a high-spending, high-taxing state, with education and health care making up more than half of total expenditures.

- The state's financial authority extends well beyond "the budget," into public authorities and various other "off-budget" areas.

$\mathbf{I}$t accounts for only 20 paragraphs or so of the state Constitution, which runs to 89 pages in the Department of State's *Legislative Manual*. But adoption of the state budget is the single most important job the governor and the Legislature perform every year.

The budget represents hundreds of separate decisions on how to raise and spend tens of billions of dollars — some $113.6 billion in the 2006-07 fiscal year. New York's elected leaders also control or influence billions of dollars outside the budget, as will be explained below. Enacting the budget and making related decisions represent the most broadly important function of state government: It raises money for public services and decides how to allocate those dollars among competing demands.

Given its overarching importance and many choices, the budget is usually the central focus of debate between the governor and the Legislature in a given year. The annual process is almost always contentious, and sometimes bitterly personal. Yet for all the *sturm und drang* between the executive and legislative branches from January until the budget is adopted, the final product always shows the imprint of the Executive Budget in both its size and content. In 2006, for instance, Governor Pataki proposed spending $110.6 billion. The final budget, reflecting changes agreed upon by the Legislature and the governor, represented an increase of 3.6 percent. As it typically does, the Legislature also reallocated some spending proposed in the Executive Budget.

This chapter will summarize both what New York State government does in its budget — the policy decisions represented in collecting and spending the taxpayers' dollars — and how those decisions are made.

Who Are the Players?

Before discussing the policy choices reflected in New York State's budgets, and the processes that shape those choices, a brief explanation of the institutions that make and implement budget decisions is in order.

Under the state Constitution, the governor is responsible for preparing the state's expenditure and revenue plans. As head of the executive branch, the governor also exercises significant influence over *how* certain public dollars are spent. He can, for instance, restrain state agencies' spending below the level appropriated by the Legislature, and decide when to send legislatively approved state aid to local governments and school districts. As recent court decisions have affirmed, the governor can write budget bills that specify how billions of dollars will be spent — and the Legislature has limited options for changing those proposals. The governor appoints a budget director, who oversees the Division of the Budget. In addition to drawing up the state's financial plan, the division's 365 or so employees serve as the executive branch's primary source of institutional expertise on issues ranging from local government finance to the operations of public authorities. The Division also coordinates much of the development and execution of state agency programs, a source of control which can extend as far as approving each agency decision to fill individual jobs.

In the Legislature, the fiscal committees — Senate Finance and Assembly Ways and Means — are each chaired by a senior legislator who plays a role in development and public promotion of the body's budget positions. Given the importance of the budget, the Senate majority leader and the Assembly speaker retain overall decision-making authority for their houses' fiscal actions. Each exercises that authority through a top staff assistant — the secretary to the fiscal committee — who reports primarily to the leader of the house rather than to the committee chair. The majority conference in each house also retains dozens of fiscal staff employees who keep almost as close watch on program spending as do their counterparts in the Budget Division. The minority conferences in the Senate and Assembly also have budget staff. However, like their principals among members of the Legislature, the minority staffs have little influence on the budget.

The comptroller has no role in adopting the budget or making the policy decisions to implement it. As the state's chief fiscal officer, however, the comptroller has an important role to play in carrying out the budget decisions made by the governor and lawmakers, as described in Chapter Four. The comptroller also has the power to attract a certain amount of media coverage of any pronouncements he makes on the policies chosen by the governor and the Legislature. For instance, Comptrollers Edward V. Regan, H. Carl McCall, and Alan Hevesi have all helped draw attention to the comparatively high level of state debt.

The national tobacco settlement reached in 1999 by attorneys general from around the country created a new, significant role in the finances of state government. Attorneys General Dennis Vacco and Eliot Spitzer, as New York's representatives in negotiations with the tobacco companies, helped determine the amount of money that the state and its localities would receive (and the amount that would be collected from smokers and tobacco-company stockholders nationwide, including those in New York). With no action by the governor or the Legislature, New York's state government played a leading role in deciding on a huge new transfer of dollars from one segment of society to another. (The governor and Legislature did decide, however, where that money would be spent — mostly on expansion of the Medicaid program, under the December 1999 legislation mentioned earlier.) The amount involved, roughly $1 billion every year for the foreseeable future, is on the scale of total tuition received by the State University or annual receipts from the state's petroleum business tax. As the state's chief lawyer, the attorney general's office periodically shapes court settlements that direct defendants to make certain levels of payments that will be spent in specified ways — without approval from the governor and legislators.

How to Measure the Budget?

How much will New York State spend this year? A good question with a handful of answers, each correct in its own way but differing by tens of billions of dollars.

The largest part of the budget is known as the General Fund. Historically, the fund was viewed as essentially the same as the overall budget — it collected all state taxes and held most of the dollars to be spent in a given year. With the advent of significant amounts of federal aid for social services and other programs, particularly since the 1960s, the General Fund has become an inadequate measure of the budget. In the fiscal year ending March 31, 2006, it represented only 45 percent of total spending, and less than two-thirds of nonfederal revenues.

A more useful picture of how much New Yorkers are paying in taxes, and how much their elected state representatives are spending on their behalf, is the "state-funds" measure. It includes all the dollars in the General Fund, but adds "special revenue funds" that receive other income directly from New Yorkers — for instance, State University tuition, Lottery collections, business fees, and payouts from the nationwide tobacco settlement. Even some tax revenues that were traditionally considered part of the General Fund now go into special revenue funds. In the 2005-06 budget, for instance, $3.2 billion in personal income tax revenues was dedicated to a special fund for the STAR school-tax refund program.

The totality of spending in the budget is called the "all-funds" budget. It includes all of the General Fund, the additional dollars that go into the state-funds measure, and federal revenues.

More Than Meets the Eye

Even that measure, however, does not provide a full picture of state government's revenues and spending in the 21st century. By 2002, the state was spending more than $1 billion a year, totally "off-budget," on health care and related programs. Much of the spending was from the state tobacco tax, while some was from fees on health-insurance policies and other sources. "On the theory that this money was never actually collected by the state, but was simply redistributed to hospitals and other health-care providers, state lawmakers had not counted these transactions as part of the budget. The money went into various 'pools' managed by a private firm under contract with the Health Department, and payments to providers, unlike most other state spending, do not pass through the comptroller's office."[1] In 2006, after some criticism of the hidden nature of the health-care fund, state leaders made it part of the regular budget.

The state's public authorities — the Metropolitan Transportation Authority, the Port Authority of New York and New Jersey, the Dormitory Authority, and others — raised and spent more than $27 billion in 2005. Only $3 billion or so of that total came from state appropriations. Nearly 90 percent of the authorities' spending was outside the state budget, most of it coming from transit fares and other user fees *(Financial data for the largest public authorities appear in Chapter Eleven.)*

Technically, these agencies are independent of the "regular" governmental structure; their boards of directors are appointed for fixed terms and could establish policies at variance with the wishes of the elected leadership. In reality, though, their actions are ultimately — and often immediately — controlled by the governor and the Legislature. One example of that came in early 2000, when the Thruway Authority proposed toll increases and then backed down in the face of public criticism and opposition by legislative leaders and Governor Pataki.

Then there are the local governments and school districts. In many ways, Albany requires and directs the spending of additional billions through their budgets. For instance, the governor and the Legislature design the state's Medicaid program, on which counties and New York City spent more than $5 billion in 2006.

---

1   William Hammond, Jr., "Enron-Style Management Comes to Albany," *New York Sun*, New York, NY, May 6, 2002, p. 6.

Then there are the dollars that state government controls for targeted purposes outside the budget.

One individual in state government, the comptroller, is in charge of even more dollars than the governor and the Legislature — albeit in a different sense than their control over the budget. State Finance Law makes the comptroller the sole trustee of the pension fund for nearly 900,000 state and local government employees and pensioners. The Common Retirement Fund's assets totaled more than $126 billion — more than one-quarter again the total of the state budget — in 2005. The Comptroller cannot simply spend those dollars, but decides how to invest them for the benefit of pension recipients, as required by state law. *(See Chapter Four.)*

Finally, the state's leaders control large funds that are subject to state law but are not available for general-purpose budgetary allocation. For example, the Labor Department administers the state's unemployment insurance program, which collected $1.6 billion in employer taxes in 1999 and paid out a similar amount in benefits to unemployed workers. Taxes that fund unemployment insurance are set by laws enacted by the governor and Legislature; the Labor Department has some authority to change tax rates depending on the balance in the fund. The State Insurance Fund, a nonprofit agency whose board is appointed by the governor, is the largest seller of workers' compensation insurance to employers in New York; it has more than $11.5 billion in assets. Although the fund has no direct connection to the state's fiscal operations, during the 1980s and early 1990s, Governor Cuomo and the Legislature removed some $1.3 billion from its assets to use as cash for the regular state budget. The money has not been (and seems unlikely to be) repaid.

What's in the Budget: The Spending Side

New York State government spent an average of $5,257 (including federal aid) for every resident during the fiscal year ending March 31, 2005, according to the Office of the State Comptroller (OSC). As shown in the nearby table, more than a third of the total, or $2,008 was devoted to public health — mainly, New York's Medicaid program. One other area — education — commands a large share of the state budget. Per-capita spending on public schools, the State and City universities, and other education programs totaled $1,531 in the 2005

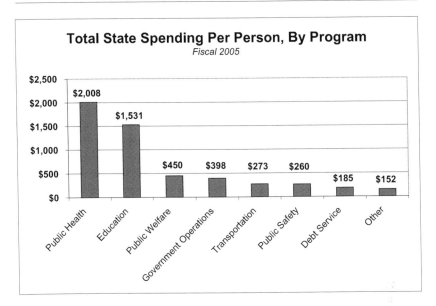

Total State Spending Per Person, By Program
Fiscal 2005

fiscal year, OSC reported. Together, those big-ticket items represented more than two-thirds of total state spending.

The two programs also illustrate the triangular structure of public spending in the Empire State: each is financed through federal, state, and local tax dollars. Localities across the state spent $8.6 billion on health programs in 2003 — again, primarily on the Medicaid program — and $31.9 billion on education.[2] The figures include assistance the localities receive from the state for Medicaid and public schools. (Data on spending by localities are not as timely as those for state government because the comptroller's office, which reports the local figures, must collect numbers from virtually every municipality and school district.)

Looking solely at state-funds spending — leaving aside federal aid — education is by far the state's highest priority, as has been the case for decades. New York is unusual among the states in devoting more total spending to Medicaid and other health programs; in most states, education remains the largest cost center even when dollars from Washington are included. In 2005, New York's state-funded spending of $25.9 billion on education (including the $3 billion STAR program) far outpaced public health, at $14.7 billion.[3]

---

2   Office of the State Comptroller, *2005 Annual Report on Local Governments*.

3   Office of the State Comptroller, *2005 Comptroller's Report on the Financial Condition of New York State*.

Education and health care are the primary reasons that combined state and local government spending in New York is among the highest in the country. In public schools, per-pupil spending from all sources was $12,930 in 2003-04, second-highest in the country, according to the Census Bureau. Medicaid spending in the state was $2,131 per capita in 2004, highest in the nation and more than twice the average for all states. That greater level of spending provides services to more residents; New York ranks sixth-highest in the nation for Medicaid recipients as a proportion of the overall population. *(See Chapters Twelve and Thirteen for further discussion of health- and education-related spending.)*

The third-largest priority for state spending — public welfare, including cash assistance and some other programs, at $450 per state resident in 2005 — receives barely a third of the amount spent on education, according to the comptroller's office. Other major spending areas include transportation and public safety.

If spending by public authorities is included in the total, however, the picture changes somewhat. Per-capita spending on transportation, for instance, rises from $273 a year to more than $800.

Priorities Change

Spending priorities can change dramatically over time, even over just a few years. Calculations by Senate Finance Committee staff showed that social-services spending increased dramatically — from 28 to 38 percent of the state's total budget — between fiscal 1990 and 1995. Because of a slowdown in Medicaid spending, welfare reform, and growth in the state's economy, social-services spending fell back to a projected 32.8 percent of total expenditures in 2000-01. During the same period, education spending rose from 21.5 to 25.3 percent of the total, according to the Senate data.[4]

The Budget Division presented a similar look at changes over time in a 1990 report for Governor Cuomo's Council on Fiscal and Economic Priorities. It showed that, from fiscal 1983 to 1990, spending on both "public protection" (including corrections) and "health" had jumped by more than 120 percent. Funding for mental health had risen by 88 percent and education by 73 percent. Meanwhile, spending on

---

4   Senate Finance Committee, *Staff Analysis of the SFY 2000-01 Executive Budget,* January 2000, p. 3.

transportation had grown by only 27 percent and general-purpose aid to localities by 5 percent. Inflation for the state-and-local-government sector during the period was 38 percent, DOB said.

Unfortunately, it is difficult to compare the state's spending priorities over historical periods. The fiscal plan does not list lump sums for "health," "transportation" or "public protection," although the budget bills have been structured along such functional lines since 1996. Instead, it provides appropriations for different agencies. Only in the last 15 years or so have the Office of the State Comptroller and the Budget Division published estimates of spending in functional categories. Still, there is no question that social services, health care, and corrections are responsible for a much higher share of spending today than several decades ago.

Where Does the Money Come From?

The state Constitution gives New York's elected leaders broad taxing discretion. Unlike charters in some other states, it includes no restrictions on the overall level of taxation or expenditure, and allows wide latitude in granting exemptions. The most significant restrictions imposed by the Constitution prohibit taxation of property used exclusively for religious, educational, or charitable purposes; taxation of pensions of public employees; and imposition of ad valorem or excise taxes related to intangible personal property.

The Constitution also gives the governor and Legislature control over the taxing authority of local governments and school districts. Localities cannot impose income taxes, sales taxes, or most other taxes without explicit statutory authorization from Albany. The Constitution does authorize local property taxes but gives the state the power to regulate those taxes.

The taxes collected by Albany generated around 48 percent of the state's total revenue in 2004-05. Another 14 percent or so came from fees, tuition, and other nontax revenue paid by state residents, and from proceeds of the Lottery and other gambling. Just more than a third, or 36 percent, was from federal grants (which in turn are funded by federal taxes that New Yorkers also pay). Roughly 2 percent of the total came from borrowing.

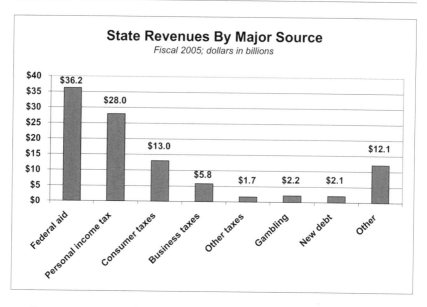

State Revenues By Major Source
Fiscal 2005; dollars in billions

State government's most lucrative tax is the personal income tax, which has provided more than half of total tax revenues in recent years. As of 2006, the tax was imposed at rates starting at 4 percent of taxable income over $8,000 for a single individual and rising to 6.85 percent for an individual's income over $20,000. (For tax years 2003 through 2005, the top rate was set at 7.5 percent for high-income individuals.)

New York State's personal income tax generally follows federal definitions of income and deductions. As with federal taxes, New Yorkers can deduct home interest payments, charitable contributions, and certain other expenses from their state taxable income. Among notable differences, the state does not tax pension income of retired government employees; it also excludes all Social Security income from taxation. The state's income tax applies to income earned in New York by residents of other states.

The state's second-largest tax is the 4 percent sales and use tax, generating some 20 percent of tax collections. ("Use" tax means that the levy applies not only to items purchased in the state, but to those bought elsewhere for use in New York — for instance, an automobile purchased in Pennsylvania by a resident of Binghamton.) Optional local sales taxes typically add another 4 percent or more to the state levy.

"As a general rule, tangible goods are taxed unless they are explicitly exempted from taxation, and services are not taxed unless they are explicitly enumerated for taxation," according to one summary of the sales tax.[5] Prescription and nonprescription drugs, most foods sold for off-premises use, and certain other tangible goods are not taxed. The Department of Taxation and Finance makes specific rulings within these broad guidelines. The sales tax law, like those in other states, has often been ridiculed for disparities in treatment of related goods — for instance, orange juice is not taxable but Tang breakfast drink is. (Occasionally, legislators criticize the tax department for such distinctions, but the department responds that it only interprets and enforces the law written by the Legislature.)

Business taxes provided roughly 5.7 percent of overall revenues in the 2004-05 fiscal year. (That does not include personal income tax revenues from owners of Subchapter S corporations, partnerships, and sole proprietorships.) The main business profits tax, known as the Article 9-A corporation franchise tax, and taxes on banks and insurance companies contribute more than half of that total. The most significant business tax preference is the investment tax credit. It allows manufacturers and securities firms to subtract from New York State tax up to 5 percent of capital investments related to core operations in the state.

Other state taxes apply to tobacco and alcoholic beverages, estates, motor fuel, wagers on horse racing, real property sales, boxing and wrestling exhibitions, and hotel room rentals.

Cutting Taxes

What many in Albany remember as the "fiscal crisis" that confronted New York City and state government in the mid-1970s was, more accurately, an extended economic crisis, as numerous businesses scaled back operations and cut jobs in New York. Total employment statewide in 1977 was lower than it had been in 1967; meanwhile, the number of jobs nationwide had grown by more than 25 percent. With economic growth lacking in New York, tax revenues collected by the city and state failed to keep pace with rising demands for spending.

State leaders identified high taxes as a core competitive problem for the Empire State. The state's top tax rate on personal income, 7 percent

---

5   Donald Boyd and James Barrese, *New York's State and Local Tax System*, paper prepared for Citizens Budget Commission, New York, NY, December 1995, p. 8. Some of this section's discussion of the general characteristics of New York State taxation is adapted from their paper.

in the mid-1950s, had been raised in steps to more than 15 percent by 1969. A surcharge brought the rate to 15.375 percent in 1972. Governor Carey signed legislation in 1977 eliminating the surcharge; he and the Legislature brought the top rate down to 12 percent the following year and to 10 percent in 1981. Governor Cuomo and the Legislature reduced the top rate further in several steps to 7.875 percent in 1989. While the top rate was declining, changes to tax brackets, deductions, and other provisions of the tax law added to savings for taxpayers.

When the state's economy faltered in 1990 and 1991, Governor Cuomo and the Legislature rewrote existing law that would have brought the top tax rate on personal income down to 7 percent. They enacted other tax increases, as well, including a 15 percent surcharge on corporate taxes.

In the last 12 years, however, most of the state's major taxes have been reduced.

In 1995, at the initiative of Governor Pataki, the Legislature reduced rates and enacted other changes to the personal income tax to return an estimated $4 billion a year to taxpayers.

Corporate tax rates, including the bank and insurance taxes, were reduced from 9 to 7.5 percent over four years under legislation enacted in 1997 and 1998 at the urging of Senate Majority Leader Joseph L. Bruno. Another tax change of primary interest to the business community was reduction of the alternative minimum tax, from 3.5 to 2.5 percent. The alternative tax applies when taxpayers use a certain amount of investment tax credit or other credits, and has the effect of reducing the value of such credits. The corporate tax surcharge first applied in 1990 was eliminated in steps from 1994 through 1996.

The rate of the state sales tax has not changed in recent years, but a major new exemption — on clothing sales — was enacted at the initiative of Assembly Speaker Sheldon Silver. The exemption was first applied for one-week periods in 1998 and 1999. It now applies, for purchases valued at $110 or less, throughout the year. (Numerous counties around the state, on the other hand, raised local sales tax rates in the late 1980s and early 1990s, largely in response to increasing Medicaid costs that critics said were driven higher by policies set in Albany.)

As of February 1, 2000, New York's estate tax was reduced to the amount that can be taken as a credit against federal estate taxes. Previously one of the highest death taxes in the nation, the levy was then as low in New York as in any other state, and lower than those in more than a dozen states. Congressional action in 2001, reducing federal estate taxes, had the unintended effect of returning New York's estate tax to life. Its maximum rate is 16 percent for larger estates.

State leaders significantly increased one tax in recent years. Governor Pataki and the Legislature raised the cigarette tax from 56 cents to $1.11 per package in 2000 as one of several new revenue sources to pay for expanding the state's Medicaid program, and added another increase in 2002 to bring the tax to $1.50 per pack, not counting any local tobacco taxes.

The Growing Role of State-Sponsored Gambling

Like many other states, New York has increasingly promoted gambling as a means of increasing revenue. Lottery tickets and other forms of gambling will produce an estimated $2.4 billion for Albany in the 2006-07 fiscal year, up nearly $1 billion from six years earlier.

New York and other states commonly used lotteries as revenue sources in the nation's first decades. In 1821, a Constitutional Convention recommended a ban on the practice in the Empire State, and voters agreed. An 1894 amendment extended the prohibition to most other forms of gambling, with pari-mutuel betting on horse races allowed starting in 1939. In 1957, voters approved an amendment allowing bingo and similar games for support of certain religious, charitable and nonprofit organizations.

Creation of the modern Lottery a decade later was controversial,[6] with many opponents arguing it was wrong for the government to encourage activity the Legislature had long outlawed because of its harmful social impact. The Regents announced their opposition to the proposal in August 1966, just weeks before voters were to decide. Supporters, including Governor Rockefeller, said the lottery would supplant illegal gambling while providing additional resources for the state. The proposal emerged after Rockefeller and the Legislature had

---

6   Voters in 43 of 62 counties rejected Amendment 7, authorizing state lotteries for the support of education. Outside New York City, the amendment was barely favored, by 1,290,325-1,200,200. Strong support in the city — with 1,174,573 "yes" and 404,494 "no" votes — carried the measure to easy statewide approval.

increased education spending significantly in the early 1960s. But spending on other programs was increasing, as well.

To help win support from voters, drafters of the amendment included a provision that proceeds would go exclusively to education. With approval from voters, state-operated gambling began in June 1967, the second modern state lottery in the nation (New Hampshire's started in 1964). Revenue was relatively modest, less than $100 million a year, for more than a decade. In 1984-85, Governor Cuomo and the Legislature approved three extended-sales periods with big prizes, stimulating higher sales. Revenue rose to $615 million that year.

In the last decade, Governor Pataki and the Legislature have enacted major new forms of state-sponsored gambling. A 1995 law allowed bars and restaurants to offer "Quick Draw" games, previously derided as "video crack," which allow bets as often as every four minutes. In 2001, the state agreed to join multijurisdictional contests such as Mega Millions — with prizes that can run into scores of millions of dollars. That year's legislation also allowed video-lottery terminals (VLTs) at selected racetracks. As of September 2006, VLTs were operating at Saratoga, Finger Lakes, Monticello, Buffalo, and Batavia raceways. Yonkers and Aqueduct raceways were expected to add the terminals within the following year, adding hundreds of millions to state revenues.

Official references such as the Executive Budget's revenue estimates refer to Lottery proceeds as "current receipts for education." The practical effect of the state's gambling proceeds is to increase the state's overall revenues, and thus allow more overall spending without tax increases. Disgruntled property taxpayers often complain that the Lottery does not fulfill its promise of providing needed revenue for schools. A 1998 report by the Office of the State Comptroller found that "...an examination of the aid formula demonstrates that the lottery does not affect total aid received by schools."[7] Evidence cited in the report included Rockefeller's use of the first-year Lottery revenues to pay part of the costs of previously enacted school-aid increases.

Recent expansions of gambling in the state have been less controversial than the 1966 amendment creating the Lottery, perhaps because the Legislature has not consulted voters. The VLT legislation, for

---

7   Office of the State Comptroller, *The New York State Lottery: Role in Financing Education*, p. 2.

Native American Gambling

The state's drive to increase revenue from gambling has played the primary role in its relations with Native American tribes in recent years. In a related issue, state leaders have tried repeatedly — but, as of mid-2006, unsuccessfully — to collect taxes on reservations' sales of cigarettes and gasoline.

In 1987, the U.S. Supreme Court ruled that states cannot prohibit gambling on Indian reservations if they allow it elsewhere. A year later, Congress passed the Indian Gaming Regulatory Act, creating rules for agreements between tribes and states regarding casinos and other gambling facilities on reservations.

The Oneida Indian Nation and Governor Cuomo signed a compact, under the framework of the federal law, in 1993. The nation opened its Turning Stone casino in Verona, Oneida County, that year. Its agreement with the state subjects the property to oversight by the State Police and the Racing and Wagering Board.

The Mohawk tribe opened a casino in Franklin County in 1999, and the Seneca Nation in Niagara Falls on New Year's Eve 2002. The 2001 legislation that allowed video lottery terminals in various locations also contemplated six additional Indian casinos. State officials and Native American tribes had also pursued establishment of casinos in Buffalo, in the Catskills and near the eastern end of Long Island, but as of September 2006 no such agreements had been reached.

As sovereign nations, Indian tribes are not required to collect state taxes on the sale of products such as cigarettes and gasoline on reservations. State leaders have tried for years to force such collections, to no avail. At $1.50 per pack, New York's cigarette tax is higher than almost any other state's; New York City's local tax of $1.50 creates the highest such tax in the nation. Fiscal staff in the Legislature estimate the state could collect $150 million or more annually with enforcement of cigarette taxes on tribal sales to non-Native Americans.

example, was enacted late at night after a quick introduction that gave legislators themselves little time to study the detailed proposal. Still, some critics have emerged.

A 2006 report by the New York Council on Problem Gambling, a nonprofit education and advocacy group, found that adolescent gambling "has taken a turn for the worse" and issued recommendations including a statewide public-awareness campaign. State Senator Frank Padavan has warned that the advent of casinos and nearly continuous Lottery drawings known as Quick Draw games harm families and individuals by enticing gamblers to lose more than they can afford (the VLT legislation prohibits such gambling in Queens, home to Padavan's district). Counseling agencies and other observers have pointed to sharp increases in problem gambling in recent years.[8] Critics also note that poorer individuals spend disproportionately on Lotto and other games, compared to middle- and upper-income residents, skewing the state's overall revenue burden more toward those who can least afford to pay. In 2000, then-Comptroller H. Carl McCall urged a moratorium on new gambling initiatives absent comprehensive plans to address problem gambling, a recommendation that Governor Pataki and the Legislature ignored.

After enactment of the 2001 legislation approving VLTs, opponents sued to block introduction of the devices, arguing they did not meet the constitutionally acceptable form of a "lottery." The Court of Appeals ruled in 2005 that the machines were permissible because, while resembling casino slot machines, VLTs are assembled into networks that constitute lottery drawings.[9]

The state acknowledges that additional gambling opportunities will lead to increased participation. The 2006-07 Executive Budget estimated that 25.8 percent of New Yorkers aged 21 or older would visit a casino in an average month. It added:

> The participation rate appears correlated with the availability of casinos, suggesting that additional participants are encouraged by access to VLT venues. Therefore, it is assumed that as more VLTs become available over time, the participation rates in New York and some surrounding states will increase to between 35 percent and 40 percent, which seems to be the norm for states with easier access to these facilities.[10]

---

8   See, for instance, Kate Gurnett, *Gambling With Lives* series in the *Times Union*, Albany, NY, January 2003. Some of the increase, especially in the last five years or so, is attributable to Internet-based poker and other games.

9   *Dalton v. Pataki,* May 3, 2005.

10 New York State Division of the Budget, *2006-07 Executive Budget: Economic and Revenue Outlook*, p. 574.

Since the mid-1990s, the state has provided modest funding for the New York Council on Problem Gambling. The Office of Alcoholism and Substance Abuse Services also supports 10 counseling centers for problem gamblers and a similar number of prevention programs.

As of 2004, New York's cumulative total of sales since creation of the modern Lottery stood at $52 billion, first among the states and more than 10 percent of the national total, according to the Tax Foundation. Cumulative prizes were $25 billion, for an average payout of 48 percent, compared to 53 percent nationwide. Total collections by the state were $21 billion.[11]

The Executive Budget Process

Since the days of Governor Franklin D. Roosevelt, New York State has operated under an Executive Budget process that makes the governor primarily responsible for state fiscal policy. Article VII of the state Constitution gives the governor:

- Exclusive power to initiate discussions about the overall budget by submitting to the Legislature a complete plan of expenditures and revenues.

- As part of that power, complete control over spending requests from executive-branch agencies.

- Authority to veto any spending the Legislature adds to his proposal, with the veto subject to legislative override that historically has been rare (although relatively common in the last years of the Pataki administration).

- Significant power over how the budget, especially that part covering state agency operations, is implemented during the fiscal year.

Before institution of the Executive Budget process, heads of state agencies applied to the Legislature for appropriations. There was no centralized "budget" in the sense of a complete account of projected

---

11 Alicia Hansen, *Lotteries and State Fiscal Policy*, Washington, DC: Tax Foundation, October 2004.

spending and revenues for a given year. A history of the Division of the Budget explains the origins of the Executive Budget this way:

> Governor Charles Evans Hughes was completing his third legislative session in 1909, and was wondering why it should be necessary to exercise his veto again and again with respect to appropriation bills that bore little relation to the missions of the agencies, were internally inconsistent, and inadequately investigated as to both need and effect. Always impressed by the virtues of orderly administration, the Governor added a postscript to a veto memorandum and inadvertently planted the seed from which the executive budget was to grow: "There should ... be provided some permanent method for comparative examination of departmental budgets and proposals for appropriations in advance of the legislative session so that the Legislature may be aided by preliminary investigation and report in determining, with just proportion, the amounts that can properly be allowed.[12]

The Legislature responded by requiring the comptroller to compile agency budget requests and present them, along with estimates of projected revenue, to the Legislature for its consideration. Still, a better-organized starting point for legislative consideration did not guarantee a better outcome. The budget remained susceptible to horse-trading and failure to devote resources where most needed. Governor Al Smith, who served as Ways and Means chairman and later pushed through the requirement for an executive budget with help from Hughes, wrote:

> Each assemblyman used his influence to put what he wanted into the appropriation bill before it left the assembly, and when it reached the senate the same thing happened. In fact, there was a story prevalent in Albany in 1915 that one of the clerks of the assembly amended the appropriation bill himself by inserting an item in it while carrying it from the assembly to the senate chamber.[13]

Governors William Sulzer, Martin H. Glynn, and Charles S. Whitman, who among them served from 1913 through 1918 (the governor then had a two-year term), followed Hughes in calling for and seeking to exercise greater executive control over the budget. The Constitutional Convention of 1915 recommended an executive budget as one of

---

12 New York State Division of the Budget, *The Executive Budget in New York State: A Half-Century Perspective*, 1981, p. 1.

13 Smith, *Up To Now*, 1929, p. 257.

several major steps to strengthen the role of the governor and, by extension, make state government more accountable. However, voters rejected the convention's proposed new Constitution that fall because of
concerns over legislative reapportionment and other issues.

After taking office in 1920, Governor Smith appointed a Reconstruction Commission to push for reform (the staff was directed by
Robert Moses, initiating his rise to appointed positions of enormous
power in both state and New York City government). After losing his
1921 bid for re-election to Nathan L. Miller, Smith returned to office in
1923 still committed to change. This time, thanks to another commission chaired by former Governor Hughes, Smith was able to convince
both the Legislature and voters to enact a revised Article VII of the
Constitution. First effective in 1929, when Governor Franklin D. Roosevelt took office, the Executive Budget system has remained fundamentally the same ever since.

How the Process Unfolds

Article VII of the Constitution calls for the governor to send the proposed budget to the Legislature by February 1 in years after a gubernatorial election. In other years, the deadline for submittal is the second
Tuesday after the first day of legislative session, which typically means
in the second or third week of January. The Constitution sets no date for
budget adoption; under the State Finance Law, the state's fiscal year
begins on April 1.

Before the governor's spending and tax proposals undergo review
by the Legislature, agency requests face close scrutiny by Budget Division staff. In November, the budget director conducts hearings on each
agency proposal. The hearings are not public. However, as the state
Constitution requires, representatives of the Legislature may participate in the division's hearings, giving lawmakers an inside look at what
the governor might propose several weeks later.

At the same time, the Budget Division's fiscal staff assesses the state
of the economy to forecast the level of revenues the state is likely to collect under existing tax laws and any contemplated changes. Through
December and into January, the governor and top advisers decide what
new priorities to pursue in the Executive Budget proposal.

Items of appropriation proposed by the governor become law upon approval by the Legislature, with no further action required by the executive. If the Legislature inserts additional appropriations or adds to proposed spending, the governor must approve; a veto eliminates the additions unless two-thirds of both houses vote to override. The Constitution favors less spending rather than more: If the Legislature strikes or reduces appropriation items submitted by the governor, the lower appropriation figure becomes law without further executive approval.

The Constitution allows the Legislature to initiate one multipurpose, supplemental budget bill after acting on the governor's proposals. (Action on other multipurpose bills can precede voting on Executive Budget bills only if the governor agrees. Recent years' practice of enacting temporary budget bills between April 1 and final enactment of the budget has relied on such gubernatorial assent.) This provision became particularly relevant in 2001, when a stalemate between Governor Pataki and the Legislature delayed action on the budget until early August. The Senate and Assembly approved scaled-down versions of the governor's bills and considered a supplemental budget. Lawmakers can pass as many appropriation bills as they desire, but except for the one supplemental bill, all such legislation must contain only "a single object or purpose."

The Constitution allows statutory language to be included in the governor's and the supplemental appropriation bills, as long as such language relates specifically, and only, to some particular item of appropriation in the bill.

The legislative acts that actually authorize state spending are called appropriations. The "all-funds" and other measures of the budget mentioned above describe the dollars expected to be spent in a given year, which differ from the total amount of appropriations. State government cannot legally spend money without a legislative appropriation. However, the state does not spend all appropriations in a given year; the Constitution allows them to be made over a two-year period.

Actual disbursements (the technical term for cash outlays) occur under the authority of appropriations, but over the course of a year total disbursements generally do not match total appropriations. Sometimes disbursements are lower, because not all the money authorized is spent or because some appropriations involve projects that stretch over more than one year. Similarly, for some categories disbursements may be higher than that year's appropriations because the spending may be based in part on a prior year's appropriations. The 2000-01 Executive Budget proposed by Governor Pataki included appropriations totaling $121 billion — more than half again as much as actual projected spending.Together, the set of estimates of actual revenues and disbursements expected for the fiscal year comprise the "financial plan."

The state's fiscal year is set in statute (not the Constitution) as April 1 through March 31. (Legislators in both houses have called unsuccessfully in recent years for the fiscal year to start in May or June, allowing them more time for review and to make timely budget adoption more likely.) The Constitution allows the governor to revise the proposal within 30 days after submitting it. Given the complex nature of the process, the executive branch starts work on the governor's proposal months earlier; individual agencies may begin internal budget deliberations in May or June of the previous year. By early fall, the agency head sends its proposals to the Budget Division.

After the Legislature approves appropriation bills and the governor acts on any changes to his original proposals, the Budget Division prepares a financial plan reflecting the final levels of spending and revenues. State agencies begin implementing programs funded by the new appropriations — hiring staff, obtaining office space, preparing requests for contracts, and so on. Throughout the year, the Budget Division keeps a close watch on the flow of revenues and expenditures, constantly comparing them to the financial plan and revising the plan quarterly as needed. Most financial transactions require approval of both the Budget Division — representing the governor — and the comptroller's office, while contracts are reviewed by the attorney general's office as well. In addition, many transactions require notification be sent to the legislative fiscal committee chairs. The result, generally speaking, is that at least two separately elected statewide officials and/or the legislative branch are informed of any expenditure of taxpayers' dollars.

The Office of the State Comptroller may use appropriations made in one fiscal year to pay vouchers for capital projects through September 30 of the following year, on charges that were incurred during the fiscal year for which the appropriation was made. Thus the "year" in which such an appropriation is made may be considered to have lasted up to 18 months from the passage of an appropriation — and as much as 27 months from when the agency first began planning the expenditure, to when the bill is finally paid.

The Legislature's Role

For members of the Legislature, work on the budget starts with simply finding out how the governor's proposal may affect important constituencies: Would school aid to local districts go up or down, and by how much? Are state institutions back home targeted for expansion or cutbacks? How would any proposed tax cuts or increases affect district residents and businesses? For lawmakers in the governor's political party, what is there to compliment in the budget? For the opposition, what is there to criticize?

Legislative staff members assigned to the Senate Finance and Assembly Ways and Means committees analyze the budget in depth, and publish detailed reports on the spending and revenue implications within two weeks or so of the budget's introduction.

Over the next several weeks, the two houses hold joint public hearings on major programs. At the hearings, executive agency leaders argue on behalf of the governor's proposals, and interest groups — mayors and other municipal leaders, state employee unions, organizations representing other providers of state-funded services, and other lobbyists ranging from environmental groups to advocates for business — speak as well. During a dozen or so public hearings, more than 100 speakers may make their case in relation to particular parts of the budget. Generally, at the start of a hearing, a half-dozen or more legislators will represent each house. However, the final speakers of the day may face an audience of only a single legislator and a few fiscal committee staff members.

Throughout the Legislature's budget review, individual lawmakers receive delegations of professional lobbyists, teachers, senior citizens, advocates for the mentally disabled, and other citizens pressing for additional funding or other changes in the budget.

Legislators and their staffs also talk to commissioners and other officials in state agencies during this time. Away from the public forum of the budget hearings, agency officials will occasionally be helpful to legislators who seek to add more funding than the Budget Division wishes to accept. Legislative fiscal staffers sometimes like to say that commissioners work for the governor until the budget is out, but they work for the Legislature after it is released. That may overstate the case, but there is some truth in it.

The "New Pork Barrel"

Almost from the state's beginning in the 18th century, members of the Legislature have viewed the annual budget process as an opportunity to bring funding back to their home districts. In recent years, the scale of appropriations for such purposes has grown dramatically, as shown in a 2005 newspaper report:

> Starting in 1997-98, Governor Pataki and legislative leaders set aside hundreds of millions of dollars each year for economic-development projects, grants to nonprofit organizations and other uses subject to decisions long after adoption of the budget. Senate Majority Leader Joseph L. Bruno and Assembly Speaker Sheldon Silver controlled funding set-asides for their respective houses, approving requests from members for projects in their communities.
>
> For example, in 2005 a Syracuse-area legislator obtained $15 million in funding for a hotel in the city, according to a newspaper report.
>
> New York state leaders this week committed state taxpayers to $15 million, plus interest, for a new convention center hotel in Syracuse without any statewide competition, with no public debate by the state Senate or Assembly, and before they set guidelines for the slush fund they plan to tap.
>
> State Sen. John DeFrancisco just asked for the money.
>
> "Go for it," Senate Majority Leader Joseph Bruno told DeFrancisco privately on the Senate floor Wednesday before the start of the day's public business.
>
> "I went for it," DeFrancisco said later, recounting the conversation.
>
> With a thumbs-up from his leader, DeFrancisco said, he got on the phone to Gov. George Pataki's staff, then to Assemblyman William Magnarelli to ask them to get their leaders to commit $5 million each.
>
> The other legislators will have no say in the spending. State taxpayers will contribute to the project. New York's taxpayers spend about $100 million a year to pay off the debt on these kinds of projects.

Source: Michelle Breidenbach, "Hotel funds from slush fund," *Post-Standard*, Syracuse, NY, February 11, 2005.

By mid-March, the majority conference in each house has established its position — a number of areas where it will seek to add to the governor's budget, perhaps a few where it might reduce funding, and its proposals for tax reductions or increases. In recent decades, the Senate majority leader and the Assembly speaker generally held private meetings with the governor, joined by one or two top assistants to each of the principals (the process known as "three men in a room"), to negotiate the final budget. Other staff from each house and the budget office negotiate detailed line items for every agency. In 1998, the Legislature adopted a joint conference committee process to organize its deliberations and reach legislative agreement on a budget. That year, the Senate and Assembly agreed on extensive increases in expenditures over Governor Pataki's proposal. The governor vetoed much of the increased spending, and there was no override. In 1999 and 2000, the two houses used the conference committee again, but also conducted leadership negotiations with the governor that avoided major vetoes. Extensive vetoes and overrides returned in 2003.

A Contentious Process

More than anything else, annual negotiations between the governor and the Legislature reflect the nature of relations between the two branches — more specifically, between the leaders. Each institution has policies it wishes to promote and political influences to address, creating institutional tensions that ebb and flow from year to year and from incumbent to incumbent.

From 1985 through 2004, the most noticeable effect of those tensions was a budget adopted weeks, or even months, after the start of the state fiscal year. The state Constitution does not specify when the budget must be adopted, but State Finance Law sets the fiscal year as April 1 through March 31. Reasons for the 20 straight years of late budgets included legislators' increasing sense of insulation from political risk; the improved technical ability of legislative fiscal staff, which reduces the hegemony of the executive branch over fiscal information; and increased constituent expectations that legislators will bring increased state assistance home to schools and community programs.

Perhaps the most fundamental reason for late budgets is that elected leaders perceive the political and policy-related costs to be less than the gains. Temporary budget bills allow most state operations and aid programs to proceed even when there is no budget in place. Legislators have found that voters do not hold them individually accountable for the problem. With the executive budget system placing most accountability in the chief executive, governors have tended to place more emphasis on the need for timely budgets. But it is difficult for governors to force the Legislature to act.

One perennial source of disagreement among the budget negotiators is the level of projected revenues. Small differences in opinion on economic forecasts can translate into differences of hundreds of millions of dollars in revenue projections. Almost without exception, members of the Legislature want to add spending to the governor's proposal; one way to justify additional expenditures is to "find" offsetting revenues. Governors, on the other hand, generally want to make sure they avoid significant budget shortfalls which could force them to take unpopular actions to reduce spending (Governor Smith and others were correct in believing the executive budget process would bring more careful budgeting). Thus, governors generally seek to limit the Legislature's spending increases above those already contained in the Executive Budget. Legislation that resulted from continually late budgets in the early 1990s calls for the executive and legislative branches to agree on projected revenues by mid-March, to allow time for final budget negotiations before the April 1 start of a new fiscal year. In practice, staff for each of the three major players — the governor and the majority conference in each house — announce their own estimates at the required time but do not officially agree on revenue estimates until the entire new budget has been negotiated. Once the governor and legislative leaders agree on broader aspects of the budget, they typically find room for compromise on revenue estimates. While the Constitution is interpreted to require a balanced-budget proposal from the governor, neither it nor the State Finance Law require that the Legislature produce a balanced plan.

The Continuing Struggle Over Budget Powers

While executive-legislative disputes over the budget process arose periodically in the decades after creation of the Executive Budget, a 1993 court case can be said to have marked the beginning of more intense debate.

In 1990, the Legislature added a statutory change to one of Governor Cuomo's appropriation bills, imposing a new fee on state-chartered banks. The New York State Bankers Association challenged the fee in court, arguing that the Constitution does not allow the Legislature to change language in an Executive Budget appropriation bill, even if the governor does not object. The Court of Appeals agreed.[14]

Two later cases, decided jointly by the Court of Appeals in December 2004, furthered the high court's line of rulings on executive and legislative budget powers and helped lay the groundwork for the 2005 Constitutional amendment on the budget process known as Proposal One. In 1998, the Legislature amended nonappropriation (so-called "Article VII") budget bills Governor Pataki had submitted as part of his Executive Budget. Many of the Legislature's amendments affected appropriations the governor had submitted, and the Legislature had approved, in that year's appropriation bills. Governor Pataki used his line-item veto on 55 such items, saying the Legislature's changes went beyond its Constitutional authority to strike out or reduce an item of appropriation. In December 2004, the Court of Appeals ruled in the governor's favor in both *Silver* v. *Pataki*, stemming from the 1998 dispute, and *Pataki* v. *New York State Assembly*, relating to the 2001 budget deliberations. The latter case emerged after Governor Pataki used his Executive Budget bills as vehicles for unusually extensive legislative proposals. The 2001 Executive Budget appropriation bills included, for instance, 17 pages of language rewriting the formulas for allocation of state aid to public schools; changes to Public Health Law provisions for computing certain Medicaid reimbursement rates; and creation of a new Office of Cultural Resources to oversee the State Museum and State Library. Legislative leaders said that such extensive inclusion of statutory changes in appropriation bills crossed the constitutional line. Among other responses, the Legislature enacted its own appropriation bills, including amounts that in some cases were identical to the governor's proposals but imposing different statutory conditions on use of the funding. With some other items, the Legislature enacted the governor's appropriation but then amended the appropriation by adopting language changes in nonappropriation budget bills.

The Court of Appeals decision in *Silver* v. *Pataki* and *Pataki* v. *Assembly* came down firmly, if in somewhat muddled fashion, on the side of executive power. In both cases, the court found that the Legislature

---

14 *New York State Bankers Association v. Wetzler*, 81 NY2d 98, 104 (1993).

The Budget Powers: No Clarity Yet

If the Court of Appeals' decision in *Pataki* v. *Assembly* is any indication, the state Constitution's division of executive and legislative budget powers remains confusing and a recipe for continuing strife between the two branches.

The ruling found only three members of the seven-judge court agreeing on the key issue of how much a governor can do to write policy changes into Executive Budget appropriation bills. Two other members of the court joined in supporting Governor Pataki's legal arguments against the Legislature in the cases at hand. But those two differed sharply from the three-vote plurality on what future governors may or may not do with budget proposals. A highly critical dissent by Chief Judge Judith Kaye — joined by one colleague — raised still further questions about the decision. On the specifics of the state's most important budget-related judicial decision in decades, the high court split 3-2-2.

In short, more than 75 years after voters approved today's Article VII, *Pataki* v. *Assembly* left the balance of powers very much up in the air.

The Legislature, which failed to persuade voters to approve one sweeping amendment on the issue, has taken the first step toward placing a related amendment on the ballot in 2007. That proposed amendment — much less complex, and likely to be less controversial, than the 2005 Proposal One — amends the existing Article VII to specify that the governor may not include legislative language in appropriation bills. Both houses gave first passage to the amendment in 2005, and could give the required second passage as early as 2007.

had altered the Governor's appropriation bills in ways not permitted by the Constitution. In *Pataki* v. *Assembly,* the court found Governor Pataki's insertion of statutory language into appropriation bills acceptable — seeming to provide broad leeway for such action until further court rulings. The latest decisions left the Legislature with few options for pursuing its budgetary wishes in the future. As has been the case since FDR's first state budget, legislators retain the power to strike or reduce any Executive Budget appropriation. As the court's decision pointed out, the Legislature also has the option of refusing to act on the governor's budget bills to induce negotiations. Then there is the final option: Amend the Constitution.

The Battle Over Proposal One

Leaders of the Legislature decided in 2005 they could address both the Court of Appeals' decision on the budget powers, and the long string of late budgets, by amending the provisions of Article VII that Governor Smith and others had initiated in the 1920s. The plan included a constitutional amendment intended to guarantee that some form of a budget would always be in place at the start of a new fiscal year, even in the absence of legislative action on the Executive Budget. That guarantee came in the form of a contingency budget, based on the previous year's appropriations, that would take effect automatically if no enacted budget were in place. The contingency proposal also dealt with the Legislature's concern over executive dominance of the budget process. In a dramatic change, the Legislature's amendment provided that, if there were no final action on the Executive Budget by the start of a new fiscal year, the governor's appropriation bills would become dead letters. The Legislature would be forbidden from acting on the Executive Budget bills, and instead would introduce its own appropriation bills — going back, at least in years with late budgets, to the system that had prevailed until 1928.

Although legislative leaders announced the outlines of their budget-reform proposal in March 2004, the actual legislation did not emerge until June 19, just days before the end of the regular legislative session. With little public review, both houses passed the bill, Senate bill S7615, three days later. The agreed-upon legislation was a mix of proposals from differing plans each house had advanced previously.

The Court of Appeals decision in December 2004 provided additional impetus for the Legislature to give second passage to Proposal One, as it became known, in 2005. In the months before Election Day 2005, several polls showed voters favoring the amendment. Joining the Senate and Assembly in support of Proposal One were three of Albany's "good-government" groups: Common Cause/NY, the League of Women Voters of New York State, and New York Public Interest Research Group (NYPIRG). Opponents included Governor Pataki, Attorney General Spitzer, fiscal analysts E.J. McMahon of the Manhattan Institute and Frank J. Mauro, political scientist Gerald Benjamin, the

Business Council of New York State, Citizens Budget Commission, and Citizens Union. Campaign-style efforts included a statewide tour by a taxpayer group displaying a pink pig statue, and advertising campaigns for and against.[15]

On Election Day, the amendment failed, with 35 percent of voters in favor and 65 percent opposed. In 2006, legislators approved a new statutory proposal that would move the state's fiscal year to May 1 and make some other changes. Governor Pataki vetoed the measure.

Who Decides, and How?

As underscored by the Court of Appeals, when it comes to directing use of the state's financial resources, New York's governor has enormous powers. This is especially true when considering not only "the budget," but the finances of the state's public authorities as well.

Once the budget is enacted, the governor has the power to limit spending by state agencies (such spending is typically less than 20 percent of the total budget), by reducing the workforce through layoffs or attrition, postponing planned contracts, and taking other steps.

The Legislature, however, is not without its own substantial ability to shape the budget. First, of course, as noted, the Senate and Assembly must act on the governor's Executive Budget. The Legislature can add spending to the budget and, if those changes are vetoed, can override the veto with a two-thirds vote in each house. When enough members of the Legislature agree, then, it has the final voice on appropriations.

While the Legislature generally prefers to negotiate rather than override a gubernatorial veto, the mere existence of such power restrains the governor's willingness to ignore the Legislature's desires. During Governor Pataki's tenure, for instance, the arm of the Legislature most supportive of his proposals to limit spending has been the Assembly Republican conference, which had more than a third of the seats in the Assembly. One might assume that the governor could veto any legislative increases and rely on the Assembly Republicans to prevent an override, which requires a two-thirds vote. However, the

---

15 For a more detailed look at Proposal One and the 2005 campaign, see Robert B. Ward, "Proposal One: 'Modest' Reform, or a 'Runaway Spending Amendment?'," in *Journal of Governmental Finance and Public Policy*, New York State Division of the Budget/Nelson A. Rockefeller Institute of Government, Albany, NY, July 2006.

administration would have had to ensure that no more than one or two Republican legislators would vote in favor of an override. It's always difficult for a governor to be certain of every member's vote in such a situation.

The Legislature often uses another important power — refusing to enact program legislation sought by the governor. Governors commonly seek changes in statutes to control spending, reshape programs, or achieve other budgetary goals. During each of his first few years in office, for example, Governor Pataki sought to amend the Social Services Law and Public Health Law to reduce Medicaid costs. The Legislature accepted some of his proposals and rejected others.

The comptroller has no part in the budget-making process, but plays a key role in actual spending of taxpayer dollars. Under the Constitution, the state cannot make any payments without pre-approval by the comptroller's office. As detailed in Chapter Four, the office's "pre-audit" function involves ascertaining whether payment vouchers are supported by valid documents which are not, on their face, unreasonable or fraudulent. Under the State Finance Law, no contract for more than $10,000 by any state agency can become effective until approved by the comptroller. The department also conducts "post-audits" of specific transactions, internal administrative controls, and the operations of agencies and programs, both in state government and in local governments.

As a result of decisions by the Court of Appeals and lower courts, the judicial branch of state government may take a direct role in a major policy decision concerning state financing for education. A group called the Campaign for Fiscal Equity sued the state, alleging that Albany's aid to local school districts fails to give all children the opportunity for the "sound basic education" that the Court of Appeals has ruled they are entitled to under the state Constitution. Similar lawsuits in a number of other states have produced judicial orders for increased spending on schools; the Campaign for Fiscal Equity seeks a similar ruling in New York. The Court of Appeals is expected to issue a final ruling in 2007.

Such judicial involvement in a major policy and funding decision had some precedent in 1975, when the state entered into a consent judgment with the New York State Association for Retarded Children and other plaintiffs who had sued in federal District Court over the care given to clients in state institutions. The Carey administration agreed to a detailed list of standards affecting staffing, space, and programming, all with financial implications. Governor Carey had taken a personal interest in improving care for the mentally disabled, but the court's involvement played a major role.

One of the most powerful influences on any year's budget is the accumulation of decisions made in previous years. As with most large organizations, particularly those in the public sector, New York State government tends to budget incrementally. Elected and appointed officials seldom question existing programs — partly because virtually every state program has legislative support and a constituency, and it is easier to block change in government than to achieve it. The question in Albany in any typical year is how large an increase each spending area will receive. Generally, the only exceptions are years when revenues fall or grow more slowly than usual. Smart administrators use those times as opportunities to focus budget-cutting efforts on programs that are least effective and most deserve to be scaled back or eliminated.

The Balance of Power

In New York, as elsewhere in America, a central element in the system of democratic government is division of power among the branches of government. The balance of that power shifts in one direction or the other from time to time.

The current Executive Budget system was created through constitutional amendment in 1927 as part of an effort, ongoing for much of the early part of this century, to make state government more responsible and accountable. It transferred significant power from the Legislature to the governor. Strong governors consolidated budgetary power even further through the middle half of the 20th century.

By the 1970s, the Legislature had begun to push back. One example was its concern over staffing levels in state agencies. Governor Carey reduced staff in various agencies, both to restrain spending and to reflect changes in priorities. For instance, significant numbers of clients living in state institutions for the mentally disabled were moving into the community. When tough economic times again reduced revenues in 1990, Governor Cuomo also cut the state payroll. The state's public-employee unions enjoy significant influence with members of the Legislature, and one result was a 1992 law requiring that the Executive Budget include estimates of how spending proposals would affect employment in each state agency.

The Legislature's perspective on the division of powers was captured in a 1991 book published by the Rockefeller Institute of Government, *The Modern New York State Legislature: Redressing The Balance*. The book's dustjacket summary declared: "In accord with the American model of democratic governance, the Legislature in New York was designed to be the principal repository of the State's powers."

In its summary of the proposed 2000-01 Executive Budget, the staff of the Senate Finance Committee raised procedural questions about the appropriation legislation submitted by the governor as part of the budget. The Finance Committee critique said the proposal used broader appropriation categories than had historically been the case. For instance, it said, "personal service" or payroll costs for entire agencies were written as one lump sum rather than broken into smaller amounts for various classifications of workers.

"As a result of this generalized structure of appropriations, the Executive now has almost blanket authority to undertake flexible levels of expenditures for programs of its choosing without legislative oversight and can even enter into multi-million dollar contracts that may change the course of the State for years to come, again without legislative oversight," the committee staff wrote. "Instead of firmly holding the purse strings, the role of the Legislature has been eroded over the years to that of observer and whistle blower after a commitment is made and in some cases after the money is spent."

How New York Compares

By almost any measure, government in New York is bigger and more costly than those in other states. The U.S. Census Bureau compiles the official measure of public spending and revenues by the states and local governments. For state fiscal years ending in 2004, New York State government's per-capita tax burden of $2,280 — including all taxes collected by Albany — was about 20 percent above the national average and eighth-highest among the states.

Most observers of state finance believe that combining state and local taxes and spending provides a better measure than state government figures alone. As of fiscal 2004, by this measure, New York was number one in both total taxes per capita, and taxes as a proportion of personal income. As suggested by those figures, the big difference between New York and other states is in local taxes. In 2004, according to the Census Bureau, New Yorkers' local taxes totaled $2,404 per person, some 83 percent above the national average. Much of the local tax burden is affected by decisions made in Albany. For instance, New York is one of the few states that require localities to pay part of the cost of Medicaid. Given the expensive nature of the program in New York, that adds up to significant costs on counties and New York City.

Another good way to compare tax burdens among states is the "tax effort" measure originally developed by the federal Advisory Commission on Intergovernmental Relations and applied most recently by the Federal Reserve Bank of Boston to 1999 Census Bureau data on state and local finances. The tax effort indicator is a more sophisticated way to answer the basic question: How heavy is a given state's tax burden compared to what its economy can support? Using that measure, New York's combined state and local tax burden was by far the highest in the nation, 43 percent higher than the national average (the second-ranking state, Connecticut, was 19 percent higher than average).[16]

High taxes in New York are driven by high spending compared to other states. In 2004, combined state and local spending in the state totaled $11,375 per person, 47 percent above the national average, driven by relatively high spending on social services and other programs.

(The latest figures from the Census Bureau are available through www.census.gov/govs/www.index.html.)

Why Is Government in New York More Expensive?

If the choices made by elected leaders over time can be assumed to reflect the wishes of the voters (at least in a general way), then it must follow that New Yorkers *want* government to provide a relatively more costly array of services than those in other states. (That philosophy appears to go beyond the state level. New York State's Congressional delegation, is more often found supporting additional federal spending than pushing for federal tax cuts.)

---

16 Robert Tannenwald and Nicholas Turner, *Interstate Fiscal Disparity in State Fiscal Year 1999*, Public Policy Discussion Papers, Boston, MA: Federal Reserve Bank of Boston, December 2004.

State leaders can hardly be blamed if they believe that voters want government to increase spending every year. During the budget season, members of the Senate and Assembly hear from hundreds — sometimes thousands — of constituents asking them to support additional funding for public schools and universities, programs for the mentally disabled, highways and mass transportation, sports facilities, and a myriad of other projects. Few voters write or visit legislators to demand reduced (or even restrained) spending.

Some measures of need indicate that government in New York must spend more than those in many other states to provide an equivalent level of services. For instance, as of 2004-05, the Census Bureau found that 14.8 percent of New Yorkers were in poverty, compared to 12.7 percent of all U.S. residents. The Federal Reserve Bank of Boston found, though, that overall need for governmental services in New York is barely above the national average. Its "index of fiscal need" for 1999 put New York at a score of 101, compared to a nationwide average need index of 100.[17]

The question of how much state government can do — and should do — underlies the debates and negotiations over every year's budget. That question is, particularly, a pressing one for governors; they, much more than legislators, bear responsibility for making sure that both the current year's and future financial plans will not require irresponsible levels of debt, politically unpopular tax increases, or spending reductions.

Each governor applies a different philosophy to resolving the question. For example, Governor Charles Evans Hughes complained once, "There is not the slightest ground for the expectation that the people of the State will permit any substantial reduction of our activities." In more recent times, Governor Rockefeller spoke of the need for "muscular" state government. Governor Carey emphasized fiscal restraint and an end to "the days of wine and roses." Governor Cuomo, seeking some new programs while avoiding expansion on the Rockefeller scale, said people must have "all the government we need, but only the government we need."

---

17 Tannenwald and Turner, p. 25.

More Transparency Under
New Accounting Rules

When a weak economy reduced revenues to Albany in the mid-1970s, the fiscal crisis that developed in state government revealed serious structural flaws in the budget process. Over a period of years under Governor Rockefeller, as spending growth outpaced revenues, the state had established annual borrowings in the spring to pay bills deferred from the final months of the prior fiscal year. In 1981, legislation initiated by the Assembly majority required that state funds be reported according to Generally Accepted Accounting Principles (GAAP). Such reporting gives a more accurate picture of the state's fiscal position by requiring revenues and spending to be recognized as they are incurred. The traditional, cash basis of accounting — still used for actual operation of the fiscal plan — is more like a household checkbook and recognizes transactions as they are received or disbursed.

The advent of GAAP accounting showed that state government had an accumulated deficit of more than $2.3 billion, largely reflected in spring borrowings. In 1990, as the state was again facing serious economic and fiscal problems, Governor Cuomo and the Legislature created the Local Government Assistance Corporation (LGAC) to issue long-term bonds, which in turn would be used to reduce the accumulated deficit and eliminate spring borrowing. As of 2005, outstanding LGAC debt totaled $4.4 billion — nearly as much as its original borrowing. Plans called for the state to continue paying debt service on the LGAC bonds — in other words, paying now for expenditures made years ago — for an additional two decades.

While the annual spring borrowing was still in place, one step by which state leaders reassured the financial markets about the state's commitment to paying off bonds was to have the comptroller (and, in certain years, the legislative leaders) certify that the budget was balanced. Since the elimination of the spring borrowing, that certification is no longer used.

The Government Accounting Standards Board (GASB) has begun requiring states to make public additional financial information in recent years. An important player in public understanding of the state's finances, and those of other states and municipalities, GASB is a private, nonprofit body that establishes accounting and financial reporting standards for the more than 84,000 governmental units in the United States outside the federal government.

Starting in 2003, GASB began requiring states to make public extensive new information about its financial health, including estimates of the value of capital assets. All capital assets, including infrastructure, are now reported along with depreciation expenses — that is, the cost of "using up" capital assets.

The new reporting requirements will give New Yorkers additional opportunity to examine the policy decisions underlying the use of their tax dollars and how well those dollars are used. As a result of including the cost of using infrastructure and the introduction of accrual accounting, citizens will have available more comprehensive information about the cost of government services. They will also be able to see what portion of a program's cost is self-supported through user charges and grants, and what share must be subsidized generally by the public with tax revenues.

Starting in 2007, New York must report the estimated, accumulated cost of health-care benefits for current and future retirees. An initial estimate in 2006 put the state's long-term liability for such costs at $47 billion to $54 billion. GASB created the new accounting requirement to nudge states and localities into more careful planning for retiree health care. Public employers in New York and elsewhere set aside reserves for employee pensions each year, but pay retiree health benefits on a cash basis.

Budget Watchdogs

For New Yorkers who have an interest in the state's spending and revenues, there are numerous excellent sources of both data and sophisticated analysis.

As noted earlier in this chapter, financial reports from both the governor's Budget Division and the comptroller's office are available on the Internet. The same is true of budget reports from the Legislature *(see www.senate.state.ny.us and www.assembly.state.ny.us).*

More than ever before, outside groups with varying perspectives publish useful analyses of state finances. The most important are Standard & Poors and Moody's Investor Services, which analyze the state's finances from the perspective of investors in state bonds. These and

Where to Find Information on the Budget

Key reports about the state's finances are available from these agencies:

- Budget Division, *www.budget.state.ny.us*. The site includes the state's official financial plan for the current year; the governor's Executive Budget, which contains highly detailed information about both spending and revenues; summaries of the state's budget process; and the capital plan.

- Office of the State Comptroller,*www.osc.state.ny.us*. Information here includes the comptroller's analyses of the current year's budget and the state's overall financial condition; monthly updates on receipts and disbursements; reports on the state pension fund; audits of state agencies and programs; and data on municipal and school district finances.

- Senate and Assembly website,*www.senate.state.ny.us* and *www.assembly.state.ny.us*. The two houses provide information on their changes to the Executive Budget, economic reports and other data.

- Department of Taxation and Finance,*www.tax.state.ny.us*. Reports cover details of the state's overall tax collections, major individual taxes such as those on income and sales, tax policy and statistics, and technical bulletins.

other nongovernmental observers of the state's fiscal practices can shape public opinion Starting in 2007, New York must report the estimated, accumulated cost of health-care benefits for current and future retirees. An initial estimate in 2006 put the state's long-term liability for such costs at $47 billion to $54 billion. GASB created the new accounting requirement to nudge states and localities into more careful planning for retiree health care. Public employers in New York and elsewhere set aside reserves for employee pensions each year, but pay retiree health benefits on a cash basis. and thereby affect the policies that elected leaders establish. In the case of the bond raters, additional influence flows from their analyses of the state's creditworthiness in the bond market. A better rating by the agencies reduces the interest costs the state must pay on its bonds; conversely, a downgrading raises the cost of borrowing. The firms exercise their ultimate power when they judge the state unlikely to repay a given debt. This occurred with the state Urban Development Corp. in 1975, and the result was financial and operational breakdown.

Other budget "watchdogs" include:

- The Citizens Budget Commission, a New York City group financed largely by businesses, law firms, and foundations.

- The Fiscal Policy Institute, based outside Albany, financed by unions and foundations.

- The Manhattan Institute, based in New York City, financed by fiscally conservative individuals and foundations.

- The Public Policy Institute, based in Albany, financed by businesses.

Chapter Eleven

STATE DEBT AND PUBLIC AUTHORITIES

Key points:

- Debt plays an appropriate role in public finance, but many experts believe New York State borrows too much, particularly for operating expenses.

- Governors and the Legislature have created public authorities in part to borrow money without seeking voter approval, which the Constitution requires for the state's own debt.

- Reform efforts are focusing on limiting the total amount of state debt and the purposes for which it can be incurred, and on improving governance of the state's public authorities.

This chapter was primarily researched and written by Brian T. Stenson, deputy director of the Rockefeller Institute of Government.

N ew York State collects over $55 billion in taxes and receives more than $35 billion in aid from the federal government each year. Like any large entity in the public or private sector, the state also borrows substantial amounts — additional billions of dollars each year. Governors and legislators have created separate agencies to borrow funds to finance spending on taxpayers' behalf. The amount of debt for which the state is responsible, how the debt is issued, and how to control the agencies that issue it are among the issues taking center stage in the reform arena in Albany.

When used appropriately, debt provides appropriate budgetary flexibility. When families and individuals build or purchase a home, they typically borrow much of the money they need. Businesses, too, go into debt for capital investments such as factories, office buildings, and major equipment. The same is true of most governments, including New York State. Government-related debt is typically secure, meaning that default cases are extremely rare (unlike corporate debt). And for the most part, New York borrows for purposes for which it is normally intended — to build roads and bridges, prisons, office buildings, college campuses, park facilities, and other projects that will be used over many years, and even decades. Because these capital projects have such a long useful life, and are extremely expensive to build, public finance experts endorse the use of bonds to finance their costs. The bonds, as with a home mortgage, are paid off over many years, usually tied to the expected life of the project. In this way, current taxpayers are not saddled with the entire cost of a road or a prison that will serve citizens for decades to come.

In incurring debt, a government, whether New York State or a small town, takes a loan from investors and issues a note promising to repay that loan. The government issuer must have the legal authorization to issue the debt and must put provisions in place to ensure its repayment. For example, is the debt to be repaid from all revenues available to the government, or only from a specified revenue stream, such as toll receipts pledged to repay the costs of building a highway?

The questions of how to issue state debt, and what kinds to issue, have been the subject of debate, reforms, and court challenges in New York for nearly 200 years, dating back to development of the most important public works project in America's first century, the Erie Canal, which was financed by state bonds. While the canal was an undeniable success, its cost and the troublingly high levels of debt that it helped produce led to a constitutional change that still has important effects more than a century and a half later.

The Limits on State Debt

Article VII of New York's Constitution lays out a seemingly simple framework for the state to incur debt. In brief, it provides that state debt must be:

- Authorized by the voters. This requirement was added in 1846 as a reaction to high levels of borrowing by the state to develop the Erie Canal and the railroads. Exceptions — reflecting the concerns of the 19th century, when the section was written — are made for borrowing needed to "repel invasion, suppress insurrection, or defend the state in war, or to suppress forest fires." For certain other purposes, including the State University and eliminating street-level railroad crossings, the Legislature may authorize debt without voter approval, but only up to amounts set out in the Constitution.

- Submitted to the voters through no more than one proposal each year. A debt referendum cannot be put before the voters at the same general election when another similar question is already on the ballot.

- Issued "for some single work or purpose."

- Paid off through annual appropriations of state moneys by the Legislature, and if the Legislature fails to make the necessary appropriations, then the state comptroller is required to divert state general revenues to make the payments, even without an appropriation. This provision means the state pledges its "full faith and credit" to repay the bonds, which are known as "general obligation" debt. Repayment of the annual principal and interest payments is backed by the state's full credit and treasury.

Although there is no maximum limit established for the amount of state debt, these constitutional provisions combine to create a daunting process for borrowing. Because only one bonding program can be proposed each year and that proposal must be somewhat narrow in scope (the "single work or purpose"), state lawmakers have tended to advance plans that can finance the capital needs of a program over several years. This necessarily drives up the size of the bond issue. Perhaps as a result, voters have not been overly kind to such ballot proposals. Since 1974, 14 borrowing questions have been put before the voters: seven have been approved, including five transportation bond issues and two environmental proposals. New Yorkers have rejected proposals for prisons, public schools, economic development, and low-rent housing, as well as environmental quality and transportation.

This puts lawmakers in a bind. They cannot, for example, incarcerate criminals (and claim to be tough on crime) without building prisons; meet transportation demands without building roads and bridges; or provide a State University system without building campuses. The prospects of securing voter approval for wholesale changes to the Constitution that would modernize, and liberalize, the issuance of general obligation state debt have long been considered slim, at best. Decades ago, state leaders decided a different vehicle had to be found to provide the capital financing required by New York's extensive public services network. That vehicle is the public authority.

The Rise of Public Authorities

In the 20th century, the state began to develop an alternative to the voter-approval process — issuing debt through the state's public authorities as authorized by the Legislature. Since then, authority debt has become by far the most-used mechanism through which the state finances the costs of its capital projects. As of 2006, according to data from the Office of the State Comptroller, for every dollar of outstanding general obligation state debt that was authorized by the voters, there was at least some $12 of other debt for which the state had a financial obligation (the exact definition of which is a matter of continuing debate, as will be seen later). Virtually all of this other debt was issued by public authorities.

Public authorities are agencies that governors and Legislatures establish outside the main structure of government. Technically, they are either "public benefit corporations" or not-for-profit corporations, which are organized to build or run a public improvement that benefits the state or the people. Authorities are created by acts of the Legislature. They differ from traditional state agencies in a number of ways and generally offer their managers a way to operate outside of the restrictions that are imposed on "regular" state agencies.

Public authorities enjoy greater autonomy from the Office of the State Comptroller and the Budget Division than do state agencies. This autonomy includes freedom from many financing restrictions, civil-service rules, and other laws. Most authorities are controlled by boards of directors appointed for fixed terms, who, in turn, appoint the executive directors and other top full-time staff. Thus, the individuals controlling these agencies often remain from one gubernatorial administration to another, at least for a time.

There are two critical features of public authorities that explain their rise to such a significant role in New York State. First, they may operate across jurisdictional boundaries. This allows them to play an important role in solving problems that require a regional, even interstate, solution. But even more important is that as authorized by the state Legislature, the authorities may issue their own debt. This debt technically is not a direct obligation of the state.

Public authorities proliferated in the first half of the 20th century, with one man, Robert Moses, generally credited (criticized by many) with creatively using the authorities to expand capital programs and his own institutional power. Moses, head of the Triborough Bridge & Tunnel Authority, used surplus revenues from the authority's operations as seed capital to help develop park and transportation facilities. Considered the "master builder," Moses used his appointive positions in state and New York City government to develop tens of billions of dollars' worth of parks, roads, and other projects, and developed more than a dozen public authorities. At his initiative, laws were enacted in the 1930s and 1940s that created individual agencies to develop Jones Beach, as well as state parks elsewhere across Long Island; the Henry Hudson and other parkways in the downstate metropolitan region; the Triborough and other bridges in and around New York City; and the New York Power Authority.

The ability of public authorities to accomplish what otherwise might never be realized can be shown in what Moses took from dream to reality: the nation's biggest parks system: hundreds of miles of highways and a dozen major bridges; huge projects such as the United Nations headquarters, Lincoln Center, and Shea Stadium; and thousands of

Longstanding Concerns
Over Public Authorities

In 1956, the Temporary State Commission on Coordination of State Authorities published a report on New York State's public authorities. In a letter of submittal to commission members, staff director William J. Ronan wrote:

> In the three and a half decades since the first public authority was established, New York State has accumulated a substantial body of experience with public authorities. The achievements of certain of these authorities account in large measure for the general popularity of the public authority as a governmental device not only in this State but elsewhere. However, these achievements should not be allowed to camouflage the very real problems that exist with respect to the proper and responsible use of the public authority as an agency of the State government. At present the State government is operating in the dark with respect to much public authority activity. This is a potentially dangerous situation. Before the public the State bears a responsibility for public authority activities, which it cannot escape.

The Ronan letter could easily have been written half a century later. In 2003, critics accused the Metropolitan Transportation Authority of failing to produce legally required long-range financial plans and hiding important elements of its financial position. The Port Authority, the oldest public authority in the state, remained in the spotlight for reformers as well.

Continuing concerns about public authorities reflect broader issues in our understanding of and desires for government. If we want government to get things done efficiently, a public authority may be a better tool for the job than a traditional state agency that has more restrictions on its work. On the other hand, if openness and accountability are the goals, public authorities are less desirable, for the same reason: They are subject to fewer such requirements than "line" agencies.

In its 1956 report, the Coordination Commission recommended nine bills for consideration by the Legislature. Two were enacted into law. Their substance suggests the reluctance — then as now — of the state's elected leaders to restrict the powers of public authorities.* One

---

*   Temporary State Commission on Coordination of State Activities, *Staff Report on Public Authorities Under New York State*, Albany, NY: Williams Press Inc., 1956. Ronan, secretary to Governor Rockefeller from 1959 to 1966, went on to serve as chairman of the MTA, and on the boards of the Port Authority and New York Power Authority.

bill increased, from five to 10 days, the period in which the governor may veto the minutes of a Port Authority meeting. The second new law initiated by the commission eliminated 13 public authorities that "had become inactive." The commission counted 33 active authorities. In 2004, the Office of the State Comptroller identified 190 "major" authorities with statewide or regional significance, and hundreds more at the state and local levels.

residential apartments. This kind of power can also have a negative impact. As government agencies, public authorities have the power of eminent domain, which allows them to seize private property for public purposes. Moses' biographer concluded that the developer's authorities' use of eminent domain and other practices displaced roughly half a million residents, most of them poor families and individuals.[1]

The power of public authorities in New York reached its zenith under Moses, who for decades was the most powerful appointed official in the state and, on numerous occasions, virtually dictated policy to elected mayors and governors and their staffs. Moses used bond covenants — contractual agreements with institutions and individuals who loan money to governmental units through bond purchases — to cement the legal power of the authorities he controlled. First appointed to high position by Governor Alfred E. Smith in 1923, Moses remained in power until Governor Rockefeller effectively pushed him out in the 1960s.

Public Authorities Today

Today, public authorities perform some of state government's crucial functions: operating and maintaining airports, highways, and transportation services; providing financing for public facilities from schools to hospitals to housing; and providing economic incentives to growing businesses. They have also provided the state with substantial resources to close budget deficits.

---

1   See Robert A. Caro, *The Power Broker: Robert Moses and the Fall of New York*, New York, NY: Alfred A. Knopf, 1974.

Why don't traditional governmental agencies perform these core services? Unlike traditional departments such as Transportation or Education, which are funded primarily by state tax dollars, most public authorities rely largely on revenue from user fees or bonds. The Metropolitan Transportation Authority (MTA) and the Port Authority receive most of their funding from the fares and fees that commuters and others pay to use the subways, buses, bridges, airports, and other facilities operated by the authorities. The "off-budget" nature of such revenues can give the agencies more freedom to use available dollars as they and/or elected officials wish. In recent years, for instance, some toll revenues collected by the Thruway Authority have been used to support maintenance and development of the canal system. Public authorities can also keep governors and legislators a step removed from controversial decisions, or float potentially unpopular proposals publicly before elected leaders take a position. Still, elected officials do not escape accountability entirely. One result is that decisions such as raising fares on the MTA or the Long Island Railroad (LIRR) seldom happen in election years.

While a larger-than-life figure like Moses could sometimes have his way even with governors, public authorities in general represent a concentration of authority in the executive branch at the expense of the Legislature. Their boards and/or chief executives are generally appointed by the governor with the consent of the Senate. Their primary power is one of finance, so that in a budgeting system dominated by the executive — such as New York's — the effect is to give the governor another financial tool. As with everything state government does (aside from constitutional changes made by the people), the Legislature has the ultimate power over public authorities. Once the Senate and Assembly cede that power to an authority, however, it can be difficult to reclaim.

The September 11, 2001, terrorist attacks on the World Trade Center in New York City thrust one public authority — the Port Authority of New York and New Jersey — into the focus of governmental and public attention. The Port Authority is a bi-state public entity whose board appointments are shared by the governors of the two states. Created in 1921 with the consent of the U.S. Congress, it oversees planning and development of terminal, transportation, and other facilities in a district of some 1,500 square miles centering on New York Harbor.

The Port Authority developed the World Trade Center in the late 1960s and early 1970s, and remains the owner of the Trade Center site.[2] An example of the largely unrecognized role played by the Port Authority and other authorities came in the days after the center's destruction, as the news media began to report discussions about potential rebuilding. For days, such coverage ignored the key role that New York State's leaders — who control the state's seats on the authority board — would play in any decisions.[3]

The original development of the World Trade Center occurred largely as the result of the efforts of David Rockefeller, chairman of Chase Manhattan Bank; and his brother Nelson, the governor. David Rockefeller had risked his own reputation and significant corporate assets building the bank's headquarters in downtown Manhattan, to jumpstart a revival of the area. Governor Rockefeller pushed the Port Authority into moving ahead with the Trade Center. In November 2001, Governor Pataki and Mayor Rudolph Giuliani named board members of a new Lower Manhattan Redevelopment Corp., a subsidiary of Empire State Development Corp., to oversee rebuilding efforts in lower Manhattan. The agency has extensive power, including the ability to acquire privately owned property through condemnation by its parent corporation. Five years after the Trade Center towers fell, new buildings for the site were still in design stages. Subway service to the site had been restored, but full redevelopment is years away.

Not all public authorities are as massive and powerful as the Port Authority. Some are localized in a particular community — the City of Albany Housing Authority, for instance. Some are more geographically spread out, but have a narrow function, like the Hudson River-Black River Regulating District. Some authorities have a broad mandate — the Dormitory Authority finances and constructs facilities for public and private colleges and hospitals. Others exist to do one specific type of transaction — the Tobacco Settlement Financing Corporation (TSFC) was created to assume future state revenues from the national tobacco litigation settlement; sell the rights to those revenues to

---

2   Some 75 Port Authority employees, including the executive director, Neil Levin, were among those who died in the terrorist attack.

3   Sixteen days after the attacks, for example, *The New York Times* carried a story headlined "State Seeks to Play a Role in the Reconstruction Effort" — as though state government did not automatically have a major role.

investors through the issuance of bonds backed by the future revenue stream; and transfer the bond proceeds back to the state.

How many public authorities are there? That depends on the definition. The Office of the State Comptroller has compiled an exhaustive list of 740 entities it considers public authorities, although its definition is broader than that used by some other observers. For example, the comptroller's list includes entities such as the auxiliary services corporations (or faculty-student associations) of the State University and City University of New York. Many of the authorities listed do not issue debt at all; most have a purely local jurisdiction, and many are subsidiaries of statutorily created authorities. The Comptroller's Office contends that all relevant entities should be listed and monitored — even those that are currently inactive or that are subsidiaries that have been informally, but not officially dissolved by their parent authority. To that end, the list offers a comprehensive illustration of the extent to which New York has used the public authority mechanism to operate programs, provide services, and in some cases issue debt. The comptroller's list is summarized below:

- 190 major authorities with statewide or regional significance. These include the Dormitory Authority, Metropolitan Transportation Authority, Thruway Authority, State University Construction Fund, and the Urban/Empire State Development Corporation and its more than 100 subsidiaries.

- 68 other entities affiliated with the state. This group includes the New York Racing Association, and the auxiliary services corporations of SUNY and CUNY.

- 474 locally based authorities. This largest group includes authorities mainly focused on housing, parking, water and sewer, and local development activities. As an example, there are at least 20 authorities located in Albany County alone.

- 8 international or interstate authorities. Primary examples are the Port Authority of New York and New Jersey and its four subsidiaries.

A quite different perspective is offered by the New York State Commission on Public Authority Reform (COPAR). The Commission was established by Executive Order of Governor Pataki and made several recommendations, many of which were incorporated in the Public Authorities Accountability Act of 2005. Using the definitions included in the Act, COPAR identified 46 statewide authorities and 246 local authorities it considered "recognized," meaning they are active and play a significant role in the operations or financing of public programs. That the commission recognized fewer than half of the authorities contained on the state comptroller's list illustrates the difficulty in developing a common definition of public authorities.

The table on the next page shows the 15 largest state authorities. Prepared by the Division of the Budget, this table illustrates not only the relative size of the authorities as measured by revenues and the amount of outstanding debt, but also differences between entities that actually operate programs and those that serve mainly as financing vehicles. For example, four of the five largest authorities — the Metropolitan Transportation Authority or MTA, the Long Island Power Authority, the Port Authority of New York and New Jersey, and the Power Authority — all show significant amounts of operating expenses, indicating they manage ongoing services and programs. In contrast, the Dormitory Authority, the Local Government Assistance Corp., and the Tobacco Settlement Financing Corp. all have relatively insignificant amounts of operating expenses, in most cases related to expenses incurred in managing the timely payment of debt service costs.

State Debt Profile

The difficulty observers have in agreeing on the definition of public authorities is matched by the task of defining state debt in clear categories. Some commonly used groupings are:

General obligation debt. This is the debt approved by voters as authorized by the Constitution. As of 2006, there was almost $3.5 billion of this debt outstanding. The debt is issued directly by the state (by the state comptroller) and carries the full faith and credit of the state. These bonds may be used only for capital purposes.

State-supported authority debt. This type of debt is issued by public authorities pursuant to authorization by the Legislature. In most cases, the Legislature establishes the maximum amount of debt the authority can issue, known as a "bond cap." The bonds are obligations of the authorities, not of the state. In cases known as "revenue bonds," such as

Major New York State Public Authorities, 2006
(ranked by revenues; all figures in millions of dollars)

Authority	Total Revenues	Operating Expenses	Bonds Outstanding*	Debt Service
Metropolitan Transportation Authority	$9,940	$8,379	$14,086	$1,340
Long Island Power Authority	3,735	3,086	7,020	574
Port Authority of NY and NJ	3,632	2,196	9,825	592
Dormitory Authority	3,265	92	31,099	3,173
New York Power Authority	2,644	2,285	1,435	373
Empire State Development Corp.	703	55	6,495	663
Environmental Facilities Corp.	673	20	6,957	647
State of New York Mortgage Agency	669	150	2,873	519
Thruway Authority	612	389	10,621	131
Housing Finance Agency	489	44	6,894	441
Tobacco Settlement Financing Corp.	440	1.7	4,278	438
Local Government Assistance Corp.	373	18	4,317	355
Energy Research and Development Authority	252	246	3,672	6
Buffalo Fiscal Stability Authority	214	1.5	99	57
Battery Park City Authority	190	33	1,068	119

*Figures for outstanding bonds are for September 30, 2005.
Source: 2006-07 Executive Budget.

the Thruway Authority's bonds for toll roads and bridge operations, and the Dormitory Authority's debt for SUNY residence halls, revenue from authority operations or contracts is more than adequate to pay associated debt service costs. However, authorities often do not have the means to meet the bonds' annual debt service requirements, so the state enacts annual budget appropriations authorizing payments to the authorities, which in turn, pay bondholders. In contrast to general obligation debt, these payments by the state can only be made if an appropriation for them is included in the state budget. Over the years, the state has utilized many features and techniques to convince investors that it has a strong, abiding interest in seeing that the debt is repaid, thereby earning a higher credit rating and lower interest rates. For example, the financing arrangements may be made pursuant to a lease, such as when the authority builds a prison and leases it to the state for its use. In other cases, the state pledges to bondholders that it will seek appropriations to pay the debt service. In still others, the state pledges or earmarks specific revenues to repay the bonds. The most recent example is the pledge of a portion of the state's personal income tax revenue to pay for debt service on certain authority bonds; this pledge is so strong that Standard and Poor's rating agency has assigned its highest rating, "AAA," to these bonds. The state's use of this "back door" to obtain debt financing for its expansive capital program has grown to the point where the back door is far larger, and used much more extensively than the "front door" of voter-approved debt. As of 2006, the amount of this outstanding debt exceeded $37.7 billion. A glance at the table reveals that a significant amount of this total debt is for what has to be considered local or regional benefit, not for state purposes such as prisons or office buildings.

> Together, general-obligation and state-supported authority debt are termed "state-supported debt" because debt service on the bonds is a direct charge against state taxes and other revenue. They totaled $41.2 billion as of March 2006.

Contingent and other debt. In addition to these state-supported debt programs, New York and its authorities have engaged in transactions where the state has a contingent obligation to pay debt service. In these cases, the state has pledged to pay the bondholders, as a form of "backup" security, if the primary source of revenue is insufficient to pay the debt service . In one form of such debt — the Job Development Authority (JDA) — the voters authorized the state to guarantee payment of the debt service if the JDA does not receive the necessary payments from the private companies it had loaned money to for job creation activities. In all other such cases, the Legislature, without voter approval, created authorities or other mechanisms to issue debt that has at least some contingent obligation by the state. The largest case of this type of debt was issued by the Tobacco Settlement Financing Corporation. The corporation has nearly $4.3 billion of its debt outstanding, and New York may be required to provide moneys to pay debt service if the stream of tobacco settlement revenue is insufficient to pay debt service on the bonds. This category of contingent and other debt has nearly $5.7 billion outstanding.

> *The two categories, state-supported debt and this contingent debt, together are known as state-related debt. There was just over $46.9 billion in state-related debt outstanding as of March 2006. According to figures from the Division of the Budget, nearly one-half of the projected total amount of this debt as of March 2007 was issued for transportation and education purposes.*

Beyond this state-related category, there is other debt issued by public authorities where the state has no obligation, even an indirect or contingent one. This so-called "conduit financing" involves a public authority issuing bonds on behalf of a nonpublic entity. For example, the Dormitory Authority also issues bonds on behalf of independent or private colleges and nonprofit hospitals. In fact, more than 45 percent of the authority's outstanding debt is attributable to bonds issued for these nonpublic entities. The state has authorized its public authorities to engage in this business so that private organizations can obtain tax-free financing for their capital expansion plans; these entities make annual payments to the authority to cover the cost of the debt service. There is no commitment by the state to pay the debt service if the private entity is unable to make its required payment to the authority.

There also is debt authorized by the state and issued by authorities to benefit local governments and for which certain state aid payments are pledged for debt service. (For example, the state authorized the establishment of a not-for-profit corporation in 2003 solely to allow New York City to refinance debt originally issued by the Municipal Assistance Corporation (MAC). The state also authorized the New York City-related Transition Finance Authority to issue school construction bonds that are backed by future state education aid payments.) The state Budget Division does not consider this debt to be state-supported as defined by state statutes, but the Office of the State Comptroller has established a category called "state-funded debt" in which it is included.

Bondholders typically receive annual interest payments on the bonds they purchase. Their initial investment is repaid when their bonds mature. The overall maturity schedule of bonds used to finance capital spending is linked to the useful life of the asset being built or purchased, but generally does not exceed 30 years. The state and its authorities then are required to make annual debt service payments — the combination of principal and interest — over the life of the bond issue. For 2006-07, the total amount of debt service payments projected by the Division of the Budget was more than $4.1 billion on the $41.2 billion in state-supported debt outstanding.

Criticisms of State Debt and Public Authorities

State borrowing practices and public authorities, have come under mounting criticism in recent years. Although there have been questions for decades about the proliferation of authorities, and state debt levels and practices have caused concern in certain quarters for many years, only recently have these concerns reached the point where debt and authorities are at the center of debate in Albany.

These concerns touch on the amount of state debt, how that debt is used, and New York's reliance on authorities rather than its own faith and credit, and the effectiveness of mechanisms to oversee those entities.

Entire books can be — and have been — written about each topic. The following section covers only a small fraction of the issues.

"New York has too much debt." By any reasonable measure, except perhaps when compared to the federal government, New York State has a lot of debt. But how much is too much? As stated above, the total amount of debt outstanding, where the state makes annual payments to cover debt service costs, was $41.2 billion as of 2006. When other debt, on which payments might be required, is included, the total of state-related debt was $46.9 billion. This has grown steadily during recent decades. The Office of the State Comptroller estimates that state-supported debt rose 215 percent from 1990 to 2004.

The state Budget Division reports various debt measures, indicating somewhat of a mixed record. Not surprisingly, given New York's relatively stagnant population, when expressed on a per capita basis, the debt load has increased sharply. However, when expressed as a percentage of total state personal income (a measure of the wealth and economic condition of a state), the broader measure of state-related debt has declined from 7.1 percent to 6.1 percent over the last decade.

When compared to the debt loads in other states, New York's indebtedness is very high. According to data from Moody's Investors Service, New York ranks fifth in both tax-supported debt per capita and debt as a percent of state personal income. Another major credit rating agency, Standard and Poor's, noted that, "Although debt levels continue to be problematic, New York's debt ratios are now within the range of other states in the Northeast."[4] Another outside monitoring group, the Citizens Budget Commission (CBC), considers New York one of eight states in a "danger zone" of unaffordable debt. The CBC's analysis is based on ability to repay debt without tax increases or service cutbacks that would make a location less attractive than competitors. The "danger zone" designation indicates that a state is "far above its competitors" in its ratio of debt to available resources.[5]

Another measure of debt burden is the relative share of the budget that is devoted to debt service, similar to the measure banks use to determine a mortgage applicant's ability to afford monthly payments out of current income. The Budget Division calculates that debt service as a percent of total state spending (from all federal and state sources) has declined from 5.7 percent in 1996-97 to an estimated 4.2 percent in 2006-07. This relative decline reflects many possible factors including growth in the state's "all funds" budget, which includes federal aid, Lottery moneys, and other revenues that cannot legally be used for debt service. Other contributing factors are a decline in the rate of growth in state debt compared to the previous decade; the low interest rate environment, which reduces costs and allows debt to be refunded; a spate of debt refundings that temporarily reduced debt service payments; improved credit ratings; and the use of alternative debt instruments (such as variable rate bonds and other more complex forms) that lower interest costs.

"New York State uses debt inappropriately." The ready availability of public authorities to issue state debt has spawned another significant development. Over the past two decades there has been a trend toward using public authority debt to finance spending where no capital asset is

4   *State Review: New York State*, Standard & Poor's, New York, NY, March 1, 2006.

5   Citizens Budget Commission, *New York's Public Authorities: Promoting Accountability and Taming Debt*, New York, NY, September 2006.

The Credit Rating Agencies

Three major credit rating agencies — Standard & Poor's, Moody's Investors Services, and Fitch Ratings — analyze the state's finances from the perspective of investors in state bonds. Rating agencies attempt to measure the likelihood that the issuer (the state, local government, or public authority) will pay all required principal and interest payments, and do so on time. Since an exceedingly small number of governments have ever defaulted on their debt or missed a required payment — New York State has never defaulted on its debt or its authority debt — the rating agencies rely largely on factors other than prior experience with an issuer. Using Wall Street's adage that "past results are no guarantee of future performance," the rating agencies instead review an issuer's overall debt load, economic condition, budgetary practices, financial management experience, and management capability — then weigh all these factors to determine a credit rating. The rating scales used by the three agencies are different, and in practice, the "raters" often assign somewhat different ratings to the same debt. In addition, the ratings for different state bonding programs, such as general obligation bonds, dedicated highway program bonds, the tobacco securitization debt, and various other programs may all be different, reflecting the assessment by the agencies of the credit structures, and repayment provisions of each. Ratings assigned by the credit rating agencies can help shape public opinion (when, for example, for years New York State's credit rating was the lowest of any state in the nation, except that of Louisiana) and influence the interest rate the issuer has to pay for the debt. The firms exercise their ultimate power when they judge the state unlikely to repay a given debt. This occurred with the state Urban Development Corp. in 1975. The result was financial and operational breakdown for the agency, and widespread perception that the state itself was on shaky ground.

involved. Back in the era of Robert Moses, public authorities were established to finance and operate capital facilities. In this way, toll roads and bridges could be built and operated by an agency that focused its attention on that project without political interference — in theory, at least.

All that has changed. In the current state fiscal environment, public authorities are used extensively to help solve state budget problems.

Current state obligations have been bonded out through public authorities. Perhaps the best known and most criticized example of the use of authority debt to cover operating costs occurred 15 years ago. In 1991, Governor Cuomo and the Legislature enacted what became the much-criticized "sale" of the Attica Correctional Facility to the Urban Development Corp. to obtain $200 million for the state's regular operations.

These "Attica bonds" may be the most notorious example of debt issued for operating purposes, but they comprise only a small fraction of such debt. In later years, through its authorities, the state has issued debt to restructure the timing of its state aid payments and eliminate annual cash flow borrowings; convert the stream of revenue received from the tobacco industry settlement into one-time, upfront payments; pay school aid claims and some pension costs from prior fiscal years; and extend debt associated with New York City's 1970's fiscal crisis. A conservative estimate of the amount of outstanding debt that was originally issued for such operating purposes is $9.3 billion, or 20 percent of the total amount of state-related debt. Independent experts on public finance say that such use of debt is appropriate only as a last resort during an extraordinary fiscal crisis, because it shifts the cost of today's services to tomorrow's taxpayers. In addition to issuing debt for operating purposes, the state has used debt to pay for any number of local projects that in prior years were paid from operating budget moneys. Member items and local economic development projects are financed routinely through bonds, in an amount the Office of the State Comptroller estimated at $2.8 billion from 1997 through 2005. Billions more were authorized at the end of the 2006 legislative session.

The state also uses debt in creative ways to achieve budget savings. For example, just as homeowners refinance their mortgages to lower their monthly payments, New York and other governments refinance debt when current interest rates are below the rates being paid on outstanding bonds. However, New York State has often refinanced debt in ways that actually *increase* total debt service costs over the life of the bonds by deferring principal payments until a future year or stretching out the debt longer than the original maturity. The most illuminating example of this technique is the debt associated with the "sale" of Attica. Debt was originally sold by an authority in 1990 and subsequently refinanced in 1995. However, these refinancing bonds were structured in such a way that payments were avoided for several years. According to the Office of the State Comptroller, the "Attica bonds" will wind up costing New York taxpayers a total of $565 million in exchange for a $200 million pot of money used to pay operating expenses and help balance the budget in 1990.

A more extensive use of debt to achieve budget savings occurred during 2002-03 and 2003-04, when the state was suffering from the recession and the effects of the September 11th terrorist attacks. The state and its authorities refunded billions of dollars of state-supported debt using debt service repayment schedules that maximized budgetary savings in those years — debt service payments on the new bonds can be delayed or paid out of bond proceeds. After this brief two-year dip, debt service costs have grown steadily and will be higher in future years than they otherwise would have been. Indeed, the latest projections from the Division of the Budget indicate that debt service costs will increase by 44 percent in four short years, raising debt service as a percentage of spending from 4.2 percent to 5.2 percent. This increase reflects not only the resumption of normal debt service costs following the temporary savings from these debt restructurings, but also the spate of new bonding programs enacted in 2006.

"New York relies too much on authorities." The combination of voter resistance to large bond issues on the ballot and the relative ease with which public authorities can be created presents a tempting recipe for the use of back door borrowing. According to the Budget Division, of the nearly $4.2 billion in state debt planned for issue in 2006-07, approximately 95 percent was to be issued by authorities. Critics say the borrowing by public authorities violates the spirit, if not the letter, of the state Constitution. The Court of Appeals has upheld the practice, however.

"The management and oversight of authorities need to be strengthened." Although they have become more common recently, the previous three criticisms have been heard for many years. But within the past few years, a renewed concern has been voiced by many observers. In the wake of corporate accounting scandals and the resulting Sarbanes-Oxley legislation at the federal level, greater scrutiny has been directed at the way in which state public authorities operate and manage their programs and finances.

Critics have cited public authorities for a lack of transparency, meaning that their activities and finances are not clearly reported to the public and watchdog groups. They also criticize authority governance practices, noting that the boards of directors generally do not exercise effective and independent control over authority staff or operations. Instead, authorities generally follow the wishes of the governor and, to a lesser extent, the Legislature.

The Office of the State Comptroller conducts audits of public authority operations and reports many instances where authorities do not follow competitive procurement guidelines. In some cases, authorities have failed to follow their own internal rules regarding purchasing and contracting. The scandal involving the New York State Canal Corporation's lease of canal-side development rights for a risibly small dollar amount was one noteworthy example of questionable purchasing and contracting practices by state authorities.

An early attempt by the state to exercise more oversight of public authorities was the establishment of the Public Authorities Control Board (PACB). The PACB was created in 1976 as a response to a financial crisis at the State Urban Development Corporation. Financial markets were resisting efforts by certain state authorities to issue much-needed debt and demanding greater state oversight. The PACB includes the executive and representatives of the majority in both the Assembly and Senate (nonvoting members from the minority in both houses bring the total membership to five). The PACB's role is very powerful: The three voting members must approve financing and construction of any project proposed by 10 specified authorities. Because the vote must be unanimous, the effect is to give the governor and the leaders of the two houses veto power over any projects undertaken by the affected agencies. In many ways, however, PACB is quite limited. It has oversight of only the 10 covered authorities, so many other public authorities, such as the Port Authority, the MTA, and the Thruway Authority are not subject to PACB control. In addition, many other activities of the covered authorities, such as contracting, hiring, and procurement, are also beyond the PACB's scope. Moreover, limiting the membership of the PACB to the three parties who also control debt authorizations for the authorities means that other important and independent voices are not considered in the board's deliberations.

Reform Efforts: Recent and Proposed

The growing chorus of calls for reform has resulted in attempts by lawmakers to address the criticisms of both state debt practices and public authorities. The State Debt Reform Act of 2000 has had little impact thus far, and the Public Authorities Accountability Act of 2005 has not yet received a fair test.

Controlling state debt. The State Debt Reform Act of 2000 was described by its primary supporter, Governor Pataki, as a major effort to rein in state borrowing practices. For the first time, a law was passed that attempted to control the amount of state debt that was issued, including authority debt. The law defined and imposed caps on state-supported debt outstanding, as expressed as a percentage of state personal income — the cap increases gradually to four percent of personal income by 2010. In addition, the law caps the amount of debt service (again, phased in) to five percent of the total (all funds) budget in 2013. Importantly, the law also required that state-supported debt could be used only for capital, and not operating, purposes.

But the law suffered from several flaws that have rendered it less effective than backers had claimed. First, the cap on debt covered only bonds issued after the passage of the law, and ignored the tens of billions of dollars of debt already on the books at that time. The cap on debt may begin to limit debt, but only in future years. Second, the law does nothing about the state's ability to use authorities to issue debt (versus voter-approved debt issued directly by the state itself). Finally, the language of the law did not prevent the state from establishing an authority to issue tobacco securitization bonds several years later, which generated more than $4.2 billion in bond moneys for the state, and was backed by a pledge of future revenues the state would have received from the tobacco settlement. There is no question that New York State faced desperate fiscal challenges after 9/11. With massive revenue shortfalls, other states joined New York in borrowing to close budget gaps. However, the ease with which the debt cap was evaded calls into question its effectiveness.

Not surprisingly, proposals for more reforms keep coming. The state comptroller, the governor, and watchdog groups like the Citizens Budget Commission have advanced plans to impose greater discipline over state debt. Most plans would impose some limit on all debt issued where the state pays or could pay debt service; allow more flexibility in seeking voter approval of state debt; consolidate and streamline debt programs; establish some debt oversight body; and impose stricter guidelines on authorities.

"Reining in" the authorities. Drawing upon the recommendations of the Commission on Public Authority Reform, and previous

proposals offered by many state officials, the state enacted the Public Authorities Accountability Act of 2005. The law seeks to improve the oversight of operations within each authority and by statewide entities. It requires that each authority appoint board committees responsible for governance and audit functions, two committees generally deemed crucial to ensuring that the board performs its oversight responsibilities diligently. In addition, authorities are required to provide more detailed reporting of debt matters. To enhance state oversight of the authorities, the new law establishes an Authority Budget Office and codifies in law the Office of the State Inspector General.

The commission has already proposed legislation to strengthen the provisions of the act by expanding reporting and accounting requirements, and mandating that if the authority issues debt that it also establish a finance committee. The proposal would also require that members of authority finance and audit committees possess appropriate experience and knowledge.

The prospects for further and more meaningful reform of state debt practices and public authorities are far from certain, especially as most of the sweeping reforms require voter approval of amendments to the Constitution. New York State's appetite for, and reliance on, public authority debt is considerable. Backdoor borrowing is used to a great extent, not only for essential capital purposes, but also for dispensing largess to local communities, and for operating budget relief. Critics of Albany's budgetary and legislative practices point out that in 2006, even in the face of growing criticism of state debt and authorities, the Legislature established several new authority bonding initiatives, including a new $2.6 billion Dormitory Authority program to fund school construction projects. Continuing a recent trend, the legislation provides that the authority will distribute the borrowed funds directly to school districts, in the words of the Office of the State Comptroller, "...bypassing the state's central accounting system and pre-audit process."

Fifty years after state leaders identified significant problems with public authorities, the reform movement still has its work cut out for it. As noted in Chapter Two, changing the rules — in this case, the laws and regulations governing authorities — is one of the ways to approach reform. Other approaches involve people and policies. Governor-elect Spitzer has promised to appoint highly qualified leaders to state authorities, refrain from inappropriate use of debt, and otherwise raise standards of accountability and efficiency in the authorities.

Chapter Twelve

HEALTH AND
MENTAL HYGIENE

Key points:

- Providing health care is New York State's single largest priority, if total spending is the measure.

- The state's Medicaid program is the most costly in the nation, and there is evidence that substantial amounts of money are not used effectively; elected officials are studying major restructuring of the health-care system in hopes of reducing costs and improving care.

- Medicaid has played a key role in expansion of services for the developmentally disabled and, to a lesser extent, individuals with mental illness.

If you have good health, the saying goes, you have everything. For society itself, as with individuals, nothing is more important than preventing illness and addressing health problems as quickly and effectively as possible. It's not surprising, then, that by at least one measure — dollars spent — providing health care and protecting public health is New York State's single highest priority. In 2004-05, state government's spending on Medicaid and other health programs totaled more than $38.6 billion, or $2,008 for every resident, according to the Office of the State Comptroller.[1] That amount, including both the state's own tax dollars and federal funds, was 31 percent more than spending in the second-biggest program area, education.

Government's role in *protecting* health in the Empire State began before the Civil War, with the development of sanitary inspections to reduce the spread of smallpox, typhus, and other infectious diseases. At the start of the 21st century, overseeing such activities remained a critically important function of the state Health Department.

In the modern era, though, state government does even more to *pay for and provide* health care and health-insurance coverage. The biggest single program in this area (and the largest cost center anywhere in state government) is Medicaid, for which nearly 4.2 million New Yorkers were eligible in 2006. These individuals — 1.5 million more than those eligible for Medicaid five years earlier — counted on the tax-payer-funded program to pay their bills for nursing home and other institutional care, as well as for hospital treatment, doctor visits, and other health care.

State government also supplements the federal nutrition program for Women, Infants and Children (WIC). The state helps senior citizens who do not qualify for other government assistance to pay for prescription drugs through the Elderly Pharmaceutical Insurance Coverage program. It sponsors television and other advertisements against smoking. And in the 2006-07 fiscal year, according to the Division of the Budget, New York State planned to spend $3.4 billion on AIDS patients and programs alone. The Health Department also provides direct care to patients through institutions such as the Helen Hayes Hospital in Rockland County, and the New York State Veterans Home in Chenango County.

New York is unusual in centralizing these varied responsibilities in a single agency, the Health Department. Medicaid, public health, oversight of health facilities, and financing of such facilities are each major concerns that many states locate in separate departments.

---

1   *2005 Comptroller's Report on the Financial Condition of New York State.*

The Health Department administers and enforces the Public Health Law and the state Sanitary Code. It has regulatory authority over all health-care facilities and general supervision of all local health authorities. It provides aid for public-health work conducted by counties and cities, and administers federal dollars allotted for health work under the Social Security Act and other programs.

The department is administered by the commissioner of health, who must be a physician with at least 10 years of experience and possess "skill and experience in public health duties and sanitary science." The commissioner is appointed by the governor with the advice and consent of the Senate. Given the wide-ranging powers of the Health Department, the commissioner is one of the most influential public-health officials in the nation. Commissioner Antonia Novello, appointed to the position in 1999 by Governor Pataki, had previously served three years as U.S. surgeon general.

State government's work of providing and overseeing health care extends beyond the Health Department. The Department of Mental Hygiene — operating through three independent agencies that deal with mental health, mental retardation/developmental disabilities, and alcoholism/substance abuse — provides and supervises services for hundreds of thousands of New Yorkers. This chapter examines the state's broad portfolio of involvement in general health issues as well as those related to mental health.

A Multi-Tiered System

All these activities to promote both physical and mental health in the Empire State involve the federal and/or local governments as well as the state. Federal taxes support half the cost of New York's Medicaid program and provide some funding for many other health-related efforts. Local governments — counties and New York City — also bear some of the cost of Medicaid. Counties and many municipalities are also deeply involved in public-health and mental-health efforts.

The federalist nature of government in the United States has important implications for publicly funded health care. Like other states, New York must follow certain rules established by Congress and federal agencies to the extent that it seeks financial assistance from Washington. For example, state officials continually make decisions regarding Medicaid programs and policies based on drawing down maximum federal matching funds, including not only routine health care for the poor and long-term care for the elderly but institutional care for individuals with mental disabilities. At the same time, leaders in Albany make decisions about how much of a given program's cost to impose on local governments.

Dividing costs among three levels of government has allowed these programs to grow far beyond the scope that state government alone could afford. Medicaid, for instance, is far more expansive in New York than in other states in part because Governor Rockefeller designed the program to include substantial financing at the local level, from New York City and counties elsewhere in the state. With three major levels of decision making, public-health programs also have greater opportunity for innovation. The federal government drove creation of Medicaid in the 1960s; states led the way into Medicaid managed care in the 1990s. Addressing public-health problems such as the West Nile virus outbreak in the New York City area in 1999 demands the expertise and varied powers of federal, state, and local officials.

Where It Began: Public Health

As with building roads, providing education, and most other public undertakings, government's interest in health began at the local level. The political decisions that expanded public-health efforts at the state level occurred because of the work of private individuals and organizations, as well as elected and appointed officials in both state and local government.

In 1795, the governor asked the state medical society to investigate an epidemic then prevailing in parts of New York City. A report issued the following year recommended improvements in environmental sanitation, including addressing "the accumulation of filth in the streets," clearing obstructed water mains, draining low-lying areas, improving dock and river shores to prevent the collection of refuse, and reducing air pollution by slaughterhouses and soap factories. "Effective implementation of these proposals was not possible, however, so long as there was no permanent health organization in the municipal government."[2]

---

2   The source of the quote and selected other historical discussion is George Rosen, *A History of Public Health, Expanded Edition*, Baltimore, MD: Johns Hopkins University Press, 1993, p. 218.

Additional impetus for creating such an agency came three years later, when an epidemic of yellow fever in New York City killed 1,600 residents. State legislation soon gave the city authority to pass its own health laws, and a city health inspector was appointed in March 1804. By the 1830s, the city had both a health officer, appointed by the state and responsible for applying quarantine laws at the port; and a resident physician, a municipal official whose job was to monitor and discover cases of communicable disease. The posts were often filled based on political considerations, and authority was divided among those two positions as well as an advisory Board of Health. State government's earliest role in provision of health care included building and operating tuberculosis hospitals in the early 19th century.

High levels of immigration and an investigation of health conditions by the state Senate in the middle of the century helped lead to formation of the Citizens Association, an activist organization that included a number of New York City's prominent physicians. In 1864, the association enlisted young doctors to conduct a sanitary survey of the city. The survey's findings aroused widespread public interest, and the physicians enlisted the aid of ministers and other community leaders; eventually, the matter became a significant political issue. In 1866, a new law established a powerful Metropolitan Board of Health. The statute was the first in the nation to create a strong governmental authority for monitoring and enforcing sanitary conditions; even England and France, which had pioneered public-health efforts in the Western world, were not far ahead. Similar laws in other large cities and states soon followed.

New York City's longstanding status as a center of world-class hospitals began when the second hospital in the United States, New York Hospital, opened in 1791 (the first was in Philadelphia, 40 years earlier). By 1825, another general hospital and the first specialty institution — an eye and ear infirmary — had opened in the city as well.

State Government's Growing Involvement

Responding to concerns around the state that echoed those in New York City, Governor Hamilton Fish and the Legislature began in 1850 to require every city and incorporated village to appoint a board of health and a health officer. An 1880 review by the state Board of Health found that most localities had failed to comply, but more counties began health-related programs in ensuing decades. In 1921, the Legislature authorized county governments to form health districts and created matching grants for building hospitals and providing nursing and other health services.[3]

In the decades just before and after the start of the 20th century, public health made huge gains across the country. Local efforts in New York City and elsewhere in the state often helped spawn worldwide advances. "Milk stations" that provided clean cow's milk to mothers who could not feed their babies were developed in New York City and Rochester. Children in New York City schools were the first to benefit broadly from school nurses, medical inspectors, and subsidized lunches. The first public-health nursing associations, forerunners of visiting nurse associations, were organized in Buffalo in 1885.

In 1929, the Legislature required local welfare districts to provide medical care to those receiving relief and to otherwise self-supporting persons who could not afford needed care. "Local governments paid all medical costs for needy persons and received reimbursement from the state for all except inpatient hospital care."[4]

Education of the public concerning how to stay healthy became a government function after both the New York City and New York State health departments created special bureaus for that purpose in 1914; dozens of other states and municipalities followed suit over the next two decades. The state agency was also the first, along with the Massachusetts Health Department, to employ nutritionists, in 1917.

Today, public-service messages on television and radio that inform Americans about the dangers of smoking and provide other health-related messages are commonplace. The first state agency in the country to broadcast regular health programs was New York's Health Department, which began in 1922 with a talk on "Keeping Well" over WGY in Schenectady.

The department's mission of informing the public about health matters is broader now than ever. The public-health agenda originally focused on keeping individuals safe from environmental pathogens and diseases such as typhus and diphtheria. Today, the agenda includes

---

3   Ellis at al., *A History of New York State*, p. 483.

4   *State-County Relations in New York: Key Partnership Issues, The Impacts of State Revenue Sharing and the Medicaid Mandate*, Buffalo, NY: Institute for Local Governance and Regional Growth, University at Buffalo, December 2000, p. 51.

encouraging New Yorkers to reduce or avoid the use of tobacco, early or "unsafe" sexual activity, and abuse of alcohol and drugs.

For half a century or more, the public-health mission of the Health Department was largely taken for granted. New Yorkers, like other Americans, assumed that water supplies would be pure, individual cases of life-threatening diseases would be rare and isolated, and public sources of food would be hygienically clean. Yet, new threats continually challenge the department to ensure these outcomes, as became clear in the summer of 1999 and again in September 2001. In 2006, Commissioner Novello unveiled a comprehensive Pandemic Influenza Plan to help protect state residents in the event of a worldwide epidemic.

A Broad Range of Powers

By the middle of the 20th century, state government's responsibility to protect public health was deemed so important that elected governors and legislatures had granted sweeping powers to the Health Department, its associated Public Health Council, and local health officers and boards of health. For instance, any individual who willfully violates the Public Health Law or any state or local health regulation may be punished by up to a year in jail for each offense.[5] The commissioner of health has the power to compel witnesses to appear and testify "in any matter or proceeding before him." Other powers include the ability to annul or change an order or regulation of a local health board when, in the commissioner's judgement, the matter may affect public health beyond that locality.

The Public Health Council consists of 15 members, including the commissioner; the other members are appointed by the governor to six-year terms with the consent of the Senate. The council advises the commissioner and establishes the state Sanitary Code. The code includes a wide range of sanitary regulations that automatically supersede any conflicting local laws. The council regulates cleanliness standards for hospitals and laboratories, designates communicable diseases that physicians must report to the department, prescribes the qualifications of both state and local health officials, requires bacteriological testing of bottled water sold in the state, and sets requirements for emergency

---

5   Public Health Law, Article 1, Section 12-b, 2002.

Public Health: What Was Old Is New Again

In late summer 1999, much of metropolitan New York was frightened by a public-health threat unlike any seen in decades. The West Nile virus, never before reported in the Western Hemisphere, was identified as the cause of seven deaths in the region from encephalitis, an inflammation of the brain. More than 50 other individuals contracted the disease but survived.

Once the West Nile threat was identified, staff of the state departments of Health, Agriculture and Markets, and Environmental Conservation worked with experts from the New York City departments of Health and Environmental Protection, local agencies from other counties in the downstate area, the federal Centers for Disease Control, Cornell and Fordham universities, and other private organizations to develop a response. Under the state Public Health Law, the Health Department has chief responsibility for addressing outbreaks of disease. Given the nature of the threat, existing programs and resources were not enough; a major new action plan had to be developed and implemented.

West Nile virus is transmitted by mosquitoes that feed on both humans and birds. To reduce the threat of infection, the Health Department and other agencies developed four approaches: educating the public, reducing habitat for mosquito larvae, killing larvae once hatched, and controlling mosquitoes that reach adulthood. Each approach entails a number of permutations. Education, for instance, ranges from teaching homeowners to eliminate standing water, to communicating techniques for avoiding mosquito bites, to updating health-care providers on the spread of the disease. Actions taken only if absolutely necessary include aerial spraying of insecticides after careful consideration of potential risks to humans. In the summer of 1999, spraying was conducted in several areas of the metropolitan region over a period of weeks. It was repeated in 2000, when another two individuals died from the virus, and in 2001. Cases of the virus in humans declined in the years thereafter; in 2006, only a few nonfatal cases were identified statewide.

The West Nile virus represented the return of infectious-disease threats similar to those that had started the public-health movement two centuries earlier. In its summary of the plan to battle the virus, the state Health Department stated: "This new infrastructure and communication network will form a cohesive multiagency approach to respond to other similar disease events. Even if West Nile virus does not recur in the northeast, there are other disease agents that pose threats to our general welfare and may require the very expertise developed as a result of this wakeup call for public health."

medical services at large public functions. The council's duties also include prescribing health and safety standards for children's camps, hotels, and motels.

The state's Public Health Law creates legal authority for local boards of health in counties, cities, towns, and villages. Outside New York City, the most important are typically county Boards of Health, appointed by the local legislature or board of supervisors.

Regulating and Providing Health Care

In recent decades, state government has taken on a major role in providing health care and health insurance, and a larger role in regulating private-sector activities in both areas.

Private health-insurance coverage first became common in the United States during World War II, when many employers began providing it as an alternative to wage increases that were limited by the federal government. As medical costs rose after the war, employer-provided health coverage became the means by which most Americans pay for medical care.

Some voices in New York and elsewhere were calling for a broad program of publicly funded health care by 1920. In 1950, President Truman and Congress provided the first federal participation in financing of state payments made to doctors and other medical providers for treatment of welfare recipients. Fifteen years later, Medicaid — a much more comprehensive program of financing health care for the poor — was established as part of President Johnson's "Great Society" expansion of government programs. At the same time, Congress and the president created Medicare to pay for medical care for the elderly (with similar names, the two programs are often confused). Medicare remains strictly a federal program. From the outset, though, Medicaid was a responsibility of both Washington and the states (and, in New York, local governments as well).

In 2004, some two-thirds of all New Yorkers — 12.8 million — were covered by private health insurance for at least part of the year, according to the Census Bureau. The great majority of those, 11.6 million, had employer-based coverage. In addition to the private coverage, some 3.3 million state residents were covered by Medicaid, while 2.7 million had Medicare (some individuals were covered by both programs, and/or had private coverage as well). Some 2.6 million New

Yorkers lacked health coverage for at least part of the year. They typically received relatively little primary or preventive medical care, instead visiting a hospital or seeing a doctor only when absolutely necessary.

Medicaid

To those who admire it, the scope of state government in New York reflects a clear-eyed recognition of social problems and an appropriate response to them, with the level of public support that a relatively wealthy economy can provide. To its detractors, government in the Empire State is enormously expensive, providing more services, and paying more on a unit basis for them, than do most other states. New York's Medicaid program exemplifies the factors that draw praise as well as those that are sometimes criticized.

Medicaid has traditionally been thought of as two programs. First, it provides health care for low-income families and individuals, including those on welfare and numerous others who do not collect cash benefits because they are employed or for other reasons. Second, the program pays the bills for elderly and disabled individuals who meet certain income and asset guidelines and need long-term care in nursing homes, other institutions, or at home. Over the last 20 years or so, Medicaid has taken on a third major role, financing much of the state's long-term care for those who are mentally ill or developmentally disabled.

Early discussion of a broad program of public health care in New York began in 1920, when Health Commissioner Hermann Biggs proposed a network of local health centers that could include hospitals, clinics for tuberculosis and other specific diseases, laboratories, and public-health nursing. The centers would provide annual physicals and regular medical care at an affordable cost, and at no charge for those who could not afford to pay. State aid would cover half the cost of buildings, treatment of indigent patients, and certain other expenses. "While a large number of community organizations supported these proposals, the Sage-Machold bill, which embodied this health center program, was defeated in the New York State Legislature. The whole idea was far ahead of public opinion, and especially of opinion in the New York medical profession."[6]

---

6   Rosen, *A History of Public Health*, p. 450.

As mentioned above, state legislation in 1929 required localities to provide medical care for those on welfare. In 1955, the mandate was expanded to require comprehensive health care, from physical exams to vision care and lab services. Within months of the federal government's creation of Medicaid a decade later, Governor Rockefeller and the Legislature created New York's version of the program. Rockefeller sent a special message to the Legislature urging that the state not lose the chance for millions of dollars in federal assistance for such an important purpose. The Senate and Assembly approved the program in 1966.

From early in its history, New York's Medicaid program has sought to balance the effort to provide a wide range of services with the need to remain affordable. Less than two years after pushing the program into creation, Rockefeller was asking the Legislature to scale it back because of the cost to both the state and local governments.

The former Department of Social Services (DSS) administered Medicaid for more than two decades, as Governor Rockefeller maintained that the agency providing the funding should not be the same as that determining the standards it should meet (Health). Governor Pataki initiated consolidation of the entire program in the Health Department in 1998 as part of a broad restructuring that eliminated DSS.

Expanding Services, and Growing Costs

Despite continual concern over costs, Medicaid grew by leaps and bounds — sometimes driven by federal expansion, often by state leaders. A quarter-century after its creation, New York's Medicaid program covered more than 3 million individuals — one in every six state residents — in the early 1990s. Coverage declined slightly, to some 2.8 million, later in the decade. After the September 11, 2001, terrorist attacks, Governor Pataki and the Legislature eased restrictions on Medicaid applications. Those steps, and an economic downturn that reduced employment statewide, resulted in a sharp increase in enrollment. In 2002, the Health Department reported a jump to 3.4 million individuals eligible for Medicaid; the 2005 figure was 4.2 million. (Many of those eligible for coverage do not obtain services in a given period; the average number of actual beneficiaries in 2005 was around 3.3 million.)

The federal government pays half the cost in New York (based on average incomes in each state, it pays a higher percentage — up to 83 percent — in most of the rest of the country). State government pays about 35 percent of the total, while localities — New York City and county governments elsewhere in the state — cover on average about 15 percent of the total (or 30 percent of the nonfederal share). The division of costs between Albany and localities varies depending on the type of care. The state pays more than 80 percent of nonfederal costs for nursing home and other long-term care, and 50 percent for most other types of care. Because long-term care represents a higher proportion of local costs outside New York City, state government pays a higher share of overall Medicaid costs in other counties than it does in the city.

The state has gradually assumed a higher proportion of the nonfederal cost of Medicaid since 1980, when those expenditures were split evenly between Albany and localities. By 1990, the state share had risen to 63.5 percent; as of 1998, it was 67.8 percent. Growth in the overall cost of the program, though, produced sharply rising costs for state government, New York City, and county governments alike.[7]

For state government after the recent turn of the century, Medicaid represented a complex combination of elements. From a pure budgetary standpoint, the program was known as the 800-pound gorilla: spending totaled more than $46 billion in 2006, a third more than that in much larger California. (That figure includes local spending not reflected in the Office of the State Comptroller data cited at the beginning of this chapter.) Following on the actions of its founder, every governor since the program's inception has called for changes to reduce its cost — *and* sponsored expansion of its services.

In addition to services required by the federal government, New York's program offers almost all services that Washington makes optional for states. Governor Cuomo, in his budget message for 1990-91, observed that he and the Legislature had expanded the program in each of the two previous years, making more than a quarter-million individuals newly eligible. He called for further expansion, providing new health insurance for an estimated 136,000 children. At the same time, Governor Cuomo said, "We must, however, continue our efforts to control the rapid increase in Medicaid expenditures." He proposed a series of cost-saving measures, including cuts in provider reimbursement rates as well as "intensified audits, detection of fraud and abuse, and enhanced controls over Medicaid payments."[8] Governor Pataki, too,

---

7 *State-County Relations in New York*, p. 66.

8 New York State Division of the Budget, *Annual Budget Message 1990-91*, pp. M43-M44.

Medicaid Spending, New York And Selected States

(millions of dollars, 2005)

State	Total Spending, 2005	Inpatient Hospital Care	Nursing Facilities	Home Health & Personal Care
New York	$43,406	$6,119	$6,937	$7,820
California	33,948	5,859	3,094	5,647
Texas	18,328	3,491	1,697	2,241
Pennsylvania	15,465	621	4,403	1,615
Florida	13,327	2,238	2,228	1,281
Ohio	11,840	1,667	2,732	1,695
Illinois	10,799	3,396	1,414	937
Massachusetts	9,598	1,018	1,687	1,345
N.Y. % of U.S. total	**14.3%**	**14.5%**	**14.8%**	**18.8%**

Source: Kaiser Family Foundation

called for reducing costs and initiated major expansion of the program. As a candidate for governor in 2006, Eliot Spitzer promised to take both steps, as well.

Despite its cost, the program has, in some ways, been a fiscal boon to Albany. Throughout the late 1980s and 1990s, sharp-eyed analysts in the Budget Division and state agencies continually found new ways to shift existing services into Medicaid and thereby draw significant amounts of new federal funding for programs that had been totally state-funded.

Medicaid poses contradictions from the public-health perspective, as well. Clearly, it is a godsend to uncounted New Yorkers who might otherwise go without medical care, or who might obtain hospital care only after health problems had advanced to an emergency nature. Yet the program has long been harshly criticized for its perceived failure to encourage preventive and primary care; the shift to managed care in recent years is partly an effort to pursue those approaches more widely. And despite repeated expansion of Medicaid and other health-care programs, the number of Empire State residents with no health insurance remains in the millions. The fees included in private health-insurance policies to help pay for Medicaid are one reason that private coverage is more expensive in New York than in most other states — which in turn discourages some employers and individuals from purchasing health coverage.

As in other states, Medicaid is New York's largest social welfare program, far larger than cash-based welfare programs. Yet a substantial share of its costs go to pay the nursing-home bills of individuals who have used gifts and trusts to distribute assets to family members, thereby establishing eligibility for support from the government. Many of the taxpayers who contribute to that public support are less wealthy than those receiving the benefits.[9] The medical-care portion of Medicaid represents a majority of recipients, but long-term care makes up a larger share of the overall cost because each individual case is far more expensive.

All told, New York's expenditures on Medicaid are by far the highest in the country. In 2005, according to federal data, New York's $43.4 billion spending represented 14.3 percent of the total for all the states —

---

9   In his campaign for Medicaid reform, Nassau County Executive Tom Suozzi publicized a constituent who arranged for his wife's nursing-home bills to go to the county, despite holding assets well over $1 million.

a proportion that was more than double the Empire State's share of the nationwide population.[10]

A study by the Citizens Budget Commission, a private think tank in New York City, found that as a share of the total population, the number of Medicaid beneficiaries in New York was about 20 percent above the national average. As a share of the poverty population, the state's Medicaid caseload was about 12 percent above the national average. Most of the relatively high spending in New York was due to high costs per beneficiary, the commission found. The discrepancy was significant for spending on both acute-care services and for long-term care, but the gap was more pronounced for the latter. New York spending per beneficiary was 58 percent above the national average for acute care, and 168 percent above the average for long-term care.[11]

Political Support

Medicaid is especially important — for reasons of human services, economics, and politics — in New York City. Medicaid expenditures there totaled more than 64 percent of all those statewide in 2004, while the city's population accounted for roughly 42 percent of the state's total. That demographic picture has generally meant that legislators from the city have been more likely to support expanding it — or, in difficult budget years, to oppose cutbacks — than members from the suburbs or upstate. The Assembly, controlled by Democrats since 1974, has been a consistently strong supporter of Medicaid during that time because a majority of its Democrat members have represented the city.

The Assembly majority initiated the expansion of Medicaid known as Family Health Plus in 1999. Leaders of hospital-worker unions and the hospital industry persuaded both Governor Pataki and the Republican Senate majority to join in enacting the program expansion. The new program was made possible, in part, by settlement of a national lawsuit that states brought against major tobacco companies, resulting in a commitment of roughly $1 billion a year to New York. The Family Health Plus legislation also included a 55-cent increase in the cigarette tax. The most powerful political push for the legislation came from

10 Kaiser Family Foundation, *www.statehealthfacts.org.*

11 Citizens Budget Commission, *Budget 2000 Project: Social Welfare Spending*, New York, NY, 1998, p. 17.

Local 1199 of the Service Employees International Union, which had raised millions of dollars from member dues to be set aside for political advertising. The 1999 legislation also included an agreement that there would be no reductions in Medicaid reimbursement for hospitals at least until 2003, after the next statewide elections. After persuading Governor Pataki and the Legislature to approve another major increase in health care funding in 2002, the head of Local 1199, Dennis Rivera, was widely regarded as the most influential lobbyist in Albany.

Hospital Funding and Long-Term Care

As a result of the creation of Medicare and Medicaid, "vast amounts of new dollars were being forced into the health system without adequate controls over costs or third-party reimbursement rates,"[12] and market forces were unable to serve their normal function of regulating costs. The result was sharp inflation in health-care costs.

Starting in the mid-1960s, concern over high and rising hospital costs prompted state leaders to enact regulations on construction of new health facilities and price controls on hospital bills paid by Medicaid and Blue Cross. In 1983, the Health Department was assigned to decide how much hospitals in each region of the state could charge private insurers, Medicaid and Blue Cross for each of several hundred types of services, from various types of surgery to laboratory tests. The rate-setting, known as the New York Prospective Hospital Reimbursement Method (NYPHRM), appeared to have some success, with some studies showing that hospital costs in New York rose less rapidly in ensuing years than in many other states. By the 1990s, however, private hospitals, as well as many employers and insurers, were complaining that the state's price controls did not allow them the freedom to negotiate rates and forced retention of an oversupply of hospital beds. The private hospitals feared increasing competition from for-profit managed-care plans, while employers and insurers who paid hospital bills saw negotiated rates as a path to restraint in rising health-care costs.

In 1996, Governor Pataki and the Legislature repealed NYPHRM and allowed most non-Medicaid payors of hospital bills to negotiate

---

12 Arthur L. Levin, "Health Care," in *Governing New York State: The Rockefeller Years*, Robert H. Connery and Gerald Benjamin, eds., New York, NY: The Academy of Political Science, 1974, p. 176.

rates with hospitals. The goal was to increase competition among hospitals and thereby encourage efficiency. Besides affecting the hospital rates charged to private payors — and thus the cost of health insurance in the state — NYPHRM determined how much the state itself would pay hospitals for services to Medicaid patients. The 1996 reform act included a number of cost-containment measures, while successor legislation in December 1999 included significant increases in state funding for hospitals.

The state retains substantial regulatory control over construction of hospitals and other health-care facilities. The department's Hospital Review and Planning Council reviews applications for the establishment of new health care entities and applications for construction or modification of existing medical facilities, acquisition of major medical equipment, change in ownership, or addition of services.

Major Changes Coming for Hospitals and Nursing Homes

For two decades or more, state Health Department officials have diagnosed New York's hospital system as too big. During that period, some hospitals closed and others reorganized to provide other forms of care. Yet, by most measures, New York's infrastructure of health-care facilities remained significantly larger and more expensive than those in other states. As of 2003, the number of hospital beds in New York was some 21 percent higher than the national average, after adjusting for population. Hospitalization rates, and the average length of stays in hospitals, are longer than average in New York. While the state spends more than $3 billion a year on programs intended to help older and disabled residents stay out of institutions, the proportion of residents living in nursing homes is higher in New York than most states, as well.

In 2005, Governor Pataki proposed the most comprehensive effort yet to restructure the state's system of acute- and long-term care. Legislation approved as part of that year's budget gave the Commission on Health Care Facilities in the 21st Century more than a year to "examine the needs and capacities of the health care system and make recommendations to right-size hospitals and nursing homes."[13] With the approach

---

13 Press release, Executive Chamber, June 2, 2005.

of its December 2006 reporting date (after statewide and legislative elections), some hospital executives who opposed likely recommendations worked to build public opposition, arguing that reducing hospital capacity would harm New Yorkers' health care.[14] The commission, chaired by former state official Stephen Berger, issued an interim report in February 2006 that included these findings:

> In the past two decades, much has changed in healthcare, especially in the areas of financing, clinical care, information technology, and delivery mechanisms. Yet today, New York is struggling to maintain a 20th century institutional structure in the face of mounting costs, excess capacity, and unmet need for community based alternatives. The existing institutional infrastructure is neither affordable nor flexible. The fiscal instability facing New York's health care providers threatens the availability of important safety-net and public good functions. Today's reality demands a realignment of resources and a reinvestment strategy.[15]

The commission was expected to recommend major industry changes — closing of some institutions, and perhaps expansion or redevelopment of others — in each region of the state. The legislation creating the commission gave the governor and the Legislature the month of December 2006 to consider rejecting its proposals. Absent such rejection, the law empowered the state health commissioner — with that office's broad powers over the health-care system — to put the commission's recommendations into effect.

During the 2006 gubernatorial campaign, both Eliot Spitzer and John Faso make supportive comments about the work of the Berger Commission. Its report was expected to play a key role in defining health-care policy in 2007 and beyond.

Medicaid Managed Care

Like Medicaid across the country, New York's program historically relied on emergency rooms and hospitals to provide a significant amount of routine care. Often, patients would see a different doctor each time

---

14 See, for example, Gary J. Fitzgerald, "Hospitals face closing after election," *The Post-Standard*, Syracuse, NY, October 8, 2006.

15 *Planning For The Future: Capacity Needs in a Changing Health Care System*, New York, NY: Commission on Health Care Facilities in the 21st Century, 2006.

they sought treatment; there was little ongoing review of patients' health status. Those problems were exacerbated by low physician fees, which kept most doctors from accepting Medicaid patients. To promote preventive and primary care, and in hopes of reducing the growth in costs, state leaders started moving some recipients into managed care in the mid-1990s. In 1997, the federal government approved the state's request for permission to enroll 2.2 million recipients, on a mandatory basis, into managed care over several years. Most other states moved into managed care more quickly; as of 1997, one study found, a majority of states had enrolled more than half of all recipients in the new type of program, while the proportion in New York was less than one-third. As of September 2006, some 2 million New Yorkers were enrolled statewide.

The nationwide popularity of managed care "has been driven both by a desire to save money on Medicaid and by the potential of managed care to enhance the accountability of the health care system in ways that were not possible under the fee-for-service system," a Rockefeller Institute of Government study explained. "Care under the fee-for-service system is provided by a host of independent providers and reimbursed one service at a time. There is no single entity that can be held responsible for the care provided to clients and little opportunity for states to influence the way care is delivered to Medicaid clients or establish standards for the appropriateness or quality of care. Managed care, by contrast, creates one organization — a health maintenance organization (HMO) or something similar — that accepts a single payment for the entire range of services to each Medicaid client. This organization can, at least in theory, be held responsible for the entire range of health care received by its enrollees, and be sanctioned in various ways if it fails to comply with specified standards of care."[16]

Within several years of its start, the managed-care program was meeting at least some of its goals. Use of primary care increased while emergency room visits and total inpatient days in hospitals declined, according to the Health Department.

The movement toward managed care in Medicaid occurred at the same time as similar shifts among private insurance plans provided by employers, and in the federal Medicare program for senior citizens. In

---

16 James W. Fossett at al., *Managing Accountability In Medicaid Managed Care: The Politics of Public Management*, Albany, NY: Rockefeller Institute of Government, 1999, p. 1.

response, the Health Department created measurements for analyzing management and performance by managed-care plans. The Quality Assurance Reporting Requirements track key indicators such as rates of immunization, lead screening, well-child visits and diabetes testing statewide as well as for individual managed-care plans.

As a result of 2005 legislation, the Health Department began a number of demonstration programs in disease management — a broad regimen of care for individuals whose treatment is especially costly because of they suffer from advanced chronic illnesses or from a variety of health problems. The demonstration programs were intended to test how much savings could be obtained from the relatively small number of Medicaid recipients who generate a disproportionately large share of overall costs.

Expanding Health Coverage

The program expansions that have generally characterized New York's publicly funded health insurance programs continued in the 1990s. At Governor Cuomo's initiative, the Legislature enacted the Child Health Plus program to provide health insurance for children whose families were not poor enough to qualify for Medicaid. The new program was expected to be cost-effective because health insurance for children is relatively inexpensive. The program became a model for the national State Children's Health Insurance Program enacted by President Clinton and Congress in 1997. Expanded in 1996 and 1998, Child Health Plus came to cover individuals up to age 19 in families earning up to 2.5 times the federal poverty level. The program pays for hospital care, doctor visits, x-rays and other lab tests, prescription drugs, dental and vision care, speech therapy, and other services.

Family Health Plus, enacted in 1999, was designed to build on the Child Health Plus program to provide a broad range of health services, including doctor visits, prescription drugs, and dental care. The program is aimed at lower-income, working adults aged 19 through 64 who do not have coverage through their employers, yet have an income high enough to disqualify them for other public programs. Another program created in 2000, Healthy NY, provides additional health-insurance options for individuals and for small businesses that do not already provide coverage for employees.

Recent Developments:
Addressing Local Costs and Fraud

As noted in Chapter Two, the increasing impact of Medicaid on property taxes across the state drove county executives and others to demand action by the Legislature starting in 2003. In 2005, Governor Pataki and legislators committed the state to paying a larger share of future cost increases. Albany has also taken over the cost of Family Health Plus, the program approved in 2001 to cover working adults with lower incomes. The shift in funding for both programs will ease fiscal concerns for counties and New York City, but add to the state's own fiscal challenges in coming years — some $3 billion as of the 2009 fiscal year.

State leaders have long recognized the potential for fraud in Medicaid, given the large number of patients served and the decentralized nature of a health-care system that includes a wide variety of institutions and care providers. The Legislature created a special bureau in the attorney general's office to prosecute Medicaid fraud in the mid-1970s. In mid-2005, though, *The New York Times* reported that such fraud was costing taxpayers billions of dollars a year due to lack of oversight from state officials.[17] The newspaper's investigation showed that unscrupulous physicians and other health-care providers were able to bill Medicaid for numerous services on the same day. Consumers were able to obtain multiple prescriptions from different doctors, and sell the taxpayer-financed drugs on the black market. The newspaper's reporters found much of their information by using computer software to look for irregularities in the state's data on Medicaid reimbursements. In 2006, a report by the inspector general of the federal Department of Health and Human Services confirmed the newspaper's findings that state leaders were not doing enough to prevent fraud and abuse.

After extensive press coverage, elected officials and candidates for office traded criticisms over the state's failure to prevent such large-scale fraud. One factor may have been the 1995 consolidation of the Medicaid program into the Health Department. Before that restructuring, utilization-review specialists in the former Department of Social Services were charged with analyzing reimbursements to hospitals, doctors, and other providers to seek out potential abuse. Once those

---

17 Clifford J. Levy and Michael Luo, "New York Medicaid Fraud May Reach Into Billions," *The New York Times*, July 18, 2005.

positions were shifted to the Health Department, some employees perceived that the different organizational culture in the new agency discouraged critical oversight of such expenditures. Clearly, no one in state government — at the Health Department or elsewhere — had been charged with managing the overall Medicaid program effectively.

The 2006 legislative session ended with agreement to create a new Medicaid inspector general, with additional powers to investigate and prosecute fraud.

Regulating Health Care

The Health Department regulates hospitals, nursing homes, and other health facilities across the state. Its oversight duties include setting standards for personnel, cleanliness, and patient nutrition, and conducting regular inspections to ensure adherence to these standards. Institutions that fail to meet the standards are subject to citations, fines, or revocation of an operating certificate. When local newspapers pay attention to state reviews of nursing homes and other institutions, publicity can provide a powerful impetus for improvement. Department staff located in regional offices perform most public health monitoring and oversee the activities of county health departments.

As in many other aspects of health care, New York's private sector was a leader in the early development of managed care. The Health Insurance Plan of Greater New York began operating in 1947 as one of the nation's first prepaid group plans offering comprehensive health services — the forerunner of today's health maintenance organizations and other managed-care plans.

By the mid-1990s, most employers — private and public — were using managed care for at least some of their health coverage, in an effort to contain costs while promoting primary and preventive care. In response to efforts to restrain cost increases, doctors and some consumer advocates complained that health-maintenance organizations were limiting patients' choices. In 1996, Governor Pataki and the Legislature created a "Bill of Rights" requiring that certain information be made available to patients and guaranteeing that insurers would not limit the ability of providers to discuss treatment options with patients. In 1999, additional legislation required managed-care plans to allow patients to obtain an independent review if their health claim is denied on the grounds that it is not medically necessary or is experimental.

Along with the Education Department, the Health Department regulates the practice of medicine and certain other health-related professions. It also monitors the availability of doctors, nurses, and other health professionals and identifies underserved areas for programs that provide training.

Health Department Institutions

The department's Wadsworth Center for Laboratories and Research investigates a wide variety of public-health concerns. Its screening programs annually report results of nearly 3 million tests to doctors and other health-care providers in areas such as HIV, tuberculosis, and genetic disorders in newborns. Ongoing research, largely funded by external grants the center wins on a competitive basis, is conducted on public-health topics such as AIDS, Lyme disease, cancer, and the toxic effects of chemical substances and radiation. Wadsworth scientists played primary roles in the state's response to the West Nile virus threats in recent summers and to the anthrax-bioterrorism emergency in 2001. In the latter case, department physicians provided the expertise local health and law-enforcement officials needed to learn how to recognize and treat anthrax contamination. The agency faxed and e-mailed notices to hundreds of hospitals and other institutions, warning of the need to look for unusual diseases or clusters of illnesses. Letters informed tens of thousands of doctors of guidelines for testing for and treating anthrax infection. Department staff analyzed hundreds of samples and answered hundreds of telephone calls from county health departments, hospitals and medical offices, and frightened members of the public.

Other important subjects of Wadsworth studies in recent years have included groundwater contamination at Brookhaven National Laboratory in Suffolk County, polychlorinated-biphenyls (PCBs) pollution in the Hudson River, and radon risks in communities throughout the state. The center also regulates more than 800 environmental laboratories and 1,800 clinical laboratories to ensure test quality and public health and safety.

Roswell Park Cancer Institute in Buffalo is among the leading cancer research and treatment centers in the world, one of 20 nationwide to be members of National Comprehensive Cancer Network. A major teaching and research facility, it employs 1,500 or so and trains more than 300 graduate students, residents, and fellows each year. Administered by the state for decades, the Institute now is operated by a public-health and research corporation, which creates greater operational and financial flexibility. Employees retained civil-service protections under the 1997 law creating the corporation, and the Institute continued to receive tens of millions of dollars in state funding each year.

The Helen Hayes Hospital, operated by the Health Department, is a physical rehabilitation and surgical center in Rockland County dedicated to preventing and reducing the harmful effects of physical disability and chronic disease. It also conducts research on clinical treatment, osteoporosis and other bone diseases, neurology, and rehabilitation technology. Established in 1900 and formerly known as the New York State Rehabilitation Hospital, today it is a modern facility whose patients in recent years have included actor Christopher Reeve.

The Health Department oversees resident care at veterans' nursing homes in Batavia, Oxford, St. Albans, and Montrose, Westchester County.

Vital Statistics and Other Responsibilities

Statistics on births, deaths, and disease began to assume a new social significance in the mid-1800s. The numbers told medical practitioners and researchers how many infants and mothers died in particular neighborhoods, and how many deaths were caused by communicable diseases — information that could be used in prevention and treatment efforts. Today the Health Department maintains extensive statistics on pregnancies, live births, spontaneous fetal deaths, induced abortions, general mortality, marriages, and divorces — with most data available by sex, age, and race. In recent years, the leading causes of death in New York have been heart diseases and cancer.

Government public-health efforts — along with medical and pharmaceutical advances by the private sector — brought dramatic progress in health. Throughout the 20th century, for instance, infant mortality rates declined sharply in New York and across the country. The Health Department's statistics make it possible to track the damage inflicted by various illnesses, and to compare key indicators of New Yorkers' health over time and to those of other states.

Besides monitoring public health, the department fulfills other major responsibilities:

- The State Board for Professional Medical Conduct engages in disciplinary proceedings against physicians charged with negligence, incompetence, and impairment by drugs, alcohol, or disability. The board submits findings to the commissioner, who can recommend license revocation or other penalty to the Board of Regents, which licenses physicians and most other professionals in the state.

- The department sets a wide range of fees for various health-related services. Examples include nursing and other services provided to sick and disabled persons in the home.

The Health Department workforce stood at approximately 5,800 as of 2006, with nearly a quarter of those individuals employed in the agency's health-care facilities. Some three-quarters of all positions are funded by federal funds or reimbursement from third parties such as insurers and private patient fees.

Deaths and Death Rates By Selected Causes, New York State, 2002		
Disease	*Number of Deaths*	*Rate per 100,000 Population*
Heart diseases	56,670	295.8
Cancer	36,499	190.5
— of respiratory system	9,988	52.1
— digestive system	9,525	49.7
— breast (female)	3,010	15.7
Pneumonia	5,428	28.3
Chronic obstructive pulmonary disease	6,997	36.5
Accidents	4,317	22.5
Suicide	1,317	6.9
Homicide	936	4.9
Source: New York State Health Department, Bureau of Biometrics		

Mental Hygiene

Not long after public efforts to promote physical health began in the early 1800s, social reformers in New York and elsewhere turned their attention to problems of mental health and mental retardation. Until the mid-19th century, state government was not involved in the care and treatment of individuals with mental illness or the mentally retarded. Most were cared for by their families, while others were committed to county poorhouses. There, such individuals typically received only minimal custodial care while remaining vulnerable to exploitation.

The first state-funded mental health institution, the State Asylum for Lunatics, opened in Utica in 1843.[18] Common wisdom held that "moral treatment," humane care and instruction, could "cure" the illness in a relatively short time. Clients deemed incurable after a year at the asylum were returned to the poorhouses in their home communities.

In the two decades before the Civil War, the reformer Dorothea Dix exposed ill treatment of mentally ill individuals and the Legislature authorized an investigation. The result, in 1865, was establishment of a state hospital for chronic mentally ill patients. The institution was named after Dr. Sylvester D. Willard, who led the investigation. As late as 1992, the Seneca County facility continued as the Willard Psychiatric Center. Due to the declining need for inpatient psychiatric care and a growing need for drug treatment for prison inmates, it was converted into a state treatment center.

As industrialization expanded both the state's population and its ability to pay for public services, 17 new state asylums opened during the latter half of the 1800s. The centers began admitting more chronically ill individuals, and their role evolved into one of custodial care and protection of the community. Treatment was given secondary consideration, at best. State government completed its assumption of responsibility for the mentally ill in 1890 with legislation that abolished county asylums and stipulated staffing levels, treatment regimens, and safety rules for state facilities. Often considered the first such statute in the country, the law established a statewide system that remained largely in place until the 1950s. It also substituted the word "hospital" for "asylum."

---

18 How times change. Today, the word "asylum" carries negative connotations, contrary to its original meaning as a place of refuge. "Lunatic" ceased being an acceptable term for individuals with mental illness decades ago.

Report by Dorothea Dix

During the 1840s and 1850s, Dorothea Dix visited prisons and alms-houses in New York and numerous other states, reporting her findings to state legislatures and asking for development of state hospitals to provide specialized care for the mentally ill. The following, an excerpt from her 1844 Memorial to the New York State Legislature, provides a chilling reminder of the conditions in which many of the mentally disabled were once kept.

It was on the afternoon of a severely cold day in November of 1842, that I visited the alms-house at Albany. Inquiring of the master who held charge of the establishment, the number of the insane then in close confinement, I was answered, "There are plenty of them; somewhere about twenty." "Will you let me see them?" "No, you can't, they're naked, in the crazy cellar." ... (After further discussion) I entered an apartment not clean, not ventilated, and over-heated: here were several females chiefly in a state of dementia; they were decently dressed, but otherwise exhibited personal neglect; the beds were sufficiently comfortable; the hot air, foul with noisome vapors, produced a sense of suffocation and sickness impossible to be long endured by one unaccustomed to such an atmosphere. I delayed here but few moments, and asked to be conducted to the dungeons....

In the cell first opened was a madman; the fierce command of his keeper brought him to the door — a hideous object; matted locks, unshorn beard, a wild wan countenance, yet more disfigured by vilest uncleanness, in a state of entire nudity, save the irritating incrustations derived from that dungeon reeking with loathsome filth: here, without light, without pure air, without warmth, without cleansing, without *anything* to secure decency or comfort, here was a human being, forlorn, abject, and disgusting it is true, but not the less a human being — nay more, an immortal being, though now the mind had fallen in ruins, and the soul was clothed in darkness...

A woman, of what age one could not conjecture, so disfigured was she by neglect and suffering, occupied a dungeon on the right. The keeper harshly summoned her "to come out," but she only moved feebly amidst the filthy straw which was the only furnishing of the place; her moans and low cries indicated both mental anguish and physical pain. In vain they tried to force her forward — she seemed powerless to raise herself upright; she, too, was unclothed....

Dorothea Dix, *On Behalf of the Insane Poor: Selected Reports*, reprinted in *Poverty, U.S.A.: The Historical Record*, New York: Arno Press & The New York Times, 1971.

In the early 1900s, aftercare services, occupational therapy, and out-patient clinics were developed. Voluntary admissions to state mental hospitals began in 1907, expanding state government's responsibility. By 1912, the census of the state system topped 31,000; the State Hospital Commission estimated that more than 40 percent of patients would require lifelong institutionalization.

In 1926, as part of their broad restructuring of state government, Governor Smith and the Legislature established the Department of Mental Hygiene to consolidate responsibility for individuals with mental illness, those with mental retardation, and those suffering from epilepsy. Construction of new psychiatric centers and admission of patients grew steadily until 1955, when the census peaked at 93,314. Legislation enacted under Governor Dewey in 1954 established local mental-health boards in each county and in New York City, formally creating a state-local partnership for delivery of mental-health services. Federal funding initiated nine years later created a new impetus for community-based mental-health services. Around the same time, psychotropic drugs pioneered at New York State's research facilities were starting to show their effectiveness, contributing to the possibility of greater use of community care for mental illness.

The number of mentally retarded individuals in state facilities continued to grow into the 1960s, reaching nearly 30,000 in the middle of the decade before starting to decline. As the institutionalized population peaked, overcrowding and other problems led to poorer care. As early as August 1965, the *Staten Island Advance* reported on deteriorating conditions in Willowbrook State School for the Mentally Retarded, the largest institution of its kind in the country, which housed some 5,700 retarded children and adults. Most residents were severely retarded and had spent the bulk of their lives at Willowbrook. Another *Advance* series of articles, updating the story in 1971, described horrific conditions such as naked, retarded boys spending their days curled on the floor for lack of any programs and others picking at untreated sores. Those stories led to television coverage, which — along with a lawsuit filed by parents, volunteer organizations, and individual residents — finally brought corrective attention from state leaders.

In 1978, Governor Carey and the Legislature reorganized the Department of Mental Hygiene in an effort to improve management of programs for those with mental illness, mental retardation, and drug/alcohol abuse. "The previous administrative structure of the department was heavily weighted in favor of mental-health programs, and it was difficult for programs in mental retardation and alcoholism/substance abuse to receive proper attention."[19] The former department remains in place, largely as a legal construct, while three autonomous agencies provide services for individuals with differing needs. The 1978 law created the Office of Mental Health, Office of Mental Retardation and Developmental Disabilities, and the Office of Alcoholism and Substance Abuse (later renamed the Office of Alcoholism and Substance Abuse Services). Each office is headed by a commissioner, appointed by the governor with consent of the Senate. The three commissioners serve on an inter-office coordinating council. Today the three agencies employ some 42,000 individuals, nearly one in four members of the executive branch's workforce.

During the 1970s, community care for both mentally ill and retarded and developmentally disabled individuals grew in importance, both because it was considered better for clients and because of the potential for cost savings. At the same time, state government took over additional responsibility for funding mental-health services from counties and New York City.

The shift from huge institutions to the community brought both benefits and new problems. A noticeable increase in the number of homeless individuals, many of them mentally ill, was often attributed in part to deinstitutionalization. On the other hand, there was no question that thousands of men and women were living better lives in the community than they had in the large state-operated centers.

Despite the movement of tens of thousands of individuals from institutional to community care, the state still maintains what some observers consider an inefficiently large number of developmental and psychiatric centers. While the state has not built new centers, and has closed a number of institutions in recent decades, facilities that are still operating have cost hundreds of millions of dollars for rebuilding and modernization.

Much of the state's activity in mental-hygiene programs in the last two decades has been aimed at maximizing federal Medicaid funding. The Office of Mental Retardation and Developmental Disabilities is almost entirely funded by Medicaid. Increases in federal funding have allowed the agency to expand both residential and

---

19 *The New York State Archives Guide to the Organization and History of State Government*, Albany, NY: The University of the State of New York, State Archives and Records Administration, 1994.

nonresidential services more rapidly than the Office of Mental Health, given that federal law makes Medicaid less easily available for care of mental illness.

Mental Health

Recent decades brought advances in treatments and medications that have made living in community settings a realistic possibility for most individuals with serious mental illness or emotional disturbance. The state's public mental-health system provides recovery-oriented services to some 630,000 New Yorkers annually, with the vast majority receiving services in community-based programs while living at home, and often working or attending school.

The gender breakdown of state psychiatric center residents has changed dramatically in the last three decades. Through the 1970s, women represented a slight majority — around 53 percent in 1972. Male residents became a majority in 1982, and have since become the overwhelming majority at nearly 70 percent as of 2000. The change occurred as overall population dwindled, clients with less serious illness were returned to the community, and centers became home mainly to clients with particularly debilitating illness.

OMH, and the services it provides and regulates, continue to evolve with increasing understanding of the most successful approaches to treatment mental illness. For instance, in recent years, recipients of services have begun to influence the design of services for recovery and rehabilitation.

In 1999, Governor Pataki and the Legislature enacted "Kendra's Law," in response to the killing of a New York City woman by a mentally disabled man who had failed to take medication prescribed for his illness. The law provides for assisted outpatient treatment and supervision for mentally ill individuals who will not regularly take the medications they need to live safely in the community. The death of Kendra Webdale and the enactment of Kendra's Law led to significant increases in funding to establish new initiatives for housing and treatment.

The agency regulates, certifies, and oversees the public mental-health system and licenses more than 2,500 mental-health programs operated by local governments and private agencies. Such programs include inpatient and outpatient services as well as emergency, community support, residential, and family-care programs. As of 2006, OMH's 17,500 employees

Award-Winning Research in Mental Health

The Office of Mental Health includes two research institutes, the New York State Psychiatric Institute in Manhattan, and the Nathan S. Kline Institute, located on the grounds of Rockland Psychiatric Center. The Psychiatric Institute performs basic research, much of which has been groundbreaking. The Kline Institute studies applications and health services for the mentally ill.

Reseachers at the psychiatric institute conducted the first genetic studies of schizophrenia in the United States and made the nation's first demonstration of the effects of certain drugs in arresting symptoms of the disease. American medical research on the use of electroconvulsive therapy (formerly known as electroshock treatment) was first undertaken at the institute, which was also home to the first childhood depression clinic in the world. Other important discoveries have included new evidence for a genetic cause of manic depression, identification of the gene that causes Huntington's disease, and early work on teen suicide and depression.

An institute scientist, Eric Kandel, received the 2000 Nobel Prize in Medicine. His discoveries, using a type of signal between nerve cells known as slow synaptic transmission, used the nervous system of sea slugs as an experimental model. Also affiliated with Columbia University, Dr. Kandel shared the honor with Paul Greengard, of Rockefeller University in New York City, and a Swedish researcher. The discoveries have been crucial in understanding normal brain function and how disturbances in communications between cells can result in neurological and psychiatric disease. The Nobel committee said the research might help produce new treatments to improve memory function in patients with dementia.

operated 25 psychiatric centers (a reduction of three institutions in the past five years), including six specifically for children and three forensic psychiatric centers treating individuals charged with crimes.

Mental Retardation

The Office of Mental Retardation and Developmental Disabilities operates state developmental centers and community-based programs, and oversees a network of nonprofit providers, for individuals with developmental disabilities that include mental retardation, epilepsy, cerebral palsy, neurological impairments, and autism.

The agency served some 140,000 persons with disabilities, with total funding of $3.4 billion, in 2006-07. While several decades ago the great majority of clients were institutionalized, today some 38,000 clients live in state-certified homes. A total of 64,000, including many who live with their families, benefit from community-based day services. Supported work programs, sheltered workshops, and other services help many individuals experience the working world. Under a program called NYS-CARES (New York State-Creating Alternatives in Residential Environments and Services), more than 12,000 individuals moved into community homes from 1998 to 2006. The program is, in part, a response to the growing number of aging parents who have cared for developmentally disabled sons and daughters at home, but are reaching stages where such care is no longer possible.

State centers were home to some 1,700 New Yorkers in 2006, a fraction of the total decades earlier. The agency works through 13 regionally based offices to oversee care and treatment for clients with developmental disabilities. The offices seek to provide specially designed assistance to each individual as requested by the client or a family. Goals include ensuring that each client has a decent place to live, employment where possible, and support services such as help with shopping and arranging medical care.

The agency operates the Institute for Basic Research on Staten Island. The institute investigates the causes of developmental disabilities, provides laboratory and clinical services, and prepares materials for public and professional education.

OMRDD also supports families in caring for some 61,000 persons by providing respite, crisis intervention, case management, recreation, home care, and other services. The agency employs 22,200 individuals, most working directly with clients.

Alcoholism and Substance Abuse

With rising concern over drug abuse in the 1960s, Governor Rockefeller and the Legislature created a Narcotic Addiction Control Commission within the Department of Mental Hygiene in 1966. Its successor agencies went through several name changes; in 1992, both antidrug and alcohol-related services were combined into the Office of Alcoholism and Substance Abuse Services (OASAS), the largest drug and alcohol prevention and treatment system in the nation. It operates 13 addiction treatment centers, licenses and evaluates service providers, and administers programs to prevent and treat alcoholism and substance abuse as well as compulsive gambling.

Men make up the majority of admissions to OASAS programs — 74 percent in 1999. While 43 percent of all those admitted were white, blacks made up a disproportionate share — 35 percent — of the total.

OASAS works with some 1,200 community-based agencies, roughly half dealing with alcoholism and the remaining with other addiction problems. The agency's programs served an estimated 300,000 individuals in 2006. Its budget was $592 million, with a workforce of just over 960 that year.

Overseeing Quality of Care

The impetus for restructuring of the Department of Mental Hygiene in the mid-1970s — to make sure that conditions such as those at Willowbrook would never arise again — also led to creation of the Commission on Quality of Care for the Mentally Disabled in 1977. The commission provides independent oversight of state institutions and state-licensed programs and facilities that collectively spend some $7 billion annually. It also makes broad recommendations to the governor and the Legislature on ensuring high-quality care, investigates allegations of patient abuse and mistreatment, and provides training and assistance to members of the Boards of Visitors at each of the state's psychiatric and developmental centers. (Boards of Visitors are empowered by state law to monitor the quality of care in such centers; many members are relatives of clients or have demonstrated concern for high-quality care.) The commission also provides advocacy services for individuals with disabilities, including legal services. It had a staff of 105 in 2006.

Chapter Thirteen

EDUCATION

Key points:

- While federal spending on public schools has risen sharply since 2000, states retain the most powerful role in deciding policy and funding for education.

- New York's Board of Regents initiated a drive for higher standards and increased accountability in the mid-1990s, and today the Education Department uses extensive statistical reporting to support that effort.

- The State University and City University are also focusing on raising academic standards and attracting higher-performing students.

More and more, in recent years, education has become a focus of bipartisan attention from the federal government. Both major political parties in Washington have pushed for, and delivered, big increases in spending on schools. The 2001 budget for the U.S. Department of

Education, $42 billion, represented not only a record in total spending at the time, but a record increase as well. Another major spending increase — and, more importantly, a new federal role in monitoring students' and schools' achievement — came the following year. Federal taxes now provide dollars to school districts for roof repairs, teacher salaries, and other needs that traditionally were funded through local and state tax dollars. Washington has become more involved, too, in setting the standards that schools and students must meet.

Day-to-day operating decisions for public schools are, of course, made at the local level. School boards and administrators hire teachers and staff, create and curtail programs, schedule bus routes, and otherwise do the hands-on work of creating a learning environment for children.

Yet, far more than Washington, and more than local school leaders, the level of government that shapes the broad outlines of children's education in New York is the state.

Overview of Education Policymaking

The Board of Regents is responsible for overall supervision of all educational institutions, public and private, in New York. The Regents and the commissioner of education determine the broad outlines of the curricula that all 2.9 million public-school students in New York follow, as well as the requirements every student must meet before winning a high-school diploma. The Legislature and the governor write the laws, and the Education Department the regulations, that specify how school leaders must hire and work with the teachers and other staff who perform the front-line work with students.

Among them, the elected officials, Regents, and Education Department staff make the rules that direct school districts' activities from the design of school buildings, to the content of cafeteria lunches, to the requirements for school-bus safety. School report cards, required by the Regents since 1996, create accountability for school districts by showing publicly how well students in each school perform on standardized tests. Not least important, state government provides some 36 percent of the money spent on public schools in New York — $14.7 billion in 2004, according to the state comptroller's office. In countless ways, the actions of both school district leaders and individual teachers are driven by the system designed, ruled, and funded from the Capitol and the stately Education Building directly across Washington Avenue in Albany.

Reorganization of state government's executive branch in the first half of the 20th century placed almost all administrative agencies under the control of the governor. Notable exceptions are the two departments headed by other statewide elected officials: Audit and Control, under the direction of the comptroller; and Law, overseen by the attorney general. The Education Department is the only other executive agency that does not report to the state's top elected official. The 16 Regents, who are collectively the head of the department, are elected by the Legislature. They, in turn, appoint the commissioner of education, and for more than a century have generally given him (no woman has served as commissioner) wide latitude to shape education policy. Given the broad authority of the office, the education commissioner influences the day-to-day lives of more New Yorkers than any other nonelected official.

The Regents: Broad Powers

The Board of Regents provides the Education Department a significant measure of insulation from political influence by the governor and legislators. That is in some contrast, for example, to the State University of New York, where the governor appoints the Board of Trustees and has often played an influential role in the broad shape of university policies. Governors have occasionally complained about the independence (or lack of responsiveness, depending on one's perspective) of the Education Department, and there have been periodic calls for eliminating the Board of Regents. Over two centuries, though, the board has remained in place. The Legislature has restricted its independence somewhat by shortening the term for which Regents are appointed to the current five years. Individual Regents who would like to serve more than one term are aware that members of the Legislature may consider the positions they have taken on the board in deciding whether to reappoint them. Members of the board who seek to continue from one term to another are generally, though not always, allowed to do so.

Although the Legislature has ceded most authority over academic matters to the Regents and education commissioners, it retains direct control over allocation of the state's dollars to individual school districts. Technically, school aid is allocated by a complex formula that reflects local wealth, the numbers of particularly needy students, and other factors. In practice, the formula is not a permanent fixture. The Senate and Assembly rewrite aid provisions of the Education Law every year, and the amounts delivered to districts reflect the political influence of different legislators as well as differing regional interests.

The powers of the Regents and the Education Department extend far beyond those of most state boards of education. The education commissioner also has quasi-judicial authority to review appeals of actions by local school boards or other officials. Such cases often involve education plans for students with special needs, and disciplinary cases against teachers and other employees. Besides their impact on primary and secondary schools, the Regents and the Education Department are responsible for:

- Overseeing postsecondary education, from New York's world-class universities to small proprietary schools.

- Certifying teachers, and certifying or licensing practitioners of 38 professions, from accounting to veterinary medicine.

- Operating the State Museum in Albany, the School for the Blind at Batavia, the School for the Deaf at Rome, and other educational and cultural institutions.

- Acting as the institutional guardians of New York's history by chartering cultural organizations, including libraries and historical societies.

- Providing vocational rehabilitation, job-placement assistance, and education for individuals with disabilities.

This chapter examines each of those areas, giving particular attention to K-12 education in public schools. The relationship between local school leaders and state officials has been important throughout the history of public education in the Empire State. The chapter explores the varying role state government has played — a role that has grown continually over two centuries.

The Constitution and the Board of Regents

Established by the Legislature in 1784, the Board of Regents is the oldest continuous state education entity in America. The Legislature's action creating the Regents occurred during its first session after the Revolution, in response to a message from Governor Clinton:

> Neglect of the education of youth is among the evils consequent on war. Perhaps there is scarce anything more worthy of your attention than the revival and encouragement of Seminaries of Learning, and nothing by which we can more satisfactorily express our gratitude to the Supreme Being for His past favors, since Piety and Virtue are generally the offspring of an enlightened understanding.[1]

Under the state Constitution, the board is formally known as The University of the State of New York. This "university" is considered to be the entire system of all education and other institutions under the jurisdiction of the Regents — elementary, secondary, and postsecondary schools; libraries and museums; public broadcasting; state records and archives; regulation of professions; vocational education services for individuals with disabilities; and other responsibilities the Legislature may assign to the Board of Regents. The similarly named and more familiar State University of New York, with its four university centers and 60 other campuses, is one part of the broader university (*more on SUNY and other institutions of higher education appears later in this chapter*).

The Board of Regents includes 16 members elected by the Legislature for five-year terms: one from each of the state's 12 judicial districts and four members who serve at large. Members are elected by the Legislature as a whole. For the past quarter-century or so, Democrats who control the state Assembly have held more than 90 seats (in recent years, more than 100). Because these represent a large proportion of the combined 212 seats in both houses, the Assembly majority has been able to choose Regents with no input from the Republican conferences in the two houses, and some limited input from Senate Democrats. Despite that, policy directions of the board do not appear to reflect the sole influence of the Assembly. Indeed, some of its major actions — such as publishing report cards for every public school in the state — would have been unlikely to pass the Assembly if proposed in the form of legislation.

Regents and education commissioners generally treat governors with a great deal of deference. Despite the governor's lack of influence

---

1   Cited in Harlan H. Horner, *University of the State of New York Bulletin: The State and Higher Education*, Albany, NY, April 15, 1939.

in appointing the education policymakers, his budgetary and other powers make the governor a key player in many issues the Regents address. Still, the Regents often take positions contrary to the governor's, on issues from school finance to structure of the state's education and cultural agencies.

Regents are unsalaried, which may also contribute to the independence of the agency — members of the board need only worry about losing prestige, not a livelihood, if they incur the Legislature's displeasure and are not re-elected. They are reimbursed for travel and related expenses.

The Regents elect one of their group as chancellor, whose duties include sharing the commissioner's duties as chief spokesman for the department, chairing monthly meetings and appointing members of committees. The committees do much of the policy-related work of the board.

The state Constitution's treatment of education is relatively brief, considering state government's huge role in the area. In addition to providing for authority of the Regents, Article XI includes only two other provisions that:

- Require the Legislature to "provide for the maintenance and support of a system of free common schools, wherein all the children of this state may be educated." The Court of Appeals has interpreted this to mean that the Legislature must provide the opportunity for every child in public schools to obtain a "sound basic education."[2]

- Prohibit the state or its subdivisions from using public money, property, or credit "directly or indirectly" to aid any school that is "wholly or in part under the control or direction of any religious denomination, or in which any denominational tenet or doctrine is taught." Exceptions are made for transportation of students, examination, and inspection. The Legislature has enacted laws, subsequently permitted by the courts, providing publicly funded textbooks to children attending private schools, on the ground that such aid goes to the student, not the institution.

---

2   New York State Constitution, Article XI, Section 1; *Campaign for Fiscal Equity, Inc., et al.* v. *State of New York*, 86 N.Y. 2d 307.

While retaining authority over the State University and other institutions of higher learning, the Regents and the Education Department devote most of their attention to K-12 public schools. Still, the board and Commissioner Richard Mills have set a goal of combining all of the assets of the "University of the State of New York" to enhance education of adults as well as children. The department's 2000 Strategic Plan included six "Regents Goals," with three related exclusively to K-12 instruction. In the 2005 Strategic Plan, only one of six goals was directed exclusively at K-12. The others focused on performance in "all educational institutions," including museums and libraries; "qualified, ethical professionals" in the professions, as well as education; and other measurements of success.

Early Public Education in New York

At the start of the 21st century, common wisdom and standard political rhetoric hold that education is more important than ever. Yet questions surrounding how the schools should be administered and funded, and what they should teach, have been among the most salient issues for New York State government since its earliest days.

Even in the late 18th century, when New York State government didn't do much of anything, it played a role in education. Just a few years after the Legislature created the Regents, starting in the 1790s, state law provided for elected town commissioners or superintendents of schools to license teachers, distribute state aid to schools, and compile statistical reports.[3]

New York's education system has roots in colonial school systems under both the Dutch and the English. The Dutch focused on providing general education to a large proportion of residents and established tax-supported schools under church and state control. The English established a system of private and church-supported academies that emphasized advanced education for the socioeconomic elite.

As originally constituted, the Board of Regents included the governor, other top state officials, the mayors of New York and Albany, and 24 other members. A 1787 statute introduced election of most of the board by the Legislature, although the governor and lieutenant

---

3   This discussion of the history of education policy relies in part on information from the Education Department's website. *www.nysed.gov.*

governor remained members. Later laws placed administrative control of public schools under a superintendent, appointed by the Council of Appointment, starting in 1812, and under the secretary of state effective in 1821.

The 1812 law established three key principles that remain today. First, while still financed primarily through local taxes and operated largely autonomously, public schools were a state function. Funding of public education was a joint responsibility of the state and local governments. Finally, the local governmental unit was the school district, rather than (as is true in some other states) the county or the town.[4]

The Legislature created a new Department of Public Instruction, under a superintendent elected by the Legislature, in 1854. The department provided increasing supervision of public elementary schools while the Board of Regents maintained general authority over higher education and private academies.

The state further codified its commitment to public education as part of the broad rewriting of the Constitution in 1894. The new document created most of today's Education article. Under Governor Theodore Roosevelt in 1901, a commission recommended abolishing the Department of Public Instruction and merging it with the administrative offices of the Regents to create the Education Department. More than a century after state government began to support and oversee educational institutions, the unifying legislation was enacted in 1904.

Concerns beyond those of a purely academic nature soon became part of the department's responsibilities. The commissioner has overseen school construction since 1904. The resulting influence can be seen, for instance, in the all-on-one-floor look many schools now display as a result of building standards the department set in the 1950s.

The advent of motor vehicles and paved roads early in the 20th century made public transportation of students to and from school possible — and, before too long, a state requirement. A 1925 statute required transport of children in most public school districts. Since 1942, the Education Department has approved bids for transportation contracts, reviewed bus routes, and established standards for drivers and vehicles.

---

4   James D. Folts, "History of the University of the State of New York and the State Education Department 1784-1996," 1996; available at *www.nysl.nysed.gov/edocs/ education.sedhist.htm*.

Toward Universal Schooling

The concept of free and universal public education arose in the 1820s. The nascent labor movement, based largely in the cities, campaigned for public schools both to improve prospects for the next generation and to reduce youthful competition for adult workers. At the same time, some rural leaders feared the decline of farming, and sought to avert it through more widespread education. The Legislature enacted a law providing for free schools for all children in 1867, along with a state-wide property tax to pay for it. Little more than a quarter-century later, the new 1894 Constitution wrote the current guarantee into the state's fundamental law.

The number of days that constituted a school year grew over time. An 1874 law required most children to attend at least 70 days a year, although many did not do so. Growing public concern about child labor translated into stronger attendance laws. In 1894, children aged 8-12 were to be in school at least 130 days (80 days for slightly older students who were employed). The school year was extended to the current 180 days in 1913. The age for mandatory attendance rose in 1916 to 15, in 1936 to 16, and in 1994 to the end of the school year in which a student turns 16. During the 2000 session, the Legislature approved a bill raising the age to 17; Governor Pataki vetoed it as an unjustified mandate on school districts.

Time in school at the other end of the age spectrum has also expanded. A 1933 foundation study suggested integrating nursery school, kindergarten, and primary school into a comprehensive program. State aid for kindergartens began in 1942, prompted in part by the need for mothers to go to work during wartime. In 1966, Governor Rockefeller and the Legislature enacted new aid for low-income children to attend preschool. At the initiative of the Assembly Democratic majority, funding for preschool increased substantially at the end of the 1990s.

While student enrollment grew almost continually for more than a century until the 1970s, the number of school districts decreased sharply during the period. The Education Department counted 9,118 districts statewide in 1930. Most were limited to K-8, including many one-room schools.

The Statewide Education System Today

During the mid-20th century, education leaders in New York and nationwide pushed for consolidation of districts to standardize and improve classroom practices; concern for efficiency and costs also influenced the move. By 1960, the number of districts in the state had dropped to 1,292; as of 2004 they numbered 699. There are also 38 Board of Cooperative Educational Services (BOCES) districts through which districts share educational and administrative services. State aid formulas today retain significant incentives for consolidation, and the number of districts continues to drop by one or two in a typical year.

By far the largest school district in the state, and among the biggest in the nation, is New York City's. In 2004, the city's schools enrolled just over 1 million students and employed some 140,000, including educational and other staff. The number of teachers in the city schools, around 75,000, was nearly double the student enrollment in the state's second-largest district, Buffalo. Seventeen districts around the state had fewer than 100 pupils as of 2004.[5] Raquette Lake, a one-building district with six students in 2004, closed its doors the following year and sent children to the nearby Indian Lake system.

Regional BOCES provide a variety of shared services for districts, including educational programs such as vocational/technical instruction; physical and occupational therapy for students with disabilities; and administrative functions such as staff development and bus maintenance. Individual districts decide whether to purchase specific services from the regional organization. As taxpayers in many areas of the state urge school districts to consolidate services, BOCES may play a growing role in coming years. BOCES superintendents serve as regional representatives of the state education commissioner; Commissioner Mills, for instance, has tasked them with driving implementation of state standards and improvement in student achievement.

Statewide student enrollment was steady, around 2.8 million, from 1998 to 2003. Public-school staffing levels were at a record highs in recent years. The Education Department counted 266,900 total professional employees — including 224,005 teachers and 42,895

---

5   A handful of these districts are essentially legal entities with no school buildings of their own; they send students to other districts on a tuition basis.

Fall Enrollment in Grades K-12, New York State			
Year	Public	Nonpublic	Total
1964	3,121,717	873,000 (est.)	3,994,717
1969	3,442,809	840,415	4,283,224
1974	3,424,873	643,812	4,068,685
1979	2,958,725	580,185	3,538,910
1984	2,631,059	547,857	3,178,916
1989	2,537,669	483,975	3,021,644
1994	2,733,913	473,212	3,207,125
1999	2,850,824	491,276	3,342,100
2003	2,826,116	476,782	3,302,898

Source: New York State Education Department

administrators, counselors, nurses and other nonsupport staff — in 2003-04; that total was up by more than 20,000 from five years earlier.[6]

All children aged 6 through 16 are required by state law to attend school or receive an equivalent education at home.[7] The public-school day is defined as five hours at the elementary level, and 5.5 hours in high school.

Academics: Curriculum, Teaching, and Assessment

Oversight of curriculum, instruction, and student assessment has been the Regents' most important role for nearly two centuries, and a wide-ranging effort to raise the quality of education is the most notable aspect of recent state education policy.

---

6   New York State Education Department, *New York, the State of Learning: Statewide Profile of the Educational System*, Albany, NY, July 2005, p. 49.

7   Seventeen states do not require children to start school until age 7, while eight begin at age 5 and two, Pennsylvania and Washington, at 8 years of age. Source: National Center for Education Statistics.

As early as 1817, the Regents specified texts or subjects that academies must teach to qualify for state aid. Such assistance was restricted to students who had passed local entrance exams in the "common branch" subjects of reading, writing, grammar, arithmetic and geography. "Unfortunately," as a department history states, "many academies lowered their standards in order to attract students and get state aid."[8]

The first Regents exams were held in 1865, and 12 years later a new law authorized the Regents to give academic exams as a standard for high-school graduation and college admission. From the start, the exams were respected as representing high standards. Studies in the 1920s and 1930s indicated that high scores on the tests were good predictors of success in college. In recent years they have often been labeled the "gold standard" among standardized secondary-school assessments in the United States.

Along with exams, the Regents published recommended curricula and teacher guides starting in the 1880s. Curricular requirements and recommendations varied over the decades. Social studies tended to stress citizenship education in the 1940s and '50s, international affairs in the 1960s and '70s, and multiple cultural perspectives in the 1980s and '90s. The teaching of science in elementary school was mandated in 1958 as part of a national reaction to the Soviet Union's success in space flight.

A quarter-century later, Americans had new cause for alarm over the quality of many children's education. Leaders in New York and nationally called for another major effort to improve learning, particularly after a 1983 report said America was "a nation at risk" because of inadequate schools.[9] A series of initiatives by several education commissioners led the Regents to undertake a broad and continuing effort to raise academic standards throughout the state's public schools. In 1984, the Regents required high-school graduates to prove basic competence in English, math, science, global studies, and U.S. history and government; students had the choice of passing local exams or generally more challenging Regents exams. In a step toward accountability, school districts were required to prepare an annual Comprehensive Assessment Report with data including student performance on state tests. In 1991, Commissioner Thomas Sobol and the Regents established the New

8   Folts, ibid.

9   National Commission on Excellence in Education, *A Nation at Risk: The Imperative for Educational Reform*, April 1983.

Compact for Learning, a broad statement of educational philosophy. The compact aimed at raising standards further, challenging all students to achieve "mastery," giving schools more authority over the ways they would meet the state's goals, and including parents — along with teachers and administrators — among those responsible for school and pupil performance.

Commissioner Richard P. Mills, appointed in 1995, took the drive for higher standards and greater accountability significantly further. In 1996, the Regents adopted new standards defining what students should know at all grade levels, including more rigorous requirements for high-school graduation. All students who entered ninth grade in September 2001 or later were required to pass Regents exams — without the option of substituting local tests — in English, math, global history, U.S. history, and science. A July 2005 report from the Regents to the governor and the Legislature commented:

> The effect of higher standards is already apparent in improved performance on many State assessments. In 2003-04, more students scored 65 or higher on Regents examinations in all five areas required for graduation than took these examinations in 1996-97. These areas are English, mathematics, global studies (or global history and geography), U.S. history and government, and biology (or living environment).... These signs of progress are encouraging, but too many students and schools have not yet shared in these successes.[10]

As the 21st century began, students in New York schools represented many of the nation's brightest and best-educated, winning national and international awards in science, writing, and other subjects and studying at the world's most prestigious universities. At the same time, as is true in every other state, tens of thousands of children were not learning as they should. The Regents reported that, in large city school districts, only 44 percent of elementary students met state standards for English language arts. Achievement in middle-level math was poorer, with 29 percent of students in large urban districts meeting the standards. A state Supreme Court judge who ruled on a case involving financing for New York City schools found: "The majority of the City's public school students leave high school unprepared for more than low-paying work, unprepared for college, and unprepared for the duties

---

10 *New York, the State of Learning*, p. v.

Regents Learning Standards

Throughout much of the 1990s, the Board of Regents and Education Department leaders and staff worked on developing specific new standards for learning in seven major curriculum areas. The standards described broad expectations regarding what students should know, understand, and be able to do as they progress through grades K-12.

As of 2005, the Regents' Learning Standards for English, for instance, set four goals. Each standard said that "students will read, write, listen and speak" for a different purpose — for information and understanding, for literary response and expression, for critical analysis and evaluation, and for social interaction. Working with teachers and administrators from throughout the state, the department prepared an in-depth English Language Arts Core Curriculum to guide educators in every school district.

Given concerns about local control, the core curriculum document carefully stated that it "respects the tradition of local choice in New York State" regarding texts and instructional strategies. There is no statewide list of reading assignments for fourth-graders, for instance, although the curriculum suggests things such as encouraging students to read at least 25 books each year and write at least 1,000 words each month.

In pre-K to first grade, students are expected to learn the difference between vowels and consonants, recognize the singular and plural of frequently used words and capitalize the first letters of sentences. By grade 6, children should be able to write interpretive essays, identify the use of symbolism and other literary devices, and develop characters in original texts. High-school seniors should "read, view, and respond independently to literary works that represent a range of social, historical, and cultural perspectives," and synthesize information from different sources in complex ways.

placed upon them by a democratic society."[11] Some critics questioned the court ruling that problems were caused largely by inadequate financing, but there was no public disagreement with the judge's finding concerning the quality of education in some schools. The worst-performing

11 *Campaign for Fiscal Equity* v. *State of New York.*

Selected New York State Curriculum Mandates		
Subject	*Section of Education Law*	*Date Enacted*
Patriotism and citizenship	801	1947
Irish potato famine	801	1996
Use of the flag/Pledge of Allegiance	802	1947
Abuse of alcohol, tobacco and other drugs	804	1977
Highway and bicycle safety/traffic regulation	806	1947
Humane treatment of animals and birds	809	1947

public schools tended to have almost exclusively nonwhite student populations.

The comments in the Regents' 2000 report to the governor and the Legislature reflected another major effort — one that, unlike the push for higher standards, had little precedent in New York or elsewhere. Schools are now required to measure their students' overall performance against similar schools elsewhere in the state, and report that comparison to the public through "school report cards" introduced in 1998.

School report cards are intended to be easily understandable to average citizens, and generally they are. For example, the district-wide reports in 2004-05 showed three years of data for both grade 4 and middle-school English language arts, mathematics, and science. Reports on individual schools provide more detailed information. Data are presented graphically to help parents and other taxpayers understand the results clearly.

The idea behind the report cards was to provoke public discussion of each school's performance, or "constructive conversations which lead to improved education for all children in the State," to cite a description Commissioner Mills used frequently. That goal, too, has been met, at least in many communities across the state.

Beyond the broad academic requirements for school districts created by the Regents, legislators and governors have enacted dozens of detailed curriculum requirements, including those shown in the nearby table.

Along with the state's report cards, school districts are subject to greater scrutiny from the federal government, as a result of President Bush's No Child Left Behind Act. The law requires extensive testing of students in elementary grades and provides public reporting on academic results as well as data related to student safety.

Use of data to measure performance throughout the education system is a major change from a decade and more ago, when schools — like institutions elsewhere in society — engaged in relatively few such comparisons. For a November 2005 "Education Summit," Education Department staff compiled an in-depth report on widely varying indicators that relate to education potential and performance. The analysis showed, for instance, that 22 percent of 2-year-olds in New York are not fully immunized, and that 73 percent of young children whose mothers had college degrees experienced reading daily, compared to 42 percent of those whose mothers did not have a high-school diploma. The summit produced agreement among teachers, administrators, state officials, unions, and business leaders to work together to raise achievement among low-performing students across the state. In September 2006, the department announced a major new data collection and reporting system that gives schools, teachers, and parents access to more detailed information on student achievement.

Operational Mandates

State government also imposes a wide variety of operational mandates — some that reflect plain common sense, and others that limit the ability of local school boards, administrators, and teachers to run schools and allocate limited dollars as they otherwise might.

The state requires, for instance, that school districts transport all students who live within certain mileage limits in the district, including those who attend private schools. The state Department of Transportation has authority to regulate safety on school buses, within (extensive) laws enacted by the Legislature. State laws provide that school buses must stop at all railroad crossings, regardless of whether students are on board; and cannot turn right on red if students are present.

Federal law requires a "free appropriate public education" for children with disabilities; New York law and regulations implement the federal requirement and sometimes go further. In some cases, the state requires local districts to pay for disabled students who attend private schools, if necessary for educational reasons.

In one important area, kindergarten education, New York allows an unusual level of local choice. Some 40 states require districts to offer half-day or full-day kindergarten; Albany requires neither.[12]

Every state mandate starts with a persuasive rationale, but school boards and superintendents argue that some have outlived their usefulness or fail to provide a reasonable balance in terms of efficiency. School boards commonly complain, for instance, about tenure provisions of the Education Law that make it difficult to remove teachers who are ineffective, or are potential dangers to students, without administrative proceedings that can take years. In some cases, teachers who were charged with sexual abuse of students have continued to receive salary and benefits even after conviction, until sentencing. Many administrators seldom attempt to dismiss teachers whose only offense is poor work, because of the difficulty of the effort. A survey by the New York State School Boards Association in the late 1990s found that the average disciplinary case against a tenured school employee took 319 days to complete and cost the district $94,527 in legal and other expenses.

School-board representatives also complain about a particular provision of the state's Taylor Law, which governs labor relations in the public sector. The provision, known as the Triborough Amendment, requires terms and conditions of union contracts to stay in effect after a contract has expired unless changed by a new contract. School administrators say the amendment, not found in other states, tilts the balance of bargaining power to unions. Union representatives respond that the Triborough Amendment is an integral part of the protections the Taylor Law gives public employees in exchange for taking away their right to strike.

School districts are also subject to construction-related rules that apply to all levels of state and local government in New York; by their nature as places where large numbers of people congregate, schools are particularly affected by such mandates. The Wicks Law requires use of

---

12 Source: National Center for Education Statistics.

at least four separate contractors on most public construction projects, making the process more complicated and — according to local officials and the state Budget Division — more expensive. State laws and regulatory practices requiring payment of "prevailing" wages — generally, union wages — on all public construction have the same effects.

Charter Schools

As mentioned above, development of school report cards was one step in the late 1990s to make schools more accountable by keeping parents and the community better informed about students' academic achievement. The push for greater accountability was part of a nationwide movement, as Americans engaged in a broad school-improvement effort.

That was the context in 1998 when Governor Pataki initiated, and the Legislature reluctantly approved, legislation to allow creation of charter schools in New York. The governor said in recommending the proposal, "Charter schools operate outside of the traditional public school structure, which frees them from the bureaucratic mandates that too often stifle the innovative spirit."[13] Supporters also argued that the new schools would provide public-school choice for families who could not afford to attend private schools or to move to better school districts. The competition, supporters said, would improve schools by encouraging administrators and teachers throughout the educational system to be more creative in improving student achievement.

Governor Pataki's initiative in creating charter schools also continued longstanding gubernatorial efforts to establish some influence over education policy. Governor Rockefeller, for instance, took several steps along these lines, including creating an Office of Education Performance Review to examine the cost-effectiveness of public schools.

The state's first five charter schools opened in 1999. As of the 2004-05 school year, 61 were open for instruction, including 32 chartered by the State University Board of Trustees, 16 by the Regents, 11 by the New York City schools chancellor and two by the Buffalo school board. Roughly one in three schools partnered with outside management companies such as Edison Schools Inc. and Victory Schools Inc.

---

13 State of the State address, January 7, 1998.

More than 1,100 students attended the largest institution, the Charter School of Science and Technology in Rochester.

Reflecting the goal of creating new choices for students and their families, the schools adopted a variety of approaches to education. In Buffalo, the Eugenio Maria de Hostos school used "dual-immersion" teaching in English and Spanish to help students learn both languages. The International Charter School of Schenectady offered an internationally oriented, college-preparatory curriculum for students focusing primarily on the core subjects of English, mathematics, sciences and languages. The Harlem Day Charter School achieved good results on math and English exams with a back-to-basics academic program using Core Knowledge curricula.

Under the New York statute, charter schools can be organized by applicants such as community groups, teachers, parents, administrators, and private businesses. Organizers must obtain a charter, or legal authority to operate, from the State University Board of Trustees, the Board of Regents, or the local school board (in New York City, the city-wide schools chancellor). The maximum term of a charter is five years, renewable in five-year increments, creating an ongoing source of pressure for the school to demonstrate good academic results.

Perhaps the most important difference between charter schools and others, including other alternative forms of public schools that exist in many of the state's cities, is that the former were the first to create competition for the state-aid dollars that all school districts depend upon. The state sends the new schools the per-pupil assistance that would otherwise go to the home district of each student enrolled. The figure does not include state aid for capital spending, transportation, school lunches, or any of the local district's own tax revenue. All those revenues remain with the district; the Charter Schools Institute of SUNY estimates that school districts retain 20 to 35 percent of per-student funding for each child who leaves a "regular" public school for a charter school. Still, in several cities where some of the first charter schools opened, the loss of revenue was enough to spark criticism from district officials as a drain on an already hard-pressed system. In response, supporters of the charter schools questioned why the existing schools could not reduce expenses as the number of students enrolled declined.

As of 2005, some 18,400 students were enrolled in charter schools — the equivalent of one of the largest urban or suburban school districts. Most students were from minority families and relatively poor, as

evidenced by qualification for free lunches. As in traditional urban public schools, many students performed well while others failed to meet
state standards. Unlike traditional schools, however, some charter
schools close when their students do not do well. Five schools failed to
win charter renewals from the SUNY board, based on student achievement. Perhaps reflecting widespread loss of faith in many urban school
districts, parents continued to show strong support for charter schools,
with new institutions opening and attracting full classes each year. As
of 2006, some 10,000 students were on waiting lists for charter schools
around the state, according to the New York Charter Schools
Association.

Under the 1998 law, the Board of Regents and SUNY board may approve 100 new charter schools. An unlimited number of existing public
schools can decide to become charter schools with the approval of a majority of both parents and teachers. In 2006, with the first 100 approvals
nearly all used, Governor Pataki proposed raising the limit on such
schools. The Legislature did not act on the proposal during the regular
legislative session.

School Finance

Assistance to local schools, financed by statewide taxes and fees collected in Albany, has been part of New York's public education system
since early in the history of state government. In 1795, the Legislature
appropriated $100,000 a year for each of the next five years to encour-
age creation of locally controlled common schools. A decade later, the
comptroller was authorized to sell certain state lands and use the proceeds as part of a permanent fund to support public schools.

State aid represented 36 percent of total revenues to districts statewide as of 2004, according to the Office of the State Comptroller. Local
property taxes were the largest source of revenue for public schools, at
$21.3 billion or 52 percent. Federal aid accounted for 8 percent of the
statewide total. That proportion was higher in most urban districts, because federal programs emphasize help for disadvantaged children, and
lower in the average suburban district. The comptroller's data showed
statewide spending on K-12 public schools that year totaled $43.2 bil-
lion, or just over $15,300 per student — a figure that was among the
highest in the nation.

For all the power that the Board of Regents and Education Department hold over education in New York, they have no authority over the annual decisions that often attract more attention than anything the Regents do: the size and structure of state aid to local school districts. The state aid budget, $16.3 billion in the 2005-06 fiscal year, is part of the overall state budget enacted by the governor and the Legislature. More than any other part of the budget, it is the product of the Senate and Assembly rather than the chief executive. Legislators have a strong sense that one of the primary jobs voters assign to them is bringing home a fair share of state spending. For most lawmakers, particularly those outside New York City, school aid is the primary focus of attention in this area.

In New York as elsewhere, aid to education is one of the most politically popular spending programs. Governors and legislators typically provide generous increases in school aid when the state can afford to do so, and do everything possible to avoid cuts in lean years when other programs face reductions. (A rare exception came in 1990, when the state's economic slowdown and revenue shortfall forced Governor Cuomo and the Legislature to reduce school aid by $190 million in the middle of the school year. Still, given the budget increase enacted earlier that year, schools received more aid in 1990 than they had in 1989.) Voters do not look on school spending with an uncritical eye, however. In 1997, they rejected a proposed state borrowing of $2.4 billion, intended largely for school construction and repairs, after state leaders and interest groups failed to mount a strong campaign in support.

The Board of Regents and the education commissioner make annual recommendations on the amount of new aid needed and how to structure assistance to school districts. Elected officials take note of these recommendations because they carry the imprimatur of the state's chief education policymakers. In the end, though, the Legislature makes its own decisions — subject to negotiations with or veto by the governor — based on the varying wishes and political needs of its members.

As with all elements of the budget, legislative action on the state aid formula is determined by the majority conferences in both houses — in recent history, Republicans in the Senate and Democrats in the Assembly. Leaders generally allot more senior members, and politically "marginal" members who need to be able to show voters that they've delivered for the district, a better share than other members. Members of the Senate from Long Island have generally demonstrated the strongest interest in bringing ever-growing amounts of state aid back to the home district. In New York City and the other largest city school districts — Buffalo, Syracuse, Rochester, and Yonkers — state education aid goes into the city budget. There, mayors and city councils determine how much to allocate to schools compared with police, street repairs, or other services. A majority-party legislator from outside the big cities typically plays an important role in determining exactly how much state aid the public schools in his or her legislative district will receive.

Discussion of aid to local schools generally centers around the statutory school-aid formula that, in theory, determines how much each district receives. As a practical matter, in recent years, allocations to most districts have been based not on the formula itself but on minimum and maximum figures for per-student aid. For decades, the need in the Legislature to satisfy members from wealthier as well as poorer districts has resulted in "save-harmless" funding, in which no district receives less aid one year than in the previous year, even when enrollment declines. In the 2000-01 fiscal year, only 54 districts received aid based strictly on their attendance, property wealth, average incomes, and other elements of the official formula, according to one estimate. Some 330 districts that would have received relatively little based on the formula received the 2 percent increase that Governor Pataki and the Legislature agreed would be the minimum for any district. Another 302 districts received an amount determined by maximum limits based on a flat 4.27 percent or other calculations.[14]

Still, the fundamental purpose of state funding — giving every district at least a minimally acceptable amount to spend on education — appears to have been met. The district with the *lowest* per-pupil spending in 2004, Marcellus in Onondaga County, spent $9,926 per student in 2004.[15] That figure was more than the *average* in most other states. State funding has also made progress toward another goal, that of bringing expenditures in poorer districts closer to those in wealthier areas. In 1999-2000, the "highest-need" districts averaged more than $6,000 per student in state aid, nearly four times the average of "low-need" districts, according to Education Department data.

Allocations for each district are further complicated by use of "categorical" aid streams directed at particular types of spending such as textbooks, prekindergarten programs and those for students with

---

14 *2000-01 Final Enacted Budget Analysis*, Albany, NY: New York State Council of School Superintendents, May 2000.

15 Based on data reported by the Office of the State Comptroller.

limited English skills. Senators and Assembly members from the large urban districts where school budgets are subject to the control of mayors and city councils support categorical funding to ensure that the Legislature's intent for those dollars will be followed.

School funding for given districts or regions is also subject to legislators' priorities for bringing state funding back home. A *New York Times* commentary observed that one reason New York City schools do not receive more aid is that state legislators from the city tend to focus their political influence on obtaining funding for hospitals and social services, while suburban and upstate legislators concentrate on school aid.[16]

Court Rulings on Education Finance

Because local revenues are a major share of total spending for each district, and because property wealth varies widely from one community to another, the total amount of spending also varies from one district to another. Twenty districts reported spending more than $40,000 per pupil in 2004, according to data they submitted to the state comptroller's office. A dozen or so reported spending less than $11,000 per student.

Efforts to narrow that disparity go back decades. In 1978, a group of Long Island school districts with relatively low property wealth — joined by New York City and other large city school districts — sued the state education commissioner in an attempt to force a new financing system for public education. In a 1982 ruling in the case, the Court of Appeals found that substantial inequities in funding did exist from district to district, but ruled that the state Constitution does not require equal funding for education. The court found that the Constitution entitles students to a "sound basic education," although it did not specify what that means.[17]

In 1993, another group of New York City community school boards and other plaintiffs filed a new lawsuit, on different grounds. The coalition filing the suit, the Campaign for Fiscal Equity, claimed that the state was failing in its simple obligation to provide the "sound basic education" that the Court of Appeals had previously ruled was required by

---

16 Steven R. Weisman, "Machiavelli and New York's School-Aid Politics," *The New York Times*, January 18, 2001, p. A-22.

17 *Board of Education, Levittown Union Free School District* v. *Nyquist*, 57 NY 2d 27.

the Constitution. In June 1995, the high court concluded that the group had grounds for a legal claim. In a decision written by Judge Carmen B. Ciparick, a four-member majority found:

> Children are entitled to minimally adequate physical facilities and classrooms which provide enough light, space, heat and air to permit children to learn. Children should have access to minimally adequate instrumentalities of learning such as desks, chairs, pencils and reasonably current textbooks. Children are also entitled to minimally adequate teaching of reasonably up-to-date curricula such as reading, writing, mathematics, science and social studies by sufficient personnel adequately trained to teach those subject areas.[18]

The case was remanded to state Supreme Court for findings of fact as to whether the state's existing funding structure for education meets the constitutional requirement. In January 2001, Supreme Court Justice LeLand DeGrasse said the education provided New York City students "is so deficient that it falls below the constitutional floor" created by the Education Article and that "the State's actions are a substantial cause of this constitutional violation." (The judge also agreed with the plaintiffs' claim that the school finance system violated the federal Civil Rights Act of 1964, prohibiting discriminatory treatment of racial minorities.) The state appealed the decision.

In June 2003, the Court of Appeals ruled mostly for the plaintiffs. In a decision written by Chief Judge Judith Kaye, the high court required state officials to:

- Determine the cost of providing a sound basic education for New York City school children;

- Ensure that every school in the city "would have the resources necessary for providing the opportunity for a sound basic education," and

- "[E]nsure a system of accountability to measure whether the reforms actually provide the opportunity for a sound basic education."

The ruling did not require the state itself to pay all additional costs, but said state leaders could require New York City to increase its local

---

18 *Campaign for Fiscal Equity Inc. et al.* v. *State of New York*, 86 NY 2d 307.

education funding as part of the solution. It gave Governor Pataki and the Legislature until July 30, 2004, to "implement the necessary measures." In each of the following three years, state leaders increased aid to schools in the city, but did not implement a plan to comply fully with the 2003 ruling. In early 2005, Judge DeGrasse issued an order with more specific requirements, including operating funding of $5.6 billion annually and additional billions for capital funding. The Appellate Division of the state Supreme Court rejected an appeal of that decision. The Court of Appeals was expected to rule on Judge DeGrasse's latest order in 2007. Meanwhile, school officials in some other urban districts planned their own lawsuits, hoping to win similar enhancements in state aid.

The Campaign for Fiscal Equity decision highlighted the ongoing controversy over the role that increased funding might play in improving student achievement in the worst-performing schools. "Although student performance in general tends to be highly correlated with increased spending, scholars are generally reluctant to suggest that increased spending necessarily makes for better education," one review of the state's education policies concluded.[19] And several studies have identified high-performing schools that have the same demographics — students of low income and minority backgrounds — as many poorly performing schools. One analysis, for example, found 126 schools in New York that had reading or math performance in the top third of those statewide, and had relatively high numbers of poor or minority students.[20]

Private Schools and Home Schooling

In its first few decades, state government subsidized the most widely available versions of secondary education, known as academies or seminaries. Some 165 such institutions operated around the state as of the 1850s. Later in the 1800s, the Legislature and the Regents provided funding for and otherwise encouraged the creation of public high schools. Most of the private academies closed or merged with the new public schools, and funding for private schools was eliminated. An 1844 statute outlawed state aid to schools under the direction of any re-

---

19 Edward Schneier, "The Politics of Local Education," in *Governing New York State*, Jeffrey M. Stonecash, ed., Albany, NY: SUNY Press, 2001, p. 226.

20 Craig D. Jerald, *Dispelling The Myth Revisited*, Washington, DC: The Education Trust, 2001.

ligious denomination, and the convention 50 years later added that provision to the state Constitution.

This so-called Blaine amendment was a central focus of the 1967 Constitutional Convention.[21] By then, some 800,000 children in New York attended Catholic schools. A 1938 revision to the Constitution allowed publicly funded transportation for such students. Federal funding established in the mid-1960s also covered certain services in parochial schools. The 1967 convention proposed repealing the Blaine amendment, among other changes, but voters rejected the convention's proposals on Election Day.

Despite the general ban on aid to sectarian education, governors and legislators have established ways to support students in private and religious schools. In addition to requiring that school districts provide transportation, state laws require that each district purchase textbooks to be loaned to children who live in the district but attend nondistrict schools. Both the Court of Appeals and the U.S. Supreme Court have ruled that such aid is permissible, because it benefits the students rather than the institutions. Courts have also upheld the state's reimbursement of nonpublic schools' costs of administering state-required examinations.

Elected leaders in a few other states have created financial assistance programs for low-income students who attend nonpublic, including sectarian, schools. A 2002 report by Attorney General Spitzer's office commented favorably on proposals such as requiring that school districts provide computers, in addition to textbooks, for students attending nonpublic schools. In 2006, Governor Pataki proposed a tuition tax credit that could be used by families with children in either public or private schools. Representatives of Catholic and Jewish schools persuaded many legislators to support the idea, and Attorney General Spitzer spoke in favor of the concept. Strong opposition from New York State United Teachers, the statewide teachers union, convinced legislative leaders not to approve the tax credit.

In the last decade or two, a growing number of parents in New York and other states have adopted another alternative to public schools: educating their children at home. The Education Department adopted

---

21 James G. Blaine, for whom the provision was named, never lived in New York. A U.S. representative from Maine, he served as speaker of the House and as U.S. secretary of state, and was the unsuccessful Republican candidate for president in 1884. He proposed a similar amendment to the U.S. Constitution. For details, see Dullea, *Charter Revision in the Empire State*.

regulations for such education in 1988. These regulations require that home-schooled students receive at least the "substantial equivalent" of the time and types of instruction provided in public schools.

New York's regulations governing both parental and school responsibilities are "more rigorous than in other states," one analysis found.[22] Parents must report quarterly to the local school district regarding each child's course of study. Annual reports of student achievement, including scores on commercially published tests or certain alternative assessments, are also required. Parents or others providing home instruction are not required to have any specific credentials; local school districts are primarily responsible for determining whether students receive an education that meets state regulations.

School districts are not required, although they are allowed, to loan textbooks to students who are schooled at home. Contrary to practice in some states, home schoolers in New York are not allowed to attend classes in the public schools because state law does not provide for part-time attendance. Also off-limits is participation in school athletics, although students may be allowed to join in intramural or other school club activities. Districts are allowed to decide whether home-schooled students may participate in school bands, use facilities such as school libraries and gyms, and borrow instructional items such as science equipment.

Some 28,000 students were home-schooled as of 2001.

Higher Education

The state's activity in education began not at the elementary and secondary levels, which dominate funding and attention today, but with higher education. The immediate purpose for creating the Board of Regents in 1784 was to redevelop King's College (later renamed Columbia College), which had been founded by a charter from King George II in 1754 and was discontinued during the Revolutionary War.[23] Many modern education watchers complain that elected officials sometimes

---

22 "Home Schooling in New York State," Westchester Institute for Human Services Research Inc., Winter 2001-02.

23 A 1787 statute gave Columbia College, the forerunner of today's Columbia University, independent status under its own board of trustees.

attempt to micromanage educators' work. The same might be said of the original statute creating the Regents. The board's duties were to include discipline of faculty; provision was made that no fine could exceed "the value of one bushel of wheat for any one offense."

Today, public higher education in New York includes two giants among American universities. The State University of New York (SUNY) is the largest single university in the nation, while City University of New York (CUNY), operating throughout New York City's five boroughs, is the largest urban public university in the country. Altogether the state is home to 271 degree-granting colleges and universities — 83 public (the SUNY and CUNY institutions), 146 independent and 42 proprietary (profit-making) — as well as some 250 nondegree, proprietary schools. More than 1.1 million students attended the degree-granting universities and colleges in 2004. That represented an increase of more than 10 percent from a decade earlier, with the additional students largely attending full-time at SUNY and independent campuses.

Both of New York's public university systems came under scrutiny in the last quarter of the 20th century for what critics said was a diminished focus on high standards. At SUNY, results have included more financial freedom for campuses within the resources provided from Albany, and budgetary allocations more closely linked to programs' success in attracting students. CUNY began several efforts to raise academic standards, including eliminating remedial courses at its four-year institutions. Both university systems now include significantly expanded programs aimed at stimulating advanced technological research as part of the state's economic-development efforts.

State funding from taxpayers provides just less than a third of the SUNY budget and a slightly smaller proportion at CUNY. Tuition is the other major source of income. Total state appropriations for college and university operating expenses are low in New York, compared to most other states, partly because of the extensive network of private institutions. The state provides limited support for private colleges and universities through what is known as Bundy aid, allocated to institutions for each graduating student, totaling some $47 million in 2000-01. That aid is based on a fixed number of dollars for each degree a given institution awards.

New York State provides some $800 million a year in financial aid for college students through the Tuition Assistance Program, an important support for low-income students at both public and private institutions. The state also allocates significant funding for capital improvements at private colleges and universities. In 2005, Governor Pataki and the Legislature approved a $150 million matching-grant program that the Commission on Independent Colleges and Universities said would help stimulate $2 billion in new capital spending by the private institutions.

The Education Department's Office of Higher Education manages licensing and certification of teachers — the largest single cohort of graduates from New York's colleges and universities. The office also administers state-funded scholarship and grant programs and develops state government's standards for higher education. The latter responsibility primarily applies to smaller and proprietary institutions. Well-established universities and colleges in New York are typically accredited by the Middle States Association of Colleges and Universities; those with programs in specialized fields such as medicine or engineering will often be accredited by organizations in those fields as well. The Education Department reviews proposed academic programs and institutions' requests for authority to issue new degrees. At times, the Regents have moved to exert more authority over higher education. In the past few years, such efforts have generally been limited to raising standards for teacher education programs, an area closely linked to the Education Department's dominant role in K-12 education.

Proprietary schools in New York enroll some 75,000 students each year in fields ranging from barbering and bartending to ultrasound operation and welding. The department monitors such schools; its power to withhold or revoke certification can affect students' ability to qualify for federal aid.

Creating SUNY

The growth of common schools in the early 1800s increased demand for teachers, and in 1844 the Legislature created a tuition-free "normal school" at Albany. Most states established public universities in the wake of the federal government's granting of land for such purposes in the 1860s. Cornell University, a private institution, was designated as the "land-grant" college in New York. Cornell was required to admit one student from each Assembly district annually, the first instance in which the state assumed direct financial responsibility for higher education other than teacher training. The delay in creating a truly public university largely resulted from the strength of private higher education in the state, which itself had enjoyed support from state government since the 1700s. Some competition between the public and private sectors for state funding and other types of support remains today.

Governor Thomas A. Dewey envisioned a state university system partly to satisfy demand among World War II veterans for higher education. A commission he and the Legislature appointed initiated the 1948 legislation creating the State University of New York, including today's network of locally sponsored community colleges. Governor Nelson A. Rockefeller, though, brought the vision to a grand reality by building new campuses and pushing through the Legislature billions of dollars in funding for operational expenses as well as construction.

At its founding, the university consolidated 29 teachers' colleges and other state-operated institutions. Today, SUNY is the largest provider of higher education services in the state, teaching more than 40 percent of all college students. As of 2003, the system enrolled nearly 410,000 students, including some 20,000 from outside the state. Fully a third of all high-school graduates in New York enroll at a SUNY campus, including community colleges. Research and advanced graduate and professional studies are conducted primarily through the four university centers at Albany, Binghamton, Buffalo, and Stony Brook (Suffolk County). SUNY includes two major health science centers offering programs in medicine and related fields, at Buffalo and Stony Brook. Other freestanding health science centers operate as part of the SUNY system in Brooklyn and Syracuse.

Besides its institutions of general education, SUNY's colleges include the College of Environmental Science and Forestry; Maritime College, which prepares future officers in the American Merchant Marine; the College of Optometry, which graduates professional optometrists; the Institute of Technology at Utica/Rome; and the College of Technology at Farmingdale. The university system has a special relationship with Cornell University, one of the nation's leading private universities, where four state-funded colleges teach agriculture and industrial/labor relations, among other subjects. A fifth such "statutory" institution, the College of Ceramics, is located at Alfred University. University colleges of technology reside in Alfred, Canton, Cobleskill, Delhi, and Morrisville. The youngest state university in the country, SUNY may also be the most complex.

Almost half of the university's campuses consist of the 30 two-year community colleges — from Suffolk County to Niagara County — that are the entry point to higher education for more than half the university's student body. These colleges provide higher education to students who do not pursue a four-year degree, and play a key role in worker training throughout the state. The institutions' boards of trustees include members appointed by the governor and by local elected officials. The state, local counties, and student tuition each provide roughly one-third of operating funding, with capital costs split by state and local tax revenues.

The largest community college — Nassau, with nearly 21,000 students in 2003 — had a higher enrollment than all but two of SUNY's four-year institutions. Community colleges in Suffolk, Monroe, Westchester, and Erie counties, and the Fashion Institute of Technology, are also larger than most of SUNY's four-year colleges.

The State University's institutions also include its public policy research arm, the Nelson A. Rockefeller Institute of Government (publisher of this book). Created by the Legislature in 1981 to bring the resources of higher education to bear on the governmental process, the Institute conducts research on the role of state and local governments in American federalism, and on the management and finances of states and localities in major areas of domestic affairs. It also undertakes a wide range of projects to assist government officials and not-for-profit groups in New York State. The Institute oversees national projects on welfare reform and other topics conducted by research networks of state and local experts in different parts of the country, and in conjunction with agencies such as the U.S. Government Accountability Office and the Department of Housing and Urban Development. *The Wall Street Journal* and other national publications regularly cite the Institute's studies of state finances throughout the United States.

The State University is governed by a Board of Trustees, with 15 members appointed by the governor on approval from the Senate. In 1975, the Legislature added a student member, the president of the Student Assembly of the State University. The trustees appoint the chancellor of the university. The Board of Regents retains overall corporate oversight of SUNY, although its exercise of that oversight has been relatively limited in recent years.

SUNY University Centers

Each of the four university centers plays a major role in the educational life and economy of its home region.

The University at Buffalo, largest of the four, was a private institution from its creation in 1846 until 1962. Granted a charter by the state Legislature partly as a result of efforts by future president Millard Fillmore, its medical department graduated its first female physician in 1876 and its first African American student in 1880. Three years later, the university recruited nationally prominent physician Roswell Park, whose name lives today in the state-funded cancer institute in Buffalo. Located in downtown Buffalo for more than a century, UB expanded to a second campus in suburban Amherst in the 1970s, contributing to a shift of population and economic activity away from the region's urban core. The university was elected to membership in the Association of American Universities, representing elite status as a research university, in 1989. In 2003, with 27,000 students and more than a dozen colleges and schools, it was the largest public university in New York or New England.

The State University can trace its roots through those of the University at Albany, whose predecessor institutions date to the normal school created by the Legislature in 1844. The school's mission was to train new teachers and improve teaching in existing public schools. The two-year institution attracted 200 to 400 students a year from throughout the state. In 1914, the normal school was upgraded to the four-year New York State College for Teachers. When Governor Rockefeller initiated expansion of the SUNY system, Albany and Stony Brook were the first developed into large university centers. Today, on three campuses, the University at Albany enrolls some 17,000 students, including graduate students, in more than 200 undergraduate, master's and doctoral programs. Areas of national distinction include criminal justice, information technology and public administration and finance.

SUNY Stony Brook was founded in 1956 to educate teachers of science and math. A 1960 report to the Regents called for its development as a major research university. Research units today specialize in marine sciences, theoretical physics, biotechnology, and other subjects. Enrolling some 22,000 students, Stony Brook fulfills major regional missions in health care, economic development, and cultural and social development; with almost 10,000 employees, it is one of the largest employers on Long Island.

Binghamton University opened its doors as Triple Cities College in 1946 as a branch of Syracuse University. Incorporated into the state university four years later, it was renamed Harpur College in honor of a colonial teacher and pioneer who helped settle the Binghamton area. Growing enrollments helped lead to the college's selection as one of the four doctorate-granting university centers in the state system. In 1965, the campus was formally designated the State University of New York at Binghamton. Enrollment in 2003 was around 13,400. The university's Thomas J. Watson School of Engineering and Applied Science — named for the founder of IBM, whose corporate roots are in the Binghamton area — enrolls 1,000 or so of the total.

City University of New York

The City University of New York dates to the creation, in 1847, of the Free Academy, which later became the City College of New York. CUNY now enrolls more than 200,000 students each year in almost 300 degree programs and 22 institutions, as well as more than 150,000 in adult and continuing education.

As the population and wealth of New York City exploded in the century following creation of the Free Academy, public colleges in the city grew as well. Manhattan's Hunter College was created in 1870. Brooklyn and Queens colleges followed in the 1930s; Staten Island Community College (now the College of Staten Island) and Bronx and Queensborough community colleges in the 1950s. State government began providing modest amounts of aid for municipal colleges in the city in 1948, as Governor Dewey and the Legislature were creating SUNY. In 1961, Governor Rockefeller and the Legislature created the City University of New York, incorporating the four-year and community colleges as well as a new graduate school, partly to balance the expansion of SUNY throughout the rest of the state.

CUNY now comprises 11 senior colleges, six community colleges, a law school and other programs. Continuing its tradition of serving many of the immigrants who journey from around the world to New York, CUNY students come from 164 countries and speak 115 native languages.

Influences on Education Policy

Few things are more important to most voters than education. As noted at the start of this chapter, while the subject has become politically important at the national level in recent years, education policy remains overwhelmingly an issue for state governments.

In New York, the Board of Regents, with its wide range of powers, is one of three centers of policy influence. The governor proposes the total amount of aid to public schools each year, by virtue of his dominance of the budget process. The executive can also initiate major changes in education policy — for instance, creation of charter schools — although such big steps happen relatively infrequently. Finally, the Legislature elects the Regents and is the primary driver determining how state aid will be apportioned to various programs and individual districts; it also plays a role, with the governor, in establishing total spending. Legislators influence educational practice by enacting laws that affect school districts' labor-management relations, require particular curricula, and otherwise tell teachers and administrators what to do and how to do it.

One organization, New York State United Teachers (NYSUT), has influence in all three centers of education policymaking. The statewide teachers' union, created in 1972 through a merger of two smaller associations, has more than 570,000 members, most of them teachers, university educators or other school employees. The unions representing faculty at the State University and City University — United University Professions and Professional Staff Congress, respectively — attract occasional news coverage when they criticize funding or policy decisions of the state's elected leaders or administration. Their political influence relies partly on that provided by NYSUT, the parent organization of both.

NYSUT's large membership makes the union politically powerful in two ways. It is perennially one of the largest donors to legislative campaigns and has the ability to sponsor expensive advertising campaigns for or against candidates. In addition, the organization uses its own newspaper and other communications to promote favored candidates, for both statewide offices and individual Senate and Assembly seats. Unlike its counterparts at the national level, NYSUT does not limit its political support to Democrats. In the 1996 state legislative elections, for instance, the union endorsed 118 Democrats and 79 Republicans, according to its web site. Union members are among the most regular visitors to legislators' offices when annual budget deliberations are underway in Albany.

Partly because of its political influence, and partly because it represents the views of many teachers, NYSUT is also a key player when the Education Department considers policy changes affecting curriculum, student assessment, and other issues.

Dozens of other associations represent particular education-related constituencies in Albany. Among the best known is the New York State School Boards Association. It often works cooperatively with NYSUT in speaking out for more school aid, while the two organizations oppose each other on many issues of labor-management relations in school districts. Other associations that lobby for funding in specific areas — for instance, school music programs — often build support through awards that proclaim helpful legislators "Friends of Music Education" or other public-relations efforts.

In the last decade or so, the Education Department has increasingly sought the views of business leaders on the types of skills required in the modern workplace and the need to raise achievement standards in the state's schools. The Business Council of New York State has been a primary player in those efforts.

Governors, legislators, and the Education Department also respond to broader public opinion, and to statistical and other indicators of school performance. As noted, one of the most important recent developments in New York education policy has been creation of school report cards. Disliked by much of the education establishment, the report cards play such an important role in the state's accountability efforts because Commissioner Mills believed they were needed. At his direction, department staff used a privately designed template to help design and implement the innovative performance measure.[24]

Broad voter sentiment includes both a general belief that education deserves strong support, and — periodically, at least — significant frustration with the cost and performance of public schools. "In New York, as in other states, education's 'halo effect' is diminished, and the demands for accountability intensify," one observer wrote in 1974.[25]

---

24 New York's school report cards are based partly on a template published in *Measuring Up In Our Schools: Improving Assessment and Accountability*, Public Policy Institute of New York State, Albany, NY, 1988.

25 Michael D. Usdan, in *Governing New York State: The Rockefeller Years*, Robert H. Connery and Gerald Benjamin, eds., Academy of Political Science, New York, NY, 1974, p. 227.

Demands for accountability today are much greater. On the other hand, the evidence appears to indicate that the "halo effect" remains strong — state aid to schools is at record levels, and voters approved 89 percent of district budget proposals in May 2006.

Regulation of Professions

Among the unique aspects of New York's Education Department is its regulation of a broad range of professions — 50 as of 2005. Most states regulate professionals such as accountants, engineers, and psychologists through a licensing agency or the equivalent of New York's Department of State. (The latter does license numerous occupations, as discussed in Chapter Eight.)

The Regents were assigned responsibility for licensing of physicians in 1891 — a logical step given the importance of medical education. Over ensuing decades, the Legislature added other health-related professions, including physician assistants, chiropractors, dentists and dental hygienists, podiatrists, optometrists, acupuncturists, veterinarians, physical therapists, pharmacists, nurses, and midwives. The department also licenses other professions requiring higher education, such as architects, engineers, and land surveyors. The Legislature has also decided to require licensing of interior designers and athletic trainers, and assigned those responsibilities to the Education Department. Licensing is often sought by well-established members of a given profession, in part to raise the standards of practice and in part to reduce competition from others who may charge lower fees.

The department's Office for the Professions relies heavily on 28 Boards for the Professions to regulate individual specialties. Each board includes members both from the profession and from outside it. Licensing, registration, and related fees fund the office, which investigates and prosecutes professional misconduct and unlicensed practice, and administers assistance for professionals with substance-abuse problems. The office's work also includes administering license examinations, reviewing qualifications and issuing credentials, and registering entities such as pharmacies and providers of continuing education.

The Office for the Professions handles many misconduct cases administratively. The Board of Regents acts on serious cases that may include fines up to $10,000 and suspension or revocation of a license. Cases involving physicians, physician assistants, and specialist assistants are investigated by the Department of Health, and final determinations made by the Regents on recommendation of the commissioner of health.

Much information about licensed professionals is available to the public. Consumers can verify a license, find whether a licensee has been disciplined, or file a complaint by contacting the Office of the Professions.

Serving Individuals with Disabilities

The Office of Vocational and Educational Services for Individuals with Disabilities promotes education for students with disabilities, assures continuity between the child and adult services systems, and provides vocational rehabilitation and independent living services. The office, known as VESID, administers 15 Early Childhood Direction Centers that help families with children with disabilities from birth to age 5 find programs and services. VESID also oversees special education services for students in public and private schools.

VESID counselors guide individuals through service programs to reach employment goals. Services may include vocational assessment, vocational counseling, assistance with transition from school to the world of work, job training and placement, and job follow-up.

State Museum and Archives

The New York State Museum, located at the Empire State Plaza in Albany, is a combination of exhibition halls dedicated to the state's natural and social history and a research center for scientists and historians. The museum was founded in 1836 as the State Geological and Natural History Survey. It is now a major research and educational institution focused on preserving the state's artistic, social, and historical legacies.

The museum's collections include more than 5 million artifacts and specimens. Its exhibits and programs attract more than 1 million visitors, more than half of whom come from outside the Capital Region. Yellow school buses are a familiar sight outside the museum.

The State Archives preserves and makes accessible essential recorded evidence of New York's governments, people, organizations, and events. It cares for more than 130 million government documents from the 1600s through the present. The Archives Partnership Trust is a tax-advantaged, public-private partnership that supports the educational initiatives, conservation efforts, exhibitions, and publications of the archives.

Chapter Fourteen

TRANSPORTATION AND ECONOMIC DEVELOPMENT

Key points:

- The state faces tens of billions of dollars in coming expenses for bridges, roads, and other infrastructure, and may consider allowing private ownership of some transportation facilities to help meet the cost.

- With business costs higher than those in many competing locations, New York uses a "coupon strategy" of providing incentives for companies to invest and create jobs in the state.

- The Empire Zone program provides economic-development incentives that are among the most sweeping in the nation, but has been criticized for funding businesses that create few or no new jobs.

DeWitt Clinton — mayor of New York, governor of New York State, and unsuccessful presidential candidate — is known to history primarily as the driving force behind the Erie Canal. His early dreams for the canal show he was also one of the clearest-eyed visionaries in the young United States of America.

"As an organ of communication between the Hudson, the Mississippi, the St. Lawrence, the Great Lakes of the north and west and their tributary rivers, it will create the greatest inland trade ever witnessed," Clinton said of his hoped-for canal in 1815. "The most fertile and extensive regions of America will avail themselves of its facilities for a market."

Then mayor of New York City, Clinton went on to say this of the changes his plan would bring about:

> The city will, in the course of time, become the granary of the world, the emporium of commerce, the seat of manufactures, the focus of great moneyed operations and the concentrating point of vast disposable, and accumulating capital, which will stimulate, enliven, extend and reward the exertions of human labor and ingenuity, in all their processes and exhibitions. And before the revolution of a century, the whole island of Manhattan, covered with inhabitants and replenished with a dense population, will constitute one vast city.

He was, of course, exactly right. Largely because of the canal once derided as "Clinton's ditch," the city of New York *did* become the world's most important center of commerce and of capital, and a manufacturing powerhouse. The resulting wealth *did* reward not only the rich but the working class and the poor as well, by providing the jobs that in turn meant survival and even progress. It made possible development of the arts, schools, and universities, as well as generous public and private services for the needy. Not only Manhattan but greater New York City became a teeming metropolis. And, not least, the canal led to the growth of Upstate New York, with major cities from its eastern terminus near Albany to Buffalo at its western end.

Even before the Erie Canal, since colonial days, transportation has been a fundamental ingredient in New York's economic growth. The same is true at the start of the 21st century, when canals play only a small role in the state's economy. This chapter examines state government's vital role in transportation and economic development, in both those early days and the present.

Early Transportation and the Great Canal

During the first decades of New York State, most goods moved either on the state's great natural waterways or on roads built by private companies. By 1821, 278 turnpike companies had received charters from the Legislature to operate toll roads and had built 4,000 miles of roads (roughly one-quarter the total length of public roads in New York today).[1] Albany, near the northern end of the navigable section of the Hudson River, was the center for turnpikes stretching west, north, and east. Much of present-day Route 20 follows the road built to the west of the capital city, and in parts is known as Western Turnpike; sections of the current Route 9W, which runs north and south near the west bank of the Hudson, still bear the old name of the Albany Post Road.

Given the road-building technology of the day, transportation over water remained far faster and cheaper, as it had been for centuries. Nearly a century before the opening of the Erie Canal in 1730, the first canal in then-colonial New York opened near Utica; other, smaller artificial waterways followed. By the start of the 1800s, leaders such as Gouverneur Morris were advocating a canal that would connect the Hudson with the hinterlands. Clinton's prescient case for building the canal came in the form of a pamphlet he published after the end of the War of 1812 allowed the state's leaders to focus on long-term progress.[2]

In 1817, then-Governor Clinton persuaded the Legislature to authorize $7 million for construction of a canal 363 miles long, 40 feet wide, and 4 feet deep. Much of the work was done by farmers who lived along the route. Some sections were open by 1820. A statewide celebration took place in October 1825 when the governor journeyed from Buffalo, along the completed canal and down the Hudson River, to New York City.

Freight rates over the canal were $10 per ton — one-tenth the overland cost. In 1829, the Erie Canal carried some 3,540 bushels of wheat down from Buffalo. By 1841 the figure had reached 1 million. All along the waterway, new enterprises needed workers to load the wheat and

---

1   Ellis et al., *A History of New York State*, p. 180.

2   George Washington was another early American leader with a strong interest in canal development. One history, written in the mid-1800s, reports that his 1784 tour through parts of Upstate New York was motivated largely by interest in canals. For links to fascinating history developed by the New York State Museum, visit the New York State Canal System website at *www.canals.state.ny.us*.

myriad other goods onto canal boats, to handle shipping transactions, to care for the boats and their crews, and to perform other jobs created by the shipping boom.

Before construction of the canal, New York City was the nation's fifth-largest seaport, behind Boston, Baltimore, Philadelphia, and New Orleans. Within 15 years of its opening, New York was by far the largest. The increase in commercial activity helped fuel development of already booming banks and other financial houses, as well as businesses involved in manufacturing and trade.

The new economic activity both upstate and down created opportunity for a population that was growing rapidly because of high birth rates and immigration — and helped stimulate even more of the latter. Cities all along the water route from New York Harbor to the Great Lakes boomed from 1825 to 1855 — New York grew from 166,000 to 630,000 residents; Albany, from 16,000 to 57,000; and Rochester, from 9,500 to 44,000. Buffalo mushroomed from a small center of 5,000 to more than 74,000 over the three decades.

As with most revolutionary economic forces, the canal created some losers as well as winners. Long-established farmers in the eastern section of the state saw their wheat lose value as western farms with rich soil no longer had to charge premium prices to cover high transportation costs. Upstate towns such as Auburn and Cazenovia that were not along the canal lost out to those that were. Hudson River port villages that had grown up as terminals for roads through the Catskills saw their growth cease as the huge increases in freight traffic no longer came on overland routes.

Growth and Decline of the Canal System

While the Erie Canal was the most important, other, smaller water routes were built and later expanded throughout much of the 1800s — the Champlain, Oswego, and Cayuga-Seneca canals among them. State government spent scores of millions of dollars on the projects. Most of the dollars were raised through the sale of bonds, leading to serious financial problems in Albany that in turn resulted in the state Constitution's limitations on debt (*see Chapter Eleven*).

During the 20th century, competition from railroads, paved roads, and motor vehicles (and, after 1959, the St. Lawrence Seaway) did away with most of the canals' usefulness as commercial traffic routes. For much of the century's latter half, state government — as well as businesses and residents — largely ignored the canals.

In 1991, Governor Cuomo and the Legislature initiated a constitutional amendment, approved by voters, that allowed long-term leasing of canal system lands to encourage business development. The following year brought legislation to transfer responsibility for operating and maintaining the canal system from the Department of Transportation (DOT) to the New York State Canal Corp., a new subsidiary of the Thruway Authority. The change made it possible to use Thruway toll revenues, rather than the tax dollars that fund DOT, to support the canals — freeing general state revenue for other needs.

A renewed focus on recreational and tourist use of the Erie Canal corridor, in particular, emerged in the 1990s. Both the state and federal governments devoted millions of dollars to develop parks, historic sites, and businesses along the canal trail.

In 1999, the Canal Corp. solicited bids from private investors for development rights along the canal. The Office of the State Comptroller eventually rejected the Canal Corp.'s agreement with a Buffalo-based company after determining that other bidders may not have had a fair opportunity to win the development rights. An interagency task force recommended in 2005 that the Canal Corp. be separated from the Thruway Authority, and financial support drawn from the general state budget rather than Thruway toll revenues. The Legislature had not acted on the proposals as of a year later.

Boaters today can cruise the 340 miles of the Erie Canal in four to five days, given the speed limit of 10 mph in force most of the way. Varying in depth from 12 to 14 feet, the canal extends from the confluence of the Mohawk and Hudson rivers at Waterford, a few miles north of Albany, to the Niagara River at Tonawanda, north of Buffalo. (For much of the first 100 miles, the canal is the Mohawk River, the original canal that paralleled the river having been abandoned.) From tidewater level at the eastern end, the canal rises through locks in the Mohawk Valley to 420 feet above sea level at Rome. Going west, it descends to 363 feet at the junction with the Oswego Canal, and then rises to 565 feet at the Niagara River. Other canals link the Erie to Lake Champlain, Lake Ontario, and two of the Finger Lakes, Cayuga and Seneca.

Changes in Administrative Structure

The growth of the canals led in 1878 to creation of the state Department of Public Works, with the primary duty of overseeing operation and maintenance of the manmade waterways. The first "state highway," called State Road Number 1, was built with a combination of town, county, and state dollars in 1898. The two-mile road was the start of what today is known as Route 7, from Schenectady to Troy. Governor Charles Evans Hughes and the Legislature created a Department of Highways, in recognition of the coming age of the automobile, 11 years later. Fulfilling their expectations, motor vehicles became more and more numerous. From 255,000 in 1915, the number of registered vehicles more than doubled over the next five years, and reached 2.3 million by 1930. (*See sidebar on the next page.*)

Governor Smith's reorganization of the state administration in 1923 included creation of a unified Department of Public Works, with responsibility for highways, canals, and public buildings. Albany imposed its first gasoline tax, 2 cents a gallon, in 1929. State spending on highways tripled, to more than $300 million, from 1930 to 1950.

The Modern Department of Transportation

Governor Nelson A. Rockefeller and the Legislature created the Department of Transportation in 1967. The declaration of policy included in the legislation stated that "adequate, safe and efficient transportation facilities and services at reasonable cost to the people are essential to the economic growth of the state and the well-being of its people." The new agency consolidated the transportation-related functions performed by the Department of Public Works and others, including responsibility for aviation that had been located in the Department of Commerce.

Today the Department of Transportation's primary operational function is maintaining highways and bridges. The agency also administers federal and state aid for local highways, airports, mass transit agencies, ports, and railways; regulates rates and service of motor and rail carriers; and inspects school and charter buses. State government spent about $3.9 billion of its own tax and fee charges, along with $1.4 billion in federal aid, on transportation in 2005. Those figures exclude

Department of Motor Vehicles

Formerly a bureau within the Department of Taxation and Finance, the Department of Motor Vehicles was established in 1959. Some 11.4 million New Yorkers were licensed drivers in 2003, making the agency the single most common point of contact between residents and their state government. The department issues licenses and vehicle registrations through 29 state offices and 101 county-clerk offices around the state.

By the early 1990s, some three decades after its founding, New York's motor vehicles agency — like those in most states — was considered an example of bureaucratic ineptitude. Long lines. Slow and sometimes discourteous service, and frustrating paperwork seemed common.

Governor Cuomo's Motor Vehicles Commissioner, Patricia Adduci, began a quality-improvement effort that involved employees as well as "customers" of the agency in studying ways to improve service. Simple steps included "take-a-number" queuing systems that allowed waiting motorists to sit rather than stand continuously in line; and electronic signs estimating how long waits might be. Mail-in renewals, on-site processing for large rental fleets, and other changes reduced waiting lines noticeably. The agency began to measure customer satisfaction, a key to pushing change through the bureaucracy, in 1993.

The Pataki administration continued improvement efforts by instituting Internet-based renewal of vehicle registrations and e-mail information services. Waiting times continued to drop. New York was one of the first states to use digital photos, allowing drivers to choose images to be imprinted on licenses. The department won widespread praise in the press and awards from groups such as the Citizens Budget Commission for innovation in public service.

Besides its registering and licensing functions, DMV keeps statistics on motor vehicle accidents. The number of individuals killed in such accidents has decreased for more than a decade, from 2,263 in 1989 to 1,431 in 2001 — a reduction of more than one-third. Nonfatal injuries also declined, though by a smaller proportion. Vehicle travel has increased sharply over the period, meaning the rates of both fatal and nonfatal injuries have fallen by a higher percentage than the absolute numbers.

DMV employed 2,775 as of 2006.

most spending by the Metropolitan Transportation, Thruway, and other authorities.

The department owns 15,020 miles of state highways, part of a combined state-and-local network totaling more than 110,000 miles. The state agency and counterparts at the local level work cooperatively in many ways. They share some facilities; in numerous locations, the state contracts with town or county highway departments to plow the snow and cut the grass and weeds along the roadside. While useful, cooperation isn't what it could be; it's not uncommon to see a state truck lift its plow blade while driving along a snowy local highway. DOT also inspects all 17,000 bridges in the state, including those that are part of local roads.

Reflecting the importance of transportation to economic growth, the department administers the Industrial Access Program and other economic-development efforts to support highway, bridge, and rail improvements that facilitate creation and retention of jobs.

DOT also maintains a Research and Development Bureau, created in 1958, that focuses on research in structures, materials, and pavement along with active technology-transfer programs to help local highway departments. Reports in the past decade have examined such things as the use of "rumble strips" that alert drivers when vehicles wander onto the edge of a highway, the use of certain types of precast beams for bridge construction, and the ability of different traffic poles to withstand wind pressure.

Reflecting rising public interest and the philosophy of a new administration, in the late 1990s the department created an Environmental Analysis Bureau. The bureau provides expertise on environmental matters and liaison to environmental agencies and groups. Commissioner Joseph Boardman said in a 1999 interview the new attention to environmental matters grew out of a conversation with Governor Pataki when the two were returning home from the funeral of former state Senator Norman J. Levy, who had served as chairman of the Senate Transportation Committee.[3] The department developed an extensive environmental initiative that included such steps as restoring wetlands diminished by previous highway projects, and retrofitting highway drainage systems to reduce water pollution from farms and other sources.

---

3   Author's interview with Commissioner Joseph Boardman, December 21, 1999.

Another management change of recent years, in response to criticism from many motorists, was legislation enacted in 1995 requiring construction projects in metropolitan New York and Long Island to be done at night whenever feasible. Many road jobs elsewhere in the state also are now performed after the hours of heaviest use.

For all the changes over the years, DOT remains, in many ways, the same engineering-focused agency its predecessors were two centuries ago. Some 4,000 of the department's approximately 10,000 employees worked in design and construction as of 2005; DOT also spends tens of millions of dollars each year hiring outside professional engineers for work on highway and other projects. Some 4,900 other employees worked in operations and maintenance, primarily running the plows and other equipment used to care for roads and bridges.

"Strictly speaking, the state of New York is not much of a highway builder. It gets them done out, like the laundry. It decides where they will go. It plans them.... It repairs them. It prints white lines along them. But the actual building is done by private enterprise" for the most part. (The quote is from a 1955 survey of state government, but remains largely true today.)[4]

Allocations of capital funding are based on requests from local officials to regional DOT offices, along with agency staff's identification of high-accident locations, connections needed for a new residential or commercial development, and roads or bridges in need of rehabilitation. Some legislators, particularly senior members of the majority conference in each house, play influential roles in directing the funding of transportation projects in their regions. The final capital program adopted each year is in the form of an agreement among DOT, the governor's office, the Legislature, and federal funding agencies. Thus the dollars available to any given region, like those for school aid and other spending, depend partly on the region's political influence in Albany.

The Thruway

Governor Herbert Lehman initiated construction of the Thruway in 1942, as the state's population continued a long boom, and use of motor vehicles became more common, and mobility more desirable. Owing

---

4   David H. Beetle, *The New York Citizen: The Guide to Active Citizenship in the Empire State*, Elsevier Press, 1955, p. 349.

partly to wartime delays, the first section opened 12 years later, with most of the Buffalo-New York City route complete by 1955. Governor Thomas E. Dewey, who was responsible for building most of the super-highway and whose name it bears today, made the decision to use tolls to pay for initial construction and maintenance.

An engineering feat of its time, the Thruway is designed for safety at high speeds — with, for instance, no curve sharp enough to reduce mo-torists' sight lines below 1,000 feet. Its construction required, among other things, the building of the grand Tappan Zee Bridge across a three-mile stretch of the lower Hudson River. (The bridge is named af-ter the local section of the river. In precolonial days, nearby lands were home to the Tappan tribe of Indians; "zee" (sea) is the Dutch name for open expanse of water.) In 1994, the bridge was rededicated as the Gov-ernor Malcolm Wilson Tappan Zee Bridge in honor of the former governor.

New York's biggest superhighway and the first of its kind in the country, the Thruway was virtually finished before the federal govern-ment began subsidizing interstate roads under President Eisenhower. The state's congressional delegations succeeded in writing federal funding formulas to repay the cost of building the Thruway. Decades after its completion, however, New York was still collecting federal aid — and the Thruway Authority was collecting tolls at higher levels than ever. The tolls remained a favorite topic of complaint for upstate motor-ists. Most agreed, though, that one big improvement had occurred in re-cent years: the quality of food and other amenities at Thruway rest stops. The Cuomo administration improved services at the rest stops by redeveloping them in partnership with McDonald's and Marriott Corp., two private companies known as worldwide leaders in the hospitality industry.

Today, the 641-mile Thruway is the longest toll superhighway sys-tem in the United States. Its mainline from New York to Albany, west to Buffalo and southwest to the Pennsylvania line at Ripley is 496 miles long. Other sections make direct connections with the Connecticut and Massachusetts turnpikes, New Jersey's Garden State Parkway and In-terstate 287, and other major expressways that lead to New England, Canada, the Midwest, and the South. Some 230 million vehicles travel more than 8 billion miles on the Thruway each year.

The Thruway Authority is a public authority whose three members are appointed by the governor, with consent of the Senate, to nine-year terms. The governor designates the chair. The authority also operates and maintains the New York State Canal System, comprised of the Erie, Champlain, Oswego, and Cayuga-Seneca canals.

Mass Transportation

Subway, bus, and light rail transportation service appears to be administered at the regional level everywhere it exists throughout the state. In fact, mass transportation is a combined state-local function, with state government providing the majority of taxpayer support and retaining ultimate authority.

More than in any other state, mass transit is a New York phenomenon. Nearly a third of the nation's transit trips each year — a total of some 2.4 billion — occur in the state, according to the Metropolitan Transportation Authority. The MTA's subways account for about half the statewide total, while buses in the city contribute almost another third. Other downstate services — the Long Island Rail Road, downstate suburban buses, the Metro-North Railroad serving New York City's northern suburbs, and the Staten Island Ferry — are also major elements of the transit total. Nine upstate regional authorities, with the largest in the Buffalo, Rochester, Syracuse, and Albany areas, provide some 70 million rides a year — roughly one trip for every 33 in the downstate region.

Mass transit originated largely as a private-sector business, modeled on bus and underground railway transportation in London, Paris, and Boston. The first New York City subway opened in October 1904; on a Sunday three days later, some 1 million city residents packed the stations. The city purchased the Interborough Rapid Transit and Brooklyn-Manhattan Transit systems in 1940, after labor and other problems made it difficult for private ownership to continue, and combined them with a city-owned system. (The IRT and BMT acronyms still appear in some subway stations, although routes have been renamed.) The MTA assumed control of city transit operations in 1968.

Today, the MTA is responsible for commuter transportation and related services within the broad downstate metropolitan region, including New York City as well as the suburban counties of Dutchess, Nassau, Orange, Putnam, Rockland, Suffolk, and Westchester. The authority's subsidiary organizations include the Long Island Rail Road; Metro-North; the New York City Transit Authority and its subsidiary, the Manhattan and Bronx Surface Transit Operating Authority; the Staten Island Rapid Transit Operating Authority; and the Triborough Bridge and Tunnel Authority.

The MTA board includes a chair and 16 other voting members, all appointed by the governor to six-year terms with the approval of the Senate. The mayor of New York City influences the MTA by recommending three members of the authority's board and, when he chooses, using the bully pulpit to create favorable or unfavorable publicity for the agency and the governor.

Fares and tolls made up some 55 percent of MTA revenues in 2005. Another important source of income is a 17 percent surcharge on state corporate income taxes paid by businesses operating in the metropolitan transit region. The authority receives other dedicated tax revenues, including proceeds from local mortgage recording taxes and the state petroleum business tax.

In addition to its operating budgets, the MTA's capital budget allocates funding for essential investments such as subway cars, track, buses, and commuter stations. The MTA Capital Program Review Board, which must approve capital spending, includes appointees of the governor, the Senate majority leader, and the Assembly speaker. Each legislative leader typically designates a legislator from the metropolitan suburbs, giving those regions a significant voice in allocating MTA capital dollars.

Other regional mass-transit authorities around the state — most of which operate bus service exclusively — formed in the 1950s and 1960s to take over failing private transportation operators. Their boards of directors are also appointed by the governor with approval of the Senate. Governors typically rely partly on nominations from local political and elected leaders, including members of other political parties, to make such appointments. Like the MTA, funding for these authorities comes from a combination of fares and state and local tax revenues.

The Niagara Frontier Transportation Authority is the largest of the upstate authorities. In addition to local bus service, it operates the Greater Buffalo and Niagara Falls International Airports, the Port of Buffalo, and a 6.4-mile light rail system linking downtown Buffalo to suburban Amherst.

Airports

When transportation is on land or on water, state and local governments play key regulatory and police roles. The same is not true of aviation, which is the province of federal regulators, primarily the Federal Aviation Administration. The state does, however, play a major role in providing and supporting the airports that make possible millions of trips each year by New Yorkers and travelers from all over the world.

By far the largest and busiest airports in the state are John F. Kennedy International Airport and LaGuardia Airport, both operated by the Port Authority of New York and New Jersey under leases with the city of New York that originated in 1948. More than 40 million passengers arrived at or departed from JFK 2005, and LaGuardia served more than 24 million. Four other airports in the state — Greater Buffalo International, Greater Rochester International, Albany International, and Syracuse-Hancock International — each had more than 1 million enplanements. JFK is by far the most important cargo airport, shipping 1.7 million tons in 2005 — roughly two-thirds of the statewide total.

JFK was known officially as New York International Airport when it opened in 1948 (unofficially as Idlewild Airport), and was renamed in honor of the late president in December 1963. Despite its size and fame, the airport has not grown as much in recent years as some counterparts elsewhere in the country, because of congestion and other factors. Starting in 1994, the Port Authority and airlines that operate from JFK undertook a long-discussed expansion of terminals and other facilities to make the airport more attractive to carriers, passengers, and shippers; that work continued in 2001. More than 35,000 people are employed at the airport. LaGuardia opened as a private flying field in 1929 under the name of Glenn H. Curtiss Airport, after the Long Island native who played a key role in developing the American aircraft industry. Later taken over by New York City, its name was changed to honor former Mayor Fiorello LaGuardia in 1947. New terminal buildings and expansions took place in the 1960s and early 1990s.

The state owns Stewart International Airport, a former military airbase near Newburgh, Orange County. In 1999, Governor Pataki signed a 99-year lease with a British firm, National Express Group, to manage the airport. The agreement for a private company to operate a major publicly owned airport was among the first in the nation. Development of the airport remains in the early stages. In 2002, Stewart saw

181,000 passengers on outbound flights, a fraction of the activity at Up-state airports such as Albany's and Buffalo's. Compared to LaGuardia or Newark Airports, with which Stewart competes for some flights, usage remains particularly light. A master plan released in 2005 called for direct access to the nearby Interstate 84 and the Metro-North Railroad's Port Jervis Line, along with a new passenger terminal and other improvements. With such developments, emplanements might rise to 1.5 million by 2022, according to the master plan. State and local officials also faced decisions that would affect commercial and industrial growth around the airport. With rapid population growth in Orange County, many residents urged strict limits on business development. Business groups argued that economic development could offset rising property taxes and provide needed jobs for the region.

Major Questions Over Future Capital Needs

In 2005, Governor Pataki and the Legislature approved a five-year transportation capital plan for maintenance and construction of assets managed by DOT, the MTA, Thruway Authority, and other agencies. State leaders identified some $70 billion in other long-term projects that were not included in the plan, such as reconstruction of the Tappan Zee Bridge over the lower Hudson River, the Second Avenue subway in New York City, and the Peace Bridge between Western New York and Canada. Pointing to experience in some two dozen other states, the Pataki administration said such large funding demands could best be met by inviting private investment to go along with state funds obtained from user fees and borrowing. As part of his 2006-07 budget proposal, Governor Pataki proposed legislation that would allow a public-private partnership for redevelopment of the Tappan Zee Bridge.

Supporters of the proposal said allowing private-sector companies to build and manage such a large project would result in earlier completion and significant cost savings, while avoiding the need for tens of billions of dollars in new state debt. Opponents said private-sector control could result in higher costs for users, lack of accountability and loss of unionized jobs. The Legislature refused to act on the Tappan Zee proposal.

In coming years, funding requirements for maintaining and improving the state's roads, bridges, mass transit, and other infrastructure will compete with demands for more spending on education, health care, and other programs. It's likely that state leaders will continue to examine whether private investment should play a role in transportation funding.

Economic Development

Organizations and regions that compete to promote economic growth strive to do two things: create and maximize competitive advantages, and reduce any disadvantages as much as possible. Digging the Erie Canal was the first large-scale effort by any state to create an economic advantage. For more than a century after DeWitt Clinton's ditch opened to traffic, the economy of the Empire State was the envy of the nation; a 1994 retrospective called that period "the First New York Century."[5] The elite of the nation's manufacturing, finance, and trading industries were headquartered in the state, as were the communications giants in publishing, broadcasting, and telephones. After more than a century of dramatic growth, New York's political strength in Washington during the early 1940s was unrivaled — the sitting president was a New Yorker, as were the presidential nominee of the other major political party, the largest bloc of votes in Congress, and the chief justice of the United States.

Even then, though, the Empire State was in the early stages of a long decline in economic and thus political power relative to the rest of the nation. The federal government began regularly counting jobs nationwide in 1939, and over the ensuing half-century annual job growth in New York was lower than the nationwide rate in more than four of every five years. Some of that difference might be explained simply by size; smaller states could be expected to experience proportionally greater growth than the largest states. That was not the only explanation, though; a 1992 study by the Federal Reserve Bank of Boston found that New York ranked last among the 48 contiguous states for overall job growth from 1969 to 1990.[6] As suggested by that study, New York's economic situation relative to other states started to become especially dire in the late 1960s and 1970s. During the latter

---

5   David F. Shaffer and Robert B. Ward, *The Comeback State*, The Public Policy Institute of New York State, Albany, NY, 1994.

6   Federal Reserve Bank of Boston, *New England Economic Review*, September/October 1992.

decade, the state was one of only two among the fifty to lose population, as residents moved elsewhere in search of opportunity.

Recognition that the state was suffering competitively was among the reasons Governor Rockefeller undertook a significant expansion of existing economic development efforts. The Department of Commerce had been created in 1944 to promote business and act as a clearinghouse for contacts between business owners and the state. Its Division of Economic Development mainly performed research and planning, including assisting localities with land-use issues and publishing statistics on the state's economy. Governor Rockefeller changed the primary function of the Commerce Department to "the creation of new job opportunities through the promotion of the continuing economic development of New York State."[7]

A related function, seldom stated publicly, was to offset the growing tendency of southern states to "raid" New York's economy by encouraging businesses to move where labor, taxes, and other costs were cheaper. Rockefeller created agencies such as the Job Development Authority, the Urban Development Corp., and the Science and Technology Foundation to play active roles in stimulating economic growth. One motivation for these efforts, it seems likely, was to offset potential economic (and political) repercussions from significant tax increases and newly strengthened regulatory activities in areas such as environmental laws. New federal programs and tax incentives aimed at job development contributed to such new approaches as well, although not all states responded to federal encouragement as much as New York did.

The Business Climate

Governor Carey continued the activist efforts begun under Rockefeller and added a new emphasis: improving the basic competitiveness of the state's business climate. His well-known 1975 declaration that "the days of wine and roses are over" was a direct reference to Albany's ability to raise and spend money — but, more fundamentally, a statement of the need to strengthen the private sector by limiting the size and cost of state government.

Over eight years, Governor Carey and the Legislature cut the top personal tax rate from over 15 percent to 10 percent. (The tax-cutting

---

7   *The New York Red Book 1971-72*, Albany, NY: Williams Press, p. 888.

had begun with a small income-tax cut introduced by Governor Malcolm Wilson, who served just more than a year after Governor Rockefeller resigned in December 1973.) The corporate tax rate rose from 9 to 10 percent (and, for two years, to 12 percent) to generate revenue during the Carey era; to help offset any damage to manufacturers, Governor Carey and the Legislature created an investment tax credit, which reduces corporate taxes for companies that make capital investments in the state. The mission of the Urban Development Corp. expanded from that of developing housing to include a broader range of economic development. To cut bureaucratic red tape that many business executives said hampered economic growth, the Carey administration created the Office of Business Permits to act as a one-stop center for permits and an advocate within government for private firms. (The office, now known as the Governor's Office of Regulatory Reform, is described in more detail in Chapter Eight.)

Governor Cuomo and the Legislature continued cutting tax rates through the economic boom of the 1980s, again with the stated goal of making New York's business climate more competitive. From 1983 through 1989, the top personal tax rate dropped in steps from 10 percent to just under 8 percent. (Some of the rate reduction was offset by a broadening of the types of income to which the tax rate applied, as a result of changes at the federal level; the federal definition of income is the basis for New York's.) The Cuomo era established other innovations such as the Centers for Advanced Technology, university-based facilities that receive state and private funding to develop marketable technologies; and the Industrial Effectiveness Program, which helps manufacturers improve management and production processes. When the state's economy foundered and Albany's revenue faltered from 1989 to 1992, Governor Cuomo and the Legislature enacted several tax increases, including a temporary surcharge on business taxes, that critics said worsened the economic downturn in New York.

Governor Pataki intensified efforts to improve the business climate. Every major state-level tax was reduced significantly starting in 1995; the resulting annual savings to taxpayers totaled nearly $10 billion, or some 20 percent of what Albany's tax collections would have been otherwise. Particularly important were reductions in tax rates on personal and corporate income. Sales tax rates in most of the state rose in the 1990s, although revenues from those increases were not as sizable as other tax reductions.

The Pataki administration adopted other policies intended to make the state more business-friendly. Regulatory agencies were directed to give greater consideration to any costs associated with new rules; potential development sites were identified, and permits for them initiated, to be ready when a major employer needed a location for a facility. Rates for workers' compensation and unemployment insurance were reduced, and electric utilities agreed with the Public Service Commission to reduce industrial energy rates and allow customers to choose electrical providers in an open marketplace.

Responding to criticisms from local economic development organizations around the state, and seeking to create a new "brand" for marketing the state to corporate executives, Governor Pataki consolidated the state's efforts under a new umbrella organization called Empire State Development. The new agency encompassed the existing Department of Economic Development, Job Development Authority, and Science and Technology Foundation as well as a new subsidiary of the Urban Development Corporation called the Empire State Development Corporation, under whose name UDC now does business. The powers of Empire State Development include the authority to issue tax-exempt and nontax-exempt bonds, override local planning and zoning codes, and take property by eminent domain for public purposes. The result of the restructuring was an approach more like those in other states that had developed successful economic development efforts in the 1980s and 1990s — a unified effort directly accountable to the governor, and therefore easier for corporate executives to understand and approach for assistance. UDC remains the legal entity through which ESD often operates; the governor appoints a nine-member board to oversee UDC, with confirmation by the Senate, and designates the chairman. (The Pataki administration retained the existing legal structure for economic-development agencies in part so new approaches would not have to be negotiated with the Legislature.)

The Pataki administration's approach to economic development differed from its predecessors in other ways as well. Governor Pataki spoke regularly with corporate chief executives to convince them of state government's willingness to support their investments in New York. More than any governor in recent memory, Pataki also spoke publicly — in State of the State addresses, and public appearances around the state — about the need to keep the state economy strong by making it possible for businesses to create jobs. That theme was a central element of the 2006 gubernatorial campaign — a reflection of the changed nature of the political debate in Albany, as well as the need for further improvement in the state's economy.

The "Coupon" Strategy

A quarter-century after Governors Wilson and Carey started cutting taxes to encourage broad-based business growth, the cost of doing business in New York was still considered generally high because of labor costs, taxes, energy costs, and other factors. To offset those disadvantages, the state continued to rely heavily on what economic development professionals sometimes call a "coupon" or "rebate" strategy — providing targeted financial incentives to overcome generally higher costs of doing business. One element of that approach was the Jobs Now fund, which set aside $40 million or so each year to be used as incentives for major new projects or business expansions. The fund was created in 1996 largely at the initiative of Senator Bruno, at a time when numerous other states were developing significant financial incentive packages to attract major employers, especially in highly paid industries such as automotive manufacturing and computer-chip fabrication.

One of the state's most frequently used economic development tools dates from 1969. That year, New York adopted legislation allowing localities to create industrial development agencies, and over the ensuing decades the IDAs' abatement of local property taxes became one of the most common elements of economic-development packages offered by the state and local organizations.

The Legislature approves creation of each agency in response to local request, and each is governed by a sponsoring municipality that appoints the agency's board of directors. For eligible projects, an IDA can purchase the relevant property, making it tax-exempt because of the agency's governmental status. The IDA then leases the property back to the business, which usually agrees to make payments in lieu of local school and other property taxes at a reduced level for 10 years or more. Project developers also can seek exemption from mortgage recording taxes on property purchases, and from sales taxes on goods used in the new facility.

While the Legislature created more than 140 IDAs over three decades, 116 were active as of 2004, with total revenues of $101.9 million, according to the Office of the State Comptroller. The reporting agencies indicated they had total outstanding obligations and conduit debt of $17 billion, with $7.3 billion of that in New York City.

Other common incentives in the 1990s and as the new century began included direct loans to businesses for a portion of project costs, loan guarantees for working capital, and cash assistance for employee training.

A Major New Incentive Program

In 2000, at the initiative of Speaker Silver, the state expanded an existing form of incentives into a dramatic new program called Empire Zones — areas within 40 designated communities around the state where new or growing businesses could operate virtually free of state and local taxes. Incentives in the zones included state reimbursement of local property taxes, exemption from sales taxes on most purchases, credits to reduce or eliminate state corporate taxes in the zone, and a state tax credit for part of the cost of employee wages. The credits could add up to significantly more than was available to companies before. When IBM announced a $2.5 billion investment in a new semiconductor plant in October 2000, the governor's office said the Empire Zone credits totaled $475 million. The zone designation was said to have been the deciding factor in other location decisions, such as a 2000 decision by Corning Incorporated to open a photonics plant in Henrietta, outside Rochester, creating more than 400 jobs.

As of 2006, the state had created 72 Empire Zones. The "zones" no longer were single, contiguous areas, but acreage — even square footage — that local zone administrators could apply to specific sites miles away from each other. Originally envisioned as targeting hard-pressed communities, the program evolved into a highly valuable economic-development tool that could be used almost anywhere in the state.

Empire Zone benefits were among the incentives state officials used to persuade Advanced Micro Devices Corp. to announce plans for a $3.2 billion computer-chip plant in Saratoga County. (The project, made public in June 2006, would also be eligible for an unusual $500 million grant to offset capital investment and $150 million in assistance for research and development costs.) The agreement was not binding on AMD. Company officials said the plant, if completed, would create 1,200 permanent, high-paid jobs and several thousand temporary construction jobs. Industry observers said the plant would be likely to stimulate several thousand jobs at suppliers, local retailers, and other businesses. Some critics said the state's assistance was too rich for the number of jobs created.[8]

The Empire Zones program has also been criticized for rewarding "new" job creation that actually involved existing jobs being moved to new corporate entities. A review by the Syracuse *Post-Standard* found that "hundreds" of companies had made such changes.

Across the state, existing companies shifted their assets or reincorporated and seemed to be new. Workers continued to make the same computers, beer, jewelry and newspapers they have produced in New York for generations....

Donald Western, who runs Onondaga County's Empire Zone, calls these kinds of moves a "change of shirt." It reminds him of turning his gym shirt inside out as a kid to play for the red team instead of the blue.[9]

Governor Pataki and the Legislature tightened the Empire Zone rules for new applicants in 2002. Benefits for companies that had already qualified were to remain in place for several additional years. The state's experience with the program illustrated the difficulty of designing business-assistance policies that would make New York companies competitive with those in other locations without providing unfair advantages to a relative few firms.

In addition to providing financial incentives and other assistance to individual businesses, ESD's major efforts include marketing the state as a business location and tourism destination. The "I Love NY" campaign developed under Governor Carey remains nationally recognized. The state has increased business marketing advertisements on broadcast media and in national financial publications to spread the word about lower taxes, a new regulatory environment, and other improvements in the business climate.

What Works in Economic Development?

The use of government-funded incentives for economic development first came under widespread criticism in many areas of the country, in-

---

8   See, for instance, Michael Marvin, "Risky business," *Times Union*, Albany, NY, July 16, 2006.

9   Michelle Breidenbach, "No small change," *The Post-Standard*, Syracuse, NY, September 24, 2006.

cluding New York, in the 1980s. As noted above, such complaints continue today. Representatives of public employee unions and other organizations that lobby for higher state spending say many of New York's tax incentives and direct financial assistance programs are unlikely to improve the state's economy and might prove harmful by reducing support for education and other services. Supporters of such programs do not argue that every individual deal makes a difference between job growth and stagnation. Business groups and economic developers point to the unquestioned increase in incentives being offered by other major states, and argue, among other things, that New York faces two choices: competing with those states, or losing more jobs and population to other states.[10]

One extensive study of industrial development agencies concluded that IDAs in New York "do appear to influence the behavior of project developers." About 30 percent of developers responding to a survey reported that projects would have moved out of New York or been canceled without IDA assistance. Others would have been altered in scale, location, or timing, while 20 percent of respondents reported that projects would have moved forward unchanged without IDA involvement. The 1998 study, conducted under a statutory directive initiated by legislators who were skeptical of some IDA projects, also found that the agencies "have added significant taxable value to local communities." It concluded, however, that effects on job creation and retention were impossible to measure definitively under existing reporting requirements.[11]

Over the last decade, state economic development officials developed a detailed analytical process to examine whether a company applying for assistance was likely to leave the state or go out of business without help, using indicators such as whether production equipment in a given facility was becoming obsolete. Applicants were required to show that they could obtain additional financing from other public or private sources. The analysis also included a comparison of costs and expected benefits, including benchmarks for incentive offers. Contracts

10 For examples of the arguments on either side, see "Taxpayers Deserve a Fair Shake From Businesses That Receive Government Subsidies," press release, Fiscal Policy Institute, Latham, NY, May 25, 1999; and *Beating Them At Their Own Game: How New York State Can Grab Its Share of 2 Million New Jobs*, The Public Policy Institute, Albany, NY, 1997.

11 Center for Governmental Research, *Evaluation of New York State Industrial Development Agencies*, Rochester, NY, 1998.

with companies receiving incentives specified how many jobs were expected after a given period, and in many cases ESD retained the right to withdraw or recoup its financial assistance if employment targets were not met.

"Many states continue to emphasize the need to be competitive with other states in attracting firms and investment with locational incentives," a 1999 review of various states' economic development policies concluded. "Given our decentralized federal system, it is hard to imagine this interstate competition disappearing completely. But it is also true that the changing nature of global competition is prompting more attention to state incentives that support innovation and growth processes rather than subsidies for specific firms."[12]

New York's Advantages and Competitive Challenges

The New York State Office of Science, Technology and Academic Research (NYSTAR) is an example of that approach. The office was created in 1999 to bring together a variety of technology-development efforts and provide increased funding for such programs. In 2001, Governor Pataki and the Legislature started devoting additional hundreds of millions of state dollars to joint university-corporate research projects in cutting-edge technologies. The intent of such Centers of Excellence is to encourage rapid commercialization of scientific breakthroughs and attraction of technology-related investment. Business and university executives joined state leaders in predicting that significant new technologies would result, and that New York would gain thousands of high-skilled, high-paid jobs. The plan was modeled largely on successful long-term economic development efforts in other states, such as Research Triangle Park in North Carolina. As of 2006, the state, universities, and private companies had created centers in Buffalo (bioinformatics and life sciences); Canandaigua (photonics); Albany (nanoelectronics); Stony Brook (information technology); and Syracuse (environmental technology).

---

12 Martin Saiz and Susan E. Clarke, "Economic Development and Infrastructure Policy," in *Politics In The American States: A Comparative Analysis*, Washington, DC: CQ Press, 1999, p. 499.

Economic developers who work to attract new businesses and jobs to New York say the state faces major competitive disadvantages such as:

- An overall tax burden generally ranked as the highest or second-highest in the nation;

- High costs for electricity (roughly 60 percent above the national average);

- Above-average costs for workers' compensation and health insurance; and

- Laws and regulations that are more favorable to organized labor than those in most states.

New York also retains important comparative advantages as a business location. For companies that sell consumer goods, one important selling point is the state's status as a center of population and disposable income. Average incomes are among the highest in the world, as are those in adjacent states such as Connecticut and New Jersey. The transportation network remains a good one, even with some signs of age. Smart, skilled workers are more important than ever; New York has both higher-than-average rates of college graduates and more-productive manufacturing workers than most states. Perhaps most fundamentally, the Empire State has a centuries-old tradition of seeking to provide a legal and social framework — for instance, in today's Business Corporation Law — that encourages entrepreneurial activity.

After declining in many respects during the 1970s and early 1990s, New York City entered a period of resurgence because of growth in the stock market, a tourist boom, and the desire of many new-media business leaders to locate in a world-class city. Still, both the city and the state as a whole continued to lag behind the U.S. average and many similar states in creating new jobs.

Chapter Fifteen

LABOR AND FAMILY ASSISTANCE

Key points:

- New York's Constitution requires public support for the needy, and the state's welfare and related assistance programs are more generous than those in most states.

- A decade after welfare reform, public assistance is aimed at helping low-income individuals enter and stay in the workforce by providing wage supplementation and support for child care, transportation, and other needs.

- Organized labor has been an important force in state politics and government for more than a century; public-employee unions are especially influential today.

For most of its first century, New York State government concentrated on erecting the legal and physical infrastructure that would allow society to operate and progress — enacting laws of corporate structure and of contracts; building roads, railroads, and canals; extending freedom by ending slavery and eliminating the freehold tenancy that made it impossible for most workers to own land.

After the Civil War, life in New York changed — as it did elsewhere in the industrializing world — and government gradually adapted with it. As outlined in previous chapters, New York State adopted more active roles in functions that promised to benefit the entire populace, from providing education for all to safeguarding public health.

Toward the end of the 19th century and the start of the 20th, population growth and an expanding, increasingly complex economy both suggested a more expansive public sector and provided the wealth that made it possible. Two new governmental roles aimed at helping particular groups emerged: providing sustenance for families and individuals who could not provide for themselves, and giving working men and women the force of new laws to balance the growing economic power of business owners.

In both areas, New York was a national leader. Its early start on government protections for the needy and for workers presaged what today are extensive laws and benefits throughout the nation.

An Overview

At the start of the 21st century, New York State provides a wide variety of social services for families and individuals who need help coping with financial and other domestic problems. This array of programs is so broad, and targeted to so many individual needs, as to have been almost unimaginable a century ago. Best-known is simple financial help, referred to at various times in recent decades as relief, welfare, public assistance, and, today, temporary assistance or safety net support. Related services include specific programs designed to make sure that no New Yorker goes without basic needs such as food, shelter, and medical care (the latter is discussed in Chapter Twelve). Every state provides these services, as do most industrialized societies around the world. Yet no other state, and few countries, surpass New York's level of services.

Formal governmental efforts to help needy families and individuals began at the community level in colonial New York. Over the course of two centuries, higher levels of government — the county, the state, and finally the federal government — assumed a share in financial responsibility and significant decision-making authority. In the last decade, Washington has begun to return some of its authority — though by no means all — to the states.

The result is an intergovernmental web of services paid for by a combination of federal, state, and local taxes. Broad policies are set by elected representatives and centralized bureaucracies in Washington and Albany. Actual services, though — financial assistance, help for a parent in asserting control over a wayward youngster, food vouchers that can be used in local grocery stores— are still provided at the county level, as has been the case since the Civil War era.

A central question for charitable organizations, government officials, policy experts, and many taxpayers has always been whether, and at what point, public assistance diminishes individual initiative. At some point, New Yorkers implicitly accepted the idea that society must bear the cost of guaranteeing every individual at least a subsistence level of income and resources. Perhaps the date of that addition to the social compact could be fixed in the early 1900s. At the latest, it must be attributed to one of the 1938 amendments to the state Constitution, Article XVII, which declares that the "aid, care and support of the needy" are a "public concern" for which the Legislature must provide.

Another balancing act — involving men and women who are or hope to be employed, labor organizations, and employers — takes place when state government makes decisions in the area of labor. New York's major labor-related policies and programs fall into three broad categories that are roughly similar to those in other states. First, the state provides for two systems of financial assistance for workers who are without a paycheck because they have been injured or laid off. Other services help workers find and train for employment, and help employers find employees. Finally, the state enacts and enforces a variety of protections for workers, ranging from job safety to wages.

The Empire State differs from many other states in the extent of legal support it gives to organized labor and workers' rights. Twenty-two states are at the opposite end of the spectrum, having enacted "right-to-work" laws that prohibit labor contracts from establishing mandatory union membership as a condition of employment. Even among states considered labor-friendly, New York has been a leader for the past century. As of 2005, the proportion of workers in the state who belonged to unions — 26.1 percent — was more than double the national rate.

This chapter examines the development and current role of New York State government's activities in family assistance, and in labor affairs. The two issues have been connected since the 1930s, when assistance programs for both unemployed workers and destitute families were created in response to the social devastation of the Great Depression. Although labor and social services are considered largely separate subjects today, links remain — for instance, the state Labor Department's role in helping welfare recipients prepare for and find employment.

Helping the Poor: Early Efforts

Dutch settlers in the colony then called New Netherland brought with them their society's attitudes and practices relating to the poor. Calvinist doctrine, the basis of the Dutch Reformed church, held that the wealthy had a responsibility to provide for the indigent. Deacons of the church collected alms from those who could afford to give and distributed assistance to the needy.

The Dutch colonial government contributed to the deacons' work. An example comes from the settlement then known as Beverwijck, later renamed Fort Orange and, eventually, Albany: "As early as 1642 ordinances provided that the deaconry should have a portion of the fines that were imposed in court sentencing. Frequently fined for slander and aggressive behavior, Jochem Wesselsz, a local baker, involuntarily contributed a considerable amount of money to poor relief in this manner."[1]

The Dutch Reformed deacons dispensed assistance with careful attention to cost-efficiency so limited funds could meet as many genuine needs as possible. Generally, they gave charity only if the needy individuals worked or were disabled, and they expected recipients to pay back what they could so others could be helped. In the case of one elderly widow whom the deacons had helped, her estate of a golden hairpin, a wedding ring, silver tableware and other items reverted to the deaconry after she died.[2] A poorhouse was established in the village in 1653.

The Dutch Reformed system also provided medical care, using an early form of what today might be considered managed care: In 1664, a

---

1 Janny Venema, "Poverty and Charity in Seventeenth-Century Beverwijck/Albany, 1652-1700," *New York History*, Cooperstown, NY: The New York State Historical Association, October 1999, p. 369.

2 Venema, p. 381.

Beverwijck surgeon was paid an annual stipend of 200 guilders to provide general care for the poor at the direction of the deacons.

After the English took control of the colony in 1664, responsibility for the poor gradually shifted to civil authorities. In New York City, the first permanent almshouse opened in 1734, when the Common Council ordered the erection of a "House of correction, workhouse and poorhouse." The combination of missions reflected the common perception that poverty and criminality were closely related. An order from the council provided that the house should provide refuge and work for "all such poor as shall be sent or committed thither and able to labour, and also all disorderly persons, parents of Bastard Children, Beggars, Servants running away or otherwise misbehaving themselves, Trespassers, Rogues, Vagabonds, poor persons refusing to work, and on their refusal to work and labour, to correct them by moderate whipping, etc."

By the 1820s, almshouses were common across the state as homes for abandoned children and poor adults who were unable to work. Around the same time, the "New England system" took hold in New York. Paupers were boarded out with friends, neighbors, and relatives at public expense. All the town paupers — people who were physically disabled, blind, mentally retarded, those who were able-bodied but poor, children, male and female alike — would be displayed and "sold" to the "purchaser" who would accept the lowest payment from local officials. Bidders were usually farmers who based their offers on how much work they might expect. "When the New England auction system finally expired in New York is not clear but its continued use in the United States was reported as late as 1926."[3]

State and County Governments Get Involved

While state government would not itself provide services for the indigent until decades later, in 1824 it focused official attention on the issue with the first comprehensive survey of local efforts to care for the poor. A report to the Legislature by Secretary of State John Yates condemned the pauper auctions as well as lack of educational facilities for poor children. Addressing themes that have resonated ever since, the report

---

3   Cornel Reinhard and William W. Culver, *The Rear Guard of Capital: Welfare Policy and the "Unfortunate" in New York State*, Rockefeller Institute Working Papers Number 14, Albany, NY: Rockefeller Institute of Government, Fall 1984.

also criticized forms of public relief that tended "to encourage the sturdy beggar and profligate vagrant to become pensioners upon the public funds." The report commented: "Without providing employment for the poor, no system can be productive of much good."[4]

The Yates report advanced the idea of making the county, rather than the town, the main unit for administering relief. The report proposed establishment of one or more houses of employment in each county, each connected with a farm, "the paupers there to be maintained and employed at the expense of the respective counties, in some healthful labor, chiefly agricultural, their children to be carefully instructed, and at suitable ages, to be put out to some useful business or trade." The Legislature responded with what may have been the first major state mandate regarding social services at the local level — a law requiring each county to appoint a superintendent of the poor and to purchase a suitable piece of land for erection of a county poorhouse. Within a few years nearly every county had a poorhouse, which soon became home to unfortunates of all ages and afflictions.

An Assembly committee investigated the county poorhouses in 1838. It found examples of severe overcrowding, such as 12 women and children in an unheated room with five beds. Gradually, other forms of institutional relief took some individuals away from the poorhouse. Local asylums for the mentally ill were created starting in the 1840s; half a century later, state law forbade confinement of any insane persons in almshouses and made most such individuals wards of the state.

Private charitable groups and philanthropic individuals also established more than 200 orphanages, "homes for the friendless," and other institutions throughout the state by the 1890s; both the state and many local governments provided some financial support. The growing sense that relief for the poor was not being provided on a consistent basis had led to creation of a state Board of Charities, under Governor Reuben Fenton, in 1867. The new Constitution written in 1894 made the board a permanent part of state government. Meanwhile, many immigrant communities created their own fraternal or trade organizations and mutual-aid societies to help financially and in other ways when members lost a job, became ill, or died.

---

4   New York Secretary of State, *Report from the Secretary of State, on the subject of the laws for the relief and settlement of the poor, 1824*, on file at the New York State Library.

During the last decades of the 1800s, "outdoor relief" — food, fuel, and cash assistance — declined in favor because critics said it reduced recipients' desire to work. Orphan asylums grew sharply in both number and size as parents broke up families to provide decent care for their children. Statewide, 65,000 children spent time in orphanages in 1895, compared with fewer than 18,000 a quarter-century earlier. A study of one orphanage found that "most children came to the Albany asylum at the behest of their parents for reasons of sickness, death, or simple poverty, and most returned to their own homes in the course of time." Parents saw the orphanage as a place where girls and boys could receive not only food and a good home, but an education as well.[5]

Cash Assistance

In 1915, future U.S. Senator Robert Wagner and future Governor Alfred E. Smith — then Democratic leaders in the state Senate and Assembly, respectively — won enactment of the precursor to today's family assistance program. The Widowed Mothers Pension Bill provided a small amount of support for families that had lost a breadwinner.

Under Governor Franklin D. Roosevelt, the Legislature went further in 1929 and 1930, extending relief and creating a general pension system for individuals who were 70 or over and met certain other restrictions. The initial New York legislation was enacted not in response to the Depression — which had not yet reached its depth — but to "years of difficulty with 19th century approaches to pauperism."[6] As the Depression settled in — cutting the number of factory jobs, for instance, from 1.1 million to 734,000 between 1929 and 1933 — the privately financed charitable organizations that were still providing the bulk of care for the needy became unable to handle the overwhelming financial and social devastation.

Roosevelt responded in August 1931 with a proposal for comprehensive relief, telling the Legislature: "In broad terms I assert that modern society, acting through its government, owes the definite obligation

---

5   Judith A. Dulberger, *"Mother Donit fore the Best": Correspondence of a Nineteenth-Century Orphan Asylum*, Syacuse, NY: Syracuse University Press, 1996, pp. 10-12.

6   Reinhard and Culver, p. 16.

to prevent the starvation or the dire want of any of its fellow men and women who try to maintain themselves but cannot.... To these unfortunate citizens aid must be extended by government — not as a matter of charity but as a matter of social duty.... When ... a condition arises which calls for measures of relief over and beyond the ability of private and local assistance to meet — even with the usual aid added by the State — it is time for the State itself to do its additional share." At Roosevelt's initiative, the Legislature enacted a major expansion of state aid to localities to establish public jobs and provide financial assistance to households. The new Temporary Emergency Relief Administration (TERA) spent some $50 million on work relief and home relief, involving an estimated 1.5 million New Yorkers, in its first 10 months of operation. The first major antipoverty program in the United States, TERA became a model for efforts by the federal government after FDR moved to the White House in 1933. After a century of emphasis on institutional settings to deal with poverty, home-based relief had returned to prominence.

Roosevelt's successor, Governor Herbert Lehman, and the Legislature made home relief permanent, with the state paying 40 percent of the cost for any individual who had lived in New York at least two years. A 1967 history of the state captured the significance of the Roosevelt-Lehman expansion of welfare: "Poverty, which had once been a mark of opprobrium, was now considered a misfortune for which the individual was not responsible. Public relief, which many people had earlier referred to as a 'dole,' was now generally accepted as a more equitable and efficacious method than private charity for relieving human misery."[7]

The crowning achievement of the movement to establish state-funded support of the needy came in 1938, with enactment of the social welfare article of the state Constitution. The article provides that "aid, care and support of the needy are public concerns and shall be provided by the state and by such of its subdivisions, and in such manner and by such means, as the legislature may from time to time determine."

In the two decades after World War II, a variety of factors drove up the costs of welfare and the number of recipients, despite a booming economy. One factor, clearly, was simply the growing acceptance of public assistance. A nationwide migration of largely poor black families and individuals from southern states to the north brought hundreds

---

7   David M. Ellis et al., *A History of New York State*, Ithaca, NY: Cornell University Press, 1967, p. 426.

of thousands of low-skilled workers to New York, among other states. As manufacturing employment in the state declined in the late 1950s and 1960s, many families had difficulty finding good-paying jobs. Additional tens of thousands of immigrants from Puerto Rico entered the state during the period; many arrived with little formal education. Throughout society, traditional assumptions about family gave way to sharp increases in divorce and childbirth outside marriage, leaving many mothers and their children in or near poverty.

The Road to Welfare Reform

During the 1960s' War on Poverty, federal policy encouraged further growth of the welfare rolls by allowing applicants simply to declare their financial status without, in most cases, being subject to investigation. Historically, the state of the overall economy had been directly linked to increases or decreases in the number of families and individuals receiving assistance. In the 1960s, though, while New York's economy grew along with that of the nation, the state's welfare caseload tripled and total payments quadrupled. Mothers who collected Aid to Families with Dependent Children were allowed to choose whether to go to work or into job training, or to stay at home with their children. Most chose to stay at home, even while many middle-class mothers entered the workforce owing to rising costs of living and changing views of the roles of men and women. The growth of welfare rolls was especially high in New York City. There, under Mayor John V. Lindsay, potential applicants were encouraged to consider public assistance an entitlement they should receive even if they might have survived without it.

Higher welfare rolls in New York State were also due in part to a relaxed approach to supervision of local districts by the Board of Social Welfare, which set eligibility standards and other key policies. "In recent years," according to one 1974 commentary, the board "tended toward a rather uncritical acceptance of the recommendations of the state commissioner whom it had itself appointed. It appeared reluctant to engage in the unpleasant combat with welfare officials throughout the state necessary to achieve strict administration of the state's welfare policies."[8] While many local officials were not disposed to be generous

---

8   Blanche Bernstein, "The State and Social Welfare," in *Governing New York State: The Rockefeller Years*, Robert H. Connery and Gerald Benjamin, eds., Academy of Political Science, New York, NY, 1974, p. 149.

with public assistance, those in New York City and some other areas were driving up statewide costs.

In 1971, the welfare caseload stood at 1.7 million — one in ten New Yorkers — even after two decades of generally strong economic growth. As he began his third term in office, Governor Rockefeller reflected growing frustration with welfare as it then existed by proposing dramatic changes. The Board of Social Welfare was stripped of all its major powers. (The board could not be eliminated by legislation because of its Constitutional status; it exists today largely as an honorary body.) Most of the board's policymaking duties were transferred to the commissioner of social services, while the Legislature and the governor would now set welfare eligibility standards through statute. The commissioner, previously appointed by the board, would be chosen directly by the governor, subject to Senate confirmation.

A quarter-century before the national welfare reforms of 1996, the Rockefeller reforms of the early 1970s included this declaration by the Department of Social Services (DSS): "The heart of the 1971 welfare reform program in New York State was the emphasis on the value of work." All employable recipients were required to report twice a month to the Labor Department's Employment Service, where their benefit checks were made available along with employment counseling and training. Mothers whose children were six or older were generally considered employable. Some 53,000 individuals lost welfare benefits for failing to meet work requirements.

Other changes included creation of an Office of Welfare Inspector General to investigate complaints of suspected fraud, and an office in DSS to audit eligibility determinations made by local districts. An audit for the second half of 1972 found a statewide ineligibility rate of 17.6 percent, "a far higher rate than ever uncovered in audits conducted by New York City or other localities."[9] DSS responded by requiring much more detailed, 11-page applications that tended to discourage some applicants and led to higher rejection rates among those who did apply.

The Role of the State Constitution

Under the social welfare clause of the state Constitution, as the Court of Appeals has made clear, the Legislature does not have a choice as to

9   Ibid., p. 151.

whether it will provide for the needy.[10] It *does* have broad discretion as to how it makes such provision. In a case involving taxpayer-supported assistance for housing, the Court of Appeals ruled: "We do not read this declaration and precept as ... commanding that, in carrying out the constitutional duty to provide aid, care and support of the needy, the State must always meet in full measure all the legitimate needs of each recipient."[11] Yet that discretion has limits. State courts have ruled, for instance, on the adequacy of publicly funded shelter allowances for the poor.[12]

In arguing for approval of the social welfare article during the Depression, supporters described it as a "charter of human protection for the underprivileged, the destitute and the handicapped of our state." Its enactment was followed by similar clauses added to constitutions in other states; it remains perhaps the strongest such provision in any state charter. Without such constitutional backing, New York's social-welfare net might be quite different today. Some observers say that in recent years the Court of Appeals has attempted "to find statutory or other means to grant relief in particular circumstances, often reversing lower courts, while at the same time maintaining a deferential posture toward the legislature."[13]

The Changing Politics of Welfare

What later became known as welfare — regular cash assistance for families, particularly single mothers living with one or more children — began on a high note as part of President Franklin D. Roosevelt's Social Security Act of 1935. The new Aid to Dependent Children (later Aid to Families with Dependent Children) was intended, among other things, to stave off the huge growth in numbers of families where parents without work surrendered children to county and municipal boarding houses for the poor. Senator Daniel Patrick Moynihan observed that Labor Secretary Frances Perkins proposed locating the new program in the Labor Department, but some in Congress opposed the idea for fear it would increase the power of labor unions. "Had the AFDC program

---

10 *Tucker* v. *Toia*, 43 NY 2d 1 (1977)

11 *Bernstein* v. *Toia*, 43 NY 2d 437 and 448-449.

12 See, for example, *Ram* v. *Blum*, 1980, 103 Misc. 2d 237, 425 NYS 2d 735, affirmed 77 A.D. 2d 278, 432 NYS 2d 892.

13 Gerald Benjamin with Melissa Cusa, "Social Policy," in *Decision 1997: Constitutional Change in New York*, 1997, p. 309.

From the New Deal to the New Welfare

The Inheritance, a 1999 book by Samuel G. Freedman, examines the political evolution of three New York families, from staunch support of FDR and the Democratic party to conviction that the New Deal had run its course and a shift to the Republican party. Among other issues, the book brings home to the Empire State the nationwide change in thinking about welfare.

One of the real-life New Yorkers the book profiles is Timothy Carey, who grew up in a lower-middle-class section of Westchester County. (Carey, whose forebears had been active in Democratic politics, later became a key player in Governor Pataki's 1994 campaign and a high-ranking official in the Pataki administration.) In 1968, Freedman writes, Carey was living in Crotonville when, for the first time, he met families who were subsisting on welfare. The book describes Carey's perception of many of the women he saw around the town:

> Some divorced, some deserted, most were taking public assistance while working off the books as barmaids or waitresses. ... The welfare system, he realized, punished people for working. It penalized them for saving. It turned the honest into cheaters. He could hardly blame the women he knew for learning the lesson well. Those wads of cash they never reported paid the baby-sitter, filled the gas tank, and took the kids to the movies. Wasn't the government supposed to help the people who wanted to help themselves? ...One night he was watching a documentary about the New Deal on public television, and there appeared footage of Harry Hopkins testifying before Congress about the WPA. He was stressing the importance of tying relief to work. That was the kind of aid Tim had heard about from his mother and grandmother, the kind that gave people not only money but also self-respect. How could it have evolved into a program that rewarded you only for sitting on your ass?

(Excerpt from Samuel G. Freedman, *The Inheritance: How Three Families and America Moved from Roosevelt to Reagan and Beyond*, Simon & Schuster, New York, NY, 1996.)

ended up in the Department of Labor, it would have been a work-oriented program from the outset," Moynihan wrote.[14]

---

14 Foreword in *The Prisoners of Charity*, Albany, NY: Public Policy Institute of New York State, 1993, p. vi.

Over the course of several decades, voters in New York and elsewhere — and even many welfare recipients themselves — began to view the program as one that created drastically wrong incentives for recipients. "Many saw that the program did not help its beneficiaries to become economically self-sufficient and, indeed, that it encouraged them to behave badly by working less, avoiding marriage, bearing children out of wedlock, and becoming dependent on governmental support, even across generations."[15]

Public assistance programs of the 1960s and 1970s created strong financial incentives for beneficiaries to avoid earning any money outside the system. Because benefits would drop as income rose, a recipient who found a job might lose up to 70 cents in assistance for every $1 in her paycheck. Despite the Rockefeller reforms and later changes, welfare costs rose slightly during the 1980s and then jumped from 1989 to 1994, when the state's income-maintenance costs reached $4.3 billion.

Welfare Reform in New York

In 1996, Congress passed changes in federal welfare laws that most political observers had considered impossible just a year or two earlier. The Personal Responsibility and Work Opportunity Reconciliation Act set, for the first time since creation of the welfare program in the 1930s, a specific limit — five years — on the time that any individual could collect benefits funded by Washington. It also created specific requirements that recipients seek employment or engage in related activities such as job training. After vetoing two earlier versions, President Clinton signed the federal legislation into law despite harsh criticism from many Democrats, including some members of his own administration and New York's senior senator, Moynihan. Public opinion polls showed consistently that most voters supported major changes in welfare. With the president seeking re-election in 1996, his signature on the bill was widely perceived as an important step toward winning a second term.

New Yorkers were like other Americans in supporting welfare reform — with some important differences. Residents of the Empire State were more likely than those from several other states to support

---

15 Mark Carl Rom, "Transforming State Health and Welfare Programs," in *Politics in the American States: A Comparative Analysis*, Washington, DC: CQ Press, 1999.

government assistance for the poor, and more concerned about how welfare reform might affect children, in an opinion survey conducted in 1999. Residents of the state ranked highest among the five studied in the importance they attached to helping poor children and helping parents pay for child care and health insurance as part of welfare reform.[16]

The 1996 act required states to change their programs to conform broadly with the new federal policies. Unlike some other states, New York provided state-funded financial assistance beyond the five-year limit for which Washington will help pay the bill. This Safety Net Assistance takes the form of cash or, in some cases, direct payment to another party (such as a landlord) or vouchers. Given the state Constitution's insistence on "aid, care and support of the needy," Governor Pataki and the Legislature had little choice but to maintain some form of assistance past the federal time limit when they enacted New York's response in 1997. As Sarah F. Liebschutz observed, "The New York State Welfare Reform Act — in its provisions for assistance to the needy through the Safety Net, expansion of the income disregard, and liberal definition of work — reaffirmed the state's historic liberalism. However, the act's limited exemption from work requirements, residency requirement, substance abuse sanctions, and 'learnfare' program represented changed public expectations about individual behavior."[17]

During the 1997 negotiations in Albany on welfare reform, the Democratic Assembly majority represented the concerns of recipients, blocking benefit cuts before the required five-year cutoff, and those of organized labor, pushing through a prohibition on welfare recipients displacing existing public employees. The Republican majority in the Senate represented the interests of county officials, most of whom were Republicans, in avoiding new costs for localities.

After Reform

The welfare system in New York changed in basic philosophy and approach as a result of both the federal and state laws enacted in the 1990s.

---

16 National Devolution Survey Conducted for the W.K. Kellogg Foundation (Virginia Beach, VA: Bonney and Co., 1999), cited in Sarah F. Liebschutz, ed., *Managing Welfare Reform in Five States: The Challenge of Devolution*, Albany, NY: Rockefeller Institute Press, 2000.

17 Sarah F. Liebschutz, "Welfare Reform in New York: A Mixed Laboratory for Change," in *Managing Welfare Reform in Five States*, ibid.

Earlier, the system had focused simply on determining each client's eligibility and distributing benefit payments. Welfare is now regarded more as it was originally: temporary income support while recipients secure employment and/or child-support payments. Now local social services workers are charged with the often more complicated tasks of "making work pay" — helping and motivating clients to find training, jobs, and child support as well as financial assistance.

A 2002 study by the Office of Temporary and Disability Assistance found that the proportion of adults in the labor force rose after welfare reform, with the largest increases in groups such as single mothers who were most likely to receive welfare payments. In 1995, 49 percent of women who were heads of households were working or engaged in related activities such as job searches or training; by 2005, the figure was 71 percent. After rising steadily before the reforms of the 1990s, teen pregnancy rates and teen births declined. Contrary to warnings by Moynihan and others, child poverty declined, especially when including the effect of the earned income tax credit (EITC), food stamps and other benefits. Such findings echoed those of some other studies nationwide. The report added:

> What is most striking about these findings is that the data clearly show that these successes cannot be solely attributed to the growth of New York State's economy between 1994-2000. Previous periods of economic prosperity — absent welfare reform — had nowhere near the results described in this report. Something else was playing a part in increasing work, raising incomes, and stopping the rise in single parent families.[18]

At the start of the 21st century, welfare was no longer near the top of the political agenda in New York or nationally. Leaders in the Democratic Party, which in past decades had supported more generous assistance policies, rarely spoke of improving conditions for recipients. Any such proposals tended to emphasize providing child care, transportation, wage supplements, or other assistance to help recipients move into the work world. The Republican Party, which had led the charge for reform, focused on other issues. In general, support for continuing existing assistance remained stronger than any desire to reduce benefits.

---

18 *Welfare Reform in New York State: Effects on Work, Family Composition, and Child Poverty*, Albany, NY: Office of Temporary and Disability Assistance, February 2002.

As of 2006, further changes in federal rules challenged New York and other states to increase the proportion of beneficiaries who are working. "Work first" efforts in the decade after the 1996 welfare-reform law had succeeded in bringing the most qualified recipients into the workforce. State officials were considering further steps to connect lower-skilled welfare recipients to training and employment, and working to identify further support mechanisms for individuals who would face the greatest difficulty in obtaining and keeping employment.

After decades of change, New York remained significantly more generous than most other states in providing assistance for the poor. In 2004, the average monthly payment under Temporary Assistance for Needy Families was $892 in New York, more than double the nation-wide average of $417 (living costs are higher in New York as well, al-though that disparity is smaller). Contrary to the picture decades earlier, the proportion of state residents receiving benefits – 1.8 percent of the population – was about the same as the national average. The number of recipients in the state fell sharply — by 70 percent — from 1996 to 2004, compared to a national drop of 61 percent.[19]

Even before the welfare reforms of the 1990s, financial assistance for the poor had become a relatively small portion of state government's social-services budget compared with Medicaid. Declining welfare caseloads and continuing growth in Medicaid during the second half of the 1990s made the funding gap between the two programs even larger. The Office of Temporary and Disability Assistance budget for 2006-07 totaled some $5.2 billion, compared with state spending of more than $45 billion for Medicaid.

The new emphasis on work has led to major policy developments that go far beyond employment requirements and time limits. Increas-ingly, state assistance goes to the "working poor," not just to those who are unemployed and likely to remain that way.

For example, child support has assumed growing importance in the so-cial-services system over the last 25 years. Government administrators at both the federal and state levels first saw enforcement of child support as a means of reducing costs for taxpayers and requiring absent fathers to take responsibility for their offspring. More recently, child support has been increasingly viewed as a means of obtaining additional

---

19 Data from the U.S. Department of Health and Human Services, Administration for Children and Families, reported in *CQ's State Fact Finder 2005*, Washington, DC: CQ Press, 2005.

income for the custodial parent and children; contrary to the former practice of reducing taxpayer-funded benefits by the amount of child support, a certain amount of such support now can be excluded for calculation of benefits.

Child support is also an example of the state's shift from categorizing families as either involved or not involved in the public-assistance system. As recently as the early 1990s, more than half of families involved in the state child-support system also received welfare benefits. By 2000, that proportion was less than one-third.

Financial assistance for child care has also risen dramatically, from less than $300 million a decade ago to nearly $1 billion. Expansion of public health-care plans such as Child Health Plus gave many parents the assurance that their children could be covered without Medicaid eligibility.

A major new source of assistance for low- and moderate-income workers, created in New York during the 1990s, further demonstrates the new consensus that public assistance should be linked to work. The EITC was established as part of the federal income tax system in 1975. The credit is "refundable," meaning that individuals who use it cannot only eliminate their income tax entirely but can receive additional refunds through their state tax returns. State Communities Aid Association, an advocacy group for low-income New Yorkers founded in 1872, built a coalition including business organizations and other nonprofit groups to convince Governor Cuomo and the Legislature to enact a New York version of the EITC in 1994.[20] The state credit later rose to 30 percent of the federal credit. As of 2006, the state credit returned an estimated $745 million to working New Yorkers. The EITC is a major reason that the Empire State's overall tax system is among the most favorable in the nation for low-income workers.

One study of the implementation of welfare reform, in New York and three other states, concluded that the historic change in approach was successful in many ways — but that support for low-income families and individuals must continue regardless of whether they remain on "welfare":

> Fortunately, the risk that TANF would throw many families into poverty has not materialized.... In focusing resources on reducing welfare caseloads, states reallocated their savings in cash assistance to their

---

20 The organization has since been renamed SCAA, the Schuyler Center for Analysis and Advocacy.

budgets for child care, transportation, and other services to support work. Maintaining caseloads at low levels will require a continuing allocation of resources to these services....

Moving families off welfare into employment changes the form of the subsidy to low-wage families from cash assistance to assistance with child care and transportation, but it does not eliminate the need for a subsidy.... While the new world of welfare has just begun to play out, experience so far points to the need for more thought about ways to increase the wages of low-skilled workers.[21]

A New Administrative Structure

Accompanying the 1997 changes to welfare was a restructuring of the state's administration of social services. The Department of Social Services was renamed the Department of Family Assistance and its major functions assigned to two separate agencies, the Office of Temporary and Disability Assistance (OTDA) and the Office of Children and Family Services (OCFS). Employment programs for welfare recipients were transferred to the Labor Department.

OTDA's major responsibilities include administering the dollars New York receives from Washington under the federal block grant program known as Temporary Assistance to Needy Families (TANF). Created as part of the 1996 federal reforms, the block grant gives states significant flexibility in deciding how to use available dollars over six years. In 2000, New York's grant totaled some $2.4 billion. The state used less than half of the total for the cash-assistance programs commonly thought of as "welfare," while other programs received the rest. For instance, TANF dollars fund much of the state's EITC.

In its first few years, the new federal approach was a fiscal boon to states because caseloads had declined since 1995-96, the years on which grant amounts were based. New York and other states were able to use federal funds to provide new services, to reduce state appropriations for existing services, and to build up federal reserves that could be drawn down if caseloads were to rise again in later years. The federal law requires states to spend, on welfare and related programs, at least 75 percent of what they spent in 1995.

---

21 Irene Lurie, *At the Front Lines of the Welfare System: A Perspective on the Decline in Welfare Caseloads*, Albany, NY: Rockefeller Institute Press, 2006, pp. 263-264.

Effective Tax Rates on
Low-Income Workers

With its multifaceted program of financial supports for low-income families and individuals, New York faces a conundrum that may become increasingly important nationally: How can government help the poor without penalizing those who rise into the middle class?

A simple example of the problem is Temporary Assistance, the primary federally supported cash-assistance program. Policy experts and elected officials have structured the program so those who are neediest receive the largest benefits, yet beneficiaries do not lose assistance on a dollar-for-dollar basis when they earn additional income. In New York, those conflicting goals are resolved with a loss of 55 cents in benefits for every added dollar of regular income, allowing recipients to retain 45 cents.

"While not a tax in the strict sense, the reduction in benefits serves as a reduction in buying power on the marginal dollar earned," David Cohen, Denard Cummings and Stuart Poole of the state Budget Division wrote in a journal article. "This person, in effect, is experiencing a marginal tax rate related to TA of 55 percent. The loss of income or benefits from TA (or any other program), therefore, has the disincentive effect of an income tax." High marginal tax rates "can serve as a disincentive to work and may be counter to program goals," the analysts wrote.*

The earned income tax credit is another example. For individuals with incomes below $11,000, the amount of earned-income credit rises by 40 cents on each dollar. At $14,000 and above, the credit declines by 20 percent for each new dollar earned — an effective marginal tax rate of 20 percent. Food-stamp recipients experience an effective marginal tax of 24 percent when income rises above $15,000. Effective marginal tax rates from loss of child-care assistance can eclipse other losses and create "a significant deterrent to additional earnings," the authors wrote. The combination of multiple lost benefits can add up to thousands of dollars at certain income levels.

---

*   David Cohen et al., "Actual Realized Earnings of Low-Income New Yorkers Due to Effective Marginal Tax Rates," in *Journal of Governmental Finance and Public Policy*, New York State Division of the Budget/Rockefeller Institute of Government, Albany, NY, 1, 1 (July 2006).

A mother of two who works 20 hours a week and earns $12,000 a year could have total income of almost $22,000 including food stamps, EITC and other benefits. "If the same mother chose to double her work effort at the same wage, her annual earned income would be $24,000, but her total income from earnings and benefits would only grow by $3,700 to a little over $25,000." In other words, $8,300 of her additional earnings — 69 percent — would effectively be lost due to reductions in benefits.

Even worse, an individual with income between $14,000 and $16,000 could lose more than she gains with added income. At that level, the effective "tax" related to Temporary Assistance is 55 percent; EITC, 27 percent; and food stamps, 24 percent — for a total marginal cost of 106 percent.

What to do about programs that effectively create large marginal tax rates for beneficiaries who work more and thus gain more income? One solution would be for all benefit programs to reach further up the income ladder, well into middle-class territory. But that would be enormously expensive, and would represent a major change in the nature of the nation's political economy.

Improving educational outcomes for low-income students and enhancing job-training opportunities for adults (both easier said than done) would help more New Yorkers attain middle-class incomes without public assistance.

The authors suggested that benefit phase-outs might be restructured so that the marginal losses to recipients from different programs would not take place at the same income levels. The federal child tax credit, available to moderate-income taxpayers, may help families who are losing other benefits, they wrote. The same may be true of a new child tax credit New York's Legislature enacted in 2006. Still, those credits would add up to less than $1,500 per child for most families — some help, but not enough to eliminate the impact of marginal "taxes" on low-income workers.

As of 2006, OTDA's responsibilities included oversight of these benefit programs:

- *Family Assistance*, the cash-benefit program formerly known as Aid to Families with Dependent Children. Families that include a minor child living with one or both parents, or a caretaker relative, are eligible. Adults may receive benefits for up to 60 months during their lifetime. Parents and other adult relatives who can work must do so, or be involved in work-related activities such as training.

- *Safety Net Assistance*, formerly known as Home Relief. Those eligible for this program include single adults, childless couples, children living apart from any adult relative, families of individuals who are unable to work because of alcohol or drug abuse, persons who have exceeded the 60-month limit on assistance, and certain noncitizens who are ineligible for Family Assistance. Recipients must engage in work activities unless they are physically or mentally disabled. Cash assistance is available for two years, after which recipients can receive noncash assistance such as vouchers.

- *Supplemental Security Income*, a federal benefit program for the aged, blind, and physically or mentally disabled who have limited or no other income. New York State supplements the federal benefit amount.

- *Food Stamps*, a federal program that issues vouchers redeemable for food at authorized retail stores. Unlike the above programs, Washington pays the total cost, along with half of the administrative expenses. There is no time limit for families with children. Formerly distributed as cash-like vouchers, food stamps now take the form of debit cards that allow better monitoring of usage and appear more like the payment methods used by the majority of consumers.

- *Home Energy Assistance Program*, which provides grants that help low-income individuals and families pay heating bills or make energy-saving home repairs.

- *Homeless services.* These include capital grants and loans to not-for-profit corporations, charitable and religious organizations, municipalities, and public corporations to acquire, build, and rehabilitate housing for homeless persons. Grants are also available for homelessness intervention services designed to stabilize homeless and at-risk households, and to support single-room-occupancy housing.

OTDA also helps custodial parents — usually mothers — collect child support from noncustodial parents. The agency helps find absent parents, establish legal fatherhood for children, obtain support orders from judges, and collect and enforce support payments. In 2006, the office helped produce some $1.5 billion in such payments to parents. Unlike most other social-services programs, child support is not heavily concentrated in New York City. The city's proportion of all cases statewide is only slightly higher than its share of the population.

Part of OTDA, the Bureau of Refugee and Immigration Affairs, serves immigrants who resettle in New York. The bureau contracts with local service providers around the state to help refugees and legal immigrants find jobs, learn English, and obtain other services. In 2001, the office created a new unit to help undocumented immigrants obtain legal residence.

A State and Local System

New York is unusual among the states in maintaining large administrative functions at both the state and local levels. OTDA does not deliver checks to recipients; local officials do that. The state agency supervises the work of local social-services districts in New York City and the other 57 counties, and provides administrative hearings to individuals who appeal denials of benefits or other decisions at the local level. Applicants are entitled to a "fair hearing" in which a state administrative law judge considers arguments from both sides. The department issues a written decision stating whether the local department of social services was right or wrong. Beyond affecting the individuals immediately involved, decisions by state administrative law judges, which often reverse local officials' rulings, can shape policy for both state and local officials to follow in future actions.

The commissioner of OTDA has the power to remove a local social-services commissioner if charges initiated by the state are substantiated. The power is rarely used. In practice, the state's ability to withhold funding temporarily or otherwise inconvenience local officials provides substantial influence over localities.

Partly because of the dual levels of bureaucracy, overall administrative costs for social services in New York are relatively high. The state's average cost to administer a TANF case was roughly two-thirds higher than the national average as of 1999.[22] The Citizens Budget Commission has estimated that reducing those administrative costs to the national average would save more than $300 million.[23] New information technology has made it possible for state and local officials to eliminate some overlapping functions, and may reduce administrative costs further in coming years.

Paralleling the devolution of responsibility for shaping public assistance programs from Washington to the states, Albany has devolved some functions to counties and New York City. In many areas, the state gives localities broader discretion in setting their own welfare policies than they have enjoyed in decades — including a block grant for child care that localities can use as they see fit, within certain restrictions. At the same time, the new federal and state rules have created some additional responsibilities for local social-services offices — they must, for instance, screen Family Assistance recipients for possible domestic violence.

Office of Children and Family Services

If the income-replacement function of the poorhouse can be thought of as the province of today's Office of Temporary and Disability Assistance, another state agency — the Office of Children and Family Services (OCFS) — might be considered, among other things, the modern successor to the old orphanage.

Under the 1997-98 restructuring of the former Department of Social Services, many programs for children and families were combined with the former Division for Youth to create a new Office of Children and Family Services. Other than cash assistance (provided through OTDA) and health care (through the Health Department), OCFS is responsible for most state-funded programs for families and children.

Most of the office's $3.3 billion budget goes to counties, New York City, and nonprofit service providers for family support and child welfare programs. Working largely through those local agencies, OCFS administers programs that attempt to make families stronger, and to deal with the sometimes tragic results of family breakdown. Those programs:

---

22 Unpublished data from U.S. Department of Health and Human Services, cited in *CQ's State Fact Finder 2001*, p. 302.

23 *Budget 2000 Project: Social Welfare Spending.*

- Help parents find quality child care services.

- Identify and protect abused and neglected children.

- Provide counseling and other services to strengthen families and enable them to avoid foster care.

- Place children in foster care when needed and, when possible, reunite them with parents.

- Find permanent adoptive parents for children who cannot return to birth parents.

- Prepare teens for independent living.

- Protect vulnerable adults from domestic violence.

The agency's other major responsibility is to provide detention and corrective services for individuals under 18 who have been convicted of crimes. The Division of Rehabilitative Services, formerly known as the Division for Youth, operates 45 residential facilities and day placement centers. The agency retains custody of some 2,000 youths, as a result of assignment from family or criminal courts, in a typical year. Rehabilitative efforts include counseling and health, education and employment, and religious services. Although it spends a relatively small share of the OCFS budget, the division represents some two-thirds of the agency's employment (*see Chapter Sixteen for details*).

Child Care

The agency's most wide-ranging program for families entails oversight of, and funding for, child care. As of December 2000, some 550,000 children were in state-certified day-care programs throughout the state, with slightly more than half of those in New York City. Child care has been one of the fastest-growing services funded by state government, owing to available federal funding and the need to help low-income mothers stay off welfare.

In general, families are eligible for state financial assistance for child care if they meet certain income guidelines and need child care to work, look for work, or attend employment training. Child care is guaranteed for individuals who are on public assistance and need to meet work participation requirements. State funding is also guaranteed for one year after public-assistance recipients leave the rolls for a job and need child care. The state sends each county, and New York City, a block grant that allows local officials to tailor expenditures to meet needs as they determine them.

OCFS provides support for people and organizations that are interested in starting day-care programs in their communities. As a general rule, any program planning to serve three or more children for more than three hours a day on a regular basis must obtain a license or registration certificate. The agency sets health and safety standards for some 30,000 day-care providers ranging from centers that care for more than six children at a time in a setting other than a home, to family day-care homes where three to six children are cared for. The agency's key regulatory responsibilities include staffing ratios, ongoing training for directors and staff, and inspections.

The state provides some funding for construction of care centers. It also distributes grants ranging from $300 to $750 to individuals who work in child care and meet certain requirements that encourage continuing education and commitment to remaining in the field. Working through some 40 child care referral agencies throughout the state, OCFS helps families find and assess day-care programs for their children.

Protecting Children

Besides promoting quality child care, OCFS works to protect children from abuse and neglect and to find new homes — temporary or permanent — when necessary. The state's child abuse hotline receives more than 330,000 calls each year — an average of some 900 each day — reporting alleged maltreatment or abuse of children. OCFS initiates investigations of each allegation by county protective-services employees and/or local law enforcement agencies; some two-thirds of reports are determined to be unfounded. Determinations are made at the local level, where most of the heartaches occur and recriminations fall when real abuse goes unrecognized.

The agency also maintains a database of those found culpable of child abuse so certain employers, such as day-care centers, can screen out potential employees with a history of abuse.

Foster Care

When families cannot or will not care for children, local judges can assign individuals up to age 17 to foster care. State funding includes financial support for children not living with their parents, payments to child-care agencies to monitor the care provided by foster parents, and funding for both OCFS and local-government efforts to oversee those agencies and make decisions about children in foster care.

Traditionally and today, state policy has attempted to balance the desire to keep families intact with the imperative of giving children a secure home when parents and other family members do not. Some 26,600 children were in foster care in 2005 in New York. That number represented a drop from nearly 54,000 in 1995; foster-care placements had risen sharply in the late 1980s and early 1990s, in part because of the growth of "crack" cocaine abuse. The great majority of foster children reside in family homes, while perhaps one in ten are in institutions and a smaller number live in group homes.

Many children in family homes live with relatives. Such "kinship care," particularly in New York City, was largely responsible for a sharp increase in the state's foster-care population during the 1980s. The rate of children in foster care rose from around 5 per 1,000 children in 1983 to more than 14 per 1,000 children in 1991. That number has since declined slightly. As of 1993, one study found, the proportion of foster-care children in New York was three times the national average. Foster-care spending in the state was nearly five times as high as in all other states, after adjusting for differences in personal income (given relatively higher incomes in the Empire State, the ratio would have been higher without such adjustment).[24]

Adoption

OCFS oversees regulation of, and in most cases assistance for, more than 4,500 adoptions in the state each year. More than two-thirds of those take place in New York City.

More than 130 adoption agencies operate statewide — one in each county government and New York City, plus more than 70 authorized

24 Ibid.

voluntary agencies. At the end of 1999, some 15,000 children were in foster care with a goal of eventual adoption.

The legal process of adoption can take six months or more from application to placement in a new home. State law requires that the child live in the home at least three additional months before the adoption may be finalized in court.

The state subsidizes adoption of most children who have a disability or are hard to place, with the amount varying depending on the age and needs of the child. Many adopted children also qualify for Medicaid.

As of mid-2006, a listing of children on the state's adoption register, including information about and photos of each child, was available on the Internet through the Office of Children and Family Services web site, *www.ocfs.state.ny.us*.

Labor Policy in New York

In the early to mid-1800s, craftspeople working in their homes and in small shops produced most goods made in the United States. In the decades after the Civil War, most manufacturing moved into factories, where the scale of production was larger and ownership more centralized. Owners of the new factories acquired more economic power, giving them greater ability to set wages and working conditions for employees. With markets no longer local in scale, owners also faced increased rivalry from competitors based in other regions, a new source of pressure to keep costs low. Workers saw a threat to their earning power from new labor-saving technologies, the rising number of available laborers (owing partly to immigration), and a shift in economic importance from those who could provide labor to those who commanded large amounts of capital.

New York was home to some of the first labor organizations to result from the new economic trends, and the state pioneered numerous governmental protections for unions and workers. In the early 1790s, crafts unions of printers, carpenters, and shoemakers formed in New York City, Philadelphia, and Boston to seek higher wages, shorter hours, exclusive union hiring, and other improvements for members. Even earlier, in 1768, New York tailors engaged in "the first authenticated strike" in America, seeking to reverse a cut in wages.[25]

As unions began to gather strength in the early 1800s, employers adopted various tactics in response. Both sides turned to government for advantage in the struggle for economic power. At first, employers were favored, as courts issued rulings hostile to unionization and legislatures ignored most of labor's requests for new laws. Courts in New York and other states held, based on longstanding common law, that unions' efforts to raise wages represented conspiracies against the public in restraint of trade. Over the course of the 19th century, unions came to be regarded as lawful, but the legality of strikes and boycotts remained in question. By the early 20th century, the picture changed dramatically, as elected leaders in Albany enacted numerous laws sought by organized labor.

Labor Starts to Gain Power

In 1829, organized labor achieved its first electoral victory when the Working Men's Party in New York City elected Ebenezer Ford, president of the Carpenters Union, to a seat in the Assembly. Still, major prolabor changes in government policy were slow in coming. Nearly a quarter-century later, in 1853, New York became the first state to legislate a maximum 10-hour day for noncontract workers. The following year, New York City became the first municipality to use public construction bonds to alleviate unemployment through public-works projects.

The rise of industrial centers during and after the Civil War, primarily in the North, led to the birth of a true national labor movement, with many roots in the Empire State. In 1864, labor won an important victory in Albany by blocking passage of a bill that would have authorized fines or imprisonment for union activity. As often happens with interest-group activity in politics and government, success in preventing unwanted legislation galvanized the movement to new strength and helped set the stage for passage of proposals favored by the group. Three years later, New York was one of the first states to authorize the eight-hour day for state workers. (In an illustration of the sometimes decisive role played by the executive branch even then, the legislation

---

25 U.S. Department of Labor, Bureau of Labor Statistics, *A Brief History of the American Labor Movement*, Bulletin 1000, 1970, p. 3.

proved an incomplete victory, as Governor Reuben Fenton refused to enforce it consistently.)

As organized labor continued to grow, so did its support in the halls of state government. In September 1882, the first Labor Day parade was held around Union Square in Manhattan. Five years later, the Legislature in Albany declared Labor Day an official holiday. Four other states did so the same year, and Congress followed suit, creating a national holiday for working men and women in 1894. Labor Day was important to unions because it symbolized official approval of the role that unions played in promoting the rights of workers. To this day, the holiday gives organized labor an annual opportunity to spark public discussion of the status of working men and women (or, in the modern parlance, "working families") and of what should be done to improve their lot.

Of more immediate importance during the 1880s and early 1890s was creation of the key statutory and administrative structures that undergird the state Labor Department and New York's labor laws today.

First came the Bureau of Labor Statistics, reflecting union leaders' recognition that progress would depend partly on dependable information about developments in the marketplace. Next came legislation providing for state inspection of factories, to protect the health and welfare of workers and enforce a new ban on child labor; and an arbitration board, to help resolve labor disputes with as little disruption to company and workers as possible.

New York forged ahead of the national government and other states in establishing a Department of Labor in 1901; the U.S. Department of Labor was created a dozen years later. Unions in the Empire State also played a leading role in building the labor movement nationwide: two of the most important labor leaders in the nation's history were New Yorkers. The first president of the American Federation of Labor was Samuel Gompers, a cigar maker from the Lower East Side of Manhattan. When the federation merged with the Congress of Industrial Organizations in 1955, the first leader of the new national organization was George Meany, a plumber from the Bronx.

Early Legislation

Although children had worked on family farms for centuries, the advent of child-labor laws reflected new concerns sparked by growing indus-

The Labor-Government Connection

Whether using economic power to work with employers, or political strength to deal with leaders in government, organized labor has relied on the power of its numbers for well over a century.

In 1864, the Senate Judiciary Committee, chaired by Senator Charles J. Folger, sent to the floor a bill that became known as the Folger Anti-Strike Bill. Workers held opposition rallies in major cities throughout the state, including one in Manhattan's Tompkins Park that drew thousands. The New York State AFL-CIO traces its history to the Trades Assembly of New York State, created in the wake of the battle over the Folger bill.

One outcome of the unions' successful fight against the legislation was a determination to defeat Senator Folger if he became a candidate for governor, as expected. In 1882, the Republican party nominated Folger. Democrat Grover Cleveland, who had union support as well as a reputation as a reformer after having served as mayor of Buffalo, won election as governor overwhelmingly.

A century later, organized labor remained an important player in state politics. Governor Cuomo credited the Civil Service Employees Association with helping him defeat New York City Mayor Edward I. Koch in the 1982 Democratic primary that led to the first of three Cuomo terms as the state's chief executive. In 2006, labor voices in the Legislature included the president of the New York Central Labor Council, Brian McLaughlin. A Democrat who represented part of Queens in the Assembly, McLaughlin was facing a federal investigation into charges of bid rigging for city lighting contracts. Unions representing government employees and other workers whose jobs depend on public funding – such as New York State United Teachers and Local 1199/SEIU – were consistently ranked among the top spenders on lobbying the Legislature and on campaign contributions to political candidates of both major parties. In addition, unions such as Local 1199 and the Communications Workers of America were closely allied with the new Working Families Party.

trialization in which young workers were supervised not by their parents, but by business managers. The general concern for working children, and union leaders' recognition of the competition they represented for available jobs, led to measures such as laws requiring boys and girls from 8 to 14 to attend school at least 14 weeks a year.

The first labor-related addition to the state Constitution came in 1894, with addition of the present Article I, Section 16, relating to wrongful deaths. Common law in England, and by extension in the United States, provided no right of recovery for survivors in case of wrongful death. Parliament enacted a provision creating such a right in 1846, and New York's Legislature followed suit a year later.

One of the most far-reaching labor laws passed during the early 20th century created government-regulated compensation for workers injured on the job. New York's Legislature enacted "the first modern American compensation law" in 1910.[26] Opposed by some employers, the law was declared unconstitutional in the state courts, although it helped to prompt similar legislation in more than 20 other states over the next two years. Perhaps the most important law ever negotiated by supporters of organized labor and business owners, the program gave injured workers the automatic right to financial compensation while prohibiting negligence lawsuits against the employer. In 1913, unions succeeded in amending the state Constitution to allow such a program, and the Legislature passed new legislation soon thereafter. For employers, the incentive of avoiding lawsuits that previously encouraged workplace safety was replaced by a more immediate incentive, as premiums for workers' compensation coverage were based partly on injury rates in particular workplaces.

The Triangle Fire Leads to More Laws

Although the Legislature created a factory-inspection bureau in 1886, and expanded staffing for the effort thereafter, one of the worst industrial tragedies in the state's history was to occur a quarter-century later. In March 1911, more than 140 workers — mostly young women — died in a fire at the Triangle Waist Company, a shirt manufacturer near Washington Square in Manhattan. The structure was fireproof, but

---

26 Rosen, *A History of Public Health*, p. 411.

some exterior doors were blocked, and most of the workers, on the top floors of a 10-story building, could not reach the single fire escape.

The tragedy drew enormous media coverage and alarmed many in the city and elsewhere. The *Daily Tribune* and *The New York Times* each devoted five pages to the Triangle story the day after the event, and continued with multiple pages on following days. An immediate local investigation revealed the prevalence of unsafe and unhealthy conditions in many factories, including a lack of fire prevention measures or escapes, and inadequate sanitary conditions. The results of this investigation and public pressure following the Triangle fire convinced the Legislature to establish a Factory Investigating Commission whose members included state Senator Wagner, Assemblyman Smith, and the AFL-CIO's Gompers. The commission conducted public hearings and other studies over more than three years, one of the most influential series of hearings and legislation in the state's history.

The Triangle fire proved a good example of advocacy for new legislation galvanized by unforeseen events. Between 1911 and 1914, the Legislature enacted dozens of labor-related laws — more than 40 in 1913 alone.[27] The tragedy dramatically changed the political landscape regarding labor legislation and led to an entirely new level of government regulation of labor conditions.

The commission's work resulted in numerous fire-safety laws as well as others relating to sanitary conditions and working hours for women and children in stores. Other achievements included laws concerning physical examination of children before authorizing their employment; prohibition of employment of children under age 14 in canneries or tenements; compulsory education; prohibition of manufacturing in tenements; sanitary eating, washing, and toilet facilities; and building inspections. The panel proposed minimum-wage legislation, but such a statute did not gain approval until 1933.

Labor's Modern Political Involvement

While labor has long been particularly active in the Democratic Party, in the last half-century or so New York Republicans have often been

---

27 New York State Department of Labor, *Stand Fast! A Chronicle of the Workers' Movement in New York State*, Albany, NY, 1993, p. 17.

supportive of union initiatives as well. Governor Dewey issued an executive order giving state employees the right to unionize and created the beginnings of formal grievance procedures. Governor Rockefeller pushed through the Taylor Law, which guaranteed all public employees the right to organize and required public employers to negotiate with employee organizations (although unions bitterly criticized the statute's retention of a ban on strikes by public workers). Rockefeller also had good relations with many private-sector unions, including construction workers, who saw thousands of jobs created by the governor's public-works projects. Governor Pataki initiated major expansion of the state's Medicaid program with strong support from unionized hospital workers in 1999 and 2002 and received key political support from that union, as well as the AFL-CIO and several other major unions. Today both Democratic and Republican incumbents in the Senate and Assembly are generally endorsed by unions representing state and local government workers; most legislators earn such support by voting consistently as the public-employee unions request.

In addition to making endorsements and contributing to political campaigns, the AFL-CIO and its major constituent unions use the work of their members as an effective way to support favored candidates. Phone banks, in which volunteer campaign workers place thousands of calls to get out the vote, represent a powerful political tool most other interest groups cannot match.

Labor's relationship with state government has grown closer as public-sector unions have achieved growing prominence in the broader labor movement. The American Federation of State, County and Municipal Employees, New York State United Teachers, the Civil Service Employees Association, the Transport Workers Union, and other public-employee unions make up roughly half of the AFL-CIO's 2.5 million members (including retirees) in New York. Tens of thousands of other union members, such as those working in hospitals, depend heavily on government funding as well. The great majority of public employees in the state are unionized. By contrast, in manufacturing, historically a powerhouse for organized labor, fewer than half of workers are now unionized.

At the national level, organized labor tilts strongly to the Democratic Party, raising millions of dollars for presidential and Congressional candidates and engaging in huge grassroots campaigns to generate opposition to Republican candidates. Such is generally not the case in

New York. Here, unions, like other organizations that seek to influence legislation and the budget, tend to support whichever party is in power.

Several public-sector unions were founding sponsors of the Fiscal Policy Institute, a think tank created in 1991 to promote higher taxes and increased spending on education, infrastructure, and other government services. In 1998, the Communications Workers of America and Service Employees International Union led a coalition of liberal organizations in creation of a new statewide political party, the Working Families Party. The party served as a source of political pressure on both Democrats and Republicans to support traditional liberal policies such as a higher minimum wage, increased government spending on education, and universal health care. Taking advantage of New York State's unique election laws, which allow parties to endorse candidates nominated by other parties, the Working Families Party was able to entice support for its proposals from legislative candidates in both major parties. In the 1998 gubernatorial election, the party attracted enough votes to secure automatic ballot status for the following four years — an important step in building political influence. The party has played an important role in convincing local elected officials in several areas of the state to enact "living wage" legislation, which requires companies receiving contracts, subcontracts, or tax subsidies to pay their employees several dollars more than the statutory minimum wage and to provide health benefits. In 2006, it persuaded many legislators to support a requirement that businesses and nonprofit organizations with 100 or more employees provide health benefits costing at least $3 an hour. The proposal dominated much of the year's debate over health care, but was not approved in either the Senate or Assembly.

The Labor Department Today

Nearly a century after the Triangle Waist Co. fire, the role of the state Labor Department was very different from that created by Robert Wagner and Al Smith. As of 2006, the department's mission statement declared: "The New York State Department of Labor supports the economic interests of the people and businesses in New York State." Traditionally, "the economic interests of ... businesses" would have been seen as antithetical to those of workers. With New York chronically lagging behind other states in job growth, the department's outlook had changed.

The evolution in the department's mission partly reflected the philosophy of the Pataki administration, but on a more fundamental level it revealed how much the labor movement had won in the past century. There was no longer any need to argue that employers owed employees a safe place to work; such requirements had been written into law decades ago. Financial protection for workers who were injured on the job or were unemployed because of economic trends beyond their control was well-established, in the form of workers compensation and unemployment insurance. The starkest representation of worker rights — efforts to prevent industrial tragedies such as the Triangle fire — had been largely taken out of state labor departments with the federal government's creation of the Occupational Safety and Health Administration in 1971. OSHA inspects private-sector workplaces and sets rules for workplace safety intended to protect against injuries and occupational diseases.

Whether cause or effect of those trends, or perhaps both, it was also true that, as the 21st century began, organized labor was a much smaller segment of the overall workforce than a few decades earlier. Nationwide 13.5 percent of workers were union members in 2000. Although New York recorded the highest percentage of union members of any state, at just over 26 percent, even that figure represented a significant decrease from several decades earlier. Only in the public sector did unions still represent a majority of workers; that reality helps explain why public-employee unions had become more politically powerful than their counterparts in manufacturing, construction and other areas of the private sector.

Today the state Labor Department's main functions include:

- Administering the unemployment compensation system through which recently unemployed workers receive financial assistance.

- Helping workers develop and maintain job skills, including managing the state's welfare-to-work efforts, while helping employers find qualified employees.

- Enforcing laws and regulations regarding wages, salaries, and other conditions of employment, as well as safety and health standards in the workplace.

- Developing labor statistics in conjunction with the federal Labor Department.

The commissioner of labor is appointed by the governor with the consent of the Senate. Governors traditionally ensure that a candidate for the commissioner's office is acceptable to the state AFL-CIO and/or leaders of major unions before making an appointment. The Labor Department maintains a number of advisory and regulatory boards; such committees often include a mix of members nominated by labor organizations and by representatives of businesses or other regulated parties.

Unemployment Insurance

Decades after the labor movement won laws intended to make the workplace safer and support individuals who had been hurt on the job, the Depression sparked efforts to help those who had lost a job. Governor Lehman and the Legislature enacted the Unemployment Insurance Law in 1935. The following year, some 103,000 employers started contributing 1 percent of covered payroll to a benefits fund; the rate rose to 2 and 3 percent in the following two years. By January 1938, when unemployed workers began collecting benefits, the fund stood at more than $100 million. Some 438,000 individuals received benefits within the first four months.[28]

UI benefit payments accounted for some $3.8 billion of the Labor Department's $4.7 billion budget in 2006. Benefits are available for up to 26 weeks to workers who have lost a job for economic reasons or, in some cases, who have been dismissed for cause. A relatively small number of workers whom the department considers unlikely to find a job quickly may be allowed to use UI benefits to start a business.

For decades, the "unemployment line" was an emblem of bad economic times. In recent years the Labor Department has established a computerized telephone claims system to determine eligibility and collect other information. As a result, individuals seeking work and UI benefits need not report regularly to an unemployment office. The telephone system processed about 85 percent of initial claims in 2000.

The UI system is administered jointly by the federal government and the states. The dual administration has implications for both policy

---

28 *The New York Red Book 1938*, p. 278.

and finances. Under President Clinton, for instance, the U.S. Labor Department issued regulations allowing states to make unemployment benefits available to workers who take family or medical leaves. New York has not chosen to do so. Federal rules include broad stipulations as to the level of reserves that states must maintain in their UI funds, but states retain certain authority over those reserves. In 1998, at the request of business groups, New York allowed a number of employers to pre-pay part of the following year's unemployment taxes. The state's reserves rose to a level that enabled the state to reduce UI tax rates, saving employers some $400 million in 1999.

Job Services

Workers who file for unemployment benefits are among those who use the department's job-placement services, which are open to all New Yorkers. In the early 1990s, the Labor Department restructured its regional employment offices into "one-stop shopping" centers for employment-related programs. Offices of the Division of Employment Services offer career-related assistance and other DOL programs in a single location. At least one office operates in almost every county; larger counties such as Erie and the boroughs of New York City have more than one. Staff at these centers have been cross-trained in various department services so they can address more completely the needs of employers and job seekers. More recently, the agency has worked with regional Workforce Investment Boards, local governments and non-profit organizations to create joint employment centers with an even broader array of services.

Jobseekers can search for work by visiting a Division of Employment Services office. Job listings are also available through the DOL web site (*www.labor.state.ny.us*), where individuals can post resumes as well. As of fall 2006, the site listed the jobs with the most expected openings in New York as construction carpenters, math and science teachers, medical and public health workers, chemical equipment controllers, and models.

The Labor Department encourages businesses to list job openings in its data bank, a free service. The department also holds job fairs around the state, typically bringing together scores of employers and hundreds of job seekers. The department can provide targeted or customized recruitment, as well as preliminary screening and testing, to meet the hiring needs of individual businesses.

Regulating Wages

While two major functions of the Labor Department — providing job services and unemployment insurance — are largely uncontroversial, the same cannot be said of another major departmental responsibility: regulating wages. As of January 1, 2006, the New York State minimum wage was $6.75 per hour, and scheduled to increase to $7.15 as of January 2007. The federal minimum was $5.15 per hour. The Legislature approved the state-level increase in 2003, over Governor Pataki's objections that a $2 premium from the federal minimum would discourage job growth in the state.

The state Labor Department's Division of Labor Standards enforces state laws concerning minimum wages, hours of work, child labor, and payment of wages. The minimum wage applies to all employees except those in occupations specified in statute, such as certain farm workers and restaurant workers for whom the legal wage may be met by including tips.

One of the most significant Labor Department activities — and a source of controversy — concerns prevailing wages for public construction projects. During and after the Depression, legislatures in many northern states enacted prevailing-wage laws to ensure that local contractors would not be underbid by out-of-state construction companies desperate to find work. Article 1, Section 17, of the state Constitution requires that workers on public projects be paid at least "the rate of wages prevailing in the same trade or occupation in the locality within the state where such public work is to be situated," and state Labor Law provides more detailed rules.

To fulfill these requirements, the Labor Department issues wage schedules, on a county-by-county basis, that contain minimum rates of pay for different work classifications. Contractors bidding on a public job must include such wages in their bid specifications and post wage schedules on the construction site so workers know the wages to which they are entitled. In practice, prevailing wages are almost always the union wage applicable in a given region of the state. On receiving a complaint that a given contractor is not paying prevailing wages, the department's Bureau of Public Work can request certified payroll records, daily time sheets, proof of payment of wages and other records from employers to determine whether the complaint is legitimate. Disagreements between workers and employers often center on classification questions, such as whether a particular part of a job must be performed by a skilled carpenter or a lower-skilled, lower-paid worker.

Prevailing wages apply not only to state government but to localities and school districts. Local officials commonly complain that the laws drive up their costs and make management of construction projects more difficult, leading to delays and other problems. Defenders of the prevailing-wage system argue that, by paying union-level scale, public entities increase the likelihood that they will avoid errors caused by inexperienced workers.

Laws affecting young workers still reflect the concern that education come first. Full-time school is compulsory for minors up to age 16. Those under 14 may not be employed at all, with certain exceptions including farming and newspaper delivery. Minors aged 14 and 15 may work after school and during vacation, but not in factory jobs. Legislation enacted in the early and mid-1990s limits the number of hours individuals aged 14 to 17 can work during school weeks.

Workers' Compensation

Alone among major labor-related programs, workers' compensation is administered outside the Labor Department, by the separate Workers' Compensation Board. The chair of the board is also its administrative head. State Workers' Compensation Law governs the system through which employees who are injured on the job are automatically entitled to financial benefits that replace lost wages. Employers pay for the benefits through insurance premiums.

Workers' compensation developed nationally in the early 1900s after worker injuries grew dramatically with the growth of industry. Before enactment of the system, some injured workers found it necessary to take employers to court. Labor advocates bitterly criticized the delays in compensation, or even lack of compensation, that sometimes resulted. Employers, on the other hand, found it costly and time-consuming to go to court to settle disputes. The 1916 legislation represented a balance of those interests.

The Workers' Compensation Board consists of 13 individuals appointed by the governor with the consent of the Senate; the governor also designates the chair and vice chair. The agency's administrative law judges hear disputed claims for compensation and render decisions; cases may be appealed to a four-member panel of the board or, in some cases, to the entire board. The board's administrative costs are funded through assessments on workers' comp premiums paid by employers.

State laws across the country require employers to provide workers' compensation coverage. Employers in New York can purchase workers' comp coverage through private insurance companies or through the State Insurance Fund. Companies also have the option of self-insuring if they demonstrate the financial ability to do so, either individually or through group trusts. Some 12,600 private- and public-sector employers were self-insured as of mid-2001, according to the Workers' Compensation Board.

The Legislature created the State Insurance Fund in 1914 to provide a government source of workers' comp coverage. Some states, in creating similar programs, allowed only government-sponsored coverage, although few states still do so. The fund is administered by a board of eight commissioners, appointed by the governor with the consent of the Senate. Governor Cuomo and the Legislature used the insurance fund as a source of general state revenue several times in the 1980s and 1990s, taking $1.3 billion from its reserves to balance the state budget. Some legislators have called unsuccessfully for privatizing the fund, so coverage would be provided exclusively by the private sector, as is the case with most other forms of insurance.

Under workers' compensation programs in New York and most other states, employees who have been injured or developed work-related illnesses receive financial benefits based on their regular wages and the type of injury. As of 2006, the maximum wage-replacement benefit in New York was $400 a week.

The state's policies toward workers' compensation are created in a legislative balancing act that takes into account two primary organizations — the New York State AFL-CIO and The Business Council of New York State Inc. — in considering the interests of workers and employers and generally combining a benefits increase sought by labor with other changes proposed by business. An exception came in 1990, when Senate and Assembly leaders negotiated benefit increases for both workers' compensation and unemployment insurance while including none of the provisions sought by employers.

Six years later, Governor Pataki pushed through the Legislature several proposals, bitterly opposed by union leaders, that were intended to reduce premiums for the compensation program. In a multiyear effort, the Business Council and other employer groups had made workers' compensation costs part of the political debate over New York's loss of more than 500,000 jobs in the early 1990s. The business representatives cited state Insurance Department figures showing that average premiums had more than doubled from 1988 to 1992, and sparked press coverage that changed the image of workers' compensation from merely a program that helped injured workers to a costly competitiveness problem for the state. After the 1996 legislation, which also created managed-care programs for workers' compensation and instituted other changes, average premiums fell by more than 30 percent over the following five years. Along with the legislation, the Insurance Department created new regulatory pressure on insurers to reduce rates; that played a role in the premium reductions, as well. During his 2006 gubernatorial campaign, Eliot Spitzer pledged to reform the workers' compensation system so benefits for injured workers could be increased, and employer premiums reduced. One step toward reducing overall costs was expected to be a time limit on benefits for "permanent partial" injuries, which constitute a small minority of claims but a majority of costs.

Chapter Sixteen

PUBLIC PROTECTION

Key points:

- Criminal law and the criminal-justice system are primarily the responsibility of states and local governments, although federal criminal law has expanded significantly in recent years.

- Crime rates are down sharply, especially in New York City, where new management approaches rely heavily on continuous performance measurement.

- The new challenge of preventing terrorist attacks makes cooperation among police and other agencies at all levels of government more important than ever — yet such teamwork is still developing.

Protecting individuals and property from harm is the fundamental responsibility of government. As mentioned in Chapter One, *making the rules* is one of the main tasks American citizens assign to their state governments. Most criminal laws, like most statutes governing business and other civil relationships, are enacted at the state level and are enforced by a combination of state and local government efforts.

One essential principle (of the American founders) was the vesting of most coercive power in the states and restriction of the authority of the federal government. That was particularly so in the case of criminal law and its enforcement. It was felt that the exercise of criminal justice was best retained by the states. There its abuse could best be controlled by the people, who, through close surveillance of an office holder and control of the ballot box, would protect individuals against the abuse of law enforcement authority.[1]

The September 11, 2001, terrorist attacks prompted a major new body of federal and state laws intended to deter further attacks. Those laws are part of an evolving mix of federal and state law-enforcement activities, under the commonly used rubric of "homeland security," that are expanding governmental power in certain areas and sharply increasing Washington's involvement in the broader field of public protection. The vital need to prevent future attacks increases the importance of one of the longstanding, fundamental challenges facing the criminal-justice system: functioning in a coordinated way, rather than as discrete organizations and individuals.

This chapter reviews the ways that state government works to protect New Yorkers from criminals, as well as from natural disasters and from the new threat of potential terrorist attacks.

Structure of the Criminal Justice System

The founders' belief that the states should write and enforce the criminal laws was reflected in early Supreme Court rulings that there could be no common-law crime against the United States: For any offense to be considered a federal crime, Congress would have to make it so by statute. The high court reinforced the division between federal and state actions in this arena as recently as 1995, saying the Constitution withholds from Congress "a plenary police power that would authorize enactment of every type of legislation."[2]

---

1   Herbert A. Johnson, *History of Criminal Justice*, Cincinatti, OH: Anderson Publishing Co., 1988, p. 197.
2   *United States* v. *Lopez*, 514 U.S. 549, 566 (1995).

In recent decades, Congress has enacted a growing body of federal criminal law. According to one study, of all federal crimes enacted since 1865, more than 40 percent have been created since 1970. The USA PATRIOT Act,[3] enacted several weeks after the September 11, 2001, terrorist attacks, significantly expanded federal criminal legislation in areas such as banking, money laundering, government surveillance, immigration and terrorism. Despite the growing body of federal statutes, only an estimated one in 20 criminal prosecutions in the country is for federal offenses.[4] The great majority of arrests — for murder, rape, and other violent crimes; property crimes such as larceny, burglary, and arson; and petty motor-vehicle offenses — are for violations of state laws. Most authority for enforcing the law is dispersed further, through the election of prosecutors and appointment of police officers at the local level.

Many nations take a very different approach. Canada, for instance, has a nationwide criminal code and a unified law enforcement agency, the Royal Canadian Mounted Police.

Public protection remains one of the essential building blocks of every community in New York, and of state government. It starts with the Legislature's determination of what constitutes a crime. Four other major centers of activity bring together the efforts of every level of government in the state — villages, towns, cities, counties, and the state itself. The four groups of actors, which together make up the criminal justice system, are:

- *Police.* Most police in the state are employed by municipalities, although more than 5,000 members of the State Police, conservation officers, and other peace officers work for state government.

- *Prosecutors and the courts.* In each of the state's 62 counties, including each of the five boroughs of New York City, voters elect district attorneys who are responsible for bringing charges against and seeking conviction of persons who are suspected of crimes. Although chosen at the local level, these public prosecutors are paid by state government. The

---

3   The full title of the law is the Uniting and Strengthening America by Providing Appropriate Tools Required to Intercept and Obstruct Terrorism Act of 2001.

4   *The Report of the ABA Task Force on the Federalization of Criminal Law*, Washington, DC: American Bar Association, 1998.

criminal courts where cases are decided also represent a combination of state and local authority, as explained in Chapter Six.

- *Prisons and jails.* The state Department of Correctional Services operates 69 correctional facilities, which house inmates serving sentences of a year or more. Each county outside New York City has its own jail for convicted criminals who are serving less than a year, while the city itself is home to the huge Rikers Island facility. Most of the local jails also hold individuals who have been arrested and are awaiting court action. Roughly 94,000 adults are incarcerated in the state, with just over two-thirds of those in state prisons.

- *Probation and parole.* Courts sometimes sentence convicted criminals to periods of official supervision known as probation, which is the responsibility of county and New York City officials. After serving time in prison, many offenders are released on parole, another form of supervised freedom, administered by state government.

Clearly, the criminal justice system includes a broad range of agencies at different levels of government. That complexity has always complicated efforts to limit and redress crime. Throughout New York's history, state policymakers have created new administrative structures in attempts to make the criminal justice system more effective, with varying degrees of success. Such efforts continue today.

New York State spent nearly $5 billion on public safety in the 2004-05 fiscal year, according to the Office of the State Comptroller. Roughly 45 percent of that was for prisons and youth rehabilitative facilities. Federal funding to the state for public safety grew sharply after the September 11, 2001, terrorist attacks — from $306 million in fiscal 2001 to $1.7 billion in fiscal 2005. The state distributes much of the new funding to local law enforcement officials and other first responders. Under longstanding aid programs, federal dollars also help pay for such things as housing felons who are illegal aliens and Medicaid, which the state increasingly has used to pay for certain youth rehabilitative services.

In 1776, when New York and other American colonies declared their independence from Great Britain, one of the most important functions of every state was to raise the militia to conduct the war effort.

After more than two centuries, the military forces of state government consisted mostly of part-time members who were called to service only during civil emergencies or natural disasters. Hundreds of such individuals reported for duty after the 9/11 terrorist attacks, and many have been engaged in active military operations in Afghanistan, Iraq, and elsewhere in the wake of those events.

Crime in New York

While much of the world has tended to see New York — New York City in particular — as crime-ridden, the reality shown by official statistics is more positive than television shows might suggest. In 2003, the state ranked 18th-highest in the country for frequency of violent crimes, adjusted for population.[5] Such offenses include murder/manslaughter, rape, and aggravated assault, for each of which New York's rate was lower than the national average; and robbery, where New York's was higher. The state's overall rate of 466 violent crimes per 100,000 residents was slightly better than the national average, and significantly better than those in the other most populous states.

The rate of property crimes in New York was also below the U.S. average — more than one-third lower. Those crimes include burglaries, larcenies, and motor-vehicle theft; New York's rate in each category was lower than the national rate.

Crime rates throughout the state fell in the late 1990s, as they did nationally. The decline in New York was among the most dramatic in the nation, driven largely — though not exclusively — by New York City. From 1998 to 2002, the city's "index crime" rate dropped by 29 percent, more than twice the average decline in counties outside the city. Many observers attributed the city's growing safety to more sophisticated crime analysis and control by the local police — one of the nation's leading users of the tool known as performance management *(see Chapter Twenty for more on performance management)*. Another factor may have been a drop in the number of young males — the population cohort most likely to commit crimes — although such demographic change also occurred in locations where crime rates did not fall as sharply.

---

5 Federal Bureau of Investigation, Crime in the United States 2004, U.S. Department of Justice, Washington, DC, 2005.

Whatever the cause, the sharp drop in crime represented a major improvement in New Yorkers' quality of life. The total number of violent crimes in 2004 was down by some 86,000 from a decade earlier — meaning a statewide average decline of more than 200 assaults, rapes, murders and other violent crimes *every day*. After such reductions, crime took a lower profile as a political issue, compared to where it had been from the late 1960s through much of the 1980s. The death penalty, for instance, was a significant campaign issue for most of that period. In 2006, although the future of capital punishment remained in question, there was little debate on the issue in statewide or legislative campaigns.

The Penal Law

Murder, rape, arson, and burglary are crimes in New York because the Legislature has decreed it so — as have legislatures in all other states, although the specifics differ. The first statutory provisions in each jurisdiction codified elements of the common law and colonial laws established by European rulers.

The broad parameters of legal definitions of most serious crimes are now well-established. Yet the government's response to such offenses continues to evolve. New York State went more than 20 years with no capital punishment statute before Governor Pataki and the Legislature enacted a new in 1995. That law, which did not result in any executions, was ruled unconstitutional by the Court of Appeals in 2004; once again, the Legislature and a new governor will decide whether to enact a new statute. New York and most other states have also created harsher penalties for young offenders who are convicted of violent crimes in recent years. Like most actions by the Legislature, such changes occur because of a combination of policy arguments and changing public attitudes. In other words, they are, in part, political decisions.

Article 1 of New York's Penal Law states its broad purposes — in effect, the purposes of the entire criminal justice system — to be:

- Proscribing conduct that "unjustifiably and inexcusably causes or threatens substantial harm to individual or public interests," and giving fair warning of such proscription and the consequences that individuals or organizations might bear for violations.

- Differentiating between "serious and minor offenses," and providing "proportionate" penalties for them.

- Providing "an appropriate public response" to individual offenses, "including consideration of the consequences of the offense" for the victim, his or her family, and the community.

- Insuring public safety by deterring offenses, rehabilitating offenders, and confining them "when required in the interests of public protection."

The purposes of criminal-justice laws and systems in every state are more or less the same, although not every state's penal statute defines the ideas as clearly as does New York's.

The current Penal Law was enacted in 1965, four years after Governor Rockefeller named an advisory commission to develop the first comprehensive revision of the statute since 1881. Such periodic recodifications of major statutes allow the Legislature to connect related sections of law that have been added piecemeal over the years, and to respond in statute to case law developed by the courts, as well as to make policy changes.

The previous statute classified crimes by alphabet, while the current law, which became effective in 1967, classifies them by subject. The new law made substantive changes such as codifying a case-law provision that criminal liability usually is not excused by a mistaken understanding of fact or law. It also created the offense of "patronizing a prostitute" to allow for prosecution of the patron as well as the prostitute.

In certain cases, individuals 18 and under who commit crimes are designated youthful offenders and have a conviction set aside. The law gives judges greater sentencing discretion in such cases, and convictions are not considered in any future prosecutions as multiple-felony offenders (*see more details later in this chapter*).

The revised New York Penal Law, based partly on proposals from the American Law Institute, influenced reforms in other states, including California, Texas, Michigan, Connecticut, and Delaware.

Felonies, Misdemeanors, and Violations

Serious criminal charges are classified either as felonies or misdemeanors. Under New York's Constitution, an "infamous crime," or felony, usually requires indictment by a grand jury. The Penal Law provides that a felony is any offense for which a prison sentence of more than a year may be imposed. Changes to the law enacted in 1965 included major revisions to the state's sentencing structure. Felonies are grouped into letter classifications from A to E and subclassifications, with A-1 felonies the most serious. The classification system allows the code to provide sentences for each group rather than a particular sentence for every crime.

Under the law, only felonies and misdemeanors are "crimes." A misdemeanor may lead to imprisonment of 15 days to a year and/or a fine. Lesser offenses are violations, which can be punished by up to 15 days in jail; and traffic infractions, as defined by the Vehicle and Traffic Law.

Evolving Concepts of
What the Law Should Proscribe

Historically, the main purpose of criminal laws in America — as in the European nations from which most of its early settlers came — was to protect life, physical safety, and property from damage inflicted by others. Laws in the Dutch and English colonies were also influenced heavily by religious and moral beliefs, so that adultery, for instance, was considered a serious crime in certain places.

Beliefs concerning which acts were so immoral as to be outlawed changed over time. When the Legislature enacted the Penal Law in 1965, the two bills repealed provisions designating adultery and consensual sodomy as crimes. Opposition to those repeals led to agreement on chapter amendments that restored the two crimes. In his approval memorandum, Governor Rockefeller wrote: "It was evident that the main bills would not have passed" in the Legislature without assurance that the crimes of adultery and consensual sodomy would be retained.[6]

---

6   Memorandum of Approval, Chapters 1037-1039, Laws of 1965.

However, the Court of Appeals ruled in 1980 that the consensual-sodomy law violated the U.S. Constitution because it outlawed such behavior for unmarried individuals but not married couples.[7] Other state laws have been effectively made moot by federal court rulings. Examples include the issue of when states may make abortion illegal, decided by the U.S. Supreme Court in *Roe* v. *Wade* and other rulings.

During the latter decades of the 20th century, governors and legislatures expanded criminal and other laws into areas that had not been contemplated earlier, displaying greater interest in restricting individual choice to promote public safety. A 1984 statute, for instance, made New York motorists the first in the nation required to wear seatbelts. Starting in 2001, the Vehicle and Traffic Law made it a traffic infraction, punishable by a fine up to $100, to drive while using a mobile phone. In 1966, the Legislature approved a ban on motorcycle riding without a helmet. The law was controversial for a number of years. In 1989, the Legislature went further, requiring helmets for bicycle passengers under age 5; five years later, the law was extended to riders under 14. In 2005, skateboarding was made subject to the helmet requirement. Critics note, among other things, that it's virtually impossible for police to enforce the bicycle and skateboarding laws consistently, creating the possibility of discriminatory enforcement.

Enforcement of many laws varies dramatically from locality to locality, and from time to time within given jurisdictions, according to local sentiments or the priorities of police leadership. In 1999, State Police leaders organized a Buckle Up New York campaign to remind motorists of the importance of wearing seatbelts. During three 10-day enforcement blitzes, police throughout the state issued more than 130,000 tickets — some 71 percent of the total for the entire previous year. The goal was to increase compliance with the state seatbelt law from 75 to 85 percent. Such a goal was not set in the seatbelt law enacted 15 years earlier by Governor Cuomo and the Legislature, but instead was determined by police leaders implementing the law.

Some laws are commonly ignored. For instance, millions of New Yorkers gamble illegally each year in football pools, poker, and other pursuits with little fear of arrest, despite a prohibition on most private

---

7   *People v. Onofre*, 1980, 51 N.Y 2d 476, 434 N.Y.S. 2d 947

gambling. (The state itself has contributed to a changed moral perception of the issue by coaxing citizens to gamble; *see Chapter Ten*.)

The Legislature enacts significant changes to the Penal Law almost every year. The 2000 session, for instance, created a new form of crime called "hate crimes." That statute provides longer sentences for individuals who commit assault, murder, and certain other crimes because of "a belief or perception" regarding the victim's race, sexual orientation, or other characteristic. That year's legislative action also included significant changes regarding sexual assault, including designation of new crimes and longer sentences for individuals repeatedly convicted of sex-related offenses. State leaders seldom undertake any systematic review of how well criminal laws are enforced, let alone what effect changes in the law have on crime. Understanding any such effects, and analyzing the need for further statutory reform, typically depend on less formal input from criminal-justice professionals.

Besides creating new fields of law, governors and the Legislature make significant adjustments in treatment of crimes. In recent years, the Penal Law's provisions regarding sex-related crimes have changed significantly. Some such changes involved toughening of penalties. New York is one of many states that has also questioned the traditional ideal of rehabilitation with regard to certain sex offenders, particularly those with records of violence.

Elected leaders have increasingly sought to personalize media coverage and public discussion of crime, in part by "naming" laws after high-profile victims. One of the first in New York was "Megan's Law," which created the state Sex Offender Registry. The law, like similar statutes in some other states, is named for a New Jersey girl who was raped and killed by a previously convicted sex offender. In 2002, "Sean's Law" commemorated Sean French, a Columbia County teenager killed in a drunk-driving accident, by allowing judges to suspend immediately a junior driver's license or permit upon a driver's first appearance in court. Kendra's Law, adopted in 1999 after a mentally ill man pushed Kendra Webdale in front of an oncoming subway train, provides for court-ordered treatment for some individuals living outside residential mental-health centers.[8]

---

8   Not all such statutes apply to the Penal Code. "Alysa's Law," Chapter 1 of the Laws of 2001, amended the Social Services Law to require barriers around swimming pools and bodies of water on the grounds of family day-care homes. Alysa Orzolick, 2 years old, died in a 2000 accident in North Tonawanda.

Another such statute is "Jenna's Law," which eliminated the possibility of parole and increased post-release supervision for certain felony offenders. Governor Pataki made the proposal a centerpiece of his 1998 State of the State address after Jenna Grieshaber, a nursing student, was murdered by a paroled felon in Albany. Pataki had proposed such changes the year before, but could not win approval in the Assembly. In 1998, with the Grieshaber family helping create public pressure, both houses of the Legislature approved the measure.

"Jenna's Law" is among various changes in recent years that have reduced judicial or administrative discretion in punishing criminals. Critics of such changes say that longer punishment will not necessarily deter future crimes, and that individual judges or parole officials should apply their experience and discretion to specific cases. Pataki and other supporters argue that New Yorkers should not be subjected to repeated violent crimes from particular individuals. Voters tend to agree with that sentiment.

The Police

At the most fundamental level, public protection in New York and elsewhere starts with the individual, the family, and other members of the community. If every police officer in the state were on duty 24 hours a day, the resulting security force would still not be enough to keep an eye on more than 19 million state residents and to ensure that none were engaging in criminal activity. The existence of civilization requires that most people behave in a law-abiding manner most of the time.

In early New York, the tendency of people to obey social norms, for reasons of self-interest as well as moral beliefs, was reinforced by the same factors that helped maintain order in the European countries whence early settlers came. In these mostly homogeneous societies, "ideals were shared and class distinctions caused deferential obedience rather than conflict." Only "moderate law enforcement needs (existed in the) agrarian and manorial society." For fully half a millennium, starting in the early 14th century, local constables and justices of the peace maintained order despite their relative inefficiency and lack of significant power.[9]

---

9   Johnson, *History of Criminal Justice*, p. 171.

Commercial and industrial development in the late 1700s and the 1800s gave people greater freedom to travel and allowed social groups to intermingle. Crime increased, as did the need for more highly developed forces of law. In 1762, the Common Council of New York City created a permanent paid force of night watchmen to replace an unpopular and inefficient system in which every able-bodied man was required to serve one night a month. In rural areas of the state, sheriffs — and, when needed, posses — were in charge of maintaining public order well into the 1800s.

Given the state's control over local affairs, the Legislature's approval was needed when New York City created a regularly paid police force in 1844. Within a few years, as appointments to the force depended on Democratic leaders in Tammany Hall, critics charged that the Municipal Police Force was filled with corruption. In addition, many residents openly disobeyed state laws prohibiting alcoholic beverages, and neither the city's elected leaders nor the police showed much interest in enforcing them. The Legislature, dominated by upstate Republican members, enacted a statute in 1857 abolishing the local force and creating a Metropolitan Police Force, with commissioners appointed from Albany. For a short time, the city had two police forces, until disputes over enforcing prohibition and other issues resulted in violent confrontation settled by the state-controlled New York National Guard. A decision by the Court of Appeals reinforced the controlling authority of the state, and the Municipal Police Force was eliminated. Local rule in the city was restored in 1870.

Over succeeding decades, other cities, towns and counties followed New York City in creating local police forces. The Nassau County Police Department, established in 1925, is now the second-largest local force in the state and among the biggest in the nation, with some 4,000 members.

Some 465 police agencies were at work throughout New York State in 2004. California, with 16 million more residents and a larger land mass, had slightly fewer police agencies than New York. Texas, on the other hand, had far more, with 996.

As of 2004, New York had more full-time, sworn police officers than any other state except California. The Empire State's 86,481 officers represented a ratio of some 45 law-enforcement personnel for every 10,000 residents — the highest level of any state's. New York City, in particular, has a high ratio of police to residents — some 60 per 10,000 residents, compared with a national average around 25.[10]

State government makes the rules under which local police departments operate. The Criminal Procedures Law governs arrests and many other police activities. As it does with other public employees, the state also governs relationships between local elected officials and the police they employ. State law requires, for instance, that contract disputes between localities and police unions be submitted to an arbitrator whose decision is binding on both parties. Many mayors complain that mandated, binding arbitration gives police unions — the rule applies to paid firefighters as well — an unfair advantage and drives up costs for uniformed services. Unions argue that such arbitration is needed to ensure fair settlements, given that strikes by public employees are illegal.

The existence of such mandates on local governments is one aspect of the politically influential role played by police unions — a role increasingly sought by other unions, such as those representing corrections officers. Candidates for office consider it advantageous to be endorsed by police groups to show that they are "tough on crime" and often seek to curry their favor while in office.

The political influence of police unions in New York began in the late 18th century. The New York City Patrolmen's Benevolent Association lobbied successfully for an eight-hour workday by 1901. Local police organizations in Buffalo and Rochester were also among the first in the country.

In general, Albany maintains little involvement in the day-to-day operations of local police and sheriff's departments. When New York City leaders decided to make major changes in the Police Department's crime-fighting approach in the mid-1990s, for instance, they needed no approval from Albany. On the other hand, the city did require statutory approval earlier in the 1990s for a tax increase devoted to paying for additional police officers. Similarly, the Genesee County sheriff's office and other local authorities created a "restorative justice" program — emphasizing restitution, victim assistance, and community-based sentencing — in the 1980s. Their ideas, representing dramatic changes from traditional practice, did not require approval from state officials other than the judges hearing each individual case. Since then, though, state law has been changed to make it easier for courts to require that

---

10 *Crime in the United States*; U.S. Census Bureau.

criminals make restitution to victims. Local control over police agencies allows different approaches that can lead to innovation and better practices. On the other hand, it may also result in significantly varying levels of professionalism from one police agency to another.

The State Police

The Legislature established the State Police in 1917 to provide protection to rural areas still served only by constables and sheriffs. New York was well behind some other states in this regard. Texas created its Rangers in 1835; Pennsylvania, the State Constabulary in 1903.

Creation of the New York State Police followed a 1913 murder during a payroll robbery in Westchester County, then a rural area with no local police department. The victim, a construction foreman named Sam Howell, identified his attackers before he died, but the suspects escaped. Howell's employer, Moyca Newell, and her friend, Katherine Mayo, initiated the movement to form a State Police department to provide police protection to rural areas. The first superintendent of the department, George Fletcher Chandler, named the agency's original training facility Camp Newayo in honor of the two women.

The Pennsylvania and New York State forces introduced higher standards for officers, including training and disciplinary requirements. Because they reported to central authorities at the state level, the two forces were better equipped than local agencies to base promotions on merit and avoid political pressure.[11]

Professionalization of the force also included creation of the Bureau of Criminal Investigation and crime laboratory. Opening in 1936, the two new offices provided important resources for assisting local police departments as well as enhancing the State Police's own investigations.

When a nationwide network of organized-crime leaders arranged a conference in Apalachin, Tioga County, in 1957, the need for specialized investigation and intelligence efforts became apparent. The division created its first Criminal Intelligence Unit the following year, with 26 members initially assigned. This was the vanguard of what would become a broader effort to fight organized crime. Today investigators in

---

11 Johnson, *History of Criminal Justice*, p. 250.

the unit work cooperatively with the Organized Crime Task Force in the attorney general's office (*see later in this chapter*).

One of the largest police agencies in the nation, the modern Division of State Police employed 5,631 as of October 2004, according to Justice Department data.[12] State-level law-enforcement agencies in California, Texas and Pennsylvania had larger staffs. Municipal agencies in New York, Chicago, Los Angeles, Philadelphia, and Houston maintained more full-time sworn officers.

State Police patrol forces operate mainly upstate, outside cities and towns with municipal police departments. (Exceptions to the general rule include Troop L, which patrols state parkways on Long Island.) As in 1917, the division is the principal law-enforcement agency in many rural areas. Its uniformed force compares with some 3,500 uniformed employees of local sheriff's departments around the state.

Conscious of potential friction with county sheriffs and municipal police departments, the State Police emphasize that the agency's mission is to serve the public in cooperation with, and in support of, local agencies. On the other hand, the very creation of the force demonstrated a belief that sheriff's departments, in at least some cases, were inadequate. Many areas of the state are still served by both troopers and deputies. Formal arrangements to minimize duplication of efforts are rare.

In the late 20th century, the spread of emergency 911 service throughout the state increased regional integration of police services. Where such cooperation works efficiently, dispatchers continually monitor the location of patrols by all police agencies in a region and contact the closest available car to respond to a call for help. Members of the public in areas served by more than one police agency are free to call whichever agency they prefer. More than 80 years after the founding of the State Police, relationships with local authorities continue to evolve.

In suburban areas, the division provides full services in areas without a local department, patrols state roads and interstate highways, and supports local departments. In the state's urban areas, virtually all of which have local police forces, the State Police are generally a small presence, concentrating on drug trafficking, violent crime, money laundering, and organized-crime activities that cross jurisdictional boundaries.

---

12 *Crime in the United States.*

State Police play the lead role in Operation Impact, a 2004 initiative by the Pataki administration to combine local, state, and federal authorities to fight crime in jurisdictions outside New York City. Task forces brought together under the program commonly target illegal guns, drugs, and gangs. Governor Pataki later expanded the initiative, with dozens more troopers assigned to the original 15 Operation Impact counties and other areas.

State law prohibits use of the State Police within a city unless the governor so directs. Generally, such assignment is only after a request by local officials.

Perhaps the most visible element of the state force is Troop T, covering 641 miles of the Thruway and associated highways. Troop T's jurisdiction is the only service area where the State Police have exclusive policing authority. It also covers the 524 miles of waterways administered by the State Canal System.

When State Police get involved in a case, uniformed troopers usually respond first to the scene of a crime and may completely investigate violations such as traffic infractions as well as misdemeanor cases such as assault, larceny and criminal mischief. More serious cases requiring extensive investigation or involving felonies are referred to the Bureau of Criminal Investigation. With more than 900 detectives and other investigative staff, the BCI is among the most highly regarded such agencies in the nation. Its crime-scene technicians, forensic specialists, laboratory staff, computer databases, and other resources help local and county law enforcement agencies that lack the investigative resources needed for major crime investigations such as homicide, sexual assault, and other violent crimes.

The bureau maintains a DNA databank with biological evidence gathered at crime scenes as well as from the blood samples of certain offenders. As a result of legislation Governor Pataki and the Legislature enacted in 1999, anyone who commits a violent felony is subject to mandatory DNA collection. Within its first seven years of use, the databank helped identify 1,665 suspects. Police have begun collecting DNA samples at sites of property crimes, vastly expanding the amount of such information that may help solve current or future cases.

Other specialized State Police units include officers who inspect hazardous materials and enforce laws on their transport and use, and units that focus on bomb disposal, computer crimes, aviation, boating, financial crimes, firearms tracing, and canine-assisted investigations.

While modern tools help the State Police investigate crime in more sophisticated ways, much of the division's work remains relatively unchanged from decades ago. Troopers help promote highway safety by issuing 900,000 or so tickets each year — including more than half of all speeding tickets in the state, although state troopers make up less than 6 percent of the state's law-enforcement personnel, according to the division. Troopers investigate a fatal accident somewhere in the state at an average of almost one every day. More than 200 times on a typical day, they assist motorists whose cars have broken down or need other help.

The division also handles a wide variety of special projects, from providing security and coordinating transportation at the 1980 Winter Olympics to directing public safety, traffic, and other aspects of the Woodstock 1999 concert in Rome.

The State Police Academy in Albany trains recruits for 25 weeks in subjects from defensive tactics and firearms, to the penal and criminal procedure laws, to accident investigation. Each year, several hundred new troopers graduate from the academy, while a total of 14,000 or so individuals — including police officers from other northeastern states — also receive some training there.

Other Police and Peace Officers

One other state-level law enforcement organization provides broad coverage around the state: the Department of Environmental Conservation, which deploys several hundred environmental conservation officers. These officers trace their history to 1880, when the Legislature authorized the governor to appoint eight "game and fish protectors" who would enforce state laws for preserving moose, wild deer, birds, and fish. They were also given a quasi-prosecutorial role, authorized to bring actions in the name of the people of the state to penalize violators. (*See Chapter Seventeen for further discussion.*)

The state Criminal Procedure Law recognizes more than 70 classifications of peace officers in state and local government, including probation and parole officers, enforcement officers of the Department of Taxation and Finance, confidential investigators of the Department of Agriculture and Markets, and agents of a duly incorporated society for the prevention of cruelty to animals. Many peace-officer classifications cover uniformed officers of local agencies such as the Mount Vernon Housing Authority and the Niagara Frontier Transportation Authority.

Peace officers retain many, but not all, of the powers held by police officers. They can make arrests without a warrant, use physical force (including deadly force) in making an arrest or preventing an escape, and perform other police-like functions.

Prosecution and the Courts

Once the police charge an individual with a crime, the suspected criminal enters the court system, where both the state and local governments play important roles.

In New York and throughout the United States, crimes are considered to have been committed not only against individual victims but against the people of the state. Thus legal proceedings in court are named "*People of the State of New York* v. *John Doe*" when Mr. Doe is charged with a crime, and the people are represented by the local district attorney's office or, in federal cases, the regional U.S. attorney's office. (The trend toward "naming" criminal laws for particular victims, described earlier in this chapter, may weaken public understanding of that traditional principle of penal codes.)

District attorneys and their assistants conduct prosecutions in New York's state and local courts. Although voters in each county elect DAs, the state court system pays their salaries. State laws, primarily the Criminal Procedure Law, create the rules that prosecutors must follow in attempting to convict accused individuals. As seen in Chapter Six, Albany is also in charge of the court system in which prosecutors and defense lawyers do their work.

Just as the state Penal Law lays out in detail what is a crime in New York, the Criminal Procedures Law governs what police, prosecutors, defense attorneys, judges, and other officials do when charging offenders with crimes, working to establish guilt or innocence, imposing sentences, and appealing convictions.

The current Criminal Procedures Law, or CPL, became effective in 1971 after several years of work by a temporary commission. The former Code of Criminal Procedure had been in existence since 1881, although an enormous amount of case law had revised the practical effects of the statute in the intervening decades.

The new law updated the bail system, expanded the use of summonses in lieu of arrest for minor offenses, and provided greater procedural protections for mentally disabled defendants. Other elements of the modern CPL cover subjects such as the types and jurisdictions of criminal courts; the timeliness and other requirements for criminal prosecution; rules of evidence; prosecution by indictment (a charge filed by a grand jury) and by information (a charge filed by a prosecutor); sentencing; proceedings after judgement; and subpoena of witnesses. The Office of Court Administration develops administrative procedures to implement the statute.

State courts disposed of 156,713 cases involving felony arrests in 2005. Two-thirds resulted in conviction. The overwhelming majority of convictions, more than 97 percent, were the results of plea bargains. Just fewer than half of all convictions resulted in incarceration (in some cases, for time already served while awaiting disposition).[13]

Protections for the Accused

Police and prosecutors hold a great and potentially devastating power — the ability to deprive individuals of their freedom, and even (in capital cases) life itself. Public opinion generally supports tough prosecutors and offers relatively little sympathy for criminal defendants, some of whom are innocent. For those reasons, laws in America have traditionally provided important procedural protections for defendants.

Among the fundamental protections for criminal defendants is the grand jury. It dates back to the earliest days in colonial America, when local inhabitants in a given area would be asked to assess whether someone they knew might possibly have committed a given crime. As a matter of law, prosecutors today must show a grand jury enough evidence to demonstrate a reasonable likelihood that a crime was committed and that a suspected criminal — whom the grand jurors do not know — has committed that crime. In practice, many observers say, grand juries have too little independent ability to judge whether a suspect should be formally charged, and often issue whatever charges a prosecutor asks. A chief judge of New York State, Sol Wachtler, famously

---

13 Data from New York State Division of Criminal Justice Services, www.*criminaljustice.state.ny.us*.

claimed that any experienced prosecutor in the state could convince a grand jury "to indict a ham sandwich."

American lawyers adopted the right against self-incrimination, and colonial legislatures created juries as a method of safeguarding those falsely accused of crime, partly to protect against what they perceived as unfair prosecution by English colonial authorities. The 1735 trial of New Yorker John Peter Zenger, freed by a jury after being charged with seditious libel for printing critical articles about Governor William Cosby, left an important legacy. It helped create a new American jurisprudence by establishing that, contrary to English law, truth was a defense against a charge of libel.

Acts that would normally be considered crimes may be noncriminal in certain circumstances outlined in the Penal Law. Self-defense and defense of others are classic examples of actions whose legal status depends on the circumstances. Other examples: Parents are legally entitled to use physical force on offspring under 21 if they reasonably believe such a step is necessary "to maintain discipline or to promote the welfare" of the son or daughter. Anyone responsible for maintaining order in a public transportation carrier may also use physical force "when and to the extent that he reasonably believes it necessary to maintain order," and can use deadly force "when he reasonably believes it necessary to prevent death or serious physical injury." Deadly force may even be used, under New York law, in the case of burglary or arson when a homeowner or renter "reasonably believes" two things — that someone is "committing or attempting" to commit the crime, and that such force is required to prevent or interrupt it.

The Penal Law sets forth several other defenses that eliminate culpability for behavior that would normally be criminal. The best-known is probably mental disease or defect. The statute says such illness means the defendant "lacked substantial capacity to know or appreciate either: 1. The nature and consequences of such conduct; or 2. That such conduct was wrong." The current mental-defect rule, enacted as part of the 1965 reforms, represented a broadening of the previous definition.

Another acceptable defense under the Penal Law is duress — the claim that a defendant performed the illegal act only because he or someone else was subject to real or threatened physical force by someone else. Mental illness, duress, entrapment, and certain other defenses are "affirmative defenses," meaning the defendant must prove them by a preponderance of the evidence. Other examples of justifiable behavior include things people do in emergencies to prevent harm. Drafters of the new Penal Law suggested, for instance, that breaking into an unoccupied home to make a telephone call that might save someone's life could be justifiable, rather than criminal, behavior.[14]

The courts attempt to place reasonable limits on the justification defense. The Appellate Division ruled in one case that someone who voluntarily joins an illegal dice game cannot cite that illegality as justification for "violent self-help in recovering his losses."[15]

Many of the protections for suspected criminals that are familiar today — such as the right to remain silent and others required by the Supreme Court's *Miranda* v. *Arizona* decision — are rooted in the immediate post-Civil War era. The 14th Amendment to the U.S. Constitution, effective in 1868, declares that Americans are not only citizens of a given state but are also "citizens of the United States." The amendment provides that no state "shall deprive any person of life, liberty or property, without due process of law...." The limits on government included in the Bill of Rights, the original ten amendments to the U.S. Constitution, mainly restricted the power of the *federal* government. But placing limits on *state* governments eventually became crucial in criminal justice, as most responsibilities in that arena are state and local rather than in the hands of Washington.

Like their colleagues in other states, criminal-justice professionals in New York today work under a myriad of rules and procedures established by, or in response to, U.S. Supreme Court decisions handed down starting in the early 1950s. Over ensuing decades lawyers and judges effectively took some control away from police and corrections authorities, causing "a nationalization of criminal procedure" in many ways.[16]

The CPL also provides numerous procedural protections for defendants. For example, it requires judges to give juries detailed instructions on subjects including presumption of innocence and the requirement that guilt be proven beyond a reasonable doubt. Juries in criminal trials must vote unanimously for guilt to be found.

---

14 William C. Donnino, "Defense of Justification: Practice Commentary," in *McKinney's Consolidated Laws of New York Annotated: Penal Law*, Thomson West, 2004, p. 195.

15 *People* v. *Coates* (2 Dept. 1978) 64 A.D. 2d 1, 407 NYS.2d 866.

16 Johnson, *History of Criminal Justice*, p. 284.

The Role of the Attorney General

Like locally elected prosecutors, the office of the state attorney general can investigate and prosecute criminal cases. Contrary to what voters might conclude from candidates running for the office, however, the attorney general's crime-related functions are in only limited areas specified under state law. Such areas include Medicaid fraud, organized crime, and environmental crimes.

Most criminal cases prosecuted by the Department of Law arise from requests by other state agencies. The Executive Law requires the attorney general to investigate and prosecute any indictable offense related to the authority of such agencies.

In addition to units that prosecute environmental and tax violations and health-care fraud, recent attorneys general have established sections such as the Capital Assistance to Prosecutors team, which assists district attorneys prosecuting capital cases, and a group to handle child pornography and other crimes committed through the Internet.

The Medicaid Fraud Control Unit investigates and prosecutes fraud arising from the billions of dollars spent on Medicaid in New York State each year. The unit prosecutes cases of patient abuse in nursing homes and fraudulent billing practices by physicians, pharmacists, and any other health-care providers and vendors using Medicaid dollars. The adequacy of the attorney general's efforts to fight Medicaid fraud came under question after a *New York Times* series of articles in 2005. The newspaper reported that fraud and abuse cost taxpayers billions of dollars a year, while the attorney general's office prosecuted cases involving only a small fraction of that amount. Then-Attorney General Eliot Spitzer and others argued that the agency depended on the state Health Department to refer cases for prosecution. Largely in response to the news coverage, state leaders proposed various ways to strengthen anti-fraud efforts, including more power for the attorney general's office. *(For more, see broader discussion of Medicaid in Chapter Twelve.)*

Governor Rockefeller and the Legislature established the Attorney General's Statewide Organized Crime Task Force (OCTF) in 1970. The task force works with local, state, and federal enforcement agencies to investigate and prosecute multicounty, multistate, and multinational organized criminal activities such as loan sharking, gambling rings, narcotic trafficking, racketeering, and money laundering.

Disposition of Offenders and Sentencing

Once an individual is convicted of a crime, judges impose a penalty based on the mandate of the Penal Law. In certain cases a judge can impose unconditional discharge — meaning that, apart from the judgment of guilt for the crime, the defendant faces no imprisonment, fine, or other sanction — but such dispositions are relatively rare.

A sentence of conditional discharge or probation means that the offender is free to go about normal life, with exceptions, but may face a tougher sentence if he violates the court's conditions.

The law generally gives judges relatively less flexibility in sentencing for more serious crimes, including violent and drug-related offenses. For example, as of September 1, 1998, conviction of a class B or C felony usually requires a *determinate* sentence, in which the judge sets a particular length of imprisonment within a range specified by the statute. The law previously allowed an *indeterminate* sentence specifying ranges of minimum and maximum terms and allowing the judge to set a specific sentence within them.

Judges can also order offenders to make restitution, in addition to any sentence, as a result of legislation Governor Carey and the Legislature enacted in 1980. Previously, such an order could be made only as a condition of probation or conditional discharge, limiting its usefulness. The statute requires that presentencing reports include a "victim impact statement," partly to enhance the likelihood that any restitution will prove satisfactory to the victim. Full restitution is more the exception than the rule, as most convicted criminals are poor.

In cases heard in the state's criminal courts, ranging from traffic tickets to murder, convicted persons are subject to a mandatory surcharge and a "crime victim assistance fee" to help defray the costs of prosecution. Such fees are waived in cases where restitution is made.

As of late 2006, the ultimate penalty — execution by the state — has not been used in New York in more than 40 years. For decades, the state had been a leader in capital punishment; its 329 executions from 1930 to the mid-1960s were more than those in any other state except Texas and Georgia. Among those whom New York authorities put to death during the 20th century were Leon Czolgosz, assassin of President McKinley; and Chester Gillette, whose murder of a lover in the Adirondacks was the basis for the novel *An American Tragedy.*

In 1963, New York became the last state in the nation to eliminate a mandatory sentence of death for premeditated, first-degree murder. In 1965, an advisory commission created by Rockefeller recommended abolishing capital punishment. The Legislature passed the bill, leaving the death penalty in place for killing a police officer in the course of duty and murder committed by an individual already serving life in prison. The governor, who had not initiated the bill and who received conflicting recommendations from his immediate staff, signed it into law without comment.[17] Remaining provisions for the death penalty were later found unconstitutional, and a death-penalty statute was not restored until Governor Pataki and the Legislature did so in 1995. That law, too, was ruled unconstitutional by the Court of Appeals, in 2004. As the 2007 legislative session approached, a new governor who supported the death penalty in some cases prepared to take office. Since enactment of the statute 12 years earlier, though, nationwide media had brought attention to apparent errors in some capital-case convictions in other states. Leaders in the Assembly, having supported the 1995 capital-punishment statute, were expressing reservations about renewing the law. Whether the death penalty would return to New York remained highly uncertain.

Under Article IV of the state Constitution, the governor has the power to grant "reprieves, commutations and pardons" after someone is convicted of any crime except treason, or in cases of impeachment. Statutory provisions related to that power appear in the Executive and Correction laws. Clemency allows sentenced inmates to apply for parole before they would otherwise be allowed to do so. Those released early by the Parole Board are subject to reimprisonment for violating terms of parole.

Governors typically use clemency power sparingly. Governor Pataki commuted sentences of 23 individuals from 1995 through 2000. Those granted clemency have typically been model prisoners, often assisting other inmates with education or physical needs.

The Prisons: Punishment and Rehabilitation

New York's Correction Law governs operations of state prisons and local jails, along with some related functions such as parole. The statute

---

17 Related by Richard Bartlett in Benjamin and Hurd, eds., *Rockefeller In Retrospect: The Governor's New York Legacy*, 1984, p. 243.

declares that state prisons — officially known, under the law, as correctional facilities — are

... for the purpose of providing places of confinement and programs of treatment for persons in the custody of the department. Such use shall be suited, to the greatest extent practicable, to the objective of assisting sentenced persons to live as law-abiding citizens.

New York State was a leader in developing innovative approaches to punishment and attempted rehabilitation of criminals during the 19th century, when much of today's American penal system was created. New York established the first juvenile reformatory, the first reformatories for men and women, and the most influential early state prison for men. These and other initiatives established correctional practices that numerous other states copied.

Correctional practices today are fairly settled in New York and nationwide. Changes that have taken place in recent years have largely consisted of longer sentences for various types of crimes — sexual assault and other violent crimes, for instance — and efforts to deal with drug and alcohol addiction. In addition, prison administrators across the country, including New York's, must cope now with a growing number of highly volatile, often younger, more violent criminals who pose a threat to corrections officers as well as other inmates. One reaction has been increasing use of solitary confinement with almost no human contact. The practice has attracted criticism as harsh and likely to make such inmates even more sociopathic; prison administrators say they have little alternative if they are to minimize the very real danger to others in the prisons. In 2006, the Legislature approved a bill that would have prohibited solitary confinement for certain inmates suffering from mental illness while funding new treatment facilities. Governor Pataki vetoed the bill, saying it would hamper prison officials' efforts to control violent inmates and that the state already provided extensive treatment for mentally ill inmates.

New York's share of all prison and jail inmates nationwide, 4.7 percent in 2003, was significantly lower than its share of the U.S. population (roughly 6.6 percent). The state, however, spends proportionately more than most states on prisons. Its $4.8 billion in 2004 expenditures — including those by local governments — represented a per capita figure that was fourth-highest in the country and 28 percent above the national average, according to the Census Bureau.

Development of Prisons in New York

Prisons in the Western world developed, over many centuries, two functions whose relative emphasis has varied over time: Imposing retribution and physically preventing the criminal from committing further offenses, on the one hand, and helping the individual improve morally, or at least to decide that crime does not pay, on the other. That tension remains very much in place today.

Around the time that New York and the nation were founded, prisons were largely for holding suspects who had not yet been tried, and for debtors. Punishment for many crimes consisted of whipping or other corporal punishments; for lesser crimes, restitution or a period of labor for the victim was typically imposed. Capital punishment was imposed not only for murder and other felonies but, on occasion, for less serious offenses. In 1768, Robert R. Livingston, Jr., a lawyer who was later a top political leader in the new state of New York, "wrote about a woman convicted of petty theft who was under sentence of death. Her execution was delayed because of her pregnancy, only to be carried out shortly after the child was born. Livingston stressed the harshness and inhumanity of a legal system that left the infant motherless."[18] By 1796, only murder and treason were to be punished by death; life imprisonment was the new and more humane sentence for other serious crimes.

The Empire State's major contribution to early penology became known as the Auburn system. Opened in 1823, the prison in the state's Finger Lakes region attracted attention from criminal-justice experts around the country and from overseas. Over more than a century, the Auburn system "wielded an enormous and preponderating influence upon prisons and reformatories throughout this country, and has made its influence constantly felt in other lands."[19]

Inmates were classified into three groups. Those considered most hardened and vicious were kept in solitary confinement; a second group alternated between such confinement and labor; a third worked together during the day and returned to individual cells at night. At night, inmates slept alone in individual cells, a major change from previous institutions that had housed criminals in large rooms, often with individuals who

---

18 Johnson, *History of Criminal Justice*, p. 139.

19 Orlando F. Lewis, *The Development of American Prisons and Prison Customs, 1776-1845*, Montclair, NJ: Patterson Smith, 1967 (reprint of original 1922), p. 77.

were institutionalized because of poverty or mental or physical disability. Discipline was strict. Inmates were to be silent, to prevent planning of escapes or other mischief, and to enhance the moral atmosphere. When going to meals or to work, inmates had to walk in lockstep. Every day was filled with work except Sunday, when inmates could rest in their cells or attend church service within the prison. The work — hard physical labor with punishment for those considered laggards — has been characterized with phrases such as "harsh and unmitigated slavery."[20]

Infractions were punished by flogging with a rawhide whip and, in more serious cases, a "cat" with six strands of twine. Such punishment was frequent, certain, and imposed quickly. Communication with the outside world was allowed only in unusual circumstances. Another hallmark of the Auburn system was the large, interior cellblock, several tiers in height with cells back-to-back.

Although flogging was outlawed in New York in 1846, much of the approach developed in Auburn — where one of New York State's largest prisons still functions — remains in place around the country.

Modern Administration of Corrections

In recent decades, state leaders have first consolidated, and then dispersed, executive-agency responsibility for various elements of correctional services. Governor Rockefeller initiated creation of the present Department of Correctional Services in 1970. It consolidated the previous Department of Correction, the Commission of Correction, and the Division of Parole. A legislative memorandum in support stated: "Efforts to reduce the rate of crime cannot be truly successful unless the entire criminal justice system, from arrest through the courts and correctional services, can be made into a more effective instrument for reducing the number of criminal repeaters."[21] In signing the bill, Governor Rockefeller said that combining institutional (prison) and field (parole) supervision of criminals under the same leadership would provide "a coordinated, consistent and continuous system of rehabilitation."[22] A

---

20 W. David Lewis, From *Newgate to Dannemora: The Rise of the Penitentiary in New York, 1796-1848*, Ithaca, NY: Cornell University Press, 1965, p. 33.

21 Memorandum of State Executive Department, *McKinney's 1970 Session Laws of New York State*, St. Paul, MN: West Publishing Co., 1970, p. 2943.

22 Approval memorandum, L. 1970, Ch. 475-479, May 8, 1970.

companion law removed the Division of Probation from the new department, making it an independent agency within the Executive Department.

Demonstrating the uncertainty over the best ways to promote rehabilitation, seven years later, Governor Carey and the Legislature restructured the bureaucracy again — this time, in the opposite direction. The Division of Parole was again removed from the department and made an independent agency. The legislation making that change included this statement of legislative findings: "The present organizational structure is not conducive to the optimum performance of the parole system. The parole board and parole officers are placed in the department of correctional services whose primary function is providing for the care and confinement of offenders in correctional institutions." Removing parole operations from the corrections department would provide the former with "the necessary measure of independence ... while providing the control over resources which is essential to the continuing improvement of the parole process."[23]

The new law made other changes in response to criticisms that parole decisions were inconsistent and unfair. It required the Parole Board to adopt written guidelines for granting release from prison and created an appeals process, for example.

Theoretically, the varied elements of the criminal justice system operate as just that — a system. In practice, the complex, sprawling nature of the work and other factors make it difficult to ensure that police, prosecutors, the courts, prison administrators, and parole and probation authorities work in consistent and mutually supportive ways. Seeking to promote a systematic approach, Governors Cuomo and Pataki each appointed a director of criminal justice to serve as chief adviser and policy maker on a wide range of issues. The director coordinates executive-branch agencies including the State Police, Department of Correctional Services, Division of Parole, and Crime Victims Board. The director also serves as commissioner of the Division of Criminal Justice Services. The division is the state research and planning agency for criminal justice, and conducts much of the state's training and other technical assistance for local police and other agencies involved in public protection. Whatever efforts state leaders have made to produce a fully cohesive criminal-justice system, however, the goal remains

---

23 Chapter 904, Laws of 1977.

elusive given the multiplicity of levels of government, variety of interest groups, huge scale of the system and other challenges.

Attica

The most important event in the modern history of New York's prison system was the inmate takeover of Attica Correctional Facility in September 1971. Inmates controlled the prison for four days, demanding major changes in correctional procedures. After negotiations with Corrections Commissioner Russell Oswald failed to produce an agreement, Governor Rockefeller ordered the State Police to retake the prison on September 13. Thirty-two inmates and 11 correctional officers were killed during the four days, and 80 wounded — most during the final hour. It was the most deadly prison uprising in American history.

Prison life at the time, many observers noted, was not much different from that of the 1800s. Inmates lived in the same big, intimidating-looking institutions as their predecessors had for more than a century. Silence was no longer required, nor was the daily Bible reading that was a staple of the early Auburn system. In other ways, daily life was largely similar, with most time spent in a small cell and other activities heavily regimented. Critics frequently used words like "dehumanizing" to describe prisons in New York and other states.

Rockefeller appointed a Select Committee on Correctional Institutions and Programs which reviewed conditions throughout the state prison system after Attica. It called for greater recognition of prisoners' civil rights, recruitment of minority staff members, designation of institutions as other than maximum security, better staff training, and improved meals and other amenities for inmates. Governor Rockefeller and the Legislature responded by enacting eight bills in 1972. The new laws created short furloughs for inmates who were within a year of release and had demonstrated good behavior, and improved the chance of parole for certain offenders. Administrative changes included fewer restrictions on visitors, mail, and reading material, and better food service. Still, the vocational program in the prison "remained inadequate."[24]

---

24 Gerald Benjamin and Stephen P. Rappaport, "Attica and Prison Reform," in *Governing New York State: The Rockefeller Years*, Albany, NY: Academy of Political Science, May 1974, p. 211.

Punishment, Reform, Warehousing

The hope of finding a correctional approach that changes criminals into contributing members of society dates back centuries. The hope remains, while measurement of progress is difficult.

In 1921, the general secretary of the American Prison Association and the Prison Association of New York wrote a history of American prisons from colonial times to 1845, with special attention to prisons in New York.* The book opened with a description of the "gray, bastile-like prison of Sing Sing," mentioning its "notorious history as a place of punishment."

"Sing Sing is passing," wrote Dr. Orlando F. Lewis, whose position marked him as one of the world's experts on prison reform. A new receiving and classification prison was then under construction next to the old facility. "From it the newcomers will be sent, after the most careful study of their individual treatment-needs, to the institutions in which they may find the best and most permanent curative and reformatory treatment. A new day has indeed arrived in American penological methods."

Three-quarters of a century later, some of the practical experts who worked inside Sing Sing Correctional Facility were not convinced that things had changed.

Ted Conover, a writer who spent a year working in the prison, recalled the advice that experienced corrections officers gave new recruits before their first day on the job.

> "You're just a forth-thousand-dollar baby-sitter," one instructor told us in summary, after describing the misbehavior of inmates.... If our job title, "correction officer," suggested a role in setting people straight (another instructor) suggested we think again. Because in reality, he said, "rehabilitation is not our job. The truth of it is that we are warehousers of human beings." And the prison was, above all, a storage unit.**

---

*   Lewis, *The Development of American Prisons and Prison Customs*.

**   Ted Conover, *Newjack: Guarding Sing Sing*, Random House, New York, NY, 2000, p. 41.

The number of inmates confined in state prisons grew dramatically in the years after Attica, partly because of tougher restrictions on the sale and possession of illegal drugs enacted at Governor Rockefeller's initiative in 1973. As the inmate population grew, governors from Rockefeller to Pataki built more prisons. Under Governor Cuomo alone, 46 new facilities capable of housing some 31,000 inmates opened, almost doubling the capacity of the state prison system.

Most of New York's prisons are in rural upstate communities that welcome them as sources of relatively well-paid jobs. Most inmates, however, are from the New York City area. The distance from home makes it harder for inmates to retain connections with families and friends outside prison — thus, some observers say, making rehabilitation less likely.

Recent Changes in Corrections

In early 2001, Corrections Commissioner Glenn S. Goord announced that the inmate population had declined by more than 2,000 from its peak of more than 71,000 a year earlier. The count was expected to drop further, and did. As of March 2006, after six consecutive years of decline, the department was responsible for 62,980 inmates.

The change in New York ran counter to nationwide trends. For the five years ending December 31, 2004, New York's state prison population declined by 11 percent while the combined population of state prisons nationally rose 7 percent, according to the commissioner.[25] Early-release programs such as "merit time," shock-incarceration and the Willard Drug Treatment Center allowed the state to avert the need for 5,300 additional prisoner beds, the department says.

Most of the reduction in inmate counts was reflected in elimination of double-bunking, changing more cells to single occupancy. One small correctional facility was closed, and Governor Pataki proposed additional closures. The Legislature rejected those proposals, in part because of opposition from the corrections officers union, New York State Correctional Officers and Police Benevolent Association. The union-influenced decision to keep prisons open was a reminder of the state's policy, from the 1970s into the 1990s, of

---

25 *Prison Safety in New York*, Albany, NY: New York State Department of Correctional Services, 2006.

maintaining large psychiatric centers even after most clients had left those facilities.

More than three decades after Attica, the department offers academic opportunities including high-school equivalency programs, adult basic education, bilingual programs, and college credit programs. Volunteer programs help expand literacy training, other tutoring, prerelease preparation, and programs for inmates with special needs. Vocational training programs are available in skills such as drafting, welding, carpentry, plumbing, optical and dental technology, and computer operation, programming, and repair.

Inmates may apply the skills taught in vocational programs in the department's correctional industries program known as Corcraft. Correctional industries employed some 2,500 inmates statewide as of 2006. The workers produce metalware, license plates, office furniture, mattresses, cleaning products, and other items, typically working seven hours a day, five days a week. Some private-sector companies that produce similar products criticize the state agency as unfair competition because inmates' wages range from 16 to 45 cents an hour. Because of such concerns, the Legislature has prohibited Corcraft from selling its products on the open market to private organizations or individuals. The inmates' products compete with those of other companies for customers among state agencies and authorities, local governments, and nonprofit organizations.

In New York as in other states, a majority of inmates have some history of substance abuse. Drug and alcohol education and treatment programs have been created to meet the needs of the growing number of addicted inmates. Still, such programs are voluntary, and many inmates emerge from incarceration with drug habits intact — having been able to continue using illegal drugs while in prison. An analysis by *The Buffalo News* found that at least 19 inmates in New York State prisons died of drug overdoses from 2000 to 2005. Inmates are subject to random drug tests. Positive tests for marijuana, heroin, and other drugs indicate substance abuse is more common in New York than in other states, the newspaper reported.[26]

Family-oriented programs have grown, particularly for family visitations, parenting education, and counseling on family violence.

---

26 Lou Michel and Susan Schulman, "Jailhouse Highs," *The Buffalo News*, Buffalo, NY, September 17, 2005.

As it has from the beginning, the prison system faces the challenge of balancing spending needs with efforts to restrain costs. A 1990 study by the Office of the State Comptroller found that prison operating costs in the Empire State were substantially higher, on a per-inmate basis, than those in seven other major states. New York's costs averaged $25,285 a year per inmate — 19 percent higher than second-place Michigan and still further above California, Illinois, Pennsylvania, and other states. Labor costs, owing largely to higher staffing levels, were the most noticeable difference among states, the study found. It said the higher spending did not appear to result in lower recidivism or more safety compared with the other states.[27] As of 2005, according to DOCS, its ratio of corrections officers to inmates was 1-to-3. In the other largest states — California, Texas and Florida — comparable ratios were 1-to-6 or more.

The department operates a training academy in Albany that graduates 1,000 or so correction officers in a typical year. Education includes classroom study of laws and rules governing inmate and staff behavior; use of chemical agents, batons, and firearms; inmate psychology; health and safety issues such as fire prevention and AIDS awareness; and on-the-job training.

In 2001, the trainee program was expanded from seven to eight weeks to improve correctional officers' ability to deal with the greater challenges of modern prisons. The additional training focuses largely on techniques for dealing with adolescent violent offenders, the mentally ill, and other special-needs inmates; evaluating and controlling aggressive inmate behavior; and coping with stress.

Despite those programs and the variety of educational and vocational services, offenders who are sent to state correctional facilities, or to local jails for sentences of less than a year, spend most of their days inside a small cell. The unstated assumption of adult corrections policy, in New York and other states, remains what it has been for decades: that years of confinement will keep offenders from repeating their crimes in the community and, ideally, provide a strong inducement against criminal behavior.

---

27 Office of the State Comptroller, Division of Management Audit, *Staff Study on The High Cost of Imprisonment in New York vs. Other States*, March 1990.

Probation and Parole

Some 63,000 individuals were on parole at some point during the 2003-04 fiscal year, according to state figures, with 40,000 or so under parole supervision at any one time. About one in six parolees returned to prison during the year, mostly for violations of parole conditions, with 3 percent convicted of new crimes.

The state's Division of Probation and Correctional Alternatives sets standards for, and administers state aid to, local probation departments in each county and in New York City. Local probation officers meet periodically with offenders who are placed on probation to supervise their activities and, when possible, counsel them on steps to a more productive lifestyle. Such supervision is widely considered to be more effective when officers can keep closer, more regular contact with probationers. For that reason, the state pays for more intensive programs in certain pilot programs involving juvenile delinquents and other special cases. Local departments that are subject to the division's oversight also provide background reports on convicted criminals to help judges make sentencing decisions.

The division contracts with some 160 programs that offer a variety of sanctions and other interventions, such as drug treatment. These alternatives to incarceration reduce taxpayers' costs for prisons and are intended to help offenders change their behavior while ensuring public safety.

Younger Offenders

Generally, under New York law, an individual must be 16 or older at the time a crime is committed to be found guilty in criminal court. Youths under 16 who are charged with serious offenses are dealt with in Family Court. Exceptions are made in the case of second-degree murder for anyone 13 to 15; and in the case of manslaughter, rape, and certain other crimes, for individuals who are 14 or 15.

Aside from those exceptions, offenders aged 13 to 15 who are found criminally responsible are classified as juvenile offenders and remanded to juvenile detention centers rather than adult prisons. A third category of troubled youths is persons in need of supervision (PINS), individuals under 16 whom family courts have determined need state oversight because they refuse to obey parents, have run away from home, skip school, or otherwise misbehave.

As in most states, New York State law establishes different systems to handle individuals who have committed crimes below the age of 18, compared with those who are older. An individual convicted of a crime committed at age 18 or below may have the conviction set aside and be designated a "youthful offender," a status which can provide more lenient sentencing options for the judge. Differing assumptions for youthful offenders are reflected in, among other things, much higher expenditures. In New York State, taxpayers spend an average of more than $80,000 a year on offenders who are committed to youth detention centers run by the Division of Rehabilitative Services within the Office of Children's and Family Services, or OCFS. Each inmate in the custody of the Department of Correctional Services, by contrast, costs taxpayers an estimated $30,000 a year.

As in adult prisons, an overwhelming majority of young offenders are male. In 2003, girls and young women composed 18 percent of those admitted to OCFS rehabilitative programs — a figure that has been rising slowly but steadily in recent years. African-American individuals were 59 percent of the total. The most common offense was assault, followed by robbery and larceny. Homicides represented less than 1 percent of the total, 18 individuals.

Like those in state prisons, a majority of youths admitted to OCFS-operated residential programs are classified as substance abusers. More than 40 percent in a 1999 study by the Division for Youth, one of the predecessors of OCFS, had a history of mental health problems. Even higher proportions — more than three-quarters — had significant family problems or educational handicaps, and had demonstrated behavior problems at school. "Damaged" was the term most often used by the staff interviewed for this study to characterize youth placed in state custody. According to staff, the agency received "the worst of the worst" and then returned them to high-risk circumstances.[28] Roughly 20 percent of agency clients have no permanent home to return to, according to OCFS figures.

---

28 Bruce Frederick, *Factors Contributing to Recidivism Among Youth Placed With The New York State Division for Youth*, Albany, NY: New York State Division of Criminal Justice Services, Office of Justice Systems Analysis, August 1999.

Tougher Punishment, More Programming

Periodic increases in juvenile crime in recent decades prompted governors and legislators, in New York and most other states, both to toughen penalties and to consider more preventive programming for teen offenders. As mentioned, the Empire State was among the first to separate juveniles convicted of a crime from other prisoners. Around the start of the 20th century, New York followed the lead of the Chicago Juvenile Court by establishing the Manhattan Children's Court, a model that spread to the rest of the state over succeeding decades.[29]

Governor Rockefeller and the Legislature created the Family Court system in 1962. New York later became the first state to statutorily recognize the category of offenders known as persons in need of supervision. Governor Carey and the Legislature enacted statutes in 1976 and 1978 to increase penalties for violent offenses by juvenile offenders. Previously, juveniles below the age of 16 could not be held criminally responsible or have their cases waived to criminal courts after a hearing in juvenile court. (On the other hand, New York had one of the lowest ages of criminal responsibility in the nation, 16.) The late-1970s statutes were enacted partly because of media attention generated by legislators who complained that the status quo neither protected the public nor helped troubled youngsters improve their lives. The fact that 1978 was an election year, and criminal justice was a potential political problem for Governor Carey because of his refusal to approve the death penalty, may have helped lead to legislation that year. One case that created a furor involved a 15-year-old who had murdered two subway passengers but under existing law could only be imprisoned until he reached 21.[30]

Nationwide, the juvenile arrest rate for violent crimes remained relatively constant from the early 1970s to the late 1980s. It then grew 64 percent from 1988 to 1994 before dropping slightly. From 1992 through 1995, all but 10 states modified their statutes, making it easier to prosecute juveniles in criminal court, according to the U.S. Office of Juvenile Justice and Prevention. Legislatures in many states added significantly to the list of offenses eligible for criminal prosecution and lowered the

---

29 Edmund F. McGarrell, *Change in New York's Juvenile Corrections System*, Working Papers No. 22, Albany, NY: Rockefeller Institute of Government, Fall 1985.

30 Ibid.

age at which certain juveniles could be tried in criminal courts. One effect of such changes, in New York and elsewhere, was to give family-court judges less authority to make decisions regarding the venue for cases involving violent or other serious crime.

As part of legislation enacted in 1995, the Legislature required the Division of Criminal Justice Services to study recidivism rates among individuals discharged from the custody of the then-Division for Youth. The report found that most youth placed in the agency's custody had been in trouble with the law several times. Within 36 months of discharge from DFY custody, fully 81 percent of males and 45 percent of females had been arrested again, the study found. (Youth detention systems in other states apparently have similar problems, it reported.)

The report lent additional impetus to reform efforts already underway at DFY and other agencies that deal with the problems of youth. It recommended focusing on approaches such as intensive after-care for young individuals released from state custody and sustained efforts to work with offenders' families as well as individuals.

Issues of recidivism and quality of care in DFY-OCFS facilities returned to the spotlight after the arrest of an individual charged with shooting three state troopers, and killing one, in 2006. Ralph "Bucky" Phillips had spent nearly a year in a DFY residence as a teenager. He fled state custody several times, apparently in part to escape attacks at the hands of other youths in the system.[31] The incident reinforced a common, if often exaggerated, perception that impressionable young individuals in state custody sometimes emerge more likely to get into trouble.

One way that state-operated detention centers for juvenile offenders seek to avoid such problems is by providing educational services intended to replace those that individuals would receive outside. A 1992 study by state researchers found that juveniles who entered the custody of the then-Division for Youth had educational attainment below roughly 85 percent of the general population the same age. The researchers found that DFY clients made statistically significant gains in reading and math achievement tests, rising above the 30th percentile on both and making greater progress than expected if they had remained in

---

31 Carl Strock, "Fugitive's life didn't start just this year," *The Sunday Gazette*, Schenectady, NY, September 10, 2006.

regular schooling.[32] About half the students had spent the research period entirely in DFY-operated classrooms, while others spent some of their time in public schools with attendance and performance monitored by DFY staff.

Commission of Correction

The 1894 state Constitution and subsequent legislation provided for a Commission of Prisons consisting of eight gubernatorial appointees. The commission was empowered to visit and inspect all penal institutions and promote their humane and efficient administration.

In 1973, the Commission of Correction was established as an independent agency within the Executive Department. The commission functioned with part-time members until 1975, when the present commission with three full-time members and staff was established.

The commission's responsibilities include monitoring the operation of all state and local correctional facilities, including writing minimum standards for the care, custody, treatment, supervision, and discipline of all inmates. It also recommends ways to develop job programs for inmates. It investigates all deaths of inmates, and can close a prison or jail it deems to be unsafe, unsanitary, or inadequate in other ways. For instance, the agency ordered the Cayuga County Jail closed in the late 1950s.

The commission exercises broad regulatory authority over local jails. Its powers include reviewing and approving any plans for constructing or renovating local facilities; creating detailed written rules that jail officials must distribute to inmates upon admission; establishing requirements for supervision and other security matters; and regulating inmate correspondence. For instance, the commission requires that inmates who cannot afford to buy their own stationery and postage must be given materials and postage for at least two pieces of regular first-class mail each week. Commission staff also train local jail officials.

Local officials often complain that the commission's requirements drive up costs, perhaps needlessly. In 2001, for example, commission

---

32 New York State Division for Youth, Bureau of Program Evaluation and Research, *Research Focus on Youth: Evaluation of Educational Services to DFY Youth*, 2, 2 (Spring 1992).

staff told Essex County officials that segregating inmates by age, risk, and other factors would effectively mean only 80 percent of cells in a new jail could be filled at any given time. That meant building a larger facility than the county would have had otherwise.[33]

The commission accredits local jails that meet certain security, program, administrative, and other criteria. About a dozen facilities in the state were accredited as of 2000. The program is voluntary, offering local officials an opportunity to measure their practices against those required for accreditation. Among other benefits, accreditation may give local jails some legal protection against liability suits by inmates.

Help for Crime Victims

Historically, governments in New York and elsewhere have dealt with crime primarily by punishing the guilty. Crime victims traditionally were not a significant concern. In 1966, Governor Rockefeller and the Legislature created state-funded financial grants for certain crime victims. Such assistance can cover unreimbursed crime-related expenses, including medical and funeral expenses, loss of earnings or income support, counseling, the costs of cleaning up a crime scene, repair or replacement of essential personal items, court transportation expenses, and the cost of using the services of a domestic violence shelter. The Crime Victims Board, which oversees the grants, also advocates for the rights of victims and provides grants to local agencies that help victims in a variety of ways. Such organizations include rape-crisis centers and programs to help victims of domestic violence and other crimes.

Under an amendment to the Criminal Procedure Law that Governor Pataki and the Legislature enacted in 1998, prosecutors must inform a victim of violent crime of the right to know when the perpetrator of the crime is released or escapes from prison. The Department of Correctional Services is responsible for notifying such victims, and the Crime Victims Board advises local agencies on helping victims make sure they receive information in a timely manner.

Victims may be awarded grants of up to $600 a week, for a maximum of $30,000, for loss of earnings or financial support, along with burial expenses up to $6,000. Assistance for other needs can add to the

---

33 Lohr McKinstry, "'Think big' keys state primer on building Essex County jail," *Press Republican*, Plattsburgh, NY, February 8, 2001.

total. Grants provided by the board are funded largely through proceeds of a $10 fee imposed on anyone convicted of a felony, misdemeanor, or violation in the state.

Homeland Security

Governor Cuomo occasionally used the phrase "my defense budget" to describe the steadily rising cost of imprisoning criminals and otherwise working to prevent and punish crime. In the aftermath of September 11, 2001, the phrase might be used in a new way with regard to state activities — one more in keeping with its traditional use in Washington, D.C.

With U.S. intelligence services warning that additional terrorist attacks would be a concern for some time after the attacks, national and state leaders called out National Guard troops to patrol airports and other potential targets across the country. In New York, more than 2,700 Army National Guard and Air National Guard members were called into service within weeks of the attacks. Those agencies, along with the New York Naval Militia, serve as reserve forces to the U.S. Army, Air Force, and Navy, respectively. Each agency can be called into service by the president or by the governor.

The state's forces also include the New York Guard, which acts as a state-level reserve force to the Army National Guard if the latter is ordered into federal service. In 1951, during the early years of the Cold War, Governor Dewey and the Legislature created the state Civil Defense Commission to help deal with the threat of nuclear attack, including coordinating development of bomb shelters. The commission was made part of the Division of Military and Naval Affairs in 1973. The reserve forces will play key roles in efforts to prevent and, if needed, respond to future terrorist incidents.

Within days of the 9/11 attacks, Governor Pataki and the Legislature enacted new Penal Law offenses targeted at individuals who commit terrorist acts, make terrorist threats, solicit or provide material support for terrorists, or hinder prosecution of terrorists. While the certainty of death did not deter the September 11 terrorists, the Anti-Terrorism Act of 2001 presumes that state laws might deter some other individuals, or at least make prosecution of future terrorists or their supporters more likely. Its legislative findings include these:

Although certain federal laws seek to curb the incidence of terrorism, there are no corresponding state laws that facilitate the prosecution and punishment of terrorists in state courts. Inexplicably, there is also no criminal penalty in this state for a person who solicits or raises funds for, or provides other material support or resources to, those who commit or encourage the commission of horrific and cowardly acts of terrorism. Nor do our criminal laws proscribe the making of terrorist threats or punish with appropriate severity those who hinder the prosecution of terrorists.... A comprehensive state law is urgently needed to complement federal laws in the fight against terrorism and to better protect all citizens against terrorist acts.[34]

In October 2001, Governor Pataki created the Office of Public Security, with a broad portfolio to assess the potential for terrorist attacks and the ability of state agencies and private entities such as utility companies to avert and/or respond to those or other threats. One of the office's first assignments was to review security at the Indian Point nuclear power plant in Westchester County, within a few miles of millions of residents. While finding security at the plant "robust," state officials recommended some additional steps in the wake of the September 11 attacks.

Both state officials and the statute governing disaster preparedness recognize that local leaders in communities throughout the state will determine much of the success of any efforts to prevent and, if needed, deal with disasters. The Executive Law section that deals with disaster preparedness starts with the declaration:

It shall be the policy of the state that ... local government and emergency service organizations continue their essential role as the first line of defense in times of disaster, and that the state provide appropriate supportive services to the extent necessary.[35]

Under legislation adopted in 2004, the agency was codified and renamed the Office of Homeland Security. Other new laws enacted in recent years include statutes requiring state officials to review security measures at chemical plants, water supplies, and energy generation and transmission facilities.

---

34 Chapter 300, Laws of 2001.
35 Executive Law, Section 20.

Debate over the nation's response to potential terrorist threats focuses almost exclusively on Washington — the policies of the president and (to a lesser extent) Congress, as well as the operations of agencies such as the Department of Homeland Security and Federal Bureau of Investigation. But officials who work in the field point out that states and localities have a crucial role to play, as well. While the New York City Police Department has won international acclaim for its antiterrorism efforts, other local agencies remain far behind. A 2003 symposium on the terrorism challenge for state and local governments produced conclusions such as:

> Balancing the need to protect the country from attack and the need to protect citizens from unwarranted police attention is a difficult, ongoing undertaking. Recent terrorist attacks are the product of well-organized activity by groups that are frequently state supported and financed and are sophisticated in organization and logistics. The investigative and technical methods available to police to identify and apprehend these individuals have not expanded adequately to address this new form of terrorism. Such problems as identity fraud remain largely unaddressed. The appropriate roles of federal, state, and local law enforcement agencies in addressing terrorism are still in a state of some flux.

> (Experts at the symposium) endorsed a "neighborhood watch" model where the investigative initiative remains largely a federal responsibility, while state and local agencies are provided with sufficient intelligence and support to allow them to follow up on contacts made via arrests, traffic stops, or unusual events. Several of the September 11th hijackers had prior contact with local police, for example, but there was no method for identifying these individuals as "persons of interest" despite the fact that they were on foreign intelligence watch lists.

> Effective sharing of information and intelligence between law enforcement agencies remains a serious problem. Intelligence collected by different federal agencies remains "stovepiped" or retained within the agencies that collected it and there are few linkages across databases. In similar fashion, there is little sharing of intelligence between federal and local agencies.[36]

---

36 James W. Fossett in *The Prevention and Detection of Terrorist Attacks: The Challenge for State and Local Government*, report on June 12, 2003, symposium at the Nelson A. Rockefeller Institute of Government, Albany, NY.

Three years later, as New Yorkers commemorated the five-year anniversary of 9/11, some progress had been made in the areas identified by the report — but, most observers would agree, far too little. Long-term success in the fight against terrorism will require successful cooperation among agencies at the federal, state and local levels.

"Homeland security," at both the federal and state levels, is often construed to include the more traditional field of responding to natural disasters and other emergencies. New York State's modern organization of emergency-related functions came in 1978, when Governor Carey and legislators created a new Article 2-B of the Executive Law. The statute's provisions include requirements that the state, as well as every county and every city, prepare disaster-preparedness plans. "Disaster" is defined to include catastrophic natural events from earthquakes to tornados, as well as fire, epidemic, air or water contamination, infestation, explosion, radiological accident, and bridge collapse. As of September 2001, the definition did not include war or terrorist attack. The 1978 law created the Disaster Preparedness Commission, a planning and coordinating group that includes the heads of most major state agencies and two local chief elected officials. The commission was charged with developing state-level plans for preventing, mitigating, and recovering from disasters, and helping localities make such plans. Since 1983, the staff to the commission has been known as the State Emergency Management Office. In recent years, it has led state-agency responses to disasters such as the crash of TWA Flight 800 off Long Island in July 1996.

Chapter Seventeen

ENVIRONMENT AND PARKS

Key points:

- New York was a leader among the states in preserving wilderness lands and developing modern environmental laws.

- Efforts to preserve and restore environmental quality continue, often in conflict with efforts to strengthen the state's economy.

- The state parks agency has a broad portfolio, including managing the nation's second-largest area of park holdings.

The story of New York State is, in many ways, the story of natural resources.

The great New York harbor, the Hudson River, millions of acres of forest, scenic mountains, and the waterways and terrain that made the

Erie Canal possible — all played essential roles in the Empire State's development as an economic powerhouse.

Population and economic growth led, in time, to overuse of some natural resources. By the mid-1800s, for instance, woodlands in parts of the Adirondacks and Catskills were stripped to the ground; by the mid-20th century, many waterways were badly polluted by household and industrial wastes.

New Yorkers adopted, earlier than most of the industrialized world, the idea that environmental problems existed and could be solved. They led the nation in declaring that some lands must be kept forever wild; they were among the first to enact laws that required cleansing of public waterways and the air. With a stronger economy providing greater public revenues than those of most other states, they devoted significantly greater resources to protecting the environment and creating parks.

The Empire State was a national leader in setting aside both huge tracts of land as wilderness, and smaller areas as parks. As of 2004, New York ranked second to Alaska in state park holdings, with 1.5 million acres.

In recent decades, in New York and elsewhere, concern for the environment has moved far beyond land preservation into regulation of many aspects of the daily life and work of individuals, businesses, local governments, and other organizations. Under the broad heading of "environmental quality," state government closely monitors and limits discharges into the air, waterways, and land. These regulatory programs extend beyond factories and powerplants to apply to products that individuals use everyday — cars, cleaning products, paints, air conditioners, and more.

Much of what state government does in this area is directed or influenced by the federal government. The majority of Albany's policies regarding hazardous waste and automotive emissions, for instance, are in direct response to laws enacted by Congress and regulations adopted by the U.S. Environmental Protection Agency. Washington also provides significant financial support, including about 20 percent of the Department of Environmental Conservation's operations budget in fiscal 2006. Still, environmental protection across the country is primarily the responsibility of state governments. Few states are more active than New York.

Long Before Earth Day

Today the state Department of Environmental Conservation (DEC) — with its blue, green, and white logo suggesting scenic beauty — embodies New York's commitment to preserving its natural resources. By the time Governor Rockefeller signed legislation creating the DEC on the first Earth Day in 1970, however, the conservation movement in New York was already more than a century old.

It began as a reaction to overuse of some of the state's forests and waterways — use that, for hundreds of years, most of western civilization had viewed simply as humans' appropriate domination of the natural world. The first European settlers of the Empire State saw the wilderness as a source of danger — something that must be tamed and then put to work so humans could survive and progress. The Dutch West India Company brought colonists to New Netherland for the express purpose of turning natural resources into profit. Within a few years of its first permanent settlement at Fort Orange (now Albany) in 1624, the company's settlers had developed a thriving trade in beaver pelts. Such trade, much of it based on business relationships with the native Iroquois, was so active that, by 1640, the beaver was virtually gone from areas around the Hudson River from Fort Orange south.

As settlement expanded outward from the port cities of New York and Albany, farming grew in importance. Frontier families had to replace forest with farmland not only to put food on the table, but to earn income to make payments on their land purchase or rental as well. A typical household might need 40 to 50 acres under plow for long-term survival.

As the colony's population grew, lumber became an increasingly valuable raw material for homes and other buildings. Colonists also burned wood for ash to help make potash, which they could sell for agricultural and other purposes in New Amsterdam or in Europe. By 1698, the Earl of Bellmont, serving as the English governor of New York, found it necessary to restrict the cutting of white pine, the most popular source of lumber.

State action to protect the environment proceeded slowly at first, then in more frequent fits and starts. The first powerful impetus for long-term environmental policy came during the 1800s. Forest harvesting in the Adirondacks, the Catskills, and elsewhere had intensified after the Revolutionary War, when the state government needed revenue to repay war debts and sold millions of acres at pennies apiece. Still, given practical inefficiencies caused by transportation and other problems, logging continued with little concern for any damage until shortly before the Civil War. Despite extensive land sales, the state was still a large landowner, owing in large part to reclamation of already logged properties for nonpayment of taxes.

"Make It a Forest Forever"

An Albany attorney who enjoyed camping in the Adirondacks issued what is often described as the first call for saving the northern forests. Samuel Hammond wrote in 1857: "Had I my way, I would mark out a circle of a hundred miles in diameter, and throw around it the protecting aegis of the constitution. I would make it a forest forever. It would be a misdemeanor to chop down a tree and a felony to clear an acre within its boundaries."[1] Others joined in the call, including Verplanck Colvin, whom the Legislature had hired to survey the Adirondacks; and Morris Jesup, president of the American Museum of Natural History and the New York Chamber of Commerce.

The state's first environmental agency was created just after the Civil War. In 1868, the Legislature created a Fisheries Commission to study the impact of logging on fish and water supplies. Four years later, a Commission on State Parks was assigned to study creation of a park in the Adirondacks. Legislation establishing the State Forest Preserve was enacted in 1885, declaring that state forests in both the Adirondacks and the Catskills "shall be forever kept as wild forest lands." That law also created a Forest Commission to oversee protection of state-owned forest preserves. Both the land set-aside and the creation of an agency in state government to protect the environment were among the first such steps by any state. The guarantee that the state forests would be forever wild was made even stronger in 1894, when it was included in the new state Constitution. It remains as the central element of Article XIV.

Water played a key role in the decision to preserve large sections of the Adirondacks. As described in Chapter Twelve, New Yorkers created the first state Department of Health in 1901. One impetus for the new agency was concern for health implications of polluted water.

---

1   Samuel H. Hammond, *Wild Northern Scenes; or Sporting Adventures with the Rifle and Rod*, New York, NY: Derby & Jackson, 1857.

Depletion of woodlands also reduced the soil's ability to hold water, allowing topsoil to erode and exacerbating natural flooding of downstream areas, including downtown Albany. Business and political leaders saw the potential loss of navigable water on the Hudson River and the Erie Canal as an important reason for preserving forests; the New York Board of Trade and Transportation helped win passage of the constitutional amendment that prohibits logging in the forest preserve.

Economic considerations also came into play in creating the Catskill Forest. A legislative commission's report on preserving forests recommended against adding Catskill areas to the preserve. "But Cornelius Hardenburgh, an assemblyman from Ulster County, deftly put about 34,000 county-owned acres in his district into the package just before Governor Hill signed the bill. Hardenburgh was not a conservationist, but he was an ardent opponent of taxes, and Ulster County had owed $40,000 in taxes to the state for those acres. His move wiped out the debt, created a perpetual revenue source for Ulster County, and — as an afterthought — began a park that now encompasses more than 1,100 square miles."[2]

The Conservation Department

Governor John Dix and the Legislature created the primary forerunner of today's DEC, the Conservation Department, in 1911. Like the state's Health Department, it was the first such agency in any state. The new agency represented an effort to improve coordination among various bureaucracies dealing with water supply, forest preservation, fish, and game. Yet overall state government was still largely a collection of uncoordinated agencies and programs. Because of natural inertia and local political involvement in administering regional bureaus, the Conservation Department continued largely as a collection of disparate offices for years.

Governor Alfred E. Smith's intense efforts to rationalize state government included a major reorganization of the conservation agency. As a result of legislation Smith signed in 1926, the department absorbed the Conservation Commission and two water-related commissions. The

---

2   Brad Edmondsen, *Environmental Affairs in New York State: An Historical Overview*, New York State Archives, *www.archives.nysed.gov/a/researchroom/rr_env_hist.shtml*.

Stream Pollution in 1903

Tanning was a major industry in the Mohawk Valley and other areas of the state for more than a century, starting in the early 1800s. The business relied on an extensive supply of animal hides, bark from hemlock trees for processing, and water for power as well as waste disposal.

A 1903 report to the state Health Department by the Gloversville Knitting Co., now on file in the State Archives, shows that large chemical discharges into waterways were more or less taken for granted as part of the process of manufacturing gloves, mittens, and linings. The document, one of numerous reports that shops and factories were required to file with the state, lists the refuse discharged into the nearby Cayadutta Creek. On a monthly basis, the mill reported, it used 750 pounds of vitriol, 710 pounds of aniline dye, 1,700 pounds of alkali, 138 pounds of ammonia, 42 pounds of caustic potash, and other substances. The company discharged about 20,000 gallons of refuse into the creek, a tributary of the Mohawk River, each day. The mill's 175 employees also used toilets that emptied into the creek.*

Today, such pollution would attract front-page headlines and quick action from DEC. A century ago, most New Yorkers considered it business as usual.

---

*   Reprinted in *Consider the Source: Historical Records in the Classroom*, Albany, NY: University of the State of New York, State Archives and Record Administration, 1995, p. 101.

legislation created a single executive office of commissioner, to be appointed by the governor.

For more than a third of a century after Smith's reorganization, the role of the department remained largely the same: protecting public lands, promoting fishing and hunting, running state parks, and overseeing allocation of natural water supplies. The department did little to limit pollution. A Bureau of Stream Pollution Prevention had been created in 1921, but it had little real power. A 1955 book on New York State government called its chapter on the Conservation Department "Men in Green," referring to the forest rangers who were the most familiar representatives of the agency. The only reference to controlling pollution reported that the department "keeps a two-man anti-pollution team running down ammonia leaks, cyanamid seepings, and other perils to fish life."[3] The official description of the department's activities at that time sounded only a bit different: "Continuous work on water pollution is carried on. This involves study of the nature of various polluting substances and their effect on aquatic life. Such knowledge has proven useful toward decrease of many serious pollution conditions."[4] Most Americans had never heard of ecology, and governments across the country did not yet make environmental protection a priority.

The Emerging Issue of Environmental Quality

The state entered the modern era of major antipollution efforts in 1957 with enactment of the Air Pollution Control Act. During the 1950s, the number of motor vehicles registered statewide passed 5 million. Industrial activity and overall use of electricity reached then-record levels; both depended heavily on burning coal and oil, with little effort made to filter the emissions released through smokestacks. Incineration was the common way to dispose of household waste. In New York and other big cities, smoke from the chimneys of large apartment buildings could have recalled scenes from Walt Disney's *Mary Poppins*.

Governor Harriman sent the Legislature a special message recommending action. The resulting law, Harriman wrote, would enable the state for the first time to "attack the increasingly serious problems of atmospheric pollution." The law created an Air Pollution Control Board, chaired by the health commissioner, with the authority to regulate air pollution and to inspect "any property or motor vehicle for the purpose of identifying pollutants." In recognition of potential economic impacts, the board's five members included the state commerce commissioner, and the law allowed variances in rules and regulations for those who could show hardship.

Eight years later, the Legislature and voters approved the Pure Waters Bond Act at Governor Rockefeller's initiative. Two years after that, the Rockefeller administration began planning creation of a new environmental super-agency.

---

3   David H. Beetle, *The New York Citizen: The Guide to Active Citizenship in the Empire State*, New York, NY: Elsevier Press, Inc., 1955.

4   Myron D. Hartman, ed., *The New York Red Book 1956*, Albany, NY: Williams Press Inc., p. 464.

DEC and the Environmental Conservation Law

In 1970, as popular concern for the environment was reaching ever higher, Governor Rockefeller proposed and the Legislature approved creation of the Department of Environmental Conservation to bring together planning and management of all environmental protection programs.

The new agency absorbed the former Conservation Department which six decades earlier had consolidated smaller offices and bureaus. DEC also absorbed functions of the Health Department related to regulation of water and air pollution and waste disposal; and functions of the Department of Agriculture and Markets related to pesticide regulation. The legislation also created an Office of Parks and Recreation, which assumed some duties of the former Conservation Department, the state Council of Parks, and other bureaus. (*For more discussion of New York State parks see later in this chapter.*)

In 1975, Governor Carey and the Legislature took a step that was even more far-reaching than creation of the new agency: enactment of the State Environmental Quality Review Act (SEQRA). The law requires state and local agencies to conduct comprehensive review of the potential environmental impact of any significant activity they undertake or approve. The impact statement must describe not only the proposal but "reasonable" alternatives such as other sites, other designs or technology, and planned steps to minimize any environmental impacts. Perhaps most important, SEQRA required government to consider environmental impacts as a "cost" to be compared against the economic and social benefits of a proposed project, in deciding whether to approve a proposed project. These provisions affect governmental projects as well as those of private enterprises, including nonprofit organizations and individuals. SEQRA includes sweeping legislative findings on the importance of protecting the environment, saying that "every citizen has a responsibility to contribute to the preservation and enhancement of the quality of the environment."

The statute has been amended over the years, with new powers granted to DEC and additional restrictions placed on enterprises and individuals. Of all New York laws, it is "perhaps the most pervasive and far-reaching in fostering public awareness of local environmental

Changing Views on the Environment

If the actions of the state's elected leaders can be assumed to reflect the will of the voters, the Air Pollution Control Act of 1957 showed that concern for the environment had risen — but was to be addressed in the context of other needs. The act stated:

> It is declared to be the policy of the state of New York to maintain a reasonable degree of purity of the air resources of the state, which shall be consistent with the public health and welfare and the public enjoyment thereof, the industrial development of the state, the propagation and protection of flora and fauna....

Just 13 years later, the law creating the Department of Environmental Conservation laid out a dramatically broader vision for protecting the state's natural resources:

> The quality of our environment is fundamental to our concern for the quality of life. It is hereby declared to be the policy of the state of New York to conserve, improve and protect its natural resources and environment and control water, land and air pollution, in order to enhance the health, safety and welfare of the people of the state and their overall economic and social well being.

Whereas the 1957 Legislature and Governor Harriman saw "industrial development of the state" as a good that must be balanced against "reasonable degree of purity of the air," by 1970 Governor Rockefeller and lawmakers declared that environmental quality was "fundamental" to the quality of life as well as essential to economic well-being. The 1970 statute also declared that it is state policy to "achieve social, economic and technological progress for present and future generations" by taking good care of the environment.

concerns and enabling the public and the government to protect a broad range of environmental values."[5]

Under the law and associated regulations created by DEC, environmental review must be thorough and public, and usually must take place in a deliberative manner to allow for input from potentially

---

5   Nicholas A. Robinson, ed., *New York Environmental Law: A Legal Treatise*, New York State Bar Association, Albany, NY, 1992, p. 384.

affected parties. A developer wishing to build, for instance, a shopping center — whether local in scale or intended to attract visitors from hundreds of miles away — must prepare in-depth analyses of any potential impacts on land, air, water, traffic, noise, and historical or archeological resources. Such analyses, which together compose the environmental impact statement, can add up to multiple volumes in the case of large development proposals.

SEQRA applies not only to physical development, with its obvious potential for environmental impact, but state and local government agencies' "policy, regulations, and procedure-making" as well. Courts have held, for example, that the law applies to a town's action to create a sewer district,[6] and to the Metropolitan Transportation Authority's decision to implement one-way tolls on the Verrazano-Narrows Bridge.[7]

While it is part of the Environmental Conservation Law, SEQRA is not solely the responsibility of DEC. Individuals, private organizations, and governmental agencies have the power to seek enforcement by the courts if they believe a developer or other entity — including a government agency — has violated SEQRA. If more than one governmental unit is involved in undertaking or approving a contemplated action, the various agencies must agree on which will be the "lead agency" with principal responsibility for fulfilling the procedural requirements of SEQRA. On the rare occasions when agencies cannot agree on which will be the lead agency, the DEC commissioner has the power to decide.[8]

Enactment of SEQRA gave New York a state-level statute similar in many ways to the National Environmental Policy Act proposed by President Nixon and enacted by Congress in 1969. Similar laws have been enacted in most other states, but New York's statute is unusual in its breadth of applicability. In numerous other ways, New York went beyond Washington as well as most other states in environmental policymaking from the 1960s through the 1980s. New York adopted the nation's first "superfund" law for cleanup of hazardous waste sites under Governor Carey in 1979. When Governor Cuomo and the Legislature enacted the Acid Deposition Control Act of 1984, imposing limits

---

6   *Tri-County Taxpayers Association Inc.* v. *Town Board of Town of Queensbury*, 55 NY2d 41, 447 NYS.2d 699, 432 N.E.2d 592 (1982)

7   *Golden* v. *Metropolitan Transportation Authority*, 126 A.D.2d 128, 512 NYS.2d 710 (2d Dept. 1987).

8   Robinson, *New York Environmental Law*, p. 386.

on air contaminants that cause acid rain, their action anticipated the federal Clean Air Act amendments of 1990.

While widely praised for promoting more careful attention to the environment, the Environmental Quality Review Act also helped prompt new attention to potential problems of over-regulation. The same year the act became law, Governor Carey and the Legislature enacted the State Administrative Procedure Act, setting clear and consistent rules for agencies to follow in regulatory activities (see Chapter Eight). Two years later, in his Annual Message to the Legislature, Governor Carey urged action to "assure that the regulatory processes fulfill their intended objectives without costly delays or attention to frivolous concerns." The result was the Uniform Procedures Act, which establishes time limits on DEC's issuance of permits.

DEC Today

By the start of the 21st century, environmental protection had become a major concern for many New Yorkers, and thus to political leaders. An entire generation of Americans had reached adulthood since the first Earth Day, many learning environmental values in school. The movement had broadened from a small collection of interest groups to one of the most widely supported in American history.

Partly because of that support, DEC's mission has grown dramatically since its founding. In 1970 the agency was still largely the conservation-oriented department created nearly seven decades earlier, with some additional responsibilities for sewage treatment, air pollution control, and recreation. According to one observer, "Prior to 1970, 'environmental quality' was a concept, not a program."[9]

The agency's priorities have evolved over time. The divisions of Fish and Wildlife, and Forests and Land, accounted for 40 percent of departmental spending in 1970. By 2000, that figure was around 25 percent.

As a result of expanded federal and state laws and a dramatic growth in state appropriations, the influence of the Department of Environmental Conservation and related state agencies today is greater than ever. In

---

9 Gary L. Spielmann, "The Evolution of the DEC: Budget and Funding Sources, 1970-1995," *Albany Law Environmental Outlook* 2, 3 (1996).

the agency's first year, staff numbered 2,140 and state-operations appropriations totaled $31 million.[10] In 2006, DEC's operating budget was $430 million, while total spending — including that for capital projects — neared $1 billion. Some 3,335 employees worked in the Albany headquarters and in nine regional offices around the state. The latter review applications for environmental permits and work to assure compliance with state and federal laws and rules.

Funding for the department has shifted over the years, from a majority of general tax revenue to charges on regulated businesses and individuals. General Fund appropriations provide roughly 25 percent of DEC's operational funding. More than half comes from fees and license revenues, with federal funds contributing the rest.

The federal government, through several major statutes and the Environmental Protection Agency, makes many of the basic rules governing environmental quality and oversees their implementation by the states. States, though, are the primary enforcers of those rules and in many instances have the power to set their own standards above and beyond those written in Washington.

In New York, DEC's major environmental-quality efforts focus on promoting cleaner air and water, assuring safe drinking water, dealing with solid and hazardous wastes being produced today, and cleaning up sites previously contaminated by hazardous wastes and oil spills.

Air: The Air Pollution Control Board created in 1957 issued its first rules in 1962, limiting emissions from major new or modified sources. The board was abolished in 1970 and the Division of Air Resources transferred to the new DEC. President Nixon and Congress enacted the national Clean Air Act that year, and along with amendments passed in later years, federal law drives much of the state's air-related regulatory activities. Most recently, congressional action in 1990 required new permitting programs for industrial facilities, electrical generating plants, and other major stationary sources of emissions, along with new emission controls for motor vehicles and other changes. Governor Cuomo and the Legislature enacted a conforming state law in 1993. A federal law provides powerful incentives for state officials to ensure compliance with the rules made in Washington. For instance, federal officials can withhold highway funding — which pays for a major share

---

10 Much of the following discussion is adapted from *The Department of Environmental Conservation: A 25th Anniversary Review*, Albany, NY: Nelson A. Rockefeller Institute of Government, February 1996.

of the state's transportation needs — if New York does not meet air-quality standards. State leaders continually grapple with clean-air issues, including the question of how to reduce acid rain and ozone pollution caused largely by air emissions in other states. In recent years, DEC has created a second, more stringent regulatory program limiting acid rain precursors from electric generating facilities. Under Governor Pataki, New York joined New Jersey and several New England states in creating the nation's first regional program to limit emissions of "greenhouse gases" that may contribute to global warming.

Water: Protecting the state's water resources is the responsibility of both DEC and the Health Department. As it has since 1885, the Health Department oversees the quality of public drinking water supplies; both agencies play a role in monitoring and regulating farming, development, and other activities that affect local watersheds. DEC's Division of Water issues permits for, and monitors the activities of, sites such as municipal sewer plants, manufacturing facilities, and utility stations that make discharges into waterways. In some 80 percent of the state's surface water bodies, the primary source of contamination is "nonpoint" pollution from large numbers of smaller sources such as homes, farms, golf courses, roads, and parking lots.[11]

The agency's other water-related responsibilities include inspecting dams and developing flood emergency response plans; and working with other states to promote improved water quality in the Great Lakes and other shared water resources. New York's Department of State is also involved in water-related regulatory activities, particularly monitoring coastal development. Federal agencies including the Environmental Protection Agency, Army Corps of Engineers, and the Coast Guard add to the list of regulators.

Solid and hazardous waste: When DEC was created in 1970, the reorganization plan did not mention waste management. The state did not allocate tax dollars for solid or hazardous waste until 1974. Greater attention and funding came after government officials and the public realized that local landfills across the state were releasing contamination into surrounding waterways and poisonous wastes were leaking from Love Canal in the late 1970s.

Well into the 1960s, the state of the art in solid waste management was to convert open dumps to sanitary landfills. The former were

---

11 *The Department of Environmental Conservation: A 25th Anniversary Review*, p. 84.

simply large pits or low-lying areas — some 1,600 around the state — where communities dumped household garbage, other trash, and debris with little concern for what would happen when the materials decomposed, trickled through the ground, or rose into the air. As many as two-thirds of the dumps burned some waste, producing ash and stench. Regulations issued by the Public Health Council in 1962 required development of sanitary landfills, which are lined with impermeable materials and include pipes to carry off, for proper disposal, both liquid and gaseous byproducts. The regulations also required operators of municipal incinerators to limit pollution. In the 1970s, DEC issued regulations governing refuse disposal and design of solid-waste management facilities. The 1986 Environmental Quality Bond Act contributed $100 million to close remaining landfills that did not meet modern standards.

The state's regulation of solid waste disposal intensified after a barge carrying garbage from Long Island spent 156 days at sea in 1987, searching for a disposal site. North Carolina, Louisiana, Alabama, Mississippi, Florida, New Jersey, the Bahamas, Mexico, and Belize all rejected the *Mobro*'s cargo. DEC eventually arranged for the barge to dock in Brooklyn, its contents to be burned at a regulated incineration plant there, and the ash buried in a regulated landfill in Islip. The following year, Governor Cuomo and the Legislature gave DEC new powers to regulate solid waste, including a mandate that every municipality start separating and recycling different forms of household and commercial waste by 1992.

The recycling mandate created one of the most far-reaching efforts ever in New York to regulate activity in every household and office. By the late 1990s, bins of recyclable newspapers, plastic, and metal containers appeared weekly outside homes across the state, and the newspaper industry had begun a major effort to encourage recycling of its product. More than 25 percent of New York's waste stream was recycled annually as of 1999, according to DEC. As market conditions fluctuated, though, much of the material ostensibly collected for recycling went to landfills. Some critics questioned whether the push in New York and elsewhere was worth the time and expense, although such views were not popular.[12]

---

12 A June 30, 1996, article in the *New York Times Magazine*, "Recycling Is Garbage," by John Tierney, attracted more letters than any article previously published in the magazine, according to the newspaper.

The number of active solid-waste disposal sites has fallen sharply over the years — from about 860 in 1970, to 220 in 1990 and just 53 in 2000, according to DEC. Disposing of household, commercial, and other solid waste remains a challenge for many communities.

Pop-culture illustration of environmental themes, such as the 2000 film *Erin Brockovich*, often focuses on issues involving hazardous wastes, perhaps because the dramatic potential is greater than that in the case of, say, recycling. Yet, for all that hazardous wastes have come to symbolize much of the environmental movement — and despite the immediacy of the dangers that can be involved — public policy came relatively late to the issue. Governor Carey and the Legislature gave DEC authority to regulate storage and discharge of hazardous substances in 1972. Much stricter regulation, from generation to disposal, followed the Love Canal crisis.

Both Congress and the New York Legislature have passed laws designed to prevent the creation of new Love Canals. The 1976 federal hazardous waste law, titled the Resource Conservation and Recovery Act (RCRA), established a "cradle-to-grave" regulatory program that includes requirements for handling, storing, transporting, and disposing of hazardous wastes. A manifest system of required reports from manufacturers and shippers allows regulators to track hazardous wastes.

In 1978, New York adopted a similar law that, among other things, allowed the federal government to delegate its authority for implementing and enforcing RCRA to DEC. The Legislature has also adopted laws governing the location of hazardous waste landfills and incinerators, and requiring businesses to develop formal plans for reducing the amount of hazardous wastes they generate.

In recent years, state leaders debated how to ensure cleanup of sites polluted years or decades earlier. The state Hazardous Waste Remedial Fund, or Superfund, was created in 1979 and received additional funding through the 1986 bond act. As was true nationwide, though, cleanups of the most contaminated sites proceeded slowly, and hundreds of sites were left untouched. By 2001, debate focused largely on whether cleanup standards should allow consideration of future site use — with industrial property given more flexible standards than residential developments, for instance — and whether owners who were not responsible for the original pollution would assume liability. New York was one of the last large states to adopt a "brownfield" law, in 2003. (The term

Environmental Incentives

As bottled beverages grew in popularity during the mid-20th century, many glass containers required consumers to "deposit" 2, 5, or 10 cents upon purchase of soda or beer. Bottlers would refund the deposits when consumers returned the bottles, and save production costs by reusing them. As the bottling industry became more regional and then national, no-deposit, no-refund sales became more common. Consumers soon threw away most soda and beer cans. Containers became common litter along streets and roadsides across the country. Environmental groups in New York and elsewhere proposed that the government impose what had been a voluntary system of deposits. Oregon passed the first such law in 1971; New York's law followed in 1982. As of 2001, nine other states also had bottle bills.

The idea behind such laws is that economic incentives for voluntary action — such as collecting and returning empty containers — can exert a powerful effect. From this perspective, the bottle bill is an unquestioned success. A commission appointed by Governor Cuomo concluded in 1985 that New York's law reduced solid waste statewide by 3 to 5 percent, measured by weight, and 8 percent by volume. Beverage container litter was cut by 70 to 80 percent, it found. Every day thousands of New Yorkers choose to return their bottles and cans, thereby reducing air contaminants because production from recycled materials requires less energy than that from virgin materials. Some studies of container-deposit legislation show that such laws can also reduce child injuries, by reducing the amount of broken glass in public playgrounds and other areas.

However, opponents criticize the increased cost to consumers. The commission's findings suggested that consumers paid new costs to beer distributors of 1.5 cents per container sold, and to retailers of 1 cent per returned container. Supporters respond that such costs would otherwise fall on taxpayers through municipal public-works spending. Perhaps more importantly, opponents of mandatory deposits point out that bottle bills rob curbside recycling programs of aluminum, which is generally more valuable than other commodities in municipal waste streams. The result is reduced revenue to — and less effectiveness on the part of — broader recycling efforts.

brownfield typically applies to any site where contamination has affected the property's use or reuse.) The 2003 legislation adopted a number of major changes intended to promote the cleanup and redevelopment of brownfield sites, including use-based cleanup standards, liability protection, and tax credits for both cleanup and redevelopment costs. Several years later, it had helped stimulate some cleanups, but many long-abandoned sites remained.

Lands and Forests

The founding purpose of New York State's conservation efforts — preserving forestlands — is fulfilled today by DEC's Division of Lands and Forests. The division manages the Forest Preserve and other protected lands totaling more than 4 million acres, or roughly 13 percent of the state's landmass. More than 2.6 million of these acres are in the Adirondack Park; some 290,000 in the Catskill Preserve; 700,000 in 470 state forests; and 165,000 in wildlife management areas. Most of the state's holdings date from the early 20th century, although some 1 million acres were added after 1950. The office also handles the state's oversight of rivers, regulating land use on designated corridors, and evaluating the impact of hydroelectric plants on the Forest Preserve and protected rivers. It is the home of DEC's forest rangers, whose responsibilities range from fighting forest fires to helping educate the public on land stewardship (*see below in this chapter*).

The forests division also promotes New York State's forest products industry, helping companies market their goods and working to attract new employers to the state. DEC's Saratoga Nursery distributes more than 1 million tree seedlings each year, with most going to private landowners and the rest to state-owned properties. The state's 12 fish hatcheries distribute some 7 million trout and salmon, and another 200 million or so warm-water fish such as walleye and their eggs, in a typical year.

Conservation Officers and Forest Rangers

Legislation enacted in 1971, the year after the agency was created, gave environmental conservation officers the status of "police officers" in the state's Criminal Procedure Law. Officers now had statewide jurisdiction to enforce all laws of the state.

By the turn of the 21st century, the force had grown to more than 200 sworn officers responsible for enforcing laws relating to hunting, fishing, trapping, license requirements, endangered species, possession and sale of fish and wildlife, sale of domestic and foreign game, and taxidermy. For instance, officers periodically inspect records at some 700 sporting goods stores and other nongovernmental license-issuing agents. In the state's coastal areas, they enforce laws restricting harvest of oysters, scallops, lobsters, crabs, and other marine life.

Other elements of the officers' broad range of responsibilities include enforcing rules governing the transportation, storage, and disposal of hazardous waste; investigating oil and chemical spills; and enforcing laws that prohibit excessive smokestack emissions and open fires. They even inspect retail stores for illegal sale of detergents containing excessive amounts of phosphorus, which can pollute waterways.

The state issued 1.5 million hunting, fishing, and trapping licenses in 2001-02. Tens of thousands of other New Yorkers enjoy the outdoors — hiking, camping, and pursuing other recreation — each year. As their numbers increase, more require the help of environmental conservation officers. DEC conducted an average of 234 search-and-rescue missions each year during the 1990s, more than double the average during the 1960s.

Environmental conservation officers are required to maintain a residence within the geographical limits of their assigned patrol area — which might be 400 square miles in the Adirondacks, or somewhere in New York City.

DEC's 130 or so forest rangers are classified as peace officers, with the power to enforce all state laws and regulations. Roughly half are assigned to the Adirondacks and other parts of the North Country. Their duties include enforcement of laws protecting state lands, open burning laws, and licensed guide regulations.

Related Agencies

The attorney general plays an important role in enforcing state environmental laws. As it does with other state agencies, the Department of

Law generally represents DEC in court. The courts have recognized inherent enforcement authority by the attorney general even in areas where statutes do not provide such power. Much of that authority is based on common law, including numerous actions to force cleanup of toxic waste sites. Local district attorneys can also prosecute criminal violations of the Environmental Conservation Law, although such actions are uncommon.

New York State offers financial and technical help for local governments, state agencies, and businesses to meet regulatory requirements through the Environmental Facilities Corporation. A public authority created in 1970, EFC manages revolving funds that make low-interest loans for projects involving water treatment, solid waste management, sewage treatment, and remediation of hazardous wastes. Technical assistance includes activities such as helping small dry-cleaning businesses limit their air emissions.

EFC's board includes three *ex-officio* members — the environmental and health commissioners and the secretary of state — and four individuals appointed by the governor with the consent of the Senate. The agency functions as an important part of any administration's efforts in environmental affairs. As a public authority with the power to borrow and other sources of revenue outside the control of the Legislature and exempt from many bureaucratic rules such as civil service law, EFC provides the governor with more flexibility in appointing staff and providing financing for desirable projects.

The Adirondacks: A Special Case

The largest wilderness in the eastern United States, New York's Adirondack Mountains were among the earliest areas in the country to attract the eyes of conservationists. Development and logging restrictions enacted in the 1880s helped lay the groundwork for conservation efforts nationwide.

In the 1960s, the state's rising affluence and construction of the Northway — the interstate highway running from Albany to the Canadian border — created new development pressure in the region. In 1971, based on an advisory commission's recommendation, Governor Rockefeller and the Legislature created the Adirondack Park Agency with extensive powers to regulate private land use — a major step beyond the longtime regulation of many activities in the state-owned lands that make up the "forever wild" forest preserve. The law represented a conclusion that local governments in the region, most with part-time leaders, could not effectively control development. The APA developed a land-use plan which the Legislature approved in 1973.

The agency has an 11-member board appointed by the governor with the consent of the Senate. At least five members must reside in, and three outside, the Adirondack Park. Besides regulating land use, the APA operates two visitors' interpretive centers in Paul Smiths, Franklin County, and Newcomb, Essex County, to provide environmental education and orientation for park visitors.

Environmental Progress

After environmental regulation expanded broadly over several decades, state government now monitors virtually every significant, ongoing source of pollution in New York. Although environmentalists and elected officials seldom celebrate the achievement, the state's natural resources have undergone a remarkable recovery. Waterways polluted with industrial and human wastes in the 1960s are clean enough for swimming and even, with normal filtering, drinking. The air is much healthier, as indicated by measurements of airborne contaminants. No longer are hazardous wastes and municipal trash dumped into the environment, as they were just three decades or so ago. Bald eagles, wild turkey, striped bass, peregrine falcons, moose, and other animals that once were rare or extinct in New York have returned.

Environmental regulation, in New York as elsewhere, often creates tension between two key social goals — preserving a beautiful and safe environment, on the one hand, and leaving citizens free to pursue economic and other activities, on the other. Many early conservation efforts were relatively easy and noncontroversial in achieving such a balance. For instance, the state acquired thousands of acres of forest preserve in the 1800s after previous owners stripped usable timber and abandoned the land as valueless. Today things are more complicated. Government acquisition of land in the Adirondacks, for example, can advance environmental goals. But, often, it also means limiting economic options — for lumber operations, tourism, or other commercial activities — in a region where unemployment is high and most family incomes are low.

Through their taxes and charges assessed on utilities and other businesses, New Yorkers have spent billions of dollars to start achieving the goal of a cleaner environment — willingly, if the success of several bond acts and continued support by elected officials are any indication. Stricter environmental regulations have had both positive and negative economic impacts on New Yorkers. A cleaner Hudson River, for instance, makes the Empire State a more attractive tourism destination, while restrictions on development in the Adirondacks has the same effect there. On the other hand, regulatory concerns probably played a role in the state's loss of 1 million manufacturing jobs from 1960 to 2000 — a drop of more than half that occurred while industrial employment nationwide rose by 10 percent. In the Adirondacks, unemployment is high partly because of strict regulations. After a century and a half of attention to environmental issues, the state continues to seek the best balance among ecological concerns and other economic and social needs.

Parks, Recreation and Historic Preservation

From Niagara Falls to Montauk Point, many of the most naturally spectacular areas in New York are set aside for the enjoyment of all, as state parks.

At the start of the 21st century, the Office of Parks, Recreation and Historic Preservation hosted some 63 million visitors a year at its varied properties across the state. Families and individuals use boat launching sites, marinas, canal parks, nature centers, and museums; many facilities offer environmental education and interpretation programs. One of the largest operators of golf courses in the country, the agency owns 28 courses, including the site of the 2002 U.S. Open at Bethpage State Park. All told, sites managed by the agency total more than 300,000 acres.

The Empire State was an early leader in identifying scenic preservation and recreation as areas where state government should play a leading role. The Adirondack and Catskill preserves helped set the stage for national action to create large national parks. Today, in New York State government, "parks" generally connotes areas where private development is forbidden, but the government actively promotes public use by providing and maintaining beaches, swimming pools, hiking trails, and other facilities. The Office of Parks, Recreation and Historic Preservation operates 176 state parks — an increase of more than a dozen in recent years — where activities include swimming, hiking, camping, and biking. The parks department's responsibilities do not, however, include the two largest state holdings — the forest preserves in the Adirondacks and Catskills, totaling nearly 3 million acres. Those areas, mostly wilderness, fall under DEC's management.

Fittingly, Niagara Falls was the center of New York's first state park. It is now the oldest in the nation (Yellowstone was the first state park, but has since become a national park). Governor Grover Cleveland signed legislation in 1883 to create a board of commissioners to choose and acquire "certain lands to preserve the scenery of the Falls of Niagara." Owners of some choice parcels sued to block the acquisition, but the state commissioners of appraisal ruled that such a natural wonder was "not subject to human proprietorship." After the Legislature approved a $1 million bond issue for acquiring property, the Niagara Reservation State Park opened two years later. Today a half-dozen other state parks are within a few miles of the falls. Among them is Fort Niagara State Park, at the mouth of the Niagara River on Lake Ontario, where the French built a fort in the 1720s on the site of an Indian town known as Ongniaahra (origin of the present-day name). Tourist visits to the falls are vital to the local economy.

On average, some 1.5 billion gallons a second flow from Lake Erie into the Niagara River. The United States and Canada agreed in a 1950 treaty to preserve the spectacular nature of Niagara Falls while maintaining electric power generation by guaranteeing a flow of at least 100,000 cubic feet per second — roughly half the natural total — during daylight hours from April through October. That flow may be halved at night during the tourist season and anytime during the rest of the year. The treaty provides that the river can be used for generation of power that is to be divided equally between the two countries. Huge underground tunnels carry much of the flow to the New York Power Authority's Robert Moses Niagara Power Plant and Lewiston Pump-Generating Plant, as well as to Canadian hydroelectric turbines on the opposite side. Besides generating low-cost power that benefits state residents and businesses, the diversion of river flow has dramatically slowed erosion of the falls.

Donations by wealthy New Yorkers were important in adding other major state parks during the 1800s. William Pryor Letchworth, whose Buffalo company dealt in harness equipment, bought parcels along the

Genesee River over nearly half a century starting in 1859. Fearing that the spectacular river gorge and easy availability of hydroelectricity would make the property a natural for industrial development, Letchworth decided to donate nearly 1,000 acres to the state in 1906. Letchworth State Park, on the border of the state's Finger Lakes and Niagara Frontier regions, now offers hikers and other visitors beautiful views of the river and falls.

Robert H. Treman, a successful banker born in Ithaca, acquired property around Enfield Falls outside the city in 1915. He arranged for 1,000 trees to be planted nearby, and several years later donated the land for the park that now bears his name. Treman also acquired, for preservation by the state, another nearby scenic gem, Buttermilk Falls. He became the founding chairman of the Finger Lakes State Parks Commission in 1923, serving 14 years. South of Albany lies Thacher Park, named for John Boyd Thacher, mayor of Albany from 1926 to 1940. Emma Treadwell Thacher, the mayor's widow, donated the property to the state. In 1910 and again in 1916, voters across the state approved bond issues to acquire land in the Bear Mountain area, additions to the Forest Preserve and other parklands.

In each of these cases, local citizens took the lead to push for parkland, often acting on their own to acquire significant acreage and assuring its preservation simply by giving it to the state. The next major step in development of the modern parks system represented, rather than local control, a top-down initiative from Albany.

Origins of the State Parks System

By the 1920s, the Industrial Revolution had matured to a point where tens of thousands of families had what their forebears might only have dreamed about: significant amounts of leisure time. "More people had more time to go to more places — and to more distant places. Inexpensive, mass-produced automobiles changed travel habits, and shorter working hours allowed more time on the road. New preferences for outdoor recreation appeared, and woods, fields, streams, mountains and beaches attracted ever greater numbers. Community parks no longer satisfied residents yearning for action or rest in the outdoors."[13]

13 *Fifty Years: New York State Parks 1924-74*, Albany, NY: Natural Heritage Trust, 1975.

Private-Sector Support

Private wealth made it possible for New York State to acquire a number of important parklands early in the 1900s, and near the end of the century state leaders turned to the private sector once again for help with the parks.

Parks Commissioner Bernadette Castro, appointed by Governor Pataki, was raised on Long Island and was familiar with both the great history and the modern challenges facing Jones Beach and other state parks. In 1997, Commissioner Castro signed an agreement with Coca-Cola to provide $2.5 million for the parks system. In return, Coke would have an exclusive contract to supply soft drinks at all state parks and historic sites — a valuable agreement, given that more than 60 million visitors come to those locations each year. Other examples of private-sector support included five playgrounds provided by the Saturn Corp., as well as hundreds of thousands of dollars from the Ford Motor Co. for nature centers and other environmental improvements to the parks system.

Issues of private enterprise within state parks can be controversial. In 1996, the Pataki administration announced a new master plan for the largest New York State park, Allegany. The plan prohibited commercial logging. Some supporters said that allowing logging could generate revenue to support park improvements, while opponents argued that such activity was simply inappropriate in a public park.

Governor Al Smith had two big reasons for creating a state parks system. Having grown up in Manhattan's Lower East Side, he understood the benefits that parks could provide for city dwellers — at the time, a majority of state voters. Second, Governor Smith had a strong urge to bring order to the scattered and confusing organization of state government. While the state had more than 40 parks and other recreational, scenic, and historic areas, there was no mechanism to coordinate their administration and financial support. Based on a plan created by Robert Moses, Governor Smith convinced the legislature to create a State Council of Parks in 1924. The council brought together leaders of the major regional parks authorities under the country's first statewide park system. Perhaps more importantly, it gave Moses — who was soon named the council's chairman and remained in that office for 35 years

— a portfolio from which to develop and acquire new parks throughout the state.

The quintessential "power broker" (as a Pulitzer Prize-winning biography was titled), Moses had developed a broad, detailed agenda of what he wanted to accomplish — and knew how to go about accomplishing it. The combination made him ultimately more influential than any other nonelected individual in the history of the state — indeed, even more influential than most New York governors. Within a relatively short time of taking office, he had removed most decision-making power from the regional councils that had controlled parks for decades and that, in many cases, had originally made it possible for the state to acquire parklands. Moses' development of New York parks may represent the greatest concentration of power over a major public function held by any individual in state history.

Besides overseeing major expansion, Moses changed the basic nature of parks. Rather than simply preserving scenic areas, state parks would provide outdoor recreation as well as transportation networks that join parks to population centers such as New York City. His influence in siting and building highways and bridges was extraordinary, as well. He gained broader power by arranging to be named the head of the Triborough Bridge Authority and the New York Power Authority, as well as several smaller agencies *(see Chapter Eleven)*. In his only bid for elective office, Moses lost the 1934 governor's race to Herbert Lehman.

Gubernatorial support for Moses ended with the election of Nelson A. Rockefeller, whose ability to set goals and determination to accomplish them were, given the power of the executive office, more than a match for the parks chairman. Moses resigned at the start of 1963 and was succeeded by the council vice chairman, the governor's brother, Laurance Rockefeller. In addition to parks and 35 highways, Moses left a legacy of 12 major bridges, Lincoln Center for the Performing Arts, Shea Stadium, the United Nations headquarters, housing projects that were home to thousands of New Yorkers, hundreds of city playgrounds, two hydroelectric dams, and the 1964 World's Fair. His work influenced large-scale planning in other U.S. cities, although that style of public projects lost favor in the 1950s and 1960s to less imposing development.

Historic Preservation

The historic preservation program within the agency preserves, develops, and operates state-owned historic sites and collections — a major undertaking, given the Empire State's rich and important history. The first publicly owned historic site in the nation, acquired by the state in 1850, was a Newburgh home that served as George Washington's Revolutionary War headquarters in 1782 and 1783. In a 2001 exhibit, the site presented artifacts such as two mammoth boom logs from Hudson River defenses during the war, a lock of Washington's hair, and muskets from the wars against England.

The historic preservation office also administers the State and National Registers of Historic Places, which include more than 80,000 properties of historical, architectural, archeological, and cultural significance throughout the state. Inclusion in the registers can help preservation efforts by providing official recognition, state funding, tax credits in the case of income-producing properties, and a measure of protection from federal and state undertakings such as nearby construction.

A Broad Agenda

In recent decades, the parks agency has helped developed major performing arts centers. Saratoga Performing Arts Center, which features top rock and pop performers as well as the Philadelphia Orchestra and New York City Ballet, opened in 1966 within the Saratoga State Park after a campaign begun by a local newspaper columnist. Duane LaFleche, a writer for *The Knickerbocker News* of Albany, read in early 1961 that the New York Philharmonic was considering making Stowe, VT, its summer residence. "It seems very wrong," he wrote in his column, "that a New York orchestra should have to look outside the state for a summer residence. Wouldn't the State Reservation at Saratoga Springs make a nice location?"

La Fleche's words prompted action by local civic, cultural, and legislative leaders, who had previously considered a Saratoga Arts Center an interesting possibility. Within weeks, discussions were under way with the Philharmonic and New York City Ballet. The Philharmonic eventually dropped out of the plans, but the ballet and the Philadelphia Orchestra are summer fixtures in Saratoga. SPAC is a nonprofit corporation, but closely linked to state government. The state provides free use of its facilities under a 100-year lease that originated in the 1960s. In 2005, after the center experienced financial problems, its board appointed Marcia White, a longtime aide to Senate Majority Leader Joseph Bruno, as president.

The parks agency runs Earl W. Brydges Artpark, named for a Senate majority leader from Niagara County. The popular site, near the Niagara River in Lewiston, opened in 1974.

The Office of Parks, Recreation and Historic Preservation sponsors the Empire State games — summer and winter events that are the largest state-sponsored amateur athletic competitions in the country. The agency also sponsors the Empire State Senior Games and the Empire State Games for the Physically Challenged, an international model for athletic programs serving disabled youth.

Chapter Eighteen

THE 3,166 LOCAL GOVERNMENTS: HISTORY AND STRUCTURE

Key points:

- New York is home to a complex, costly local-government structure dating from colonial times and early U.S. history.

- The number and variety of municipal units reflect broad desire for local control, but the state imposes numerous operational mandates that limit local officials' flexibility.

Where road networks are established before an area is settled, the result tends to look like the common-sense grid that covers most of Manhattan from Greenwich Village north. Through Midtown, east and west of Central Park, in Harlem and Upper Manhattan, streets form a pattern that is user-friendly and efficient. On the other hand, where people move in before such planning, streets tend to follow pedestrian lanes, cowpaths, and routes of least resistance from the terrain. Older streetscapes have their own charms, but simplicity and efficiency of use are not among them. So it is with local governments.

In much of the United States, local government is streamlined and spare compared to New York's. Here, it is a complicated, costly, sprawling, and often confusing mix. Twenty-three of the 29 states that are geographically larger than New York have fewer governmental units.[1] Florida, with almost as many residents, has two-thirds fewer local governments. Of the two states with larger populations than New York, California has fewer governments in relation to population, while Texas has more.

In New York as in other states, a local government is a legal entity, a corporation. Early on, such corporations were essentially a mixture of governmental entity and private business enterprise. From colonial times into the 1800s, individual corporations — whether private companies, or local governments — were formed by individual acts of royal authorities or the Legislature. Enactment of general authority for creation of municipalities, eliminating the need for special legislation in every instance, was a step forward for local control, just as general corporate laws represented expansion of private investors' ability to operate independently of the power of elected officials.

Today, New York State government's relationship with 3,166 local-government units is intimate, and often controversial. This chapter will examine state-local relations including:

- The wide range of structures of local-government units, including major variations within classes such as counties and cities, and state-authorized "private neighborhoods" such as condominiums and cooperatives.

- The responsibilities and challenges facing local governments in the early 21st century, including the question of local-government consolidation.

The next chapter will examine:

- The perpetual struggle for control between local elected and appointed officials, and those at the state level.

---

1   Author's calculation, using U.S. Census Bureau figures for governmental units.

- Albany's role in determining how localities can raise and spend taxpayer dollars, providing funding for local services, and forcing municipalities and school districts to use resources in ways they otherwise might not.

- Localities' powers — broad, yet still subject to state regulation — over land use.

Four Types of General Government

How many local governments are there in New York? The answer is complicated. One commonly cited figure is more than 10,000, but that number includes entities most citizens would not consider actual governments.

The Empire State has four types of general governments at the local level: counties, cities, towns, and villages. That means 1,604 chief elected officials and local councils with broad powers to influence residents' lives, including the power to impose taxes and to enact laws regulating personal behavior and business activity. These are what most people would think of as "government."

Yet taxing authority is a quintessential characteristic of government, and it goes beyond the four classes of general local government. New York has 699 school districts, each with its own taxing and other powers, as well as control over one of the most important of governmental functions. The Office of the State Comptroller classifies school districts and the four types of entities mentioned above as municipal corporations — 2,303 in all.

Fire districts also have the power to levy taxes, and deliver a basic public service. Adding the 863 districts completes the picture, shown in the nearby table, of 3,166 independent governmental units.

The comptroller's office counts another 810 "independent and discrete" special-purpose units of local government, as of 2000.[2] These include solid waste districts (with expenditures of $163 million); libraries ($159 million); off-track betting corporations ($153 million); water authorities ($106 million); industrial development agencies, housing

---

2   Office of the State Comptroller, *Comptroller's Special Report on Municipal Affairs: Data on Fire Districts and Special Purpose Units*, Albany, N.Y., November 2002.

authorities and others. The degree of independence varies; local library systems often have separately elected boards of trustees, while solid-waste districts are generally controlled by board members appointed by local elected officials.

Then, OSC says, there are 6,525 town-only special districts, legal entities that can be thought of as subsidiaries of the municipal corporations known as towns. Local officials create such entities so they can budget separately for (and charge costs to users of) services such as water, street lights, fire protection, drainage, parks, and other purposes. Counting them as governmental units brings the number to well over 10,000.

Summary of Finances for Major Classes of Local Government, 2003 *Dollars in Millions*				
	Units	*Population*	*Tax Revenue*	*Total Spending*
Counties	57	10,968,179	$8,167	$17,418
Cities	61	2,265,897	1,502	3,571
New York City	1	8,008,278	23,345	61,790
Towns	932	8,692,132	3,116	5,603
Villages	553	1,871,947	952	2,009
School districts	699	—	13,623	27,527
Fire districts	863	—	416	489
Total	**3,166**	**18,976,457**	**$51,122**	**$118,407**

Figures for counties, cities and school districts exclude New York City.
Counties' population includes cities, towns and villages.
Source: Office of the State Comptroller, *2005 Annual Report on Local Governments*

Adding to the complexity of New York's local governments, units within each class differ dramatically from each other in structure. Some counties have elected chief executives; others have appointed executives, while some have no executive at all. Cities have varying structures, too: An elected "strong mayor" whose appointment and budgetary powers are analogous to the state's governor; or a "weak mayor" who is first among equals on a city council.

Some of those differences among classes of localities are spelled out in the state Constitution and statutes. There's still more variation from one county to another, and one city to another, in the individual charters that govern dozens of local-governmental units in New York. Such charters vary in treatment of major issues such as succession to elected office, relations with unionized employees, and establishment of departments to perform various functions.

Why All These Local Governments?

The complexity of local government reflects two contrasting historical influences. State-level officials originally established counties to serve as regional administrative units throughout the state, because communication and transportation in the Revolutionary era made administration difficult from afar. Similar thinking lay behind division of the counties into towns. Today, that rationale is less compelling, especially when the state itself has regional offices for departments such as labor, environmental conservation, and parks.

The existence of cities and villages represents an impetus quite different from that behind counties and towns: The state's willingness to allow people in different areas to make different decisions on some issues.

School districts reflect still a third stream of development. Wherever people formed communities, they created schoolhouses, and eventually larger educational institutions. These were already in place throughout much of the state before the Legislature first provided some state funding for self-governing common school districts in 1812. For a century now, school districts have been accountable to Albany — yet they still retain significant local control.

For purposes of general government, every square mile of New York State is included in a county, and in either a town or city. More than half of state residents live in cities. Still, the geographic majority of the state lies within towns that include neither a city nor a village.

Some of New York's local-government entities predate the state itself. The first local administrative units emerged under the Dutch and British colonial rulers more than a century before the Revolutionary

War. In 1646, the Dutch West India Company, which oversaw the colony then known as New Netherland, "granted what appear to have been certain municipal privileges" to the Village of Breuckelen, predecessor of today's Brooklyn.[3] New Amsterdam, forerunner of New York City; and Fort Orange, later known as Albany, received similar approval to perform municipal functions within the following two decades.

After control of New Netherland passed from the Dutch to the English in 1664, Governor Richard Nicolls convened delegates from English-majority areas of the colony in Hempstead, Nassau County.[4] At Nicolls' initiative, delegates adopted what became known as the Duke of York's laws, which included recognition of 17 towns and creation of the county of Yorkshire, covering present-day Long Island, Staten Island and Westchester.

The first formally recognized cities, New York and Albany, were chartered in 1686. "Freemen," adult white males who met property and other requirements, were allowed to elect aldermen and constables, although appointment of the mayor was left to the governor and council.

The first New York State Constitution, adopted in 1777, recognized counties, towns, and cities as the only units of local government. In the 1790s, the Legislature effectively created what today is recognized as the village form of government by allowing certain hamlets in Rensselaer and Saratoga counties to establish police and land-use powers.

Major Units of Local Government: Counties

Early in the development of New York, state legislators took two steps to establish local governments in a comprehensive, planned way — dividing the state into counties, and then the counties into towns. The colonial General Assembly convened by Governor Thomas Dongan in 1683 divided the then-province of New York into 12 counties to serve as the basis for legislative representation and a new system of courts.

---

3 New York State Department of State, *Local Government Handbook, 5th Edition*, Albany, NY, 2000.

4 Presumably, the governor could count on representatives from those areas to approve his proposals. Critics of the modern New York Legislature say its members determine patterns of legislative representation to preserve their own power. Some things never change.

(The 12 included Cornwall, now part of Maine; and Dukes, now much of the coastal area of Massachusetts.) The remaining counties were established by acts of the Legislature that separated sections of the original 10, reducing the size of counties and thus bringing them closer to the people.

The Legislature's last creation of a new county came in 1914, when Bronx County was organized separately from New York County. The five counties that make up New York City, also known as boroughs, retain some vestiges of county status — for instance, each has a locally elected district attorney. But, unlike other counties, the five in New York City do not have independent fiscal or legislative powers. The state's largest city government centralizes most county-type functions for its five boroughs.

Structure of County Governments

The concept of county governments as arms of the state government was reflected in such acts of the Legislature as the requirement that each county establish poor houses to care for the needy, and the overlapping state-local control of county courts. Today's friction between Albany and localities over funding of health-care and other programs reflects both the historical function of counties as local arms of the state government, and policy choices by state leaders such as the decision to create an expansive Medicaid system that required revenue beyond the state's own.

Before the 1930s, counties across the state outside New York City had similar forms of government. Elected leaders of municipalities met as the supervisors of the county to create the county budget, appoint department heads and make major policy decisions. New York developed that county supervisor form of government, which was later adopted by states such as New Jersey and Michigan.[5] Growth in the size and complexity of county governments' responsibilities in social welfare, health, and other spheres, gradually gave rise to calls for stronger, more unified leadership.

The first counties to experience significant suburban growth, Nassau and Westchester, received special charters from the Legislature to

---

5   Charles R. Adrian, *State and Local Governments*, New York, NY: McGraw-Hill, 1967, p. 209.

The Role of Counties

County governments in New York and other states have played major roles in the daily lives of local residents, especially outside metropolitan areas. Charles R. Adrian described that role this way:

> Until the advent of the auto and the telephone, the county was the largest government with which the citizen could hope to have direct, personal contact. Especially in rural areas, a legion of social organizations were established using the county as the area of focus. It became a center for the administration of health, welfare, and educational programs, for the dispensing of justice, for the paying of taxes (even state taxes), for the election of legislative representatives, for the agricultural extension program, for voluntary social agencies, for such colorful bits of Americana as the county fair, for the keeping of vital statistics and of land ownership and debt records, for the maintenance of roads, and for a thousand other things, governmental and otherwise. The county seat was a prize sought, sometimes in bitter fashion, by every community. The winning community became a trade center, the seat of the local bureaucracy, the home of governmental hangers-on such as lawyers and members of abstract companies, the location for the county fair (usually), the recreation and business center, and the home of retired farmers. The county was not an impersonal administrative unit of the state with arbitrary boundaries. It was rather a real, an important, social and political center.*

---

*   Adrian, *State and Local Governments*, ibid.

establish new forms of government in the 1930s. In 1959, voters approved a constitutional amendment giving all counties the right to adopt a charter without special authorization. Nineteen counties now have individual charters, with Rockland the most recent to adopt in 1983. Ulster County was considering adoption of a county charter in 2006.

One common argument in favor of charter status for counties is the ability to create the office of county executive, which is seen as bringing stronger leadership and greater accountability to county government. New York State, its towns, and most cities and villages have an elected chief executive, while only 16 of the state's most populated counties did as of early 2006. Thirty-one counties outside New York City had an appointed county manager or administrator, selected by the legislative body. Ten mostly smaller, rural counties retained the chair of the legislature (or of the board of supervisors) as the chief administrative officer, and "strong committee" systems with legislative committees overseeing county policy and departments.[6]

The 20th century also saw most counties change from boards of supervisors to legislatures whose members are elected independently and serve only as county officials. Some 17 counties retained the supervisors form (as opposed to legislatures). At the start of the 21st century, though, some local officials wondered whether New York's multiple layers of local government might work better with a return to the board of supervisors approach.

> Participants noted that a legislative body comprised of supervisors lives with local problems every day. They understand the issues intimately.... Furthermore, serving on a board of supervisors helps local government managers think more in terms of partnership in regional governance, and less in terms of competition with surrounding jurisdictions. In the regional meetings, participants from counties with boards of supervisors reported a higher level of cooperation around difficult issues than those with other forms of county governance.[7]

Counties in the 21st Century

Today, counties (including, for these purposes, New York City) play particularly important roles in these areas, subject to direction of the state:

- **Providing and overseeing health and human services.** Local social-services agencies determine eligibility — and in some cases deliver benefits for — Medicaid, Food Stamps, child care, and other federal and state assistance programs covering some 4 million New Yorkers. Each county has a health commissioner, who has broad powers analogous to those of the state health commissioner (see Chapter Twelve). Health departments provide some publicly funded medical services directly, and arrange others, for

---

6   Jeff Osinski, *County Government Organization in New York State*, Albany, NY: New York State Association of Counties, December 2005.

7   Sydney Cresswell, Terrence Maxwell, and Jordan Wishy, *Municipal Leaders Talk About Governing New York's Communities*, Albany, NY: Intergovernmental Solutions Program, Nelson A. Rockefeller College of Public Affairs & Policy, 2006.

needy individuals and families. Many counties provide general services for the aging; 43 operate their own nursing homes. Counties oversee taxpayer-funded mental-health and substance-abuse treatment programs. They bear the primary responsibility for protecting children in troubled families from abuse and neglect, and for seeing that noncustodial parents pay child support.

- **Prosecuting, trying, punishing, and helping rehabilitate suspected and convicted criminals.** Municipal police forces make most arrests (county sheriff's offices play a lesser role, as do the State Police). Once an individual is arrested, though, unless and until he goes to state prison, most criminal-justice activity is a function of county government. The district attorney's office prosecutes the case in county-level or municipal court, or negotiates a plea bargain; if the accused cannot afford a lawyer, the county public defender's office provides one. Individuals sentenced to a year or less in prison serve their time in county or New York City jails. If sentenced to probation, they are under the supervision of a county probation department. County coroners and medical examiners determine cause of death in cases of suspected homicide. Increasingly, counties are responsible for centralizing and overseeing emergency-response efforts.

- **Creating transparency, and preventing and settling conflicts, in private business dealings.** County clerk's offices serve as repositories for deeds that reveal publicly who owns a given property in the county; when and by whom its ownership has been transferred; and for what purchase price (deed filings must show payment of transfer tax, which indicates the selling price). County clerks also hold, and make publicly available, filings in civil cases heard by resident state Supreme Court justices. Surrogate's courts in each county settle contested wills and estates.

- **Building and maintaining essential physical infrastructure.** Counties own and maintain 20,382 miles of roads in the state, second only to towns. Most sewer and water authorities in the state were established by counties and operate countywide.

- **Encouraging business and job growth.** In the past four decades, with development of business-incentive programs,
  counties have played a growing role in helping local entre-
  preneurs and potential outside investors make use of federal,
  state, and local incentive and assistance programs.

County boards of elections oversee voting in federal, state, and local
elections. Civil-service commissions conduct exams for competitive
appointments in local governments. Other functions include processing
drivers' licenses and vehicle registrations; and operating parks, libraries, and cooperative-extension offices.

Major Units of Local Government: Cities, Towns, and Villages

Cities and villages in New York arose from residents' needs for police
and fire protection, physical infrastructure such as streets and water
systems, and other services. During the mid- to late 20th century, new
residents streaming into towns often demanded similar services outside
the urban borders. Two centuries after the Legislature mapped towns all
across the state, the three classes of municipal government provide similar types of services. With some variation, the range of functions in cities, towns, and villages includes:

- **Police and fire protection.** At 20 and 14 percent of total
  spending, respectively, such services made up more than a
  third of costs for cities outside New York in 2004. Public
  safety represented 14 percent of towns' spending, and 23
  percent for villages, according to the Office of the State
  Comptroller.

- **Street and road maintenance.** Towns are in charge of more
  than half of all road mileage in New York. Highways represented the largest share of their costs — 18.4 percent — in
  2003.

- **Regulation of land use.** The three classes of government
  make most land-use decisions through planning and zoning
  appeals boards, and building departments that issue permits
  and conduct inspections of individual properties.

- **Courts for less serious crimes.** Most misdemeanors and violations (the lowest level of crimes, such as speeding) are adjudicated in municipal courts.

- **Parks and recreation.** For most New Yorkers, the closest park is owned by a city, town, or village.

- **Water and sewer service.** An early impetus to creation of many municipalities, provision of such infrastructure remains one of the most basic tasks for local governments today. Many cities have aging water systems that will require costly capital investment in coming years; some growing towns face tough choices as they near the capacity of systems designed for smaller populations.

- **Property assessment for taxing purposes.** The methods that local policymakers and assessors must use to determine individual tax bills are set in Albany, but the actual decisions are made by local officials who use their own judgement — subject to review by the courts.

Cities

The Empire State's 62 cities today represent a small minority of local-government units in New York. But for the first two centuries or more of the state's existence, "local government" mostly meant government by cities or their municipal cousins, villages.

Today, slightly more than half of state residents live in cities — with the great bulk of those in New York City, which by itself represents 42 percent of the state's population. Residents of the nation's largest city might be more likely to think of "local government" as their community board, given that the mayor and City Council claim as many constituents as governors and legislatures in 39 states. Outside the Big Apple, cities represent a relatively small and shrinking proportion of state population, 12 percent as of the 2000 census. Still, cities remain dominant players in the economic and social lives of most regions. Long after retail centers moved to the suburbs, major communications, cultural, and governmental headquarters remain concentrated in the cities. In most metro areas, more residents live outside the city limits than inside — yet the local newspaper, perhaps the single leading exemplar of community identity, remains in the city.[8]

Like counties, cities in New York come in various governmental forms. The most common is the familiar mayor-council structure, used in 45 cities. But there are different forms within this category. In "strong mayor" cities, the chief executive has significant power over major appointments and the budget — and, in some cases, veto power over legislation approved by the council. "Weak" mayors are members of the city council and serve as ceremonial leaders, but the council as a whole — often with strong committees — develops the budget and appoints department heads.

In New York as throughout the country, weak mayors were more common a century and more ago than they are today. The same imperatives that drove strengthening of the governor's office and creation of county executives — sharp increases in the responsibilities and complexity of government—led most communities to conclude they would be better served with a strong elected executive. Weak-mayor systems remain primarily in smaller cities. There, voters may be more able to assess the performance of the municipal government, and thus see less need to vest control and accountability in a strong executive.

Fourteen cities have councils and an appointed city manager, typically invested with chief-executive powers similar to those of strong mayors (except veto authority). As of 2006, three smaller cities — Saratoga Springs, Mechanicville, and Sherrill — still elected commissioners to oversee major functions such as finance and public works; those commissioners together, along with the mayor, formed the city council. A charter-revision commission in Saratoga Springs recommended a change to a strong-mayor form in 2006. Voters were to decide the issue that November.

In thinking about cities in New York State, as in so many other ways, there are two categories: New York City, and everything else.

Downstate Vitality — New York City

If one of the central themes in state government is Albany's often troubled relationships with localities, the most consequential example is New York City. The state's largest city rightfully thinks of itself in a

---

8   The capital city's newspaper, the Albany *Times Union*, is one notable exception.

global context — most of its residents know and care little about state government. The political-social establishment looks down its nose at Albany; once a year or so, the city's most influential newspaper writes about the state capital as if conducting an anthropological study. The mayor of New York City is a major media figure, able to command a bully pulpit often exceeding that of the governor.

Yet Albany matters a great deal to the Big Apple. City leaders must seek the Legislature's approval for a myriad of decisions involving budgetary, policy, and operational choices. Often, the city's desires are ignored; even when they are not, city leaders must negotiate with legislators from other regions who may have little incentive to be helpful.

As is true with all localities, state officials also have the affirmative power to enact major policy decisions that New York City leaders oppose strenuously. In 1999, legislators eliminated the city commuter tax, a levy of up to 0.65 percent on income earned by out-of-town residents who work in the five boroughs. City leaders opposed the change, which cut receipts by $400 million or more a year. Their arguments failed because legislative leaders believed that eliminating the tax might help candidates for a suburban seat in the Senate.

New York City and Upstate New York have viewed each other with suspicion for much of the state's history. One example: Residents in each area tend to believe that their tax dollars subsidize the other. Detailed studies of the state's revenues and spending show that Upstate receives more in state appropriations than it pays in taxes, and that New York City pays more than it receives, at least when Wall Street is doing well.[9] When Governor Rockefeller successfully pushed for creation of the state's Medicaid program in the 1960s, the state required local cost-sharing in large part because Upstate legislators feared New York City residents would benefit most under the program. The local-share requirement was an effort to ensure that city officials would impose some limits on the program. It's uncertain the results were as intended.

---

9   See, for example, Kent Gardner, *Balance of Revenue & Expenditure Among New York State Regions*, Rochester, NY: Center for Governmental Research, 2004. Because the state's tax system is designed to redistribute wealth from richer to poorer individuals, the suburban areas of Long Island and Westchester-Rockland send billions more to Albany than they receive — an experience similar to New York State's with regard to the federal budget.

While Albany does much to shape governmental decisions in New York City, it's also true that the city always holds the potential to reshape state-government policy.

As a result of the Campaign for Fiscal Equity lawsuit brought by city residents, Albany legislators decided in 2006 to send $1.8 billion in construction aid, and hundreds of millions in new operating aid, to the city school system. The decision was, among other things, an affirmation of the bully pulpit held by the mayor of New York, and a reminder of the power of the city's strong representation in the Legislature. In 2003, public pressure from Mayor Bloomberg helped persuade state legislators to provide additional budget assistance to the city. Legislative leaders sought to avoid including such a cost in the pending year's financial plan. Instead, they agreed that the state would take over the obligation for $170 million in bonds that the city's Municipal Assistance Corporation had originally issued in the wake of the mid-1970s fiscal crisis, and that were scheduled to be fully paid in 2008. The effect was to transfer to taxpayers around the state the burden of repaying debt the city had incurred nearly three decades earlier (to pay for operational expenses such as city employees' salaries). The new bonds would last decades longer, delaying ultimate repayment to 63 years from the time of the original expense.

From the era of Boss Tweed in the mid-1800s to that of Mayor Lindsay in the 1960s, New York City has been easy to caricature for corruption, carefree spending and other governmental ills. Yet, thanks partly to Albany's intervention in the fiscal crises of the mid-1970s, and partly to reformist initiatives from its own citizens, the city's governmental structures and practices include much to recommend elsewhere.

The city charter establishes a strong mayor's office, an important accountability measure in a municipality of more than 8 million residents. The mayor's fiscal powers, for instance, include authority to determine the amount of revenue available for each year's budget. That power, which New York governors do not possess, effectively means the mayor can limit the size of the budget — thus reducing the chances of irresponsible spending, many analysts believe.

The charter also institutionalizes performance measurement in various ways. The best known, the annual mayor's management report, provides grades on cleanliness of parks, average response time to fires, timeliness of subways and buses, and other indicators related to city services. A separate report on social indicators presents and analyzes "the social, economic and environmental health of the city," with current and five-year data on unemployment, poverty, child welfare, housing quality, and other measures, along with national and/or regional comparisons and plans for responding to "significant problems" shown in the data. Some observers believe the city charter requires too many such reports — a total of more than 30.[10] But the state, and other major municipalities, could benefit from some of the same types of reporting.

Fiscal reforms resulting from the mid-1970s crisis left New York City with a budgetary system more transparent and accountable than that of any other municipality or the state itself. Two state agencies — a special unit of the Office of the State Comptroller, and the Financial Control Board — are charged with monitoring the city budget. Each reports periodically on the balance between revenues and expenditures, with an eye on potential gaps. From 1975 to mid-1986, the city was required to win the control board's approval for its budgets. The law establishing the board still provides for reinstatement of that requirement if the city fails to pay debt service when due or shows other signs of financial failure. The city has also established a local Independent Budget Office as another source of fiscal oversight and policy analysis.

More than a century after the consolidation of some 40 municipalities (including Brooklyn and Staten Island) into the greater City of New York, the city retains smaller, "local" governments in the form of five boroughs and 59 community boards. Borough presidents' powers include monitoring service delivery and budgetary priorities in their respective locales, and appointing representatives to the city Planning Commission and other policy-making boards. Community boards have advisory powers relating to land use and zoning, the city budget, delivery of municipal services and other matters. Their members, elected but unpaid, are often politically involved and able to influence other elected officials informally as well as through official channels.

Upstate Decline

New York State was the unquestioned economic powerhouse of the nation for most of the 19th century, and half of the 20th. Cities both Up-

---

10 See, for instance, Jacob B. Ukeles, *Toward a Performance and Accountability Management System for New York City Government*, report submitted to the New York City Charter Revision Commission, July 2005.

state and Downstate boomed, thanks to factors such as the opening of the Erie Canal, the flowering of the Industrial Revolution, and continuing streams of international immigration.

The majority of cities in the Empire State, 50 or so, are north and west of the downstate metropolitan area. They developed as industrial and social centers in the late 1700s and early 1800s. Most saw rapid growth again in the early 1900s as European immigrants, and then African-Americans from the South, moved into the state.

After 1950, most cities in the state started a downward spiral that was to continue for half a century. Buffalo lost half its population from 1950 to 2000, the fourth-highest decline among large cities nationwide. Rochester and Syracuse lost one in three residents during the period. Economic losses contribute to major budgetary pressures, as city tax bases fail to provide revenue increases normally enjoyed by areas outside the urban centers. *(See Chapter Three.)*

Not all the state's cities are struggling. As of 2000, the poverty rate in Rye (Westchester County) was 2.5 percent, less than one-quarter the national rate. Cities such as Glen Cove, Saratoga Springs, and White Plains also had poverty rates well below the national average. Contrary to the picture in most Upstate cities, Saratoga's population rose 31 percent from 1970 to 2000.

Towns

They don't get as much media attention as the cities. They don't tax and spend nearly as much as school districts. But by some measures, towns are the dominant local-government entities in New York. There are more of them — 932 — than any other class of local governments. They cover nearly 98 percent of the state's land mass, with cities and Indian reservations making up the rest. (Villages are all within towns.) Their total population, around 8.7 million, is almost four times that of the cities outside New York City, and only a few hundred thousand behind the big city itself. Towns elect more local officials than villages, cities, counties or school districts — more than 4,000 supervisors and council members, and thousands more clerks, justices, highway superintendents, assessors, and tax collectors.

One of the first acts by the young New York State Legislature, in 1788, was to divide every county into towns (119 had already been established by then).[11] Most of the state's cities and villages were chartered later from within the towns.

Today, towns vary dramatically in size and character. Hempstead — the largest, with 755,924 residents in 2000 — has more in common with many cities than with small or medium-sized towns. Much of it has an urban feel (there is a "downtown" Hempstead), and the town's population dropped noticeably from 1970 to 2000, like those in many cities. Still, its low poverty rate — 5.8 percent in 2000 — also reflected the presence of wealthier suburban neighborhoods not found in the state's troubled cities.

At the other end of the spectrum, the town of Red House in Cattaraugus County had 38 residents as of the last national census. Nearly half the geographic size of Hempstead, Red House raised just $50,856 in property taxes in 2004, less than the total bill on some individual properties in Hempstead.

With early settlement concentrated in small areas that developed into modern urban centers, New York State's towns historically were home to a relatively small share of the state's population. As recently as 1920, 83 percent of residents were classified as urban, and the remainder rural.[12] From the 1950s through the 1980s, suburban towns experienced dramatic growth, like those throughout the nation. By 1980, only 54 percent of New Yorkers lived in the cities. Long Island, with 13 towns and two small cities, added 1.7 million residents from 1950 to 1980, nearly two-thirds of the state's growth during the period. Westchester, the suburban county immediately north of New York City, boomed as well. Farther Upstate, towns such as Amherst (Erie County) also grew sharply.

While overall town growth moderated in the last two decades of the 20th century, issues related to development remain among the most pressing for many towns — including, for the first time, "exurban" areas that are the next step beyond urban centers and suburbs. The 1990s saw some inner suburban towns, where urban residents had moved decades earlier, shrinking while previously rural areas attracted new growth.

---

11 Gerald Benjamin, "Town government," entry in *The Encyclopedia of New York State*, ibid.

12 James Malcolm, ed., *The New York Red Book*, Albany, NY: J.B. Lyon Co., 1923; p. 597.

In the last quarter of the 20th century, numerous towns acted to restrict development with steps such as increasing minimum lot sizes for new homes, purchasing and setting aside undeveloped land for long-term preservation, enacting temporary development moratoria, and adopting comprehensive land-use plans for the first time.

Villages

If it's true, as many critics say, that New York's broad array of local governments is anachronistic, the state's 553 villages may best illustrate the problem. Most were incorporated in the 19th century, when population patterns and limits on the powers of towns made creation of a village the only way for residents to avail themselves of local-government services.

The new Constitution adopted in 1846 directed the Legislature to "provide for the organization of cities and incorporated villages." A general Village Law was adopted the following year, but the Legislature continued to enact special charters into the 1870s, when another constitutional amendment eliminated the practice.

Movement of residents from cities to suburbs, and resulting demand for services such as water and sewers, led to creation of 160 villages in the first half of the 20th century.[13] Gerald Benjamin writes that the state originally created towns "with limited powers to ensure the delivery of local services required in rural areas: highways, criminal justice, fence maintenance, and animal regulation." Legislation in 1890 gave selected towns authority to build water and sewer systems, dispose of garbage and provide other services. Not until 1932 did larger towns receive the automatic right to provide such services; only in the 1960s did the Legislature extend such power to all towns.[14] Authorization for towns to create special water and sewer districts eliminated the need for creation of villages for such purposes. Today, land-use issues are a common concern for residents who seek to form new villages.

As towns have developed services once not permitted outside village boundaries, the need for separate village governments has declined. Most villages could transfer existing services to the local town

---

13 New York State Department of State, *Local Government Handbook*, Albany, NY.

14 Gerald Benjamin, "Town government," entry in *The Encyclopedia of New York State*.

government, but dissolution is rare. In 2003, Governor Pataki proposed a way to encourage dissolution of villages while preserving local identity by allowing designation of the same geographic area as a hamlet. The Legislature did not approve the change.

With concern about property taxes continuing to rise around the state, numerous villages and towns have discussed consolidating services such as police and highway departments. Yet even those steps — less ambitious than consolidation of governmental units — occur each year in only a handful of municipalities around the state.

Five villages in the state are coterminous with towns. Some created dual governmental structures to attract state revenue-sharing assistance due to both units of government; others wanted to avoid annexation into a nearby city. In Scarsdale, Westchester County, the same local officials serve as town and village leaders, meeting separately in each role.

Fire Districts

Benjamin Franklin is popularly credited with creating America's first volunteer fire company in Philadelphia, in 1736. (Boston had mutual fire-protection organizations earlier, but such groups generally served only members.) By the mid-1800s, some cities had created paid, full-time fire departments. Outside cities, as mentioned above, clusters of residents in many communities created villages for the purpose of providing fire, police and other services. In the geographic majority of the state, though, volunteer services remained the norm. At first, it was neighbors joining in "bucket brigades." Eventually, modern volunteer fire companies developed with operations as sophisticated as those of paid fire departments.

Volunteer fire departments in New York are organized either as fire districts, which are public corporations with legal status separate from other municipalities; or as fire protection districts, areas which a municipality designates as receiving fire protection from a particular organization. The state's 863 fire districts have the power to impose property taxes and to borrow. While most are small, 13 districts had budgets over $5 million in 2004, according to data reported by the Office of the State Comptroller. The Eastchester district, 20 miles north of New York City, collected $10.3 million in property taxes — more than the tax levy in half the school districts in the state. The department's firefighting staff includes both paid and volunteer firefighters; other paid positions include those of an attorney and department secretary.

In the latter half of the 20th century, many fire companies began providing ambulance service to take individuals to hospitals in nearby cities during health emergencies. Eventually, emergency medical technicians became part of the equation, so that emergency treatment could be provided before a trip to the hospital. Some 70 to 80 percent of EMS squads in the state are affiliated with fire departments.[15]

By the 1990s, volunteer services were straining to do the job they'd performed for more than a century. More residents outside the cities meant more calls for assistance. The decline of farming, and concentration of employment in urban and suburban centers, meant most individuals found it difficult or impossible to volunteer.

Another cause of the decline, town officials say, has been sharply increasing regulation by federal and state authorities. Long-tenured emergency personnel complain that rules for maintaining certification require more training than original certification did years ago. Some volunteers should be allowed to serve with basic training in first aid and transport, the New York State Association of Towns suggests. The state Health Department has authorized "no-test" pilot programs under which some volunteers could begin service before receiving certification.

At the start of the 21st century, volunteer emergency services in the state were facing a potential choice between dramatic increases in taxpayer costs or elimination of services. Roughly 110,000 New Yorkers served as volunteer firefighters, and 40,000 as volunteer emergency personnel.[16] Replacing those volunteers with paid staff could cost $7 billion a year, according to the Firemen's Association of the State of New York. That would represent roughly a one-third increase in property taxes outside the state's 62 cities.

As staffing pressure on volunteer emergency services grew, efforts to create new incentives for volunteers increased. Some departments now offer health insurance, retirement plans, and other incentives. In 2006, the Legislature created a $200 income-tax credit for volunteer firefighters and ambulance workers.

---

15 Association of Towns of the State of New York, "Volunteer Emergency Medical Services" report.

16 Association of Towns of New York State, "Volunteer Emergency Services: A System in Crisis," Albany, NY, 2005.

Meanwhile, town and volunteer services are examining potential new revenue sources. One option would be user fees for some emergency and rescue services, intended partly to discourage what some officials consider needless use of hard-pressed volunteer services. Some local officials are also considering countywide emergency services, crossing traditional municipal lines and potentially increasing efficiency.

Condos, Coops, and Other "Private Neighborhoods"

If a governmental unit can be defined as an entity that makes and enforces decisions for raising revenue and providing services in a given location, entities that are variously described as residential community associations or private neighborhoods may fit the bill.

By one industry estimate, one in three new housing units built in the United States since 1970 has been part of a private community association — a condominium, homeowners association, or cooperative. Some 226,000 residential units in New York State were assessed as condominiums in 2005, according to the state Office of Real Property Services (ORPS). Around 8,000 buildings were classified as cooperatives. Local assessors, who report the data to ORPS, do not count individual units within coop buildings.

Such associations are, in important ways, their own very localized governments. They charge fees, the equivalent of taxes, for maintenance of common areas such as recreational areas and streets, as well as for services such as trash collection and snow plowing. Membership in the association is mandatory for anyone choosing to live within its boundaries. There are rules, analogous to municipal zoning, as to what can and can't be done with individually owned property. Residents elect leaders who make key decisions for the group. Like municipalities, the associations exist as a function of state laws. They're created, however, through binding covenants on real-estate transactions, rather than as municipal corporations by acts of the Legislature. Such covenants and restrictions are attached to deeds on the real property, making them permanent and enforceable by the courts.

In traditional condominiums, each resident owns a particular space and a share in ownership of the land, structures, and facilities such as central electrical systems, stairways, roofs, and recreational space.

Such ownership can apply not only in apartment-style buildings, but — increasingly common — in groups of detached, single-family homes.

Unlike the condo structure, a homeowner association is a separate legal entity that holds title to common areas; enforces deed covenants regarding structural changes and other matters; and involves individual owners as shareholders of the association.

In cooperatives, residents share ownership of the entire property, including individual units. Coops make up a relatively small number of residential community associations, in New York and nationally.

Condominium ownership rose across the United States after the federal government began allowing mortgage insurance on such properties in the early 1960s. New York's Condominium Act was enacted in 1964. Amendments enacted in 1974 led to development of more commercial and professional-office condominiums. As of 2005, the state Office of Real Property Services reported some 226,000 condo units statewide, based on data supplied by local assessors. Cooperative buildings are assessed as single units, so data on total units were not available.

Some observers lament the growth of homeowner associations as a breakdown of community bonds and self-segregation by the wealthy. Others see such growth as expansion of individuals' rights to live as they choose. The former Advisory Commission on Intergovernmental Relations pointed to these advantages of residential community associations:

> Generally, RCAs allow developers to produce more attractive and marketable homes, which include a livable environment, not just a house. The RCA also gives the developer options to cut costs and to work within a more flexible regulatory framework. Homeowners receive a range of choices in communities and service packages.... In some communities, owners can gain comparatively affordable housing. RCAs also permit home ownership in urban locations that would be beyond the means of most middle class buyers. Thus, goals for meeting the needs of special market niches are facilitated by RCA development. When RCAs are significantly self-financing, local governments find their tax base expanded, potentially without comparable expansion in the demand for those public services the RCA provides itself.[17]

---

17 Advisory Commission on Intergovernmental Relations, *Residential Community Associations: Questions and Answers for Public Officials*, Washington, DC, July 1989.

Apart from the philosophical debate, condominiums in particular present an increasing fiscal challenge for local governments in parts of New York. State laws governing condos require that the assessments on individual units not exceed the valuation that the condo property as a whole would have if assessed as one parcel. The effect is to assess individual properties as if they were rental units, which results in lower valuations (and thus tax payments). The savings to homeowners, and loss to localities and schools, can be 50 percent or more of taxes on a comparable single-family home. The Legislature enacted the requirement to give localities an incentive to limit conversion of rental units to condominium status.

In recent years, increasing numbers of developers in New York City, its immediate suburbs, and parts of Upstate New York have been selling new homes as condominium units to reduce the property tax on purchasers. The effect is to shift part of the tax burden to other taxpayers, both residents and businesses. Localities in Western New York, including the towns of Amherst and Hamburg and the city of Lockport, have asked the Legislature to revise the law, according to the state Office of Real Property Services.[18] A 1997 statute gave municipalities the power to adopt a local law prohibiting condominium tax exemptions for property converted to such status. The law does not apply to newly built homes.

Cutting Across Local-Government Barriers

After a quarter-millennium of creating more general-purpose local governments, in the last decades of the 20th century New Yorkers started thinking seriously about consolidating government entities and services. School districts went through waves of consolidation in the early 20th century, partly due to a combination of carrots and sticks preferred by Albany. The total number of districts dropped by more than 90 percent from the 10,625 counted in 1905 to today's figure of fewer than 800.

State leaders have not been willing to force consolidation of local-government entities. For more than a decade, the state has offered incentives for localities to work cooperatively and to consider consolidation of services. In 2006, Governor Pataki and the Legislature went

---

18 Office of Real Property Services, "Municipalities suffering growing pains with spread of condominiums," *The Uniform Standard*, Albany, N.Y., March 2005.

further, expanding from \$2.75 million to \$25 million a program known as Shared Municipal Services Incentives. The same year, citizen activists in Broome County started a campaign to persuade local governments to merge, as a means of reducing costs. Significant steps to consolidate services and units of government are still rare, however.

The state Constitution creates daunting hurdles to consolidation of local governments. The "Bill of Rights for local governments" in Article IX protects localities from annexation by requiring majority approval of the people in a territory to be annexed, as well as the governing boards of both the annexed and annexing units. Richard Briffault suggests that reducing or eliminating such hurdles might be a useful step toward greater flexibility in rationalizing New York's complicated system of local governments.[19]

In the absence of such constitutional change, consolidating units of government or services requires broad support and absence of organized opposition. Gerald Benjamin notes key reasons for the lack of consolidation to date:

> Although the layering and complexity of local government in New York increases costs and reduces the accountability of elected officials to the citizenry, efforts to reduce the number of local governments have met with little success. Such reform threatens the jobs of local employees and elected officials and creates uncertainty about property values and the quality of local services after the proposed change. Furthermore, citizens identify existing local government structures with their idea of community and resist linkage to places that might be less affluent or more racially and ethnically diverse. Thus reformers have come to advocate consolidating local services as an alternative to restructuring.[20]

In 1996, the Legislature authorized consolidation of county water, sewer, and garbage districts, and gave counties the power to engage in service contracts with other counties for such purposes. Other recent changes have included legislation to guarantee that dissolution of a village or other entity would not diminish state aid to local residents.

19 Richard Briffault, "Local Governments and the State Constitution: A Framework for Analysis," in *Decision 1997: Constitutional Change in New York,* Albany, NY: Rockefeller Institute Press, 1997, p. 190.

20 Gerald Benjamin, "Local government jurisdictions," entry in *The Encyclopedia of New York State,* Peter Eisenstadt, ed., Syracuse, NY: Syracuse University Press, 2005; p. 918.

Despite those and other steps, the potential for cooperative efforts remains far greater than the reality. Many observers still note the common sight of a state, county, or municipal snowplow traveling with its plow blade in the air, missing the virtually cost-free opportunity to clear roads while on the way to a section of highway owned by the government entity that owns the plow. Equally common is the presence of police officers from two, three, or even four local entities (the State Police, county sheriff's deputies, town, and village police) on a given highway.

Local Government Finance

Albany's power over local governments is plenary. But by one key measure — taxing and spending — local governments in New York are more influential than the state. In fiscal 2003, New York State's tax revenues were $40.7 billion. Those imposed by New York City, other municipal entities, and school districts totaled $51.1 billion.

As a matter of simple arithmetic, local taxes are more to blame for New York's highest-in-the-nation tax burden than are the taxes Albany imposes. As of fiscal 2002, local taxes per capita in the Empire State were 83 percent higher than average, while state-level taxes were 20 percent above average. As local officials would be quick to note, though, Medicaid and other costs imposed by Albany explain some of the difference.

As noted earlier, while the state's personal income tax generates the lion's share of Albany's tax revenue, the property tax represents nearly two-thirds of tax revenue for localities. Outside New York City, with its unique mix of local taxes, the reliance on property taxes is even higher.

Localities throughout the state spent $118.4 billion in fiscal 2003 (again, far above Albany's $89.4 billion expenditures for the year). That total includes federal and state aid, as well as local tax dollars and nontax revenue such as fees for parks, waste removal, and other services.

The biggest chunk of local spending goes to education. School districts, including New York City's, spent $41.4 billion in 2003, according to the Office of the State Comptroller. Health and social services combined for almost one in four dollars, while employee benefits (not counting wages and salaries) made up the third-largest cost for local taxpayers.

Local Government Expenditures by Function, 2003 *(dollars in millions)*		
	Amount	*Percent of Total*
General Government	$4,765	4.8%
Public Safety	9,681	9.8%
Health	8,620	8.8%
Sanitation	2,499	2.5%
Highways	1,792	1.8%
Social Services	14,104	14.4%
Culture and Recreation	1,471	1.5%
Education	31,881	32.4%
Employee Benefits	12,598	12.8%
All Other	10,871	11.1%
Total	**$98,282**	**100%**

Data include all major classes of local government (counties, cities, towns, villages, school districts, and fire districts).
Source: Office of the State Comptroller

The Property Tax: Who Pays, and How Much?

Most working people pay far more in federal and state income taxes than in local property tax. Those other taxes are imposed from far away, though. And, like the sales tax, they usually are collected in relatively small amounts throughout the year. Both factors help make the property tax even less popular than other revenue sources.

Further, who pays how much in property taxes is public information. One neighbor can find another's property assessment, and resulting tax, just by visiting Town Hall (or, increasingly, using the Internet). Given human nature, many residents see inequity if their tax bills are higher than some others, while perceiving no problem in their own bills being lower than some of their neighbors. For these and other reasons, public-opinion surveys commonly rank the property tax as the most objectionable. In most of New York, property taxes are relatively higher than those in other states, fueling the criticism here.

Property-tax levies are highest in the Long Island and mid-Hudson regions. But property values are higher there than in most of the state, as well. When adjusted for market value, property taxes are highest in Upstate counties where lack of economic growth has hurt property values — Allegany, Montgomery, and Broome, for example.[21]

The tax on an individual property results from two factors. First is the total tax rate from all the units of local government — the county, the town or city, perhaps a village, library, and fire district. Second is the taxable value of the property, as assessed by local elected or appointed officials.

Because of their direct impact on voters' finances, property assessments have long been one of the most controversial actions of local government — and one of the most susceptible to political favoritism. Well-oiled political machines such as the Republican organization in Nassau County and its Democratic counterpart in Albany County made "helping" taxpayers with their assessments a staple of the favors they granted to supporters — and, at least by implication, withheld from others. Aside from such outright favoritism, property assessing in New York and other states represented government's failure to keep up with the times. As some property values rose and others fell, even an assessment roll that was fair and accurate at one time became less so within a few years. Local political leaders saw such changes as increasing their power to grant or withhold favors in the form of assistance with assessment challenges. Most municipalities went years, or even decades, without full updates to assessment rolls, relying instead on updates when properties changed hands. Such an approach rewarded longtime property owners, who were also more likely to be loyal supporters of the party in power. Assessors were elected, rather than appointed, contributing to the politicization of assessments.

In the 1970s and 1980s, after property owners were increasingly successful at winning court challenges to inequitable assessments, the Legislature and local officials made numerous changes. Towns were given the option to convert from elected to appointed assessors. Minimum qualifications were established for such positions, including state certification for assessors in many localities. Starting in 1977, the state

21 Office of the State Comptroller, *Property Taxes in New York State*, April 2006, p. 9.

has offered financial incentives for localities to modernize property tax systems, including a program to encourage annual reassessments.

Since the state's earliest days, property-tax law had required that all parcels be assessed at full value. Most local assessors ignored the requirement and, among other inequities, imposed higher assessments on commercial and industrial property than on homeowners. In 1975, a Long Island resident named Julius Hellerstein won a ruling from the Court of Appeals that required the town of Islip and other localities around the state to follow the law. The result would have been elimination of higher assessments on businesses, and either a sharp reduction in property-tax collections or a shift of the burden to homeowners. In 1981, the Legislature enacted, over Governor Carey's veto, a law that repealed the full-value requirement. Instead, the new legislation said, local assessors must assess all property at the same percentage of full value. While the new law essentially codified existing practices, it was followed by legislative and administrative steps that brought actual practice closer to the ideal.

While inequities remain, New York's overall assessment practices have improved in the last two decades. In 2003, more than 330 taxing jurisdictions, representing more than 47 percent of taxable parcels in the state, conducted reassessments, according to the state Office of Real Property Services. State law requires local assessors to certify that assessments represent a uniform percentage of market value. Individual property-tax bills must state the percentage of market value that all local assessments represent, and the full value of the taxpayer's property. That requirement increases taxpayer awareness of potential inequities.[22]

New York's assessing system remains more complicated and cumbersome than those in most states. Elsewhere, assessing is typically done at the county level; in New York, nearly 1,000 municipalities do the job. The large number of municipalities and school districts means that a single district may include segments of a dozen or more villages, towns, and cities. That makes apportioning tax levies among the municipalities difficult.

Almost every other state requires a uniform, statewide level of assessment for all properties. In New York, that requirement applies to all

---

22 Thomas G. Griffen, "Crossroads or U-Turn?," in *The Uniform Standard*, newsletter of the New York State Office of Real Property Services, Albany, NY, August 2003.

parcels within each assessing unit. But school districts that include more than one municipality must use equalization rates established by the state to apportion the tax burden equitably among localities.

Finally, the state does not enforce its law requiring equitable or up-to-date assessments. Albany offers financial incentives for periodic reassessments to keep distribution of the property-tax burden within given localities at least relatively fair. As a practical matter, though, localities are free to leave outmoded assessments in place for years or decades.

Tough Fiscal Challenges
for Localities and Taxpayers Alike

New York State government's fiscal strength ebbs and flows depending on the strength of the economy, particularly the financial sector centered on Wall Street. The personal income tax, the state's largest source of tax revenue, rises sharply in boom years. But when the economy and income-tax revenue slow, spending decisions legislators have made in the good years tend to produce budget gaps.

Compared to the state, most local governments have relatively stable finances from year to year. Their major sources of tax revenue — property and sales taxes — are less volatile; as a result, spending decisions vary less dramatically from one year to the next. (New York City, with its own taxes on personal income and real-property gains as key revenue sources, is an exception.)

While their finances are more predictable than Albany's, many of New York's local governments have had significant problems balancing their budgets in recent years. Localities' overall spending jumped by 30 percent, or more than twice the rate of inflation, from 1998 to 2003, according to the Office of the State Comptroller.

Wages and salaries, Medicaid and health care costs, and employee benefits were major spending drivers.[23]

Continual increases in property taxes imposed by all local governments pose a special problem for school districts, which (unlike other local entities) must submit proposed budgets to taxpayers. In 2005,

---

23 New York State Office of the State Comptroller, *2005 Annual Report on Local Governments*, p. 5.

voters defeated 112 school budgets around the state; the resulting 84 percent passage rate was the lowest in a decade. The 2006 votes were more favorable for schools, with 89 percent of budgets passing. Still, school leaders in regions such as Long Island and the lower Hudson Valley, and in smaller pockets around the state, perceived stronger taxpayer resistance than they had in years.

Governor-elect Spitzer has promised a major expansion of the STAR program that uses the state's broader tax base (taxes on personal income, sales, businesses and so on) to offset some of the school property tax for most homeowners. If such expansion occurs, it may reduce voter concern about property taxes, at least for a few years. Without other steps to limit future growth in school taxes, the issue is likely to remain on the agenda for years to come.

Regional Planning: Not Much

Just as many government-reform advocates are pushing localities to work across or eliminate municipal boundaries in providing services as a means of reducing costs, other voices urge both state and local officials to expand opportunities for regional land use planning and decision making.

The same concerns that have led to new municipal limits on development have stimulated discussion at the state level about more comprehensive regional planning.

In New York, there are 1,530 cities, towns, and villages, most of which possess authority for local land use planning and decision making. The impact of this planning and resultant decision making, however, is not confined to the arbitrary political boundaries which delineate these municipalities. In addition, many of today's problems are regional in nature. Therefore, without a requirement for some coordination, cooperation, and consistency in local planning at some higher level, New York can never achieve sound, regional planning which is needed to address myriad social and environmental concerns.[24]

Recommendations for statewide and regional planning go back at least as far as the wide-ranging efforts by Governors Smith and

---

24 Patricia E. Salkin, "Regional Planning in New York State," *Pace Law Review*, 13, 505, Fall 1993, p. 1; available via Government Law Center website, *http://www.governmentlaw.org*.

Roosevelt to expand the role of state government in the 1920s and 1930s. Under Governor Rockefeller, there were serious efforts in the 1960s — including, at one point, both a Bureau of Planning in the state Commerce Department and a Division of State Planning in the Department of State. A successor agency, the Office of Planning Coordination, prepared a statewide comprehensive plan that was intended to guide development of regional plans with more authority over actual development. Local officials generally resisted the idea of such state involvement, and helped block passage of implementing legislation as well as a related proposal that emerged from a joint legislative committee in 1970.[25]

In the 1990s, rising concerns over the decline of most cities, and continued expansion of development in the suburbs, led to discussions of "smart growth" in New York and many others states. Advocates urged new government restrictions, or incentives, to push more business and residential growth into the cities rather than outside urban borders. Opponents criticize some such proposals as likely to bring harmful restrictions on development to areas already suffering from inadequate economic activity, particularly in hard-pressed Upstate regions.

Some supporters of such restrictions have pointed to Portland, OR, as a model, although critics said that city's land-use policies had led to higher housing prices and other problems. Despite some attention from the Pataki administration and some members of the Legislature, the issue of "smart growth" seemed to fade from the agenda in Albany in the last few years. In addition to concerns about potential economic impacts, the very multiplicity of local governments and officials that helped fuel concern over lack of comprehensive planning may have hindered serious action.

One area of the state, the Adirondacks, has a regional planning process. As outlined in Chapter Seventeen, the Adirondack Park Agency (APA) — part of state government — operates as a regionwide regulator of local development. It establishes a regional land use and development plan, and must approve any project with regional "significance." Municipalities within the park that have local land-use laws review smaller projects with only local impact. The APA is often criticized for lack of sensitivity to the need for economic growth in the region. Some

---

25 Ibid., p. 4.

observers say that sort of criticism would be likely to spread if stringent regional planning were imposed elsewhere.

Initiative and Referendum

For years, voices of reform in Albany have suggested that New York join numerous other states in giving voters the opportunity for direct democracy via the processes of initiative and referendum. Such a change would require amendment of the state Constitution — and, thus, either approval by the Legislature or calling of a constitutional convention by the people. Most legislators oppose the idea of granting direct democratic powers to the voters, so the idea has gone nowhere. At the state level, voters grant all policymaking power to governors and legislators except for approval of state bond issues and constitutional amendments.

At the local-government level, though, voters have more opportunities to initiate and/or vote on major issues.

Most familiar to many voters is the annual vote on school budgets in districts across the state. Municipalities are usually required to seek voter approval for changes in the basic structure of government, such as county or city charters.

Localities may use, and in some cases are required to use, permissive referenda to give voters a chance to reject an action by elected officials. One popular form of such action is for the local council to act on a proposal and make it effective at a future date, with voters given the option of submitting a petition demanding a referendum in the meantime. Few such proposals result in voter opposition.

By obtaining enough signatures on petitions, citizens can require voter approval of certain actions by elected officials. In 2006, for instance, residents of Schenectady collected signatures on a proposed ballot question that would have reversed the city council's approval of a pay raise for the mayor. Supporters of the pay raise prepared to challenge the petition, but media attention to the controversial issue led to rescission of the increase, rendering a plebiscite moot.

A few localities in New York have provisions for voter initiative of charter provisions. Suffolk County — New York's own version of California, where unusual policy proposals are often considered first — is one. The New York City charter also gives voters the power to initiate such amendments. Most notably, the provision has resulted in term limits for the mayor and members of the City Council.

Serious students of government argue about whether such results are good or bad. Clearly, the initiative power results in some major policy changes that elected representatives would not enact on their own. Whether such results are good or bad at the local level can inform future discussions of direct democracy in Albany.

Chapter Nineteen

THE STATE-LOCAL PARADOX: HOME RULE AND STATE MANDATES

Key points:

- New York's constitutional and statutory provisions regarding home rule are more extensive than those in many states. At the same time, paradoxically, Albany imposes its will and the cost of its decisions on localities more than most other state governments.

- Municipalities and school districts complain about a variety of mandates from the state, but are less concerned about such rules if the state provides additional aid.

- Albany is assuming more of the local cost for Medicaid, and further mandate relief for localities will be on the agenda in 2007.

The state government is there when the mayor of Buffalo gives the State of the City address. It's at work when Onondaga County legislators adopt each year's budget. It's there when 1.2 million state residents pay rent that's regulated by Albany; when the Hempstead school board negotiates the teachers' contract; and when officials in Orange County consider how to manage rapid residential and commercial growth.

Each unit of local government involved in those activities is, to use the common phrase, a creature of the state. Although local-government activities in much of New York predate the state government itself, today's structure of counties, cities, towns, villages, school districts, and special districts exists because state law makes it so. Not only that structure, but rules great and small for operation of each locality are written in the General Municipal Law, Local Finance Law, Municipal Home Rule Law, and separate statutes governing each class of local governments — as well as specific municipal charters that make one county, for instance, different from every other. Decisions by local officials are also governed by laws of general application such as the Civil Service Law and Tax Law. Localities have only those powers given them by the State of New York, and cannot do things Albany says they may not do.

Municipalities and school districts build their *budgets* within rules set by the state. The Constitution limits local taxes and debt (although the effectiveness of the latter is open to question). If a city or town seeks to impose a tax other than the property tax, Albany must approve.[1] State officials require local leaders to spend billions of dollars on programs created in Albany with little or no consultation from back home. The Legislature tells local assessors what they must do in deciding the taxable value of homes, businesses and other properties. At the same time, localities depend heavily on state financing. State government provides 38 percent of the revenue school districts use to educate 3 million young New Yorkers, for instance.[2]

The state's influence over local government *operations* is vast, as well. County and municipal officials in charge of local jails, courts, sewer and water systems, parks, building inspections, and zoning all must follow rules handed down from Albany.

School districts must have the state Education Department approve building plans, even though they hire licensed architects and engineers to design, and oversee construction of, new school buildings. State

---

1   Localities may, however, charge fees for services such as garbage collection and water, without specific approval from the Legislature.

2   2003 data, including New York City; Office of the State Comptroller, *2005 Annual Report on Local Governments*, Albany, NY, September 2005.

officials give thumbs up, or thumbs down, on localities' plans to link local roads to state highways, and tell local emergency responders how much training they must have before heading out in an ambulance.

The Municipal Home Rule Law

On April 30, 1963, Governor Rockefeller signed the Municipal Home Rule Law that he had proposed to the Legislature earlier in the year. The new statute and a companion amendment to the state Constitution would, Rockefeller said, "strengthen the governments closest to the people so that they may help meet the present and emerging needs of our time."[3]

Adoption of the law, and that November's approval by voters of Article IX of the Constitution, represented the high-water mark of home rule in New York — at least symbolically.

Less than three years later, Rockefeller pushed through a Medicaid program that required counties and New York City to share in the cost. Some local officials complained bitterly about the new expense. By January 1968, less than five years after initiating historic home-rule legislation, Rockefeller was lamenting the cost his own Medicaid program imposed on localities. Rising expenses, and lower-than-expected federal aid, had forced some counties to raise property taxes by 50 percent, and helped push 28 counties into creating or raising sales taxes, the governor said.[4] Today, county and New York City officials point to the state's design of Medicaid as one of the clearest examples of hegemonic behavior from Albany.

Article IX, including a "Bill of Rights" for local governments, and related statutes do not protect local governments against mandates from the state. Instead, they grant municipalities rights to adopt local laws, establish cooperative agreements, guard against unwanted annexation and undertake certain other activities.

Throughout the United States, the long-established legal understanding of state-local relations is known as Dillon's Rule, after an 1868 court decision in Iowa that emphasized the limited nature of

---

3   Memorandum of approval, cc. 843 and 844, Laws of 1963.

4   Address to the New York State Women's Legislative Forum, January 9, 1968; in *Public Papers of Governor Rockefeller*. Albany, NY: The State of New York, pp. 1273-74.

local-government powers. The doctrine holds that a local government may exercise only powers that are expressly granted by the state; necessarily implied in a charter or act of incorporation; or indispensable (not simply convenient) in carrying out the locality's assigned responsibilities. New York's home-rule laws and tradition of activist government have moved the state away from adherence to Dillon's Rule, but it remains a touchstone for modern debates over state-local relations.

In New York, the historical divide in political sensibilities between Upstate and New York City contributed to the built-in tension between state and local officials, as legislators from rural areas enacted policies that city representatives saw as almost colonial in nature *(see "New York City is Pie for the Hayseeds," Chapter Five)*.

Immigration-driven population booms and rising statewide political influence for New York and other cities helped lead to a 1923 constitutional amendment that restricted Albany's power to impose special laws on cities. A statute adopted the following year gave cities the power to adopt charters on their own, without seeking individual approval from the Legislature. A 1963 amendment extended home-rule power to towns and villages, and expanded the powers of local governments generally to adopt and amend laws relating to their "property, affairs or government," as well as certain other specific areas such as employees' compensation and hours of work.

Still, to the chagrin of many local officials, the Constitution imposes few limits on Albany's power over localities. Article IX forbids enactment of laws that affect only one local government unless elected officials there have requested such action. But statutes that affect all localities — or all school districts or towns, for example — are permissible. Some 25 states have statutory and/or constitutional limitations on their ability to impose mandates on local governments.[5] Although some legislators have introduced such proposals in New York, none have received even first passage by the Legislature. Reasons for such inaction may include certain interest groups' preference for concentration of power in Albany, and lack of leadership on the issue.

New York's courts have a long tradition of endorsing Albany's firm control over localities. In 1983, for instance, the Court of Appeals ruled against the Chemung County Legislature's attempt to fill a vacancy in

---

5 Joseph F. Zimmerman, "State Mandate Relief: A Quick Look," *Intergovernmental Perspective* 20, 2 (Spring 1994): 28.

the sheriff's office. While county officials said they were acting under a provision of the county charter, the court held that the sheriff's job included enforcing state laws, and thus appointment to the office was subject to state law, which required a different process.[6] In a 1989 case, the Court of Appeals referred to the Legislature's "untrammeled primacy of the Legislature to act" with respect to matters of state concern. Even where the Legislature has not enacted a law that specifically conflicts with a local provision, the state's "intent to occupy the field" may preempt local decisions, the court has held:

> Where the State has preempted the field, a local law regulating the same subject matter is deemed inconsistent with the State's transcendent interest, whether or not the terms of the local law actually conflict with a State-wide statute. Such local laws, were they permitted to operate in a field pre-empted by State law, would tend to inhibit the operation of the State's general law and thereby thwart the operation of the State's overriding policy concerns.[7]

The Fiscal Connection

Much, though not all, of the perpetual conflict between Albany and New York's local governments stems from arguments about money. A brief outline of the fiscal connections between the two levels of government helps show why — starting with the basic reality that localities may only raise or spend money as Albany allows.

The small, local units of government that arose before the founding of the state followed the lead of the governments they knew in European homelands, making the property tax their first general-purpose tax. Imposition of today's personal-income tax, sales tax, and other local taxes came much later, in the 20th century.

Today, counties, cities, towns, villages, school districts, and fire districts all impose property taxes, which totaled 63 percent of all local tax revenues in the state in 2003. Some libraries and other special districts impose the tax, as well.

Article VIII of the state Constitution imposes limits on property taxes, as well as highly detailed restrictions on localities' power to

6   *Cuomo* v. *Chemung County Legislature*, 122 Misc. 2d 42, 469 N.Y.S. 2d 868 (1983).

7   *Jancyn Mfg. Corp.* v. *County of Suffolk*, 71 N.Y. 2d 91, 97

borrow. Generally, counties, cities, and villages are limited to total real-property tax of 2 percent of full valuation.

Localities can also impose taxes for which the Legislature has granted general or special authorization. When Governor Rockefeller initiated a 2 percent state sales tax in 1965, the highest local sales tax was 3 percent, for a total of 5 percent. As of 2006, the average combined rate across the state was 8.25 percent, compared to a national average of 5.93 percent, according to the comptroller's office.

Other local taxes for which the Legislature has granted broad authority include city utility taxes of up to 3 percent, and mortgage recording taxes. The cities of New York and Yonkers impose local income taxes. New York City also collects other taxes including those on business income, certain commercial rents, real property sales, and unincorporated businesses.

Local-government entities also must follow Albany's rules to borrow money, starting with the constitutional limits on debt. Such limits have proven especially inconvenient for New York City, with infrastructure needs driven by far more school children, motor-vehicle traffic, and general human activity than any other locale in the state. Governors and the Legislature have taken numerous steps that effectively allow the state's largest city to escape its constitutional limit on debt with creation of separate entities that have their own borrowing powers. In 1997, for instance, Governor Pataki and legislators created the Transitional Finance Authority, to borrow money that would pay for some capital projects over the ensuing 10 years. The authority was originally empowered to borrow up to $7.5 billion. Three years later, the Legislature added another $4 billion in bonding authorization. State and local officials' discussion of such borrowing power tends to focus on the spending programs it supports, with little regard for the voters' mandate in the Constitution to limit municipal borrowing.

Those limits illustrate a historical low regard for local officials' fiscal practices, Peter Galie notes. In the case of debt, at least, there is little reason to believe Albany has forced localities to be any more responsible than the state itself.

The assumption underlying the restrictions embodied in Article VIII is that local governments cannot be trusted to act responsibly, especially in incurring debt and contingent liability that will not have to be paid until future years. The state must assume primary responsibility for regulation of local finance because fiscal irresponsibility on the part of local government implicates the financial position of the state itself.... In spite of the labyrinth of provisions, there is some doubt as to whether these restrictions have fostered sound fiscal practices in local governments. One reason for this doubt has been the willingness (by governors and legislators) to pile exemption on constitutional exemption when the need arises. A second reason is the creation of public benefit corporations (authorities), which enable local governments to raise their de facto debt limits to many times the constitutional limits.[8]

Other recent developments show that elected officials at the state level remain willing to impose new costs on their counterparts at the local level (and thus, taxpayers), while gaining political credit. In 2000, Governor Pataki and the Legislature enacted major improvements to pensions for most public employees, including permanent cost-of-living adjustments and elimination of employee contributions after 10 years of employment. Virtually every elected state official had endorsed the pension improvements; then-Comptroller H. Carl McCall was among the most insistent. Supporters justified the benefit enhancements, in part, by pointing to pension funds' record gains from the late-1990s jump in the stock market. Yet, even before the benefit improvements were signed into law, Wall Street's major indices had started to decline. Required employer contributions to the pension funds, from localities as well as the state itself, rose by billions of dollars in succeeding years.

The Mandate Problem

Throughout history, governmental leaders in locales far from centers of power have complained about decisions from above. Certainly that was true of pre-Revolutionary New Yorkers. Along with their neighbors in the other American colonies, they chafed at laws from rulers an ocean away. Two hundred and thirty years after colonial Americans declared their independence from far-off rulers, the tension between Albany and the state's local governments remains the single most contentious issue for localities.

Like states, local governments are subject to the supremacy of the federal government, under the 14th Amendment to the U.S. Constitution. Local officials in New York find reason to criticize mandates from Washington. School districts, for instance, complain about requirements of the

---

8   Galie, *The New York State Constitution: A Reference Guide*, pp. 184-5.

Medicaid: A Sign of Change
in the State-Local Balance?

In recent years, one issue has overshadowed all others for most counties in New York: the high and rising cost of Medicaid. Unlike most states, New York requires localities to pay a significant share of Medicaid costs — some 15 percent of the total, in 2006-07.

County and New York City officials started criticizing the cost of Medicaid not long after Governor Rockefeller persuaded the Legislature to create the program in 1966. After a decade of continually rising costs, Governor Carey and the Legislature relieved localities of some of the cost of long-term care in the early 1980s.

Later that decade, rapid cost escalation returned. With the state's economy suffering in the early 1990s, Medicaid helped drive significant tax increases at the state and local levels. Complaints from county and New York City officials grew louder, and political pressure stronger. The Medicaid issue emerged as the most important among others that local leaders characterized as "unfunded mandates" and "Big Brother"-style government in Albany.

By 2003, the complaints reached a crescendo as county executives throughout the state used their bully pulpits to blame Albany for rising property taxes. More than a dozen counties raised sales taxes in the past decade. At one point, Oneida County imposed a total 9.75 percent rate, including the state's share — a level that was far above those previously considered politically or economically acceptable. Beyond the tax increases, the rising cost of Medicaid led many counties to cut back on other services such as sheriff's patrols and libraries — steps that also would have been considered politically untenable just a few years earlier.

The county executives' campaign, supported by many business groups, paid off in 2005 as Governor Pataki and the Legislature enacted a limit on future growth in local Medicaid costs. Counties were guaranteed the state would pay for future cost increases above 3 percent a year, as of 2008. The 2005 statute also gave counties the option of shifting their entire Medicaid cost to Albany, along with a share of local sales-tax revenue. It created accountability measures for local social-services districts, authorizing the state health commissioner to review districts' management of Medicaid and to impose sanctions on districts that fail to monitor utilization diligently. While representing a significant change, the 2005 legislation did not eliminate all future cost increases, much less reverse those of previous years.

Local officials' noisemaking over Medicaid also helped persuade the Legislature to increase general aid to localities in 2006. But there was little indication of a long-term change in Albany's expectation that local taxes would continue to fund a major share of New York's expansive social-services programs for the foreseeable future.

No Child Left Behind education law, saying it imposes costly requirements without equivalent funding. Clearly, though, most county, municipal, and school leaders see Albany as their primary antagonist in the intergovernmental conflict.

There's no question, on the other hand, that some state mandates on localities are appropriate, improve the quality of government services and even quality of life for New Yorkers. Examples range from broad policy matters such as financial reporting requirements, to specific rules such as those covering municipal landfills. Arguably, at least, the state should go much further with mandates in some areas — such as education and training requirements for judges in small municipal courts.[9]

Virtually every year, the Legislature adds some mandates with more narrow focus. Starting around 2000, for the first time in decades, local officials forced the state-local relationship to the top of the agenda in Albany. Results include one significant victory for localities, in financing of the vast Medicaid program, and smaller concessions such as increases in general municipal aid.

Mayors, supervisors, school-board members, and other local officials say there is a long list of ways in which Albany forces them to adopt policies — and to spend taxpayer dollars — in ways they otherwise would not. Besides Medicaid, other major issues are:

Prevailing wages. When localities (or the state itself) engage in public-works projects such as building or road construction, they must pay workers the wage that is "prevailing" in a given region. For decades, under both Democratic and Republican governors, the state

9   See William Glaberson, "Broken Bench: How a Reviled Court System Has Outlasted Critics," *The New York Times*, September 27, 2006.

Labor Department has implemented the requirement to consider union wages "prevailing" even when union workers are a minority in a particular area. Local officials say the requirement drives costs up needlessly because contractors must pay higher wages than needed to obtain experienced workers, especially outside metropolitan areas. It also makes project management more difficult; contractors must classify every worker in a particular category and keep extensive records on such classifications that are subject to challenge by employees or unions. A worker who does both carpentry work and window installation, for instance, must be treated differently for the hours spent on each task, even though the pay difference is relatively small.

The "Wicks Law." State law requires governmental entities to issue four separate construction contracts for most work on public buildings, rather than hiring a general contractor who will oversee all the work. A 1987 study by the state Division of the Budget estimated that repealing the law could save Albany and local governments a combined $400 million annually — a figure that would be much higher today. Governors Cuomo and Pataki both proposed repealing or substantially reducing the impact of the law. A relatively small group of contractors and unions benefits from the contractual requirements of the law, however. As of 2006, the law stood unchanged despite two decades of efforts to eliminate it. Reform advocates had managed to eliminate the law for some individual school districts, including those in New York City and Niagara Falls. For the most part, though, the Wicks Law remained intact as a testament to the ability of highly interested groups to affect policy in Albany.

The Triborough Amendment to the Taylor Law. The amendment, which the Legislature enacted in 1982 over Governor Carey's veto, provides that terms of a public-employee union contract continue after the contract expires, unless a new agreement is reached. Employees continue to receive experience-based pay raises and all contractual fringe benefits. In recent years, as municipalities and school districts have attempted to share rising health-care costs with employees, the Triborough Amendment has forced public employers to keep the status quo until workers could be persuaded to agree on a new contract. The law has particularly significant impacts on school districts because teacher contracts often include as many as 20 years of "step" increases that continue after a labor agreement has expired. The New York State School Boards Association estimates repealing the amendment could reduce costs by $50 million or more a year.

Binding arbitration for police and firefighters. In 1999, a state-appointed arbitrator ruled in a dispute between Nassau County and the union representing police sergeants, lieutenants, and captains. The officers were already among the higher-paid in the nation; the county was facing a major budget gap; and inflation for the years covered by the contract was projected at 2 to 3 percent a year. The arbitrator imposed a 24 percent pay increase over five years. Although Nassau officials, a taxpayers' group, and credit-rating agencies criticized the ruling, the county was required to accept it under state law that provides mandatory binding arbitration for police and firefighters. The New York Conference of Mayors and other local-government associations have asked state leaders to repeal the provision or to require that arbitrators give more consideration to the locality's ability to pay. Governor Pataki proposed such a change several times, but the Legislature would not accept the provision.

All four issues are driven largely by the Legislature's desire to avoid taking steps opposed by New York's influential unions, including both public-sector organizations such as New York State United Teachers and private-sector groups such as construction trade unions. At first glance, the Wicks Law and prevailing-wage rules from Albany seem to violate the spirit of local-government protection in Article IX of the Constitution, which provides that each locality has the power to adopt laws relating to "the wages or salaries, the hours of work or labor, and the protection, welfare and safety of persons employed by any contractor or sub-contractor performing work, labor or services for it." But Albany gives power to localities with one hand, and takes it away with another; Article IX says any such laws must not be inconsistent with general state laws, such as those regulating prevailing wages and construction contracts.

While continuing to complain about what they consider unfair mandates from Albany, local officials have seen state leaders enact other changes that drive up local costs, such as mandated enhancement of public-employee pensions. Public-employee unions continue to push the Legislature for more and better benefits, as well as changes to the Taylor Law that would enhance their position at the bargaining table. Local officials, as well as taxpayer organizations and political candidates seeking to capitalize on antitax sentiment, are likely to push for further action on the laws by which the state tells counties, municipalities, school districts, and special districts what to do and/or how to do it.

Localities are subject to regulation by state agencies, and sometimes complain about such oversight, just as private-sector businesses and other organizations do. In 2006, for instance, the New York State School Boards Association questioned an OSC directive that school-board members file reports on personal financial holdings, with the reports subject to public disclosure. The comptroller's office refused to change the new rule, saying the need to assure integrity and public confidence in school districts must overcome any concern for volunteer board members' privacy.

A Changing Fiscal Relationship

As a new gubernatorial administration takes over in Albany for the first time in 12 years, the fiscal relationship between the state and localities is changing significantly in one significant area, that of Medicaid finance. Even more changes than those already taking place may be coming.

The cap on counties' and New York City's share of Medicaid changes the fiscal impact of future increases in spending on the program, now concentrated on the state. That, in turn, is likely to mean shifting attitudes about the desirability of such increases. In past years, when governors proposed cost-saving reforms to Medicaid, they would note that such changes would reduce costs for hard-pressed local taxpayers as well as the state itself. Such arguments can be politically powerful because property taxes are unpopular everywhere, and perhaps more so in New York than in most states. Supporters of increased Medicaid spending have the advantage of being able to cast their arguments in another politically popular light, that of improving and protecting health care. An analysis of Governor Pataki's proposed 2006-07 budget by the Office of the State Comptroller showed one aspect of the changing nature of the debate over Medicaid spending as a result of the cap on local contributions.

> Executive Budget recommendations of $1.3 billion in General Fund savings would have a significant effect, not only on the State's overall financial picture, but on the State's health care industry as well. When considering the impact of the Executive's proposed actions on the federal share of Medicaid spending, the State's health care industry would suffer a loss of $1.8 billion in revenue. Because of the cap on local Medicaid expenditures, any savings from the Executive Budget recommended cost control measures would no longer accrue to local governments, but only to the State and the federal government. By the same token, if the Legis-

lature rejects any of the Executive Budget recommended cost control measures, additional costs would no longer be borne by local governments, but only by the State and the federal government.[10]

Taxpayer anxiety about property taxes helped drive Albany to change Medicaid financing. The next step may be significant change in financing of local school districts — particularly if state leaders do take significant steps to limit future increases in Medicaid spending, and thus free more resources for use in education and other services.

Next: Changing School Finance?

School taxes are especially high on Long Island and in much of the lower Hudson Valley region. Legislators from those areas have taken the lead in proposing steps to ease the burden on property owners (at least, residential property owners). Several legislators proposed eliminating school property taxes entirely and replacing the revenue with new or higher income taxes, at either the state or local level. Governor Cuomo suggested an optional local income tax for school districts in the early 1990s. Then and more recently, the idea has failed to attract broad support or serious attention in the Legislature.

Governor Pataki's STAR program now provides more than $3 billion in annual funding for school-tax reduction. Funding is from the state's general revenues — meaning mostly from income taxes and the remainder from sales, business and other taxes. When first proposing STAR in 1997, Pataki included a recommendation that the measure include a legal limit on annual school property-tax increases, with the cap linked to the inflation rate. The Legislature refused to approve the tax limit. Comptroller Hevesi concluded in a 2006 report that the net impact of STAR may have been to raise overall taxes.

While STAR indisputably provides property tax relief for those receiving it, its long-term impact may well be an overall increase in State and local taxes. The reason for this is that STAR lowers the effective tax rate on homeowners — the largest group of people who vote on and otherwise influence local school budgets. For many seniors, STAR effectively eliminated their school tax burden. By reducing the local tax share paid for greater school spending, STAR actually provides an in-

10 Office of the State Comptroller, *2006-07 Budget Analysis: Review of the Executive Budget*, Albany, NY, February 2006; p. 144.

centive to increase school spending — an impact which has been described in several studies. This incentive is strongest, ironically, in the some of the highest spending areas — where high taxes and high home values combine to provide the highest STAR benefits.[11]

While campaigning for governor in 2006, Eliot Spitzer suggested that the state could "move toward" more reliance on income-tax revenues, rather than the property tax, to fund public schools. As a candidate for governor, he also said he would not raise taxes. It would be possible for Albany to provide significantly more funding for schools over time, relying on normal growth in its existing tax base. State aid already rises by hundreds of millions of dollars each year, however. Increasing those amounts by enough to make a substantial difference in property taxes would require either significant new revenues for the state or new restraint elsewhere in the state budget.

Land Use: Power for Localities
But Still Subject to State Regulations

Should new homes require a minimum lot size of half an acre or three acres — or none at all? Which is more important to a declining Upstate city — preserving historic structures, or encouraging redevelopment? Should a suburban town encourage business growth to ease the property-tax burden on homeowners, or limit commercial and industrial development for aesthetic reasons?

These are among the most contentious questions facing cities, towns, and villages, which make most decisions about land use in New York. (Some counties have planning boards, but such agencies generally provide loosely defined coordinating functions and do not exercise decision-making authority in individual planning and zoning cases.)

The basic structure of municipal land-use regulation is contained in the various local-government statutes. Every city, and most villages and towns, also have local zoning laws that provide where various types of development can take place. Such laws also establish detailed rules, such as minimum lot sizes, for new homes or maximum height for commercial buildings. Municipal planning boards advise local legislative bodies on design and amendment of zoning laws, and on specific

---

11 Office of the State Comptroller, *Property Taxes in New York State*, Albany, NY, April 2006; p. 13.

Rent Control

Besides regulating land use, state law regulates rents for many residential units in New York City and certain other localities. The continuation of rent control and rent stabilization, long past the "emergency" in housing markets that led to creation of the practice immediately after World War II, is a recurring source of tension between Albany and the state's largest city.

Rental rates for more than 1 million apartments in New York City are subject to regulation. In addition, the overall proportion of renters is far higher in the city — more than two of every three — than in almost any other area of the country, making rent regulation an especially potent political issue.

Some 50 other municipalities in the state impose some rent controls, according to the Division of Housing and Community Renewal: Albany; Buffalo; and various other cities, towns, and villages in Albany, Erie, Nassau, Rensselaer, Schenectady, and Westchester counties. In most of those localities, however, the number of rent-regulated housing units is small.

President Roosevelt signed the first federal Emergency Price Control Act, which froze rents in most of the state, in 1942. The federal law expired in 1947. New York's Legislature enacted its own comprehensive law in 1951, allowing New York City to extend the previous regime of rent regulation. As of the mid-1990s, half of all rental units in the city were subject to price controls.

The Legislature enacted laws in 1993 and 1997 that resulted in thousands of apartments moving from regulated to market-based rent or to individual ownership as condominiums or cooperatives. The new laws particularly targeted higher-end apartments, renting for $2,000 or more per month, after critics pointed out that many well-off residents of New York City were benefiting from rent control. Other changes including tightening notoriously loose rules for succession of tenant rights, with the elimination of nieces, nephews, aunts, and uncles from such provisions.

In New York City, the municipal government determines maximum allowable rent increases under rent control. Elsewhere, the state's DHCR does so.

The Assembly, dominated by New York City representatives who tend to be ideologically supportive of government intervention in the marketplace, generally pushes for continuation or strengthening of legal protections for current tenants. The Senate, traditionally more in favor of market capitalism than the Assembly, has tended to push for diminution of rent regulation. Senate Majority Leader Joseph Bruno championed the 1997 revisions to rent-control laws, the most important in a generation. The differing positions of the two houses prevent any permanent resolution to Albany's rent-regulation laws. As a result, the state retains an important role in a matter that many tenant advocates say should be left up to local elected officials.

From a profederalism perspective, the tenants' argument makes sense. Yet most economists, and many students of housing policy, believe rent regulation ultimately hurts working people by reducing the supply of affordable housing.* In New York City, at least, political concerns may trump economic arguments; the number of potential voters living in price-regulated units is greater than the number of actual votes in most state-level elections.

---

* See, e.g., Peter D. Salins and Gerard C.S. Mildner, *Scarcity By Design: The Legacy of New York City's Housing Policies*, Cambridge, MA: Harvard University Press, 1992.

proposals for rezoning. Zoning boards of appeals give homeowners and businesses an opportunity to seek variances from zoning standards and interpretations of the local zoning law that may override an administrative decision.

In recent decades, concerns over potential overdevelopment has led some suburban towns and counties to adopt or revise comprehensive plans in ways that further restrict future growth. One common approach has been to expand minimum lot sizes for new homes. That reduces the potential for new educational and other costs associated with rising population, but also reduces the housing supply, thus creating upward pressure on prices and potentially reducing housing options for working families. Other localities have purchased undeveloped land for conservation, or worked with private conservation groups that can use various legal and financial methods to prevent development.

Chapter Twenty

THE PEOPLE'S GOVERNMENT

Key points:

- Individuals can and do affect public policy in New York, especially as part of organizations that develop expertise and win the respect of elected officials over time.

- The number of lobbyists, and the amount they spend on lobbying and political contributions, has expanded sharply in the past decade.

- Making government accountable to the people requires not only open meetings and records, as envisioned since the 1970s, but measurement of government performance in the many areas affected by state policies.

As we have seen, New York State government performs, directs, and pays for a wide range of essential activities.

How much are the people — in whose name those actions are taken, who are the intended beneficiaries, and who pay for the services — involved in deciding what state government does, and how? And to what extent is state government accountable for achieving the results the people want?

The answer to both questions is — more than ever, but not as much as we'd like.

As is true throughout America, most voting-age New Yorkers do not even exercise their basic right to cast a ballot on Election Day. Some 70 percent of state residents 18 or older were registered voters in 2002, a gubernatorial election year, but fewer than one in three actually cast a ballot. The proportion of New Yorkers registered to vote was the same as the national average, while turnout was nearly 5 percentage points below the national figure.[1] Both in New York and across the country, the percentage of adults who were registered to vote was significantly *higher* — but the proportion who turned out to vote was significantly *lower* — than in 1960.

State government is more accountable than ever before to its citizens, particularly those with Internet access. With a reasonable amount of effort, New Yorkers can find state agency reports with detailed information on numerous important topics. Examples include the academic performance of local public schools, comparisons of New Yorkers' tax burden with those in other states, and how state-regulated health-care plans perform on various indicators of quality and efficiency.[2]

In any democratic society, it's important that citizens be involved as much as possible in governmental decisions, and that government be accountable to the people. The larger the scope and power of government, the more important those issues become. New York's tradition of activist government makes citizen participation and government accountability especially important.

This chapter examines the role of the people in shaping state government policies and programs, starting with the basic act of voting. Some

---

1   Formerly available from the Federal Election Commission, data on voter registration and turnout are now reported by the U.S. Election Assistance Commission, *www.eac.gov.*

2   School report cards are available at *http://emsc32.nysed.gov/repcrd2005/;* the *New York State Tax Sourcebook* at *www.tax.state.ny.us/statistics;* and annual Quality Assurance Reporting Requirement data from the Health Department at *www.health.state.ny.us.*

of the most highly motivated citizens seek to influence government by influencing the election of state leaders — working within established political parties or even creating new ones devoted to particular causes. More commonly, groups and individuals work with whichever leaders have emerged from electoral contests. This form of influence seeking is, to a large extent, organized and exerted by people who are paid to be influential in Albany — lobbyists.

The chapter also explores one of the most important issues for any student of government — that of accountability. Under our system of government, the press plays a key role in keeping elected officials and public agencies accountable; the chapter discusses the interplay of the news media and state government. Finally, it examines New York State's use of performance measurement, an increasingly common tool for promoting accountability in governments throughout the United States.

Voting

New Yorkers are about as likely as other Americans to participate in the fundamental democratic activity of voting — in other words, they often don't bother. Laws affecting citizens' right to vote in the Empire State are among the most liberal in the country. Voting hours for regular elections are 6 A.M.to 9 P.M.; polling places in other states typically close at 7 or 8 P.M., and most open later. The state's Election Law allows voters to register up to 25 days before an election; many states end registration at 30 days before elections (although some, including Connecticut and Massachusetts, allow voters more time than New York).

Some 20 states permanently bar voting by convicted felons, although in many of those states individuals can restore voting rights through legal appeals. Like a number of other states, New York allows voting by all except those currently incarcerated or on parole for a felony conviction. Unlike some 16 states, New York does not allow party-line voting; voters must choose candidates in each race individually.

In 2000, more than 6.9 million New Yorkers voted in the presidential election between George W. Bush and Al Gore — an increase of half a million from four years earlier, when the Bill Clinton-Bob Dole race was not considered competitive. Just over 50 percent of eligible adults voted in New York, slightly less than the national average, despite an 82 percent registration rate that was higher than the nation's.

New York's registration and voting rates are, to a greater extent than the national figures, depressed by the state's relatively higher proportion of residents who are recent immigrants and unable to vote. Voter turnout tends to be lower in gubernatorial election years than in other even-numbered years; the latter are presidential election years.

As of April 2006, some 47 percent of voters in the state were enrolled as Democrats, while 27 percent were Republicans and 20 percent were not enrolled in any party (others were enrolled in minor parties). The Democratic enrollment edge has grown slowly but steadily in recent years, increasing by three percentage points since 1996.[3] Voters in most cities tend to be Democrats; New York City, in particular, has an overwhelming 5-to-1 ratio of Democrats to Republicans. Residents of upstate areas outside urban centers are more likely to be Republicans. The two largest suburban counties, Nassau and Suffolk, retain Republican pluralities among the electorate, though recent margins were smaller than those that existed throughout most of the 20th century.

To be sure, enrollment advantages do not guarantee electoral success. New York City elected Republican candidates for mayor in four straight elections from 1993 to 2005, and both Nassau and Suffolk counties have elected Democratic as well as Republican county executives in recent decades.

Political Parties

In New York, as across the country, ideological and policy differences between the two major political parties exist but are seldom absolute. Generally, for instance, Republicans in the state are more likely than Democrats to favor stricter criminal laws. It is somewhat more common for Democrats to favor governmental solutions to social problems, and for Republicans (at least in recent years) to propose tax reductions. Again, these are generalizations with plenty of exceptions — for instance, Governor Nelson A. Rockefeller, a Republican, did more to expand the size and cost of government than any Democratic governor in the state's history.

At the most basic level, New Yorkers influence state policy by choosing elected leaders. Contrary to the common, cynical view that politicians are all the same, elections have enormous impact on public

---

3   Data from the New York State Board of Elections, *www.elections.state.ny.us.*

policy. For example, Lewis Lehrman, a conservative Republican, narrowly lost the 1982 gubernatorial race to Democrat Mario M. Cuomo. Lehrman almost certainly would have implemented policies quite different from those of Governor Cuomo, who quickly became one of the nation's most acclaimed voices of traditional liberalism. Twelve years later, many of the state's policies changed significantly after Governor Cuomo lost to another Republican, George E. Pataki.

Some New Yorkers have influenced the ideological approaches of the two major parties by creating "minor" political parties. Unlike most states, New York's Election Law allows a candidate to place his or her name on the ballot as the representative of more than one party. Under state Election Law, candidates appear on the ballot under the name of the party nominating them. The parties are placed in order of public support, as measured by the number of votes their gubernatorial candidates received in the most recent election. In 1998 and 2002, Governor Pataki received more votes on the Republican line than Peter Vallone and H. Carl McCall drew as the Democratic candidates. Thus, from 1999 through 2006, the Republican party was listed as Row A on all ballots in the state, and the Democratic party on Row B. From 2007 through 2010, the Democratic party will appear in Row A, as a result of candidate Eliot Spitzer receiving more votes than Republican John Faso in November 2006.

From 1999 through 2006, Row C was held by the Independence Party. Its candidate for governor, Thomas Golisano, attracted the third-highest number of votes in 1998, edging out the Conservative party. Golisano devoted millions of dollars to his candidacy; in the 2000 Senate race, with a lower-profile candidate, the party received only the sixth-highest number of votes. Golisano proposed reforms such as cutting taxes and limiting the power of insiders in Albany. The party has not had a consistent policy platform, and its endorsements in legislative races have gone to candidates with varying positions on major issues.

New York's Conservative Party was formed in 1962 in reaction to what its founders perceived as the liberal shift of state Republicans under Governors Dewey and Rockefeller. The party elected candidates to both the U.S. Senate (James L. Buckley in 1970) and House of Representatives (William Carney, from 1978 through 1984). The party has also elected members of the state Legislature. Its dual nomination of Republican candidates has helped elect numerous GOP officials, including Governor Pataki and Attorney General Dennis Vacco in 1994. The Conservative Party continues to play an ideological role in state politics and government by endorsing candidates who support lower taxes, oppose unlimited abortion rights, and promote tougher penalties for criminals. It supports some Democratic candidates, although most of its nominees are Republicans. (In 2002, 65 GOP members of the Legislature, and nine Democrats, had been elected with Conservative endorsement.) In 2002, the Conservative line drew 176,848 votes for Republican Governor George Pataki.

As mentioned in Chapter Fifteen, some union leaders and other organizations created the Working Families Party in 1998 to press for a higher minimum wage and more government support for health care and education. In 2002, endorsing McCall, the party drew the fifth-highest number of votes.

Two other parties won automatic placement on ballots from 1999 through 2002 as a result of having received at least 50,000 votes in the 1998 gubernatorial elections. The Right to Life Party nominates candidates who support prohibition of, or limits on, abortion. Typically drawing between 1 and 2 percent of the vote statewide, the party sometimes endorses Republican or Democratic candidates who meet its ideological requirements, and more often nominates others who run on its line alone. The Green Party was first officially recognized as a statewide party after the 1998 election, when it nominated a former actor, Al Lewis (best known for his role on the 1960s television show *The Munsters*), for governor. The resulting media attention played a key role in the party's successful drive to achieve more than the minimum; its official total was 52,533 votes. The party urges more attention to environmental and social-justice issues. Neither the Right to Life nor the Green party reached the 50,000 minimum in 2002; both lost their automatic ballot status for the succeeding four years.

The state Liberal Party played an important role in state politics for half a century after World War II. It was founded in 1944 as an anti-Communist offshoot of the American Labor Party. Many of its earliest members were former Democrats who had become disgusted with what they perceived as corrupt party machines in their own party and a Republican Party controlled by special interests. Historically a force on issues such as rent control and abortion rights, by the 1990s the party was seen as less ideological and more interested in perpetuating itself through patronage. In 2002, having been displaced as a political force by the Working Families Party, the Liberal Party failed to attract 50,000 votes in the gubernatorial election and lost its permanent place on the state ballot.

Lobbying

After Election Day, our democratic system of government relies on winning candidates to carry out the will of the people, at least in broad form. One way individuals and interest groups communicate the will of the people (or, at least, some of the people) is through the organized process known as lobbying.

"Lobbying" has come to have a negative connotation in American government. The term derives from the places — the lobbies of legislative chambers in Washington and state capitals — where representatives of various interests have sought to influence lawmakers since the early 1800s. Lobbying is often seen as a bad or even corrupt practice that diverts elected officials from doing things the people want and need.

Political observer and linguist William Safire observes: "During the politically venal 1800s, lobbying and lobbyists earned a bad name from which their professional descendants today, no matter how pure in motive and deed, have yet to clear themselves completely." Safire adds: "Most lobbyists now operate openly as registered advocates for their employers and clients, appearing before legislative committees and regulatory agency proceedings, where they are often useful in supplying information on complex issues."[4]

Clearly, abuses still occur — some by lobbyists; others by individuals who do not register as lobbyists but seek to influence government with monetary or other favors; and others by corrupt officials. Still, a review of current thinking on lobbying by two academic specialists cited scandals in Arizona and South Carolina in the 1990s, and commented that such abuses "are less extensive than is generally believed.... Interest groups perform functions essential to the democratic process, including representation, providing information to policy makers and the public, and offering opportunities for people to acquire political training."[5]

The right of the people "to petition the Government for a redress of grievances" is guaranteed by the First Amendment to the U.S.

---

4   William Safire, *Safire's New Political Dictionary*, New York, NY: Random House, 1993.

5   Clive S. Thomas and Ronald J. Hrebenar, "Interest Groups in the States," in *Politics in the American States: A Comparative Analysis*, Seventh Edition, Virginia Gray et al., eds., Washington, DC: CQ Press, 1999.

Constitution. Similarly, New York State's Constitution forbids any law "abridging the rights of the people peaceably to assemble and to petition the government, or any department thereof." Government may not, then, outlaw lobbying. It does, however, make rules for lobbyists, as detailed later in this chapter.

New York State's Lobbying Act, part of the Legislative Law, says that "the operation of responsible democratic government requires that the fullest opportunity be afforded to the people to petition their government for the redress of grievances and to express freely to appropriate officials their opinions on legislation and governmental operations." The act further states that "to preserve and maintain the integrity of the governmental decision-making process in this state, it is necessary [to ensure disclosure of] the identity, expenditures and activities" of anyone who seeks to influence legislation or the regulatory activity of state government.

Citizen petitioning of state government is most visible on many Tuesdays during the legislative session. Because members of the Senate and Assembly are in Albany most Tuesdays during the weeks they are in session, dozens of organizations that seek funding or legislation choose that day to send groups — often large delegations of citizens — to the Legislative Office Building and the Capitol. Streets next to the two buildings are clogged with buses that bring teachers, hospital workers, tenants, welfare and environmental activists, and others to the seat of state government. Elevators in the legislative building are filled to capacity; those who are able walk up or down as many as nine flights of stairs to lawmakers' offices. Food sellers with trucks and carts on the streets do a brisk business.

Bringing organization members to Albany is a long-established, and effective, lobbying strategy. It demonstrates to elected officials that a significant number of voters care about a particular issue. Such visits can also attract media attention, often helpful in promoting action by elected leaders.

Regulation of Lobbying

The original impetus for government oversight of lobbyists in New York State emerged a century ago from legislative investigation into insurance companies in New York City. The investigation, led by Charles Evans Hughes as counsel, resulted in legislation enacted in 1905 requiring that lobbyists register and make public the nature of their work. For the next 72 years, lobbyists were required to register with the Secretary of State's office, although the agency had no regulatory authority and could not initiate investigations. In 1977, Governor Carey and the Legislature created the Temporary State Commission on Regulation of Lobbying. Three decades later, the commission is still "temporary," although "Regulation" is no longer part of its title.

The Lobbying Act requires that lobbyists register with, and disclose certain information to, the Temporary State Commission on Lobbying. The commission's six members are appointed by the governor and legislative leaders. It in turn appoints an executive director and other staff members.

The Lobbying Act requires that the commission monitor and make public the identities, activities, and expenditures of those seeking to influence legislation, rules, regulations, and rate-making actions of New York State government. The commission's powers include conducting investigations and random audits of lobbyists, and subpoenaing witnesses and records. The commission conducts private and public hearings, prepares reports and statements required by the act, and issues advisory opinions. It reports annually to the governor and the Legislature.

The commission's members serve two-year terms and can be reappointed. The four legislative leaders each recommend one member for appointment by the governor, who makes two appointments of his own who must be from different political parties. Members elect a chairman and vice chairman, who also must be from different parties. Under revisions enacted in 1999, the commission must meet at least six times each year.

The commission has traditionally taken the position that its registration and disclosure requirements of the Lobbying Act do not amount to regulation. In its 2005 Annual Report, the commission's description of its responsibilities and activities stated:

> While protecting the constitutional right of the people to petition government and seek redress of grievances, the Lobbying Act does not limit or regulate lobbying. However, it does require public disclosure of the identities, activities and expenditures of those who seek to lobby New York State and local government. The function of the Commission is to monitor the activities of those persons and groups attempting to lobby, and in so doing, to keep the public fully informed of these activities. The Act

also provides the Commission with the broad enforcement powers needed to ensure proper oversight and compel necessary disclosure.[6]

The Lobbying Act includes a section that requires the commission to publish explanation of what the statute calls "lobbying regulation."[7] Whether the commission does or does not "regulate" lobbying, it clearly exercises more control over lobbyists than any government agency does with regard to the press. Freedom of the press and the right of citizens to petition the government have the same protection under the First Amendment to the U.S. Constitution, but the two rights are treated quite differently in practice. Newspaper editors and publishers would react with outrage if subjected to the requirements imposed on lobbyists — and would no doubt take their objections to court, where they would probably be successful in overturning any law creating such requirements.

New Rules for Lobbying

In 1999, Governor Pataki and the Legislature enacted stricter registration and reporting requirements. The action followed newspaper articles on lobbyists — representing the Philip Morris companies, among others — who had treated legislators and executive-branch officials to expensive dinners and gifts.

Under the law, any individual or organization spending more than $2,000 a year on lobbying activities must register with the commission and file periodic reports on such activity. The law makes it illegal for a lobbyist or client to provide a public official with a gift valued at more than $75. Such gifts include food and entertainment; exceptions include charitable events, plaques, other ceremonial items, and campaign contributions.

Lobbyists are required to report eight times a year on the specific bills, rules, and rate-making proceedings that they seek to influence. Lobbyists who fail to file timely statements, file false reports, or exceed the $75 limit on gifts to public officials may be guilty of a Class A misdemeanor for a first offense or a Class E felony for subsequent offenses. The latter could be punished by up to four years in jail.

---

6   The report is available via the commission website, *www.nylobby.state.ny.us*.
7   Legislative Law, Sec. 1-q.

Government Lobbying Government

Local and state government agencies in New York spend millions of taxpayers' dollars each year on lobbying. Much of that activity is devoted to seeking additional funding from state taxpayers.

Seventy-eight governmental corporations, including municipalities such as Westchester County and agencies such as the New York City Board of Education, registered with the Lobbying Commission as of 2005. Several of state government's own agencies — including the State University Construction Fund, the Thruway Authority, and the Dormitory Authority — were also among the registered lobbyists.

Each of the various classes of municipalities has its own organization in Albany that represents local officials' views regarding the state budget and legislation. The New York State Association of Counties reported spending more than $165,000 on lobbying in 2001, while the Conference of Mayors and Other Municipal Officials spent more than $70,000 and the Association of Towns more than $55,000. Each association maintained an overall budget several times the amount reported for direct lobbying expenses.

All three associations lobby each year for additional state funding. Each also seeks to reduce costs to local taxpayers by eliminating or reforming state-mandated rules regarding civil service, hiring of public contractors, and other operational matters.

The law also gives the commission the power to impose civil penalties. In 2000, Trump Hotels and Casino Resorts Inc. and associated organizations were fined $250,000 for omitting certain expenses from reports filed with the commission. The organizations agreed to publish in various media outlets an apology for "misleading the public" by placing newspaper advertisements on the issue of casino gambling without disclosing the source of the ads. (The company, which owns casino operations in New Jersey, opposed legislation that would have allowed casino gambling in New York.) Perhaps indicating the complex nature of the reporting requirements, Common Cause — a nonprofit organization with a long record of lobbying for honest government — was fined $500 in 2001 for failing to file a particular report with the commission.

The 1999 changes also broadened the Lobbying Act to cover attempts to influence laws or regulations adopted by local governments representing 50,000 or more residents. Many groups complained that these changes might expose them to significant penalties for well-intentioned involvement in mundane matters. The local-government regulations took effect in 2002.

In 2005, Governor Pataki and the Legislature further extended the commission's oversight to procurement contracts issued by state and local-government entities.

A Variety of Interests in Albany

More than 4,200 lobbyists, representing 2,578 clients, registered with the commission in 2005. They reported activities on 14,941 bills before the Legislature, and 1,625 rules, regulations, and rates pending before state agencies. The highest-compensated lobbyist in 2005 — for the ninth straight year — was a law firm, Wilson Elser Moskowitz Edelman & Dicker, whose more than 60 clients included business associations, individual companies, hospitals, and other health-care organizations. The firm's staff included several former high-ranking employees in state government. The firm's total compensation and reimbursed expenses for lobbying in 2005 topped $6.9 million, according to the commission. Besides publishing such information on lobbyists, the commission also reports the organizations that spend the most as lobbying clients.

The highest-spending lobbying clients were three companies — Cablevision, Madison Square Garden, and the New York Jets — with competing interests in the possible construction of a new football stadium on Manhattan's West Side. Other leading spenders on lobbying included the Oneida Indian Nation, public-employee unions, and organizations interested in state health-care funding. The broad category of health and mental hygiene attracted the largest total spending on lobbying, at $19.9 million, according to the commission. Trade associations were second, at $11.9 million.

Overall spending by lobbyists has risen sharply since the lobbying commission started keeping records in 1978, with particularly big increases coming in the mid- to late 1990s. Lobbying expenses totaled less than $6 million in 1978 and rose to $39 million in 1994 before jumping to $149 million in 2005, according to commission data.

Top Lobbying Clients, 2005 *(ranked by total lobbying expenses)*	
1. CSC Holdings Inc.	$12,692,477
2. Madison Square Garden, LP	$6,114,302
3. Jets LLC (NY) (Jets Development, LLC)	$3,482,413
4. Oneida Indian Nation	$2,082,043
5. Jets, LLC (NY)	$2,011,247
6. Public Employees Federation	$1,743,963
7. Healthcare Association of New York State	$1,452,111
8. Civil Service Employees Association	$1,448,427
9. New York State United Teachers	$1,246,012
10. Medical Society of the State of New York	$1,222,577

Source: New York Temporary State Commission on Lobbying, *2005 Annual Report.*

The spending record for a single lobbying effort was set in 1999, when a coalition of health workers, hospitals, and other organizations spent roughly $15 million to support expansion of the state Medicaid program, increased funding for hospitals, and related programs. The coalition, led by Local 1199 of the Service Employees International Union, "rewrote the rules by which powerful interest groups can operate in the future," with television and radio advertisements and outreach to voters through focus groups, direct mailings, and telephone banks.[8] In its 2000 annual report, the commission said it expects advocacy advertising to increase in coming years and "intends to continually monitor these expenditures to ensure full disclosure."

A 2005 survey found that New York's lobbying regulations are stricter than those in most states. Lobbying restrictions in South Carolina, Alaska, Maine, Texas, and Washington were ranked as most restrictive, with New York's not far behind. Least restrictive were North Dakota, Wyoming, and Virginia, according to the study.[9]

---

8   "Lobbyists' Big Bucks Pay Off," *Newsday*, March 31, 2000.
9   Adam J. Newmark, "Measuring State Legislative Lobbying Regulation, 1990-2003," in *State Politics and Policy Quarterly* 5, 2 (Summer 2005): 182.

Requiring public disclosure of lobbying expenditures is the state's way of attempting to ensure that citizens are informed of such influence. Such information is intended to help create a balance between the desires of the citizenry as a whole and the representatives of interests who devote time and resources to lobbying.

Campaign Contributions

In addition to lobbying, many interest groups seek to influence state government by helping candidates win election to statewide or legislative office. Just as the Lobbying Act seeks to keep the public informed about who is lobbying whom, New York's Election Law requires public disclosure of monetary contributions to, and expenditures by, political candidates and committees.

In 1997, the Legislature passed and Governor Pataki signed legislation requiring the state Board of Elections to develop an electronic filing system under which candidates for office record their campaign contributions and other financial data, which the board then posts on the Internet. A year later, before the board's system was in place, a consortium of 19 newspapers across the state hired a consultant to copy and keyboard thousands of pages of data related to the 1998 elections for state office. The result "makes possible perhaps the most comprehensive examination ever of who contributes to candidates for New York state office, and how," according to one participating newspaper.[10] (The Board of Elections' data are available through *www.elections.state.ny.us*.)

The New York Public Interest Research Group analyzed campaign contributions by interest groups in 2004. The top donor to political campaigns, by far, was New York State United Teachers, with $1.3 million in contributions. Others in the top 10 were Local 1199/SEIU, representing health-care workers; the state Trial Lawyers Association; the state Medical Society; Empire Dental PAC; the New York State Correctional Officers Police Benovolent Association; Healthcare Association of New York State; the state AFL-CIO; Public Employees Federation; and New York City District Council of Carpenters.[11]

---

10 John Caher, "As state drags feet, newspaper steps in," *Times Union*, Albany, NY, February 15, 1998, p. A-1.

11 "PAC-ing It In: Political Action Committees' Contributions in New York State 2004," available at *www.nypirg.org*.

Another report, by Common Cause of New York, found that the Greater New York Hospital Association (GNYHA) Management Corp. gave more than $1 million in "soft money" to the state Senate Republican Campaign Committee and the Democratic Assembly Campaign Committee in recent years.[12] Such large contributions by GNYHA and the Healthcare Association of New York State (HANYS) reflected a growing trend for nonprofit organizations to make political contributions to, and engage in lobbying of, elected officials who control large portions of their budgets. HANYS' contributions of $312,150 in 2004 were more than those of organizations that traditionally have been heavily involved in politics, such as the state AFL-CIO and the Rent Stabilization Association, which represents landlords concerned about rent-control laws. Those organizations rely on member dues for most of their income, while taxpayer funding and charitable contributions make up significant portions of nonprofit hospitals' revenues.

The Election Law limits the amount individuals and corporations may contribute to statewide candidates, state legislative candidates, and state party committees. The limits on individual contributions are adjusted every four years to reflect changes in the Consumer Price Index. In 1999, the maximum contribution for statewide elections and New York City-wide general (as opposed to primary) elections was $30,700. For state Senate general elections, the limit was $7,700. For contributions to a state party committee, the maximum was $76,500. Other limits apply to primary races and Assembly campaigns. As of 2001, there were no limits on "soft money" contributions to party "housekeeping" accounts, which originally were established to pay for rent and other administrative expenses but are increasingly used for political activities.

What Purpose Do Political Contributions Serve?

Organizations and individuals who contribute significant amounts to political campaigns do so to support candidates who already share their philosophy, or to develop relationships that might influence elected leaders' positions.

---

12 *The Life of the Party: Hard Facts on Soft Money in New York State*, Albany, NY: Common Cause/NY, August 2006.

Former New York City Mayor Edward I. Koch commented that contributors to his political campaigns could gain "access" but not necessarily "influence."[13] He and some other elected officials have noted what would seem obvious to many — that a phone call or letter from a significant donor is almost certain to get a response, while such contact from another citizen might not. That conclusion does not necessarily mean that the response to the donor will be favorable. On the other hand, no access means no influence.

Clearly, each of the organizations identified by NYPIRG as the biggest spenders in Albany can claim major legislative victories in recent years. New York State United Teachers, for example, seeks, and usually wins, both large increases in school aid and funding for its priorities such as teacher training centers. The state medical society has successfully promoted continued funding of extra medical malpractice insurance coverage for physicians.

On the other hand, no organization gets everything it wants in Albany. As discussed in Chapter Thirteen, for example, NYSUT lost its battle to prevent the advent of charter schools in New York (the union did win some limited concessions in rules for operating such schools). The teachers' union is widely perceived as one of the most influential lobbying organizations at the Capitol because it has both resources for political contributions and significant numbers of members, many of whom take the union's positions into account when voting.

Often, major contributors to an elected official's campaign are on opposite sides of an important issue and essentially battle to a stalemate. One example in recent years is the issue of tort reform. The medical society, employer associations, local governments, and some nonprofit groups seek stricter limits on lawsuits, complaining that frivolous suits drive up costs to society beyond any benefit to injured individuals. The New York State Trial Lawyers Association and some other organizations oppose such limits. They seek wider opportunities for lawsuits, arguing that such a step will induce doctors, manufacturers, and municipal officials to promote safer products and services. Both sides have worked actively on the issue for a decade, with little resulting legislation in either direction.

---

13 Cited in, for instance, "Why Give Politicians $50,000?," *The New York Times*, January 30, 1986, p. A-20.

What Can a Citizen Do?

Citizens who seek to influence the actions of government should start by voting. Elected officials differ in many ways, but in one way they are all alike: they are well informed about, and highly sensitive to, the political attitudes of those who can vote for or against them.

The classic illustration of this point is the difference in the way that elected officials treat voters who are most faithful about going to the polls. Both Democrats and Republicans in national, state, and local offices court senior citizens, who are more likely than individuals of any other age group to go to the polls. Americans over the age of 18 were given the right to vote by the Twenty-sixth Amendment to the U.S. Constitution in 1971. Unfortunately, most younger citizens do not exercise the right. In 2000, some 68 percent of eligible voters over age 65 went to the polls, along with 64 percent of those aged 45 to 64, according to the federal Election Assistance Commission. Among eligible voters who were 18 to 24, only 32 percent did so. White individuals are most likely to vote, followed by black, Hispanic, and Asian citizens.

One illustration of how New York's elected officials pay particular attention to senior citizens is the STAR program Governor Pataki and the Legislature enacted in 1997 to reduce school property taxes for homeowners. The program provides especially generous benefits for those aged 65 and older. The program reflects the concern that older homeowners, many on fixed incomes, were finding it difficult to meet the continually rising cost of school taxes. Senior-citizen activists had not mounted a campaign for property-tax relief. But despite significant cost to the state, there was virtually no opposition in the Legislature.

Enrolling in a political party allows a citizen to vote for the same office twice in years when more than one candidate seeks his or her party's nomination and a primary election is held. Residents of New York City may choose to enroll in the Democratic party for a practical reason: In most city elections, the Democratic nomination is tantamount to election (despite GOP victories in mayoral contests). The same is true of the Republican party in many rural areas. Other citizens may wish to enroll in one of the minor parties that can play an influential role with its nominations. A single vote in a primary election typically is more influential than one in a general election because turnout tends to be much lower in primaries than in November.

The Role of Interest Groups

Many, if not most, of the bills that members of the Senate and Assembly introduce each year are at least partly the work of citizens who are organized into interest groups. Legislators and their staffs, along with policymakers in the executive branch, consider many lobbyists sources of policy expertise as well as guidance for how important constituent groups will react to particular proposals.

Given the wide influence and broad array of lobbying organizations, the first step for individuals who want to help shape public policy directly should be to determine whether others are already involved in the issue. Voluntary nonprofit groups that lobby on important issues in Albany are as disparate as the Adirondack Council and the Coalition of New York State Alzheimers' Associations, or the Poultry Association Inc. and the Uniformed Firefighters Association.

While hundreds of organizations represent particular interests, no organized lobbying groups exclusively represent the broad range of New Yorkers as citizens and consumers. Some organizations describe themselves as lobbying for "good government" or for consumers; the New York Public Interest Research Group, Common Cause, and the League of Women Voters are examples. All three have worked actively on issues that seek to advance democratic representation — for instance, reforming New York's laws that famously favor incumbents in achieving ballot status. Each of these groups also has its own ideas as to what "the people" want, priorities that do not necessarily correspond to those of all, or even most, New Yorkers. Each group can fairly be described as leaning, in varying degrees, toward the liberal end of the political spectrum — judging from positions on issues such as mandatory deposits on beverage containers (the "bottle bill"), more government regulation of health-care plans, abortion rights, and public funding for higher education, child care, and other programs.

For decades, New York had no organization speaking exclusively on behalf of New York taxpayers. Some broad-based business groups, such as the Business Council of New York State and the National Federation of Independent Business, regularly advocate for lower taxes. They also, however, devote resources to other issues that affect employers. An organization called United Taxpayers of New York was organized in 2006, promising to speak for taxpayer interests.

Ideally, voters elect people to represent the broad spectrum of interests in the state. The governor, other statewide elected officials, and members of the Legislature represent all New Yorkers in their many roles — as taxpayers and consumers; as students, workers, and business owners; as users of public roads, schools, and other services; as residents of upstate and downstate, in communities large and small. By definition, voters choose those who will represent their interests. If elected officials do not do so, voters have the power to choose new representatives.

Strategies for Influencing Policy

Individuals who want to advance an issue should consider time-tested strategies, including:

- *Learn the issue.* In politics generally, and in lobbying in particular, knowledge is power. Knowing as much as — and preferably more than — the government officials who make decisions helps any lobbyist or active citizen develop the confidence of those in office. Such confidence leads to greater access; ultimately, officeholders and their staffs will develop the habit of reaching out to the expert for information. Understanding the facts of how an issue affects voters also helps clarify political opportunities and obstacles.

- *Identify key actors and stakeholders.* Individuals and institutions both inside and outside of government are likely to be important. In many cases, one or more officials in the executive branch will make the key decisions; in others, one or more legislators will do so. Understanding how these leaders approach the issue at the outset, and exploring fully what might persuade them in a certain direction, makes success more likely. It's important to analyze how to minimize opposition from other players, and to broaden the base of support.

- *Consider a wide range of potential outcomes, including goals that are highly ambitious.* It can be hard to get something done in American government — blocking action is generally much easier. Often, starting with an ambitious proposal may make it possible to win a scaled-back but still de-

sirable outcome, or help block contrary proposals. At the
same time, it's essential to have realistic goals and to be
ready to bargain.

- *Personalize the issue.* Public officials, the media, and voters
  will lend support more readily if beneficiaries are clearly
  identified. A recent version of this approach is for legislators
  to name crime bills, for instance, "Kendra's Law," after a
  victim.

- *Assess the political landscape.* The status of the economy,
  whether state officials are up for election, and issues domi-
  nating the attention of the news media are some of the conditions that are likely to play a role in your issue.

- *Find a champion.* For action that requires legislation (including budget issues), one or more of the three major players — the governor and the two majority conferences in the
  Legislature — must be willing to bring the issue to the negotiating table. Perhaps a high-level official in the executive
  branch can push the issue onto the governor's agenda; perhaps a handful of legislators can persuade their leadership to
  make the issue a priority. With regard to regulatory issues,
  the governor's Executive Chamber staff and the Governor's
  Office of Regulatory Reform can be important players along
  with the agency directly involved in the issue. If the goal is to
  advance or stop a proposed regulation, legislators who are
  close to the administration — or who are in the opposite
  party and talented at attracting press attention — may be
  good champions to try to interest in your issue.

Accountability

Many voters have at least a general idea of what they want state government to accomplish. Like people everywhere, they want good schools,
high-quality health care, a sound transportation system, and other services — all at a cost they can afford.

State leaders often announce the enactment of a new law, or appropriation of millions of dollars, to achieve "desired" results. How do

citizens know whether their state government is doing what they want? Is New York State government accountable?

Accountability was the major argument for the relatively strong governorship created by the state's first Constitution. In the early decades of the 20th century, citizen reformers joined with elected leaders such as Charles Evans Hughes and Al Smith to strengthen the chief executive's office further, with accountability to the voters playing a key role in the debate. As outlined in Chapter Four, New York's governor today has greater power than governors of most other states.

The state Constitution creates other accountability mechanisms by investing power in the elective offices of comptroller, attorney general and the Legislature. Each of these separately elected officials has the power to point out instances in which a governor and executive agencies are not serving what that official believes are proper goals or the people's interests. In a similar vein, to assure fiscal accountability, state statutes established the auditing role the comptroller exercises (*see Chapter Four*).

Standing committees of the Senate and Assembly have the legal power and political standing to exercise oversight of the executive branch, but do so relatively rarely. Any such oversight is more likely to emerge from whichever party is not in the governor's office at a given time. The Legislature created the bipartisan Legislative Commission on Expenditure Review in 1969 to monitor executive-branch agencies' implementation of laws and programs, but has not provided funding for the commission since the early 1990s.

Open Government

Accountability to the voters requires information. The mid-1970s, when public confidence in government was shaken by events that included the Vietnam War and the Watergate scandal, brought New York State two major laws that promote accountability by opening governmental operations to public view. In 1974, the Legislature enacted the Freedom of Information Law, guaranteeing public access to most governmental records. Three years later, the Open Meetings Law was adopted, requiring that governmental bodies deliberate and make decisions during sessions that are open to the public.

The state's Freedom of Information Law, modeled on a federal law enacted in 1966, declares as its basic rationale that "...a free society is maintained when government is responsive and responsible to the public, and when the public is aware of governmental actions. The more open a government is with its citizenry, the greater the understanding and participation of the public in government."[14] Governor Malcolm Wilson, in signing the law, put the idea simply: "Government is the people's business."[15]

The law was not without its opponents, however. The Legislature needed three separate pieces of legislation — a main bill and two amending statutes — to decide which records would be open to the public and which would not. Under the statute today, records of any state or local government agency are presumed to be open unless they fall under a specific exemption. Examples of the latter include those that would create "an unwarranted invasion of personal privacy," such as medical histories or the personal references of someone applying for employment; and disclosures that would interfere with law enforcement.

New York's Freedom of Information Law provides for the Committee on Open Government within the Department of State to issue advisory opinions to government agencies and members of the public on implementing the statute as well as the related Open Meetings Law.[16] The committee promulgates regulations on how government agencies are required to comply with the law. The committee members include the lieutenant governor, the secretary of state, two other state officials, an elected local government official appointed by the governor, and six members of the public, at least two of whom must represent the news media.

The Open Meetings Law gives the public the right to attend meetings of public bodies. The public must receive notice of meetings in advance. The law can be viewed as an expansion of the state Constitution's requirement that all meetings of the houses of the Legislature be open to the public.

As the Committee on Open Government summarizes the Open Meetings Law, "Any time a quorum of a public body gathers for the

---

14 Public Officers Law, Section 84.

15 Memorandum of approval, May 29, 1974.

16 Before enactment of the Open Meetings Law, the agency was known as the Committee on Public Access to Records.

purpose of discussing public business, the meeting must be convened open to the public, whether or not there is an intent to take action, and regardless of the manner in which the gathering may be characterized." As with public records, meetings of public bodies are presumed to fall under the requirement of openness unless specific exceptions apply. Exceptions include matters that will imperil the public safety if disclosed; discussions regarding proposed, pending, or current litigation; and collective bargaining with public employee unions. The Open Meetings Law also requires that minutes of every meeting be compiled and made available to the public.

As mentioned above, the Freedom of Information Law generally presumes that state and local governmental records are public, and lists exceptions to that general rule. With regard to their own activities, lawmakers created the opposite presumption: the statute provides a list of records that are open to the public, and others are presumed to be beyond the scope of the law.

Both laws have contributed to a gradual but noticeable change in the way many governmental bodies operate. Before the Open Meetings Law, local government boards would commonly meet behind closed doors for "work meetings" or "study sessions" to discuss land-use issues and school budgets. Now governing boards seldom question the idea that discussions as well as votes must take place in public. (Some observers would argue that the requirement is one of the factors that has made it harder for government to get things done.)

The Committee on Open Government has encouraged members of the news media and citizens to use the open-government laws to full advantage. This is in part a reflection of the influence of the executive director of the committee for more than 25 years, Robert Freeman, who made the office an outspoken ally for reporters and others seeking access to records and meetings.

The News Media

One of the fundamental ideas of modern democracy is that a free press will inform citizens of their government's actions. The media devote significant resources to covering New York State government. For a variety of reasons, though, they pay relatively little attention to — and therefore most of the public learns little about — the actual performance of state government, a subject addressed in more detail below.

More than two dozen news organizations assigned journalists to regular coverage of the state Capitol. Most of those organizations are daily newspapers. Others include the Associated Press, news services for the Gannett and Ottaway newspaper chains, special-interest publications such as *NY Business Environment*; and television and radio outlets including the public-television program *Inside Albany*.

Still, most of the state's news media tend to give state government relatively low-profile coverage. Newspapers usually award front-page attention to stories with the greatest national or local, rather than statewide, importance. Most Capitol reporters see a front-page byline a handful of times during the year, typically when covering major news concerning the state budget or controversial legislation. Good "play" — on the front page or in another prominent place — may also be given to articles reporting on perceived mismanagement or a scandal.

Coverage of individual legislators from major cities is, typically, particularly skimpy. Most New York City residents who read *The New York Times, Daily News*, or *New York Post* can go an entire lifetime without seeing their state lawmakers' names in the paper. Articles in those newspapers — as in others across the state — generally focus on the governor and the two major legislative leaders because of their dominance of the policymaking process. Many weekly newspapers do print articles about local legislators, but such articles are usually based on, or simply reprint, press releases issued by legislators' staff. All four conferences in the Legislature employ public-relations staff whose duties include arranging favorable coverage of members.

When news media do pay attention to state government, coverage tends to focus on debates over the proposed budget, political developments, and policy proposals made by the governor or legislators. Relatively little attention goes to one of the most important questions regarding state government: How well is it implementing policies and programs intended to improve public health, educate the children of the state, and meet other essential goals?

Coverage of political campaigns, too, tends to focus on nonsubstantive matters: The latest reports on candidates' fundraising efforts, polls of potential voters, or speculation about how certain policy proposals might help or hurt a candidate. In races for Senate and Assembly seats, in particular, the news media generally ignore policy issues. Dan Lynch discovered this problem after he left the newspaper business in 2000 and won the Democratic nomination for Assembly, challenging a three-term Republican incumbent. Lynch had been managing editor of the Albany *Times Union* for 16 years, overseeing news coverage by the daily paper in the state's capital city. His conclusion about the news media and political campaigns echoes the conclusion of some other political activists: "Its almost total lack of attentiveness has made the press virtually irrelevant in informing the voters who the candidates are and what they really stand for."[17]

Unlike most other large states, New York has never had widely available television coverage of state government. As of 2001, among the 10 largest states, all but New York and Illinois offered televised broadcasts of legislative sessions; Illinois began providing such coverage in 2003. A study by Common Cause New York argued that gavel-to-gavel coverage of the Legislature is needed to "induce wider and more accurate news reporting on state affairs."[18] From 1983 to 1992, cable television systems in the Capital Region carried the New York State Community Affairs Network, broadcasting legislative and other proceedings for cable subscribers. The broadcasts were not distributed statewide, and ended during a budget stalemate between Governor Cuomo and legislative leaders. Cable broadcasts of the legislative session were once again available statewide starting in 2006.

Performance Measurement in New York

In a democratic system, public opinion can play a decisive role in changing government policies and programs. Most voters, however, do not have the time or inclination to find out how well government works. A promising tool for promoting public awareness of the effectiveness of government programs is performance measurement, which provides reliable data on the results of work performed by government agencies.

Performance measurement reflects the belief that the most common method of measuring government activity — how much it spends on various programs — is not adequate in judging success or failure. It focuses on outcomes or results — for instance, how well children are reading or how many welfare recipients have obtained jobs — rather

---

17 Dan Lynch, *Running With The Machine: A Journalist's Eye-Opening Plunge Into Politics*, Albany, NY: Whitston Publishing Co. Inc., 2001, p. 286.

18 David Evan Markus and Rebecca Medina, "Lights! Camera! Action!" Common Cause New York, April 16, 2001.

than outputs or efforts, which might be, for example, the number of students served or job-training classes held. Performance *measurement* is one facet of a broader concept known as performance *management* (also described with rubrics such as managing for results) which includes such steps as setting specific goals for governmental policies and programs, reporting on performance relative to predetermined benchmarks, and allocating resources based on specified results. While growing in use today, the idea is not new. The progressive government-reform movement in the early decades of the 20th century promoted similar concepts to improve efficiency and economy. The two Hoover Commissions that recommended management reforms for the federal government after World War II spread awareness of the concept.

New York State's best known and most successful use of performance measurement has been introduction of school report cards by the state Education Department. As outlined in Chapter Thirteen, the department prepares and publicizes annual reports on the academic performance of students in every school district and every school. The report cards have achieved the first goal of performance measurement: focusing attention on areas that need improvement. There is evidence that the report cards are stimulating improvements in performance.

The Health Department has begun several major efforts to measure the performance of doctors and health-care organizations it regulates, with an eye to promoting improvement. In 1989, the department began publishing data on the outcomes of coronary artery bypass surgery. Heart disease is by far the leading cause of death in New York and nationally, and one of the most common forms is coronary artery disease. Bypass graft surgery on coronary arteries is a common type of surgery (an average of 40 such operations were performed in New York each day in 2003); it can make a life-or-death difference. This made it an excellent first choice for the department's effort to measure performance. The department publishes mortality rates for patients operated on by particular surgeons, as well as the record of cardiac-care centers across the state; the data are adjusted to account for factors such as the severity of patients' illness. Department officials believe the reports have helped cut mortality rates by more than half since 1989.[19]

The Health Department also publishes an annual report on the performance of managed-care plans licensed to operate in the state. Data

---

19 "State Health Department Releases New Cardiac Surgery Data," press release, New York State Health Department, Oct. 28, 2005.

on health-care quality, access, utilization, and customer satisfaction are included, and both nonprofit and profit-making plans are covered. The data largely parallel those used by the National Committee for Quality Assurance, an independent nonprofit organization run by representatives of health-care organizations, employers, organized labor, academia, and consumers. The ratings given to managed-care plans have spurred press coverage, although not nearly as much as the school report cards. The department says the report is part of its overall strategy to improve quality of care by managed care plans by increasing public accountability.

In 2006, the Health Department introduced another major tool for tracking performance: report cards on hospitals. A 1996 state law that mainly dealt with hospital financing also charged the department with developing reports, similar to those on cardiac surgery, on hospital performance for other procedures. Hospital administrators raised questions about the methods used for weighing results — similar to those that often arise in connection with New York's report cards on schools and cardiac surgery. Delays in implementing the hospital assessments reflected the political opposition that performance measurement can engender. Years after their scheduled introduction, the hospital report cards began to give consumers more information on health outcomes in institutions across the state.

At the state Labor Department, subjects of performance measures include the Rapid Response and Business Retention System, which works with employers that announce plans to close facilities with 50 or more jobs. The department's measures include the number of individuals who averted layoffs after such warnings, and attainment of new skills that might help laid-off workers find other jobs.

One of the most widely known examples of performance measurement is New York City's Compstat — the New York Police Department system that uses computer-generated statistics to assess law enforcement at the neighborhood level. Precinct commanders use these data to target problems as they develop; department administrators, in turn, use the same data to hold precinct commanders accountable. Many observers believe Compstat played a significant role in the city's dramatic reduction in crime rates during most of the 1990s. In 2003, state criminal-justice officials expanded analysis of crime statistics as part of an effort to reduce crime statewide.

The 2006 Executive Budget documents included a first-ever sprinkling of performance measures for key areas in each of four broad policy areas: education, public assistance and children's services; health care and mental hygiene; environment, recreation and transportation; and criminal justice.[20] Some of the indicators provided information about performance of state programs and social conditions that may be influenced by those programs — such as student achievement in math and English, teen pregnancy rates, water quality, crime rates, and consumer satisfaction with state mental-hygiene services. Other measurements simply showed how much the state was spending in various areas, from local school aid to open-space preservation. Such indicators provide useful context. But performance measurement is primarily intended to illustrate *performance* — the results that government achieves in a given area, rather than how many dollars it spends, how many individuals in enrolls in its programs, or the laws and regulations it enacts.

As state government reports more performance measures publicly, another key step will be expanded use of such measures by elected and appointed officials to guide efforts at improving performance.

Does Measurement Improve Performance?

Some public policy analysts believe that performance measurement can bring real improvement in the provision of public services, while others are skeptical. With regard to the broader issue of performance management, former New York State Budget Director Dall W. Forsythe, for instance, has cautioned:

> Performance management initiatives in government face difficulties in implementation in the best of circumstances. At their worst, they create incentives for unexpected or even undesirable behavior by agency managers and front-line personnel.... Confusion about the goals or audiences or performance information, inattention to measurement challenges, and poor choices of incentives are all sources of difficulties for PM systems.[21]

---

20 New York State Division of the Budget, *2006-07 Executive Budget: Agency Presentations*, Albany, NY, 2006.

21 Dall W. Forsythe, in *Quicker Better Cheaper? Managing Performance in American Government*, Albany, Rockefeller Institute Press, 2001, pp. vii and 520.

New York State government has had its unsuccessful experiences with performance management. In 1981, for instance, the Legislature enacted a Key Item Reporting System (KIRS) requiring agencies to report on performance indicators specified in statute. As Forsythe recalled, "The budget office complained about the legislature's choice of agencies, programs, and indicators for monitoring, and simply refused to take the statute seriously. Nearly ten years after its enactment, as New York State suffered through its worst economic downturn since the 1930s, the executive branch stopped providing the required data. After a brief dust-up in the press over this noncompliance, the governor persuaded the legislature to repeal the KIRS requirement."[22]

Performance Measurement
on the Rise Nationally

Like most states, New York has not yet made a full commitment to performance measurement. At the national level, the Government Performance and Results Act enacted in 1993 pushes federal government agencies to focus on results. The law requires agencies to develop strategic plans and goals, and create performance measures to track progress toward those goals. A 2000 review of the act's implementation found that "GPRA has produced widespread improvements in strategic planning and performance measurement throughout the federal government.[23]

A number of other states have adopted broad performance-measurement programs. The Oregon Progress Board, appointed by the governor and legislative leaders, tracks 100 or so indicators known as the Oregon Benchmarks — a wide range of indicators of social, economic and environmental health. Minnesota Milestones sets 19 goals for the state's future and uses 70 indicators to measure progress toward those goals. Texas has institutionalized the use of performance measures for all major state agencies, with oversight shared by various elected state officials. In New York City, the City Charter requires the mayor to issue

22 Forsythe, pp. 530-531.
23 Dall W. Forsythe, *Performance Management Comes to Washington: A Status Report on the Government Performance and Results Act*, Albany, NY: Nelson A. Rockefeller Institute of Government, February 2000.

annual management reports that include measurements of a wide range of public services.

Certain federally funded programs created or amended in recent years establish financial incentives for states to achieve results. Under the 1996 federal welfare reform act, the U.S. Department of Health and Human Services awards $200 million annually in "high-performance" bonuses for results in placement and retention of former welfare recipients in paid employment. New York received a bonus in fiscal 1999.

Federal incentives such as those enacted as part of welfare reform increase pressure on state and local governments to engage more seriously in measuring performance. An initiative by the Government Accounting Standards Board (GASB) creates further attention to the issue. (The board sets standards for accounting and financial reporting by state and local governments.) GASB is studying whether to require the financial reports that New York and other states issue each year to include performance measures. Such a requirement would attempt to make such measures the norm rather than the exception for government agencies.

Governments — New York State and others — should continue to make information on results more available. Citizens demand a growing level and variety of services from state governments. They need more information to assess those services and the governmental institutions and leaders who provide them. New York's experience with school report cards and other measurement tools shows that performance measurement can help state government deliver services better and more cost-effectively.

FEDERALISM:
WHAT IS THE ROLE OF
STATE GOVERNMENTS?

Throughout this book's portrayal of one state government, in the background looms a larger subject: American federalism. For citizens, it is one of the least understood aspects of U.S. government. Millions who can barely spare the time to consider a vote for president have little understanding of, or interest in, the subject. Yet, if voters are to hold elected officials accountable, they must know who's in charge of improving schools, responding to natural disasters, regulating business relationships and other important jobs.

Contrary to what seemed to be the case just two or three decades ago, federalism is very much alive in the United States. The argument over the proper role of state governments within the federal system has dramatic implications for both the *policies* of government — in education, taxes, the environment, and other major areas — and the *extent of the power* it exercises over individuals and the economy.

In common usage, the phrase *federal government* refers to the national government based in Washington, D.C. — the president, agencies such as the Department of State and the Internal Revenue Service, Congress, and the Supreme Court. More broadly, theorists since before the American Revolution have used the term *federal* to describe a two-level form of government. "Under the U.S. Constitution, each citizen is a citizen of two governments, national and state."[1]

Canada with its provinces, and Switzerland with its cantons, are examples of federal systems. By contrast, *unitary* governments in countries such as France and Great Britain are not constitutionally required to share power in this way, although in practice they grant significant authority to local governments.

> It is only Washington that sends out and receives ambassadors, coins money, owns guided missiles and aircraft carriers, and tries to "fine-tune" the economy through control of the money supply. On the other hand, the federal government does not as a general rule arrest speeders, grant divorces, or probate wills; it does not pass zoning ordinances or run school districts; it does not foreclose mortgages, repossess television sets, or put people on trial for robbing gas stations. It does not do most of the ordinary, workaday jobs of the law.[2]

The founders of the United States of America were suspicious of centralized political authority, having been driven to the extreme step of declaring independence from a distant and sometimes hostile monarch. They recognized that separate colonies would have little chance to win separation from the great power of the British crown. Thus, alliance among the new states was essential. Yet they reflected their suspicion of concentrated power in the first structure they created for the new government, the Articles of Confederation, which gave the national government limited ability to act without the states' assent.

After adoption of the Articles, difficulties in prosecuting the war against Britain and carrying out other governmental duties convinced many of the founders to push for a stronger central authority. New York State's first Constitution was one model for the national charter adopted at the Philadelphia convention in 1787. After Congress submitted the proposed Constitution to the states, New York's Alexander Hamilton persuaded James Madison and John Jay to join him in writing newspaper articles supporting ratification. The articles were later published collectively under the title *The Federalist*.

---

1   Richard P. Nathan, "Federalism," in *The Oxford Companion to Politics of the World*, 2nd ed., Joel Krieger, ed., New York, NY: Oxford University Press, 2001.

2   Lawrence M. Friedman, *American Law: An Introduction*, New York, NY: W.W. Norton & Co., 1998, p. 147.

New York State's political leadership and voters reflected divided opinion nationally. Most of the state's large landowners and merchants favored the stronger Constitution because they thought it would improve the domestic economy and foreign trade. Other New Yorkers, however, including future Governor DeWitt Clinton and small farmers, feared a strong national government and opposed the Constitution. When a state convention held at Poughkeepsie in July 1788 voted on the proposal, it carried 30-27. All the delegates from "upstate" — north of Orange and Dutchess counties — voted against ratification, while all except one of the delegates from "downstate" were in favor. New York's vote of approval was accompanied by a resolution of "confidence" that other states would support amendments to preserve individuals' rights. That resolution helped lead to the important protections contained in the Bill of Rights.

Hamilton and others succeeded in their effort to create a much stronger central government than provided for in the Articles of Confederation. But their product, the Constitution, continued — and still retains — significant limits on the powers of the national government. It also provides for internal checks and balances, which prevent Washington from using its full powers without broad political consensus.

The federal-state division of powers acts as a brake on the natural tendency of government to acquire more power over time. That balance of power is dynamic — a good thing, Hamilton argued. He said the Constitution preserves liberty by allowing citizens to shift their support between the state and the federal levels as needed to guard against heavy-handed government: "If [the people's] rights are invaded by either, they can make use of the other as the instrument of redress."[3] As explained later in this chapter, some experts believe the opposite has proven true: Federalism has promoted growth, not restraint, in the size and power of government.

Shifts in the Balance of Powers

Chapter One observed that government changes dramatically over time in response to the will of the people and choices by elected and appointed leaders. Often, those changes take place as a result of shifts in the federal-state relationship. In 1974, for instance, Congress required

---

3   From *Federalist 28.*

states to enact 55-mph speed limits to reduce gasoline consumption (New York had already imposed the lower limit). In 1987, federal lawmakers reversed course by allowing speeds of 65 on certain rural highways while maintaining the lower limit on most roads; eight years later, President Clinton signed a law repealing the federal requirement entirely. Throughout the changes, states retained the right to ignore Washington's directives. Rather than enacting outright mandates on the states, Congress wrote the speed limits into funding measures. Any state willing to forego federal transportation assistance could have made its own decisions on speed limits. All decided to accept Washington's funding — along with its mandates.

Just two decades ago, the common wisdom among political scientists held that federalism was little more than history. The New Deal in the 1930s, court decisions such as *Brown* v. *Board of Education* in the 1950s, and creation of major new agencies such as the Environmental Protection Agency in the 1970s all shifted the balance of power to Washington. The concept of "states' rights" was considered little more than an excuse for reaction against federal enforcement of individual civil rights, particularly for African-Americans. One textbook on American government stated flatly: "It would be only a mild overstatement ... to say that the doctrine of dual federalism is virtually extinct and that, provided it has a good reason for wanting to do so, Congress can pass a law that will regulate, constitutionally, almost any kind of economic activity located anywhere in the country."[4]

Yet even as that book was published, Washington was starting to cut back its regulatory oversight of major industries such as energy and transportation. In succeeding years, President Reagan's judicial appointees gave the federal courts a much greater philosophical interest in federalism; federal judges and Supreme Court justices selected by President George W. Bush continued the pattern. In 1995, for instance, the U.S. Supreme Court overturned a 1990 federal law that outlawed possession of firearms in a school zone. The decision did not mean that the justices favored guns in or near schools. Rather, the court said, the statute "forecloses the states from experimenting and exercising their own judgement in an area to which states lay claim by right of history and expertise."[5] The decision, written by Chief Justice Rehnquist, cited

---

4   James Q. Wilson, *American Government: Institutions and Policies*, Lexington, MA: D.C. Heath & Co., 1980, p. 52.

5   *U.S.* v. *Lopez*, 514 U.S. 549.

Madison in *Federalist 45*: "The powers delegated by the proposed Constitution to the federal government are few and defined. Those which are to remain in the state governments are numerous and indefinite."

Federalism Today

More than two centuries after states ratified the Constitution, most of its provisions regarding the powers of the national government and of states remain unchanged. Under Article 1, for instance, states cannot make treaties with other nations, coin money, issue paper currency, or (except in the case of invasion or imminent danger) engage in war without Congressional approval. The Civil War and ratification of the 14th Amendment to the Constitution left the national government clearly supreme, with its sovereignty deriving directly from the people rather than from state governments.

Yet, states remain powerful in their own right — not only in matters of governance, but in making decisions that influence the federal government itself. Legislatures write the rules, and the district lines, for the elections that members of Congress must face every two years. As many Americans learned after Election Day 2000, state legislatures have the authority under the Constitution to play a deciding role in allocating electoral votes, influencing the election of the nation's president and vice president. In 2004, Republicans gained four seats in the House of Representatives — an important addition to their small margin of control — because the Texas Legislature had redistricted the state's Congressional seats.

States also retain what could be considered the ultimate trump card over Washington: Two-thirds of the legislatures can call for a convention to amend the Constitution, and any resulting amendments take effect upon ratification by three-fourths of the states with no action by Congress. (Congress can also propose amendments with a two-thirds vote in each house.)

Long before the federal government did so, states played large roles in education, transportation, public health, and caring for the disabled. In the decades after the Depression, the national government assumed significant powers in each of those areas. But states, along with local governments, remain key players. Direct service provision, particularly, is a function first of local governments, secondly of the states, and in only a few instances of the national government (for example, veterans' health services). Localities employ the largest proportion of public employees. In New York State, 1.1 million individuals work for local governments (including some 525,000 in public schools), roughly 265,000 for the state government and its authorities, and some 128,000 for the Postal Service and various branches of the federal government.[6]

In fiscal 2004, states and their local governments collected more than $1 trillion in taxes for the first time, according to U.S. Census Bureau figures. That was almost the same as the federal government's take from general taxes (not counting those for social insurance and retirement).[7]

Both the national government and states can claim credit for important accomplishments in recent decades. Washington has acted to protect the rights of citizens with federal laws and Supreme Court decisions in areas such as voting rights, equal access to public schools, and criminal defense. States led the way on welfare reform and expanded taxpayer-funded health coverage for children, ultimately sparking federal action.

In addition to serving as a check on the powers of the central government, supporters of federalism say, it increases citizen participation, encourages innovation as states try different solutions to similar problems, and preserves local and regional identity. Critics of the federal system "criticize its slowness to respond to new challenges, its perceived inability to take advantage of technological advances, and the allegedly cumbersome nature of its governmental decision-making and implementation processes."[8]

The Bottom Line: Expanding the Public Sector?

Some experts argue that, regardless of the cycles of power between states and Washington, in the long run federalism has one overriding impact: Expanding the size of the public sector, particularly in domestic social services. Richard P. Nathan explains:

---

6   U.S. Bureau of Labor Statistics data.

7   Washington collected $1.1 trillion in individual income tax; corporate income tax; excise taxes on highway usage, alcohol, tobacco and other goods and services; and estate tax. Receipts from payroll taxes for Social Security, Medicare, unemployment, and related programs added another $600 billion or so.

8   Nathan, "Federalism."

Going back to the nineteenth century and the first part of the twentieth century, the states — not all the states, but some states — have been the sources of expansion of the public sector in conservative periods. When conservative coalitions controlled national offices, programs that were incubated, tested, and debugged in liberal states became the basis for later national action. In such periods, client and provider groups also played a strong role in protecting existing programs, making retrenchment harder to achieve than otherwise would have been the case.[9]

There's little question that expansion of the overall public sector occurs continually. Reasons include voters' desires for more services, elected officials' incentive to respond to voter desires, self-interest on the part of public employees and contractors, and the tendency of bureaucracies to accrete power and resources over time. A federalist system gives proponents of any policy a variety of opportunities to seek support. Those who seek public-sector expansion tend to have a strong interest in the issue. Even if a majority of voters oppose a given policy change, few have much incentive to work against it.

Federalism allows programs created by the state and national governments to build on each other. In 1997, President Clinton and Congress created the State Children's Health Insurance Program, based partly on New York's already existing Child Health Plus program and state-level experiments elsewhere. Washington's adoption of a program that had been tested at the state level led to all states offering such coverage, to 4 million children nationwide as of 2005. The program itself remains an illustration of federalism, allowing states to make very different choices on how many participants are covered, whether premiums or enrollment fees are required, and other matters.

Interstate Activities

By reserving significant powers to the state, the American system of government gives states the opportunity to work together in ways that might not occur if all decisions came from Washington. Article I of the U.S. Constitution says states may not "enter into any Agreement or Compact with another state" without Congressional approval. Interested in their own power, and influenced by policy or political concerns

9   Richard P. Nathan, "There Will Always Be a New Federalism," *Journal of Public Administration Research and Theory*, February 14, 2006.

that may differ from the states', members of Congress may delay or impose conditions on interstate compacts. But Congress generally avoids blocking regional agreements that do not impinge on the rights of other states.

One significant agreement involving New York and other states is the Great Lakes Compact. In 1955, five states bordering the Great Lakes — Illinois, Indiana, Michigan, Minnesota, and Wisconsin — agreed to work on joint environmental and economic issues related to the watershed of the lakes, including the St. Lawrence and other rivers. Forty percent of New York State's land mass lies in the Great Lakes basin, and the state joined the compact as a result of legislation enacted in 1960. Pennsylvania and Ohio are also members, while the Canadian provinces of Ontario and Quebec are associate members.

The compact did not have full force and effect until Congress gave its approval. "Numerous bills" were introduced in Washington started in 1956, but passage did not come until 1968. Even then, parts of the interstate agreement were not approved. The law enacted by Congress reserved the right to alter or repeal the compact and included conditions such as this:

> **SEC. 2.** The consent herein granted does not extend to paragraph B of article II or to paragraphs J, K, and M or article VI of the compact, or to other provisions of article VI of the compact which purpose to authorize recommendations to, or cooperation with, any foreign or international governments, political subdivisions, agencies or bodies. In carrying out its functions under this Act the Commission shall be solely a consultative and recommendatory agency which will cooperate with the agencies of the United States. It shall furnish to the Congress and to the President, or to any official designated by the President, copies of its reports submitted to the party states pursuant to paragraph O of article IV of the compact.[10]

The compact binds New Yorkers to obey regulatory decisions from a body that is neither the state nor the federal government, but a group of state officials — the majority of whom have no electoral accountability to New York voters. Given that, states enter into regional compacts only when the subject is one that attracts broad support.

---

10 Quotes and relevant history are from the website of the Great Lakes Commission, *www.glc.org*, accessed June 23, 2006.

Leaders of the nine states and provinces in the Great Lakes pact have made other major agreements that build on the original compact, most recently in December 2005. Under those agreements, New York's Department of Environmental Conservation and other agencies in the region work cooperatively on issues such as:

- Tracking and managing withdrawals from lakes and rivers in the Great Lakes basin;

- Reducing contaminants;

- Promoting power generation, transportation and recreation; and

- Cleaning up particularly polluted "areas of concern" such as the Buffalo River and Oswego River and Harbor.

In keeping with the interstate and international agreement, state law and DEC regulations limit how municipalities, power plants, manufacturers, and other users draw on the huge, yet limited, resources of the Great Lakes and their tributaries. States must report annually to the Great Lakes Commission on all significant withdrawals from those sources. DEC must consult with the other states if a New York user seeks to consume more than 5 million gallons per day. The compact generally forbids diversions of water out of the Great Lakes basin. Under the agreement, for instance, New York's Legislature could not pass a law sending Lake Ontario water to New York City.

The U.S. Constitution gives Congress the power to "regulate Commerce ... among the several States." But, in addition to making formal interstate compacts with the approval of Congress, states conduct joint activities in a variety of regulatory and law-enforcement areas.

For example, attorneys general in New York and other states have filed several lawsuits against the federal government, challenging regulatory decisions by the Environmental Protection Agency. Sixteen states sued in the U.S. Court of Appeals for the D.C. Circuit in 2005, seeking to block mercury-emission rules based on the federal Clean Air Act. EPA agreed to a formal reconsideration of the challenged regulations. It announced in May 2006 that it planned to go forward, and the states filed a successor lawsuit weeks later. Such lawsuits do not require the approval of the governor or the Legislature.

Continuing Debate Over the Balance of Power

Public debate over proposals to assign expanded powers to Washington tends to start from the presumption that any such change would be for the better. In the 1970s, teacher unions and other supporters of increased government involvement in education lobbied Congress to create a separate federal Department of Education from the then-Department of Health, Education and Welfare. President Jimmy Carter signed such a measure into law in 1979. Conservatives decried the new agency as inappropriate federal intrusion in an area that historically had been left to the states and localities. Proposals to abolish the new agency continued to arise during the Reagan administration in the 1980s and after Republicans took control of Congress in the mid-1990s. But, as President Reagan often noted, "The nearest thing to immortality on earth is a government program," and the department was never seriously threatened.

Under President George W. Bush, federal spending on — and power over — public schools across the country expanded sharply. A quarter-century after liberals won creation of the federal Department of Education, they harshly criticized new mandates from Washington. School boards and others viewed the second Bush administration's No Child Left Behind program as creating too many new tasks for local educators, with too little funding to make such mandates worthwhile. Still, there were few — if any — new calls for abolishing the federal Department of Education.

As noted in Chapter Thirteen, members of Congress frequently call for expanding federal criminal statutes, and have enacted dozens of such changes in recent decades. If Representative Jones announces a proposal to increase penalties for a particular crime, his or her constituents are unlikely to reflect on whether state laws already provide tough penalties, or whether locally elected prosecutors and judges might be better administrators of justice than those appointed from Washington.

Voters may reflexively support increased federal action on a given issue simply because they do not understand which level of government is responsible. After Hurricane Katrina devastated New Orleans in August 2005, local residents and national news media criticized Washington's handling of the crisis. Much of the criticism was justified, but first responsibility lay with local and state officials who controlled evacuation efforts, police and other public-safety officers, and the National Guard.

Is it good that significant powers are reserved to the states? One way to answer that question is to ask another: Is it valuable for New York to make decisions concerning Medicaid — or gun control, taxes, and the allocation of transportation dollars — that may differ from decisions made in Georgia or California? Most Americans would say that to pose the question is to answer it in the affirmative: The reservation of rights to the states is a good thing because people across the vast United States have different values, different ideas about the role of government.

States' rights to enact laws that differ from those of their neighbors can have important economic, social, and even moral implications. One example was the October 2001 decision by Governor Pataki and the Legislature to expand casino gambling in the state. Supporters had argued for years that New Yorkers were spending money gambling at casinos in places such as Connecticut and Niagara Falls, Ontario. They said economically depressed areas such as the Catskills and Niagara Falls, NY, would gain jobs — and the state government would gain revenue — if those dollars instead went to casinos in the Empire State. Opponents argued that economic gains would be offset by losses in other tourism and recreation venues, and that it is wrong for government to promote an activity that harms many citizens. The revenue argument ultimately carried the day in New York. The same has been true in numerous other states that have legalized various forms of gambling in recent years. Yet, in an illustration of the importance of federalism, not all states have done so.

As many observers have noted, for much of the 20th century support for federalism was considered a central plant in the conservative platform — but more recently is associated with liberals and others who favor activist government. While serving as New York's attorney general, Eliot Spitzer commented often on the importance of state-level regulatory activities. In a 2004 essay, he wrote:

> As a law student, I was dubious of the New Federalism. I didn't think that it made sense for the federal government to say to New York: "You enforce the securities laws. You enforce the antitrust laws. You enforce the civil rights laws. We are not going to do it." I believed that regulatory uniformity was important, that in our nationally integrated economy, there should be one set of rules enforced by one centralized authority, not by fifty separate states.

Despite my apprehension, the New Federalism prevailed. . .

Law enforcement isn't the remedy for all the inequalities that we see in housing, employment and education.... I believe that standing up for people in this sort of situation should be one of the federal government's primary roles. Right now, they are not assuming their role, and that is too bad. But if the federal government won't take action, we at the state level will.[11]

The Future of Federalism

This book — like any on American government — is about decisions made and actions carried out in a political context. The ebb and flow of federalism involves constant jockeying for power between elected and appointed officials in the national government and those at the state level.

In the wake of the September 11, 2001, terrorist attacks, many scholars predicted that the power of the national government would grow as America conducted its new war on terrorism. One scholar summarized a popular conclusion among political scientists by saying, "Whenever you see a national emergency, federalism disappears."[12] The Bush administration and Congress did create significant new investigatory and prosecutorial powers for federal agencies. Yet, those did not come at the expense of states, many of which adopted their own new laws that give law-enforcement officials greater, more intrusive powers. While the new federal Patriot Act and related laws came under criticism from many Americans, states did not act as the "instrument of redress" Hamilton envisioned at the nation's founding.

National crises often leave Washington stronger. A prime example was FDR's response to the Great Depression, creating major new federal responsibilities for regulating commerce and supporting the needy. On the other hand, the growing tendency among many Americans to view nationally imposed solutions with suspicion did not disappear after September 11. Some questioned the idea of making all airport

---

11 Eliot Spitzer, "Federal Efforts to Curtail State Protection of Consumer Interests," *Government, Law and Policy Journal*, New York State Bar Association, Albany, NY, Spring 2004, p. 17.

12 Robert C. Post, a law professor at the University at California at Berkeley, quoted in "Will the Court Reassert National Authority," *The New York Times*, September 30, 2001, Sec. 4, p. 14.

security personnel federal employees by pointing out, for instance, that Israel — with extensive experience in battling terrorism — had experimented with full government control of airport security and later returned some of the responsibility to the private sector. Questions about the effectiveness of security at many airports, after federal agencies took control, added to the debate.

Whatever the trend may be at any given time, the battle over federalism remains vitally important to almost every major issue of public policy. Discussion of three examples, among many, follows.

Education Policy

In January 2002, President Bush signed into law his signature education initiative, the No Child Left Behind Act. As outlined in Chapter 12, the new law dramatically expanded Washington's role in funding and setting rules for K-12 public schools. From 2000 to 2004, federal funding for New York State school districts rose by two-thirds, to $3.2 billion, according to the Office of the State Comptroller.

Such funding increases helped persuade many leading Democrats to support the bill. For the President and many supporters, the more important elements of the law created mechanisms to measure student performance, to hold schools accountable for such outcomes, and to create new educational opportunities for children whose schools do not meet certain measures of success.

Among other things, the law requires annual testing in grades 3 through 8, with results reported publicly. Supporters say that requirement forces states and school districts to confront the reality that many children — hundreds of thousands in New York — are not learning adequately. The law allows states to set the standards that define success. Critics say the standardized tests used for NCLB are unfair to some children. Washington has failed to provide enough funding for states to provide the support failing children need, they argue.

The Role of Lobbyists and "Earmarking" in Federal Funding

Local governments and school districts in New York have long worked through associations such as the New York Conference of Mayors and the New York State School Boards Association to lobby state leaders on budget and other issues. Similar organizations work in Washington on behalf of states and localities across the country.

In recent years, municipalities and states have increasingly turned to contract lobbyists in Washington to augment the work of their associations, particularly when seeking targeted funding through the Congressional "earmarking" process. The number of public entities hiring private lobbying firms nearly doubled from 1998 to 2004. Many top lobbying firms count state, local, and tribal governments as their largest client sector, according to the Center for Public Integrity, a nonpartisan research organization.[13]

New York State spent $3.4 million to hire lobbying firms in the nation's capital from 1998 through 2004, according to the center. That did not include the state's support for organizations such as the National Governors Association and the National Conference of State Legislatures. The State University of New York and two of its campuses — Binghamton University and the College for Environmental Science and Forestry — reported hiring lobbyists during the period as well. So did four state agencies or authorities; the City of New York; the New York City Council; three New York City departments; Westchester County; and the Association of Fire Districts of the State of New York.

State and local leaders continue to rely on direct contact with U.S. Senate and House members for major issues such as rebuilding assistance for the World Trade Center site. But the increasing use of private lobbyists reflects a change in relationships between Washington and local officials. Hamilton and other founders saw the states providing a check on the powers of the federal government. When mayors or governors go hat in hand to members of Congress, seeking funding for bridges or other projects, they will not feel as free as they otherwise would to engage in public criticism of the members whose favor they seek. The loss of such voices diminishes the national debate on key policy issues.

Insurance Regulation

As outlined in Chapter Eight, some insurance companies and members of Congress are proposing a much greater role for the federal government in regulating insurance. Health, life, auto, and other insurance pol-

---

13 Jodi Rudoren and Aron Pilhofer, "Hiring Lobbyists for Federal Aid, Towns Learn That Money Talks," *The New York Times*, July 2, 2006, p. 1.

icies are among the most important purchases most Americans make each year. The companies that issue such policies are regulated mainly by the states, as has been the case since government regulation of the industry began in the mid-1800s.

A 1999 federal law, the Gramm-Leach-Bliley Financial Services Modernization Act, reaffirmed the states' primary role in regulating insurance activities — whether conducted by companies whose primary business is insurance, banking or securities. The federal law helped spur more uniformity among state licensing and other laws.

Interest in federal regulation of insurers heightened in the 1980s as a result of concerns about the effectiveness of state solvency regulations, after several major bankruptcies. More recently, industry voices have called for either regulation at the federal level, or increased uniformity in state laws, as the broad financial-services sector has become more national and international in scope. A move away from state-only regulation would likely reduce government-set price controls, and increase the power of market forces to determine what kinds of policies consumers can buy.

Voters who care about those and other issues — education, health care, the power of government, to name a few — should recognize that federalism matters.

What is the future of federalism — the role of New York and other states, relative to that of Washington, in the great issues of the 21st century? It seems safe to say that states will continue to play a major role. The nation's Constitution requires it. As a result of a well-planned and carefully executed strategy by conservative Republicans, federal courts generally favor greater deference to states than was the case a generation ago. Equally important, support for the idea is now bipartisan — witness the perspective of Governor-elect Spitzer.

Governors, legislators, and elected leaders at the federal level will continue to push their own institutions and each other in their efforts to control the policy debate. Such competition over ideas and political influence will serve all Americans — as long as an informed citizenry is a full partner in the conversation.

A LEGISLATIVE CASE STUDY: DOMESTIC RELATIONS LAW

The Legislature makes hundreds of changes to New York State laws every year. While the press and public pay attention only to a relative handful, many other laws have dramatic, if less noticed, effects on the lives of New Yorkers. Each of these is enacted with the governor's signature, but most arise because one or two legislators have taken a particular interest in the issue. Collectively, they represent the major impact the Legislature has on New Yorkers — writing the rules under which society operates. Often, a statute enacted in one year adds to or otherwise amends legislative action of a few years earlier, in response to social developments and/or judicial action.

The Domestic Relations Law is one example of a major statute that affects thousands of New Yorkers directly, and is subject to regular change by the Legislature. Dating to the recodification of New York law in 1896, it governs a broad range of family issues including marriage and divorce; adoption; child support; domestic violence; and the problems of neglected and delinquent children. With its broad scope affecting highly personal aspects of family life, the Domestic Relations Law is the subject of thousands of court cases each year. One particular aspect of the law that has seen shifting statutory definition and judicial interpretation in recent decades is Section 72, governing grandparents' rights to visit their grandchildren.

Under the English and colonial common law, "grandparents had no standing to assert rights of visitation against a custodial parent: a petition seeking such relief would necessarily have been dismissed."[1] One of the earliest such cases to advance in the courts came in 1949, when Julius Noll asked a state Supreme Court justice in Syracuse to order his widowed daughter-in-law, Margaret Ann Weiskotten Noll, to allow visits with his grandson. The boy's mother opposed the request because of "altercations and unpleasantness on earlier visitations," according to the ultimate decision in the Appellate Division of state Supreme Court. The lower court granted the grandparents permission to visit the three-year-old, Kenneth, for an hour every two months at their daughter-in-law's home. The Appellate Division reversed that decision, ruling that "where the mother was the proper, natural and legal custodian of her child and unwilling to have visitation by paternal grandparents, and the welfare, contentment, peace of mind and happiness of the child did not make such continued contact essential, a court of equity could not interfere."[2]

In 1966, though, the Legislature decided that grandparents at least should have some right to ask a court to intervene. Section 72 of the Domestic Relations Law granted grandparents standing — the legal right to ask a court for help — in visitation matters. The right was limited, though, to cases in which the grandparents' child had died. Grandma and Grandpa's rights, in other words, derived from those of the deceased parent.

Changing social norms relating to families helped nudge the Legislature into amending the law in 1975. The law, signed by Governor Carey, provided that grandparents could apply to the court for visitation rights not only when one parent had died, but also in cases "where circumstances show that conditions exist which equity would see fit to intervene" — an almost direct rebuttal to the *Noll* decision two decades earlier. In other words, judges would have broad discretion in deciding whether the best interests of the child would be served by requiring parents to allow grandparents' visitation.

The 1975 law was not a major issue for Governor Carey, as evidenced by the lack of a gubernatorial approval memo upon its signing into law. That year, after all, the then-new governor was focused on saving New York City from bankruptcy, dealing with the state's own fiscal

---

1   *Emanuel S.* v. *Joseph E.*, 573 N.Y.S.2d 36 (Ct.App 1991).
2   *Matter of Noll* v. *Noll*, 277 App.Div 286, 98 N.Y.S.2d 938.

problems and addressing critical issues such as poor conditions in state developmental centers. Nor did the new law seem important to the news media; an extensive summary of that year's legislative action published in *The New York Times* does not mention the statute. In Albany, it was significant mainly to the bill's sponsors in the Senate and Assembly — Senator Leon Giuffreda, a Suffolk County Republican; and Assemblyman Charles Schumer, a Brooklyn Democrat (and future U.S. Senator). They initiated its drafting and convinced the leadership and senior staff in their respective houses to put the bill on committee and floor calendars. As is usually the case, in the absence of particularly significant reasons to vote no, a majority of their colleagues voted in favor once the bill came to the floor.

The Legislature revisited the issue in 1986. Where existing law had given grandparents the right to seek a habeas corpus ruling, the 1986 amendment provided that such a request could also be made through a court action known as a special proceeding. Such a change gave petitioners another, potentially "less dramatic" and more convenient option for legal action.

Two years later, the Legislature added another procedural option, allowing grandparents to apply to Family Court rather than only to Supreme Court as had been the case previously. This change was part of a broader bill that focused mainly on parents' rights to visit their children in foster care.

By the year 2000, New York State's law on grandparents' rights to visit their grandchildren seemed well settled. The sensitive nature of the issue had produced dozens of court rulings on various specific aspects. (As with judicial decisions involving other statutes, the more important cases are summarized in the volumes of *McKinney's Consolidated Laws* on the Domestic Relations Law.) The right to visitation was not absolute, but grandparents did have the right to petition the courts for an order allowing them to visit grandchildren even if parents objected. Judges, in turn, maintained wide discretion to decide what was best for the children.

"...the tendency in the courts is not to force visitation over the concerted opposition of both parents," Alan D. Scheinkman wrote in 1999. "To compel visitation over the objections of both parents does raise serious constitutional and human rights issues as it invades the rights of the parents to rear their children without state interference. For the courts to invade parental rights, the case must be clear-cut and compelling. Not surprisingly, few cases are."[3]

Despite this record, the legal provisions and their impact on individual New Yorkers may be threatened by a U.S. Supreme Court decision in early 2000 striking down a wide-ranging visitation-rights law in the state of Washington. In *Troxel v. Granville*, the nation's highest court struck down a statute that permitted anyone to petition for visitation rights and that authorized courts to grant visitation whenever doing so "may serve the best interests of the child." The plurality decision, written by Justice Sandra Day O'Connor, said the Washington statute unconstitutionally infringed on the fundamental right of parents to rear their children as they see fit.[4]

Among the New Yorkers for whom the U.S. Supreme Court decision had immediate importance was a Brooklyn grandfather, Sheldon Hertz. Following marital difficulties, he and his wife separated, after which his three children and their spouses refused to allow him to visit their 15 children. Mr. Hertz took the case to court, citing Section 72 of the Domestic Relations Law; the grandchildren's parents argued that the statute represented an infringement of their fundamental rights to direct the care and custody of their children. A state Supreme Court justice agreed that the law is unconstitutional on that basis, and granted the parents' request to dismiss the case. In February 2002, however, the Appellate Division — while expressing no opinion on the merits of the Hertz case itself — reversed the lower-court decision regarding constitutionality. Unlike the Washington statute, the Appellate Division said, New York's law has been interpreted to accord deference to parents' wishes, as the U.S. Supreme Court's *Troxel* decision ruled is required.

"The litigation in New York is illustrative of what is going on around the country," Joanna Grossman commented. "Litigants are petitioning for rehearings to consider the impact of *Troxel*; courts are reconsidering the validity of their own states' statutes; and family members with acrimonious relationships are living in a state of uncertainty."[5]

---

3   "Custody and Wages of Children: Practice Commentaries," in *McKinney's Consolidated Laws of New York Annotated, Domestic Relations Law*, West Group, 1999, p. 294.

4   *Troxel v. Granville*, 530 US 57.

5   "Can The Fifty States' Grandparent Visitation Statutes Survive in the Wake of the Supreme Court's Decision in *Troxel v. Granville*?", available at
     http://writ.findlaw.com/grossman/20020312.html.

The Legislature acted in 2003 to provide some certainty with regard to grandparents' rights in a related area, custody cases. A statute adopted that year included these legislative findings:

> The legislature hereby finds that, with 413,000 children living in grandparent headed households in New York state, grandparents play a special role in the lives of their grandchildren and are increasingly functioning as care givers in their grandchildrens' (sic) lives. In recognition of this critical role that many grandparents play in the lives of their grandchildren, the legislature finds it necessary to provide guidance regarding the ability of grandparents to obtain standing in custody proceedings involving their grandchildren.[6]

The law gives grandparents the right to ask a court, upon showing of "extraordinary circumstances," to grant custody rights. Such circumstances include "an extended disruption of custody," such as when a parent voluntarily separated from a child for at least 24 months.

Senate and Assembly members introduced proposals for other changes to the Domestic Relations Law's provisions regarding grandparents' rights in recent years. In this area, as in many others, the Legislature's work is never done.

---

6   Chapter 657, Laws of 2003.

Made in the USA
Middletown, DE
02 February 2021

32897042R00351